Better Crit

Connect History ng skills through
"Critical Mission n a pivotal moment in time
and ask them to read and examine sources, maps, and timelines and develop a
historical argument.

Critical Mission | Experience History | **Truman and the Atomic Bomb**

learn about your mission

I have been president for only a few months, assuming the
position of Commander-in-Chief for a nation involved a long,
global war. New technology has provided me with an atomic
bomb-the world's first nuclear weapon-which could forever
change the face of warfare. Now, I must decide whether to use
this devastating new weapon to end the war with Japan. One
group of advisors, including my chief advisor and long-time
mentor, Secretary of State James F. Byrnes, is encouraging me
to approve the plan. Another group, including the Under-
Secretary of State and expert on Japanese diplomacy, Joseph
Grew, advises against it. Here is what I need you to do:

1. Review the information on the following
   pages-the timeline, the maps, and the documents;
2. Identify important themes and evidence that my
   advisors have considered in offering their
   opinions;
3. Write your recommendation of whether or not I
   should use the atomic bomb on Japan, including
   the themes and evidence to support your
   conclusion.

This is a decision that will shape the future for all humanity;
consider it well!

President Harry S Truman

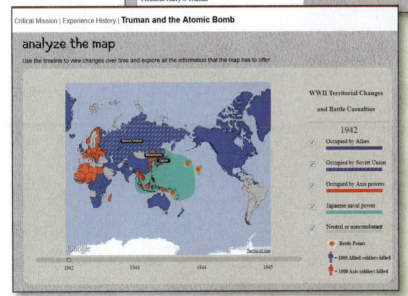

Critical Mission | Experience History | **Truman and the Atomic Bomb**

analyze the map

Use the timeline to view changes over time and explore all the information that the map has to offer.

WWII Territorial Changes
and Battle Casualties

1942

☑ Occupied by Allies

☑ Occupied by Soviet Union

☑ Occupied by Axis powers

☑ Japanese naval power

☑ Neutral or noncombatant

✹ Battle Points

= 1000 Allied soldiers killed

= 1000 Axis soldiers killed

Better Geography Skills

Embedded narrated map video learning resources in SmartBook support geographical as well as historical thinking.

Better Grades

Connect History offers a number of powerful reports and charts to give you the information you need to easily evaluate performance and keep students on a path to success. Connect Insight—now available for both students and instructors—is a series of visual data displays that provide at-a-glance information regarding student performance. Either quick review or in-depth, these reports remove the guesswork so you can focus on what matters most.

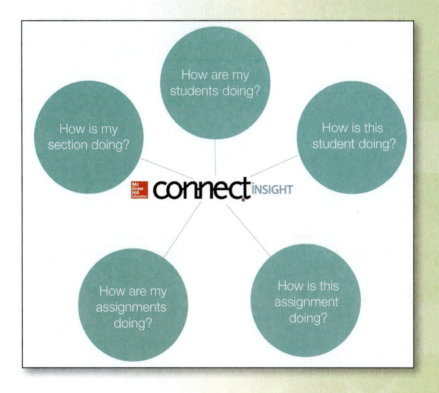

THE UNFINISHED NATION

A Concise History of the
American People
Volume 2: From 1865

THE UNFINISHED NATION

A Concise History of the American People
Volume 2: From 1865

Eighth Edition

ALAN BRINKLEY
Columbia University

with Contributions from

JOHN GIGGIE
University of Alabama

ANDREW HUEBNER
University of Alabama

THE UNFINISHED NATION: A CONCISE HISTORY OF THE AMERICAN PEOPLE, VOLUME 2, EIGHTH EDITION

Published by McGraw-Hill Education, 2 Penn Plaza, New York, NY 10121. Copyright © 2016 by McGraw-Hill Education. All rights reserved. Printed in the United States of America. Previous editions © 2014, 2010, and 2008. No part of this publication may be reproduced or distributed in any form or by any means, or stored in a database or retrieval system, without the prior written consent of McGraw-Hill Education, including, but not limited to, in any network or other electronic storage or transmission, or broadcast for distance learning.

Some ancillaries, including electronic and print components, may not be available to customers outside the United States.

This book is printed on acid-free paper.

5 6 7 8 9 10 QVS 21 20 19 18

ISBN 978-1-259-28475-5
MHID 1-259-28475-1

Senior Vice President, Products & Markets: *Kurt L. Strand*
Vice President, General Manager, Products & Markets: *Michael Ryan*
Vice President, Content Design & Delivery: *Kimberly Meriwether David*
Managing Director: *Gina Boedeker*
Brand Manager: *Jason Seitz*
Director, Product Development: *Meghan Campbell*
Lead Product Developer: *Rhona Robbin*
Product Developer: *Cynthia Ward*
Executive Marketing Manager: *April Cole*
Marketing Manager: *Alexandra Schultz*
Executive Market Development Manager: *Stacy Ruel*

Digital Product Developer: *David Chodoff*
Director, Content Design & Delivery: *Terri Schiesl*
Program Manager: *Marianne Musni*
Content Project Managers: *Susan Trentacosti, Marianne Musni, Karen Jozefowicz*
Buyer: *Susan K. Culbertson*
Design: *David Hash*
Content Licensing Specialists: *Carrie Burger, Ann Marie Jannette*
Cover Image: © *Bettmann/Corbis;* © *Charles Knowles/Alamy (RF)*
Compositor: *Aptara®, Inc.*
Printer: *LSC Communications*

Library of Congress Cataloging-in-Publication Data

Brinkley, Alan.
  The unfinished nation: a concise history of the American people / Alan Brinkley, Columbia University; with contributions from John Giggie, University of Alabama; Andrew Huebner, University of Alabama. — Eighth edition.
      pages cm
  ISBN 978-0-07-351333-1 (alkaline paper) — ISBN 0-07-351333-4 (alkaline paper)
  1. United States—History. I. Giggie, John Michael, 1965- II. Huebner, Andrew. III. Title.
  E178.1.B827 2016
  973—dc23

                                                                    2015025264

The Internet addresses listed in the text were accurate at the time of publication. The inclusion of a website does not indicate an endorsement by the authors or McGraw-Hill Education, and McGraw-Hill Education does not guarantee the accuracy of the information presented at these sites.

mheducation.com/highered

ABOUT THE AUTHORS

ALAN BRINKLEY is the Allan Nevins Professor of History at Columbia University. He served as university provost at Columbia from 2003 to 2009. He is the author of *Voices of Protest: Huey Long, Father Coughlin, and the Great Depression*, which won the 1983 National Book Award; *American History: Connecting with the Past; The End of Reform: New Deal Liberalism in Recession and War; Liberalism and Its Discontents; Franklin D. Roosevelt;* and *The Publisher: Henry Luce and His American Century*. He is board chair of the National Humanities Center, board chair of the Century Foundation, and a trustee of Oxford University Press. He is also a member of the Academy of Arts and Sciences. In 1998–1999, he was the Harmsworth Professor of History at Oxford University, and in 2011–2012, the Pitt Professor at the University of Cambridge. He won the Joseph R. Levenson Memorial Teaching Award at Harvard and the Great Teacher Award at Columbia. He was educated at Princeton and Harvard.

JOHN GIGGIE is associate professor of history and African American studies at the University of Alabama. He is the author of *After Redemption: Jim Crow and the Transformation of African American Religion in the Delta, 1875–1917,* editor of *America Firsthand*, and editor of *Faith in the Market: Religion and the Rise of Commercial Culture*. He is currently preparing a book on African American religion during the Civil War. He has been honored for his teaching, most recently with a Distinguished Fellow in Teaching award from the University of Alabama. He received his PhD from Princeton University.

ANDREW HUEBNER is associate professor of history at the University of Alabama. He is the author of *The Warrior Image: Soldiers in American Culture from the Second World War to the Vietnam Era* and has written and spoken widely on the subject of war and society in the twentieth-century United States. He is currently working on a study of American families and public culture during the First World War. He received his PhD from Brown University.

BRIEF CONTENTS

PREFACE XXIII

15 RECONSTRUCTION AND THE NEW SOUTH 351

16 THE CONQUEST OF THE FAR WEST 380

17 INDUSTRIAL SUPREMACY 404

18 THE AGE OF THE CITY 427

19 FROM CRISIS TO EMPIRE 454

20 THE PROGRESSIVES 487

21 AMERICA AND THE GREAT WAR 518

22 THE NEW ERA 543

23 THE GREAT DEPRESSION 563

24 THE NEW DEAL 587

25 THE GLOBAL CRISIS, 1921–1941 611

26 AMERICA IN A WORLD AT WAR 628

27 THE COLD WAR 653

28 THE AFFLUENT SOCIETY 678

29 THE TURBULENT SIXTIES 707

30 THE CRISIS OF AUTHORITY 736

31 FROM "THE AGE OF LIMITS" TO THE AGE OF REAGAN 766

32 THE AGE OF GLOBALIZATION 789

APPENDIX 823
GLOSSARY 851
INDEX 855

CONTENTS

PREFACE XXIII

15 RECONSTRUCTION AND THE NEW SOUTH 351

THE PROBLEMS OF PEACEMAKING 352
The Aftermath of War and Emancipation 352
Competing Notions of Freedom 352
Plans for Reconstruction 354
The Death of Lincoln 355
Johnson and "Restoration" 357

RADICAL RECONSTRUCTION 358
The Black Codes 358
The Fourteenth Amendment 358
The Congressional Plan 359
The Impeachment of Andrew Johnson 362

THE SOUTH IN RECONSTRUCTION 362
The Reconstruction Governments 362
Education 364
Landownership and Tenancy 364
Incomes and Credit 364
The African American Family in Freedom 365

THE GRANT ADMINISTRATION 366
The Soldier President 366
The Grant Scandals 367
The Greenback Question 367
Republican Diplomacy 368

THE ABANDONMENT OF RECONSTRUCTION 368
The Southern States "Redeemed" 368
Waning Northern Commitment 369
The Compromise of 1877 369
The Legacy of Reconstruction 371

THE NEW SOUTH 371
The "Redeemers" 371
Industrialization and the New South 372
Tenants and Sharecroppers 373
African Americans and the New South 373
The Birth of Jim Crow 374

Debating the Past: Reconstruction 356

Consider the Source: Southern Blacks Ask for Help, 1865 360

Patterns of Popular Culture: The Minstrel Show 376

CONCLUSION 378
KEY TERMS/PEOPLE/PLACES/EVENTS 379
RECALL AND REFLECT 379

16 THE CONQUEST OF THE FAR WEST 380

THE SOCIETIES OF THE FAR WEST 381
The Western Tribes 381
Hispanic New Mexico 382
Hispanic California and Texas 382
The Chinese Migration 383

    Anti-Chinese Sentiments 385
    Migration from the East 386

THE CHANGING WESTERN ECONOMY 386
    Labor in the West 387
    The Arrival of the Miners 387
    The Cattle Kingdom 388

THE ROMANCE OF THE WEST 390
    The Western Landscape and the Cowboy 390
    The Idea of the Frontier 391

THE DISPERSAL OF THE TRIBES 393
    White Tribal Policies 394
    The Indian Wars 395
    The Dawes Act 397

THE RISE AND DECLINE OF THE WESTERN FARMER 398
    Farming on the Plains 398
    Commercial Agriculture 399
    The Farmers' Grievances 401
    The Agrarian Malaise 402

Debating the Past: The Frontier and the West 392

Consider the Source: Walter Baron Von Richthofen, *Cattle Raising on the Plains in North America*, 1885 400

CONCLUSION 402
KEY TERMS/PEOPLE/PLACES/EVENTS 403
RECALL AND REFLECT 403

17 INDUSTRIAL SUPREMACY 404

SOURCES OF INDUSTRIAL GROWTH 405
    Industrial Technologies 405
    The Technology of Iron and Steel Production 406
    The Automobile and the Airplane 407
    Research and Development 408
    The Science of Production 408
    Railroad Expansion and the Corporation 410

CAPITALIST CONSERVATISM AND ITS CRITICS 412
    Survival of the Fittest 412
    The Gospel of Wealth 413
    Alternative Visions 417
    The Problems of Monopoly 419

THE ORDEAL OF THE WORKER 419
    The Immigrant Workforce 419
    Wages and Working Conditions 420
    Emerging Unionization 421
    The Knights of Labor 422
    The American Federation of Labor 422
    The Homestead Strike 423
    The Pullman Strike 424
    Sources of Labor Weakness 424

Consider the Source: *Andrew Carnegie Explains the Gospel of Wealth*, 1889 414

Patterns of Popular Culture: The Novels of Horatio Alger 416

CONCLUSION 425
KEY TERMS/PEOPLE/PLACES/EVENTS 425
RECALL AND REFLECT 426

18 THE AGE OF THE CITY 427

THE NEW URBAN GROWTH 428
The Migrations   428
The Ethnic City   429
Assimilation and Exclusion   431

THE URBAN LANDSCAPE 433
The Creation of Public Space   434
The Search for Housing   435
Urban Technologies: Transportation and
   Construction   436

STRAINS OF URBAN LIFE 436
Fire and Disease   437
Environmental Degradation   437
Urban Poverty, Crime, and Violence   438
The Machine and the Boss   438

THE RISE OF MASS CONSUMPTION 440
Patterns of Income and Consumption   440
Chain Stores, Mail-Order Houses, and Department Stores   441
Women as Consumers   441

LEISURE IN THE CONSUMER SOCIETY 443
Redefining Leisure   443
Spectator Sports   444
Music, Theater, and Movies   445
Patterns of Public and Private Leisure   446
The Technologies of Mass Communication   447
The Telephone   447

HIGH CULTURE IN THE URBAN AGE 448
Literature and Art in Urban America   448
The Impact of Darwinism   449
Toward Universal Schooling   450
Universities and the Growth of Science and Technology   450
Medical Science   451
Education for Women   452

America in the World: Global Migrations 432

Consider the Source: John Wanamaker, the Four Cardinal Points of the
Department Store, 1874 442

CONCLUSION   452
KEY TERMS/PEOPLE/PLACES/EVENTS   453
RECALL AND REFLECT   453

19 FROM CRISIS TO EMPIRE 454

THE POLITICS OF EQUILIBRIUM 455
The Party System   455
The National Government   456
Presidents and Patronage   457
Cleveland, Harrison, and the Tariff   458
New Public Issues   459

THE AGRARIAN REVOLT 460
The Grangers   460
The Farmers' Alliances   460
The Populist Constituency   462
Populist Ideas   462

THE CRISIS OF THE 1890s 462
The Panic of 1893   463

The Silver Question   464
"A Cross of Gold"   465
The Conservative Victory   466
McKinley and Recovery   466

STIRRINGS OF IMPERIALISM 468
The New Manifest Destiny   468
Hawaii and Samoa   468

WAR WITH SPAIN 472
Controversy over Cuba   472
"A Splendid Little War"   473
Seizing the Philippines   476
The Battle for Cuba   476
Puerto Rico and the United States   478
The Debate over the Philippines   478

THE REPUBLIC AS EMPIRE 481
Governing the Colonies   481
The Philippine War   482
The Open Door   484
A Modern Military System   485

America in the World: Imperialism 470

Patterns of Popular Culture: Yellow Journalism 474

Consider the Source: Platform of the American Anti-Imperialist League, 1899 480

CONCLUSION   485
KEY TERMS/PEOPLE/PLACES/EVENTS   486
RECALL AND REFLECT   486

20 THE PROGRESSIVES 487

THE PROGRESSIVE IMPULSE 488
The Muckrakers and the Social Gospel   489
The Settlement House Movement   491
The Allure of Expertise   492
The Professions   492
Women and the Professions   493

WOMEN AND REFORM 493
The "New Woman"   494
The Clubwomen   494
Woman Suffrage   495

THE ASSAULT ON THE PARTIES 496
Early Attacks   496
Municipal Reform   497
Statehouse Progressivism   497
Parties and Interest Groups   498

SOURCES OF PROGRESSIVE REFORM 498
Labor, the Machine, and Reform   499
Western Progressives   501
African Americans and Reform   501

CRUSADES FOR SOCIAL ORDER AND REFORM 503
The Temperance Crusade   503
Immigration Restriction   503
The Dream of Socialism   504
Decentralization and Regulation   504

THEODORE ROOSEVELT AND THE MODERN PRESIDENCY 505
The Accidental President   505

The "Square Deal" 506
Roosevelt and the Environment 507
Panic and Retirement 509

THE TROUBLED SUCCESSION 510
Taft and the Progressives 510
The Return of Roosevelt 510
Spreading Insurgency 511
Roosevelt versus Taft 512

WOODROW WILSON AND THE NEW FREEDOM 512
Woodrow Wilson 512
The Scholar as President 514
Retreat and Advance 515

America in the World: Social Democracy 490

Debating the Past: Progressivism 500

Consider the Source: John Muir on the Value of Wild Places, 1901 508

CONCLUSION 516
KEY TERMS/PEOPLE/PLACES/EVENTS 516
RECALL AND REFLECT 517

21 AMERICA AND THE GREAT WAR 518

THE "BIG STICK": AMERICA AND THE WORLD, 1901–1917 519
Roosevelt and "Civilization" 519
Protecting the "Open Door" in Asia 520
The Iron-Fisted Neighbor 520
The Panama Canal 521
Taft and "Dollar Diplomacy" 522
Diplomacy and Morality 522

THE ROAD TO WAR 524
The Collapse of the European Peace 524
Wilson's Neutrality 524
Preparedness versus Pacifism 525
Intervention 525

"OVER THERE" 527
Mobilizing the Military 527
The Yanks Are Coming 529
The New Technology of Warfare 530
Organizing the Economy for War 532
The Search for Social Unity 533

THE SEARCH FOR A NEW WORLD ORDER 535
The Fourteen Points 535
The Paris Peace Conference 536
The Ratification Battle 536

A SOCIETY IN TURMOIL 537
The Unstable Economy 537
The Demands of African Americans 538
The Red Scare 540
Refuting the Red Scare 540
The Retreat from Idealism 541

Consider the Source: Race, Gender, and World War I Posters 528

Patterns of Popular Culture: George M. Cohan, "Over There," 1917 534

CONCLUSION 541
KEY TERMS/PEOPLE/PLACES/EVENTS 542
RECALL AND REFLECT 542

22 THE NEW ERA 543

THE NEW ECONOMY 544

Technology, Organization, and Economic Growth   544
Workers in an Age of Capital   545
Women and Minorities in the Workforce   548
Agricultural Technology and the Plight of the Farmer   551

THE NEW CULTURE 551

Consumerism and Communications   551
Women in the New Era   554
The Disenchanted   555

A CONFLICT OF CULTURES 556

Prohibition   556
Nativism and the Klan   557
Religious Fundamentalism   558
The Democrats' Ordeal   558

REPUBLICAN GOVERNMENT 559

Harding and Coolidge   559
Government and Business   560

Consider the Source: America's Early Telephone Network 546

America in the World: The Cinema 552

CONCLUSION   562
KEY TERMS/PEOPLE/PLACES/EVENTS   562
RECALL AND REFLECT   562

23 THE GREAT DEPRESSION 563

THE COMING OF THE DEPRESSION 564

The Great Crash   564
Causes of the Depression   565
Progress of the Depression   567

THE AMERICAN PEOPLE IN HARD TIMES 568

Unemployment and Relief   569
African Americans and the Depression   570
Hispanics and Asians in Depression America   570
Women and Families in the Great Depression   573

THE DEPRESSION AND AMERICAN CULTURE 574

Depression Values   574
Radio   574
The Movies   575
Literature and Journalism   578
The Popular Front and the Left   579

THE ORDEAL OF HERBERT HOOVER 581

The Hoover Program   581
Popular Protest   582
The Election of 1932   584
The "Interregnum"   585

America in the World: The Global Depression 566

Consider the Source: Mr. Tarver Remembers the Great Depression 572

Patterns of Popular Culture: The Golden Age of Comic Books 576

CONCLUSION   586
KEY TERMS/PEOPLE/PLACES/EVENTS   586
RECALL AND REFLECT   586

24 THE NEW DEAL 587

LAUNCHING THE NEW DEAL 588
Restoring Confidence 588
Agricultural Adjustment 589
Industrial Recovery 590
Regional Planning 591
The Growth of Federal Relief 592

THE NEW DEAL IN TRANSITION 593
The Conservative Criticism of the New Deal 593
The Populist Criticism of the New Deal 596
The "Second New Deal" 598
Labor Militancy 598
Organizing Battles 599
Social Security 600
New Directions in Relief 601
The 1936 "Referendum" 602

THE NEW DEAL IN DISARRAY 603
The Court Fight 603
Retrenchment and Recession 603

LIMITS AND LEGACIES OF THE NEW DEAL 606
African Americans and the New Deal 606
The New Deal and the "Indian Problem" 607
Women and the New Deal 607
The New Deal and the West 608
The New Deal, the Economy, and Politics 608

Debating the Past: The New Deal 594

Consider the Source: Franklin D. Roosevelt Speaks on the Reorganization of the Judiciary 604

CONCLUSION 609
KEY TERMS/PEOPLE/PLACES/EVENTS 610
RECALL AND REFLECT 610

25 THE GLOBAL CRISIS, 1921–1941 611

THE DIPLOMACY OF THE NEW ERA 612
Replacing the League 612
Debts and Diplomacy 613
Hoover and the World Crisis 613

ISOLATIONISM AND INTERNATIONALISM 616
Depression Diplomacy 616
The Rise of Isolationism 617
The Failure of Munich 618

FROM NEUTRALITY TO INTERVENTION 619
Neutrality Tested 619
The Campaign of 1940 623
Neutrality Abandoned 623
The Road to Pearl Harbor 625

America in the World: The Sino-Japanese War, 1931–1941 614

Patterns of Popular Culture: Orson Welles and the "War of the Worlds" 620

Consider the Source: Joint Statement by President Roosevelt and Prime Minister Churchill 624

CONCLUSION 626
KEY TERMS/PEOPLE/PLACES/EVENTS 627
RECALL AND REFLECT 627

26 AMERICA IN A WORLD AT WAR 628

WAR ON TWO FRONTS 629
Containing the Japanese   629
Holding Off the Germans   630
America and the Holocaust   631

THE AMERICAN ECONOMY IN WARTIME 633
Prosperity and the Rights of Labor   633
Stabilizing the Boom and Mobilizing
  Production   634
Wartime Science and Technology   634

RACE AND ETHNICITY IN WARTIME AMERICA 635
African Americans and the War   635
Native Americans and the War   636
Mexican American War Workers   637
The Internment of Japanese Americans   637
Chinese Americans and the War   639

ANXIETY AND AFFLUENCE IN WARTIME CULTURE 639
Home-Front Life and Culture   639
Love, Family, and Sexuality in Wartime   640
The Growth of Wartime Conservatism   642

THE DEFEAT OF THE AXIS 643
The European Offensive   644
The Pacific Offensive   646
The Manhattan Project and Atomic Warfare   649

Consider the Source: The Face of the Enemy 638

Debating the Past: The Decision to Drop the Atomic Bomb 648

CONCLUSION   651
KEY TERMS/PEOPLE/PLACES/EVENTS   652
RECALL AND REFLECT   652

27 THE COLD WAR 653

ORIGINS OF THE COLD WAR 654
Sources of Soviet–American Tension   654
Wartime Diplomacy   655
Yalta   655

THE COLLAPSE OF THE PEACE 658
The Failure of Potsdam   658
The China Problem and Japan   659
The Containment Doctrine   659
The Conservative Opposition to Containment   659
The Marshall Plan   660
Mobilization at Home   661
The Road to NATO   661
Reevaluating Cold War Policy   663

AMERICA AFTER THE WAR 663
The Problems of Reconversion   663
The Fair Deal Rejected   665
The Election of 1948   666
The Fair Deal Revived   667
The Nuclear Age   668

THE KOREAN WAR 669
The Divided Peninsula   669

From Invasion to Stalemate   671
Limited Mobilization   671

THE CRUSADE AGAINST SUBVERSION 672

HUAC and Alger Hiss   672
The Federal Loyalty Program and the Rosenberg Case   673
McCarthyism   673
The Republican Revival   676

Debating the Past: The Cold War 656

Consider the Source: National Security Council Paper No. 68 (NSC-68) 664

Debating the Past: McCarthyism 674

CONCLUSION   676
KEY TERMS/PEOPLE/PLACES/EVENTS   677
RECALL AND REFLECT   677

28 THE AFFLUENT SOCIETY 678

THE ECONOMIC "MIRACLE" 679

Economic Growth   679
The Rise of the Modern West   680
Capital and Labor   681

THE EXPLOSION OF SCIENCE AND TECHNOLOGY 682

Medical Breakthroughs   682
Pesticides   683
Postwar Electronic Research   684
Postwar Computer Technology   684
Bombs, Rockets, and Missiles   684
The Space Program   685

PEOPLE OF PLENTY 686

The Consumer Culture   687
The Suburban Nation   687
The Suburban Family   687
The Birth of Television   688
Travel, Outdoor Recreation, and Environmentalism   689
Organized Society and Its Detractors   692
The Beats and the Restless Culture of Youth   692
Rock 'n' Roll   693

THE OTHER AMERICA 694

On the Margins of the Affluent Society   694
Rural Poverty   695
The Inner Cities   695

THE RISE OF THE CIVIL RIGHTS MOVEMENT 696

The *Brown* Decision and "Massive Resistance"   696
The Expanding Movement   697
Causes of the Civil Rights Movement   698

EISENHOWER REPUBLICANISM 698

"What Was Good for . . . General Motors"   699
The Survival of the Welfare State   699
The Decline of McCarthyism   699

EISENHOWER, DULLES, AND THE COLD WAR 700

Dulles and "Massive Retaliation"   700
France, America, and Vietnam   700
Cold War Crises   701
The U-2 Crisis   702

Patterns of Popular Culture: On the Road 690

Consider the Source: Eisenhower Warns of the Military–Industrial Complex 704

CONCLUSION 705
KEY TERMS/PEOPLE/PLACES/EVENTS 706
RECALL AND REFLECT 706

29 THE TURBULENT SIXTIES 707

EXPANDING THE LIBERAL STATE 708
John Kennedy 708
Lyndon Johnson 710
The Assault on Poverty 711
Cities, Schools, and Immigration 712
Legacies of the Great Society 712

THE BATTLE FOR RACIAL EQUALITY 713
Expanding Protests 713
A National Commitment 716
The Battle for Voting Rights 717
The Changing Movement 717
Urban Violence 720
Black Power 720

"FLEXIBLE RESPONSE" AND THE COLD WAR 721
Diversifying Foreign Policy 721
Confrontations with the Soviet Union 722
Johnson and the World 723

THE AGONY OF VIETNAM 724
America and Diem 724
From Aid to Intervention 725
The Quagmire 725
The War at Home 727

THE TRAUMAS OF 1968 729
The Tet Offensive 731
The Political Challenge 731
Assassinations and Politics 732
The Conservative Response 733

Debating the Past: The Civil Rights Movement 714

Consider the Source: Fannie Lou Hamer on the Struggle for Voting Rights 718

Patterns of Popular Culture: The Folk-Music Revival 728

America in the World: 1968 730

CONCLUSION 734
KEY TERMS/PEOPLE/PLACES/EVENTS 734
RECALL AND REFLECT 735

30 THE CRISIS OF AUTHORITY 736

THE YOUTH CULTURE 737
The New Left 737
The Counterculture 739

THE MOBILIZATION OF MINORITIES 740
Seeds of Indian Militancy 741
The Indian Civil Rights Movement 741
Latino Activism 742
Gay Liberation 744

THE NEW FEMINISM 745

The Rebirth 745
Women's Liberation 746
Expanding Achievements 746
The Abortion Issue 747

ENVIRONMENTALISM IN A TURBULENT SOCIETY 747

The New Science of Ecology 748
Environmental Advocacy 748
Earth Day and Beyond 749

NIXON, KISSINGER, AND THE VIETNAM WAR 750

Vietnamization 750
Escalation 750
"Peace with Honor" 751
Defeat in Indochina 753

NIXON, KISSINGER, AND THE WORLD 753

The China Initiative and Soviet–American Détente 753
Dealing with the Third World 754

POLITICS AND ECONOMICS IN THE NIXON YEARS 755

Domestic Initiatives 755
From the Warren Court to the Nixon Court 758
The 1972 Landslide 759
The Troubled Economy 759
The Nixon Response 760

THE WATERGATE CRISIS 761

The Scandals 761
The Fall of Richard Nixon 763

Consider the Source: Demands of the New York High School Student Union 738

America in the World: The End of Colonialism 756

Debating the Past: Watergate 762

CONCLUSION 764
KEY TERMS/PEOPLE/PLACES/EVENTS 765
RECALL AND REFLECT 765

31 FROM "THE AGE OF LIMITS" TO THE AGE OF REAGAN 766

POLITICS AND DIPLOMACY AFTER WATERGATE 767

The Ford Custodianship 767
The Trials of Jimmy Carter 769
Human Rights and National Interests 769
The Year of the Hostages 770

THE RISE OF THE NEW CONSERVATIVE MOVEMENT 771

The Sunbelt and Its Politics 771
Religious Revivalism 771
The Emergence of the New Right 773
The Tax Revolt 774
The Campaign of 1980 774

THE "REAGAN REVOLUTION" 775

The Reagan Coalition 777
Reagan in the White House 779
"Supply-Side" Economics 779
The Fiscal Crisis 780
Reagan and the World 781

AMERICA AND THE WANING OF THE COLD WAR 782

The Fall of the Soviet Union   782

The Fading of the Reagan Revolution   783

The Presidency of George H. W. Bush   784

The Gulf War   785

The Election of 1992   786

Consider the Source: Ronald Reagan on the Role of Government 776

CONCLUSION   787

KEY TERMS/PEOPLE/PLACES/EVENTS   788

RECALL AND REFLECT   788

32 THE AGE OF GLOBALIZATION 789

A RESURGENCE OF PARTISANSHIP 790

Launching the Clinton Presidency   790

The Republican Resurgence   791

Clinton Triumphant and Embattled   793

Impeachment, Acquittal, and Resurgence   793

The Election of 2000   794

The Presidency of George W. Bush   795

The Election of 2008   796

Obama and His Opponents   800

Obama and the Challenge of Governing   801

SCIENCE AND TECHNOLOGY IN THE NEW ECONOMY 802

The Digital Revolution   803

The Internet   803

Breakthroughs in Genetics   804

A CHANGING SOCIETY 805

A Shifting Population   805

African Americans in the Post–Civil Rights Era   805

The Abortion Debate   807

AIDS and Modern America   808

Gay Americans and Same-Sex Marriage   809

The Contemporary Environmental Movement   813

AMERICA IN THE WORLD 815

Opposing the "New World Order"   815

Defending Orthodoxy   816

The Rise of Terrorism   816

The War on Terror   818

The Iraq War   818

America after the Iraq War   820

Patterns of Popular Culture: Rap 798

Consider the Source: Same-Sex Marriage, 2015 810

America in the World: The Global Environmental Movement 812

CONCLUSION   821

KEY TERMS/PEOPLE/PLACES/EVENTS   822

RECALL AND REFLECT   822

APPENDIX 823

GLOSSARY 851

INDEX 855

THE title *The Unfinished Nation* is meant to suggest several things. It is a reminder of America's exceptional diversity—of the degree to which, despite all the many efforts to build a single, uniform definition of the meaning of American nationhood, that meaning remains contested. It is a reference to the centrality of change in American history—to the ways in which the nation has continually transformed itself and continues to do so in our own time. And it is also a description of the writing of American history itself—of the ways in which historians are engaged in a continuing, ever unfinished, process of asking new questions.

Like any history, *The Unfinished Nation* is a product of its time and reflects the views of the past that historians of recent generations have developed. The writing of our nation's history—like our nation itself—changes constantly. It is not, of course, the past that changes. Rather, historians adjust their perspectives and priorities, ask different kinds of questions, and uncover and incorporate new historical evidence. There are now, as there have always been, critics of changes in historical understanding who argue that history is a collection of facts and should not be subject to "interpretation" or "revision." But historians insist that history is not simply a collection of facts. Names and dates and a record of events are only the beginning of historical understanding. Writers and readers of history interpret the evidence before them, and inevitably bring to the task their own questions, concerns, and experiences.

Our history requires us to examine the many different peoples and ideas that have shaped American society. But it also requires us to understand that the United States is a nation whose people share many things: a common political system, a connection to an integrated national (and now international) economy, and a familiarity with a powerful mass culture. To understand the American past, it is necessary to understand both the forces that divide Americans and the forces that draw them together.

It is a daunting task to attempt to convey the history of the United States in a single book, and the eighth edition of *The Unfinished Nation* has, as have all previous editions, been carefully written and edited to keep the book as concise and readable as possible.

In addition to the content and scholarship updates that are detailed on pages xxix–xxx, we have strengthened the pedagogical features with an eye to the details. We added a glossary of historical terms and bolded those terms within the text where significantly discussed. These terms, along with key names, places, and events, are listed at the end of chapters to help students review. All of the Consider the Source features now include concise introductions that provide context for the documents. Every Consider the Source, Debating the Past, Patterns of Popular Culture, and America in the World feature is referenced within the narrative, for a clearer indication of how the different lines of inquiry work together to create a vivid and nuanced portrait of each period. Margin notes have been reinstated as well, at the request of reviewers who missed this feature from earlier editions.

It is not only the writing of history that changes with time—the tools and technologies through which information is delivered change as well. New learning resources include:

- **McGraw-Hill Connect®**—an integrated educational platform that seamlessly joins superior content with enhanced digital tools (including SmartBook®) to deliver a personalized learning experience that provides precisely what students need—when and how they need it. New visual analytics, coupled with powerful reporting, provide immediate performance perspectives. Connect makes it easy to keep students on track.

- **SmartBook®**—an adaptive eBook that makes study time as productive and efficient as possible. It identifies and closes knowledge gaps through a continually adapting reading experience that provides personalized learning resources such as narrated map videos; key point summaries; time lines; and labeling activities at the precise moment of need. This ensures that every minute spent with SmartBook is returned to the student as the most value-added minute possible.

- **Critical Missions**—an activity within Connect History that immerses students in pivotal moments in history. As students study primary sources and maps, they advise a key historical figure on an issue of vital importance—for example, should President Truman drop the atomic bomb on Japan?

- **Primary Source Primer**—a video exercise in Connect History with multiple-choice questions. The primer teaches students the importance of primary sources and how to analyze them. This online "Introduction to Primary Sources" is designed for use at the beginning of the course, to save valuable class time.

- **Create**™—a service that allows professors to create a customized version of *The Unfinished Nation* by selecting the chapters and additional primary source documents that best fit their course, while adding their own materials if desired. Register at www.mcgrawhillcreate.com to build a complimentary review copy.

- **McGraw-Hill Campus**—a first-of-its-kind institutional service that provides faculty with true, single sign-on access to all of McGraw-Hill's course content, digital tools, and other high-quality learning resources from any learning management system (LMS). This innovative offering allows secure, deep integration and seamless access to any of our course solutions, including McGraw-Hill Connect, McGraw-Hill LearnSmart, McGraw-Hill Create, and Tegrity. McGraw-Hill Campus covers our entire content library, including eBooks, assessment tools, presentation slides, and multimedia content, among other resources. This open and unlimited service allows faculty to quickly prepare for class, create tests or quizzes, develop lecture material, integrate interactive content, and much more.

ALAN BRINKLEY

ACKNOWLEDGMENTS

WE are grateful to the many advisers and reviewers who generously offered comments, suggestions, and ideas at various stages in the development of this project. Our thanks go to:

Academic Reviewers

Tramaine Anderson, *Tarrant County College, Northeast*

Darlene Antezana, *Prince George's Community College*

Maj. Paul Belmont, *U.S. Military Academy, West Point*

Peter Belser, *Ivy Tech Community College*

Robert Bender, *Eastern New Mexico University, Roswell*

Tiffany Bergman, *Missouri Valley College*

Devan Bissonette, *Excelsior College*

Blanche Brick, *Blinn College*

Brian Cervantez, *Tarrant County College, Northwest*

Sharon Courmier, *Lamar University*

Keith D. Dickson, *Old Dominion University*

Kevin Eades, *North Central Texas College*

Angela S. Edwards, *Florence-Darlington Technical College*

Ron Enders, *Ashland Community College*

Amy Essington, *California State University, Long Beach*

Glen Findley, *Odessa College*

Brandon Franke, *Blinn College*

Mary E. Frederickson, *Miami University of Ohio*

Joy Giguere, *Ivy Tech Community College*

Howell H. Gwin Jr., *Lamar University*

Donn Hall, *Ivy Tech Community College*

Maj. Adrienne Harrison, *U.S. Military Academy, West Point*

Andrew Hollinger, *Tarrant County College, Northeast*

Volker Janssen, *California State University, Fullerton*

Brian Johnson, *Tarrant County College, South*

Philbert Martin, *San Jacinto College, South*

Linda McCabe, *Tarrant County College, Northeast*

Maureen A. McCormick, *Florida State College at Jacksonville*

Brian Craig Miller, *Emporia State University*

Amanda Lea Miracle, *Emporia State University*

Josh Montandon, *North Central Texas College*

Wesley Moody, *Florida State College*

Rebekkah Morrow, *Western Oklahoma State College*

Simone de Santiago Ramos, *North Central Texas College*

Matt Schaffer, *Florence-Darlington Technical College*

Jason Scheller, *Vernon College*

Rebecca Seaman, *Elizabeth City State University*

Dennis Spillman, *North Central Texas College*

Eddie Weller, *San Jacinto College, South*

Ann K. Wentworth, *Excelsior College*

Cody Whitaker, *Drury University*

Christina A. Wilbur, *Lamar University*

Geoffrey Willbanks, *Tyler Junior College*

Martin W. Wilson, *East Stroudsburg University*

Cary Wintz, *Texas Southern University*

Connect Board of Advisors

Michael Downs, *University of Texas–Arlington*

Jim Halverson, *Judson University*

Reid Holland, *Midlands Technical College*

Stephen Katz, *Rider University*

David Komito, *Eastern Oregon University*

Wendy Sarti, *Oakton Community College*

Linda Scherr, *Mercer County Community College*

Eloy Zarate, *Pasadena City College*

Symposium and Digiposium Attendees

Gisela Ables, *Houston Community College*

Sal Anselmo, *Delgado Community College*

Mario A. J. Bennekin, *Georgia Perimeter College*

C. J. Bibus, *Wharton County Junior College*

Olwyn M. Blouet, *Virginia State University*

Michael Botson, *Houston Community College*

Cathy Briggs, *Northwest Vista College*

Brad Cartwright, *University of Texas–El Paso*

Roger Chan, *Washington State University*

June Cheatham, *Richland College*

Keith Chu, *Bergen Community College*

Karl Clark, *Coastal Bend College*

Bernard Comeau, *Tacoma Community College*

Kevin Davis, *North Central Texas College*

Michael Downs, *Tarrant County College*

Tim Draper, *Waubonsee Community College*

Laura Dunn, *Brevard Community College*

Arthur Durand, *Metropolitan Community College*

Amy Forss, *Metropolitan Community College*

Jim Good, *Lone Star College*

R. David Goodman, *Pratt Institute*

Wendy Gunderson, *Colin County Community College*

Debbie Hargis, *Odessa College*

Jim Harper, *North Carolina Central University*

Matt Hinckley, *Eastfield College*

John Hosler, *Morgan State University*

James Jones, *Prairie View A&M University*

Philip Kaplan, *University of North Florida*

Carol A. Keller, *San Antonio College*

Greg Kelm, *Dallas Baptist University*

Michael Kinney, *Calhoun Community College*

Jennifer Lang, *Delgado Community College*

Meredith R. Martin, *Collin College*

Thomas Massey, *Cape Fear Community College*

Linda McCabe, *North Lake College*

Sandy Norman, *Florida Atlantic University*

Michelle Novak, *Houston Community College*

Jessica Patton, *Tarrant County College*

Robert Risko, *Trinity Valley Community College*

Gary Ritter, *Central Piedmont Community College*

Esther Robinson, *Lone Star College*

Geri Ryder, *Ocean County College*

Horacio Salinas, *Laredo Community College*

Linda Scherr, *Mercer County Community College*

Jeffrey Smith, *Lindenwood University*

Rachel Standish, *San Joaquin Delta College*

Connie B. Thomason, *Louisiana Delta Community College*

Roger Ward, *Colin County Community College*

Don Whatley, *Blinn College*

David White, *McHenry County College*

Geoffrey Willbanks, *Tyler Junior College*

Scott M. Williams, *Weatherford College*

Carlton Wilson, *North Carolina Central University*

Chad Wooley, *Tarrant County College*

Focus Group Participants

Simon Baatz, *John Jay College*

Manu Bhagavan, *Hunter College*

David Dzurec, *University of Scranton*

Mark Jones, *Central Connecticut State University*

Stephen Katz, *Philadelphia University*

Jessica Kovler, *John Jay College*

David Lansing, *Ocean County College*

Benjamin Lapp, *Montclair State University*

Julian Madison, *Southern Connecticut State University*

David Marshall, *Suffolk Community College*

George Monahan, *Suffolk Community College*

Tracy Musacchio, *John Jay College*

Mikal Nash, *Essex County College*

Veena Oldenburg, *Baruch College*

Edward Paulino, *John Jay College*

Craig Pilant, *County College of Morris*

Susan Schmidt Horning, *Saint John's University*

Donna Scimeca, *College of Staten Island*

Matthew Vaz, *City College of New York*

Christian Warren, *Brooklyn College*

The Unfinished Nation makes history relevant to students through a series of engaging features:

CONSIDER THE SOURCE FEATURES

In every chapter, Consider the Source features guide students through careful analysis of historical documents and prompt them to closely examine the ideas expressed, as well as the historical circumstances. Among the classic sources included are John Muir's essay on the value of wild places, a radio address from FDR, Fannie Lou Hamer's testimony on the struggle for voting rights, and Ronald Reagan's inaugural speech on the role of government. Concise introductions provide context, and concluding questions prompt students to understand, analyze, and evaluate each source.

DEBATING THE PAST FEATURES

Debating the Past essays introduce students to the contested quality of much of the American past, and they provide a sense of the evolving nature of historical scholarship. From examining changing conceptions of the West and the frontier, the legacy of the New Deal, and the significance of Watergate, these essays familiarize students with the interpretive character of historical understanding.

AMERICA IN THE WORLD FEATURES

AMERICA IN THE WORLD

IMPERIALISM

America in the World essays focus on specific parallels between American history and those of other nations and demonstrate the importance of the many global influences on the American story. Topics such as global migrations, the global depression of the 1920s, and the turmoil of 1968 provide concrete examples of the connections between the history of the United States and the history of other nations.

PATTERNS OF POPULAR CULTURE FEATURES

PATTERNS OF POPULAR CULTURE

THE MINSTREL SHOW

Patterns of Popular Culture essays bring fads, crazes, hangouts, hobbies, and entertainment into the story of American history, encouraging students to expand their definition of what constitutes history and gain a new understanding of what popular culture reveals about a society.

WHAT'S NEW TO *THE UNFINISHED NATION,* EIGHTH EDITION

We have revised the narrative and the features throughout this eighth edition for clarity and currency. On a chapter-by-chapter basis, major changes include:

Chapter 15, Reconstruction and the New South

- New Patterns of Popular Culture: "The Minstrel Show."
- Expanded discussion of plans to give land to freed slaves as a first step in Reconstruction.
- New editorial cartoon on critics' view of Reconstruction.

Chapter 16, The Conquest of the Far West

- New painting, *American Progress,* illustrating the American idea of the frontier.
- New painting of a Tejanos-run ranch in Texas.
- New painting of Little Bighorn, from a Native American artist's perspective.

Chapter 17, Industrial Supremacy

- New photograph of child laborers and information about Lewis Hine's investigative photography.

Chapter 19, From Crisis to Empire

- New Patterns of Popular Culture: "Yellow Journalism."
- Revised discussion of the factors motivating American imperialism, introducing the concept of "jingoes" and the connection to ideas about the nation's masculinity.
- Revised discussion of the range of American reactions to the Cuban rebellion and the Teller Amendment.
- New discussion of race in the context of the Philippine War.
- New editorial cartoon of Chester Arthur feeling heat of competing interest groups.
- New pro-imperialism editorial cartoon.
- New photograph and information about Populist orator Mary Lease.

Chapter 20, The Progressives

- New Consider the Source: "John Muir on the Value of Wild Places."
- New photograph and information about the suffrage pageant in Washington, D.C., on the eve of Wilson's inauguration.

Chapter 21, America and the Great War

- New Consider the Source: "Race, Gender, and World War I Posters."

- Revised discussion of European alliances and the start of World War I.
- New "Intervention" subsection with a revised discussion of what compelled Wilson to enter the war.
- Revised discussion of the American contribution to the Allies' victory.
- New descriptions of American troops and how Progressive ideas were employed in basic training.
- Reorganized and revised discussion of war casualty numbers.

Chapter 22, The New Era

- New Consider the Source: "America's Early Telephone Network."

Chapter 23, The Great Depression

- Revised discussion of Depression-era literature, and addition of Richard Wright's *Native Son.*

Chapter 24, The New Deal

- New editorial cartoon of an optimistic FDR steering the nation toward recovery.
- New photo and information on the Memorial Day Massacre.
- New photo and information on Eleanor Roosevelt's role in the New Deal.

Chapter 25, The Global Crisis, 1921–1941

- New Patterns of Popular Culture: "Orson Welles and the 'War of the Worlds.'"

Chapter 26, America in a World at War

- New Consider the Source: "The Face of the Enemy."
- New scholarship on wartime culture, including two new sections: "Home-Front Life and Culture" and "Love, Family, and Sexuality in Wartime."
- Updated war casualty numbers.

Chapter 27, The Cold War

- New information on the Rosenberg case.
- Additional information on Ellen Schrecker's *Many Are the Crimes.*
- Revised discussion of Cold War attitudes.

Chapter 28, The Affluent Society

- New Patterns of Popular Culture: "On the Road."
- Expanded explanations of postwar economic growth as well as the decline in farm prices.

Chapter 29, retitled The Turbulent Sixties

- New Patterns of Popular Culture: "The Folk-Music Revival."
- New Consider the Source: "Fannie Lou Hamer on the Struggle for Voting Rights."
- Expanded discussions of the 1964 Civil Rights Act; Malcolm X; the Cuban missile crisis.

Chapter 30, The Crisis of Authority

- Additional information on the extent of the draft and resistance; the history of gay rights; the consequences of the 1973 OPEC embargo.
- New photos showing the Native American occupation of Alcatraz; Robert Kennedy with César Chávez; Nixon in China.
- New graph on the gender income gap.

Chapter 31, From the "Age of Limits" to the Age of Reagan

- New Consider the Source: "Ronald Reagan on the Role of Government."

Chapter 32, The Age of Globalization

- Thoroughly updated and reorganized chapter and illustrations to reflect events up to press time. In addition to content changes in every section:
- New Patterns of Popular Culture: "Rap."
- New Consider the Source: "Same-Sex Marriage, 2015."
- New graph on immigration trends from 1850 to the present.
- Updated discussion of environmental catastrophes, including Deepwater Horizon.

15 RECONSTRUCTION AND THE NEW SOUTH

THE PROBLEMS OF PEACEMAKING

RADICAL RECONSTRUCTION

THE SOUTH IN RECONSTRUCTION

THE GRANT ADMINISTRATION

THE ABANDONMENT OF RECONSTRUCTION

THE NEW SOUTH

LOOKING AHEAD

1. What were the various plans for Reconstruction proposed by Lincoln, Johnson, and Congress? Which plan was enacted and why?
2. What were the effects of Reconstruction for blacks and whites in the South?
3. What were the political achievements and failures of the Grant administration?

FEW PERIODS IN THE HISTORY of the United States have produced as much bitterness or created such enduring controversy as the era of Reconstruction—the years following the Civil War during which Americans attempted to reunite their shattered nation. To many white Southerners, Reconstruction was a vicious and destructive experience—a period when vindictive Northerners inflicted humiliation and revenge on the defeated South. Northern defenders of Reconstruction, in contrast, argued that their policies were the only way to prevent unrepentant Confederates from restoring Southern society to what it had been before the war.

To most African Americans at the time, and to many people of all races since, Reconstruction was notable for other reasons. Neither a vicious tyranny, as white Southerners charged, nor a thoroughgoing reform, as many Northerners hoped, it was instead an important first step in the effort to secure civil rights and economic power for the former slaves. Reconstruction did not provide African Americans with either the enduring legal protections or the material resources to ensure anything like real equality. Most black men and women still had little formal power to overturn their oppression for many decades.

And yet for all its shortcomings, Reconstruction did help African Americans create new institutions and some important legal precedents that helped them survive and that ultimately, well into the twentieth century, became the basis of later efforts to win greater freedom and equality.

1863

Lincoln announces
Reconstruction plan

1864

Lincoln vetoes
Wade-Davis Bill

1865

Confederacy surrenders

Lincoln assassinated;
Johnson is president

Freedmen's Bureau

Joint Committee on
Reconstruction

1866

Republicans gain in
congressional elections

1867

Congressional
Reconstruction begins

1868

Johnson impeached and
acquitted

14th Amendment
ratified

Grant elected president

1869

Congress passes 15th
Amendment

1872

Grant reelected

1873

Panic and depression

1877

Hayes wins disputed
election

Compromise of 1877
ends Reconstruction

1883

Supreme Court
upholds segregation

1890s

Jim Crow laws in South

1895

Atlanta Compromise

1896

Plessy v. Ferguson

THE PROBLEMS OF PEACEMAKING

Although it was clear in 1865 that the war was almost over, the path to actual peace was not yet clear. Abraham Lincoln could not negotiate a treaty with the defeated government; he continued to insist that the Confederacy had no legal right to exist. Yet neither could he simply readmit the Southern states into the Union.

THE AFTERMATH OF WAR AND EMANCIPATION

The South after the Civil War was a desolate place. Towns had been gutted, plantations burned, fields neglected, bridges and railroads destroyed. Many white Southerners—stripped of their slaves through emancipation and of capital invested in now worthless Confederate bonds and currency—had almost no personal property. More than 258,000 Confederate soldiers had died in the war, and thousands more returned home wounded or sick. Some white Southerners faced starvation and homelessness.

If the physical conditions were bad for Southern whites, they were far worse for Southern blacks—the three and a half million men and women now emerging from bondage. As soon as the war ended, hundreds of thousands of them left their plantations in search of a new life in freedom. But most had nowhere to go, and few had any possessions except the clothes they wore.

COMPETING NOTIONS OF FREEDOM

For blacks and whites alike, Reconstruction became a struggle to define the meaning of the war and, above all, the meaning of freedom. But the former slaves and the defeated whites had very different conceptions of what freedom meant.

For most white Southerners, freedom meant the ability to control their own

RICHMOND, 1865 By the time Union forces captured Richmond in early 1865, the Confederate capital had been under siege for months and much of the city lay in ruins, as this photograph reveals. On April 4, President Lincoln, accompanied by his son Tad, visited Richmond. As he walked through the streets of the shattered city, hundreds of former slaves emerged from the rubble to watch him pass. "No triumphal march of a conqueror could have equalled in moral sublimity the humble manner in which he entered Richmond," a black soldier serving with the Union army wrote. "It was a great deliverer among the delivered. No wonder tears came to his eyes." (The Library of Congress)

destinies without interference from the North or the federal government. And in the immediate aftermath of the war, this meant trying to restore their society to its antebellum form. When these white Southerners fought for what they considered freedom, they were fighting above all to preserve local and regional autonomy and white supremacy.

For African Americans, freedom meant independence from white control. In the wake of advancing Union armies, millions of black Southerners sought to secure that freedom with economic opportunity, which for many meant landownership. An African American man in Charleston told a Northern reporter, "Gib us our own land and we take care ourselves."[1] For a short while during the war, Union generals and federal officials cooperated, awarding confiscated land to the former slaves who had worked it.

Early in the war, when Union forces occupied the Sea Islands of South Carolina, the islands' white property owners fled to the mainland, and 10,000 former slaves seized control of the vacated land. Later in the war, a delegation of freed slaves approached General William Sherman for outright possession of the land. Sherman acceded. He issued Special Field Order No. 15 on January 16, 1865, granting former Confederate land in *Special Field Order No. 15* coastal Georgia and South Carolina (including the Sea Islands) to the region's ex-slaves. Within five months, nearly 400,000 acres had been distributed to 40,000 freed people.

In the war's immediate aftermath, the federal government attempted to help ex-slaves forge independent lives by establishing the Bureau of Refugees, Freedmen, and Abandoned Lands, which Congress authorized in March 1865. The Freedmen's Bureau, *Freedmen's Bureau*

1 Foner, *Reconstruction*, p. 104.

as it became known, helped feed, clothe, educate, and provide medical care for ex-slaves. It also settled land disputes and set labor contracts between freedmen and white property owners. Headed by General Oliver O. Howard, the Freedman's Bureau operated on a shoestring budget with fewer than 1,000 agents, some of whom were corrupt, yet it still emerged as a key federal institution shaping black and white life in the South after the war.

The Freedmen's Bureau, for a while at least, also supported the redistribution of land, overseeing the allocation of 850,000 acres of confiscated land to former slaves. General Howard instructed his agents in his famous "Circular 13" to lease the land in 40-acre plots to former slaves with the intention of eventually selling it to them. A small number of freedmen *Land Redistribution* purchased land outright under the Southern Homestead Act of 1866 that Howard had championed; the act made 46 million acres of public land for sale in 160-acre plots in Alabama, Arkansas, Florida, Louisiana, and Mississippi. (The law was repealed before many ex-slaves were able to take advantage of it.) Some of Howard's officials and other army personnel secured mules for freed people as well, fulfilling the common wisdom that 40 acres and a mule were the building block of any stable household. The Bureau also settled land disputes and set labor contracts between freedmen and white property owners.

PLANS FOR RECONSTRUCTION

Political control of Reconstruction rested in the hands of the Republicans, who were deeply divided in their approach to the issue. Conservatives within the party insisted that the South accept abolition, but they proposed few other conditions for the readmission of *The Radical Republicans* the seceded states. The Radicals, led by Representative Thaddeus Stevens of Pennsylvania and Senator Charles Sumner of Massachusetts, urged a much harsher course, including disenfranchising large numbers of Southern whites, protecting black civil rights, confiscating the property of wealthy whites who had aided the Confederacy, and distributing the land among the freedmen. Republican Moderates rejected the most stringent demands of the Radicals but supported extracting at least some concessions from the South on black rights.

President Lincoln favored a lenient Reconstruction policy, believing that Southern Unionists (mostly former Whigs) could become the nucleus of new, loyal state governments in the South. Lincoln announced his Reconstruction plan in December 1863, more than a year before the war ended. It offered a general amnesty to white Southerners—other than high officials of the Confederacy—who would pledge an oath of loyalty to the government and accept the abolition of slavery. When 10 percent of a state's total number of voters in 1860 took the oath, those loyal voters could set up a state government. Lincoln also proposed extending suffrage to African Americans who were educated, owned property, or had served in the Union army. Three Southern states—Louisiana, Arkansas, and Tennessee, all under Union occupation—reestablished loyal governments under the Lincoln formula in 1864.

Outraged at the mildness of Lincoln's program, the Radical Republicans refused to admit representatives from the three "reconstructed" states to Congress. In July 1864, they *Wade-Davis Bill* pushed their own plan through Congress: the Wade-Davis Bill. Named for Senator Benjamin Wade of Ohio and Representative Henry Davis of Maryland, it called for the president to appoint a provisional governor for each conquered state. When a majority of the white males of a state pledged their allegiance to the Union, the governor could summon a state constitutional convention, whose delegates were to be elected by voters who had never borne arms against the United States. The new state constitutions would be required to abolish slavery, disenfranchise Confederate civil and military leaders, and repudiate debts accumulated by the state governments during the war. Only then would Congress readmit the states to the Union. Like the president's proposal, the Wade-Davis Bill left the question of political rights for blacks up to the states.

Congress passed the bill a few days before it adjourned in 1864, but Lincoln disposed of it with a pocket veto that enraged the Radical leaders, forcing the pragmatic Lincoln to recognize he would have to accept at least some of the Radical demands. The debate between Congress and Lincoln over the proper course of Reconstruction and its purpose and objectives was one that scholars would soon pick up. Indeed, beginning in the latter stages of Reconstruction, historians struggled to make sense of its meaning to America. They continue to do so today. (See "Debating the Past: Reconstruction.")

THE DEATH OF LINCOLN

What plan the president might have produced no one can say. On the night of April 14, 1865, Lincoln and his wife attended a play at Ford's Theater in   *Lincoln's Assassination* Washington. John Wilkes Booth, an actor fervently committed to the Southern cause, entered the presidential box from the rear and shot Lincoln in the head. Early the next morning, the president died.

ABRAHAM LINCOLN   This haunting photograph of Abraham Lincoln, showing clearly the weariness and aging that four years as a war president had created, was taken in Washington only four days before his assassination in 1865. (The Library of Congress)

Johnson revealed his plan for Reconstruction—or "Restoration," as he preferred to call *Johnson's Reconstruction Plan* it—soon after he took office and implemented it during the summer of 1865 when Congress was in recess. Like Lincoln, he offered some form of amnesty to Southerners who would take an oath of allegiance. In most other respects, however, his plan resembled the Wade-Davis Bill. The new president appointed a provisional governor in each state and charged him with inviting qualified voters to elect delegates to a constitutional convention. To win readmission to Congress, a state had to revoke its ordinance of secession, abolish slavery and ratify the Thirteenth Amendment, and repudiate Confederate and state war debts.

By the end of 1865, all the seceded states had formed new governments—some under Lincoln's plan, others under Johnson's—and awaited congressional approval of them. But Radicals in Congress vowed not to recognize the Johnson governments, for, by now, Northern opinion had become more hostile toward the South. Delegates to the Southern conventions had angered much of the North by their apparent reluctance to abolish slavery and by their refusal to grant suffrage to any blacks. Southern states had also seemed to defy the North by electing prominent Confederate leaders to represent them in Congress, such as Alexander Stephens of Georgia, the former vice president of the Confederacy.

RADICAL RECONSTRUCTION

Reconstruction under Johnson's plan—often known as "presidential Reconstruction"—continued only until Congress reconvened in December 1865. At that point, Congress refused to seat the representatives of the "restored" states and created a new Joint Committee on Reconstruction to frame a policy of its own. The period of "congressional," or "Radical," Reconstruction had begun.

THE BLACK CODES

Meanwhile, events in the South were driving Northern opinion in still more radical directions. Throughout the South in 1865 and early 1866, state legislatures enacted sets of laws known as the **Black Codes,** which authorized local officials to apprehend unemployed blacks, fine them for vagrancy, and hire them out to private employers to satisfy the fines. Some codes forbade blacks to own or lease farms or to take any jobs other than as plantation workers or domestic servants, jobs formerly held by slaves. Former slaves raised an alarm immediately and called for swift intervention by the federal troops and for new legislation to protect them. (See "Consider the Source: Southern Blacks Ask for Help.")

Congress first responded to the Black Codes by passing an act extending the life and expanding the powers of the Freedmen's Bureau so that it could nullify work agreements forced on freedmen under the Black Codes. Then, in April 1866, Congress passed the first *Johnson's Vetoes* Civil Rights Act, which declared blacks to be fully fledged citizens of the United States and gave the federal government power to intervene in state affairs to protect the rights of citizens. Johnson vetoed both bills, but Congress overrode him on each of them.

THE FOURTEENTH AMENDMENT

In April 1866, the Joint Committee on Reconstruction proposed the Fourteenth Amendment to the Constitution. Congress approved it in early summer and sent it to the states for ratification. It offered the first constitutional definition of American citizenship. Everyone born in the United States, and everyone naturalized, was automatically a citizen and entitled to all the "privileges and immunities" guaranteed by *Citizenship for African Americans* the Constitution, including equal protection of the laws by both the state and national governments. There could be no other requirements for citizenship. The amendment also imposed penalties on states that denied suffrage to any adult male inhabitants. (Supporters of woman suffrage were dismayed by the addition of the word *male* to the amendment.) Finally, it prohibited former members of Congress or other former federal officials who had aided the Confederacy from holding any state or federal office unless two-thirds of Congress voted to pardon them.

Congressional Radicals offered to readmit to the Union any state whose legislature ratified the Fourteenth Amendment. Only Tennessee did so. All the other former Confederate states, along with Delaware and Kentucky, refused, leaving the amendment temporarily without the necessary approval of three-fourths of the states.

But by now, the Radicals were growing more confident and determined. Bloody race riots in New Orleans and other Southern cities were among the events that strengthened their hand. In the 1866 congressional elections, Johnson actively campaigned for Conservative candidates, but he did his own cause more harm than good with his intemperate speeches. The voters returned an overwhelming majority of Republicans, most of them Radicals, to Congress. In the Senate, there were now 42 Republicans to 11 Democrats; in the House, 143 Republicans to 49 Democrats. Congressional Republicans were now strong enough to enact a plan of their own even over the president's objections.

The Congressional Plan

The Radicals passed three Reconstruction bills early in 1867 and overrode Johnson's vetoes of all of them. These bills finally established, nearly two years after the end of the war, a coherent plan for Reconstruction.

Under the congressional plan, Tennessee, which had ratified the Fourteenth Amendment, was promptly readmitted. But Congress rejected the Lincoln–Johnson governments of the other ten Confederate states and, instead, combined those states into five military districts. A military commander governed each district and had orders to register qualified voters (defined as all adult black males and those white males who had not participated in the rebellion). Once registered, voters would elect conventions to prepare new state constitutions, which had to include provisions for black suffrage. Once voters ratified the new constitutions, they could elect state governments. Congress had to approve a state's constitution, and the state legislature had to ratify the Fourteenth Amendment. Once enough states ratified the amendment to make it part of the Constitution, the former Confederate states could be restored to the Union.

By 1868, seven of the ten remaining former Confederate states had fulfilled these conditions and were readmitted to the Union. Conservative whites held up the return of Virginia and Texas until 1869 and Mississippi until 1870. By then, Congress had added an additional requirement for readmission—ratification of another *Fifteenth Amendment* constitutional amendment, the Fifteenth, which forbade the states and the federal government to deny suffrage to any citizen on account of "race, color, or previous condition of servitude." Ratification by the states was completed in 1870.

To stop Johnson from interfering with their plans, the congressional Radicals passed two remarkable laws of dubious constitutionality in 1867. One, the Tenure of Office Act,

CONSIDER THE SOURCE

SOUTHERN BLACKS ASK FOR HELP, 1865

Even before the war ended, groups of former slaves gathered in conventions to petition the federal government for steady support for black civil rights, including the use of the U.S. Army to subdue unrepentant ex-Confederates. In this example, African Americans from Virginia publicly air their hopes and fears only three months after Appomattox.

We, the undersigned members of a Convention of colored citizens of the State of Virginia, would respectfully represent that, although we have been held as slaves, and denied all recognition as a constituent of your nationality for almost the entire period of the duration of your Government, and that by your *permission* we have been denied either home or country, and deprived of the dearest rights of human nature; yet when you and our immediate oppressors met in deadly conflict upon the field of battle—the one to destroy and the other to save your Government and nationality, we, with scarce an exception, in our inmost souls espoused your cause, and watched, and prayed, and waited, and labored for your success. . . .

When the contest waxed long, and the result hung doubtfully, you appealed to us for help, and how well we answered is written in the rosters of the two hundred thousand colored troops now enrolled in your Service; and as to our undying devotion to your cause, let the uniform acclamation of escaped prisoners, "whenever we saw a black face we felt sure of a friend," answer.

Well, the war is over, the rebellion is "put down," and we are *declared* free! Four fifths of our enemies are paroled or amnestied, and the other fifth are being pardoned, and the President has, in his efforts at the reconstruction of the civil government of the

States, late in rebellion, left us entirely at the mercy of these subjugated but unconverted rebels, in *everything* save the privilege of bringing us, our wives and little ones, to the auction block. *We know* these men—know them well—and we assure you that, with the majority of them, loyalty is only "lip deep," and that their professions of loyalty are used as a cover to the cherished design of getting restored to their former relations with the Federal Government, and then, by all sorts of "unfriendly legislation," to render the freedom you have given us more Intolerable than the slavery they intended for us.

We warn you in time that our only safety is in keeping them under Governors of the *military persuasion* until you have so amended the Federal Constitution that it will prohibit the States from making any distinction between citizens on account of race or color. In one word, the only salvation for us besides the power of the Government, is in the *possession of the ballot.* Give us this, and we will protect ourselves. . . . But, 'tis said we are ignorant. Admit it. Yet who denies we *know* a traitor from a loyal man, a gentleman from a rowdy, a friend from an enemy? . . . All we ask is an *equal chance* with the white *traitors* varnished and japanned with the oath of amnesty. Can you deny us this and still keep faith with us? . . .

We are "sheep in the midst of wolves," and nothing but the military arm of the Government prevents us and all the *truly* loyal white men from being driven from the land of our birth. Do not then, we beseech you, give to one of these "wayward sisters" the rights they abandoned and forfeited when they rebelled until you have secured our rights by the aforementioned amendment to the Constitution.

UNDERSTAND, ANALYZE, & EVALUATE

1. What did the authors of this petition emphasize in the first two paragraphs, and why did they feel this was important?

2. Why did the authors emphasize that they had been "declared" free? What dangers to their prospect of freedom did they observe?

3. What federal legal responses did they propose? Can you recognize these suggestions in the constitutional changes that came with Reconstruction?

Source: "Proceedings of the Convention of the Colored People of Virginia, Held in the City of Alexandria, August 2, 3, 4, 5, 1865" (Alexandria, Va., 1865), in W. L. Fleming (ed.), *Documentary History of Reconstruction* (Cleveland, Ohio, 1906), vol. 1, pp. 195–196; located in "Southern Blacks Ask for Help (1865)," in Thomas A. Bailey and David M. Kennedy (eds.), *The American Spirit*, vol. 1, 7th ed. (Lexington, Mass., 1991), pp. 466–467.

forbade the president to remove civil officials, including members of his own cabinet, without the consent of the Senate. The principal purpose of the law was to protect the job of Secretary of War Edwin M. Stanton, who was cooperating with the Radicals. The other law, the Command of the Army Act, prohibited the president from issuing military orders except through the commanding general of the army (General Grant), who could not be relieved or assigned elsewhere without the consent of the Senate.

Limits on Presidential Powers

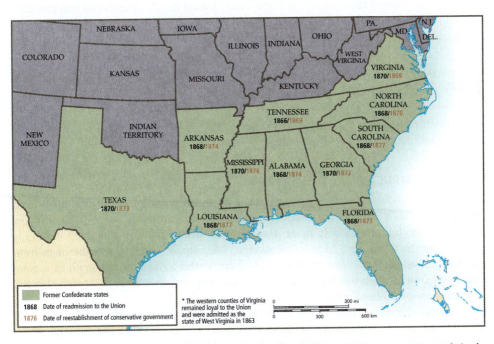

RECONSTRUCTION, 1866–1877 This map provides the date when each former Confederate state was readmitted by presidential order to the Union, as well as the date when a traditional white conservative elite took office as a majority in each state—an event white Southerners liked to call "redemption." • *What had to happen for a state to be readmitted to the Union? What had to happen before a state could experience "redemption"?*

The congressional Radicals also took action to stop the Supreme Court from interfering with their plans. In 1866, the Court had declared in the case of *Ex parte Milligan* that military tribunals were unconstitutional in places where civil courts were functioning. Radicals in Congress immediately proposed several bills that would require two-thirds of the justices to support any decision overruling a law of Congress, would deny the Court jurisdiction in Reconstruction cases, would reduce its membership to three, and would even abolish it. The justices apparently took notice. Over the next two years, the Court refused to accept jurisdiction in any cases involving Reconstruction.

THE IMPEACHMENT OF ANDREW JOHNSON

President Johnson had long since ceased to be a serious obstacle to the passage of Radical legislation, but he was still the official charged with administering the Reconstruction programs. As such, the Radicals believed, he remained a major impediment to their plans. Early in 1867, they began looking for a way to remove him from office, and a search for grounds for **impeachment** began. Republicans found it, they believed, when Johnson dismissed Secretary of War Stanton despite Congress's refusal to agree. Elated Radicals in the House quickly impeached the president and sent the case to the Senate for trial.

The trial lasted throughout April and May 1868. The Radicals put heavy pressure on all the Republican senators, but the Moderates vacillated. On the first three charges to *Johnson Acquitted* come to a vote, seven Republicans joined the Democrats and independents to support acquittal. The vote was 35 to 19, one vote short of the constitutionally required two-thirds majority. After that, the Radicals dropped the impeachment effort.

THE SOUTH IN RECONSTRUCTION

Reconstruction may not have immediately accomplished what its framers intended, but it did have profound effects on the South.

THE RECONSTRUCTION GOVERNMENTS

Critics labeled Southern white Republicans with the derogatory terms *scalawags* and *"Scalawags" and "Carpetbaggers"* carpetbaggers. Many of the scalawags were former Whigs who had never felt comfortable in the Democratic Party or farmers who lived in remote areas where there had been little or no slavery. The carpetbaggers were white men from the North, most of them veterans of the Union army who looked on the South as a more promising frontier than the West and had settled there at war's end as hopeful planters, businessmen, or professionals.

The most numerous Republicans in the South were the black freedmen, few of whom had any previous experience in politics. They tried to build institutions through which they could learn to exercise their power. In several states, African American voters held their own conventions to chart their future course. Their newfound religious independence from white churches also helped give them unity and self-confidence.

African Americans played significant roles in the politics of the Reconstruction South. They served as delegates to the constitutional conventions and held public

THE "STRONG" GOVERNMENT 1869—1877.

CRITICS' VIEW OF RECONSTRUCTION This Reconstruction-era cartoon expresses the view held by Southern white Democrats that they were being oppressed by Northern Republicans. President Grant (whose hat bears Abraham Lincoln's initials) rides in comfort in a giant carpetbag, guarded by bayonet-wielding soldiers, as the South staggers under the burden in chains. Evidence of military occupation is in the scarred background. (© Granger, NYC—All Rights Reserved.)

offices of practically every kind. Between 1869 and 1901, twenty blacks served in the United States House of Representatives, two in the Senate. Blacks served, too, in state legislatures and in various other state offices. Southern whites *Freedmen in Politics* complained loudly about "Negro rule," but in the South as a whole, the percentage of black officeholders was small—and always far lower than the percentage of blacks in the population.

The record of the Reconstruction governments is mixed. Critics at the time and later denounced them for corruption and financial extravagance, and there is some truth to both charges. But the corruption in the South, real as it was, was hardly unique to the Reconstruction governments. Corruption had been rife in some antebellum and Confederate governments, and it was at least as rampant in the Northern states. And the large state expenditures of the Reconstruction years were huge only in comparison with the meager budgets of the antebellum era. They represented an effort to provide the South with desperately needed services that antebellum governments had never provided.

EDUCATION

Perhaps the most important accomplishment of the Reconstruction governments was a dramatic improvement in Southern education. Much of the impetus for educational reform in the South came from outside groups—the Freedmen's Bureau, Northern private philanthropic organizations, the many Northern white women who traveled to the South to teach in freedmen's schools—and from African Americans themselves. Over the opposition of many Southern whites, who feared that education would give blacks "false notions of equality," these reformers established a large network of schools for former slaves—4,000 schools by 1870, staffed by 9,000 teachers (half of them black), teaching 200,000 students. In the 1870s, Reconstruction governments began to build a comprehensive public school system. By 1876, more than half of all white children and about 40 percent of all black children were attending schools in the South (although almost all such schools were racially segregated). Several black "academies," offering more advanced education, also began operating. Gradually, these academies grew into an important network of black colleges and universities.

LANDOWNERSHIP AND TENANCY

The most ambitious goal of the Freedmen's Bureau, and of some Republican Radicals *Land Reform Thwarted* in Congress, was to reform landownership in the South. The effort failed. By June 1865, the bureau had settled nearly 10,000 black families on their own land—most of it drawn from abandoned plantations in areas occupied by the Union armies. By the end of that year, however, Southern plantation owners were returning and demanding the restoration of their property. President Johnson supported their demands, and the government eventually returned most of the confiscated lands to their original white owners.

Even so, the distribution of landownership in the South changed considerably in the postwar years. Among whites, there was a striking decline in landownership, from 80 percent before the war to 67 percent by the end of Reconstruction. Some whites lost their land because of unpaid debt or increased taxes; others left the marginal lands they had owned to move to more fertile areas, where they rented. Among blacks, during the same period, the proportion of landowners rose from virtually none to more than 20 percent.

Still, most blacks, and a growing minority of whites, did not own their own land during Reconstruction and, instead, worked for others in one form or another. Many black agricultural laborers—perhaps 25 percent of the total—simply worked for wages. Most, however, became tenants of white landowners—that is, they worked their own plots of land and paid their landlords either a fixed rent or a share of their crops (hence the term **sharecropping**). As tenants and sharecroppers, blacks enjoyed at least a physical independence from their landlords and had the sense of working their own land, even if in most cases they could never hope to buy it. But tenantry also benefited landlords in some ways, relieving them of the cost of purchasing slaves and of responsibility for the physical well-being of their workers.

INCOMES AND CREDIT

In some respects, the postwar years were a period of remarkable economic progress for African Americans in the South. The per capita income of blacks (when the material benefits of slavery are counted as income) rose 46 percent between 1857 and 1879, while the per capita income of whites declined 35 percent. African Americans were also able to work less than they had under slavery. Women and children were less likely to labor in the fields, and adult men tended to work shorter days. In all, the black labor force worked about one-third fewer hours during Reconstruction than it had been compelled to work under slavery—a reduction that brought the working schedule of blacks roughly into accord with that of white farm laborers.

But other developments limited these gains. While the black share of profits was increasing, the total profits of Southern agriculture were declining. Nor did the income redistribution of the postwar years lift many blacks out of poverty. *Persistent Black Poverty* Black per capita income rose from about one-quarter of white per capita income (which was itself low) to about one-half in the first few years after the war. After this initial increase, however, it rose hardly at all.

Blacks and poor whites alike found themselves virtually imprisoned by the **crop-lien system.** Few of the traditional institutions of credit in the South—the *The Crop-Lien System* "factors" and banks—returned after the war. In their stead emerged a new credit system, centered in large part on local country stores—some of them owned by planters, others owned by independent merchants. Blacks and whites, landowners and tenants—all depended on these stores. And since farmers did not have the same steady cash flow as other workers, customers usually had to rely on credit from these merchants to purchase what they needed. Most local stores had no competition and thus could set interest rates as high as 50 or 60 percent. Farmers had to give the merchants a lien (or claim) on their crops as collateral for the loans (thus the term *crop-lien system*). Farmers who suffered a few bad years in a row, as many did, could become trapped in a cycle of debt from which they could never escape.

As a result of this burdensome credit system, some blacks who had acquired land during the early years of Reconstruction, and many poor whites who had owned land for years, gradually lost it as they fell into debt. Southern farmers also became almost wholly dependent on cash crops—and most of all on cotton—because only such marketable commodities seemed to offer any possibility of escape from debt. The relentless planting of cotton ultimately contributed to soil exhaustion, which undermined the Southern agricultural economy over time.

THE AFRICAN AMERICAN FAMILY IN FREEDOM

A major reason for the rapid departure of so many blacks from plantations was the desire to find lost relatives and reunite families. Thousands of African Americans *Families Reunited* wandered through the South looking for husbands, wives, children, or other relatives from whom they had been separated. Former slaves rushed to have their marriages, previously without legal standing, sanctified by church and law.

Within the black family, the definition of male and female roles quickly came to resemble that within white families. Many women and children at first ceased working in the fields. Such work, they believed, was a badge of slavery. Instead, many women restricted themselves largely to domestic tasks. Still, economic necessity often compelled black women to engage in income-producing activities: working as domestic servants, taking in laundry, even helping their husbands in the fields. By the end of Reconstruction, half of all black women over the age of sixteen were working for wages.

LABORING OVER LAUNDRY One of the most common occupations of women recently emancipated from slavery was taking in laundry from white families who no longer had enslaved servants. This photograph illustrates how arduous a task laundry was. (The Library of Congress)

THE GRANT ADMINISTRATION

American voters in 1868 yearned for a strong, stable figure to guide them through the troubled years of Reconstruction. They turned trustingly to General Ulysses S. Grant.

THE SOLDIER PRESIDENT

Grant could have had the nomination of either party in 1868. But believing that Republican Reconstruction policies were more popular in the North, he accepted the Republican nomination. The Democrats nominated former governor Horatio Seymour of New York. *Grant Elected* The campaign was a bitter one, and Grant's triumph was surprisingly narrow. Without the 500,000 new black Republican voters in the South, he would have had a minority of the popular vote.

Grant entered the White House with no political experience, and his performance was clumsy and ineffectual from the start. Except for Hamilton Fish, whom Grant appointed secretary of state, most members of the cabinet were ill equipped for their tasks. Grant relied chiefly on established party leaders—the group most ardently devoted to patronage, and his administration used the spoils system even more blatantly than most of its predecessors. Grant also alienated the many Northerners who were growing disillusioned with the Radical Reconstruction policies, which the president continued to support. Some

Republicans suspected, correctly, that there was also corruption in the Grant administration itself.

By the end of Grant's first term, therefore, members of a substantial faction of the party—who referred to themselves as Liberal Republicans—had come to oppose what they called "Grantism." In 1872, hoping to prevent Grant's reelection, they bolted the party and nominated their own presidential candidate: Horace Greeley,   *Opposition from Liberal Republicans* veteran editor and publisher of the *New York Tribune*. The Democrats, somewhat reluctantly, named Greeley their candidate as well, hoping that the alliance with the Liberals would enable them to defeat Grant. But the effort was in vain. Grant won a substantial victory, polling 286 electoral votes to Greeley's 66.

THE GRANT SCANDALS

During the 1872 campaign, the first of a series of political scandals came to light that would plague Grant and the Republicans for the next four years. It involved the French-owned Crédit Mobilier construction company, which had helped build the Union Pacific Railroad. The heads of Crédit Mobilier had used their positions as Union Pacific stockholders to steer large fraudulent contracts to their construction company, thus bilking the Union Pacific of millions. To prevent investigations, the directors had given Crédit Mobilier stock to key members of Congress. But in 1872, Congress conducted an investigation, which revealed that some highly placed Republicans—including Schuyler Colfax, now Grant's vice president—had accepted stock.

One dreary episode followed another in Grant's second term. Benjamin H. Bristow, Grant's third Treasury secretary, discovered that some of his officials and a group of distillers operating as a "whiskey ring" were cheating the government   *The "Whiskey Ring"* out of taxes by filing false reports. Then a House investigation revealed that William W. Belknap, secretary of war, had accepted bribes to retain an Indian-post trader in office (the so-called Indian ring). Other, lesser scandals also added to the growing impression that "Grantism" had brought rampant corruption to government.

THE GREENBACK QUESTION

Compounding Grant's problems was a financial crisis, known as the Panic of 1873. It began with the failure of a leading investment banking firm, Jay Cooke   *The Panic of 1873* and Company, which had invested too heavily in postwar railroad building. There had been panics before—in 1819, 1837, and 1857—but this was the worst one yet.

Debtors now pressured the government to redeem federal war bonds with greenbacks, which would increase the amount of money in circulation. But Grant and most Republicans wanted a "sound" currency—based solidly on gold reserves—which would favor the interests of banks and other creditors. There was approximately $356 million in paper currency issued during the Civil War that was still in circulation. In 1873, the Treasury issued more in response to the panic. But in 1875, Republican leaders in Congress passed the Specie Resumption Act, which provided that after January 1, 1879, greenback dollars would be redeemed by the government and replaced with new certificates, firmly pegged to the price of gold. The law satisfied creditors, who had worried that debts would be repaid in paper currency of uncertain value. But "resumption" made things more difficult for debtors, because the gold-based money supply could not easily expand.

In 1875, the "Greenbackers" formed their own political organization: the National
National Greenback Party   Greenback Party. It failed to gain widespread support, but the
money issue was to remain one of the most controversial and enduring issues in
late-nineteenth-century American politics.

REPUBLICAN DIPLOMACY

The Johnson and Grant administrations achieved their greatest successes in foreign affairs
as a result of the work not of the presidents themselves but of two outstanding secretaries
of state: William H. Seward and Hamilton Fish.

An ardent expansionist, Seward acted with as much daring as the demands of
Reconstruction politics and the Republican hatred of President Johnson would permit.
He accepted a Russian offer to buy Alaska for $7.2 million, despite criticism from
Seward's Purchase of Alaska   many who derided the purchase as "Seward's Folly." In 1867,
Seward also engineered the American annexation of the tiny Midway Islands, west
of Hawaii.

Hamilton Fish's first major challenge was resolving the long-standing controversy over
the American claims that Britain had violated neutrality laws during the Civil War by
permitting English shipyards to build ships (among them the *Alabama*) for the Confederacy.
American demands that England pay for the damage these vessels had caused became
Hamilton Fish and the "Alabama Claims"   known as the "*Alabama* claims." In 1871, after a number of failed efforts, Fish forged an agreement, the Treaty of Washington, which provided
for international arbitration.

THE ABANDONMENT OF RECONSTRUCTION

As the North grew increasingly preoccupied with its own political and economic problems,
interest in Reconstruction began to wane. By the time Grant left office, Democrats had
taken back seven of the governments of the former Confederate states. For three other
states—South Carolina, Louisiana, and Florida—the end of Reconstruction had to wait
for the withdrawal of the last federal troops in 1877.

THE SOUTHERN STATES "REDEEMED"

In the states where whites constituted a majority—the states of the upper South—
overthrowing Republican control was relatively simple. By 1872, all but a handful of
Southern whites had regained suffrage. Now a clear majority, they needed only to organize
and elect their candidates.

In other states, where blacks were a majority or where the populations of the two races
were almost equal, whites used outright intimidation and violence to undermine the
Ku Klux Klan   Reconstruction regimes. Secret societies—the Ku Klux Klan, the Knights of
the White Camellia, and others—used terrorism to frighten or physically bar blacks from
voting. Paramilitary organizations—the Red Shirts and White Leagues—armed themselves
to "police" elections and worked to force all white males to join the Democratic Party.
Strongest of all, however, was the simple weapon of economic pressure. Some planters
refused to rent land to Republican blacks; storekeepers refused to extend them credit;
employers refused to give them work.

The Republican Congress responded to this wave of repression with the Enforcement Acts of 1870 and 1871 (better known as the Ku Klux Klan Acts), which *Enforcement Acts* prohibited states from discriminating against voters on the basis of race and gave the national government the authority to prosecute crimes by individuals under federal law. The laws also authorized the president to use federal troops to protect civil rights—a provision President Grant used in 1871 in nine counties of South Carolina. The Enforcement Acts, although seldom enforced, discouraged Klan violence, which declined by 1872.

WANING NORTHERN COMMITMENT

But this Northern commitment to civil rights did not last long. After the adoption of the Fifteenth Amendment in 1870, some reformers convinced themselves that their long campaign on behalf of black people was now over, that with the *Flagging Interest in Civil Rights* vote blacks ought to be able to take care of themselves. Former Radical leaders such as Charles Sumner and Horace Greeley now began calling themselves Liberals, cooperating with the Democrats, and even denouncing what they viewed as black-and-carpetbag misgovernment. Within the South itself, many white Republicans now moved into the Democratic Party as voters threw out Republican politicians whom they blamed for the financial crisis.

The Panic of 1873 further undermined support for Reconstruction. In the congressional elections of 1874, the Democrats won control of the House of Representatives for the first time since 1861. To appeal to southern white voters, Grant even reduced the use of military force to prop up the Republican regimes in the South.

THE COMPROMISE OF 1877

Grant had hoped to run for another term in 1876, but most Republican leaders—shaken by recent Democratic successes and scandals by the White House—resisted. Instead, they settled on Rutherford B. Hayes, three-time governor of Ohio and a champion of civil service reform. The Democrats united behind Samuel J. Tilden, the reform governor of New York, who had been instrumental in overthrowing the corrupt Tweed Ring of New York City's Tammany Hall.

Although the campaign was a bitter one, few differences of principle distinguished the candidates from one another. The election produced an apparent Democratic victory. Tilden carried the South and several large Northern states, and his popular *Disputed Election* margin over Hayes was nearly 300,000 votes. But disputed returns from Louisiana, South Carolina, Florida, and Oregon, whose electoral votes totaled 20, threw the election in doubt. Hayes could still win if he managed to receive all 20 disputed votes.

The Constitution had established no method to determine the validity of disputed returns. The decision clearly lay with Congress, but it was not obvious with which house or through what method. (The Senate was Republican, and the House was *Victory for Hayes* Democratic.) Members of each party naturally supported a solution that would yield them the victory. Finally, late in January 1877, Congress tried to break the deadlock by creating a special electoral commission composed of five senators, five representatives, and five justices of the Supreme Court. The congressional delegation consisted of five Republicans and five Democrats. The Court delegation would include two Republicans, two Democrats, and the only independent, Justice David Davis. But when the Illinois legislature elected Davis to the United States Senate, the justice resigned from the

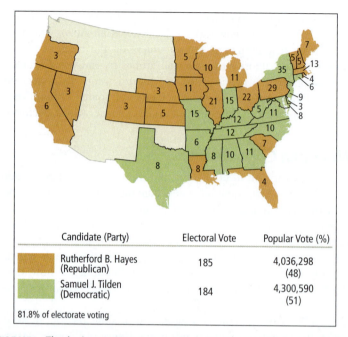

Candidate (Party)	Electoral Vote	Popular Vote (%)
Rutherford B. Hayes (Republican)	185	4,036,298 (48)
Samuel J. Tilden (Democratic)	184	4,300,590 (51)

81.8% of electorate voting

THE ELECTION OF 1876   The election of 1876 was one of the most controversial in American history. As in the elections of 1824, 1888, and 2000, the winner of the popular vote—Samuel J. Tilden—was not the winner of the electoral vote, which he lost by one vote. The final decision as to who would be president was not made until the day before the official inauguration in March. • *How did the Republicans turn this apparent defeat into a victory?*

commission. His seat went instead to a Republican justice. The commission voted along straight party lines, 8 to 7, awarding every disputed vote to Hayes.

Behind this seemingly partisan victory, however, lay a series of elaborate and sneaky compromises among leaders of both parties. When a Democratic filibuster threatened to derail the electoral commission's report, Republican Senate leaders met secretly with Southern Democratic leaders. As the price of their cooperation, the Southern Democrats exacted several pledges from the Republicans: the appointment of at least one Southerner to the Hayes cabinet, control of federal patronage in their areas, generous internal improvements, federal aid for the Texas and Pacific Railroad, and most important, withdrawal of the remaining federal troops from the South.

In his inaugural address, Hayes announced that the South's most pressing need was the restoration of "wise, honest, and peaceful local self-government," and he soon withdrew the troops and let white Democrats take over the remaining Southern state governments. *Federal Troops Withdrawn*   That produced charges that he was paying off the South for acquiescing in his election—charges that were not wholly untrue. The outcome of the election created such bitterness that not even Hayes's promise to serve only one term could mollify his critics.

The president and his party hoped to build up a "new Republican" organization in the South committed to modest support for black rights. Although many white Southern leaders sympathized with Republican economic policies, resentment of Reconstruction was so deep that supporting the party became politically impossible. The "solid" Democratic South, which would survive until the mid-twentieth century, was taking shape.

THE LEGACY OF RECONSTRUCTION

Reconstruction made important contributions to the efforts of former slaves to achieve dignity and equality in American life. There was a significant redistribution of income and a more limited but not unimportant redistribution of landownership. Perhaps most important, African Americans themselves managed to carve out a society and culture of their own and to create or strengthen their own institutions.

Reconstruction was not as disastrous for Southern white elites as most believed at the time. Within little more than a decade after a devastating war, the white South had regained control of its own institutions and, to a great extent, restored its traditional ruling class to power. The federal government imposed no drastic economic reforms on the region and, indeed, few lasting political changes of any kind other than the abolition of slavery.

Reconstruction was notable, finally, for its limitations. For in those years, the United States failed in its first serious effort to resolve its oldest and deepest social problem—the problem of race. The experience so disillusioned white Americans that it would be nearly a century before they would try again to combat racial injustice.

Given the odds confronting them, however, African Americans had reason for considerable pride in the gains they were able to make during Reconstruction. And future generations would be grateful for the two great charters of freedom—the Fourteenth and Fifteenth Amendments to the Constitution—which, although widely ignored at the time, would one day serve as the basis for a "Second Reconstruction" that would renew the drive to bring freedom to all Americans.

THE NEW SOUTH

The Compromise of 1877 was supposed to be the first step toward developing a stable, permanent Republican Party in the South. In that respect at least, it failed. In the years following the end of Reconstruction, white southerners established the Democratic Party as the only viable political organization for the region's whites. Even so, the South did change in some of the ways the framers of the Compromise had hoped.

THE "REDEEMERS"

Many white southerners rejoiced at the restoration of what they liked to call "home rule." But in reality, political power in the region was soon more restricted than at   *"Home Rule"* any time since the Civil War. Once again, most of the South fell under the control of a powerful, conservative oligarchy, whose members were known variously as the "Redeemers" or the "Bourbons."

In some places, this post-Reconstruction ruling class was much the same as the ruling class of the antebellum period. In Alabama, for example, the old planter elite retained much of its former power. In other areas, however, the Redeemers constituted a genuinely new ruling class of merchants, industrialists, railroad developers, and financiers. Some of them were former planters, some of them northern immigrants, some of them ambitious, upwardly mobile white southerners from the region's lower social tiers. They combined a defense of "home rule" and social conservatism with a commitment to economic development.

The various Bourbon governments of the New South behaved in many respects quite similarly. Virtually all the new Democratic regimes lowered taxes, reduced spending, and drastically diminished state services. One state after another eliminated or reduced its support for public school systems.

INDUSTRIALIZATION AND THE NEW SOUTH

Many white southern leaders in the post-Reconstruction era hoped to see their region develop a vigorous industrial economy, a "New South." Henry Grady, editor of the *Atlanta Constitution,* and other New South advocates seldom challenged white supremacy, but they did promote the virtues of thrift, industry, and progress—qualities that prewar southerners had often denounced in northern society.

Southern industry did expand dramatically in the years after Reconstruction, most visibly in textile manufacturing. In the past, southern planters had usually shipped their cotton to manufacturers in the North or in Europe. Now textile factories appeared in the *Textiles, Tobacco, and Iron* South itself—many of them drawn to the region from New England by the abundance of water power, the ready supply of cheap labor, the low taxes, and the accommodating conservative governments. The tobacco processing industry similarly established an important foothold in the region. In the lower South, and particularly in Birmingham, Alabama, the iron (and, later, steel) industry grew rapidly.

Railroad development also increased substantially in the post-Reconstruction years. Between 1880 and 1890, trackage in the South more than doubled. And in 1886, the South changed the gauge (width) of its trackage to correspond with the standards of the North. *Substantial Railroad Development* No longer would it be necessary for cargoes heading into the South to be transferred from one train to another at the borders of the region.

Yet southern industry developed within strict limits, and its effects on the region were never even remotely comparable to the effects of industrialization on the North. The southern share of national manufacturing doubled in the last twenty years of the century, but it was still only 10 percent of the total. Similarly, the region's per capita income increased 21 percent in the same period, but average income in the South was still only 40 percent of that in the North; in 1860 it had been more than 60 percent. And even in those industries where development had been most rapid—textiles, iron, railroads—much of the capital had come from, and many of the profits thus flowed to, the North.

The growth of southern industry required the region to recruit a substantial industrial workforce for the first time. From the beginning, a high percentage of the factory workers were women. Heavy male casualties in the Civil War had helped create a large population of unmarried women who desperately needed employment. Hours were long (often as much as twelve hours a day), and wages were far below the northern equivalent; indeed, one of the greatest attractions of the South to industrialists was that employers were able *Worker Exploitation* to pay workers there as little as one-half of what northern workers received. Life in most mill towns was rigidly controlled by the owners and managers of the factories, who rigorously suppressed attempts at protest or union organization. Company stores sold goods to workers at inflated prices and issued credit at exorbitant rates (much as country stores did in agrarian areas), and mill owners ensured that no competing merchants were able to establish themselves in the community.

Some industries, such as textiles, offered virtually no opportunities to African American workers. Others—tobacco, iron, and lumber, for example—did provide some employment

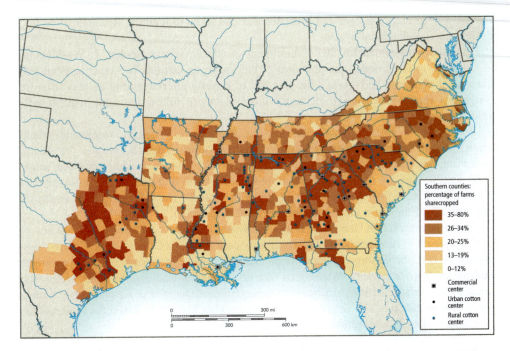

THE CROP-LIEN SYSTEM IN 1880   In the years after the Civil War, more and more southern farmers—white and black—became tenants or sharecroppers on land owned by others. This map shows the percentage of farms that were within the so-called crop-lien system, the system by which people worked their lands for someone else, who had a claim (or "lien") on a part of the farmers' crops. Note the high density of sharecropping and tenant farming in the most fertile areas of the Deep South, the same areas where slaveholding had been most dominant before the Civil War. • *How did the crop-lien system contribute to the shift in southern agriculture toward one-crop farming?*

for blacks. Some mill towns, therefore, were places where the black and white cultures came into close contact, increasing the determination of white leaders to take additional measures to protect white supremacy.

TENANTS AND SHARECROPPERS

The most important economic problem in the post-Reconstruction South was the impoverished state of agriculture. The 1870s and 1880s saw an acceleration of *Growth of Tenantry* the process that had begun in the immediate postwar years: the imposition of systems of tenantry and debt peonage on much of the region; the reliance on a few cash crops rather than on a diversified agricultural system; and increasing absentee ownership of valuable farmlands. During Reconstruction, perhaps a third or more of the farmers in the South were tenants; by 1900, the figure had increased to 70 percent.

AFRICAN AMERICANS AND THE NEW SOUTH

The "New South creed" was not the property of whites alone. Many African Americans were attracted to the vision of progress and self-improvement as well. Some former slaves (and, as the decades passed, their offspring) succeeded in elevating themselves into the middle class, acquired property, established small businesses, or entered professions. Believing strongly that education was vital to the future of their people, they expanded the network of black colleges and institutes that had taken root during Reconstruction into an important educational system.

The chief spokesman for this commitment to education was Booker T. Washington, *Booker T. Washington* founder and president of the Tuskegee Institute in Alabama. Born into slavery, Washington had worked his way out of poverty after acquiring an education (at Virginia's Hampton Institute). He urged other blacks to follow the same road to self-improvement.

Washington's message was both cautious and hopeful. African Americans should attend school, learn skills, and establish a solid footing in agriculture and the trades. Industrial, not classical, education should be their goal. Blacks should, moreover, refine their speech, improve their dress, and adopt habits of thrift and personal cleanliness; they should, in short, adopt the standards of the white middle class. Only thus, Washington claimed, could they win the respect of the white population.

In a famous speech in Georgia in 1895, Washington outlined a controversial philosophy of *Atlanta Compromise* race relations that became widely known as the Atlanta Compromise. Blacks, he said, should forgo agitation for political rights and concentrate on self-improvement and preparation for equality. Washington offered a powerful challenge to those whites who wanted to discourage African Americans from acquiring an education or winning any economic gains. But his message was also intended to assure whites that blacks would not challenge the emerging system of segregation.

THE BIRTH OF JIM CROW

Few white southerners had ever accepted the idea of racial equality. That the former slaves acquired any legal and political rights at all after emancipation was in large part the result of their own efforts and crucial federal support. That outside support all but vanished after 1877, when federal troops withdrew and the Supreme Court stripped the Fourteenth and Fifteenth Amendments of much of their significance. In the so-called civil rights cases of 1883, the Court ruled that the Fourteenth Amendment prohibited state governments from discriminating against people because of race but did not restrict private organizations or individuals from doing so. Popular culture reflected these frightening political developments. The rise of minstrel shows—slapstick dramatic representations of black culture—typically embodied racist ideas. "Corked-up" whites (or whites using heavy makeup to appear black) grossly caricatured African American culture as silly, unintelligent, sensual, and immoral. Late in the 1800s, however, blacks founded their own minstrel shows in part to modify these stereotypes, though with only modest success. (See "Patterns of Popular Culture: The Minstrel Show.")

Eventually, the Court also validated state legislation that institutionalized the separa-*Plessy v. Ferguson* tion of the races. In *Plessy v. Ferguson* (1896), a case involving a Louisiana law that required segregated seating on railroads, the Court held that separate accommodations did not deprive blacks of equal rights if the accommodations were equal. In *Cumming v. County Board of Education* (1899), the Court ruled that communities could establish schools for whites only, even if there were no comparable schools for blacks.

Even before these dubious decisions, white southerners were working to separate the races to the greatest extent possible, and were particularly determined to strip African Americans of the right to vote. In some states, disenfranchisement had begun almost as soon as Reconstruction ended. But in other areas, black voting continued for some time after Reconstruction—largely because conservative whites believed they could control the black electorate and use it to beat back the attempts of poor white farmers to take control of the Democratic Party.

In the 1890s, however, franchise restrictions became much more rigid. During those years, some small white farmers began to demand complete black   *Black Disenfranchisement* disenfranchisement—because they objected to the black vote being used against them by the Bourbons. At the same time, many members of the conservative elite began to doubt their ability to influence black voters and fear that poor whites might unite politically with poor blacks to challenge them.

In devising laws to disenfranchise black males, the southern states had to find ways to evade the Fifteenth Amendment, which prohibited states from denying anyone the right to vote because of race. Two devices emerged before 1900 to accomplish this goal: the poll tax, or some form of property qualification (few blacks were prosperous enough to meet such requirements); and the "literacy" or "understanding" test, which required voters to demonstrate an ability to read and to interpret the Constitution. Even those African Americans who could read had a hard time passing the difficult test white officials gave them, which often required them to interpret an arcane part of the Constitution to the satisfaction of a white elected official. (The laws affected poor white voters as well as blacks.) By the late 1890s, the black vote had decreased by 62 percent, the white vote by 26 percent.

Laws restricting the franchise and segregating schools were only part of a network of state and local statutes—collectively known as the Jim Crow laws—that by   *Jim Crow Laws* the first years of the twentieth century had institutionalized an elaborate system of racial hierarchy reaching into almost every area of southern life. Blacks and whites could not ride together in the same railroad cars, sit in the same waiting rooms, use the same washrooms, eat in the same restaurants, or sit in the same theaters. Blacks had no access to many public parks, beaches, or picnic areas; they could not be patients in many hospitals. Much of the new legal structure did no more than confirm what had already been widespread social practice in the South. But the Jim Crow laws also stripped blacks of many of the modest social, economic, and political gains they had made in the late nineteenth century.

More than legal efforts were involved in this process. The 1890s witnessed a dramatic increase in white violence against blacks, which, along with the Jim Crow laws, served to inhibit black agitation for equal rights. The worst such violence—lynching of blacks by white mobs—reached appalling levels. In the nation as a whole in the 1890s, there was an average of 187 lynchings each year, more than 80 percent of them in the South. The vast majority of victims were black. Those who participated in lynchings often saw their actions as a legitimate form of law enforcement, and some victims of lynchings had in fact committed crimes. But lynchings were also a means by which whites controlled the black population through terror and intimidation.

The rise of lynchings shocked the conscience of many white Americans in a way that other forms of racial injustice did not. In 1892, Ida B. Wells, a committed   *Ida B. Wells* black journalist, published a series of impassioned articles after the lynching of three of her hometown friends in Memphis, Tennessee; her articles launched what became an international antilynching movement. The movement gradually attracted substantial support from whites in both the North and the South (particularly from white women). Its goal was a federal antilynching law, which would allow the national government to do what state and local governments in the South were generally unwilling to do: punish those responsible for lynchings.

THE MINSTREL SHOW

The minstrel show was one of the most popular forms of entertainment in America in the second half of the nineteenth century. It was also a testament to the high awareness of race (and the high level of racism) in American society both before and after the Civil War. Minstrel performers were mostly white, usually disguised as black. But African American performers also formed their own minstrel shows and transformed them into vehicles for training black entertainers and developing new forms of music and dance.

Before and during the Civil War, when minstrel shows consisted almost entirely of white performers, performers blackened their faces with cork and presented grotesque stereotypes of the slave culture of the American South. Among the most popular of the stumbling, ridiculously ignorant characters invented for these shows were such figures as "Zip Coon" and "Jim Crow" (whose name later resurfaced as a label for late-nineteenth-century segregation laws). A typical minstrel show presented a group of seventeen or more men seated in a semicircle facing the audience. The man in the center ran the show, played the straight man for the jokes of others, and led the music—lively

MINSTRELSY AT HIGH TIDE   The Primrose & West minstrel troupe—a lavish and expensive entertainment that drew large crowds in the 1800s—was one of many companies to offer this brand of entertainment to eager audiences all over the country. Although minstrelsy began with white musicians performing in blackface, the popularity of real African American minstrels encouraged the impresarios of the troupe to include groups of white and black performers alike. (The Library of Congress)

dances and sentimental ballads played on banjos, castanets, and other instruments and sung by soloists or the entire group.

After the Civil War, white minstrels began to expand their repertoire. Drawing from the famous and successful freak shows of P. T. Barnum and other entertainment entrepreneurs, some began to include Siamese twins, bearded ladies, and even a supposedly 8-foot 2-inch "Chinese giant" in their shows. They also incorporated sex, both by including women in some shows and, even more popularly, by recruiting female impersonators. One of the most successful minstrel performers of the 1870s was Francis Leon, who delighted crowds with his female portrayal of a flamboyant "prima donna."

One reason white minstrels began to move in these new directions was that they were now facing competition from black performers, who could provide more-authentic versions of black music, dance, and humor. They usually brought more talent to the task than white performers. The Georgia Minstrels, organized in 1865, was one of the first all-black minstrel troupes, and it had great success in attracting white audiences in the Northeast for several years. By the 1870s, touring African American minstrel groups were numerous. The black minstrels used many of the conventions of the white shows. There were dances, music, comic routines, and sentimental recitations. Some black performers even chalked their faces to make themselves look as dark as the white blackface performers with whom they were competing. Black minstrels sometimes denounced slavery (at least indirectly) and did not often speak demeaningly of the capacities of their race. But they could not entirely escape caricaturing African American life as they struggled to meet the expectations of their white audiences.

The black minstrel shows had few openly political aims. They did help develop some important forms of African American entertainment and transform them into a part of the national culture. Black minstrels introduced new forms of dance, derived from the informal traditions of slavery and black community life. They showed the "buck and wing," the "stop time," and the "Virginia essence," which established the foundations for the tap and jazz dancing of the early twentieth century. They also improvised musically and began experimenting with forms that over time contributed to the growth of ragtime, jazz, and rhythm and blues.

Eventually, black minstrelsy—like its white counterpart—evolved into other forms of theater, including the beginnings of serious black drama. At Ambrose Park in Brooklyn in the 1890s, for example, the celebrated black comedian Sam Lucas (a veteran of the minstrel circuit) starred in the play *Darkest America,* which one black newspaper later described as a "delineation of Negro life, carrying the race through all their historical phases from the plantation, into reconstruction days and finally painting our people as they are today, cultured and accomplished in the social graces, [holding] the mirror faithfully up to nature."

But interest in the minstrel show did not die altogether. In 1927, Hollywood released *The Jazz Singer,* the first feature film with sound. It was about the career of a white minstrel performer, and its star was one of the most popular singers of the twentieth century: Al Jolson, whose career had begun on the blackface minstrel circuit years before. ●

UNDERSTAND, ANALYZE, & EVALUATE

1. How did minstrel shows performed by white minstrels reinforce prevailing attitudes toward African Americans?
2. Minstrel shows performed by black minstrels often conformed to existing stereotypes of African Americans. Why?
3. Can you think of any popular entertainments today that carry remnants of the minstrel shows of the nineteenth century?

A LYNCH MOB, 1893 A large, almost festive crowd gathers to watch the lynching of a black man accused of the murder of a three-year-old white girl. Lynchings remained frequent in the South until as late as the 1930s, but they reached their peak in the 1890s and the first years of the twentieth century. Lynchings such as this one—publicized well in advance and attracting whole families who traveled great distances to see them—were relatively infrequent. Most lynchings were the work of smaller groups, operating with less visibility. (The Library of Congress)

But the substantial southern white opposition to lynchings stood as an exception to the general white support for suppression of African Americans. Indeed, just as in the antebellum period, the shared commitment to white supremacy helped dilute class animosities between poorer whites and the Bourbon oligarchies. Economic issues tended to play a secondary role to race in southern politics, distracting people from the glaring social inequalities that afflicted blacks and whites alike.

CONCLUSION

Reconstruction was a profoundly important moment in American history. Despite the bitter political battles in Washington and throughout the South, culminating in the unsuccessful effort to remove President Andrew Johnson from office, the most important result of the effort to reunite the nation after its long and bloody war was a reshaping of the lives of ordinary people in all regions.

In the North, Reconstruction solidified the power of the Republican Party. The rapid expansion of the northern economy accelerated, drawing more and more of its residents into a burgeoning commercial world.

In the South, Reconstruction fundamentally rearranged the relationship between white and black citizens. African Americans initially participated actively and effectively in southern politics. After a few years of widespread black voting and significant black officeholding, however, the forces of white supremacy shoved most African Americans to the margins of the southern political world, where they would mostly remain until the 1960s.

In other ways, however, the lives of southern blacks changed dramatically and permanently. Overwhelmingly, they left the plantations. Some sought work in towns and cities. Others left the region altogether. But the great majority began farming on small farms of their own—not as landowners, except in rare cases, but as tenants and sharecroppers on land owned by whites. The result was a form of economic bondage, driven by debt, only scarcely less oppressive than the legal bondage of slavery. Within this system, however, African Americans managed to carve out a much larger sphere of social and cultural activity than they had ever been able to create under slavery. Black churches proliferated in great numbers. African American schools and printing presses emerged in some communities, and black colleges began to operate in the region. Some former slaves owned businesses and flourished.

Strenuous efforts by "New South" advocates to advance industry and commerce in the region produced impressive results in a few areas. But the South on the whole remained what it had always been: a largely rural society with a sharply defined class structure. It also maintained a deep commitment among its white citizens to the subordination of African Americans—a commitment solidified in the 1890s and the early twentieth century when white southerners erected an elaborate legal system of segregation (the Jim Crow laws). Tragically, the promise of the great Reconstruction amendments to the Constitution—the Fourteenth and Fifteenth—remained largely unfulfilled in the South as the century drew to its close.

KEY TERMS/PEOPLE/PLACES/EVENTS

Andrew Johnson 357
Atlanta Compromise 374
Black Codes 358
Booker T. Washington 374
carpetbagger 362
Compromise of 1877 369
crop-lien system 365
Enforcement Acts 369
Fourteenth Amendment 358

Fifteenth Amendment 359
Freedmen's Bureau 353
Ida B. Wells 375
impeachment 362
Jim Crow laws 375
Ku Klux Klan 368
New South 372
Panic of 1873 367
Plessy v. Ferguson 374

Radical Republicans 354
Reconstruction 354
Redeemers 371
scalawag 362
sharecropping 364
Thaddeus Stevens 354
Wade-Davis Bill 354
William H. Seward 368

RECALL AND REFLECT

1. What were the principal questions facing the nation at the end of the Civil War?
2. What were the achievements of Reconstruction? Where did it fail and why?
3. What new problems arose in the South as the North's interest in Reconstruction waned?
4. What was the Compromise of 1877, and how did it affect Reconstruction?
5. How did the New South differ from the South before the Civil War?

16 THE CONQUEST OF THE FAR WEST

THE SOCIETIES OF THE FAR WEST
THE CHANGING WESTERN ECONOMY
THE ROMANCE OF THE WEST
THE DISPERSAL OF THE TRIBES
THE RISE AND DECLINE OF THE WESTERN FARMER

LOOKING AHEAD

1. What various ethnic and racial groups populated the American West, and how were the cultural characteristics of these groups reflected in the West?
2. How did the arrival and settlement of substantial numbers of Anglo-Americans transform the society and economy of the West?
3. What role did the federal government play in shaping the development of the West?

BY THE MID-1840s, WHITE AMERICAN migrants, along with many others, from the eastern regions of the nation had settled in the West in substantial numbers. Farmers, ranchers, and miners all found opportunity in the western lands. By the end of the Civil War, the West had become legendary in the eastern states. No longer the Great American Desert, it was now widely viewed as the "frontier": an empty land awaiting settlement and civilization; a place of wealth, adventure, opportunity, and untrammeled individualism.

In fact, the real West of the mid-nineteenth century bore little resemblance to its popular image. It was a diverse land, with many different regions, climates, and stores of natural resources. And it was extensively populated. The English-speaking migrants of the late nineteenth century did not find an empty, desolate land. They found Indians, Mexicans, African Americans, French and British Canadians, Asians, and others, some of whose families had been living in the West for generations.

THE SOCIETIES OF THE FAR WEST

The Far West was in fact a composite of many lands. It contained both the most arid regions and some of the wettest and lushest areas of the United States. It contained the flattest plains and the highest mountains. It also contained many peoples.

THE WESTERN TRIBES

The Indian tribes made up the largest and most important western population group before the great white migration. Some were members of eastern tribes who had been forcibly resettled west of the Mississippi. But most were members of indigenous tribes whose roots stretched back generations.

More than 300,000 Indians (among them the Serrano, Chumash, Pomo, Maidu, Yurok, and Chinook) had lived on the Pacific Coast before the arrival of Spanish settlers. They supported themselves through a combination of fishing, foraging, and simple agriculture. The Pueblos of the Southwest had long lived largely as farmers and had established permanent settlements there.

The most widespread Indian groups in the West were the Plains Indians. They were, in fact, made up of many different tribal and language groups. Some lived more or less sedentary lives as farmers, but many subsisted largely through hunting buffalo. Riding small but powerful horses, the tribes moved through the grasslands following the herds, constructing tepees as temporary dwellings. The buffalo, or bison, provided the economic basis for the Plains Indians' way of life. The flesh of the large animal was their principal source of food, and its skin supplied materials for clothing, shoes, tepees, blankets, robes, and utensils. "Buffalo chips"—dried manure—provided fuel; buffalo bones became knives and arrow tips; buffalo tendons formed the strings of bows.

TIME LINE

1862
Homestead Act

1865–1867
Sioux Wars

1869
Transcontinental railroad completed

1873
Barbed wire invented

1874
Black Hills gold rush

1876
Battle of the Little Bighorn

1877
Desert Land Act

1882
Chinese Exclusion Act

1885
Twain's *Huckleberry Finn*

1887
Dawes Act

1889
Oklahoma opened to white settlement

1890
Battle of Wounded Knee

1893
Turner thesis

The Plains warriors proved to be the most formidable foes the white settlers had encountered. But the tribes were usually unable to unite against white aggression. At times, tribal warriors even faced white forces who were being assisted by guides and even fighters from rival tribes. Some tribes, however, were able to overcome their divisions and cooperate effectively. By the mid-nineteenth century, for example, the Sioux, Arapaho, *Plains Warriors' Vulnerabilities* and Cheyenne had forged a powerful alliance that dominated the northern plains. That proved no protection, however, against the greatest danger to the tribes: ecological and economic decline. Indians were highly vulnerable to eastern infectious diseases, such as the smallpox epidemics that decimated the Pawnee in Nebraska in the 1840s. And the tribes were, of course, at a considerable disadvantage in any long-term battle with an economically and industrially advanced people.

HISPANIC NEW MEXICO

For centuries, much of the Far West had been part of the Spanish Empire and, later, the Mexican Republic. When the United States acquired its new lands there in the 1840s, it also acquired many Mexican residents.

In New Mexico, the centers of Spanish-speaking society were farming and trading communities established in the seventeenth century. Descendants of the original Spanish settlers (and more recent migrants from Mexico) engaged primarily in cattle and sheep ranching. When the United States acquired title to New Mexico in the aftermath of the Mexican War, General Stephen Kearny—who had commanded the American troops in the region—tried to establish a territorial government out of the approximately 1,000 Anglo-Americans in the region, ignoring the more than 50,000 Hispanics. There were widespread fears among Hispanics and Indians that the new American rulers would con-fiscate their lands. In 1847, before the new government had established itself, Taos Indians *Taos Indian Rebellion* rebelled, killing the new governor and other Anglo-American officials before being subdued by United States Army forces. New Mexico remained under military rule for three years, until the United States finally organized a territorial government there in 1850. The United States Army finally broke the power of the Navajo, Apache, and other tribes in the region. The defeat of the tribes led to substantial Hispanic migration into other areas of the Southwest and as far north as Colorado.

The Anglo-American presence in the Southwest grew rapidly once the railroads pen-etrated the region in the 1880s and early 1890s. With the railroads came extensive new ranching, farming, and mining. This expansion of economic activity attracted a new wave of Mexican immigrants, who moved across the border in search of work. The English-speaking proprietors of the new enterprises, however, commonly restricted most Mexicans to the lowest-paying and least stable jobs.

HISPANIC CALIFORNIA AND TEXAS

In California, Spanish settlement began in the eighteenth century with a string of Catholic missions along the Pacific Coast. The missionaries and the soldiers who accompanied them gathered most of the coastal Indians into their communities, some forcibly and oth-ers by persuasion. In the 1830s, after the new Mexican government began reducing the power of the church, the mission society largely collapsed. In its place emerged a secular Mexican aristocracy, which controlled a chain of large estates in the fertile lands west of the Sierra mountains. For them, the acquisition of California by the United States was

***TEJANO RANCHERS, 1877*, BY JAMES WALKER** The Spanish term *Tejano* or *Texano* refers to Texans of Mexican descent. The mounted rancher has roped a white mustang; a saddle is ready nearby. Small independent ranches were well established in south Texas before large Anglo-American enterprises moved in. (Private Collection/ © Peter Newark Pictures/Bridgeman Images)

disastrous. So vast were the numbers of English-speaking immigrants that the *californios* (as the Hispanic residents of the region were known) had little power   **Plight of Californios** to resist the onslaught. English-speaking prospectors organized to exclude them, sometimes violently, from the mines during the gold rush. Many *californios* also lost their lands—either through corrupt business deals or through outright seizure.

Increasingly, Mexicans and Mexican Americans became part of the lower end of the state's working class, clustered in *barrios* in Los Angeles or elsewhere or laboring as migrant farmworkers. Even small Hispanic landowners who managed to hang on to their farms found themselves unable to raise livestock, as once-communal grazing lands fell under the control of powerful Anglo ranchers.

A similar pattern occurred in Texas after it joined the United States. Many Mexican landowners lost their land—some as a result of fraud and coercion, others   **Mexicans in Texas** because even the most substantial Mexican ranchers could not compete with the emerging Anglo-American ranching kingdoms. In 1859, angry Mexicans, led by the rancher Juan Cortina, raided the jail in Brownsville and freed all the Mexican prisoners inside. But such resistance had little long-term effect. As in California, Mexicans in southern Texas became an increasingly impoverished working class, relegated largely to unskilled farm or industrial labor.

THE CHINESE MIGRATION

At the same time that ambitious or impoverished Europeans were crossing the Atlantic in search of opportunities in the New World, many Chinese were crossing the Pacific in hopes of better lives. Not all came to the United States. Many Chinese—some   ***"Coolies"*** as "coolies" (indentured servants whose condition was close to slavery)—moved to Hawaii, Australia, Latin America, South Africa, and even the Caribbean.

A CHINESE FAMILY IN SAN FRANCISCO This portrait of Chun Duck Chin and his seven-year-old son Chun Jan Yut was taken in a studio in San Francisco in the 1870s. Both father and son appear to have dressed up for the occasion, in traditional Chinese garb, and the studio—which likely took many such portraits of Chinese families—provided a formal Chinese backdrop. The son is holding what appears to be a chicken, perhaps to impress relatives in China with the family's prosperity. (National Archives and Records Administration)

A few Chinese traveled to the American West even before the gold rush, but after 1848 the flow increased dramatically. By 1880, more than 200,000 Chinese had settled in the United States. Almost all came as free laborers. For a time, white Americans welcomed the Chinese as a conscientious, hardworking people. Very quickly, however, white opinion turned hostile—in part because the Chinese were so industrious and successful that some white Americans began considering them rivals.

In the early 1850s, large numbers of Chinese immigrants joined the hunt for gold. Many of them were well-organized, hardworking prospectors, and for a time some enjoyed considerable success. But opportunities for the Chinese to prosper in the mines were fleeting. In 1852, the California legislature began trying to exclude the Chinese from gold mining by enacting a "foreign miners" tax. Gradually, the effect of the discriminatory laws, the hostility of white miners, and the declining profitability of the surface mines drove most Chinese out of prospecting.

As mining declined as a source of wealth and jobs for the Chinese, railroad employment grew. Beginning in 1865, over 12,000 Chinese found work building the transcontinental railroad, forming 90 percent of the labor force of the Central Pacific. *Railroad Workers* The company preferred them to white laborers because they worked hard, made few demands, and accepted relatively low wages.

Work on the Central Pacific was arduous and often dangerous. In the winter, many Chinese tunneled into snowbanks at night to create warm sleeping areas for themselves, even though such tunnels frequently collapsed, suffocating those inside. In the spring of 1866, 5,000 Chinese railroad workers rebelled against the terrible conditions and went on strike to demand higher wages and a shorter workday. The company isolated them, surrounded them with strikebreakers, and starved them into submission.

In 1869, the transcontinental railroad was completed, and thousands of Chinese lost their jobs. Some moved into agricultural work, usually in menial positions. Increasingly, however, the Chinese flocked to cities. By far the largest single Chinese community was in San Francisco. Much of community life there, and in other "Chinatowns" throughout the West, revolved around organizations, somewhat like *"Chinatowns"* benevolent societies, that filled many of the roles that political machines often served in immigrant communities in eastern cities. Often led by prominent merchants (in San Francisco, the leading merchants—known as the "Six Companies"—often worked together to advance their interests in the city and state), these organizations became, in effect, employment brokers, unions, arbitrators of disputes, defenders against outside persecution, and dispensers of social services. They also organized elaborate festivals and celebrations that were a conspicuous and important part of life in Chinatowns.

Other Chinese organizations were secret societies, known as "tongs." Some of the tongs were violent criminal organizations, involved in the opium trade and prostitution. Few people outside the Chinese communities were aware of their existence, except when rival tongs engaged in violent conflict (or "tong wars").

In San Francisco and other western cities, the Chinese usually occupied the lower rungs of the employment ladder. Many worked as common laborers, servants, and unskilled factory hands. Some established their own small businesses, especially laundries. There were few commercial laundries in China, but they could be started in America with very little capital and required only limited command of English. By the 1890s, Chinese constituted over two-thirds of all the laundry workers in California.

During the earliest Chinese migrations to California, virtually all the relatively small number of women who made the journey did so because they had been sold into prostitution. As late as 1880, nearly half the Chinese women in California were *Chinese Families* prostitutes. Gradually, however, the number of Chinese women increased, and Chinese men in America became more likely to seek companionship in families.

ANTI-CHINESE SENTIMENTS

As Chinese communities grew larger and more visible, anti-Chinese sentiment among white residents intensified. Anti-Chinese activities, some of them bloody, reflected the resentment of many white workers toward Chinese laborers for accepting lower wages. As the political value of attacking the Chinese grew in California, the Democratic Party took up the call. So did the Workingmen's Party of California—founded in 1878 by Denis Kearney, an Irish immigrant—which gained significant power in the state largely because of its hostility to the Chinese. By the mid-1880s, anti-Chinese agitation and violence had spread up and down the Pacific Coast and into other areas of the West.

In 1882, Congress responded to the political pressure and the growing racial violence *Chinese Exclusion Act* by passing the Chinese Exclusion Act, which banned Chinese immigration into the United States for ten years and barred Chinese already in the country from becoming naturalized citizens. Congress renewed the law for another ten years in 1892 and made it permanent in 1902. It had a dramatic effect on the Chinese population, which declined by more than 40 percent in the forty years after the act's passage.

MIGRATION FROM THE EAST

The scale of post–Civil War white migration to the American West dwarfed everything that had preceded it. In previous decades, the settlers had come in thousands. Now they came in millions. Most of the new settlers were from the established Anglo-American societies of the eastern United States, but substantial numbers—over 2 million between 1870 and 1900—were foreign-born immigrants from Europe: Scandinavians, Germans, Irish, Russians, Czechs, and others.

They came to the West for many reasons. Settlers were attracted by gold and silver deposits, by the short-grass pasture for cattle and sheep, and ultimately by the rich sod of the plains and the meadowlands of the mountains. The completion of the great transcontinental railroad line in 1869, and the construction of the many subsidiary lines that spidered out from it, encouraged rapid settlement. So did the land policies of the federal *Homestead Act* government. The Homestead Act of 1862 permitted settlers to buy plots of 160 acres for a small fee if they occupied the land they purchased for five years and improved it.

Supporters of the Homestead Act believed it would create new markets and new outposts of commercial agriculture for the nation's growing economy. But a unit of 160 acres, while ample in much of the East, was too small for the grazing and grain farming of the Great Plains. Eventually, the federal government provided some relief. The Timber Culture Act (1873) permitted homesteaders to receive grants of 160 additional acres if they planted 40 acres of trees on them. The Desert Land Act (1877) allowed claimants to buy 640 acres at $1.25 an acre, provided they irrigated part of their holdings within three years. These and other laws ultimately made it possible for individuals to acquire as much as 1,280 acres of land at little cost.

Political organization followed on the hard heels of settlement. By the mid-1860s, territorial *New Western States* governments were in operation in the new provinces of Nevada, Colorado, Dakota, Arizona, Idaho, Montana, and Wyoming. Statehood rapidly followed. Nevada became a state in 1864, Nebraska in 1867, and Colorado in 1876. In 1889, North and South Dakota, Montana, and Washington won admission; Wyoming and Idaho entered the next year. Congress denied Utah statehood until its Mormon leaders convinced the government in 1896 that polygamy (the practice of men taking several wives) had been abandoned. At the turn of the century, only Arizona, New Mexico, and Oklahoma remained outside the Union.

THE CHANGING WESTERN ECONOMY

The great wave of Anglo-American and European settlement transformed the economy of the Far West and tied the region firmly to the growing industrial economy of the East.

LABOR IN THE WEST

As commercial activity increased, many farmers, ranchers, and miners found it necessary to recruit a paid labor force—not an easy task given the small labor pool compared to that found in established cities. This labor shortage led to higher wages for some workers than were typical in the East. But working conditions were often treacherous, and job security was almost nonexistent. Once a railroad was built, a crop harvested, a herd sent to market, a mine played out, hundreds and even thousands of workers could find themselves suddenly unemployed.

The western working class was highly multiracial. English-speaking whites worked alongside African Americans and immigrants from southern and   *Multiracial Working Class* eastern Europe, as they did in the East. Even more, they worked with Chinese, Filipinos, Mexicans, and Indians. But the workforce was highly stratified along racial lines. In almost every area of the western economy, white workers (whatever their ethnicity) occupied the upper tiers of employment: management and skilled labor. The lower tiers— unskilled work in the mines, on the railroads, or in agriculture—were filled overwhelmingly by nonwhites.

The western economy was, however, no more a single entity than the economy of the East. In the late nineteenth century, the region produced three major industries, each with distinctive history and characteristics: mining, ranching, and commercial farming.

THE ARRIVAL OF THE MINERS

The first economic boom in the Far West was the result of mining. The mining boom began around 1860 and flourished until the 1890s. Then it abruptly declined.

At first it was news of a gold or silver strike that would start a stampede. The California gold rush of 1849 was the first and most famous gold rush. But it was followed by others. Individual prospectors would pan for gold, extracting the first shallow deposits of ore largely by hand, a method known as placer mining. After these surface deposits dwindled, corporations moved in to engage in lode or quartz mining, which dug deeper beneath the surface. Then, as those deposits dwindled, commercial mining declined, and ranchers and farmers moved in and established a more permanent economy.

The first great mineral strikes (other than the California gold rush) occurred just before the Civil War. In 1858, gold was discovered in the Pike's Peak district of what would soon be the territory of Colorado; the following year, 50,000 prospectors stormed in. Denver and other mining camps blossomed into "cities" overnight. Almost as rapidly as they had developed, the booms ended. Later, the discovery of silver near Leadville supplied a new source of mineral wealth.

While the Colorado rush of 1859 was still in progress, news of another strike drew miners to Nevada. Gold had been found in the Washoe district. Even more plentiful and more valuable was the silver found in the great Comstock Lode (first   *Comstock Lode* discovered in 1858 by Henry Comstock) and other Washoe veins. The first prospectors to reach the Washoe fields came from California, and from the beginning, Californians dominated the settlement and development of Nevada. A remote desert without railroad transportation, the territory produced no supplies of its own, and everything had to be shipped from California to Virginia City, Carson City, and other roaring camp towns. When the first placer (or surface) deposits ran out, Californian and eastern capitalists bought the claims of the pioneer prospectors and began to use the more difficult process of quartz mining, which enabled them to retrieve silver from deeper veins. For a few years, these outside owners reaped tremendous profits: from 1860 to 1880, the Nevada lodes yielded bullion worth $306 million. After that, the mines quickly played out.

The next important mineral discoveries came in 1874, when gold was found in the Black Hills of southwestern Dakota Territory. Prospectors swarmed into the remote area. Like the others, the boom flared for a time, until surface resources faded and corporations took over—above all, the enormous Homestake Mining Company—and came to dominate the fields. The Dakotas, like other boom areas of the mineral empire, ultimately developed a largely agricultural economy.

The gold and silver discoveries generated the most popular excitement. But less glamorous natural resources proved more important to western development. The great Anaconda copper mine, launched by William Clark in 1881, marked the beginning of an industry that would remain important to Montana for many decades. In other areas, mining operations had significant success with lead, tin, quartz, and zinc.

Gender Disparity　Men greatly outnumbered women in the mining towns, and younger men in particular had difficulty finding female companions of comparable age. Those women who did gravitate to the new communities often came with their husbands. Single women, or women whose husbands were earning no money, did work for wages at times, as cooks, laundresses, and tavernkeepers. And in the sexually imbalanced mining communities, there was always a ready market for prostitutes.

The thousands of people who flocked to the mining towns in search of quick wealth and failed to find it often remained as wage laborers in corporate mines after the boom period, working in almost uniformly terrible conditions. In the 1870s, one worker in every thirty was disabled in the mines, and one in every eighty was killed. That rate fell later in the nineteenth century, but mining remained one of the most dangerous and arduous working environments in the United States.

THE CATTLE KINGDOM

A second important element of the changing economy of the Far West was cattle ranching. The open range—the vast grasslands of the public domain—provided a huge area on the Great Plains where cattle raisers could graze their herds.

Mexican Roots　The western cattle industry was Mexican and Texan by ancestry. Long before citizens of the United States entered the Southwest, Mexican ranchers had developed the techniques and equipment that the cattlemen and cowboys of the Great Plains later employed: branding, roundups, roping, and the gear of the herders—their lariats, saddles, leather chaps, and spurs. Americans in Texas, with the largest herds of cattle in the country, adopted these methods and carried them to the northernmost ranges of the cattle kingdom. From Texas, too, came the small, muscular horses (broncos and mustangs) that enabled cowboys to control the herds.

At the end of the Civil War, an estimated 5 million cattle roamed the Texas ranges. Eastern markets offered good prices for steers. The challenge facing the cattle industry lay in getting the animals from the range to the railroad centers. Early in 1866, some Texas cattle ranchers began driving their combined herds, up to 260,000 steers, north to Sedalia, Missouri, on the Missouri Pacific Railroad. The caravan suffered heavy losses. But the drive proved that cattle could be driven to distant markets and pastured along the trail. This earliest of the **long drives** established the first, tentative link between the isolated cattle breeders of west Texas and the booming urban markets of the East.

THE CATTLE KINGDOM, ca. 1866–1887 Cattle ranching and cattle drives are among the most romanticized features of the nineteenth-century West. But they were also hardheaded businesses, made possible by the growing eastern market for beef and the availability of reasonably inexpensive transportation—thanks to the dense network of trails and railroads—to take cattle to the urban markets. • *Why was the open range necessary for the great cattle drives, and what eventually ended the cattle trails?*

Market facilities soon grew up at Abilene, Kansas, on the Kansas Pacific Railroad, and for years the town reigned as the railhead of the cattle kingdom. But by the mid-1870s, agricultural development in western Kansas had eaten away at the open-range land. Cattlemen had to develop other trails and other market outlets. As the railroads reached farther west, other locations began to rival Abilene as major centers of stock herding: Dodge City and Wichita in Kansas, Ogallala and Sidney in Nebraska, Cheyenne and Laramie in Wyoming, and Miles City and Glendive in Montana.

There had always been an element of risk and speculation in the open-range cattle business. Rustlers and Indians frequently seized large numbers of animals. But as the settlement of the plains increased, new forms of competition arose. Sheep breeders from

California and Oregon brought their flocks onto the range to compete for grass. Farmers ("nesters") from the East threw fences around their claims, blocking trails and breaking *"Range Wars"* up the open range. A series of "range wars"—between sheepmen and cattlemen, ranchers and farmers—erupted out of the tensions among these competing groups.

Accounts of the lofty profits to be made in the cattle business tempted eastern, English, and Scottish capital to the plains. Increasingly, the structure of the cattle economy became *Decline of the Open-Range Industry* corporate; in one year, twenty corporations with a combined capital of $12 million were chartered in Wyoming. The result of this frenzied, speculative expansion was that the ranges, already shrunk by the railroads and the farmers, became overstocked. There was not enough grass to support the crowding herds or sustain the long drives. Two severe winters, in 1885–1886 and 1886–1887, and a searing summer between them scorched the plains. Streams and grass dried up. Hundreds of thousands of cattle died. Princely ranches and costly investments disappeared in a season.

The open-range industry never recovered, and the long drive finally disappeared for good. Railroads displaced the trail as the route to market for livestock. But some established cattle ranches survived, grew, and prospered, eventually producing more beef than ever.

THE ROMANCE OF THE WEST

The rapidly developing West occupied a special place in the Anglo-American imagination. Many white Americans continued to consider it a romantic place, a wilderness where individuals could experience true freedom. But such thinking was more fiction than fact.

THE WESTERN LANDSCAPE AND THE COWBOY

Part of the attraction of the West was its spectacular natural landscape. Painters of the *"Rocky Mountain School"* new "Rocky Mountain school"—of whom the best known were Albert Bierstadt and Thomas Moran—celebrated the new West in grandiose canvases, some of which toured the eastern and midwestern states and attracted enormous crowds, eager for a vision of the Great West.

Gradually, paintings and photographs inspired a growing wave of tourism among people eager to see the natural wonders of the region. In the 1880s and 1890s, resort hotels began to spring up near some of the region's most spectacular landscapes.

Even more appealing was the rugged, free-spirited lifestyle that many Americans associated with the West. Many nineteenth-century Americans came especially to idealize the figure of the cowboy. Western novels such as Owen Wister's *The Virginian* (1902) roman- *Cowboys in Fiction* ticized the cowboy's supposed freedom from traditional social constraints, his affinity with nature, even his supposed propensity for violence. Wister's character— one of the most enduring in popular American literature—was a semi-educated man whose natural decency, courage, and compassion made him a powerful symbol of the supposed virtues of the "frontier." But *The Virginian* was only the most famous example of a type of literature that soon swept throughout the United States. Novels and stories glorified the West and the lives of cowboys in particular, in boys' magazines, pulp novels, theater, and serious literature.

Among the reasons for the widespread admiration of the cowboy were the remarkably popular Wild West shows that traveled throughout the United States and Europe. Most successful were the shows of Buffalo Bill Cody, a former Pony Express rider, Indian fighter, and hero of popular dime novels for children. Cody's Wild West show, which spawned dozens of imitators, exploited his own fame and romanticized the life of the cowboy through reenactments of Indian battles and displays of horsemanship and riflery (many of them by the famous sharpshooter Annie Oakley). Buffalo Bill and his imitators confirmed the popular image of the West as a place of romance and glamour and helped keep that image alive for later generations.

THE IDEA OF THE FRONTIER

It was not simply the particular character of the new West that resonated in the nation's imagination. It was also that many Americans considered it the last natural frontier. Since the earliest moments of European settlement in America, the image of uncharted territory to the west had always comforted and inspired those who dreamed of starting life anew.

Mark Twain gave voice to this romantic vision of the frontier in a *Mark Twain* series of novels and memoirs. In *The Adventures of Tom Sawyer* (1876) and *The Adventures of Huckleberry Finn* (1885), he produced characters who repudiated the constraints of organized society and attempted to escape into a more natural world. (For Huck Finn, the vehicle of escape was a small raft on the Mississippi.) This yearning for freedom reflected a larger vision of the West as the last refuge from the constraints of civilization.

AMERICAN PROGRESS, 1872 The Brooklyn artist John Gast painted this image of hardy settlers marching toward the frontier for western travel guides. The goddess of progress, holding a schoolbook and telegraph line, leads the way. Native Americans, buffalo, and a bear are pushed off to the margins by the pioneers' approach.
(The Library of Congress)

THE FRONTIER AND THE WEST

The emergence of the history of the American West as an important field of scholarship can be traced to a paper Frederick Jackson Turner delivered to the American Historical Association in 1893: "The Significance of the Frontier in American History." Turner stated his thesis simply. The settlement of the West by white Americans—"the existence of an area of free land, its continuous recession, and the advance of American settlement westward"—was the central story of the nation's history. The process of westward expansion had transformed a desolate and savage land into modern civilization and had continually renewed American ideas of democracy and individualism.

In the first half of the twentieth century, virtually everyone who wrote about the West echoed at least part of Turner's argument. Ray Allen Billington's *Westward Expansion* (1949) was almost wholly consistent with the Turnerian model. In *The Great Plains* (1931) and *The Great Frontier* (1952), Walter Prescott Webb similarly emphasized the bravery and ingenuity of white settlers in the Southwest.

Serious efforts to displace the Turner thesis as the explanation of western American history began after World War II. In *Virgin Land* (1950), Henry Nash Smith examined many of the same heroic images of the West that Turner and his disciples had presented; but he treated those images less as descriptions of reality than as myths. Earl Pomeroy challenged Turner's notion of the West as a place of individualism, innovation, and democratic renewal. "Conservatism, inheritance, and continuity bulked at least as large," he claimed. Howard Lamar, in *Dakota Territory, 1861–1889* (1956) and *The Far Southwest*

(1966), emphasized the highly diverse character of the West.

The western historians who emerged since the late 1970s launched an even more emphatic attack on the Turner thesis and the idea of the "frontier." "New western historians" such as Richard White, Patricia Nelson Limerick, William Cronon, Donald Worster, Peggy Pascoe, and many others challenged the Turnerians on a number of points.

Turner saw the nineteenth-century West as "free land" awaiting the expansion of Anglo-American settlement and American democracy. The more recent western historians reject the concept of an empty "frontier," emphasizing instead the elaborate and highly developed civilizations that already existed in the region. White, English-speaking Americans, they have argued, did not so much "settle" the West as conquer it. And they continued to share the region not only with the Indians and Hispanics who preceded them there, but also with African Americans, Asians, Latin Americans, and others who flowed into the West at the same time they did.

The Turnerian West was a place of heroism, triumph, and above all progress, dominated by the feats of brave white men. The West that the new western historians describe was a less triumphant (and less masculine) place in which bravery and success coexisted with oppression, greed, and failure; in which decaying ghost towns, bleak Indian reservations, impoverished barrios, and ecologically devastated landscapes have been as characteristic of western development as great ranches, rich farms, and prosperous cities.

To Turner and his disciples, the nineteenth-century West was a place where rugged individualism flourished and replenished American democracy. The newer scholars point out that the region was inextricably tied to a national and international capitalist economy. Westerners depended on government-subsidized railroads for access to markets, federal troops for protection from Indians, and (later) government-funded dams and canals for irrigating their fields and sustaining their towns.

And while Turner defined the West as a process—a process of settlement that came to an end with the "closing of the frontier" in the late nineteenth century—the newer historians see the West as a region. Its distinctive history did not end in 1890 but continues into our own time. •

UNDERSTAND, ANALYZE, & EVALUATE

1. How and why did the portrayal of the West by the newer western historians differ from the West that Turner described?
2. Why did the newer western historians challenge Turner's views, and why has their depiction of the west, in turn, provoked such controversy?

One of the most beloved and successful artists of the nineteenth century was Frederic Remington, a painter and sculptor whose works came to represent the *Frederic Remington* romance of the West. He portrayed the cowboy as a natural aristocrat, much like Wister's *The Virginian,* living in a natural world in which all the normal supporting structures of "civilization" were missing.

Theodore Roosevelt also contributed to the romanticizing of the West. He traveled to the Dakota badlands in the mid-1880s to recover from the sudden death of his young wife. In the 1890s, he published a four-volume history, *The Winning of the West,* with a heroic account of the spread of white civilization into the frontier.

Perhaps the most influential statement of the romantic vision of the frontier came from the young historian Frederick Jackson Turner, in a memorable paper he delivered as a thirty-two-year-old in Chicago in 1893 titled "The Significance of the Frontier in American History." In it he boldly claimed that the experience of western expansion had stimulated individualism, nationalism, and democracy; kept opportunities for advancement alive; and made Americans the distinctive people that they were. "Now," Turner concluded portentously, "the frontier has gone and with its going has closed the first period of American history." The **Turner thesis** was widely accepted by his contemporaries, but later historians have *Turner Thesis* challenged it. (See "Debating the Past: The Frontier and the West.")

In accepting the idea of the "passing of the frontier," many Americans were acknowledging the end of one of their most cherished myths. As long as it had been possible for them to see the West as an empty, open land, it was possible to believe that there were constantly revitalizing opportunities in American life. But by the end of the nineteenth century, there was a vague and ominous sense of opportunities foreclosed.

THE DISPERSAL OF THE TRIBES

Having imagined the West as a "virgin land" awaiting civilization by white people, many Americans tried to force the region to match their image of it. That meant, above all, ensuring that the Indian tribes would not be obstacles to the spread of white society.

A third grievance concerned prices. A farmer could plant a large crop at a moment when its price was high and find that by the time of the harvest the price had declined. Farmers' fortunes rose and fell in response to unpredictable forces. But many farmers became convinced (often with some reason) that "intermediaries"—speculators, bankers, regional and local agents—were conspiring with one another to fix prices so as to benefit themselves at the growers' expense. Many farmers also came to believe (again, not entirely without reason) that manufacturers in the East were colluding to keep the prices of farm goods low and the prices of industrial goods high. Although farmers sold their crops in a competitive world market, they bought manufactured goods in a domestic market protected by tariffs and dominated by trusts and corporations.

THE AGRARIAN MALAISE

These economic difficulties helped produce social and cultural resentments. Among them was the isolation of farm life. Farm families in some parts of the country were virtually cut off from the outside world. During the winter months, the loneliness and boredom could *Reasons for Discontent* become nearly unbearable. Many farmers lacked access to adequate education for their children. They had few or no proper medical facilities. There were few organized recreational or cultural activities. Older farmers felt the sting of watching their children leave the farm for the city. They felt the humiliation of being ridiculed as "hayseeds" by the new urban culture that was coming to dominate American life.

This sense of isolation and obsolescence led to a growing malaise among many farmers, a discontent that helped create a great national political movement in the 1890s. It found reflection, too, in some of the literature that emerged from rural America. Writers in the late nineteenth century might romanticize the rugged life of the cowboy and the western miner. For the farmers, however, the image of the agricultural world was different. Hamlin Garland, for example, reflected the growing disillusionment in a series of novels and short stories. In the introduction to his novel *Jason Edwards* (1891), he wrote that in the past, the agrarian frontier had seemed to be "the Golden West, the land of wealth and freedom and happiness." Now, however, the bright promise had faded. The trials of rural life were crushing the human spirit. "So this is the reality of the dream!" a character in *Jason Edwards* exclaims, "A shanty on a barren plain, hot and lone as a desert. My God!" Once, sturdy yeoman farmers had viewed themselves as the backbone of American life. Now they were becoming painfully aware that their position was declining in relation to the rising urban-industrial society to the east.

CONCLUSION

To many Americans in the late nineteenth century, the West seemed an untamed "frontier" in which hardy pioneers were creating a new society. The reality of the West in these years, however, was very different from this enduring image. White Americans moved into the vast regions west of the Mississippi at a remarkable rate in the years after the Civil War, and many of them indeed settled in lands far from any civilization they had ever known. But the West was not an empty place. It contained a large population of Indians, with whom the white settlers sometimes lived uneasily and with whom they sometimes battled; but almost always in the end, the Indians were pushed aside and (with help from the federal government) relocated onto lands whites did not want. There were significant numbers of Mexicans in some areas, small populations of Asians in others, and African Americans moving in from the South in search of land and freedom. The West was no barren frontier but a place of many cultures.

The West was also closely and increasingly tied to the emerging capitalist-industrial economy of the East. The miners who flooded into California, Colorado, Nevada, the Dakotas, and elsewhere were responding to the demand in the East for gold and silver, but even more for iron ore, copper, lead, zinc, and quartz. Cattle and sheep ranchers produced meat, wool, and leather for eastern consumers and manufacturers. Farmers grew crops for sale in national and international commodities markets. The West certainly looked different from the East. But the growth of the West was very much a part of the growth of the rest of the nation. And the culture of the West, despite the romantic images of pioneering individuals embraced by easterners and westerners alike, was at its heart as much a culture of economic growth and capitalist ambition as was that of the rest of the nation.

KEY TERMS/PEOPLE/PLACES/EVENTS

Californios 383
Chief Joseph 397
Chinese Exclusion
  Act 386
concentration policy 394
coolies 383
Dawes Severalty Act 398

Frederick Jackson
  Turner 393
Frederic Remington 393
George A. Custer 395
Geronimo 397
Homestead Act 386
Little Bighorn 396

long drive 388
Mark Twain 391
Plains Indians 381
range wars 390
Rocky Mountain school 390
Turner thesis 393
Wounded Knee 397

RECALL AND REFLECT

1. How did the ethnic, racial, and cultural prejudice affect western society?
2. What were the three major industries involved in the development of the West, and how did these industries transform the western economy?
3. What was the romantic image of the West, and how was this image expressed in art, literature, and popular culture?
4. How did actions and policies of the federal government affect the fate of Indians in the West?

17 INDUSTRIAL SUPREMACY

SOURCES OF INDUSTRIAL GROWTH
CAPITALIST CONSERVATISM AND ITS CRITICS
THE ORDEAL OF THE WORKER

LOOKING AHEAD

1. What factors drove America's industrial expansion in the late nineteenth and early twentieth centuries?

2. Who were the critics of America's new industrial economy, what were their criticisms, and what solutions did they propose?

3. How did the conditions and characteristics of the workforce change during this period of rapid industrialization?

"TWENTY-FIVE YEARS AFTER THE DEATH of Lincoln, America had become, in the quantity and value of her products, the leading manufacturing nation of the world. What England had accomplished in a hundred years, the United States had achieved in half the time." So boasted the historians Charles and Mary Beard in the 1920s, expressing the amazement many Americans felt when they considered the remarkable expansion of their industrial economy in the late nineteenth century.

In fact, America's rise to industrial supremacy was not as sudden as such observers suggested. The nation had been building a manufacturing economy since early in the nineteenth century. But Americans were clearly correct in observing that the accomplishments of the last three decades of the nineteenth century overshadowed all the earlier progress.

The remarkable growth did much to increase the wealth and improve the lives of many Americans. But such benefits were very unequally shared. While industrial titans and a growing middle class were enjoying a prosperity without precedent in the nation's history, workers, farmers, and others were experiencing an often painful ordeal that slowly edged the United States toward a great economic and political crisis.

SOURCES OF INDUSTRIAL GROWTH

Many factors contributed to the growth of American industry: abundant raw materials, a large and growing labor supply, a surge in technological innovation, the emergence of a talented and often ruthless group of entrepreneurs, a federal government eager to assist the growth of business, and an expanding domestic market for the products of manufacturing.

INDUSTRIAL TECHNOLOGIES

The rapid emergence of new technologies, together with the discovery of new materials and productive processes, was one of the principal sources of late-nineteenth-century industrial growth. Some of the most important innovations were in communications. In 1866, Cyrus W. Field laid a transatlantic telegraph cable to Europe. During the next decade, Alexander Graham Bell developed the first telephone with commercial capacity. By 1900, there were 1.35 million telephones, and by 1920, 13.3 million. And the Italian inventor Guglielmo Marconi was taking the first steps toward the development of radio in the 1890s; the technology he developed quickly found its way to the United States. Other inventions that speeded the pace of business organization were the typewriter (by Christopher L. Sholes in 1868), the cash register (by James Ritty in 1879), and the calculating, or adding, machine (by William S. Burroughs in 1891).

Among the most revolutionary innovations was the introduction in the 1870s of electricity as a source of light and power. The pioneers of electric lighting included Charles F. Brush, who devised the arc lamp for street illumination, and Thomas A. Edison, who invented the incandescent lamp (or lightbulb). Edison and others designed improved generators and built large power plants to furnish electricity to

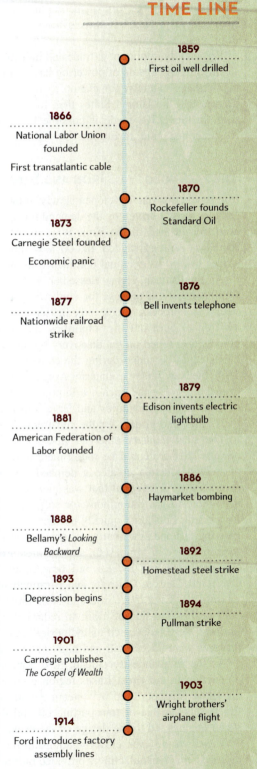

TIME LINE

1859
First oil well drilled

1866
National Labor Union founded

First transatlantic cable

1870
Rockefeller founds Standard Oil

1873
Carnegie Steel founded

Economic panic

1876
Bell invents telephone

1877
Nationwide railroad strike

1879
Edison invents electric lightbulb

1881
American Federation of Labor founded

1886
Haymarket bombing

1888
Bellamy's *Looking Backward*

1892
Homestead steel strike

1893
Depression begins

1894
Pullman strike

1901
Carnegie publishes *The Gospel of Wealth*

1903
Wright brothers' airplane flight

1914
Ford introduces factory assembly lines

whole cities. By the turn of the century, electric power was becoming commonplace in street railway systems, in the elevators of urban skyscrapers, in factories, and increasingly in offices and homes.

Particularly important to trade and industry was the development of new high-efficiency steam engines capable of powering larger ships at faster speeds than ever before. The new high-speed freighters, for example, made it cheaper for Britain to buy wheat grown in Canada and the United States than to grow it at home. The introduction of refrigerated ships in the 1870s made it possible to transport meat from North America, and even Australia and Asia, to Europe.

THE TECHNOLOGY OF IRON AND STEEL PRODUCTION

Iron production had developed slowly in the United States through most of the nineteenth century, mostly driven by the demand for iron rails; steel production had developed hardly at all by the end of the Civil War. In the 1870s and 1880s, however, iron production soared as railroads added 40,000 new miles of track, and steel production made great strides toward its eventual dominance in the metals industry.

An Englishman, Henry Bessemer, and an American, William Kelly, developed, almost simultaneously, a process for converting iron into the much more durable and versatile steel. (The process, which took Bessemer's name, consisted of blowing air through molten iron to burn out the impurities and create a much stronger metal.) The Bessemer process also relied on the discovery by the British metallurgist Robert Mushet that ingredients could be added during the conversion process to give steel additional strength. In 1868, the New Jersey ironmaster Abram S. Hewitt introduced from Europe another method of making steel—the open-hearth process. These techniques made possible the production of steel in great quantities and large dimensions, for use in the manufacture of locomotives, rails, and girders for the construction of tall buildings.

The steel industry emerged first in western Pennsylvania and eastern Ohio, partly because iron ore could be found there in abundance. It was also because the new forms of steel production created a demand for new kinds of fuel—and particularly for the anthracite (or hard) coal that was plentiful in Pennsylvania. Later, new techniques made it possible to use bituminous (or soft) coal, also easily mined in western Pennsylvania. As a result, Pittsburgh quickly became the center of the steel world. But the industry was growing fast and new sources of ore soon emerged. The upper peninsula of Michigan, the Mesabi Range in Minnesota, and the area around Birmingham, Alabama, became important ore-producing locales and new centers of steel production grew up near them: Cleveland, Detroit, Chicago, and Birmingham, among others.

Until the Civil War, iron and steel furnaces were mostly made of stone and usually built against the side of a hill to reduce construction demands. By the 1870s, however, furnaces were redesigned as cylindrical iron shells lined with brick. These massive new furnaces were 75 feet tall and higher and could produce over 500 tons a week.

As the steel industry spread, new transportation systems emerged to serve it. Steel production in the Great Lakes region produced steam freighters that could carry ore on the lakes. Shippers used new steam engines to speed the unloading of ore. The demand for vessels capable of transporting oil and the development of new and more powerful steam engines led to the design of larger and heavier freighters.

There was an even closer relationship between the emerging steel companies and the railroads. Steel manufacturers provided rails and parts for cars; railroads were both markets

PIONEER OIL RUN, 1865   The American oil industry emerged first in western Pennsylvania, where speculators built makeshift facilities almost overnight. An oil field on the other side of the hill depicted here had been producing 600 barrels a day, and the wells quickly spilled over the hill and down the slope shown in the photograph. (The Library of Congress)

for and transporters of manufactured steel. But the relationship soon became more intimate than that. The Pennsylvania Railroad, for example, actually created the *Steel and Railroads* Pennsylvania Steel Company.

The steel industry's need for lubrication for its machines helped create another important new industry in the late nineteenth century—oil. (Not until later did oil become important primarily for its potential as a fuel.) The existence of petroleum reserves in western Pennsylvania had been common knowledge for some time. The Pennsylvania businessman George Bissell showed that the substance could be burned in lamps and that it could also yield such products as paraffin, naphtha, and lubricating oil. Bissell raised money to begin drilling; and in 1859, Edwin L. Drake, one of Bissell's employees, established the first oil well near Titusville, Pennsylvania, which soon produced 500 barrels of oil a month. Demand for petroleum grew quickly, and promoters soon developed other oil fields in Pennsylvania, Ohio, and West Virginia.

THE AUTOMOBILE AND THE AIRPLANE

Among the most important technological innovations was the invention of the automobile. Two technologies led to its development. First was the creation of gasoline (or petrol), the product of an extraction process developed in the late nineteenth century in the United States by which lubricating oil and fuel oil were removed separately from crude oil. The second technology was the development of a self-contained engine. As early as the 1870s, designers in France, Germany, and Austria had begun to develop an "internal combustion engine," which used the expanding power of burning gas to drive pistons. A German, Nicolaus August Otto, created a gas-powered "four-stroke" engine in the mid-1860s, which was a precursor to automobile engines. But he did not develop a way to untether it from gas lines to be used portably in machines. One of Otto's former employees, Gottfried Daimler, later perfected an engine that could be used in automobiles.

The American automobile industry developed rapidly in the aftermath of these European breakthroughs. Charles and Frank Duryea built the first gasoline-driven motor vehicle in *Henry Ford* America in 1893. Three years later, Henry Ford produced the first of the famous cars that would bear his name. In 1895, there were only four automobiles on the American highways. By 1917, there were nearly 5 million.

The search for a means of human flight, as old as civilization, had been almost entirely futile until the late nineteenth century, when engineers, scientists, and tinkerers in both the United States and Europe began to experiment with a wide range of aeronautic devices. Balloonists began to consider ways to make dirigibles useful vehicles of transportation. Others experimented with kites and gliders.

Two brothers in Ohio, Wilbur and Orville Wright, began to construct a glider in 1899 *The Wright Brothers* that could be propelled through the air by an internal combustion engine. Four years later, Orville made a celebrated test flight near Kitty Hawk, North Carolina, in which an airplane took off by itself and traveled 120 feet in 12 seconds under its own power before settling back to earth. By the fall of 1904, the Wright brothers had improved the plane to the point where they were able to fly over 23 miles, and in the following year they began to take a few passengers on their flights with them.

Although the first working airplane was built in the United States, aviation technology was slow to gain a foothold in America. Most of the early progress in airplane design occurred in France, where there was substantial government funding for research and development. The U.S. government created the National Advisory Committee on Aeronautics in 1915, twelve years after the Wright brothers' flight, and American airplanes became a significant presence in Europe during World War I. But the prospects for commercial flight seemed dim until the 1920s, when Charles Lindbergh's famous solo flight from New York to Paris electrified the nation and the world.

RESEARCH AND DEVELOPMENT

New industrial technologies persuaded many businesses to build their own research operations. The corporate research-and-development (R&D) laboratories coincided with a decline in government support for research, helping corporations attract skilled researchers. It also decentralized the sources of research funding and ensured that inquiry would move in many directions, and not just along paths determined by the government.

A rift began to emerge between scientists and engineers. Engineers—both inside and outside of universities—became increasingly tied up with the R&D agendas of corporations. Many scientists continued to scorn this "commercialization" of knowledge and preferred to stick to basic research that had no immediate practical applications. But many American scientists were more closely connected to practical challenges than were their European counterparts, and some joined engineers in corporate R&D laboratories, which over time began to sponsor both practical and basic research.

THE SCIENCE OF PRODUCTION

Central to the growth of the automobile and other industries were changes in the techniques of production. By the turn of the century, many industrialists were embracing the

WOMEN ON THE ASSEMBLY LINE   This photograph, from 1902, shows women at work on the lock and drill department assembly line at the National Cash Register Company in Dayton, Ohio. (© Everett Collection Historical/Alamy)

new principles of "scientific management," often known as "Taylorism" after   *"Taylorism"*
its leading theoretician, Frederick Winslow Taylor. Taylor and his many admirers argued that scientific management made human labor compatible with the demands of the machine age. He persuaded employers to take control of the workplace. Taylor also urged employers to reorganize the production process by subdividing tasks. This sped up production and made workers more interchangeable, thus diminishing a manager's dependence on any particular employee. If properly managed by trained experts, he claimed, workers using modern machines could perform simple tasks at much greater speed, greatly increasing productive efficiency.

The most important change in industrial technology was the emergence of mass production and, along with it, the moving assembly line, which Henry Ford   *Assembly Line*
introduced in his automobile plants in 1914. The assembly line was a particular place—a factory through which automobiles moved as they were assembled by workers who specialized in particular tasks. It was also a concept. The concept stressed the complete interchangeability of parts. General Motors adopted the same philosophy. Automobile production relied on other technologies, too, in particular the intensive use of electricity—to drive the assembly line, to light the factories, and to run the critical ventilating systems that kept dust from interfering with the machines. The revolutionary assembly-line technique enabled Ford to raise wages and reduce hours while cutting the base price of his Model T from $950 in 1914 to $290 in 1929. It became a standard for many other industries.

RAILROAD EXPANSION AND THE CORPORATION

The principal agent of industrial development in the late nineteenth century was still the expansion of the railroads. Railroads gave industrialists access to distant markets and remote sources of raw materials. They were America's biggest investors, stimulating economic growth through their own enormous expenditures on construction and equipment and sale of their vast tracks of land.

Total railroad trackage increased from 30,000 miles in 1860 to 193,000 in 1900. *Importance of Government Subsidies* Subsidies from federal, state, and local governments (along with foreign loans and investments) were vital to this expansion. Equally important was the emergence of great railroad "combinations" (mergers), many of them dominated by one or two individuals. The achievements (and excesses) of these tycoons—Cornelius Vanderbilt, James J. Hill, Collis P. Huntington, and others—became symbols to much of the nation of concentrated economic power. But railroad development was less significant for the individual barons it created than for its contribution to the growth of a new institution: the modern corporation.

There had been various forms of corporations in America since colonial times, but the modern corporation emerged as a major force only after the Civil War. By then, railroad magnates and other industrialists realized that their great ventures could not be financed by any single person.

Under the laws of incorporation passed in many states in the 1830s and 1840s, business organizations could raise money by selling stock to members of the public; after the Civil War, one industry after another began doing so. What made these stocks appealing was that investors now had only "limited liability"—they risked only the amount of their

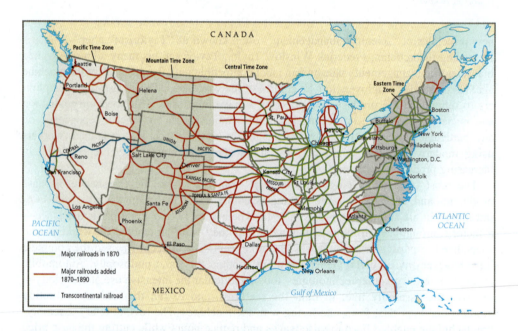

RAILROADS, 1870–1890 This map illustrates the rapid expansion of railroads in the late nineteenth century. In 1870, there was already a dense network of rail lines in the Northeast and Midwest, illustrated here by the green lines. The red lines show the further expansion of rail coverage between 1870 and 1890, much of it in the South and the areas west of the Mississippi River. • *Why were railroads so essential to the nation's economic growth in these years?*

investments and were not liable for any debts the corporation might accumulate beyond that point. The ability to sell stock to a broad public made it possible for entrepreneurs to gather vast sums of capital and undertake great projects with manageable financial risk.

The Pennsylvania and other railroads were among the first to adopt the new corporate form of organization. But incorporation quickly spread beyond the railroad industry. Andrew Carnegie, a Scottish immigrant, worked his way up from modest beginnings and, in 1873, opened his own steelworks in Pittsburgh. Soon he dominated the industry. With his associate Henry Clay Frick, he bought up coal mines and   *Carnegie, Frick, and Morgan* leased part of the Mesabi iron range in Minnesota, operated a fleet of ore ships on the Great Lakes, and acquired railroads. He financed his vast undertakings not only out of his own profits but also out of the sale of stock. Then, in 1901, he sold out for $450 million to the banker J. Pierpont Morgan, who merged the Carnegie interests with others to create the giant United States Steel Corporation—a $14 billion enterprise that controlled almost two-thirds of the nation's steel production.

Other industries developed similarly. Gustavus Swift forged a relatively small meatpacking company into a great national corporation. Isaac Singer patented a sewing machine in 1851 and created I. M. Singer and Company—one of the first modern manufacturing corporations.

Large, national business enterprises needed systematic administrative structures. As a result, corporate leaders introduced managerial techniques that relied on the systematic division of responsibilities. Companies built carefully designed hierarchies of control, strict cost-accounting procedures, and a new breed of business executives: the "middle managers," who formed a layer of command between workers and owners. Efficient administrative capabilities helped make possible another major feature of the modern corporation: consolidation.

Businessmen created large consolidated organizations primarily through two methods. **Horizontal integration** combined a number of firms engaged in the same enterprise into a single corporation such as the consolidation of many different railroad lines into one company. Through **vertical integration,** a company took over all the different businesses on which it relied for its primary function, for example, Carnegie Steel, which came to control not only steel mills but also mines, railroads, and other enterprises.

The most celebrated corporate empire of the late nineteenth century was John D. Rockefeller's Standard Oil. Shortly after the Civil War, Rockefeller   *Rockefeller's Standard Oil* launched a refining company in Cleveland and immediately began trying to eliminate his competition. Allying himself with other wealthy capitalists, he formed the Standard Oil Company of Ohio in 1870, which in a few years had acquired twenty of the twenty-five refineries in Cleveland, as well as plants in Pittsburgh, Philadelphia, New York, and Baltimore.

So far, Rockefeller had expanded only horizontally—buying many refineries. But soon he began expanding vertically as well. He built his own barrel factories, terminal warehouses, and pipelines. Standard Oil owned its own freight cars and developed its own marketing organization. By the 1880s, Rockefeller had established such dominance within the petroleum industry that to much of the nation he served as a leading symbol of monopoly.

Rockefeller and other industrialists saw consolidation as a way to cope with what they believed was the greatest curse of the modern economy: "cutthroat competition." Most businessmen claimed to believe in free enterprise and a competitive marketplace, but in fact they feared that substantial competition could spell instability and ruin for all.

As the movement toward consolidation accelerated, new vehicles emerged to facilitate it. The railroads began with so-called pool arrangements—informal agreements among various companies to stabilize rates and divide markets (arrangements that would, in later years, be known as cartels). But the pool arrangements were too weak and could not ensure cost stability.

The failure of the pools led to new techniques of consolidation. The next effort to *Trusts* stabilize prices was the creation of the "trust"—pioneered by Standard Oil in the early 1880s and the banker J. P. Morgan. Under a trust agreement, stockholders in individual corporations transferred their stocks to a small group of trustees in exchange for shares in the trust itself. Owners of trust certificates often had no direct control over the decisions of the trustees; they simply received a share of the profits of the combination. The trustees themselves, on the other hand, might literally own only a few companies but could exercise effective control over many.

In 1889, the state of New Jersey helped produce a third form of consolidation by changing its laws of incorporation to permit companies to buy up rivals. Other states soon followed. Once actual corporate mergers were permitted, the original trusts became unnecessary. Rockefeller, for example, quickly relocated Standard Oil to New Jersey and created *Holding Companies* what became known as a "holding company"—a central corporate body that would buy up the stock of various members of the Standard Oil trust and establish direct, formal ownership of them.

By the end of the nineteenth century, 1 percent of the corporations in America were able to control more than 33 percent of the manufacturing. A system of economic orga- *Concentration of Power* nization was emerging that lodged enormous power in the hands of very few men—the great bankers of New York such as Morgan, industrial titans such as Rockefeller (who himself gained control of a major bank), and others.

The industrial giants of the era clearly contributed to substantial economic growth. They were also creating the basis for one of the greatest public controversies of their era: a raging debate over concentrated economic and political power that continued well into the twentieth century.

CAPITALIST CONSERVATISM AND ITS CRITICS

The inequality of the roaring capitalism of the late nineteenth century was not without its critics. Farmers, workers, middle-class businessmen, and many others considered the new capitalism to be a threat to their own destinies. But the industrial titans built a powerful defense for the new corporate economy.

SURVIVAL OF THE FITTEST

The new rationale for capitalism was based on the belief of individualism—an ideology *Ideology of Individualism* that would remain at the heart of American conservatism for many decades. Wealthy capitalists defended their wealth by saying that they had earned their wealth and power through their own hard work and their acquisitiveness and thrift. Those who failed had only themselves to blame—a result of ignorance, stupidity, or laziness.

Conservative social theories helped support the belief that through "survival of the fittest" wealthy capitalists deserved their success. Among them was the theory of **Social Darwinism.** Darwin's theories argued that the fittest forms of life survived over thousands of years because of their biological fitness. Social Darwinism argued that individuals rose or fell in society because of their innate "fitness." (Darwin himself, along with most scientists, debunked Social Darwinism, but many Americans embraced it nevertheless.) The English philosopher and biologist Herbert Spencer introduced the theory of Social Darwinism in his book *Principles of Biology* (1864). Society, he argued, benefited from the elimination of the unfit and the survival of the strong and talented. William Graham Sumner, a sociologist at Yale, borrowed from Spencer's theory and created a theory of his own in his famous 1906 book *Folkways*. Those who failed, he argued in a 1913 essay, were unfit for success: "Before the tribunal of nature a man has no more right to life than a rattlesnake; he has no more right to liberty than any wild beast; his right to pursuit of happiness is nothing but a license to maintain the struggle for existence." Wealthy corporate leaders were attracted to the ideas of Spencer and Sumner. Their success confirmed their own virtues and "fitness."

Capitalists argued that they earned their wealth through the honest, all-American virtues of competition and the free market. But critics of the industrial and financial titans claimed that they earned their wealth not because of the innate fitness of those who succeeded, but because they replaced the natural workings of the marketplace by building great monopolies that would protect them from competition.

The Gospel of Wealth

Some businessmen attempted to temper the harsh philosophy of Social Darwinism with a gentler, if in some ways equally self-serving, idea: the "**gospel of wealth**." People of great wealth, they argued, had not only great power but also a great responsibility to use their riches to advance social progress. Elaborating on this creed in his 1889 article "The Gospel of Wealth," and elaborated on in the 1901 book of the same title, Andrew Carnegie wrote that people of wealth should consider all revenues in excess of their own needs to be "trust funds" used for the good of the community. (See "Consider the Source: Andrew Carnegie Explains "The Gospel of Wealth."") Carnegie was only one of many industrialists who devoted large parts of their fortunes to philanthropic works.

The idea of private wealth as a public blessing existed alongside another popular concept: the notion of great wealth as something available to all. Russell H. Conwell, a Baptist minister, became one of the most prominent spokesmen for the idea by delivering one lecture, "Acres of Diamonds," more than 6,000 times between 1880 and 1900. Conwell told a series of stories, which he claimed were true, of individuals who had found opportunities for extraordinary wealth in their own backyards. (One such story involved a modest farmer who discovered a vast diamond mine in his own fields.) Most of the millionaires in the country, Conwell claimed (inaccurately), had begun on the lowest rung of the economic ladder and had worked their way to success.

But the most famous promoter of the success story was Horatio Alger. He was originally a minister in a small town in Massachusetts but was driven from his *Horatio Alger* pulpit as a result of sexual scandals. He moved to New York, where he wrote over 100 celebrated novels—all of them tributes to social mobility and the ability of Americans to rise from "rags to riches." (See "Patterns of Popular Culture: The Novels of Horatio Alger.")

If Alger's rags-to-riches tales captured the aspiration of many men, Louisa May Alcott's enormously popular novels helped give voice to the often unstated *Louisa May Alcott* ambitions of many women. Alcott was the daughter of a noted New England reformer,

ANDREW CARNEGIE EXPLAINS "THE GOSPEL OF WEALTH," 1889

Writing for a general audience in the literary and culture magazine *The North American Review*, billionaire Andrew Carnegie made one of the industrial age's most famous arguments about the inherent justness of the unequal distribution of economic power and wealth.

The problem of our age is the proper administration of wealth, that the ties of brotherhood may still bind together the rich and poor in harmonious relationship. The conditions of human life have not only been changed, but revolutionized, within the past few hundred years. In former days there was little difference between the dwelling, dress, food, and environment of the chief and those of his retainers. The Indians are today where civilized man then was. . . . The contrast between the palace of the millionaire and the cottage of the laborer with us to-day measures the change which has come with civilization. This change, however, is not to be deplored, but welcomed as highly beneficial. It is well, nay, essential, for the progress of the race that the houses of some should be homes for all that is highest and best in literature and the arts,—and for all the refinements of civilization, rather than that none should be so. Much better this great irregularity than universal squalor. . . . The "good old times" were not good old times. Neither master nor servant was as well situated then as to-day. A relapse to old conditions would be disastrous to both—not the least so to him who serves—and would sweep away civilization with it. But whether the change be for good or ill, it is upon us, beyond our power to alter, and, therefore, to be accepted and made the best of. It is a waste of time to criticize the inevitable.

It is easy to see how the change has come. . . . In the manufacture of products we have the whole story. . . . To-day the world obtains commodities of excellent quality at prices which even the preceding generation would have deemed incredible. The poor enjoy what the rich could not before afford. What were the luxuries have become the necessaries of life. The laborer has now more comforts than the farmer had a few generations ago. The farmer has more luxuries than the landlord had, and is more richly clad and better housed. The landlord has books and pictures rarer and appointments more artistic than the king could then obtain.

The price we pay for this salutary change is, no doubt, great. . . . Under the law of competition, the employer of thousands is forced into the strictest economies, among which the rates paid to labor figure prominently, and often there is friction between the employer and the employed, between capital and labor, between rich and poor. Human society loses homogeneity.

The price which society pays for the law of competition, like the price it pays for cheap comforts and luxuries, is also great; but the advantages of this law are also greater still than its cost—for it is to this law that we owe our wonderful material development, which brings improved conditions in its train. But, whether the law be benign or not, we must say of it, as we say of the change in the conditions of men to which we have referred: It is here; we cannot evade it; no substitutes for it have been found; and while the law may be sometimes hard for the individual, it is best for the race, because it insures the survival of the fittest in every department.

What is the proper mode of administering wealth after the laws upon which civilization is founded have thrown it into the hands of the few? . . .

There remains . . . only one mode of using great fortunes; in this we have the true antidote for the temporary unequal distribution of wealth, the reconciliation of the rich and the poor—a reign of harmony. . . . It is founded upon the present most intense Individualism, and the race is prepared to put it in practice by degrees whenever it pleases. Under its sway we shall have an ideal State, in which the surplus wealth of the few will become, in the best sense, the property of the many, because administered for the common good; and this wealth, passing through the hands of the few, can be made a much more potent force for the elevation of our race than if distributed in small sums to the people themselves. Even the poorest can be made to see this, and to agree that great sums gathered by some of their fellow-citizens and spent for public purposes, from which the masses reap the principal benefit, are more valuable to them than if scattered among themselves in trifling amounts through the course of many years. . . .

Poor and restricted are our opportunities in this life, narrow our horizon, our best work most imperfect; but rich men should be thankful for one inestimable boon. They have it in their power during their lives to busy themselves in organizing benefactions from which the masses of their fellows will derive lasting advantage, and thus dignify their own lives. The highest life is probably to be reached, not by such imitation of the life of Christ as Count Tolstoi gives us, but, while animated by Christ's spirit, by recognizing the changed conditions of this age, and adopting modes of expressing this spirit suitable to the changed conditions under which we live, still laboring for the good of our fellows, which was the essence of his life and teaching, but laboring in a different manner.

This, then, is held to be the duty of the man of wealth: To set an example of modest, unostentatious living, shunning display or extravagance; to provide moderately for the legitimate wants of those dependent upon him; and, after doing so, to consider all surplus revenues which come to him simply as trust funds, which he is called upon to administer, and strictly bound as a matter of duty to administer in the manner which, in his judgment, is best calculated to produce the most beneficial results for the community—the man of wealth thus becoming the mere trustee and agent for his poorer brethren, bringing to their service his superior wisdom, experience, and ability to administer, doing for them better than they would or could do for themselves. . . .

[T]he best means of benefiting the community is to place within its reach the ladders upon which the aspiring can rise—free libraries, parks, and means of recreation, by which men are helped in body and mind; works of art, certain to give pleasure and improve the public taste; and public institutions of various kinds, which will improve the general condition of the people; in this manner returning their surplus wealth to the mass of their fellows in the forms best calculated to do them lasting good.

Thus is the problem of rich and poor to be solved. The laws of accumulation will be left free, the laws of distribution free. Individualism will continue, but the millionaire will be but a trustee for the poor, intrusted for a season with a great part of the increased wealth of the community, but administering it for the community far better than it could or would have done for itself. . . .

Such, in my opinion, is the true gospel concerning wealth, obedience to which is destined some day to solve the problem of the rich and the poor, and to bring "Peace on earth, among men good will."

UNDERSTAND, ANALYZE, & EVALUATE

1. What did Carnegie think of the inequality of wealth in industrial America? What were the wealthy supposed to do in this inequality of wealth, and what role did Andrew Carnegie envision for the poor?
2. What was the price of this new inequality?

Source: Andrew Carnegie, "Wealth," *North American Review* (1889), located in: Michael P. Johnson, *Reading the American Past: Selected Historical Documents, vol. 2: From 1865*, 5th ed. (Boston: Bedford St. Martin's, 2012), pp. 52–55.

THE NOVELS OF HORATIO ALGER

A young boy, perhaps an orphan, makes his way through life on the rough streets of the city by selling newspapers or peddling matches. One day, his energy and determination catch the eye of a wealthy man, who gives him a chance to improve himself. Through honesty, charm, hard work, and aggressiveness, the boy rises in the world to become a successful man.

That, in a nutshell, is the story that Horatio Alger presented to his vast public in novel after novel—over 100 of them in all—for over forty years. During his lifetime, Americans bought millions of copies of his novels. After his death in 1899, his books (and others written in his name) continued to sell at an astonishing rate. Even today, when the books themselves are largely forgotten, the name Horatio Alger has come to represent the idea of individual advancement through (in a phrase Alger coined) "pluck and luck."

Alger was born in 1832 into a middle-class New England family, attended Harvard, and spent a short time as a Unitarian minister. In the mid-1850s, he turned to writing stories and books, and he continued to do so for the rest of his life. His most famous novel, *Ragged Dick*, was published in 1868. Almost all of his books were fables of a young man's rise "from rags to riches." The purpose of his writing, he claimed, was twofold. He wanted to "exert a salutary influence upon the class of whom [he] was writing, by setting before them inspiring examples of what energy, ambition, and an honest purpose may achieve." He also wanted to show his largely middle-class readers "the life and experiences of the friendless and vagrant children to be found in all our cities."

Most Americans of the late nineteenth and early twentieth centuries were attracted to Alger's stories because the stories helped them believe in one of the most cherished national myths: that with willpower and hard work, individuals could rise in the world. That belief was all the more important in the late nineteenth century when large-scale corporate industrialization was making it increasingly difficult for individuals to control their own fates.

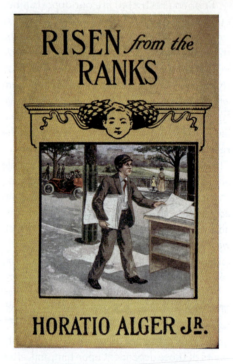

A NEWSBOY'S STORY Alger's novels were even more popular after his death in 1899 than they had been in his lifetime. This reprint of one of his many rags-to-riches stories—about a New York newsboy's rise to wealth and success—was typical of his work. (© Granger, NYC—All Rights Reserved.)

Alger placed great emphasis on the moral qualities of his heroes; their success was a reward for their virtue. But many of his readers ignored the moral message and clung simply to the image of sudden and dramatic success. After the author's death, his publishers abridged many of Alger's works, eliminating the parts of his stories where the heroes do good deeds and focusing solely on the success of Alger's heroes in rising in the world.

Alger himself had very mixed feelings about the new industrial order he described. His books were meant to reveal not just the opportunities for advancement it sometimes created, but also its cruelty. That was one reason that in almost all his books, his heroes triumphed not just because of their own virtues or efforts, but because of some amazing stroke of luck. To Alger, at least, the modern age did not guarantee success through hard work alone; there had to be some providential assistance as well. Over time, however, Alger's admirers ignored his own misgivings about industrialism and portrayed his books purely as celebrations of (and justifications for) laissez-faire capitalism and the accumulation of wealth.

An example of the transformation of Alger into a symbol of individual achievement is the Horatio Alger Award, established in 1947 by the American Schools and Colleges Association to honor "living individuals who by their own efforts [have] pulled themselves up by their bootstraps in the American tradition." Among its recipients have been Presidents Dwight D. Eisenhower and Ronald Reagan, evangelist Billy Graham, and Supreme Court Justice Clarence Thomas. •

UNDERSTAND, ANALYZE, & EVALUATE

1. How do Alger's novels both defend industrial capitalism and criticize it?
2. According to the essay, Alger placed great emphasis on the moral qualities of his heroes, but his publishers later eliminated that aspect of the novels. Why?

but her family nevertheless experienced considerable hardship. After serving as a nurse in the Civil War and writing a series of popular adventure novels (under a pen name, A. M. Barnard, that disguised her gender), she became a major literary figure with the publication of *Little Women* in 1869 and two sequels over the next twenty years. The main character in these novels, Jo March, struggles to build a life for herself that is not defined by conventional women's roles and ambitions. She spurns a conventional marriage and eventually weds a professor who appears to support her literary ambitions. "Girls write to ask who the little women marry, as if that was the only end and aim of a woman's life," Alcott wrote a friend. "I won't marry Jo to Laurie [the attractive, wealthy neighbor who proposes to her] to please any one." Alcott's female characters, in some ways like Alger's male ones, are remarkable for their independence and drive. Jo March is willful, rebellious, stubborn, ambitious, and often selfish—far from the posed, romantic, submissive women in most popular sentimental novels of Alcott's time aimed at female audiences.

ALTERNATIVE VISIONS

Alongside the celebrations of competition and the justifications for great wealth stood a group of alternative philosophies, challenging the corporate ethos and, at times, capitalism itself.

One such philosophy came from the sociologist Lester Frank Ward. In *Dynamic Sociology* (1883) and other books, he argued that civilization was not governed by natural selection but by human intelligence, which could shape society as it wished. In contrast to

"MODERN COLOSSUS OF (RAIL) ROADS"   Cornelius Vanderbilt, known as the "Commodore," accumulated one of America's great fortunes by consolidating several large railroad companies in the 1860s. His name became a synonym not only for enormous wealth but also (in the eyes of many Americans) for excessive corporate power—as suggested in this cartoon, showing him standing astride his empire and manipulating its parts. (© Niday Picture Library/Alamy)

Sumner, who believed that state intervention to remodel the environment was futile, Ward thought that an active government engaged in positive planning was society's best hope.

Other Americans adopted more-radical approaches to reform. Some dissenters found a home in the Socialist Labor Party, founded in the 1870s and led for many years by Daniel De Leon, an immigrant from the West Indies. Although De Leon attracted a following in the industrial cities, the party never became a major political force and never polled more than 82,000 votes. A dissident faction of De Leon's party, eager to forge stronger ties with organized labor, broke away and in 1901 formed the more *American Socialist Party* enduring American Socialist Party.

Other radicals gained a wider following. Among them was the California writer and activist Henry George. His angrily eloquent *Progress and Poverty,* published in 1879, *Henry George* became one of the best-selling nonfiction works in American publishing history. George blamed social problems on the ability of a few monopolists to grow wealthy as a result of rising land values. An increase in the value of land, he claimed, was not a result of any effort by the owner, but an "unearned increment," produced by the growth of society around the land. Such profits were rightfully the property of the community. And so George proposed a "single tax" on land, to replace all other taxes, which would return the increment to the people. The tax, he argued, would destroy monopolies, distribute wealth more equally, and eliminate poverty.

Rivaling George in popularity was Edward Bellamy, whose utopian novel *Looking Backward,* published in 1888, sold more than 1 million copies. It described *Edward Bellamy* the experiences of a young Bostonian who went into a hypnotic sleep in 1887 and awoke in the year 2000 to find a new social order in which want, politics, and vice were unknown. The new society had emerged through a peaceful, evolutionary process: the large trusts of the late nineteenth century had continued to grow in size and to combine with one another until ultimately they formed a single, great trust, controlled by the government, which distributed the abundance of the industrial economy equally among all the people. "Fraternal cooperation" had replaced competition. Class divisions had disappeared. Bellamy labeled the philosophy behind this vision "nationalism."

THE PROBLEMS OF MONOPOLY

Relatively few Americans shared the views of those who questioned capitalism itself. But as time went on, a growing number of people were becoming deeply concerned about the growth of **monopoly.**

By the end of the century, a wide range of groups had begun to assail monopoly and economic concentration. In the absence of competition, they argued, monopolistic industries could charge whatever prices they wished. Railroads, in particular, charged very high rates along some routes because they knew their customers had no choice but to pay them. Beginning in 1873, the economy fluctuated erratically, producing severe recessions every five or six years, each worse than the last.

THE ORDEAL OF THE WORKER

Most workers in the late nineteenth century experienced a real rise in their standard of living. But they did so at the cost of arduous and often dangerous working conditions, diminishing control over their own work, and a growing sense of powerlessness.

THE IMMIGRANT WORKFORCE

The industrial workforce expanded dramatically in the late nineteenth century as a result of massive migration into industrial cities. Rural Americans continued to flow into factory towns and cities—people disillusioned with or bankrupted by life on the farm. There was also a great wave of immigration from abroad (primarily from Europe, but also from Asia, Canada, Mexico, and other areas) in the decades following the Civil War—an influx greater than that of any previous era. The 25 million immigrants who arrived in the United States between 1865 and 1915 were more than four times the number who had arrived in the previous fifty years.

In the 1870s and 1880s, most of the immigrants came from England, Ireland, and northern Europe. By the end of the century, however, the major sources of immigrants had shifted, with large numbers of southern and eastern Europeans (Italians, Poles, Russians, Greeks, Slavs, and others) moving into the country and into the industrial workforce.

The new immigrants came to America in part to escape poverty and oppression in their homelands. But they were also attracted by expectations of new opportunities. Railroads lured immigrants into their western landholdings by distributing misleading advertisements overseas. Industrial employers actively recruited immigrant workers under the Labor Contract Law, which—until its repeal in 1885—permitted them to pay for the passage of workers in advance and deduct the amount later from their wages. Even after the repeal of the law, employers continued to encourage the immigration of unskilled laborers, often with the assistance of foreign-born labor brokers, such as the Greek and Italian *padrones,* who recruited work gangs of their fellow nationals.

The arrival of these new groups heightened ethnic tensions within the working class. *Job Competition*   Low-paid Poles, Greeks, and French Canadians began to displace higher-paid British and Irish workers in the textile factories of New England. Italians, Slavs, and Poles emerged as a major source of labor for the mining industry. Chinese and Mexicans competed with Anglo-Americans and African Americans in mining, farmwork, and factory labor in California, Colorado, and Texas.

WAGES AND WORKING CONDITIONS

At the turn of the century, the average income of the American worker was $400 to $500 a year—below the $600 figure that many believed was required to maintain a reasonable level of comfort. Nor did workers have much job security. All were vulnerable to the boom-and-bust cycle of the industrial economy and the instability caused by technological advances. Even those who kept their jobs could find their wages suddenly and substantially cut in hard times. Few workers, in other words, were ever very far from poverty.

Many first-generation workers, accustomed to the patterns of agrarian life, had trouble adjusting to the nature of modern industrial labor: routine, repetitive tasks on a strict and monotonous schedule. Skilled artisans, whose once-valued tasks were now performed by machines, found the new system impersonal and demeaning. Most factory laborers worked ten hours a day, six days a week; in the steel industry they worked twelve hours a day. Industrial accidents were frequent.

The decreasing need for skilled work in factories induced many employers to increase the use of women and children, whom they could hire for lower wages than adult males. By 1900, 20 percent of all manufacturing workers were women. Women labored in all areas of industry, even in some of the most arduous jobs. Most women, however, worked in a few industries where unskilled and semiskilled machine labor (as opposed to heavy manual labor) prevailed. The textile industry remained the largest single industrial employer of women. (Domestic service, though, remained the most common female occupation overall.) Women worked for wages well below the minimum necessary for survival (and well below the wages paid to men working the same jobs).

SPINDLE BOYS Young boys, some of them barefoot, clamber among the great textile machines in a Georgia cotton mill, mending broken threads and replacing empty bobbins. Many of them were the children or siblings of women who worked in the plant. The photograph is by Lewis Hine, who traveled around the country documenting abuses for the National Child Labor Committee. (© Bettmann/Corbis)

At least 1.7 million children under sixteen years of age were employed in factories and fields; 10 percent of all girls aged ten to fifteen, and 20 percent of all boys, held jobs. Under public pressure, thirty-eight states passed child labor laws in the late *Child Labor* nineteenth century. But 60 percent of child workers were employed in agriculture, which was typically exempt from the laws. For children employed in factories, the laws merely set a minimum age of twelve years and a maximum workday of ten hours, standards that employers often ignored in any case.

EMERGING UNIONIZATION

Laborers attempted to fight back against such conditions by creating national unions. By the end of the century, however, their efforts had met with little success.

There had been craft unions in America, representing small groups of skilled workers, since well before the Civil War. But most unions could not hope to exert significant power in the economy. And during the turbulent recession years of the 1870s, unions faced the additional problem of widespread public hostility. When labor disputes with employers turned bitter and violent, as they occasionally did, much of the public instinctively blamed the workers for the trouble, rarely the employers. Particularly alarming to middle-class Americans was the emergence of the "Molly Maguires," *Molly Maguires* an Irish secret society, in the anthracite coal region of western Pennsylvania. This militant labor organization sometimes used violence and even murder in its battle with coal operators.

Excitement over the Molly Maguires paled beside the near hysteria that gripped the *Railroad Strike of 1877* country during the railroad strike of 1877, which began when the eastern railroads announced a 10 percent wage cut and soon expanded into something approaching a class war. Strikers disrupted rail service from Baltimore to St. Louis, destroyed equipment, and rioted in the streets of Pittsburgh and other cities. State militias were called out, and in July President Hayes ordered federal troops to suppress the disorders. In Baltimore, eleven demonstrators died and forty were wounded in a conflict between workers and militiamen. In Philadelphia, the state militia killed twenty people when the troops opened fire on thousands of workers and their families who were attempting to block the railroad crossings. In all, over 100 people died before the strike finally collapsed several weeks after it had begun. The great railroad strike was America's first major national labor conflict.

THE KNIGHTS OF LABOR

In the first major effort to create a genuinely national labor organization, the Noble Order of the Knights of Labor was founded in 1869 under the leadership of Uriah S. Stephens. Membership was open to all who "toiled," a definition that included all workers, most business and professional people, and virtually all women—whether they worked in factories, as domestic servants, or in their own homes. Only lawyers, bankers, liquor dealers, and professional gamblers were excluded. The Knights of Labor championed an eight-hour workday and the abolition of child labor, but they were more interested in long-range reform of the economy. The Knights hoped to replace the "wage system" with a new "cooperative system," in which workers would themselves control their workplaces.

For several years, the Knights remained a secret fraternal organization. But in the late 1870s, under the leadership of Terence V. Powderly, the order moved into the open and entered a period of spectacular expansion. By 1886, it claimed a total membership of over 700,000. Local unions or assemblies associated with the Knights launched a series of railroad and other strikes in the 1880s in defiance of Powderly's wishes. Their failures to win any meaningful concessions helped discredit the organization. By 1890, membership of the Knights had shrunk to 100,000. A few years later, the organization disappeared altogether.

THE AMERICAN FEDERATION OF LABOR

Even before the Knights began to decline, a rival association appeared. In 1881, representatives of a number of craft unions formed the Federation of Organized Trade and Labor Unions of the United States and Canada. Five years later, this body took the name it has borne ever since, the American Federation of Labor (AFL).

Rejecting the Knights' idea of one big union for everybody, the federation was an association of essentially autonomous craft unions that represented mainly skilled workers. *Samuel Gompers* Samuel Gompers, the powerful leader of the AFL, concentrated on labor's immediate objectives: wages, hours, and working conditions. As one of its first objectives, the AFL demanded a national eight-hour workday and called for a general strike if the goal was not achieved by May 1, 1886. On that day, strikes and demonstrations for a shorter workday took place all over the country.

In Chicago, a center of labor and radical strength, a strike was already in progress at the McCormick Harvester Company. City police had been harassing the strikers, and labor and radical leaders called a protest meeting at Haymarket Square on May 1. *Haymarket Bombing* When the police ordered the crowd to disperse, someone threw a bomb that killed seven policemen and injured sixty-seven others. The police, who had killed four strikers the day before, fired into the crowd and killed four more people. Conservative, property-conscious Americans—frightened and outraged—demanded retribution. Chicago officials finally rounded up eight anarchists and charged them with murder, on the grounds that their statements had incited whoever had hurled the bomb. All eight scapegoats were found guilty after a remarkably injudicious trial. Seven were sentenced to death. One of them committed suicide, four were executed, and two had their sentences commuted to life imprisonment.

To most middle-class Americans, the Haymarket bombing was an alarming symbol of social chaos and radicalism. "Anarchism" now became in the public mind a code word for terrorism and violence, even though most anarchists were relatively peaceful. For the next thirty years, the specter of anarchism remained one of the most frightening concepts in the American imagination. Business owners exploited it to smear labor leaders and disrupt their activities. It became a constant obstacle to the goals of the AFL and other labor organizations, and it did particular damage to the Knights of Labor. However much they tried to distance themselves from radicals, labor leaders were always vulnerable to accusations of anarchism, as the violent strikes of the 1890s occasionally illustrated.

THE HOMESTEAD STRIKE

The Amalgamated Association of Iron and Steel Workers was the most powerful trade union in the country in the late 1800s. Its members were skilled workers, in great demand by employers, and they had long been able to exercise significant power in the workplace. In the mid-1880s, however, demand for skilled workers declined as new production methods changed the steelmaking process. In the streamlined Carnegie system, which was coming to dominate the steel industry, the union was able to maintain a foothold in only one of the corporation's three major factories—the Homestead plant near Pittsburgh.

By 1890, Carnegie and his chief lieutenant, Henry Clay Frick, had decided that the Amalgamated "had to go." Over the next two years, they repeatedly cut wages at Homestead. At first, the union acquiesced, aware that it was not strong enough to wage a successful strike. But in 1892, when the company stopped even discussing its decisions with the union and gave it two days to accept another wage cut, the Amalgamated called for a strike.

Frick abruptly shut down the plant and called in 300 guards from the Pinkerton Detective Agency, well known as strikebreakers, to enable the company to hire *Pinkertons* nonunion workers. They approached the plant by river, on barges, on July 6, 1892. The strikers poured gasoline on the water, set it on fire, and then met the Pinkertons at the docks with guns and dynamite. After several hours of fighting, which killed three guards and ten strikers and injured many others, the Pinkertons surrendered and were escorted roughly out of town.

But the workers' victory was temporary. The governor of Pennsylvania, at the company's request, sent the state's entire National Guard contingent, some 8,000 men, to

Homestead. Production resumed, with strikebreakers now protected by troops. And public opinion turned against the strikers when a radical made an attempt to assassinate Frick. Slowly, workers drifted back to their jobs, and finally—four months after the strike began—the Amalgamated surrendered. By 1900, every major steel plant in the Northeast had broken with the Amalgamated. Its membership shrank from a high of 24,000 in 1891 (two-thirds of all eligible steelworkers) to fewer than 7,000 a decade later.

THE PULLMAN STRIKE

A dispute of greater magnitude, if less violence, was the Pullman strike in 1894. The Pullman Palace Car Company manufactured railroad sleeping and parlor cars at a plant near Chicago. There the company constructed a 600-acre town, Pullman, and rented its trim, orderly houses to the employees. George M. Pullman, owner of the company, saw the town as a model—a solution to the problems of industrial workers. But many residents chafed at the regimentation (and the high rents). In the winter of 1893–1894, the Pullman Company slashed wages by about 25 percent, citing its own declining revenues in the depression, without reducing the rent it charged its employees. Workers went on strike and persuaded the militant American Railway Union, led by Eugene V. Debs, to support *Eugene V. Debs and the Railway Union* them by refusing to handle Pullman cars and equipment. Within a few days, thousands of railroad workers in twenty-seven states and territories were on strike, and transportation from Chicago to the Pacific Coast shut down.

Unlike most elected politicians, the governor of Illinois, John Peter Altgeld, was a man with demonstrated sympathies for workers and their grievances. He refused to call out the militia to protect employers. Infuriated, railroad operators bypassed Altgeld and asked the federal government to send regular army troops to Illinois, using the pretext that the strike was preventing the movement of mail on the trains. In July 1894, President Grover Cleveland ordered 2,000 troops to the Chicago area. A federal court issued an injunction forbidding the union to continue the strike. When Debs and his associates defied it, they were arrested and imprisoned. With federal troops protecting the hiring of new workers and with the union leaders in a federal jail, the strike quickly collapsed.

SOURCES OF LABOR WEAKNESS

In the last decades of the nineteenth century, labor made few real gains despite militant organizing efforts. Industrial wages rose hardly at all. To be sure, labor leaders won a few legislative victories—the abolition of the Contract Labor Law, the establishment of an eight-hour day for government employees, compensation for some workers injured on the job, and others. But many such laws were not enforced. Widespread strikes and pro-tests, and many other working-class forms of resistance, large and small, led to few enduring gains. The end of the century found most workers with less political power and less control of the workplace than they had had forty years before.

Workers failed to make greater gains for many reasons. The principal labor organiza-tions represented only a small percentage of the industrial workforce; the AFL, the most important, blatantly excluded unskilled workers and most women, blacks, and recent immigrants. Divisions within the workforce, such as tensions among different ethnic and racial groups, contributed further to union weakness.

Another source of labor weakness was the shifting nature of the workforce. Many immigrant workers came to America intending to earn some money and then return home.

The assumption that they had no long-range future in the country tamed their enthusiasm to organize. Other workers were in constant motion, moving from one job to another, one town to another, seldom in a single place long enough to establish any institutional ties or exert any real power.

Above all, perhaps, workers made few gains in the late nineteenth century because they faced corporate organizations of vast wealth and power, which were generally determined to crush any efforts by workers to challenge their prerogatives. And as the Homestead and Pullman strikes suggest, the corporations usually had the support of local, state, and federal authorities, who were willing to send in troops to "preserve order" and crush labor uprisings on demand.

Despite the creation of new labor unions and a wave of strikes and protests, workers in the late nineteenth century failed on the whole to create successful organizations or to protect their interests. In the battle for power within the emerging industrial economy, almost all the advantages seemed to lie with capital.

CONCLUSION

In the four decades after the Civil War, the United States propelled itself into the forefront of the industrializing nations of the world. Large areas of the nation remained overwhelmingly rural, to be sure. But even so, America's economy, and along with it the nation's society and culture, was being profoundly transformed.

New technologies, new forms of corporate management, and new supplies of labor helped make possible the rapid growth of the nation's industries and the construction of its railroads. The factory system contributed to the growth of the nation's cities. Immigration provided a steady supply of new workers for the growing industrial economy. The result was a steady increase in national wealth, rising living standards for much of the population, and the creation of great new fortunes.

But industrialization did not spread its fruits evenly. Large areas of the country, most notably the South, and large groups in the population, most notably minorities, women, and recent immigrants, profited relatively little from economic growth. Industrial workers experienced arduous conditions of labor. Small merchants and manufacturers found themselves overmatched by great new combinations.

Industrialists strove to create a rationale for their power and to persuade the public that everyone had something to gain from it. But many Americans remained skeptical of modern capitalism, and some—workers struggling to form unions, reformers denouncing trusts, socialists envisioning a new world, and many others—created broad and powerful critiques of the new economic order. Industrialization brought both progress and pain to late-nineteenth-century America. Controversies over its effects defined the era and would continue to define the first decades of the twentieth century.

KEY TERMS/PEOPLE/PLACES/EVENTS

American Federation of Labor 422

American Socialist Party 419

Andrew Carnegie 411

Edward Bellamy 419

Eugene V. Debs 424

gospel of wealth 413

Haymarket bombing 423

Henry Clay Frick 411

Henry Ford 408

Henry George 419

Homestead Strike 423

Horatio Alger 413

horizontal integration 411

John D. Rockefeller 411

J. P. Morgan 411

Knights of Labor 422

Louisa May Alcott 413

Molly Maguires 421

monopoly 419

Pullman strike 424

Samuel Gompers 422

Social Darwinism 412

Taylorism 409

vertical integration 411

Wilbur and Orville
 Wright 408

RECALL AND REFLECT

1. Who were some of the business and industrial titans of the late nineteenth century, and what did they contribute to America's industrial growth?
2. What changes took place in corporate organization in the late nineteenth century, and how did these changes affect the nation's economy?
3. What was the gospel of wealth?
4. How did Social Darwinism attempt to justify the social consequences of industrial capitalism?
5. How did workers respond to the expansion of industrialization and the new industrial economy?

18 | THE AGE OF THE CITY

THE NEW URBAN GROWTH

THE URBAN LANDSCAPE

STRAINS OF URBAN LIFE

THE RISE OF MASS CONSUMPTION

LEISURE IN THE CONSUMER SOCIETY

HIGH CULTURE IN THE URBAN AGE

LOOKING AHEAD

1. What were some of the problems that resulted from rapid urbanization, and how did urban governments respond to these problems?

2. How did the sources of immigration to America shift in the late nineteenth century, and what was the native response to the change?

3. How did the rise of mass consumption affect leisure and entertainment?

THE FACE OF AMERICAN SOCIETY was transformed in countless ways by the growth of industry and commerce. But no change was more profound than the growing size and influence of cities. Having begun its life as a primarily agrarian republic, the United States in the late nineteenth century was becoming an urban nation.

1869

First intercollegiate football game

1870

NYC opens first elevated railroads

1871

Boston and Chicago fires

1872

Boss Tweed convicted

1876

Baseball's National League founded

1882

Congress restricts Chinese immigration

1884

First "skyscraper" in Chicago

1890

Riis's *How the Other Half Lives*

1891

Basketball invented

1894

Immigration Restriction League formed

1897

Boston opens first subway in America

1899

Chopin's *The Awakening*

1901

Baseball's American League founded

1903

First World Series

THE NEW URBAN GROWTH

Although the great movement of people to the city was not unique to the United States, Americans found urbanization particularly jarring. The urban population increased sevenfold in the half century after the Civil War. And in 1920, the census revealed that for the first time, a majority of the American people lived in "urban" areas—defined as communities of 2,500 people or more.

Natural increase accounted for only a small part of the urban growth. Families in cities experienced a high rate of infant mortality, a declining fertility rate, and a high death rate from disease. It was immigration, rather, that expanded the urban population so dramatically.

THE MIGRATIONS

In the late nineteenth century, Americans left the declining agricultural regions of the East at a dramatic rate. Some moved to the newly developing farmlands of the West. But almost as many moved to the growing cities of the East and the Midwest.

Among those leaving rural America for industrial cities in the 1880s were black men and women trying to escape the poverty, debt, violence, and oppression they faced in the rural South. They were also seeking new opportunities in cities. Factory jobs for African Americans were rare and professional opportunities almost nonexistent. Urban blacks tended to work in service occupations as cooks, janitors, domestic servants, and so on. Because many such jobs were considered women's work, black women often outnumbered black men in the cities.

The most important source of urban population growth, however, was the great number of new immigrants from abroad—part of a larger pattern of mobility around the world. (See "America in the World: Global Migrations.") Some came from Canada, Latin America, and—particularly on the West Coast—China and Japan. But the greatest number came from Europe. After 1880, the flow of new arrivals began to include large numbers of people from southern and eastern Europe. By the 1890s, more than half of all immigrants came from these regions.

In earlier years, most new immigrants from Europe (particularly Germans and Scandinavians) had arrived with at least some money and education. Most of them arrived at one of the major port cities on the Atlantic Coast (the greatest number landing at New York's immigrant depot at Castle Garden) and then headed west. But the new immigrants of the late nineteenth century generally lacked the capital to buy farmland and lacked the education to establish themselves in professions. So, like similarly poor Irish immigrants before the Civil War, they settled overwhelmingly in industrial cities, where they worked largely in unskilled jobs.

THE ETHNIC CITY

By 1890, most of the population of the major cities consisted of immigrants: 87 percent of the population in Chicago, 80 percent in New York, 84 percent in Milwaukee and

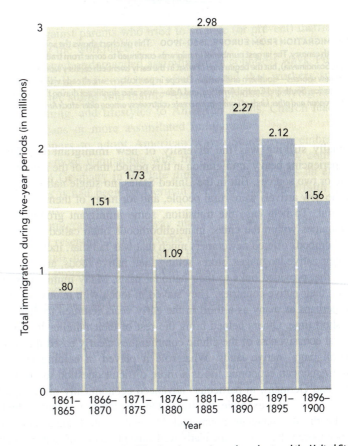

TOTAL IMMIGRATION, 1861–1900 Over 10 million immigrants from abroad entered the United States in the last forty years of the nineteenth century, with particularly high numbers arriving in the 1880s and 1890s. This chart shows the pattern of immigration in five-year intervals. • *What external events might help explain some of the rises and falls in the rates of immigration in these years?*

of leisure in *The Theory of Prosperity* (1902), *The New Basis of Civilization* (1910), and other works. He challenged the centuries-old assumption that the normal condition of civilization was a scarcity of goods. In earlier times, Patten argued, fear of scarcity had caused people to place a high value on thrift, self-denial, and restraint. But in modern industrial societies, new economies could create enough wealth to satisfy not just the needs but also the desires of all.

As Americans became more accustomed to leisure as a normal part of life, they began to look for new experiences and entertainments. Mass entertainment occasionally bridged differences of class, race, and gender. But it could also be sharply divided. Saloons and some sporting events tended to be male preserves. Shopping and going to tea rooms and luncheonettes were more characteristic of female leisure. Theaters, pubs, and clubs were often specific to particular ethnic communities or particular work groups. When the classes did meet in public spaces—as they did, for example, in city parks—there was often considerable conflict over what constituted appropriate public behavior. Elites in New York City, for example, tried to prohibit anything but quiet, "genteel" activities in Central Park, while working-class people wanted to use the public spaces for sports and entertainments.

SPECTATOR SPORTS

Among the most important responses to the search for entertainment was the rise of *Baseball* organized spectator sports, especially baseball. A game much like baseball—known as "rounders" and derived from cricket—had enjoyed limited popularity in Great Britain in the early nineteenth century. Versions of the game began to appear in America in the early 1830s. By the end of the Civil War, interest in the game had grown rapidly.

THE AMERICAN NATIONAL GAME   Long before the modern major leagues began, local baseball clubs were active throughout much of the United States, establishing the game as the "national pastime." This print of a "grand match for the championship" depicts an 1866 game at Elysian Fields, a popular park just across the river from New York City in Hoboken, New Jersey. (© Photo Reproduction by Transcendental Graphics/Getty Images)

More than 200 amateur or semiprofessional teams and clubs existed, many of which joined a national association and proclaimed a set of standard rules. As the game grew in popularity, it offered opportunities for profit. The first salaried team, the Cincinnati Red Stockings, was formed in 1869. Other cities fielded professional teams, and in 1876 the teams banded together in the National League. A rival league, the American Association, appeared and collapsed, but in 1901 the American League emerged to replace it. And in 1903, the first modern World Series was played, in which the American League's Boston Red Sox beat the National League's Pittsburgh Pirates. By then, baseball had become an important business and a national preoccupation.

Baseball had great appeal to working-class males. The second most popular game, football, appealed at first to a more elite segment of the male population, in part because it originated in colleges and universities. The first intercollegiate football game in America occurred between Princeton and Rutgers in 1869. Early intercollegiate football bore only an indirect relation to the modern game; it was more similar to present-day rugby. By the late 1870s, however, the game was becoming standardized and was taking on the outlines of its modern form.

Basketball was invented in 1891 in Springfield, Massachusetts, by Dr. James A. Naismith, a Canadian working as an athletic director for a local college.   *Basketball Invented* Boxing, which had long been a disreputable activity concentrated primarily among the urban lower classes, became by the 1880s a more popular and, in some places, more reputable sport.

Participation in the major sports was almost exclusively the province of men, but several sports emerged in which women became involved. Golf and tennis both attracted more and more relatively wealthy men and women. Bicycling and croquet also enjoyed widespread popularity in the 1890s among women as well as men. Women's colleges introduced their students to more strenuous sports as well—track, crew, swimming, and (beginning in the late 1890s) basketball.

Music, Theater, and Movies

Other forms of popular entertainment also developed in the cities. Many ethnic communities maintained their own theaters, which presented plays in the languages of the immigrant communities. Urban theaters in the heart of the cities attracted a much broader audience. They introduced new and distinctively American entertainment forms: the musical comedy, which evolved gradually from the comic operettas of Europe; and vaudeville, a   *Vaudeville* form of theater adapted from French models, which remained the most popular urban entertainment into the first decades of the twentieth century. It consisted of a variety of acts (musicians, comedians, magicians, jugglers, and others) and was, at least in the beginning, inexpensive to produce. As the economic potential of vaudeville grew, some promoters—most prominently Florenz Ziegfeld of New York—staged much more elaborate spectacles.

Vaudeville was also one of the few entertainment media open to black performers, who brought to it elements of the minstrel shows they had earlier developed for black audiences in the late nineteenth century. Some minstrel singers (including the most famous, Al Jolson) were white performers wearing heavy makeup (or "blackface"), but most were black. Entertainers of both races performed music based on the gospel and folk tunes of the plantation and on the jazz and ragtime of black urban communities. Performers of both races also tailored their acts to prevailing white prejudices, ridiculing African Americans by acting out demeaning stereotypes.

American popular entertainment was transformed with the emergence of motion picture shows. Thomas Edison and others had created the technology underpinning the motion picture in the 1880s. Soon after that, short films became available to individual viewers watching peepshows in pool halls, penny arcades, and amusement parks. Soon, larger projectors made it possible to display the images on big screens, which permitted substantial audiences to see films in theaters. By 1900, Americans were becoming attracted *Silent Films* in large numbers to these early movies—usually plotless films of trains or waterfalls or other spectacles. The director D. W. Griffith carried the motion picture into a new era with his silent epics—*The Birth of a Nation* (1915), *Intolerance* (1916), and others—which introduced serious (if notoriously racist) plots and elaborate productions to filmmaking. Motion pictures were the first truly mass entertainment medium.

PATTERNS OF PUBLIC AND PRIVATE LEISURE

Particularly striking about popular entertainment in the late nineteenth and early twentieth centuries was its public quality. Many Americans spent their leisure time in places where they would find not only entertainment but also other people. Thousands of working-class New Yorkers spent evenings in dance halls, vaudeville houses, and concert halls. More affluent New Yorkers enjoyed afternoons in Central Park, where a principal attraction was seeing other people (and being seen by them). Moviegoers were attracted not just by the movies themselves but also by the energy of the audiences at lavish new "movie palaces," just as sports fans were drawn by the crowds as well as by the games.

Perhaps the most striking example of popular public entertainment in the early twen-*Coney Island* tieth century was Coney Island, the famous and self-consciously fabulous amusement park and resort on a popular beach in Brooklyn. Luna Park, the greatest of the Coney Island attractions, opened in 1903 and provided rides, stunts, and lavish reproductions of exotic places and spectacular adventures: Japanese gardens, Venetian canals with gondoliers, a Chinese theater, a simulated trip to the moon, and reenactments of such disasters as burning buildings and earthquakes. A year later, a competing company opened Dreamland, which tried to outdo even Luna Park with a 375-foot tower, a three-ring circus, chariot races, and a Lilliputian village from *Gulliver's Travels.* The popularity of Coney Island in these years was phenomenal. Thousands of people flocked to the large resort hotels that lined the beaches. Many thousands more made day trips out from the city by train and (after 1920) subway. In 1904, the average daily attendance at Luna Park alone was 90,000 people.

Most people found Coney Island appealing in part because it provided an escape from the genteel standards that governed so much of American life at the time. In the amusement parks of Coney Island, decorum was often forgotten, and people delighted in finding themselves in situations that in any other setting would have seemed embarrassing or improper: women's skirts blown above their heads with hot air; people pummeled with water and rubber paddles by clowns; hints of sexual freedom as strangers were forced to come into physical contact with one another on rides and amusements.

Not all popular entertainment, however, involved public events. Many Americans *Dime Novels* amused themselves privately by reading novels and poetry. The so-called dime novels, cheaply bound and widely circulated, became popular after the Civil War, with detective stories, tales of the Wild West, sagas of scientific adventure, and novels of "moral uplift." Publishers also distributed sentimental novels of romance, which developed a large audience among women, as did books about animals and about young children growing up. Louisa May Alcott's *Little Women,* most of whose readers were female, sold more than 2 million copies.

THE TECHNOLOGIES OF MASS COMMUNICATION

American journalism experienced dramatic change in the decades following the Civil War. Between 1870 and 1910, the circulation of daily newspapers increased nearly ninefold (from under 3 million to more than 24 million), a rate three times as great as the rate of population increase. And while standards varied widely from one paper to another, American journalism was developing the beginnings of a professional identity. Salaries of reporters increased; many newspapers began separating the reporting of news from the expression of opinion; and newspapers themselves became important businesses.

This transformation was to a large degree a result of new technologies of communication. The emergence of national press services, for example, was a product of the telegraph, which made it possible to supply papers with news and features from around the nation and the world. By the turn of the century, important newspaper chains had emerged as well, linked together by their own internal wire services. The most powerful was owned by William Randolph Hearst, who by 1914 controlled *William Randolph Hearst* nine newspapers and two magazines. New printing technologies were making possible more elaborate layouts, the publication of color pictures, and, by the end of the century, the printing of photographs. These advances not only helped publishers make their own stories more vivid; they also made it possible for them to attract more advertisers.

THE TELEPHONE

The most important new technology of communication in the late nineteenth century was the telephone, which Alexander Graham Bell had first demonstrated in 1876. In its first years, the telephone was a relatively impractical tool. Those who subscribed to telephone service had to have direct wire links to everyone else they wished to call. In 1878, the first "switchboard" opened in New Haven, Connecticut, opening the way for more practical uses of the telephone. Once there was a switchboard, a telephone subscriber needed only a line to the central telephone office from which connections could be made to any other subscriber. A new occupation—the "telephone operator"—was born. The Bell System, which controlled all American telephone service, hired young white women to work as operators, hoping that a pleasant female voice would make the experience of using the telephone (and the inconvenience of the frequent technological problems that accompanied it) less irritating to customers. Telephone signals were very weak at first, and callers could seldom reach anyone more than a few miles away. In an effort to increase the range of telephones, engineers created the "repeater," which periodically strengthened the signal as it moved over distances. By 1914, the repeaters had improved to the point that it was now practical to envision a transcontinental line.

In its early years, the telephone was an almost entirely commercial instrument. Of the nearly 7,400 telephone customers in the New York–New Jersey area in 1891, 6,000 were businesses and organizations. Even the residential telephones tended to belong to doctors or business managers.

The growing reach of the telephone in the early years of the twentieth century made the Bell System (formally named American Telephone and Telegraph, or *The Bell System* AT&T) one of the most powerful corporations in America and a genuine monopoly.

Central to its success was an early decision by executives that the company would exclusively build and own all telephone instruments and then lease them to subscribers. That made it possible for AT&T to control both the equipment and the telephone service itself, and to exclude any competitors in either field. It also gave AT&T effective control over the local telephone companies allied with it and made the nation's telephone system into an effective cartel.

HIGH CULTURE IN THE URBAN AGE

In addition to the important changes in popular culture that accompanied the rise of cities and industry, there were profound changes in the realm of "high culture." The distinction between "highbrow" and "lowbrow" culture was largely new to the industrial era. In the early nineteenth century, most cultural activities had targeted people of all classes. By the late nineteenth century, however, elites were developing a cultural and intellectual life quite separate from the popular amusements of the urban masses.

LITERATURE AND ART IN URBAN AMERICA

One of the strongest impulses in American literature was the effort to recreate urban *Literary Realism*   social reality. This trend toward realism found an early voice in Stephen Crane, who—although perhaps best known for his novel of the Civil War, *The Red Badge of Courage* (1895)—created a sensation in 1893 when he published *Maggie: A Girl of the Streets,* a grim picture of urban poverty and slum life. Theodore Dreiser, Frank Norris, and Upton Sinclair were similarly drawn to social issues as themes. Kate Chopin, a southern writer who explored the oppressive features of traditional marriage, encountered widespread public abuse after the publication of her shocking 1899 novel, *The Awakening,* which described a young wife and mother who abandoned her family in search of personal fulfillment. William Dean Howells, in *The Rise of Silas Lapham* and other works, described what he considered the shallowness and corruption in ordinary American lifestyles.

American art through most of the nineteenth century had been overshadowed by that of Europe. By 1900, however, a number of American artists broke from Old World traditions and experimented with new styles. Winslow Homer brought a distinctive approach to his paintings of New England maritime life and other American subjects. James McNeil Whistler was one of the first Western artists to introduce Asian themes into American and European art.

By the first years of the new century, some American artists were turning decisively away from the traditional academic style (a style perhaps most identified in America by the brilliant portraitist John Singer Sargent). Members of the so-called Ashcan school *Ashcan School*   produced work startling in its naturalism and stark in its portrayal of the social realities of the era. John Sloan portrayed the dreariness of American urban slums; George Bellows caught the vigor and violence of his time in paintings and drawings of prizefights; Edward Hopper explored the starkness and loneliness of the modern city. The Ashcan artists were also among the first Americans to appreciate expressionism and abstraction; and they showed their interest in new forms in 1913, when they helped stage *Armory Show*   the famous "Armory Show" in New York City, which displayed works of the French postimpressionists and of some American moderns.

DEMPSEY AND FIRPO The artist George Bellows began painting fight scenes in the first years of the twentieth century, when boxing appealed primarily to working-class audiences. By 1924, when he painted this moment from a famous prizefight, boxing had become one of the most popular sports in America. (© Whitney Museum of American Art, New York, USA/Bridgeman Images)

THE IMPACT OF DARWINISM

One of the most profound intellectual developments in the late nineteenth century was the widespread acceptance of the theory of evolution, associated most prominently with the English naturalist Charles Darwin. Darwin argued that the human species had evolved from earlier forms of life through a process of "natural selection." History, Darwin suggested, was not the working out of a divine plan. It was a natural process dominated by the fiercest or luckiest competitors.

The theory of evolution met widespread resistance at first from educators, theologians, and even many scientists. By the end of the century, however, the evolutionists had converted most members of the urban professional and educated classes. Even many middle-class Protestant religious leaders had accepted the doctrine, making significant alterations in theology to accommodate it. The rise of Darwinism, however, *Divisions over Darwinism* contributed to something unseen by most urban Americans at the time: a deep schism between the new, cosmopolitan culture of the city and the more traditional, provincial culture of some rural areas. Thus the late nineteenth century saw not only the rise of a liberal Protestantism in tune with new scientific discoveries but also the beginning of an organized Protestant fundamentalism.

Darwinism helped spawn other new intellectual currents. There was the Social Darwinism of William Graham Sumner and others, which industrialists used so enthusiastically to justify their favored position in American life. But there were also more sophisticated philosophies, among them a doctrine that became known as "pragmatism."

William James, a Harvard psychologist (and brother of the novelist Henry James), was the most prominent publicist of the new theory, although earlier intellectuals such as Charles S. Peirce and later ones such as John Dewey were also important to its develop-
"Pragmatism" ment and dissemination. According to the pragmatists, modern society should rely for guidance not on inherited ideals and moral principles but on the test of scientific inquiry. No idea or institution (not even religious faith) was valid, they claimed, unless it "worked," unless it stood the test of experience.

A similar concern for scientific inquiry was influencing the social sciences. Sociologists such as Edward A. Ross and Lester Frank Ward urged applying the scientific method to the solution of social and political problems. Historians such as Frederick Jackson Turner and Charles Beard argued that economic factors more than spiritual ideals had been the governing force in historical development. John Dewey proposed a new approach to education that placed less emphasis on the rote learning of traditional knowledge and more on flexible, democratic schooling.

The implications of Darwinism also promoted the growth of anthropology and encouraged some scholars to begin examining other cultures in new ways. Some white Americans began to look at Indian society, for example, as a coherent culture with its own norms and values that were worthy of respect and preservation, even though they were different from those of white society.

TOWARD UNIVERSAL SCHOOLING

The growing demand for specialized skills and scientific knowledge naturally created a growing, and changing, demand for education. The late nineteenth century, therefore, was a time of rapid expansion and reform of American schools and universities.

Free public primary and secondary education spread rapidly. By 1900, compulsory school attendance laws existed in thirty-one states and territories. Education was still far from universal. Rural areas lagged far behind urban-industrial ones in funding public education. In the South, many African Americans had no access to schools at all. But for many white men and women, educational opportunities were expanding rapidly.

Educational reformers tried to extend educational opportunities to the Indian tribes as well, in an effort to "civilize" them and help them adapt to white society. In the 1870s, reformers recruited small groups of Indians to attend Hampton Institute (a primarily black college). In 1879, they organized the Carlisle Indian Industrial School in Pennsylvania. Like many black colleges, Carlisle emphasized practical "industrial" education. Ultimately, however, these reform efforts failed, in part because they were unpopular with their intended beneficiaries.

UNIVERSITIES AND THE GROWTH OF SCIENCE AND TECHNOLOGY

Colleges and universities also proliferated rapidly in the late nineteenth century. The Morrill Land Grant Act of 1862, by which the federal government had donated public land to states for the establishment of colleges, led to the creation of sixty-nine "land-grant" institutions in the last decades of the century—among them the state university systems of California, Illinois, Minnesota, and Wisconsin. Other universities, including Chicago, Columbia, Harvard, Northwestern, Princeton, Syracuse, and Yale, benefited from millions of dollars contributed by business and financial titans such as Rockefeller and Carnegie. Other philanthropists founded new universities or reorganized older ones to perpetuate their family names—for example, Vanderbilt, Johns Hopkins, Cornell, Duke, Tulane, and Stanford.

These and other universities played a vital role in the economic development of the United States in the late nineteenth century and beyond. The land-grant institutions were specifically mandated to advance knowledge in "agriculture *Higher Education and the Economy* and mechanics." From the beginning, therefore, they were committed not just to abstract knowledge but to making discoveries that would be of practical use to farmers and manufacturers. As they evolved into great state universities, they retained that tradition and became the source of many of the great discoveries that helped American industry and commerce advance. Private universities emerged that served many of the same purposes: the Massachusetts Institute of Technology, founded in 1865, soon became the nation's premier engineering school; Johns Hopkins University in Baltimore, founded in 1876, did much to advance medical scholarship, as did the Rockefeller Institute for Medical Research in New York (later Rockefeller University) and the Carnegie Institution. By the early twentieth century, older and more traditional universities were beginning to form relationships with the private sector and the government, doing research that did not just advance knowledge for its own sake but that was directly applicable to practical problems of the time.

MEDICAL SCIENCE

Both the culture of and the scientific basis for medical care were changing rapidly in the early twentieth century. Most doctors were beginning to accept the new medical assumption that there were underlying causes to particular symptoms—that a symptom was not itself a disease. They were also beginning to make use of new or improved technologies—the X-ray, improved microscopes, and other diagnostic devices—that made it possible to classify, and distinguish among, different diseases. Laboratory tests could now identify infections such as typhoid and dysentery. These technologies were a critical first step toward the effective treatment of diseases. At about the same time, pharmaceutical research began to produce some important new medicines. Aspirin was first synthesized in 1899. Other researchers experimented with chemicals that might destroy diseases in the blood, an effort that eventually led to the various forms of chemotherapy that are still widely used in treating cancer. In 1906, an American surgeon, G. W. Crile, became the first physician to use blood transfusion in treatment, which revolutionized surgery. In the past, patients often lost so much blood during operations that extensive surgery could be fatal for that reason alone. With transfusions, it became possible to conduct much longer and more elaborate operations.

The widespread acceptance by the end of the nineteenth century of the germ theory of disease had important implications. Physicians quickly discovered that *Germ Theory Accepted* exposure to germs did not by itself necessarily cause disease, and they began looking for the other factors that determined who got sick and who did not. Among the factors they eventually discovered were general health, previous medical history, diet and nutrition, and eventually genetic predisposition. The awareness of the importance of infection in spreading disease also encouraged doctors to sterilize their instruments, use surgical gloves, and otherwise purify the medical environment.

By the early twentieth century, American physicians and surgeons were generally recognized as among the best in the world, and American medical education *Declining Mortality* was beginning to attract students from many other countries. These improvements in medical knowledge and training, along with improvements in sanitation and public health, did much to reduce infection and mortality in most American communities.

EDUCATION FOR WOMEN

The post–Civil War era saw an important expansion of educational opportunities for women, although such opportunities continued to lag far behind those available to men and were almost entirely denied to black women.

Most public high schools accepted women readily, but opportunities for higher education were fewer. At the end of the Civil War, only three American colleges were coeducational. After the war, many of the land-grant colleges and universities in the Midwest and such private universities as Cornell and Wesleyan began to admit women along with men. But coeducation was less crucial to women's education in this period than was the creation of a network of women's colleges. Mount Holyoke in central Massachusetts had begun its life in 1836 as a "seminary" for women; it became a full-fledged college in the 1880s, at about the same time that entirely new female institutions were emerging: Vassar, Wellesley, Smith, Bryn Mawr, Wells, and Goucher. A few of the larger private universities created separate colleges for women on their campuses (Barnard at Columbia and Radcliffe at Harvard, for example).

The female college was part of an important phenomenon in the history of modern American women: the emergence of distinctive women's communities outside the family. Most faculty members and many administrators were women (usually unmarried). And college life produced a spirit of sorority and commitment among educated women that had important effects in later years. Most female college graduates ultimately married, but they married at a more advanced age than their noncollege counterparts. A significant minority, perhaps over 25 percent, did not marry at all, but devoted themselves to careers. The growth of female higher education clearly became for some women a liberating experience, persuading them that they had roles other than those of wives and mothers to perform in their rapidly changing urban-industrial society.

CONCLUSION

The extraordinary growth of American cities in the last decades of the nineteenth century led to both great achievements and enormous problems. Cities became centers of learning, art, and commerce and produced great advances in technology, transportation, architecture, and communications. They provided their residents—and their many visitors—with varied and dazzling experiences, so much so that people increasingly left the countryside to move to the city.

But cities were also places of congestion, filth, disease, and corruption. With populations expanding too rapidly for services to keep up, most American cities in this era struggled with makeshift techniques to solve the basic problems of providing water, disposing of sewage, building roads, running public transportation, fighting fire, stopping crime, and preventing or curing disease. City governments, many of them dominated by political machines and ruled by party bosses, were often models of inefficiency and corruption—although in their informal way they also provided substantial services to the working-class and immigrant constituencies who needed them most. Yet they also managed to oversee great public projects: the building of parks, museums, opera houses, and theaters, usually in partnership with private developers.

The city brought together races, ethnic groups, and classes of extraordinary variety—from the families of great wealth that the new industrial age was creating to the vast working class, much of it consisting of immigrants, who crowded into densely packed neighborhoods divided by nationality. The city also spawned temples of consumerism: shops, boutiques, and, above all, the great department stores. And it created forums for public recreation and entertainment: parks, theaters, athletic fields, amusement parks, and, later, movie palaces.

Urban life created anxiety among those who lived within the cities and among those who observed them from afar. But in fact, American cities adapted reasonably successfully over time to the great demands their growth made of them and learned to govern themselves if not entirely honestly and efficiently, at least enough to allow them to survive and grow.

KEY TERMS/PEOPLE/PLACES/EVENTS

Armory Show 448
Ashcan school 448
city beautiful
  movement 434
Coney Island 446
consumerism 440
Darwinism 449

Jacob Riis 436
Kate Chopin 448
National Consumers
  League 443
Public Health Service 437
Tammany Hall 440
tenements 436

Theodore Dreiser 438
vaudeville 445
William James 450
William M. Tweed 440
William Randolph
  Hearst 447

RECALL AND REFLECT

1. What groups of people were most likely to move to the cities of late-nineteenth-century America, and why?
2. What was the relationship between immigration and urbanization in the late nineteenth century?
3. How did the new consumer economy affect roles and expectations for women?
4. What was Darwinism, and what was its impact on American intellectual life?

19 FROM CRISIS TO EMPIRE

THE POLITICS OF EQUILIBRIUM

THE AGRARIAN REVOLT

THE CRISIS OF THE 1890s

STIRRINGS OF IMPERIALISM

WAR WITH SPAIN

THE REPUBLIC AS EMPIRE

LOOKING AHEAD

1. What were the major social and economic problems that beset the United States in the late nineteenth century, and how did the two major political parties respond to these problems?

2. What was Populism, what were its goals, and to what degree were these goals achieved?

3. How did the United States become an imperial power?

THE UNITED STATES APPROACHED the end of the nineteenth century as a fundamentally different nation from what it had been at the beginning of the Civil War. With rapid change came cascading social and political problems—problems that the weak and conservative governments of the time showed little inclination or ability to address.

A catastrophic economic depression that began in 1893 created devastating hardship for millions of Americans. Farmers responded by creating an agrarian political movement known as Populism. American workers, facing massive unemployment, staged large and occasionally violent strikes. Not since the Civil War had American politics been so polarized and impassioned. The election of 1896, which pitted the agrarian hero William Jennings Bryan against the solid conservative William McKinley, was dramatic but anticlimactic. Supported by the mighty Republican Party and many eastern groups who looked with suspicion and unease at the agricultural demands coming from the West, McKinley easily triumphed.

McKinley did little in his first term in office to resolve the problems and grievances of his time, but the economy revived nevertheless. Having largely ignored the depression, however, McKinley focused on another great national cause: the plight of Cuba in its war with Spain. In the spring of 1898, the United States declared war on Spain and entered the conflict in Cuba—a brief but bloody war that ended with an American victory four months later.

454 ·

The conflict had begun as a way to support Cuban independence from the Spanish, but a group of fervent and influential imperialists worked to convert the war into an occasion for acquiring overseas possessions. Despite a powerful anti-imperialist movement, the acquisition of the former Spanish colonies proceeded—only to draw Americans into yet another imperial war, this one in the Philippines, where the Americans, not the Spanish, were the targets of local enmity.

THE POLITICS OF EQUILIBRIUM

The enormous social and economic changes of the late nineteenth century strained not only the nation's traditional social arrangements but its political institutions as well. Searching for stability and social justice, Americans looked to the government for leadership. Yet that government during much of this period was ill equipped to confront these new challenges. As a result, problems and grievances festered and grew.

THE PARTY SYSTEM

The most striking feature of late-nineteenth-century politics was the stability of the party system. From the end of Reconstruction until the late 1890s, the electorate was divided almost evenly between the Republicans and the Democrats. Sixteen states were solidly and consistently Republican, and fourteen states (most in the South) were solidly and consistently Democratic. Only a handful of states were usually in doubt, and they generally decided the results of national elections, often on the basis of voter turnout. The Republican Party captured the presidency in all but two of the elections of the era, but in the five presidential elections beginning in 1876, the average popular-vote margin separating the Democratic and Republican candidates was 1.5 percent. The congressional

TIME LINE

1867
National Grange founded

1876
Hayes elected president

1880
Garfield elected president

1881
Garfield assassinated; Arthur becomes president

1884
Cleveland elected president

1887
Interstate Commerce Act

U.S. gains base at Pearl Harbor

1888
Benjamin Harrison elected president

1890
Sherman Antitrust Act

Sherman Silver Purchase Act

McKinley Tariff

1892
Cleveland elected president again

People's Party formed

1893
Revolution in Hawaii

Economic depression begins

Sherman Silver Purchase Act repealed

1894
Coxey's Army marches on Washington, D.C.

1896
McKinley elected president

1898
War with Spain

Treaty of Paris

U.S. annexes Hawaii, Puerto Rico, Philippines

1898–1902
Philippines revolt

1899
Open Door notes

1900
Boxer Rebellion

McKinley reelected

1901
Platt Amendment

balance was similarly stable, with the Republicans generally controlling the Senate and the Democrats generally controlling the House.

High Voter Turnout Despite the relatively modest differences, most eligible Americans had strong loyalties to their chosen party. Voter turnout in presidential elections between 1860 and 1900 averaged over 78 percent of all eligible voters. Large groups of potential voters were disenfranchised in these years: women in most states and almost all blacks and many poor whites in the South. But for adult white males, there were few restrictions on voting.

Reasons for Party Loyalties What explains this extraordinary loyalty to the two political parties? It was not that the parties took distinct positions on important public issues. They did so rarely. Party loyalties reflected other factors. Region was perhaps the most important. To white southerners, loyalty to the Democratic Party—the vehicle by which they had triumphed over Reconstruction and preserved white supremacy—was a matter of unquestioned faith. Republican loyalties were equally intense in the North. To many, the party of Lincoln remained a bulwark against slavery and treason.

Religious and ethnic differences also shaped party loyalties. The Democratic Party attracted most of the Catholic voters, recent immigrants, and poorer workers. The Republican Party appealed to northern Protestants, citizens of old stock, and much of the middle class. Among the few substantive issues on which the parties took clearly different stands were immigration matters. Republicans tended to support immigration restriction and to favor temperance legislation, which many believed would help discipline immigrant communities. Catholics and immigrants viewed such proposals as assaults on them and their cultures, and the Democratic Party followed their lead.

Party identification, then, was usually more a reflection of cultural inclinations than a calculation of economic interest. Individuals might affiliate with a party because their parents had done so or because it was the party of their region, their church, or their ethnic group.

The National Government

One reason the parties avoided most substantive issues was that the federal government did relatively little. The government in Washington was responsible for delivering the mail, maintaining a military, conducting foreign policy, and collecting tariffs and taxes. It had few other responsibilities and few institutions capable of undertaking additional responsibilities even if it had chosen to do so.

First Pension System There was one significant exception. From the end of the Civil War to the early twentieth century, the federal government administered a system of annual pensions for retired Union Civil War veterans and their widows. At its peak, this pension system was making payments to a majority of the male citizens (black and white) of the North and to many women as well. Some reformers hoped to make the system permanent and universal, others found it corrupt and expensive. When the Civil War generation died out, the pension system died with it.

In most other respects, the United States in the late nineteenth century was a society without a modern national government. The most powerful institutions were the two political parties (and the bosses and machines that dominated them) and the federal courts.

PRESIDENTS AND PATRONAGE

Presidents in the late nineteenth century had great symbolic importance, but they were unable to do very much except distribute government appointments. A new president and his tiny staff had to make almost 100,000 appointments.

It sometimes proved impossible for a president to avoid factional conflict, as the presidency of Rutherford B. Hayes demonstrated. By the end of his term, two groups—the Stalwarts, led by Roscoe Conkling of New York, and the Half-Breeds,   *Stalwarts and Half-Breeds* captained by James G. Blaine of Maine—were competing for control of the Republican Party. Rhetorically, the Stalwarts favored traditional, professional machine politics, while the Half-Breeds favored reform. In fact, both groups were mainly interested in a larger share of patronage. Hayes tried to satisfy both and ended up satisfying neither.

The battle over patronage overshadowed all else during Hayes's unhappy presidency. His one important, substantive initiative—an effort to create a civil service system—attracted no support from either party. And his early announcement that he would not seek reelection only weakened him further.

The Republicans managed to retain the presidency in 1880 in part because they agreed on a ticket that included a Stalwart and a Half-Breed. They nominated James A. Garfield, a veteran congressman from Ohio and a Half-Breed, for president and Chester A. Arthur of New York, a Stalwart, for vice president. The Democrats nominated General Winfield Scott Hancock, a minor Civil War commander with no national following. Benefiting from the end of the recession of 1879, Garfield won a decisive electoral victory, although his popular-vote margin was thin.

GETTING HOT ENOUGH FOR HIM.

PRESIDENT CHESTER A. ARTHUR   Although originally a Stalwart, Arthur attempted to reform the spoils system. In this *Puck* cartoon, he is catching heat from a variety of Republican factions, including the Stalwarts and Half-Breeds. (The Library of Congress)

Garfield began his presidency by defying the Stalwarts and supporting civil service reform. He soon found himself embroiled in an ugly public quarrel with Conkling and the Stalwarts. The dispute was never resolved. On July 2, 1881, only four months after *Garfield Assassinated* his inauguration, Garfield was shot twice while standing in the Washington railroad station by an apparently deranged gunman (and unsuccessful office seeker) who shouted, "I am a Stalwart and Arthur is president now!" Garfield lingered for nearly three months but finally died.

Garfield's successor, Chester A. Arthur, had spent his political lifetime as a devoted, skilled, and open spoilsman and a close ally of the New York political boss Roscoe Conkling. But on becoming president, he tried—like Hayes and Garfield before him—to follow an independent course and even to promote reform. To the dismay of the Stalwarts, Arthur kept most of Garfield's appointees in office and supported civil service reform. In *Pendleton Act* 1883, Congress passed the first national civil service measure, the Pendleton Act, which required that some federal jobs be filled by competitive written examinations rather than by patronage. Relatively few offices fell under civil service at first, but its reach steadily widened.

Cleveland, Harrison, and the Tariff

In the unsavory election of 1884, the Republican candidate for president was Senator James G. Blaine of Maine—known to his admirers as the "Plumed Knight" but to many others as a symbol of seamy party politics. A group of disgruntled "liberal Republicans," known by their critics as the "mugwumps," announced that they would bolt the party and support an honest Democrat. Rising to the bait, the Democrats nominated Grover Cleveland, the reform governor of New York.

In a campaign filled with personal invective, what may have decided the election was the last-minute introduction of a religious controversy. Shortly before the election, a delegation of Protestant ministers called on Blaine in New York City; their spokesman, Dr. Samuel Burchard, referred to the Democrats as the party of "rum, Romanism, and rebellion." Blaine was slow to repudiate Burchard's indiscretion, and Democrats quickly *Cleveland Elected* spread the news that Blaine had tolerated a slander on the Catholic Church. Cleveland's narrow victory probably resulted from an unusually heavy Catholic vote for the Democrats in New York.

Grover Cleveland was respected, if not often liked, for his stern and righteous opposition to politicians, grafters, pressure groups, and Tammany Hall. He embodied an era in which few Americans believed the federal government could, or should, do very much. Cleveland had always doubted the wisdom of protective tariffs (taxes on imported goods designed to protect domestic producers). The existing high rates, he believed, were responsible for the annual surplus in federal revenues, which was tempting Congress to pass "reckless" and "extravagant" legislation, which he frequently vetoed. In December 1887, therefore, he asked Congress to reduce the tariff rates. Democrats in the House approved a tariff reduction, but Senate Republicans defiantly passed a bill of their own, actually raising the rates. The resulting deadlock made the tariff an issue in the election of 1888.

The Democrats renominated Cleveland and supported tariff reductions. Endorsing protection, Republicans settled on former senator Benjamin Harrison of Indiana, who was obscure but respectable (and the grandson of President William Henry Harrison). It was *Harrison Elected* one of the most corrupt elections in American history. Cleveland won the popular vote by 100,000, but Harrison won an electoral majority of 233 to 168.

New Public Issues

Benjamin Harrison's record as president was little more substantial than that of his grandfather, who had died a month after taking office. Harrison had few visible convictions, and he made no effort to influence Congress. And yet during Harrison's passive administration, public opinion was beginning to force the government to confront some of the pressing social and economic issues of the day, most notably the power of trusts.

By the mid-1880s, fifteen western and southern states had adopted laws prohibiting combinations that restrained competition. But corporations found it easy to escape limitations by incorporating in states, such as New Jersey and Delaware, that offered them special privileges. If antitrust legislation was to be effective, its supporters believed, it would have to come from the national government. In July 1890, both houses of Congress passed the Sherman Antitrust Act, almost without dissent. For over a   *Sherman Antitrust Act* decade after its passage, the Sherman Act—indifferently enforced and steadily weakened by the courts—had no impact. As of 1901, the Justice Department had instituted many antitrust suits against unions, but only fourteen against business combinations.

The Republicans were more interested in the issue they believed had won them the 1888 election: the tariff. Representative William McKinley of Ohio and Senator Nelson W. Aldrich of Rhode Island drafted the highest protective measure ever proposed to Congress. Known as the McKinley Tariff, it became law in October 1890. But Republican leaders   *McKinley Tariff* apparently misinterpreted public sentiment. Many voters saw the high tariff as a way to enrich producers and starve consumers. The party suffered a stunning reversal in the 1890 congressional election. The Republicans' substantial Senate majority was slashed to 8; in the House, the party retained only 86 of the 332 seats, losing its majority in that chamber. Nor were the Republicans able to recover over the next two years. In the presidential election of 1892, Benjamin Harrison once again supported protection; Grover Cleveland, renominated by the Democrats, once again opposed it. A new third party, the People's Party, with James B. Weaver as its candidate, advocated substantial economic reform. Cleveland won 277 electoral votes to Harrison's 145 and had a popular margin of 380,000. Weaver ran far behind.

The policies of Cleveland's second term were much like those of his first. Again, he supported a tariff reduction, which the House approved but the Senate weakened. Cleveland denounced the result but allowed it to become law as the Wilson-Gorman Tariff.

Public pressure had been growing since the 1880s for other reforms, among them regulation of the railroads. Farm organizations in the Midwest (most notably the Grangers) had persuaded several state legislatures to pass regulatory legislation in the early 1870s. But in 1886, the Supreme Court—in *Wabash, St. Louis, and Pacific Railway Co. v. Illinois,* known as the *Wabash* case—ruled one of the Granger Laws in Illinois unconstitutional. According to the Court, the law was an attempt to control interstate commerce and thus infringed on the exclusive power of Congress. Later, the courts limited the powers of the states to regulate commerce even within their own boundaries.

Effective railroad regulation, it was now clear, could come only from the federal government. Congress responded to public pressure in 1887 with the   *Interstate Commerce Act* Interstate Commerce Act, which banned discrimination in rates between long and short hauls, required that railroads publish their rate schedules and file them with the government, and declared that all interstate rail rates must be "reasonable and just." A five-person agency, the Interstate Commerce Commission (ICC) was to administer the act. But it had to rely on the courts to enforce its rulings. For almost twenty years after its passage, the Interstate Commerce Act—which was, like the Sherman Act, haphazardly enforced and narrowly interpreted by the courts—had little practical effect.

THE AGRARIAN REVOLT

No group watched the performance of the federal government in the 1880s with greater dismay than American farmers. They helped produce the Populist upheaval—one of the most powerful movements of political protest in American history.

THE GRANGERS

Farmers had been making efforts to organize politically for several decades before the 1880s. The first major farm organization was the National Grange of the Patrons of Husbandry, founded in 1867. From it emerged a network of local organizations that tried to teach new scientific agricultural techniques to their members. When the depression of 1873 caused a sharp decline in farm prices, membership rapidly increased and the direction of the organization changed. Granges in the Midwest began to organize marketing cooperatives and to promote political action to curb monopolistic practices by railroads and warehouses. At their peak, Grange supporters controlled the legislatures in most of the midwestern states. The result was the Granger Laws of the early 1870s, by which many states imposed strict regulations on railroad rates and practices. But the destruction of the new regulations by the courts, combined with the political inexperience of many Grange leaders and the return of prosperity in the late 1870s, produced a dramatic decline in the power of the association.

THE FARMERS' ALLIANCES

As early as 1875, farmers in parts of the South were banding together in so-called Farmers' Alliances just as the Granges were weakening. By 1880, the Southern Alliance had more than 4 million members; a comparable Northwestern Alliance was taking root in the plains states and the Midwest, largely replacing the Grange.

Like the Granges, the Alliances formed cooperatives and other marketing mechanisms. They established stores, banks, processing plants, and other facilities to free their members from dependence on the hated "furnishing merchants" who kept so many farmers in debt. Some Alliance leaders, however, saw the movement in larger terms: as an effort to build a society in which economic competition might give way to cooperation. Alliance lecturers traveled throughout rural areas, lambasting the concentrated power of great corporations and financial institutions.

Although the Alliances quickly became far more widespread than the Granges had ever been, they suffered from similar problems. Their cooperatives did not always work well, partly because of mismanagement and partly because of the strength of opposing market forces. These economic frustrations helped push the movement into a new phase at the end of the 1880s: the creation of a national political organization.

In 1889, the Southern and Northwestern Alliances agreed to a loose merger. The next year the Alliances held a national convention at Ocala, Florida, and issued the so-called *Ocala Demands* Ocala Demands, which were, in effect, a party platform. In the 1890 off-year elections, candidates supported by the Alliances won partial or complete control of the legislatures in twelve states. They also won six governorships, three seats in the U.S. Senate, and approximately fifty in the U.S. House of Representatives. Many of the successful Alliance candidates were Democrats who had benefited—often passively—from

MARY E. LEASE The fiery Populist orator Mary E. Lease was a fixture on the Alliance lecture circuit in the 1890s. She made some 160 speeches in 1890 alone. Her critics called her the "Kansas Pythoness," but she was popular among farmers with her denunciations of banks, railroads, and "middlemen," and her famous advice to "raise less corn and more hell." (© Corbis)

Alliance endorsements. But dissident farmers drew enough encouragement from the results to contemplate further political action.

Alliance leaders discussed plans for a third party at meetings in Cincinnati in May 1891 and St. Louis in February 1892. Then, in July 1892, 1,300 exultant delegates poured into Omaha, Nebraska, to proclaim the creation of the new party, approve an official set of principles, and nominate candidates for the presidency and vice *People's Party Established* presidency. The new organization's official name was the People's Party, but the movement was more commonly referred to as **Populism.**

The election of 1892 demonstrated the potential power of the new movement. The Populist presidential candidate—James B. Weaver of Iowa, a former Greenbacker—polled more than 1 million votes. Nearly 1,500 Populist candidates won election to seats in state legislatures. The party elected three governors, five senators, and ten congressmen. It could also claim the support of many Republicans and Democrats in Congress who had been elected by appealing to Populist sentiment.

THE POPULIST CONSTITUENCY

Already, however, there were signs of the limits of Populist strength. Populism had great appeal to farmers, particularly to small farmers with little long-range economic security. But Populism failed to move much beyond that group. Its leaders made energetic efforts to include labor within the coalition by courting the Knights of Labor and adding a labor plank to its platform. But Populism never attracted significant labor support, in part because the economic interests of labor and the interests of farmers were often at odds.

In the South, white Populists struggled with the question of whether to accept African Americans into the party. There was an important black component to the movement—a network of "Colored Alliances" that by 1890 numbered over 1.25 million members. But most white Populists accepted the assistance of African Americans only as long as it was clear that whites would remain indisputably in control. When southern conservatives began to attack the Populists for undermining white supremacy, the interracial character of the movement quickly faded.

POPULIST IDEAS

The Populists spelled out their program first in the Ocala Demands of 1890 and then, more clearly, in the Omaha platform of 1892. They proposed a system of "subtreasuries," a network of government-owned warehouses where farmers could deposit their crops, to allow them to borrow money from the government at low rates of interest until the price *The Populists' Reform Program* of their goods went up. In addition, the Populists called for the abolition of national banks (which they believed were dangerous institutions of concentrated power), the end of absentee ownership of land, the direct election of United States senators (which would weaken the power of conservative state legislatures), and other devices to improve the ability of the people to influence the political process. They called as well for regulation and (after 1892) government ownership of railroads, telephones, and telegraphs. And they demanded a system of government-operated postal savings banks, a graduated income tax, the inflation of the currency, and, later, the remonetization of silver.

Some Populists were anti-Semitic, anti-intellectual, anti-eastern, and antiurban. But bigotry was not the dominant force behind Populism. It was, rather, a serious and usually responsible effort to find solutions to real problems. Populists emphatically rejected the laissez-faire orthodoxies of their time, including the idea that the rights of ownership are absolute, and in fact called on the federal government to promote a dramatic redistribution of wealth and power. In short, the Populists raised one of the most overt and powerful challenges of the era to the direction in which American industrial capitalism was moving.

THE CRISIS OF THE 1890s

The agrarian protest was only one of many indications of the national political crisis emerging in the 1890s. There was a severe depression, widespread labor unrest and violence, and the continuing failure of either major party to respond to the growing distress. Grover Cleveland, who took office for the second time just as the economy was collapsing, remained convinced that any government action would be a violation of principle.

THE PANIC OF 1893

The Panic of 1893 launched the most severe depression the nation had ever experienced. It began in March 1893, when the Philadelphia and Reading Railroad, unable to meet payments on loans, declared bankruptcy. Two months later, the National Cordage Company failed as well. Together, these two corporate failures triggered a stock market collapse. And since many of the major New York banks were heavy investors in the market, a wave of bank failures soon began. That caused a contraction of credit, which meant that many of the new, aggressive, and loan-dependent businesses soon went bankrupt.

The depression reflected, among other things, the degree to which all parts of the American economy were now interconnected. And it showed how dependent the economy was on the health of the railroads, which remained the nation's most powerful corporate and financial institutions. When the railroads suffered, as they did beginning in 1893, everyone suffered.

Once the panic began, it spread with startling speed. Within six months, more than 8,000 businesses, 156 railroads, and 400 banks failed. Already low agricultural prices tumbled further. Up to 1 million workers, 20 percent of the labor force, lost their jobs. The depression was unprecedented not only in its severity but also in its persistence. Although conditions improved slightly beginning in 1895, prosperity did not fully return until 1901.

The depression produced widespread social unrest, especially among the enormous numbers of unemployed workers. In 1894, Jacob S. Coxey, an Ohio businessman and Populist, began advocating a massive public works program to create jobs for the unemployed.

COXEY'S ARMY   Jacob S. Coxey leads his "army" of unemployed men through the town of Allegheny, Pennsylvania, in 1894, en route to Washington, where he hoped to pressure Congress to approve his plans for a massive public works program to put people back to work.   (© Photo by Fotosearch/Getty Images)

When it became clear that Congress was ignoring his proposals, Coxey organized a march *"Coxey's Army"* of the unemployed (known as "Coxey's Army") to Washington, D.C., to present his demands to the government. Congress continued to ignore them.

To many middle-class Americans, the labor turmoil of the time—the Homestead and Pullman strikes, for example (see Chapter 17)—was a sign of a dangerous instability, even perhaps a revolution. Labor radicalism—some of it real, more of it imagined by the frightened middle class—heightened the general sense of crisis among the public.

The Silver Question

The financial panic weakened the government's monetary system. President Cleveland believed that the instability of the currency was the primary cause of the depression. The "money question," therefore, became one of the burning issues of the era.

The debate centered on what would form the basis of the dollar, what would lie behind it and give it value. Today, the value of the dollar rests on little more than public confidence in the government. But in the nineteenth century, many people believed that currency was worthless if there was not something concrete behind it—precious metal (specie), which holders of paper money could collect if they presented their currency to a bank or to the Treasury.

During most of its existence as a nation, the United States had recognized two metals—gold and silver—as a basis for the dollar, a system known as "bimetallism." In the 1870s, however, that had changed. The official ratio of the value of silver to the value of gold for purposes of creating currency (the "mint ratio") was 16 to 1: sixteen ounces of silver equaled one ounce of gold. But the actual commercial value of silver (the "market ratio") was much higher than that. Owners of silver could get more by selling it for manufacture into jewelry and other objects than they could by taking it to the mint for conversion into coins. So they stopped taking it to the mint, and the mint stopped coining silver.

In 1873, Congress passed a law that seemed simply to recognize the existing situation by officially discontinuing silver coinage. Few objected at the time. But later in the 1870s, the market value of silver fell well below the official mint ratio of 16 to 1. Silver was suddenly available for coinage again, and it soon became clear that Congress had foreclosed a potential method of expanding the currency. Before long, many Americans concluded that a conspiracy of big bankers had been responsible for the "demonetization" of silver and referred to the law as the "Crime of '73."

Two groups of Americans were especially determined to undo the Crime of '73. One consisted of the silver-mine owners, now understandably eager to have the government take their surplus silver and pay them much more than the market price. The other group consisted of discontented farmers, who wanted an increase in the quantity of money—an inflation of the currency—as a means of raising the prices of farm products and easing payment of the farmers' debts. The inflationists demanded that the government return at once to the "free and *"Free Silver" Advocates* unlimited coinage of silver" at the old ratio of 16 to 1. Congress responded weakly to these demands with the Sherman Silver Purchase Act of 1890, which required the government to purchase silver and pay for it in gold. But the government allowed only existing silver coinage. It did not allow any newly minted silver money.

At the same time, the nation's gold reserves were steadily dropping. President Cleveland believed that the chief cause of the weakening gold reserves was the Sherman Silver Purchase Act. Early in his second administration, therefore, Congress responded to his request and repealed the Sherman Act—although only after a bitter and divisive battle that helped create a split in the Democratic Party.

"A CROSS OF GOLD"

Republicans, watching the failure of the Democrats to deal effectively with the depression, were confident of success in 1896. Party leaders, led by the Ohio boss Marcus A. Hanna, settled on former congressman William McKinley, author of the 1890 ==*McKinley Nominated*== tariff act and now governor of Ohio, as the party's presidential candidate. The tariff, they believed, should be the key issue in the campaign. But they also opposed the free coinage of silver, except by agreement with the leading commercial nations (which everyone realized was unlikely). Thirty-four delegates from the mountain and plains states walked out of the convention in protest and joined the Democratic Party.

BEARING THE CROSS OF GOLD   The cartoonist Grant Hamilton created this image of William Jennings Bryan shortly after he made his famous "Cross of Gold" speech at the Democratic National Convention, which subsequently nominated him for president. The cartoon highlights two of the most powerful images in Bryan's speech—a "crown of thorns" and a "cross of gold," both biblical references and both designed to represent the oppression that the gold standard imposed on working people. (© Granger, NYC—All Rights Reserved.)

The Democratic Convention of 1896 was unusually tumultuous. Southern and western delegates, eager for a way to compete with the Populists, were determined to seize control of the party from conservative easterners, incorporate some Populist demands—among them free silver—into the Democratic platform, and nominate a pro-silver candidate.

Defenders of the gold standard seemed to dominate the debate, until William Jennings Bryan, a handsome, thirty-six-year-old congressman from Nebraska, mounted the podium to address the convention. His great voice echoed through the hall as he delivered what became one of the *Bryan's "Cross of Gold" Speech* most famous political speeches in American history. The closing passage sent his audience into something close to a frenzy: "Having behind us the producing masses of this nation and the world, supported by the commercial interests, the laboring interests and the toilers everywhere, we will answer their demand for a gold standard by saying to them: 'You shall not press down upon the brow of labor this crown of thorns; you shall not crucify mankind upon a cross of gold.'" It became known as the "Cross of Gold" speech.

In the glow of Bryan's speech, the convention voted to adopt a pro-silver platform. And the following day, Bryan (as he had eagerly and not entirely secretly hoped) was nominated for president on the fifth ballot.

The choice of Bryan and the Democratic platform created a quandary for the Populists. They had expected both major parties to adopt conservative programs and nominate conservative candidates, leaving the Populists to represent the growing forces of protest. But now the Democrats had stolen much of their thunder. The Populists faced the choice of naming their own candidate and splitting the protest vote or endorsing Bryan and losing their identity as a party. Many Populists argued that "fusion" with the Democrats would destroy their party. But the majority concluded that there was no viable alternative. Amid considerable acrimony, the convention voted to nominate Bryan as the Populist candidate.

The Conservative Victory

The campaign of 1896 produced panic among conservatives. The business and financial community, frightened beyond reason at the prospect of a Bryan victory, contributed lavishly to the Republican campaign. From his home in Canton, Ohio, McKinley conducted a traditional "front-porch" campaign by receiving pilgrimages of the Republican faithful, organized and paid for by Hanna.

Bryan showed no such restraint. He became the first presidential candidate in American history to stump every section of the country systematically. He traveled 18,000 miles and addressed an estimated 5 million people.

On election day, McKinley polled 271 electoral votes to Bryan's 176 and received 51.1 percent of the popular vote to Bryan's 47.7. Bryan carried the areas of the South and West where miners or struggling staple farmers predominated. The Democratic program, like that of the Populists, had been too narrow to win a national election.

For the Populists and their allies, the election results were a disaster. They had gambled *End of the People's Party* everything on their fusion with the Democratic Party and lost. Within months of the election, the People's Party began to dissolve.

McKinley and Recovery

The administration of William McKinley saw a return to relative calm. One reason was the exhaustion of dissent. Another reason was the shrewd character of the McKinley administration itself, committed as it was to reassuring stability. Most important, however, was the gradual easing of the economic crisis, a development that undercut many of those who were agitating for change.

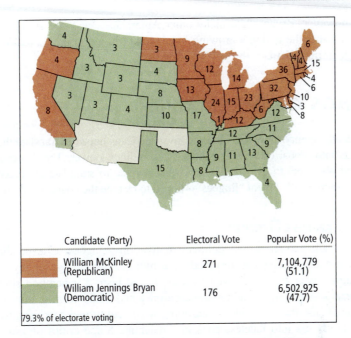

Candidate (Party)	Electoral Vote	Popular Vote (%)
William McKinley (Republican)	271	7,104,779 (51.1)
William Jennings Bryan (Democratic)	176	6,502,925 (47.7)

79.3% of electorate voting

THE ELECTION OF 1896 The results of the presidential election of 1896 are, as this map shows, striking for the regional differentiation they reveal. William McKinley won the election by a comfortable if not enormous margin, but his victory was not broad-based. He carried all the states of the Northeast and the industrial Midwest, along with California and Oregon, but virtually nothing else. Bryan carried the entire South and almost all of the agrarian West. • *What campaign issues in 1896 helped account for the regional character of the results?*

McKinley and his allies committed themselves fully to only one issue: the need for higher tariff rates. Within weeks of his inauguration, the administration won approval of the Dingley Tariff, raising duties to the highest point in American history. The administration dealt more gingerly with the explosive silver question (an issue that McKinley himself had never considered very important). He sent a commission to Europe to explore the possibility of a silver agreement with Great Britain and France. As he and everyone else anticipated, the effort produced nothing. The Republicans then enacted the Currency, or *Gold Standard Act* Gold Standard, Act of 1900, which confirmed the nation's commitment to the gold standard.

And so the "battle of the standards" ended in victory for the forces of conservatism. Economic developments at the time seemed to vindicate the Republicans. Prosperity began to return in 1898. Foreign crop failures drove farm prices upward, and American business entered another cycle of expansion. Prosperity and the gold standard, it seemed, were closely allied.

But while the free-silver movement had failed, it had raised an important question for the American economy. In the quarter century before 1900, the countries of the Western world had experienced a spectacular growth in productive facilities and population. Yet the supply of money had not kept pace with economic progress. Had it not been for a dramatic increase in the gold supply in the late 1890s (a result of new techniques for extracting gold from low-content ores and the discovery of huge new gold deposits in Alaska, South Africa, and Australia), Populist predictions of financial disaster might in fact have proved correct. In 1898, two and a half times as much gold was produced as in 1890, and the currency supply was soon inflated far beyond anything Bryan and the free-silver forces had anticipated.

By then, however, Bryan—like many other Americans—was becoming engaged with another major issue: the nation's growing involvement in world affairs and its increasing flirtation with **imperialism.**

STIRRINGS OF IMPERIALISM

As the nineteenth century drew to a close, many Americans hoped to translate the era's great industrial feats into global economic, political, and military power. The depression of 1893 further pushed observers to call for greater overseas trade to stimulate the economy. These expansionists—some called them "**jingoes**"—hoped to resume the course of Manifest Destiny.

THE NEW MANIFEST DESTINY

In addition to their economic and political motivations, jingoes believed that domestic tensions in the country might be resolved by a more robust foreign policy and stronger American nationalistic spirit—or even by war. It had been a generation since the Civil War, and some jingoes felt the nation's masculinity had withered in the meantime. Mass industrial wage labor, the same line of reasoning went, had turned American workers from independent producers into faceless cogs in a machine. Some critics of woman suffrage thought it threatened to feminize and weaken the traditional male preserve of politics. Waves of immigration and wars of labor had divided the country. A more stout assertion of power abroad, jingoes hoped, might restore American vitality and unity.

Expansionists were also driven by competitive impulses. Americans were well aware of the imperialist fever that was raging through Europe, leading the major powers to partition much of Africa among themselves and to turn eager eyes on the Far East and the Chinese Empire. (See "America in the World: Imperialism.") Some Americans feared that their nation would soon be left out of all these potential markets. Scholars and others found a philosophic justification for expansionism in Charles Darwin's theories. They contended that nations or "races," like biological species, struggled constantly for existence and that only the fittest could survive. For strong nations to dominate weak ones was, therefore, in accordance with the laws of nature.

The most effective apostle of imperialism was Alfred Thayer Mahan, a captain and, later, admiral in the United States Navy. Mahan's thesis, presented in *The Influence of* *Sea Power upon History* (1890) and other works, was simple: countries with sea power were the great nations of history. Effective sea power required, among other things, colonies. Mahan believed that the United States should, at the least, acquire defensive bases in the Caribbean and the Pacific and take possession of Hawaii and other Pacific islands. He feared that the United States did not have a large enough navy to play the great role he envisioned. But during the 1870s and 1880s, the government launched a shipbuilding program that by 1898 had moved the United States to fifth place among the world's naval powers, and by 1900 to third place.

Sea Power and Colonies

HAWAII AND SAMOA

The islands of Hawaii in the mid-Pacific had been an important way station for American ships in the China trade since the early nineteenth century. By the 1880s, officers of the expanding United States Navy were looking covetously at Pearl Harbor on the island of

Oahu as a possible permanent base for U.S. ships. The growing number of Americans who had taken up residence on the islands also pressed for an increased American presence in Hawaii.

Settled by Polynesian people beginning in about 1500 B.C., Hawaii had developed an agricultural and fishing society in which different islands (and different communities on the same islands), each with its own chieftain, lived more or less self-sufficiently. When the first Americans arrived in Hawaii in the 1790s on merchant ships from New England, there were perhaps half a million people living there. Battles among rival communities were frequent, as ambitious chieftains tried to consolidate power over their neighbors. *First Sugar Plantation* In 1810, after a series of such battles, King Kamehameha I established his dominance, welcomed American traders, and helped them develop a thriving trade between Hawaii and China. But Americans soon wanted more than trade. Missionaries began settling there in the early nineteenth century; and in the 1830s, William Hooper, a Boston trader, became the first of many Americans to buy land and establish a sugar plantation on the islands.

The arrival of these merchants, missionaries, and planters was devastating to traditional Hawaiian society. The newcomers inadvertently brought infectious diseases to which the Hawaiians, like the American Indians before them, were tragically vulnerable. By the mid-nineteenth century, more than half the native population had died. The Americans brought other incursions as well. Missionaries worked to replace native religion with Christianity. Other white settlers introduced liquor, firearms, and a commercial economy, all of which eroded the traditional character of Hawaiian society. By the 1840s, American planters had spread throughout the islands; and an American settler, G. P. Judd, had become prime minister of Hawaii under King Kamehameha III, who had agreed to establish a constitutional monarchy. Judd governed Hawaii for over a decade.

In 1887, the United States negotiated a treaty with Hawaii that permitted it to open a naval base at Pearl Harbor. By then, growing sugar for export to America had become the basis of the Hawaiian economy—as a result of an 1875 agreement allowing Hawaiian sugar to enter the United States duty-free. The American-dominated sugar plantation system displaced native Hawaiians from their lands and relied heavily on Asian immigrants, whom the Americans considered more reliable and more docile than the natives.

Native Hawaiians did not accept their subordination without protest. In 1891, they elevated a powerful nationalist to the throne: Queen Liliuokalani, who *Queen Liliuokalani* set out to challenge the growing American control of the islands. But she remained in power only two years. In 1890, the United States had eliminated the exemption from American tariffs in Hawaiian sugar trade. The result was devastating to the economy of the islands, and American planters concluded that the only way for them to recover was to become part of the United States (and, hence, exempt from its tariffs). In 1893, they staged a revolution and called on the United States for protection. After the American minister ordered marines from a warship in Honolulu harbor to go ashore to aid the American rebels, the queen yielded her authority.

A provisional government, dominated by Americans, immediately sent a delegation to Washington to negotiate a treaty of annexation. Debate over the treaty *Hawaii Annexed* continued until 1898, when Congress finally approved the agreement.

Three thousand miles south of Hawaii, the Samoan islands had also long served as a way station for American ships in the Pacific trade. As American commerce with Asia increased, business groups in the United States regarded Samoa with new interest, and the American navy began eyeing the Samoan harbor at Pago Pago. In 1878, the Hayes administration extracted a treaty from Samoan leaders for an American naval station at Pago Pago.

IMPERIALISM

Empires were not, of course, new to the nineteenth century, when the United States acquired its first overseas colonies. They had existed since the early moments of recorded history, and they have continued into our own time.

But in the second half of the nineteenth century, the construction of empires took on a new form, and the word *imperialism* emerged for the first time to describe it. In many places, European powers now created colonies not by sending large numbers of migrants to settle and populate new lands, but instead by creating military, political, and business structures that allowed them to dominate and profit from the existing populations. This new imperialism changed the character of the colonizing nations, enriching them greatly and producing new classes of people whose lives were shaped by the demands of imperial business and administration. It changed the character of colonized societies even more, drawing them into the vast nexus of global industrial capitalism and introducing Western customs, institutions, and technologies to the subject peoples.

As the popularity of empire grew in the West, efforts to justify it grew as well. Champions of imperialism argued that the acquisition of colonies was essential for the health, even the survival, of their own industrializing nations. Colonies were sources of raw materials vital to industrial production; they were markets for manufactured goods; and they were suppliers of cheap labor. Defenders of empire also argued that imperialism was good for the colonized people. Many saw colonization as an opportunity to export Christianity to "heathen" lands, and new missionary movements emerged in Europe and America in response. More secular apologists argued that imperialism

helped bring colonized people into the modern world.

The invention of steamships, railroads, telegraphs, and other modern vehicles of transportation and communication; the construction of canals (particularly the Suez Canal, completed in 1869, and the Panama Canal, completed in 1914); the creation of new military technologies (repeating rifles, machine guns, and modern artillery)—all contributed to the ability of Western nations to reach, conquer, and control distant lands.

The greatest imperial power of the nineteenth century was Great Britain. By 1800, despite its recent loss of the colonies that became the United States, it already possessed vast territory in North America, the Caribbean, and the Pacific. In the second half of the nineteenth century, Britain greatly expanded its empire. Its most important acquisition was India, one of the largest and most populous countries in the world and a nation in which Great Britain had long exerted informal authority. In 1857, when native Indians revolted against British influence, British forces brutally crushed the rebellion and established formal colonial control over India. British officials, backed by substantial military power, now governed India through a large civil service staffed mostly by people from England and Scotland but with some Indians serving in minor positions. The British invested heavily in railroads, telegraphs, canals, harbors, and agricultural improvements, to enhance the economic opportunities available to them. They created schools for Indian children in an effort to draw them into British culture and make them supporters of the imperial system.

The British also extended their empire into Africa and other parts of Asia. The great imperial champion Cecil Rhodes expanded a small existing British colony at

THE BRITISH RAJ   The Drum Corps of the Royal Fusiliers in India poses here for a formal portrait, taken in 1877. Although the drummers are British, an Indian associate is included at top left. This blending of the dominant British with subordinate Indians was characteristic of the administration of the British Empire in India—a government known as the "raj," from the Indian word for "rule." (© Photo by Time Life Pictures/Mansell/Getty Images)

Capetown into a substantial colony that included much of what is now South Africa. In 1895, he added new British territories to the north, which he named Rhodesia (and which today are Zimbabwe and Zambia). Others spread British authority into Kenya, Uganda, Nigeria, and much of Egypt. British imperialists also extended the empire into East Asia, with the acquisition of Singapore, Hong Kong, Burma, and Malaya; and they built a substantial presence—although not formal colonial rule—in China.

Other European states, watching the vast expansion of the British Empire, quickly jumped into the race for colonies. France created colonies in Indochina (Vietnam and Laos), Algeria, west Africa, and Madagascar. Belgium moved into the Congo in west Africa. Germany established colonies in the Cameroons, Tanganyika, and other parts of Africa, and in the Pacific islands north of Australia. Dutch, Italian, Portuguese, Spanish, Russian, and Japanese imperialists created colonies as well in Africa, Asia, and the Pacific—driven both by a calculation of

their own commercial interests and by the frenzied competition that had developed among rival imperial powers. In 1898, the United States was drawn into the imperial race, in part inadvertently as an unanticipated result of the Spanish-American War. But the drive to acquire colonies resulted as well from the deliberate efforts of home-grown proponents of empire (among them Theodore Roosevelt), who believed that in the modern industrial-imperial world, a nation without colonies would have difficulty remaining, or becoming, a true great power.   •

UNDERSTAND, ANALYZE, & EVALUATE

1. What motivated the European nations' drive for empire in the late nineteenth century?
2. Why was Great Britain so successful in acquiring its vast empire?
3. How do the imperial efforts and ambitions of the United States at the end of the nineteenth century compare with those of European powers?

Great Britain and Germany were also interested in the islands, and they, too, secured treaty rights from the native princes. For the next ten years, the three powers jockeyed for *Samoa Divided* dominance in Samoa, finally agreeing to create a tripartite protectorate over Samoa, with the native chiefs exercising only nominal authority. The three-way arrangement failed to halt the rivalries of its members, and in 1899, the United States and Germany divided the islands between them, compensating Britain with territories elsewhere in the Pacific. The United States retained the harbor at Pago Pago.

WAR WITH SPAIN

Imperial ambitions had thus begun to stir within the United States well before the late 1890s. But a war with Spain in 1898 turned those stirrings into overt expansionism.

CONTROVERSY OVER CUBA

Spain's once-formidable empire had grown rickety, but still included two prized island possessions: Cuba, ninety miles off the shores of Florida, and the Philippines, in Asia. As in many imperial holdings, the native peoples in these regions objected to the presence of European colonizers and occasionally waged insurrections. One rebellion in Cuba had ended in 1878 with Spanish rule intact. Nominal Cuban control over the economy followed, but the depression of the 1890s led Spain to withdraw even that privilege. In 1895 *Cuban Revolt* Cuban revolutionaries mounted a new insurrection, led by the revolutionary poet José Martí and military heroes of the earlier wars of liberation.

The rebellion soon attracted the sympathies of people in the United States. Popular newspapers reported horrific atrocities committed by the Spanish against Cuban rebels and civilians. The Spanish governor since 1896, General Valeriano Weyler, was rounding up Cubans in detention camps to isolate rebels in the countryside, and then destroying agriculture to starve them out. These policies of "the Butcher" led to the deaths of tens of thousands of Cuban civilians. The conflict also imperiled the American-owned sugar plantations in Cuba and regional commerce more broadly. And ever since the articulation of the Monroe Doctrine in 1823, Americans had dreamed of ridding North and South America of European colonizers. Some hoped to replace the Spanish with a heavy American presence in the region, while others, including William Jennings Bryan and other prominent Democrats and members of Congress, wished only to liberate Cuba and leave it to the Cubans.

The conflict in Cuba came at a particularly opportune moment for the publishers of some American newspapers: Joseph Pulitzer with his *New York World* and William Randolph Hearst with his *New York Journal.* In the 1890s, Hearst and Pulitzer were engaged in a ruthless circulation war, and they both sent batteries of reporters and illustrators to Cuba with orders to provide accounts of Spanish atrocities. This sort of sensationalist reporting was known as **yellow journalism**. (See "Patterns of Popular Culture: Yellow Journalism.")

Although President Cleveland worried about the potential disruptions of American trade, he did not intervene. Nor, at first, did his successor, William McKinley. Both men shared the commercial and humanitarian concerns, but sought to avoid war with a European power. An irritated Theodore Roosevelt, the assistant secretary of the navy, excoriated President McKinley for his un-masculine weakness, charging that he had "no more backbone than a chocolate éclair."

The situation changed in early 1898. In January pro-Spanish Cubans rioted in Havana against the idea of a free Cuba, or *Cuba libre*, which the two American political parties had at least rhetorically supported even as successive U.S. administrations remained neutral. Thus the riots carried anti-American undertones, and President McKinley, under pressure from the popular media after unfulfilled promises from Spain, sent the U.S.S. *Maine* to Havana harbor to protect American citizens. On February 15, 1898, *The Maine* the ship exploded, killing 266 Americans. Although later investigations revealed it likely an accident, most Americans, egged on by the jingoistic press, blamed the Spanish.

For all the earlier arguments about humanity, commerce, and geopolitical strategy, the destruction of the *Maine* challenged American honor. A Democrat in the House voted for war "to defend the honor and maintain the dignity of this republic"; a Republican sought "peace with honor." On April 25, Congress passed a resolution calling for war against the Spanish. It included the Teller Amendment, named for Democratic senator *Teller Amendment* Henry T. Teller from Colorado, which swore off any intentions to occupy, possess, or control Cuba after a future victory against the Spanish.

"A Splendid Little War"

The American ambassador to England, John Hay, called the ensuing Spanish-American conflict "a splendid little war," an opinion that most Americans—with the exception of many of the enlisted men who fought in it—seemed to share. Declared in April, it was over in August, in part because Cuban rebels had already greatly weakened the Spanish resistance, making the American intervention in many respects little more than a "mopping-up" exercise. Only 460 Americans were killed in battle or died of wounds, although some 5,200 others perished of disease: malaria, dysentery, and typhoid, among others. Casualties among Cuban insurgents, who continued to bear the brunt of the fighting, were much higher.

The American war effort was not without difficulties. United States soldiers faced serious supply problems: a shortage of modern rifles and ammunition, uniforms too heavy for the warm Caribbean weather, inadequate medical services, and skimpy, almost indigestible food. The regular army numbered only 28,000 troops and officers, most of whom had experience in quelling Indian outbreaks but none in larger-scale warfare. That meant that, as in the Civil War, the United States had to rely heavily on National Guard units, organized by local communities and commanded for the most part by local leaders without military experience.

A significant proportion of the American invasion force consisted of black soldiers. Some were volunteer troops put together by African American communities. Others were members of the four black regiments in the regular army, who had been stationed on the frontier to defend white settlements against Indians and were now transferred east to fight in Cuba. As the black soldiers traveled through the South toward the training camps, some resisted the rigid segregation to which they were subjected. African American soldiers in Georgia deliberately made use of a "whites only" park; in Florida, they beat a soda-fountain operator for refusing to *Racial Tensions in the Military* serve them; in Tampa, white provocations and black retaliation led to a nightlong riot that left thirty wounded.

Racial tensions continued in Cuba. African Americans played crucial roles in some of the important battles of the war (including the famous charge at San Juan Hill) and won many medals. Nearly half the Cuban insurgents fighting with the Americans were themselves black,

including one of the leading insurgent generals, Antonio Maceo. The sight of black Cuban soldiers fighting alongside whites as equals gave African Americans a stronger sense of the injustice of their own position.

SEIZING THE PHILIPPINES

By an accident of history, the assistant secretary of the navy during the Cuban revolution was Theodore Roosevelt, an ardent Anglophile eager to see the United States join the British and other nations as imperial powers. Roosevelt was, in fact, a relatively minor figure in the Navy Department, but he was determined to expand his power. British friends had persuaded him that the war in Cuba gave the United States a rare opportunity to expand the American empire. Roosevelt responded by sending the Navy's Pacific fleet to the Philippines, with orders to attack as soon as America declared war. On May 1, 1898, Commodore George Dewey led the fleet into Manila harbor, quickly destroyed the aging Spanish fleet, and forced the Spanish government to surrender Manila with hardly a shot fired. He became the first American hero of the war.

THE BATTLE FOR CUBA

Cuba remained the principal focus of American military efforts. At first, the American commanders planned a long period of training before actually sending troops into combat. But when a Spanish fleet under Admiral Pascual Cervera slipped past the American navy into Santiago harbor on the southern coast of Cuba, plans changed quickly. The American Atlantic fleet quickly bottled Cervera up in the harbor. And the U.S. Army's commanding general, Nelson A. Miles, hastily altered his strategy and left Tampa in June with a force of 17,000 to attack Santiago.

General William R. Shafter, the American commander, moved toward Santiago, which he planned to surround and capture. On the way he met and defeated Spanish forces at Las Guasimos and, a week later, in two simultaneous battles, El Caney and San Juan Hill. At the center of the fighting (and on the front pages of the newspapers) during many of

The Rough Riders   these engagements was a cavalry unit known as the Rough Riders. Nominally commanded by General Leonard Wood, its real leader was Colonel Theodore Roosevelt, who had resigned from the Navy Department to get into the war and who had struggled with an almost desperate fury to get his regiment into the fighting. His passion to join the war undoubtedly reflected the decision of his beloved father, Theodore Roosevelt Sr., not to fight in the Civil War, a source of private shame within the family that his son sought to erase.

Roosevelt rapidly emerged as a hero of the conflict. His fame rested in large part on his role in leading a bold, if perhaps reckless, charge up Kettle Hill (a minor part of the larger battle for the adjacent San Juan Hill) directly into the face of Spanish guns. Roosevelt himself emerged unscathed, but nearly a hundred of his soldiers were killed or wounded. He remembered the battle as "the great day of my life."

Although Shafter was now in position to assault Santiago, his army was so weakened by sickness that he feared he might have to abandon his position. But unknown to the Americans, the Spanish government had by now decided that Santiago was lost and had ordered Cervera to evacuate. On July 3, Cervera tried to escape the harbor. The waiting American squadron destroyed his entire fleet. On July 16, the commander of Spanish ground forces in Santiago surrendered. At about the same time, an American army landed

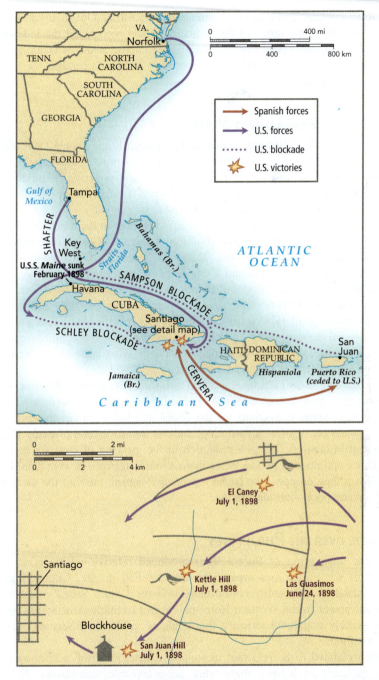

THE SPANISH-AMERICAN WAR IN CUBA, 1898 The military conflict between the United States and Spain in Cuba was a brief affair. The Cuban rebels and an American naval blockade had already brought the Spanish to the brink of defeat. The arrival of American troops was simply the final blow. In the space of about a week, U.S. troops won four decisive battles in the area around Santiago in southeast Cuba—one of them (the Battle of Kettle Hill) the scene of Theodore Roosevelt's famous charge up the adjacent San Juan Hill. This map shows the extent of the American naval blockade, the path of American troops from Florida to Cuba, and the location of the actual fighting. • *What were the implications of the war in Cuba for Puerto Rico?*

in Puerto Rico and occupied it against virtually no opposition. On August 12, an armistice ended the war. Under the terms of the armistice, Spain recognized the independence of

Puerto Rico Occupied   Cuba, ceded Puerto Rico and the Pacific island of Guam to the United States, and accepted continued American occupation of Manila pending the final disposition of the Philippines.

PUERTO RICO AND THE UNITED STATES

The island of Puerto Rico had been a part of the Spanish Empire since 1508. By the early seventeenth century, the native people of the island, the Arawaks, had largely disappeared as a result of infectious diseases, Spanish brutality, and poverty. Puerto Rican society developed, therefore, with a Spanish ruling class and a large African workforce for the coffee and sugar plantations that came to dominate its economy.

Puerto Rican resistance to Spanish rule began to emerge in the nineteenth century. The resistance prompted some reforms: the abolition of slavery in 1873, representation in the Spanish parliament, and other changes. Demands for independence continued to grow, and in 1898, Spain granted the island a degree of independence. But before the changes had any chance to take effect, control of Puerto Rico shifted to the United States. American military forces occupied the island during the Spanish-American War, and they remained

Foraker Act   in control until 1900, when the Foraker Act ended military rule and established a formal colonial government. Agitation for independence continued, and in 1917, Congress passed the Jones Act, which declared Puerto Rico to be United States territory and made all Puerto Ricans American citizens.

The Puerto Rican sugar industry flourished as it took advantage of the American market that was now open to it without tariffs. As in Hawaii, Americans from the mainland began establishing large sugar plantations on the island and hired natives to work them. The growing emphasis on sugar as a cash crop, and the transformation of many Puerto Rican farmers into paid laborers, led to a reduction in the growing of food for the island and greater reliance on imported goods. When international sugar prices were high, Puerto Rico did well. When they dropped, the island's economy sagged, pushing the many plantation workers—already poor—into destitution.

THE DEBATE OVER THE PHILIPPINES

Although the annexation of Puerto Rico produced relatively little controversy, the annexation of the Philippines created an impassioned debate. Controlling a nearby Caribbean island fit reasonably comfortably into the United States' sense of itself as the dominant power in the Western Hemisphere. But to many Americans, controlling a large and densely populated territory thousands of miles away seemed very different and more ominous.

McKinley claimed to be reluctant to support annexation. But, according to his own accounts, he came to believe there were no acceptable alternatives. Returning the

The Philippines Question   Philippines to Spain would be "cowardly and dishonorable," he claimed. Turning them over to another imperialist power (France, Germany, or Britain) would be "bad business and discreditable." Granting them independence would be irresponsible because the Filipinos were "unfit for self government." The only solution was "to take them all and to educate the Filipinos, and uplift and Christianize them, and by God's grace do the very best we could by them."

MEASURING UNCLE SAM FOR A NEW SUIT   In this *Puck* cartoon, President McKinley is favorably depicted as a tailor, meaning his client for a suit is large enough to accommodate the new possessions the United States obtained in the aftermath of the Spanish-American War. The stripes on Uncle Sam's pants bear the names of earlier, less controversial acquisitions, such as the Louisiana Purchase. (The Library of Congress)

The Treaty of Paris, signed in December 1898, confirmed the terms of the armistice and brought a formal end to the war. American negotiators had startled the Spanish by demanding that they also cede the Philippines to the United States, but an American offer of $20 million for the islands softened their resistance. They accepted all the American terms.

In the United States Senate, however, resistance was fierce. During debate over ratification of the treaty, a powerful anti-imperialist movement arose to oppose acquisition of the Philippines. The anti-imperialists included some of the   *Anti-Imperialist League* nation's wealthiest and most powerful figures: Andrew Carnegie, Mark Twain, Samuel Gompers, Senator John Sherman, and others. Some anti-imperialists believed that imperialism was immoral, a repudiation of America's commitment to human freedom. Others feared "polluting" the American population by introducing "inferior" Asian races into it. Industrial workers feared being undercut by a flood of cheap laborers from the new colonies. Conservatives worried about the large standing army and entangling foreign alliances that they believed imperialism would require and that they feared would threaten American liberties. Sugar growers and other anti-imperialists feared unwelcome competition from the new territories. The Anti-Imperialist League, established late in 1898 by upper-class Bostonians, New Yorkers, and others to fight against annexation, waged a vigorous campaign against ratification of the Paris treaty (See "Consider the Source: Platform of the Anti-Imperialist League.").

But favoring ratification was an equally varied group. There were the exuberant imperialists such as Theodore Roosevelt, who saw the acquisition of empire as a way to reinvigorate the nation. Some businessmen saw opportunities to dominate the Asian trade. Most Republicans saw partisan advantages in acquiring valuable new territories through a war fought and won by a Republican administration. Perhaps the   *Arguments for Annexation* strongest argument in favor of annexation, however, was that the United States already possessed the islands.

PLATFORM OF THE AMERICAN ANTI-IMPERIALIST LEAGUE, 1899

As part of their campaign against the annexation of the Philippines by the United States, members of the Anti-Imperialist League circulated this party platform. Here they argue that American political ideals are not compatible with imperialist actions.

We hold that the policy known as imperialism is hostile to liberty and tends toward militarism, an evil from which it has been our glory to be free. We regret that it has become necessary in the land of Washington and Lincoln to reaffirm that all men, of whatever race or color, are entitled to life, liberty, and the pursuit of happiness. We maintain that governments derive their just powers from the consent of the governed. We insist that the subjugation of any people is "criminal aggression" and open disloyalty to the distinctive principles of our Government.

We earnestly condemn the policy of the present National Administration in the Philippines. It seeks to extinguish the spirit of 1776 in those islands. We deplore the sacrifice of our soldiers and sailors, whose bravery deserves admiration even in an unjust war. We denounce the slaughter of the Filipinos as a needless horror. We protest against the extension of American sovereignty by Spanish methods.

We demand the immediate cessation of the war against liberty, begun by Spain and continued by us. We urge that Congress be promptly convened to announce to the Filipinos our purpose to concede to them the independence for which they have so long fought and which of right is theirs.

The United States have always protested against the doctrine of international law which permits the subjugation of the weak by the strong. A self-governing state cannot accept sovereignty over an unwilling people. The United States cannot act upon the ancient heresy that might makes right.

Imperialists assume that with the destruction of self-government in the Philippines by American hands, all opposition here will cease. This is a grievous error. Much as we abhor the war of "criminal aggression" in the Philippines, greatly as we regret that the blood of the Filipinos is on American hands, we more deeply resent the betrayal of American institutions at home. The real firing line is not in the suburbs of Manila. The foe is of our own household. The attempt of 1861 was to divide the country. That of 1899 is to destroy its fundamental principles and noblest ideals.

Whether the ruthless slaughter of the Filipinos shall end next month or next year is but an incident in a contest that must go on until the Declaration of Independence and the Constitution of the United States are rescued from the hands of their betrayers. Those who dispute about standards of value while the Republic is undermined will be listened to as little as those who would wrangle about the small economies of the household while the house is on fire. The training of a great people for a century, the aspiration for liberty of a vast immigration are forces that will hurl aside those who in the delirium of conquest seek to destroy the character of our institutions.

We deny that the obligation of all citizens to support their Government in times of grave national peril applies to the present situation. If an Administration may with impunity ignore the issues upon which it was chosen, deliberately create a condition of war anywhere on the face of the globe, debauch the civil service for spoils to promote the adventure, organize a truth-suppressing censorship and demand of all citizens a suspension of judgment and their unanimous support while it chooses to continue the fighting, representative government itself is imperiled.

We propose to contribute to the defeat of any person or party that stands for the forcible subjugation of any people. We shall oppose for reelection all who in the White House or in Congress betray American liberty in pursuit of un-American gains. We still hope that both of our great political parties will support and defend the Declaration of Independence in the closing campaign of the century.

Source: "Platform of the American Anti-Imperialist League," in *Speeches, Correspondence, ard Political Papers of Carl Schurz*, vol. 6, ed. Frederick Bancroft (New York: G.P. Putnam's Sons, 1913), p. 77, note 1.

UNDERSTAND, ANALYZE, & EVALUATE

1. On what grounds did the Anti-Imperialist League oppose U.S. expansion, and where were these principles ratified?
2. What were the costs of imperial expansion for the United States and what losses were Filipinos to incur?
3. How did the prospect of an American empire affect the nation's democratic principles?

When anti-imperialists warned of the danger of acquiring heavily populated territories whose people might have to become citizens, the jingoes had a ready answer: the nation's long-standing policies toward Indians—treating them as dependents rather than as citizens— had created a precedent for annexing land without absorbing people.

The fate of the treaty remained in doubt for weeks, until it received the unexpected support of William Jennings Bryan, a fervent anti-imperialist. He backed ratification because he hoped to move the issue out of the Senate and make it the subject of a national referendum in 1900, when he expected to be the Democratic presidential candidate again. Bryan persuaded a number of anti-imperialist Democrats to support the treaty so as to set up the 1900 debate. The Senate ratified it finally on February 6, 1899.

But Bryan miscalculated. If the election of 1900 was in fact a referendum on the Philippines, as Bryan expected, it proved beyond a doubt that the nation   *Election of 1900* had decided in favor of imperialism. Once again Bryan ran against McKinley; and once again McKinley won—even more decisively than in 1896. It was not only the issue of the colonies, however, that ensured McKinley's victory. The Republicans benefited from growing prosperity—and also from the colorful personality of their vice presidential candidate, Theodore Roosevelt, the hero of San Juan Hill.

THE REPUBLIC AS EMPIRE

The new American empire was small by the standards of the great imperial powers of Europe. But it embroiled the United States in the politics of both Europe and the Far East in ways the nation had always tried to avoid in the past. It also drew Americans into a brutal war in the Philippines.

GOVERNING THE COLONIES

Three American dependencies—Hawaii, Alaska, and Puerto Rico—presented relatively few problems. They received territorial status (and their residents American citizenship) relatively quickly: Hawaii in 1900, Alaska in 1912, and Puerto Rico in 1917. The navy took control of the Pacific islands of Guam and Tutuila. The United States simply left alone some of the smallest, least populated Pacific islands now under its control. Cuba was a thornier problem. American military forces, commanded by General Leonard Wood, remained there until 1902 to prepare the island for independence. Americans built roads, schools, and hospitals; reorganized the legal, financial, and administrative systems; and introduced medical and sanitation reforms. But the United States also laid the basis for years of American economic domination of the island.

Platt Amendment When Cuba drew up a constitution that made no reference to the United States, Congress responded by passing the Platt Amendment in 1901 and pressuring Cuba into incorporating its terms into its constitution. The Platt Amendment barred Cuba from making treaties with other nations; gave the United States the right to intervene in Cuba to preserve independence, life, and property; and required Cuba to permit American naval stations on its territory. The amendment left Cuba with only nominal political independence.

American capital made the new nation an American economic appendage as well. American investors poured into Cuba, buying up plantations, factories, railroads, and refineries. Resistance to "Yankee imperialism" produced intermittent revolts against the Cuban government—revolts that at times prompted U.S. military intervention. American troops occupied the island from 1906 to 1909 after one such rebellion; they returned again in 1912 to suppress a revolt by black plantation workers. As in Puerto Rico and Hawaii, sugar production—spurred by access to the American market—increasingly dominated the island's economy and subjected it to the same cycle of booms and busts that plagued other sugar-producing appendages of the United States economy.

THE PHILIPPINE WAR

Like other imperial powers, the United States soon discovered that subjugating another people was not an easy task. The American experience in the Philippines began with a long and bloody war.

The conflict in the Philippines is the least remembered of all American wars. It was also one of the longest. It lasted from 1898 to 1902, and it was one of the most vicious. It involved 200,000 American troops and resulted in 4,300 American deaths. The number of Filipinos killed in the conflict has long been a matter of dispute, but it seems likely that at least 50,000 natives (and perhaps many more) died. The American occupiers faced brutal guerrilla tactics in the Philippines, and they soon found themselves drawn into the same pattern of brutality that had outraged so many Americans when Weyler had used them in the Caribbean.

The Filipinos had rebelled against Spanish rule before 1898, and as soon as they realized the Americans had come to stay, they rebelled against them as well. Ably led by *Emilio Aguinaldo* Emilio Aguinaldo, who claimed to head the legitimate government of the nation, Filipinos harried the American army of occupation from island to island for more than three years. At first, American commanders believed the rebels had only a small popular following. But by early 1900, General Arthur MacArthur, an American commander in the islands (and father of General Douglas MacArthur), was writing: "I have been reluctantly compelled to believe that the Filipino masses are loyal to Aguinaldo and the government which he heads."

To MacArthur and others, that realization was not a reason to moderate American tactics or conciliate the rebels, but rather to adopt much more severe measures. Gradually, the American military effort became more systematically vicious and brutal. Captured Filipino

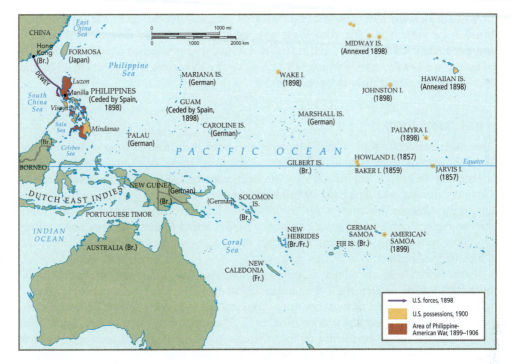

THE AMERICAN SOUTH PACIFIC EMPIRE, 1900   Except for Puerto Rico, all of the colonial acquisitions of the United States in the wake of the Spanish-American War occurred in the Pacific. The new attraction of imperialism persuaded the United States to annex Hawaii in 1898. The war itself gave America control of the Philippines, Guam, and other, smaller Spanish possessions in the Pacific. When added to the small, scattered islands that the United States had acquired as naval bases earlier in the nineteenth century, these new possessions gave the nation a far-flung Pacific empire, even if one whose total territory and population remained small by the standards of the other great empires of the age.   •   *What was the reaction in the United States to the acquisition of this new empire?*

guerrillas were treated not as prisoners of war but as murderers. Many were summarily executed. On some islands, entire communities were evacuated—the residents forced into concentration camps while American troops destroyed their villages. A spirit of savagery grew among some American soldiers, who came to view the Filipinos as almost subhuman and, at times, seemed to take pleasure in arbitrarily killing them.

The racial undertones of the war—American soldiers called the Filipinos "niggers"— were particularly grating for African American troops serving in segregated units. They were hardly unaware that at home, southern states and lynch mobs were in the process of disenfranchising and terrorizing black people. Some noticed a resemblance between the attitude of the American military and government toward the Filipino natives and popular attitudes toward African Americans and Native Americans.

By 1902, reports of the brutality and of the American casualties had soured the American public on the war. But by then, the rebellion had largely exhausted itself and the occupiers had established control over most of the islands. The key to their victory was the March 1901 capture of Aguinaldo, who later signed a document urging his followers to stop fighting and declared his own allegiance to the United States. Fighting continued intermittently until as late as 1906, but American possession of the Philippines was now secure. In the summer of 1901, the military transferred authority over the islands

to William Howard Taft, who became their first civilian governor and gave the Filipinos broad local autonomy. The Americans also built roads, schools, bridges, and sewers; instituted major administrative and financial reforms; and established a public health sys-
Gradual Shift to Self-Rule   tem. Filipino self-rule gradually increased, and on July 4, 1946, the islands finally gained their independence.

THE OPEN DOOR

The American acquisition of the Philippines increased the already strong U.S. interest in Asia. Americans were particularly concerned about the future of China, which provided a tempting target for exploitation by stronger countries. By 1900, England, France, Germany, Russia, and Japan were beginning to carve up China among themselves, pressuring the Chinese government for "concessions" that gave them effective control over various regions of China. In some cases, they simply seized Chinese territory and claimed it as their own. Many Americans feared that the process would soon cut them out of the China trade altogether.

Eager for a way to advance American interests in China without risking war, McKinley issued a statement in September 1898 saying the United States wanted access to China but no special advantages there. "Asking only the open door for ourselves, we are ready to accord the open door to others." The next year, Secretary of State John Hay translated those words into policy when he addressed identical messages—which
Hay's "Open Door Notes"   became known as the "Open Door notes"—to England, Germany, Russia, France, Japan, and Italy. He asked that each nation with a "sphere of influence" in China allow other nations to trade freely and equally in its sphere. The principles Hay outlined would allow the United States to trade freely with China without fear of interference.

Europe and Japan received the **Open Door** proposals coolly. Russia openly rejected them; the other powers claimed to accept them in principle but to be unable to act unless all the other powers agreed. Hay refused to consider this a rebuff. He boldly announced that all the powers had accepted the principles of the Open Door in "final and definitive" form and that the United States expected them to observe those principles.

No sooner had the diplomatic maneuvering over the Open Door ended than the Boxers, a secret Chinese martial-arts society with highly nationalist convictions (and a somewhat mystical vision of their invulnerability to bullets), launched a revolt against foreigners in
Boxer Rebellion   China. The Boxer Rebellion spread widely across eastern China, attacking Westerners wherever they could find them—including many Christian missionaries. But the climax of the revolt was a siege of the entire Western foreign diplomatic corps, which took refuge in the British embassy in Peking. The imperial powers (including the United States) sent an international expeditionary force into China to rescue the diplomats. In August 1900, it fought its way into the city and broke the siege.

The Boxer Rebellion became an important event for the role of the United States in China. McKinley and Hay had agreed to American participation in quelling the Boxer Rebellion in order to secure a voice in the settlement of the uprising and prevent the partition of China by the European powers. Hay now won support for his Open Door approach from England and Germany and induced the other participating powers to accept compensation from the Chinese for the damages the Boxer Rebellion had caused. Chinese territorial integrity survived at least in name, and the United States retained access to its lucrative China trade.

A Modern Military System

The war with Spain had revealed glaring deficiencies in the American military system. Had the United States been fighting a more powerful foe, disaster might have resulted. After the war, McKinley appointed Elihu Root, an able corporate lawyer in New York, as secretary of war to supervise a major overhaul of the armed forces.

Root's reforms enlarged the regular army from 25,000 to a maximum of 100,000. They established federal army standards for the National Guard, ensuring that never again would the nation fight a war with volunteer regiments trained and equipped differently than those in the regular army. They sparked the creation of a system of officer training schools, including the Army Staff College (later the Command and General Staff School) at Fort Leavenworth, Kansas, and the Army War College in Washington. And in 1903, a general staff (named the Joint Chiefs of Staff) was established to act as military advisers to the secretary of war. As a result of the new reforms, the United States entered the twentieth century with something resembling a modern military system.

CONCLUSION

For nearly three decades after the end of Reconstruction, American politics remained locked in a rigid stalemate. The electorate was almost evenly divided, and the two major parties differed on only a few issues. A series of unimposing if respectable presidents presided over this political system as unwitting symbols of its stability and passivity.

Beneath the calm surface of national politics, however, social issues were creating deep tensions: battles between employers and workers, growing resentment among American farmers facing declining prosperity, outrage at what many voters considered corruption in government and excessive power in the hands of corporate titans. When a great depression began in 1893, these social tensions exploded.

The most visible sign of the challenge to the political stalemate was the Populist movement, an uprising of American farmers demanding far-reaching changes in politics and the economy. In 1892, they created their own political party, the People's Party, which for a few years showed impressive strength. But in the climactic election of 1896, in which the Populist hero William Jennings Bryan became the presidential nominee of both the Democratic Party and the People's Party, the Republicans won a substantial victory—and, in the process, helped create a great electoral realignment that left the Republicans with a clear majority for the next three decades.

The crises of the 1890s helped spur the United States' growing involvement in the world. In 1898, the United States intervened in a colonial war between Spain and Cuba, won a quick and easy military victory, and signed a treaty with Spain that ceded significant territory to the Americans. A vigorous anti-imperialist movement failed to stop the imperial drive. But taking the colonies proved easier than holding them. In the Philippines, American forces became bogged down in a brutal four-year war with Filipino rebels. The conflict soured much of the American public, and the annexation of colonies in 1898 proved to be both the beginning and the end of American territorial expansion.

KEY TERMS/PEOPLE/PLACES/EVENTS

Benjamin Harrison 458
Boxer Rebellion 484
Chester A. Arthur 457
Coxey's Army 464
Farmers' Alliances 460
Free silver 464
Grangers 460
Grover Cleveland 458
Half-Breeds 457

imperialism 468
Interstate Commerce
  Act 459
James A. Garfield 457
jingoes 468
Open Door 484
Panic of 1893 463
Populism 461
Puerto Rico 484

Queen Liliuokalani 469
Rutherford B. Hayes 457
Sherman Antitrust Act 459
Spanish-American
  War 478
Stalwarts 457
William Jennings Bryan 481
William McKinley 459
yellow journalism 472

RECALL AND REFLECT

1. How and why did the federal government attempt to regulate interstate commerce in the late nineteenth century?
2. What efforts did farmers undertake to deal with the economic problems they faced in the late nineteenth century?
3. What was the "silver question"? Why was it so important to so many Americans? How did the major political parties deal with this question?
4. How did the Spanish-American War change America's relationship to the rest of the world?
5. What were the main arguments of those who supported U.S. imperialism and those who opposed the nation's imperial ambitions and efforts?

20 THE PROGRESSIVES

THE PROGRESSIVE IMPULSE

WOMEN AND REFORM

THE ASSAULT ON THE PARTIES

SOURCES OF PROGRESSIVE REFORM

CRUSADES FOR SOCIAL ORDER AND REFORM

THEODORE ROOSEVELT AND THE MODERN PRESIDENCY

THE TROUBLED SUCCESSION

WOODROW WILSON AND THE NEW FREEDOM

LOOKING AHEAD

1. What role did women and women's organizations play in the reforms of the progressive era? How did progressive era reforms affect women?
2. What changes to politics and government did progressive reformers advocate at the local, state, and federal levels? How did government change as a result of their reform efforts?
3. How did Woodrow Wilson's progressivism differ from that of Theodore Roosevelt? In what ways was it similar to Roosevelt's?

WELL BEFORE THE END OF the nineteenth century, many Americans had become convinced that rapid industrialization and urbanization had created a growing crisis. The nation's most pressing need, they claimed, was to impose order and justice on a society that seemed to be approaching chaos. By the early years of the twentieth century, this outlook had acquired a name: progressivism.

Not even those who called themselves progressives could agree on what the term meant, for it was a phenomenon of great scope and diversity. But despite or perhaps because of its great diversity, the progressive movement generated a remarkable wave of political and social innovation. From the late nineteenth century until at least the end of World War I, progressive reformers brought into public debate such issues as the role of women in society, racial equality, the rights of labor, and the impact of immigration and cultural diversity.

Progressivism began as a series of local movements and encompassed many different efforts to improve the working of society. Slowly but steadily, these efforts became national

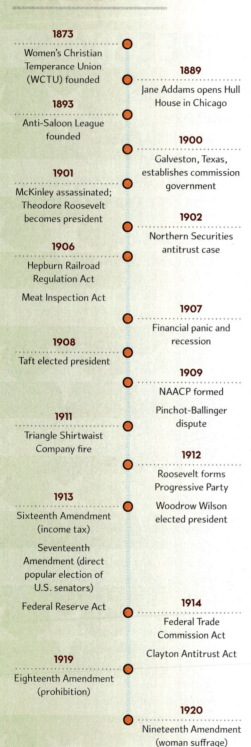

1873

Women's Christian Temperance Union (WCTU) founded

1889

Jane Addams opens Hull House in Chicago

1893

Anti-Saloon League founded

1900

Galveston, Texas, establishes commission government

1901

McKinley assassinated; Theodore Roosevelt becomes president

1902

Northern Securities antitrust case

1906

Hepburn Railroad Regulation Act

Meat Inspection Act

1907

Financial panic and recession

1908

Taft elected president

1909

NAACP formed

Pinchot-Ballinger dispute

1911

Triangle Shirtwaist Company fire

1912

Roosevelt forms Progressive Party

Woodrow Wilson elected president

1913

Sixteenth Amendment (income tax)

Seventeenth Amendment (direct popular election of U.S. senators)

Federal Reserve Act

1914

Federal Trade Commission Act

Clayton Antitrust Act

1919

Eighteenth Amendment (prohibition)

1920

Nineteenth Amendment (woman suffrage)

efforts. Ultimately it was the presidency, not the Congress, that became the most important vehicle of national reform—first under the dynamic leadership of Theodore Roosevelt and then under the disciplined, moralistic guidance of Woodrow Wilson. By the time America entered World War I in 1917, the federal government—which had exercised limited powers prior to the twentieth century—had greatly expanded its role in American life.

THE PROGRESSIVE IMPULSE

Progressives believed, as their name implies, in the idea of progress. They were optimistic that society was capable of improvement and that continued growth and advancement were the nation's destiny. But progressives believed, too, that growth and progress could not continue to occur recklessly, as they had in the late nineteenth century. The "natural laws" of the marketplace, and the doctrines of laissez-faire and Social Darwinism that dominated those laws, were not sufficient. Direct, purposeful human intervention was essential to ordering and bettering society. These ideas percolated in the United States as well as many other industrializing parts of the world. (See "America in the World: Social Democracy.")

Progressives did not always agree on the form their interventions should take, and the result was a variety of reform impulses. One powerful impulse was the spirit of "antimonopoly," the fear of concentrated power and the urge to limit and disperse authority and wealth. Another progressive impulse was a belief in the importance of social cohesion: the belief that individuals are part of a great web of social relationships, that each person's welfare is dependent on the welfare of society as a whole. Still another impulse was a deep faith in knowledge—in the possibilities of applying to society the principles of natural and social sciences. Most progressives believed, too, that a modernized government could—and must—play an important role in the process of improving and stabilizing society.

The Muckrakers and the Social Gospel

Among the first people to articulate the new spirit of national reform were crusading journalists who began to direct public attention toward social, economic, and political injustices. Known as the **muckrakers,** after Theodore Roosevelt accused them of raking up muck through their writings, they were committed to exposing scandal, corruption, and injustice.

Their first major targets were the trusts and, particularly, the railroads, which the muckrakers considered powerful and deeply corrupt. Exposés of the great corporate organizations began to appear as early as the 1860s, when Charles Francis Adams Jr. and others uncovered corruption among the railroad barons. Decades later, journalist Ida Tarbell produced a scorching study of the Standard Oil trust. By the turn of the century, many muckrakers were turning their attention to government and particularly to the urban political machines. Among the most influential was Lincoln Steffens, a reporter for *McClure's* magazine. His portraits of "machine government" and "boss rule" in cities, written in a tone of studied moral outrage, helped arouse sentiment for urban political reform. By presenting social problems to the public with indignation and moral fervor, they helped inspire other Americans to take action.

Growing outrage at social and economic injustice committed many reformers to the pursuit of **social justice.** (*Social justice* is a term widely used around the world to promote a kind of justice that goes beyond the individual but, instead, seeks justice for whole

THE BOSSES OF THE SENATE (1889), BY JOSEPH KEPPLER Keppler was a popular political cartoonist of the late nineteenth century who shared the growing concern about the power of the trusts—portrayed here as bloated, almost reptilian figures standing menacingly over the members of the U.S. Senate, to whose chamber the "people's entrance" is "closed." (© Granger, NYC—All Rights Reserved.)

SOCIAL DEMOCRACY

Enormous energy, enthusiasm, and organization drove the reform efforts in America in the late nineteenth and early twentieth centuries, much of it a result of social crises and political movements in the United States. But the "age of reform," as some have called it, was not an American phenomenon alone. It was part of a wave of social experimentation that was occurring throughout much of the industrial world. "Progressivism" in other countries influenced the social movements in the United States. American reform, in turn, had significant influence elsewhere as well.

Several industrializing nations adopted the term *progressivism* for their efforts—not only the United States, but also England, Germany, and France. But the term that most broadly defined the new reform energies was *social democracy*. Social democrats in many countries shared a belief in the betterment of society through the accumulation of knowledge. They favored improving the social condition of all people through reforms of the economy and government programs of social protection. And they believed that these goals could be achieved through peaceful political change, rather than through radicalism or revolution. Political parties committed to these goals emerged in several countries: the Labour Party in Britain, social democratic parties in various European nations, and the short-lived Progressive Party in the United States. Intellectuals, academics, and government officials across the world shared the knowledge they were accumulating and observed one another's social programs. American reformers at the turn of the century spent much time visiting Germany, France, Britain, Belgium, and the Netherlands, observing the reforms in progress there; and Europeans, in turn, visited the United States. Reformers from both America and Europe were also fascinated by the advanced social experiments in Australia and, especially, New Zealand—which the American reformer Henry Demarest Lloyd once called "the political brain of the modern world." But New Zealand's dramatic experiments in factory regulation, woman suffrage, old-age pensions, progressive taxation, and labor arbitration gradually found counterparts in many other nations as well. William Allen White, a progressive journalist from Kansas, said of this time: "We were parts of one another, in the United States and Europe. Something was welding us into one

THE PARIS EXPO, A PROGRESSIVE SYMBOL The Paris Expositions of 1889 and 1900, symbolized by the Eiffel Tower and enormous globe, drew progressive experts as well as tourists with the vision of progress through industrial innovation. During the Expos, an international group of progressives held meetings to share ideas for bettering society. (© Archives Charmet/Bridgeman Images)

social and economic whole with local political variations . . . [all] fighting a common cause."

Social democracy—or, as it was sometimes called in the United States and elsewhere, social justice or the social gospel—was responsible for many public programs. Germany began a system of social insurance for its citizens in the 1880s while simultaneously undertaking a massive study of society that produced over 140 volumes of "social investigation" of almost every aspect of the nation's life. French reformers pressed in the 1890s for factory regulation, assistance to the elderly, and progressive taxation. Britain pioneered the settlement houses in working-class areas of London—a movement that soon spread to the United States—and, like the United States, witnessed growing challenges to the power of monopolies at both the local and national levels.

In many countries, social democrats felt pressure from the rising worldwide labor movement and from the rise of socialist parties in many industrial countries as well. Strikes, sometimes violent, were common in France, Germany, Britain, and the United States in the late nineteenth century. The more militant workers became, the more unions seemed to grow. Social democrats did not always welcome the rise of militant labor movements, but they took them seriously and used them to support their own efforts at reform.

The politics of social democracy represented a great shift in the character of public life all over the industrial world. Instead of battles over the privileges of aristocrats or the power of monarchs, reformers now focused on the social problems of ordinary people and attempted to improve their lot. "The politics of the future are social politics," the British reformer Joseph Chamberlain said in the 1880s, referring to efforts to deal with the problems of ordinary citizens. That belief was fueling progressive efforts across the world in the years that Americans have come to call the "progressive era." •

UNDERSTAND, ANALYZE, & EVALUATE

1. What is social democracy? How does it differ from socialism?
2. What progressive era reforms in American social and political life can be seen in other nations as well?

groups or even societies. Advocates of social justice are likely to believe in a more egalitarian society.) That impulse helped create the rise of what became known as the "Social Gospel," the effort to make faith into a tool of social reform. The Social Gospel movement was chiefly concerned with redeeming the nation's cities.

The Salvation Army, which began in England but soon spread to the United States, was one example of the fusion of religion with reform. A Christian social welfare organization with a vaguely military structure, it had recruited 3,000 "officers" and 20,000 "privates" by 1900 and was offering both material aid and spiritual service to the urban poor. In addition, many ministers, priests, and rabbis left traditional parish work to serve in the troubled cities. Charles Sheldon's book *In His Steps* (1898), the story of a young minister who abandoned a comfortable post to work among the needy, sold more than 15 million copies. The Social Gospel was never the dominant element in the movement for urban reform. But the engagement of religion with reform helped bring to progressivism a powerful moral commitment to redeem the lives of even the least favored citizens.

THE SETTLEMENT HOUSE MOVEMENT

An element of much progressive thought was the belief in the influence of the environment on individual development. Nothing produced greater distress, many urban reformers

21 | AMERICA AND THE GREAT WAR

THE "BIG STICK": AMERICA AND THE WORLD, 1901–1917

THE ROAD TO WAR

"OVER THERE"

THE SEARCH FOR A NEW WORLD ORDER

A SOCIETY IN TURMOIL

LOOKING AHEAD

1. What were the most important events that led up to the United States declaring war on Germany?

2. How did U.S. participation in the Great War affect the nation's economy and society, both during the war and after the conflict ended?

3. Why did the Great War fail to become the "war to end all wars"?

THE "GREAT WAR," AS IT was known to a generation unaware that a greater war would soon follow, began quietly in August 1914 when Austria-Hungary invaded the tiny Balkan nation of Serbia. Within weeks, however, the conflict had grown into a conflagration engaging the armies of most of the major nations of Europe. Americans looked on with horror as the war became what many people claimed was the most savage in history. It dragged on, brutally and inconclusively, for over four years. Most Americans also believed at first that the conflict had little to do with them. They were wrong. After nearly three years of attempting to affect the outcome of the conflict without becoming embroiled in it, the United States formally entered the war in April 1917.

THE "BIG STICK": AMERICA AND THE WORLD, 1901–1917

To most of the American public, foreign affairs remained largely remote in the early twentieth century. But to Theodore Roosevelt and later presidents, that remoteness made foreign affairs appealing. Overseas, the president could act with less regard for Congress and the courts.

ROOSEVELT AND "CIVILIZATION"

Theodore Roosevelt believed in using American power in the world (a conviction he once alluded to by citing the proverb, "Speak softly, and carry a big stick"). But he had two different standards for using that power.

Roosevelt believed that an important distinction existed between the "civilized" and "uncivilized" nations of the world. "Civilized" nations, as he defined them, were predominantly white and Anglo-Saxon or Teutonic; "uncivilized" nations were generally nonwhite, Latin, or Slavic. Civilized nations were also, by Roosevelt's definition, producers of industrial goods. Uncivilized nations were suppliers of raw materials and markets for industrial products. Roosevelt believed that a civilized society had the right and duty to intervene in the affairs of "backward nations" to preserve order and stability—for the sake of both nations. That belief, the obligation of a "civilized" nation to, in effect, police the world, was one important reason for Roosevelt's early support of the development of American sea power. By 1906, the American navy had attained a size and strength surpassed only by that of Great Britain.

TIME LINE

1914
World War I begins
Panama Canal opened

1915
U.S. troops in Haiti
Lusitania torpedoed
Wilson supports preparedness

1916
Wilson reelected
U.S. troops in Mexico

1917
German unrestricted submarine warfare
U.S. enters World War I
Selective Service Act
War Industries Board created

1918
Sedition Act
Wilson's Fourteen Points
Armistice ends war
Paris Peace Conference

1919
Senate rejects Treaty of Versailles
Race riots in Chicago and other cities
Steel strike and other labor actions

1920
Palmer raids and Red Scare
Harding elected president

1927
Sacco and Vanzetti executed

THE ROAD TO WAR

By 1914, the European nations had created an unusually precarious international system. It careened into war very quickly on the basis of what seemed to be a minor series of provocations.

THE COLLAPSE OF THE EUROPEAN PEACE

The major powers of Europe were organized by 1914 in two great, competing alliances. The "Triple Entente" linked Britain, France, and Russia. The "Triple Alliance" united Germany, the Austro-Hungarian Empire, and Italy.

The conflict emerged most directly out of a controversy involving nationalist movements within the Austro-Hungarian Empire. On June 28, 1914, Archduke Franz Ferdinand, heir to the throne of the tottering empire, was assassinated while paying a state visit to Sarajevo, the capital of Bosnia, then a province of Austria-Hungary. Slavic nationalists wished to annex Bosnia to neighboring Serbia. The killer of the archduke and his wife Sophie was a Serbian nationalist.

Austria immediately blamed Serbia for the murders and issued impossible ultimatums. Russia, Serbia's Slavic ally and a seeker of greater influence in the Balkans, mobilized its armies along the border with Austria-Hungary. The Germans, faced with that provocation against their ally and concerned about a two-front war against Russia and France, declared war against both. Germany's subsequent assault on France ran through neutral Belgium, prompting Britain to declare war on Germany.

The coalitions soon changed in name and membership. On one side were the Central Powers: Germany and Austria-Hungary, joined in the fall by the Ottoman Empire. On the *Allies and Central Powers* other side were the Allies, made up of Britain, France, and Russia. Hoping to seize territory from the Central Powers, Italy and Japan soon threw in their lot with the Allies.

As these changes suggest, the alliance system did not necessarily *bind* nations to act as they did. Leaders made the decision for war based on their own interests and ambitions, on the assumption that national self-defense required it, and on the erroneous belief that their objectives could be met quickly. What the alliance system did was provide a framework within which the choices for war were made. As tragic as those choices seem in retrospect, no one expected or wanted the ghastly world war that followed.

WILSON'S NEUTRALITY

Wilson called on his fellow citizens in 1914 to remain "impartial in thought as well as deed." But that was impossible. Most Americans sympathized with Britain. Lurid reports of German atrocities in Belgium and France, sometimes (but not always) exaggerated by British propagandists, strengthened the hostility of many Americans toward Germany.

Economic realities also made it impossible for the United States to deal with the belligerents on equal terms. The British had imposed a naval blockade on Germany to prevent munitions and supplies from reaching the enemy. As a neutral, the United States had the right, in theory, to trade with Germany, but the British blockade made that impossible. A truly neutral response to the blockade would have been to stop trading with Britain as well. But while the United States could survive an interruption of its relatively modest trade with the Central Powers, it could not easily weather a break in its much more extensive trade with the Allies. So America tacitly accepted the blockade of Germany and continued trading with Britain. By 1915, the United States had *Continued Trade with Britain* gradually transformed itself from a neutral power into the arsenal of the Allies.

The Germans, in the meantime, were resorting to a new and, in American eyes, barbaric tactic: submarine warfare. Unable to challenge British domination on *Sinking of Lusitania* the ocean's surface, the Germans announced early in 1915 that they would sink enemy vessels on sight. Months later, on May 7, a German submarine (or U-boat, a name derived from the German *Unterseeboot*) sank the British passenger liner *Lusitania* without warning, causing the deaths of 1,198 people, 128 of them Americans. The ship was carrying both passengers and munitions, but most Americans considered the attack an unprovoked act on civilians.

Wilson angrily demanded that Germany promise not to repeat such outrages, and the Germans reluctantly agreed. But early in 1916, in response to an announcement that the Allies were now arming merchant ships to sink submarines, Germany proclaimed that it would fire on such vessels without warning. A few weeks later, it attacked the unarmed French steamer *Sussex,* injuring several American passengers. Again, Wilson demanded that Germany abandon its "unlawful" tactics; again, the German government relented.

PREPAREDNESS VERSUS PACIFISM

Despite the president's increasing bellicosity in 1916, he was still far from ready to commit the United States to war. One obstacle was American domestic politics.

The question of whether America should make military and economic preparations for war sparked a heated debate between pacifists and interventionists. Wilson at first denounced the idea of an American military buildup as needless and provocative. In the fall of 1915, however, he endorsed an ambitious proposal by American military leaders for a large and rapid increase in the nation's armed forces.

Still, the peace faction wielded considerable political strength, as became clear at the Democratic National Convention in the summer of 1916. The convention became especially enthusiastic when the keynote speaker punctuated his list of the president's diplomatic achievements with the chant, "What did we do? What did we do? . . . We didn't go to war! We didn't go to war!" That speech helped produce one of the most prominent slogans of Wilson's reelection campaign: "He kept us out of war." During the campaign, Wilson did nothing to discourage those who argued that the Republican candidate, the progressive New York governor Charles Evans Hughes, was more likely than he to lead the nation into war. Wilson ultimately won reelection by fewer than 600,000 popular votes and only 23 electoral votes. But he was uncomfortable about a slogan that had aided his victory. "Any little German lieutenant," he said of the U-boat situation, "can put us into the war at any time by some calculated outrage."

INTERVENTION

Wilson was right—but it was the German leadership that provoked him. In January 1917 Germany made a desperate gamble, declaring unrestricted submarine warfare against all maritime traffic in the hopes of defeating the Allies before Wilson could mobilize an army. Meanwhile, the German foreign secretary Arthur Zimmermann *Zimmermann Telegram* sent a telegram to the German ambassador in Mexico instructing him to offer the Mexicans a deal: if they would join a military alliance, Germany would help Mexico take back

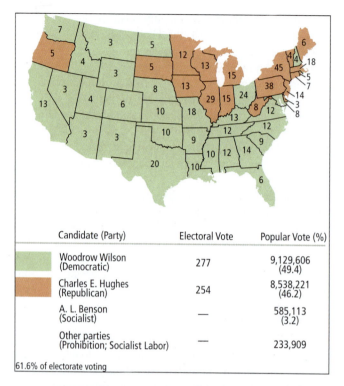

Candidate (Party)	Electoral Vote	Popular Vote (%)
Woodrow Wilson (Democratic)	277	9,129,606 (49.4)
Charles E. Hughes (Republican)	254	8,538,221 (46.2)
A. L. Benson (Socialist)	—	585,113 (3.2)
Other parties (Prohibition; Socialist Labor)	—	233,909

61.6% of electorate voting

THE ELECTION OF 1916   Woodrow Wilson had good reason to be concerned about his reelection prospects in 1916. He had won only about 42 percent of the vote in 1912, and the Republican Party—which had been divided four years earlier—was now reunited around the popular Charles Evans Hughes. In the end, Wilson won a narrow victory over Hughes with just under 50 percent of the vote and a similarly narrow margin in the electoral college. Note the striking regional character of his victory. • *How did Wilson use the war in Europe to bolster his election prospects?*

territory in the present states of Texas, New Mexico, and Arizona. By March, when Wilson released the intercepted and decoded telegram—and after three United States ships were torpedoed by U-boats—war with Germany seemed imminent.

Although German crimes on the seas, the offer to Mexico, and the threats to American commerce provided the immediate causes for war, Wilson had broader purposes in mind as well. The president hoped that American intervention, by earning him a seat at the postwar negotiating table, would usher in a new era. In the place of militarism, secret alliances, violence, and autocracy would come democracy, freedom of travel and commerce, open diplomacy, and self-determination.

President Wilson articulated this vision on the rainy evening of April 2, 1917, when he asked Congress for a declaration of war. German U-boat warfare had claimed American
Wilson's War Message   lives and treasure. The country's honor could not tolerate such affronts. But aware of divisions in public opinion, Wilson sought to invest the moment with higher meaning. The war would make the world "safe for democracy" and safeguard "the rights of mankind." America would not fight for material gain or territory, the president said, but to guarantee a future of free trade, self-governance, peace, and justice. Opposition to the war would not be tolerated. "If there should be disloyalty," he warned, "it will be dealt with a firm hand of repression."

Wilson's view carried the session, but dissenters spoke up. Some midwesterners and southerners saw corporate profits, not honor, at stake in the Atlantic. A few pacifists, including the first woman elected to Congress, Jeannette Rankin, a Republican from Montana, argued that no war was worth the costs. Still others argued the United States should stay out of Europe's affairs. When the declaration of war finally passed on April 6, six senators and fifty representatives voted against it.

"OVER THERE"

European armies on both sides of the conflict were decimated and exhausted by the time of Woodrow Wilson's declaration of war. The Allies looked desperately to the United States for help in breaking the stalemate.

MOBILIZING THE MILITARY

By the spring of 1917, Great Britain was suffering such vast losses from German submarines that its ability to receive vital supplies from across the Atlantic was in jeopardy. Within weeks of joining the war, the United States had begun to alter the balance. A fleet of American destroyers aided the British navy in attacking the U-boats and planting anti-submarine mines in the North Sea. The results were dramatic. Sinkings of Allied ships had totaled nearly 900,000 tons in the month of April 1917; the figure dropped to 350,000 by December 1917 and to 112,000 by October 1918.

Many Americans had hoped that providing naval assistance alone would be enough to end the war, but it quickly became clear that a major commitment of American ground forces would be necessary as well. Britain and France had few remaining reserves. After the Bolshevik Revolution in November 1917, a new communist *Bolshevik Revolution* government, led by V. I. Lenin, negotiated a hasty and costly peace between Russia and the Central Powers. That freed German troops to fight on the western front.

The United States did not have a large enough standing army to provide the necessary ground forces in 1917. Even amid recruitment efforts (see "Consider the Source: Race, Gender, and World War I Posters"), enlistments proved inadequate. Only a national draft could provide the needed men. Despite protests, Wilson won passage of the Selective Service Act in mid-May. From a prewar total of 121,000 enlisted soldiers, the army *Selective Service Act* grew to more than 4 million, 2 million of whom went to France. Draftees comprised 72 percent of all American soldiers in the war—a far higher percentage than on either side of the Civil War.

The typical American soldier (or doughboy) in the Great War was a white, single, poorly educated draftee in his early twenties. Women were barred from regular military *The Doughboy* service, but could sign up for things like nursing, clerical work, and telephone operation. As many as 400,000 African Americans joined the military, the vast majority conscripted. But this was a strict Jim Crow army. Units were segregated, white officers were in charge, and blacks generally performed menial labor. Yet two combat divisions, the Ninety-Second and Ninety-Third, were composed entirely of African American soldiers.

In training camps around the country, selectees learned how to be soldiers. They marched and drilled and practiced maneuvers. In case they weren't sure what *Basic Training* they were fighting for, every backpack contained a copy of Wilson's war message. For the huge number of foreign-born soldiers—approaching 20 percent of the wartime army, speaking forty-six different languages—military service acted as a tool of assimilation, to

RACE, GENDER, AND WORLD WAR I POSTERS

Much can be learned about a society's values from how it handles the mobilization of the home front during wartime. Nations typically clarify the terms of citizenship and service—asking some people to fight, and some to stay home and support the effort in other ways. As part of the broad national campaign to mobilize public opinion and service during World War I, American officials disseminated the two posters reproduced here. One urged enlistment, the other the purchase of war bonds.

UNDERSTAND, ANALYZE, & EVALUATE

1. How do the posters use images of women or the home to encourage either enlistment or financial support for the war?

2. What do these posters say about contemporary understandings of gender roles? What did the state and society expect from men? What did they expect from women?

3. Like almost all recruiting posters of World War I, these two depict white people—despite the fact that many African Americans and ethnic minorities served as well. What does that say about mainstream attitudes toward race and ethnicity during World War I?

(The Library of Congress)

(The Library of Congress)

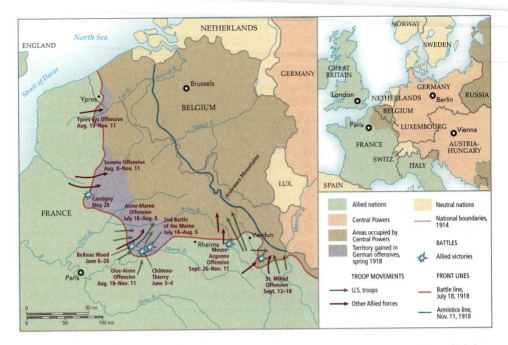

AMERICA IN WORLD WAR I: THE WESTERN FRONT, 1918 These maps show the principal battles in which the United States participated in the last year of World War I. The small map on the upper right helps locate the area of conflict within the larger European landscape. The larger map at left shows the long, snaking red line of the western front in France—stretching from the border between France and southwest Germany all the way to the northeast border between Belgium and France. Along that vast line, the two sides had been engaged in murderous, inconclusive warfare for over three years by the time the Americans arrived. Beginning in the spring and summer of 1918, bolstered by reinforcements from the United States, the Allies began to win a series of important victories that finally enabled them to begin pushing the Germans back. American troops, as this map makes clear, were decisive along the southern part of the front. • *At what point did the Germans begin to consider putting an end to the war?*

the delight of nativists. The draftees received moral instruction as well. Progressives in the government, as well as thousands of American parents, worried about the sexual purity of the soldier. One social hygiene poster implored the soldier to "Remember—the folks at home. Go back to them physically fit and morally clean. Don't allow a whore to smirch your record."

THE YANKS ARE COMING

The United States had sent the first units of the American Expeditionary Forces (AEF) to France in June 1917 under the leadership of General John J. Pershing, but American soldiers weren't heavily implicated in the fighting until the next year. In March 1918, the Germans launched nimble thrusts into the Allied defenses. Under the French commander of Allied forces, Ferdinand Foch, Pershing's troops halted the German offensive at Cantigny and Château-Thierry. Then the American Second Division, including a brigade of marines, lost 9,800 casualties in a savage but successful fight to drive the Germans from Belleau Wood, a place that would live on in Marine Corps lore. In July the Germans attacked again, and at the Second Battle of the Marne, the Allies fought together to repulse them. Over the course of that summer, the influx of American divisions helped the Allies push the German army back roughly to its original position.

By September, with American troops plentiful and the Germans depleted, the Allies prepared to advance toward Germany. Pershing withdrew many of his divisions to the Americans' own sector on the southern edge of the front. From that position, the dough-boys took the Saint-Mihiel salient, a bulge into Allied lines that the Germans had held for years. Foch then ordered Pershing's divisions to their place in the war's final Allied *The Meuse-Argonne Offensive* push, the Meuse-Argonne offensive. Beginning on September 26, more than a million American doughboys—the great majority of them seeing combat for the first time—advanced against the Germans, while to the northwest the British and French undertook coordinated campaigns. The Germans sagged but held, and something like trench warfare set in again. September and October were terrible months for the Americans, with 27,000 men killed. "Those of us who still lived," wrote one doughboy, "who were able to move, in body if not in spirit, wanted to drop to our knees and implore God to stop this horrible slaughter of mankind."

By November the Germans had been worn down, their civilian population suffering from an increasingly effective blockade, their soldiers captured by the hundreds of thousands, their U-boats more or less neutralized by a convoy system, and their rear harassed *Armistice* by airplane bombardment. Facing invasion, the Germans sought an armistice. Early on the morning of November 11, 1918, while men along the front were still dying, representatives of the warring parties signed an armistice in a railway car in the French forest. The four-year "war to end all wars" shuddered to a close.

THE NEW TECHNOLOGY OF WARFARE

World War I was a proving ground for a range of new military technologies. The trench *Trench Warfare* warfare that characterized the conflict was a result of the enormous destructive power of newly improved machine guns and higher-powered artillery. It was no longer feasible to send troops out into an open field. The new weaponry would slaughter them in an instant. Trenches sheltered troops while allowing limited, and usually inconclusive, fighting. But technology overtook the trenches, too, as mobile weapons—tanks and flamethrowers—proved capable of piercing entrenched positions. Most terrible of all, perhaps, new chemical weapons—poisonous mustard gas, which required troops to carry gas masks at all times—made it possible to attack entrenched soldiers without direct combat.

The new forms of technological warfare required elaborate maintenance. Faster machine guns needed more ammunition. Motorized vehicles required fuel, spare parts, and mechanics capable of servicing them. The logistical difficulties of supply became a major factor in planning tactics and strategy. Late in the war, when the Allied armies were advancing toward Germany, they frequently had to stop for days at a time to wait for their equipment to catch up with them.

World War I was the first conflict in which airplanes played a significant role. The planes themselves were relatively simple and not very maneuverable; but antiaircraft technology was not yet highly developed either, so their effectiveness was still significant. Planes began to be constructed to serve various functions: bombers, fighters (planes that would engage in "dogfights" with other planes), and reconaissance aircraft.

The most "modern" part of the military during World War I was the navy. Battleships emerged that made use of new technologies such as turbine propulsion, hydraulic gun controls, electric light and power, wireless telegraphy, and advanced navigational aids. Submarines, which had made a brief appearance in the American Civil War, now became

LIFE IN THE TRENCHES   For most British, French, German, and, to a lesser extent, American troops in France, the most debilitating part of World War I was the misery of life in the trenches. Some young men lived in these cold, wet, muddy dugouts for months, even years, surrounded by filth, sharing their space with vermin, eating mostly rotten food. Occasional attacks to try to dislodge the enemy from its trenches usually ended in failure and became the scenes of terrible slaughter. (National Archives and Records Administration)

significant weapons (as the German U-boat campaign in 1915 and 1916 made clear). The new submarines were driven by diesel engines that were more compact than steam engines and used fuel that was less explosive than that of gasoline engines.

The new technologies were responsible for the war's truly stunning statistics of death. Russia lost 1.8 million soldiers; Germany, 2 million; France, 1.4 million; *Appalling Casualties* the British Empire, 1 million; Austria-Hungary, 1.5 million; Italy, 460,000. Something like 5 million civilians died under the stress of war—by violence or slower means—though the exact number is hard to know. The United States lost 116,000 soldiers, about half of those in combat, the others to disease. Some perished in the 1918 influenza pandemic that ultimately claimed an estimated 50 to 100 million lives worldwide.

Although only in the war briefly, the Americans had played a significant role in the victory. Their casualty rates in the periods of intense fighting approximated or exceeded those of their Allies. The prospect of more doughboys arriving in the future surely affected the German leadership's capitulation in 1918. The British, Russian, and French contributions, of course, dwarfed the American one in sheer numbers. But Wilson's army had acquitted itself well enough to earn him a seat at the negotiating table—one of his ambitions all along.

ORGANIZING THE ECONOMY FOR WAR

By the time the war ended, the federal government had appropriated $32 billion for war expenses—a staggering sum at the time. The entire federal budget had seldom exceeded $1 billion before 1915, and as recently as 1910 the nation's entire gross national product had been only $35 billion. To raise the money, the government relied on two devices. First, it launched a major drive to solicit loans from the American people by selling *"Liberty Bonds"* "Liberty Bonds" to the public. By 1920, the sale of bonds, accompanied by elaborate patriotic appeals, had produced $23 billion. At the same time, new taxes were bringing in an additional sum of nearly $10 billion—some of it coming from levies on the "excess profits" of corporations but much of it coming from new, steeply graduated income and inheritance taxes that ultimately rose as high as 70 percent in some brackets.

An even greater challenge was to organize the economy to meet war needs. In 1916, Wilson established the Council of National Defense, composed of members of his cabinet, and the Civilian Advisory Commission, which set up local defense councils in every state and locality. But this early administrative structure soon proved completely unworkable, and members of the council urged a more centralized approach. The administrative structure that slowly emerged was dominated by a series of "war boards," one to oversee the railroads, one to supervise fuel supplies (largely coal), another to handle food (a board that elevated to prominence the brilliant young engineer and business executive Herbert Hoover). The boards generally succeeded in meeting essential war needs without paralyzing the domestic economy.

The War Industries Board (WIB) was created in July 1917 to coordinate government *War Industries Board* purchases of military supplies. Casually organized at first, it stumbled badly until March 1918, when Wilson restructured it and placed it under the control of the Wall Street financier Bernard Baruch. Baruch decided which factories would convert to the production of which war materials, and he set prices for the goods they produced. When materials were scarce, Baruch decided to whom they should go. When corporations were competing for government contracts, he chose among them.

Baruch viewed himself, openly and explicitly, as a partner of business; and within the WIB, businessmen themselves—the so-called dollar-a-year men, who took paid leave from their corporate jobs and worked for the government for a token salary—supervised the affairs of the private economy.

The National War Labor Board, established in April 1918, served as the final mediator of labor disputes. It pressured industry to grant important concessions to workers: an

WOMEN INDUSTRIAL WORKERS In World War II, such women were often called "Rosie the Riveter." Their presence in these previously all-male work environments was no less startling to Americans during World War I. These women are shown working with acetylene torches to bevel armor plate for tanks. The photographer was Margaret Bourke-White, who herself broke gender boundaries as the first female photojournalist for *Life* magazine and the first female war correspondent. (Photo by Margaret Bourke-White/© The LIFE Picture Collection/Getty Images)

eight-hour day, the maintenance of minimal living standards, equal pay for women doing equal work, recognition of the right of unions to organize and bargain collectively. In return, it insisted that workers forgo strikes and that employers not engage in lockouts.

THE SEARCH FOR SOCIAL UNITY

Government leaders were painfully aware that public sentiment about the war was sharply divided. The most conspicuous official effort to support the war was a vast propaganda campaign orchestrated by the Committee on Public Information (CPI), *Wartime Propaganda* under the direction of the progressive journalist George Creel. The CPI supervised the distribution of over 75 million pieces of printed material and controlled much of the information available for newspapers and magazines. Creel encouraged journalists to exercise "self-censorship" when reporting war news, and most complied by covering the war largely as the government wished. By 1918, government-distributed posters and films were offering lurid (and exaggerated) portrayals of the savagery of the Germans. In this climate, songwriters and other artists produced popular works that heavily favored the war. (See "Patterns of Popular Culture: George M. Cohan, 'Over There,' 1917.")

The government also began efforts to suppress dissent. CPI-financed advertisements in magazines implored citizens to report to the authorities any evidence among their neighbors of disloyalty, pessimism, or yearning for peace. The Espionage Act of 1917 gave the government new tools with which to combat spying, sabotage, or obstruction of the war effort (crimes that were often broadly defined). The Sabotage Act and the Sedition Act,

GEORGE M. COHAN, "OVER THERE," 1917

Music was one of the richest forms of American popular culture in the early twentieth century, much of it emanating from New York City companies in a neighborhood known as Tin Pan Alley. Lyricists and composers, eager to peddle their sheet music widely, had long captured popular attitudes toward the issues of their day. In 1915, with men dying in the Great War at a staggering rate, songwriters churned out such antimilitarist numbers as "I Didn't Raise My Boy to Be a Soldier" and "Don't Take My Darling Boy Away!"

In April 1917, however, President Wilson's demand for unanimity changed Tin Pan Alley's tune. Songs now demonized Kaiser Wilhelm II, the emperor of Germany, glorified the American *doughboy* (a term dating to the mid-nineteenth century but of mysterious origins) and sentimentalized the home-front family. Other tunes became anthems of American confidence and strength, none more so than George M. Cohan's "Over There." Even before that hit—which became the best-known song of the war—Cohan was a leading figure in the American entertainment industry, a prolific creator and performer of Broadway productions, and the composer of hundreds of original songs, including classics such as "Yankee Doodle Boy."

Written just after Wilson's war address of April 2, "Over There" offered a jaunty soundtrack for American intervention. It was sung on the home front and in basic training; doughboys in France found it in songbooks issued by various civilian agencies. "Over There" represented a prominent strain in public culture of 1917—deeply patriotic, optimistic, and sentimental—even as many Americans worried quietly about what this new war would mean for them and their families.

Johnnie, get your gun,
Get your gun, get your gun,
Take it on the run,
On the run, on the run.
Hear them calling, you and me,
Every son of liberty.
Hurry right away,
No delay, no delay,
Make your daddy glad
To have had such a lad.
Tell your sweetheart not to pine,
To be proud her boy's in line.

Chorus
Over there, over there
Send the word, send the word over there
That the Yanks are coming,
The Yanks are coming,
The drums rum-tumming
Ev'rywhere.
So prepare, say a pray'r,
Send the word, send the word to beware.
We'll be over, we're coming over,
And we won't come back till it's over
Over there.
Johnnie get your gun,
Get your gun, get your gun,
Johnnie show the Hun
Who's a son of a gun.
Hoist the flag and let her fly,
Yankee Doodle do or die.

22 THE NEW ERA

THE NEW ECONOMY
THE NEW CULTURE
A CONFLICT OF CULTURES
REPUBLICAN GOVERNMENT

LOOKING AHEAD

1. How did the technological innovations of the early twentieth century affect industry and American social life of the 1920s?
2. What were some of the cultural conflicts of the 1920s, and what caused them?
3. Is the term the *New Era* a fitting description of the 1920s?

IN POPULAR CULTURE, THE 1920s are often remembered as an era of affluence, conservatism, and cultural frivolity. In reality, however, the decade was a time of significant, even dramatic social, economic, and political change. The American economy not only enjoyed spectacular growth but also developed new forms of organization. Many Americans reshaped themselves to reflect the increasingly urban, industrial, consumer-oriented society of the United States. And American government experimented with new approaches to public policy. That was why contemporaries liked to refer to the 1920s as the "New Era"—an age in which America was becoming a modern nation.

At the same time, however, the decade saw the rise of a series of spirited, and at times effective, rebellions against the transformations in American life. The intense cultural conflicts that characterized the 1920s showed that much of American society remained unreconciled to the modernizing currents of the New Era.

TIME LINE

1914–1920
Great Migration of blacks to the North

1920
Prohibition begins

Harding elected president

1922
Lewis's *Babbitt*

1923
Harding dies; Coolidge becomes president

Harding administration scandals revealed

1924
National Origins Act passed

Coolidge elected president

Ku Klux Klan membership peaks

1925
Fitzgerald's *The Great Gatsby*

Scopes trial

1927
First sound motion picture, *The Jazz Singer*

1928
Hoover elected president

THE NEW ECONOMY

After the recession of 1921–1922, the United States began a period of almost uninterrupted prosperity and economic expansion. Less visible at the time, but equally significant, was the survival (and even the growth) of inequalities and imbalances.

TECHNOLOGY, ORGANIZATION, AND ECONOMIC GROWTH

No one could deny the remarkable feats of the American economy in the 1920s. The nation's manufacturing output rose by more than 60 percent. Per capita income grew by a third. Inflation was negligible. A mild recession in 1923 briefly interrupted the pattern of growth; but when it subsided early in 1924, the economy expanded with even greater vigor.

The economic boom was a result of many things, but one of the most important was technology. As a result of the development of the assembly line and other innovations, automobiles now became one of the most important industries in the nation, stimulating growth in such related industries as steel, rubber, and glass, tool companies, oil corporations, and road construction. The increased mobility that the automobile made possible increased the demand for suburban housing, fueling a boom in the construction industry.

Radio contributed as well to the economic growth. Early radio had been able to broadcast little besides pulses, which meant that radio communication could occur only through the Morse code. But with the discovery of the theory of modulation, pioneered by the Canadian scientist Reginald Fessenden, it became possible to transmit speech and music. Many people built their own radio sets at home for very little money, benefiting from the discovery that inexpensive crystals could receive signals over long distances (but not very well over short ones). These "shortwave" radios, which allowed individual owners to establish contact with one another, marked the beginning of what later became known as "ham radio." Once commercial broadcasting began, families flocked to buy more conventional radio sets powered by reliable vacuum tubes and capable of receiving high-quality signals over short and medium distances. By 1925, there were 2 million sets in American homes, and by the end of the 1920s, almost every family had one.

Commercial aviation developed slowly in the 1920s, beginning with the use of planes to deliver mail. On the whole, airplanes remained curiosities and sources of *Commercial Aviation* entertainment. But technological advances—the development of the radial engine and the creation of pressurized cabins—laid the groundwork for the great increase in commercial travel in the 1930s and beyond. Electronics, home appliances, plastics and synthetic fibers (such as nylon), aluminum, magnesium, oil, electric power, and other industries fueled by technological advances—all grew dramatically. Telephones continued to proliferate. By the late 1930s, there were approximately 25 million telephones in the United States, roughly one for every six people. (See "Consider the Source: America's Early Telephone Network.")

The seeds of future technological breakthroughs were also visible. In both England and America, scientists and engineers were working to transform primitive calculating machines into devices capable of performing more complicated tasks. By the early *Early Computing* 1930s, researchers at MIT, led by Vannevar Bush, had created an instrument capable of performing a variety of complicated tasks—the first analog computer. A few years later, Howard Aiken, with financial assistance from Harvard and MIT, built a much more complex computer with memory, capable of multiplying eleven-digit numbers in three seconds.

Genetic research had begun in Austria in the mid-nineteenth century through the work of Gregor Mendel, a Catholic monk who performed experiments on the *Genetic Research* hybridization of vegetables in his monastery garden. His findings attracted little attention during his lifetime, but in the early twentieth century they were discovered by several investigators and helped shape modern genetic research. Among the American pioneers was Thomas Hunt Morgan of Columbia University and, later, Cal Tech, whose experiments with fruit flies revealed how several genes could be transmitted together. He also revealed the way in which genes were arranged along the chromosome. His work helped open the path to understanding how genes could recombine—a critical discovery that led to more advanced experiments in hybridization and genetics.

Large sectors of American business accelerated their drive toward national organization and consolidation. Certain industries—notably those dependent on large-scale mass production, such as steel and automobiles—seemed to move naturally toward concentrating production in a few large firms. Other industries—less dependent on technology and less susceptible to great economies of scale—proved more resistant to consolidation.

The strenuous efforts by industrialists throughout the economy to find ways to curb competition reflected a strong fear of overcapacity. Even in the booming 1920s, industrialists remembered how too-rapid expansion and overproduction had helped produce recessions in 1893, 1907, and 1920. The great unrealized dream of the New Era was to find a way to stabilize the economy so that such collapses would never occur again.

WORKERS IN AN AGE OF CAPITAL

Despite the remarkable economic growth, more than two-thirds of the American people in 1929 lived at no better than what one major study described as the "minimum comfort level." Half of those were at or below the level of "subsistence and poverty."

CONSIDER THE SOURCE

AMERICA'S EARLY TELEPHONE NETWORK

Alexander Graham Bell received a patent for the invention of the telephone in 1876. By 1914, telephone exchanges linked more than 70,000 places and 8 million subscribers in the United States. This map, part of an advertisement for the American Telephone and Telegraph Company, shows the extent of telephone coverage that year.

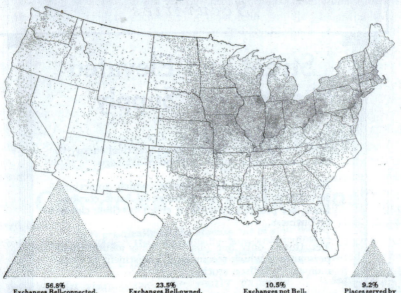

What the Telephone Map Shows

56.8%	23.5%	10.5%	9.2%
Exchanges Bell-connected, but not Bell-owned.	Exchanges Bell-owned.	Exchanges not Bell-owned or connected.	Places served by two companies.

EVERY dot on the map marks a town where there is a telephone exchange, the same sized dot being used for a large city as for a small village. Some of these exchanges are owned by the Associated Bell companies and some by independent companies. Where joined together in one system they meet the needs of each community and, with their suburban lines, reach 70,000 places and over 8,000,000 subscribers.

The pyramids show that only a minority of the exchanges are Bell-owned, and that the greater majority of the exchanges are owned by independent companies and connected with the Bell System.

At comparatively few points are there two telephone companies, and there are comparatively few exchanges, chiefly rural, which do not have outside connections.

The recent agreement between the Attorney General of the United States and the Bell System will facilitate connections between all telephone subscribers regardless of who owns the exchanges.

Over 8,000 different telephone companies have already connected their exchanges to provide universal service for the whole country.

 AMERICAN TELEPHONE AND TELEGRAPH COMPANY
AND ASSOCIATED COMPANIES

One Policy   *One System*   *Universal Service*

For our Mutual Advantage mention Popular Electricity and Modern Mechanics when writing to Advertisers.

(*Popular Electricity and Modern Mechanics*, September, 19, 1914).

1. In what area of the United States was the concentration of telephone exchanges the heaviest? Why do you think there were more exchanges in this part of the country than in other areas?
2. The text accompanying the map explains that the same-sized dots are used for large cities as for small villages. Would the use of different-sized dots to indicate larger cities or smaller towns make the map more representative of U.S. telephone usage in 1914?
3. This map is part of an advertisement produced by the American Telephone and Telegraph Company. How does that fact influence a reading of the information provided in the map and accompanying text?

American labor experienced both the successes and the failures of the 1920s. On the one hand, most workers saw their standard of living rise during the decade. Some employers adopted paternalistic techniques that came to be known as **welfare capitalism.**

THE STEAMFITTER Lewis Hine was among the first American photographers to recognize his craft as an art. In this carefully posed photograph from the mid-1920s, Hine made a point that many other artists were making in other media: the rise of the machine could serve human beings, but might also bend them to its own needs. (© New York Public Library, USA/Bridgeman Images)

Henry Ford, for example, shortened the workweek, raised wages, and instituted paid vacations. By 1926, nearly 3 million industrial workers were eligible for at least modest pensions upon retirement. When labor grievances surfaced despite these efforts, workers could voice them through the so-called company unions that emerged in many industries—workers' councils and shop committees, organized by the corporations themselves. But welfare capitalism, in the end, gave workers no real control over their own fates. Company unions were feeble vehicles. And welfare capitalism survived only as long as industry prospered. After 1929, with the economy in crisis, the entire system collapsed.

Welfare capitalism affected only a relatively small number of firms in any case. Most laborers worked for employers who were interested primarily in keeping their labor costs low. Workers as a whole, therefore, received wage increases that were proportionately far below the growth of the economy. At the end of the decade, the average annual income of a worker remained below $1,500, when $1,800 was considered necessary to maintain a minimally decent standard of living. Only by relying on the combined earnings of several family members could many working-class families make ends meet.

The New Era was a bleak time for labor organization, in part because many unions themselves were relatively conservative and failed to adapt to the realities of the modern economy. The American Federation of Labor (AFL), led after Samuel Gompers's death by the cautious William Green, sought peaceful cooperation with employers and remained wedded to the concept of the craft union. In the meantime, the rapidly rising number of unskilled industrial workers received little attention from the craft unions.

But whatever the unions' weaknesses, the strength of the corporations was the principal reason for the absence of effective labor organization in the 1920s. After the turmoil of 1919, corporate leaders worked hard to spread the doctrine that a crucial element of democratic capitalism was the protection of the "open shop" (a shop in which no worker could be required to join a union). The crusade for the open shop, euphemistically titled *"American Plan"* the "American Plan," became a pretext for a harsh campaign of union-busting. As a result, union membership fell from more than 5 million in 1920 to under 3 million in 1929.

WOMEN AND MINORITIES IN THE WORKFORCE

A growing proportion of the workforce consisted of women, who were concentrated in what have since become known as "pink-collar" jobs—low-paying service occupations. Large numbers of women worked as secretaries, salesclerks, and telephone operators and in other nonmanual service capacities. Because technically such positions were not industrial jobs, the AFL and other labor organizations were uninterested in organizing these workers. Similarly, the half-million African Americans who had migrated from the rural South into the cities during the Great Migration after 1914 had few opportunities for union representation. The skilled crafts represented in the AFL usually excluded black workers. Partly as a result of that exclusion, most blacks worked in jobs in which the AFL took no interest at all—as janitors, dishwashers, garbage collectors, and domestics and in other service capacities. A. Philip Randolph's *Brotherhood of Sleeping Car Porters* Brotherhood of Sleeping Car Porters was one of the few important unions dominated and led by African Americans.

AFRICAN AMERICAN WORKER PROTESTING The frail union movement among African Americans in the 1920s, led by A. Philip Randolph and others, slowly built up a constituency within the black working class. Here, an aspiring dairy worker draws attention to the unjust treatment of African American men who had demonstrated their patriotism during the war. (© Photo by John Vachon/Anthony Potter Collection/Getty Images)

In the West and the Southwest, the ranks of the unskilled included considerable numbers of Asians and Hispanics. In the wake of the Chinese Exclusion Acts, Japanese immigrants increasingly replaced the Chinese in menial jobs in California. They worked on railroads, construction sites, farms, and in many other low-paying workplaces. Some Japanese managed to escape the ranks of the unskilled by forming their own small businesses or setting themselves up as truck farmers; and many of the Issei (Japanese immigrants) and *Issei and Nisei* Nisei (their American-born children) enjoyed significant economic success—so much so that California passed laws in 1913 and 1920 to make it more difficult for them to buy land. Other Asians—most notably Filipinos—also swelled the unskilled workforce and generated considerable hostility. Anti-Filipino riots in California beginning in 1929 helped produce legislation in 1934 virtually eliminating immigration from the Philippines.

Mexican immigrants formed a major part of the unskilled workforce throughout the Southwest and California. Nearly half a million Mexicans entered the United States in the 1920s. Most lived in California, Texas, Arizona, and New Mexico; and by 1930, most lived in cities. Large

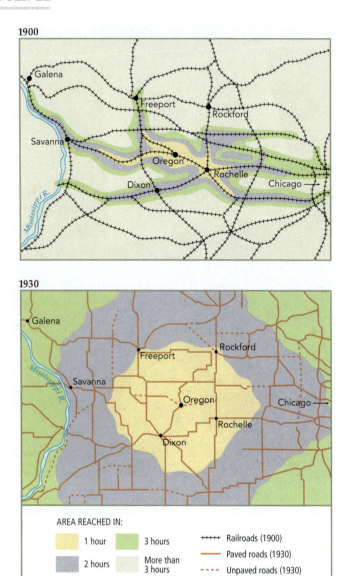

BREAKING DOWN RURAL ISOLATION: THE EXPANSION OF TRAVEL HORIZONS IN OREGON, ILLINOIS
This map uses the small town of Oregon, Illinois—west of Chicago—to illustrate the way in which first railroads and then automobiles reduced the isolation of rural areas in the early decades of the twentieth century. The gold and purple areas of the two maps show the territory that residents of Oregon could reach within two hours. Note how small that area was in 1900 and how much larger it was in 1930, by which time an area of over 100 square miles had become easily accessible to the town. Note, too, the significant network of paved roads in the region by 1930, few of which had existed in 1900. • *Why did automobiles do so much more than railroads to expand the travel horizons of small towns?*

Mexican barrios grew up in Los Angeles, El Paso, San Antonio, Denver, and many other urban
Rising Mexican Immigration   centers. Some of the residents found work locally in factories and shops; others traveled to mines or did migratory labor on farms but returned to the cities between jobs. Mexican workers, too, faced hostility and discrimination from the Anglo population of the region, but there were few efforts actually to exclude them. Employers in the relatively underpopulated West needed this ready pool of low-paid and unorganized workers.

Agricultural Technology and the Plight of the Farmer

Like industry, American agriculture in the 1920s embraced new technologies. The number of tractors on American farms quadrupled during the 1920s, especially after they began to be powered by internal combustion engines (like automobiles) rather than by the cumbersome steam engines of the past. They helped open 35 million new acres to cultivation. Increasingly sophisticated combines and harvesters proliferated, making it possible to produce more crops with fewer workers.

Agricultural researchers worked on other innovations: the invention of hybrid corn (made possible by advances in genetic research), which became available to farmers in 1921 but was not grown in great quantities for a decade or more; and the creation of chemical fertilizers and pesticides, which also had limited use in the 1920s but proliferated quickly in the 1930s and 1940s.

The new technologies greatly increased agricultural productivity, but the demand for agricultural goods was not rising as fast as production. As a result, *Declining Food Prices* there were substantial surpluses, a disastrous decline in food prices, and a severe drop in farmers' incomes beginning early in the 1920s. More than 3 million people left agriculture altogether in the course of the decade. Of those who remained, many lost ownership of their lands and had to rent instead from banks or other landlords.

In response, some farmers began to demand relief in the form of government price supports. One price-raising scheme in particular came to dominate agrarian demands: the idea of "parity." Parity was a complicated formula for setting an adequate price for *Parity* farm goods and ensuring that farmers would earn back at least their production costs no matter how the national or world agricultural market might fluctuate. Champions of parity urged high tariffs against foreign agricultural goods and a government commitment to buy surplus domestic crops at parity and sell them abroad.

The legislative expression of the demand for parity was the McNary-Haugen Bill, which required the government to support prices at parity for grain, cotton, tobacco, and rice. It was introduced repeatedly between 1924 and 1928. In 1926 and again in 1928, Congress approved the bill. President Calvin Coolidge vetoed it both times.

THE NEW CULTURE

The urban and consumer-oriented culture of the 1920s helped Americans in all regions live their lives and perceive their world in increasingly similar ways. That same culture exposed them to a new set of values. But different segments of American society experienced the new culture in different ways.

Consumerism and Communications

The United States of the 1920s was a consumer society. More people than ever before could buy items not just because of need but also for convenience and pleasure. Middle-class families purchased electric refrigerators, washing machines, and vacuum cleaners. People wore wristwatches and smoked cigarettes. Women purchased cosmetics and mass-produced fashions. Above all, Americans bought automobiles. By the end of the decade, there were more than 30 million cars on American roads.

No group was more attuned to the emergence of consumerism (or more responsible for creating it) than the advertising industry. In the 1920s, partly as a *Advertising Industry* result of techniques pioneered by wartime propaganda, advertising came of age. Publicists

THE CINEMA

There is probably no cultural or commercial product more closely identified with the United States than motion pictures—or, as they are known in much of the world, the cinema. Although the technology of cinema emerged from the work of inventors in England and France as well as the United States, the production and distribution of films has been dominated by Americans almost from the start. The United States was the first nation to create a film "industry," and it did so at a scale vaster than that of any other country. With 700 feature films a year in the 1920s, Hollywood produced ten times as many movies as any other nation; and even then, its films were dominating not only the huge American market but much of the world's market as well. Seventy percent of the films seen in France, 80 percent of those seen in Latin America, and 95 percent of the movies viewed in Canada and Great Britain were produced in the United States in the 1920s. As early as the 1930s, the penetration of other nations by American movies was already troubling many governments. The Soviet Union responded to the popularity of Walt Disney's Mickey Mouse cartoons by inventing a cartoon hero of its own—a porcupine, designed to entertain in a way consistent with socialist values and not the capitalist ones that they believed Hollywood conveyed. During World War II, American films were banned in occupied France (prompting some antifascist dissidents to screen such American films as Frank Capra's *Mr. Smith Goes to Washington* in protest).

American dominance was a result in part of World War I and its aftermath, which debilitated European filmmaking just as movies were vigorously growing in the United States. By 1915, the United States had gained complete control of its own vast market and had so saturated it with movie theaters that by the end of World War I, half the theaters of the world were in America. Two decades later, after an extraordinary expansion of theaters in other nations, the United States continued to have over 40 percent of the world's cinemas. And while the spread of theaters through other areas of the world helped launch film industries in many other countries, it also increased the market (and the appetite) for American films and strengthened American supremacy in their production. "The sun, it now appears," the *Saturday Evening Post* commented in the mid-1920s, "never sets on the British Empire and the American motion picture." Movies were then, and perhaps remain still, America's most influential cultural export. Even American popular music, which has enormous global reach, faces more significant local competition than American movies do in most parts of the world.

Despite this American dominance, however, filmmaking has flourished—and continues to flourish—in many countries around the world. India's fabled "Bollywood," for example, produces an enormous number of movies for its domestic market—almost as many as the American industry creates—although few of them are widely exported. This global cinema has had a significant impact on American filmmaking. The small British film industry had a strong early influence on American movies, partly because of the quality and originality of British films and partly because of the emigration of talented actors, directors, and screenwriters

VALENTINO The popularity of the film star Rudolph Valentino among American women was one of the most striking cultural phenomena of the 1920s. Valentino was slight and delicate, not at all like the conventional image of "manliness." But he developed an enormous following among women, in part—as this poster is obviously intended to suggest—by baring his body on screen. Valentino was Italian, which made him seem somehow strange and foreign to many older-stock Americans, and he was almost always cast in exotic roles, never as an American. His sudden death in 1926 (at the age of 31) created enormous outpourings of grief among many American women. (© United Artists/Photofest)

generation of highly individualistic directors in the United States. Asian cinema—especially the thriving film industry in Hong Kong with its gritty realism—helped lead to some of the powerfully violent American films of the 1980s and beyond, as well as the genre of martial-arts films that has become popular around the world. German, Italian, Swedish, Dutch, Japanese, Spanish, Australian, and Indian filmmakers also had enormous influence on Hollywood—and over time perhaps even greater influence on the large and growing "independent film" movement in the United States.

In recent decades, as new technologies and new styles have transformed films around the world, the American movie industry has continued to dominate global cinema. But national boundaries no longer adequately describe moviemaking in the twenty-first century. It is becoming as truly global as other commercial ventures. "American" films today are often produced abroad, often have non-American directors and actors, and are often paid for with international financing. Hollywood still dominates worldwide filmmaking, but Hollywood itself is now an increasingly global community. •

to the United States. The great Alfred Hitchcock, for example, made his first films in London before moving to Hollywood, where he spent the rest of his long career. After World War II, French "new wave" cinema helped spawn a new

UNDERSTAND, ANALYZE, & EVALUATE

1. Did American movies, as the Soviet Union claimed in the 1930s, promote capitalism?
2. Why has the American movie industry continued to dominate global cinema?

no longer simply conveyed information; they sought to identify products with a particular lifestyle. They also encouraged the public to absorb the values of promotion and salesmanship and to admire those who were effective "boosters" and publicists. One of the most successful books of the 1920s was *The Man Nobody Knows,* by the advertising executive Bruce Barton. It portrayed Jesus as not only a religious prophet but also a "super salesman." Barton's message, one sensitive to the new spirit of the consumer culture, was that Jesus had been concerned with living a full and rewarding life in this world and that twentieth-century men and women should do the same.

The advertising industry made good use of new vehicles of communication. Newspapers were absorbed into national chains. Mass-circulation magazines attracted broad national audiences. Movies in the 1920s became an ever more popular and powerful form of mass communication. Over 100 million people saw films in 1930, as compared to 40 million in 1922. The addition of sound to motion pictures—beginning in 1927 with the first *The Jazz Singer* feature-length "talkie," *The Jazz Singer* starring Al Jolson—greatly enhanced film's appeal. A series of scandals in the early 1920s led to the creation of the new Motion Picture Association, which imposed much tighter controls over the content of films. The result was safer, more conventionally acceptable films, which may in fact have broadened the appeal of movies generally. (See "America in the World: The Cinema.")

An equally important communications vehicle was the radio. The first commercial radio station in America, KDKA in Pittsburgh, began broadcasting in 1920, and the first national radio network, the National Broadcasting Company, was formed in 1927. That same year, Congress passed the Radio Act, which created a Federal Radio Commission to regulate the public airwaves used by private companies. (In 1935, it became the Federal Communications Commission, which survives today.)

WOMEN IN THE NEW ERA

College-educated women were no longer pioneers in the 1920s. There were now two and even three generations of graduates of women's or coeducational colleges and universities, and some were making their presence felt in professional areas that in the past women had rarely penetrated. The "new professional woman" was a vivid and widely publicized figure in the 1920s. In reality, however, most employed women were still nonprofessional, lower-class workers. Middle-class women, in the meantime, remained largely in the home.

Yet the 1920s constituted a new era for middle-class women nonetheless. In particular, the decade saw a redefinition of motherhood. Shortly after World War I, John B. Watson and other behavioralists began to challenge the long-held assumption that women had an *Motherhood Redefined* instinctive capacity for motherhood. Maternal affection was not, they claimed, sufficient preparation for child rearing. Instead, mothers should rely on the advice and assistance of experts and professionals: doctors, nurses, and trained educators.

For many middle-class women, these changes devalued what had been an important and consuming activity. Many attempted to compensate through what are often called "companionate marriages," which elevated the importance of compatibility and love between partners. Some women now openly considered their sexual relationships with their husbands not simply as a means of procreation, as earlier generations had been taught, but as important and pleasurable experiences in their own right, the culmination of romantic love.

One result of the new era for women was growing interest in birth control. The pioneer *Margaret Sanger* of the American birth-control movement, Margaret Sanger, began her career as a promoter of the diaphragm and other birth-control devices out of a concern for working-class women; she believed that large families contributed to poverty and distress in poor communities. By the 1920s, she was becoming more effective in persuading middle-class women to see the benefits of birth control. Nevertheless, some birth-control devices remained illegal in many states (and abortion remained illegal nearly everywhere).

To the consternation of many longtime women reformers and progressive suffragists, some women concluded that in the New Era it was no longer necessary to maintain a rigid, Victorian female "respectability." They could smoke, drink, dance, wear seductive

THE FLAPPER By the mid-1920s, the flapper—the young woman who challenged traditional expectations—had become not only a social type but a movement in fashion as well. Here, Catherine Dear is shown posing in a "beach costume," a fashion a long way from the rigid "respectability" of Victorian-age styles. (©Bettmann/Corbis)

clothes and makeup, and attend lively parties. Those assumptions were reflected in the emergence of the "flapper"—the modern woman whose liberated lifestyle found *"Flappers"* expression in dress, hairstyle, speech, and behavior. The flapper lifestyle had a particular impact on urban lower-middle-class and working-class single women, who were filling new jobs in industry and the service sector. At night, such women flocked to clubs and dance halls in search of excitement and companionship. Many more affluent women soon began to copy the flapper style.

Despite all the changes, most women remained highly dependent on men and relatively powerless when men exploited that dependence. The National Woman's Party, under the leadership of Alice Paul, attempted to fight that powerlessness through its campaign for the Equal Rights Amendment, although it found little support in Congress. Responding to the suffrage victory, women organized the League of Women Voters and the women's auxiliaries of both the Democratic and Republican Parties. Female-dominated consumer groups grew rapidly and increased the range and energy of their efforts.

Women activists won a brief triumph in 1921 when they helped secure passage of the Sheppard-Towner Act, which provided federal funds to states to establish prenatal and child health-care programs. From the start, however, the act produced controversy. Alice Paul and her supporters opposed the measure, complaining that it classified all women as mothers. More important, the American Medical Association fought Sheppard-Towner, warning that it would introduce untrained outsiders into the health-care field. In 1929, no longer worried about women voting as a bloc, Congress terminated the program.

THE DISENCHANTED

The generation that lived through (and in many cases fought in) the Great War quickly came to see the conflict as a useless waste of lives lost for no purpose. For many young people in the 1920s, disenchantment with the war contributed to a growing disenchantment with the United States. The newly prosperous and consumer-driven era they encountered seemed meaningless and vulgar to many artists and intellectuals in particular. As a result, they came to view their own culture with contempt. Rather than trying to influence and reform their society, they isolated themselves from it and embarked on a restless search *The "Lost Generation"* for personal fulfillment. The American writer Gertrude Stein once referred to the young Americans emerging from World War I as a "Lost Generation."

Many artists and intellectuals coming of age in the 1920s experienced that fundamental disenchantment with modern America, reflected in a series of savage critiques of *Modern Society Critiqued* modern society by a wide range of writers, some of whom were known as the "debunkers." Among them was the Baltimore journalist H. L. Mencken, who delighted in ridiculing religion, politics, the arts, even democracy itself. Sinclair Lewis published a series of savage novels—*Main Street* (1920), *Babbitt* (1922), *Arrowsmith* (1925), and others—in which he lashed out at one aspect of modern bourgeois society after another. Intellectuals of the 1920s claimed to reject the "success ethic" they believed dominated American life. The novelist F. Scott Fitzgerald, for example, attacked the American obsession with material success in *The Great Gatsby* (1925). The roster of important American writers active in the 1920s may have no equal in any other period. It included Fitzgerald, Lewis, Ernest Hemingway, Thomas Wolfe, John Dos Passos, Ezra Pound, T. S. Eliot, Gertrude Stein, Edna Ferber, William Faulkner, and Eugene O'Neill and a remarkable group of African American artists. In New York City, a new generation of black intellectuals created a flourishing artistic life widely described as the "Harlem *"Harlem Renaissance"* Renaissance." The Harlem poets, novelists, and artists drew heavily from their African roots in an effort to prove the richness of their own racial heritage and assert resistance against white racism and stereotyping. The ethos was captured in a single sentence by the poet Langston Hughes: "I am a Negro—and beautiful." Other black writers in Harlem and elsewhere—James Weldon Johnson, Countee Cullen, Zora Neale Hurston, Claude McKay, Alain Locke—as well as black artists and musicians helped establish a thriving and at times highly politicized culture.

A CONFLICT OF CULTURES

The modern, secular culture of the 1920s did not go unchallenged. It grew up alongside an older, more traditional culture, with which it continually and often bitterly competed.

PROHIBITION

When the prohibition of the sale and manufacture of alcohol went into effect in January 1920, it had the support of most members of the middle class and most of those who considered themselves progressives. Within a year, however, it had become clear that the *Failure of Prohibition* "noble experiment," as its defenders called it, was not working well. At first, prohibition did substantially reduce drinking in most parts of the country. But it also produced conspicuous and growing violations. Before long, it was almost as easy to acquire illegal alcohol in many parts of the country as it had once been to acquire legal alcohol. And since an enormous, lucrative industry was now barred to legitimate businessmen, organized crime took it over.

Many middle-class progressives who had originally supported prohibition soon soured on the experiment. But a large constituency of provincial, largely rural Protestant Americans continued vehemently to defend it. To them, prohibition represented the effort of an older

America to protect traditional notions of morality. Drinking, which they associated with the modern city and Catholic immigrants, became a symbol of the new culture they believed was displacing them.

As the decade proceeded, opponents of prohibition (or "wets") gained steadily in influence. Not until 1933, however, when the Great Depression added weight to their appeals, were they finally able to challenge the "drys" effectively and win repeal of the Eighteenth Amendment.

Nativism and the Klan

Agitation for a curb on foreign immigration had begun in the nineteenth century and, as with prohibition, had gathered strength in the years before the war largely because of the support of middle-class progressives. In the years immediately following the war, as immigration's association with radicalism intensified and migration from Europe resumed, popular sentiment on behalf of restriction grew rapidly.

In 1921, Congress passed an emergency immigration act, establishing a quota system by which annual immigration from any country could not exceed 3 percent of the number of persons of that nationality who had been in the United States in 1910. The new law cut immigration from 800,000 to 300,000 in any single year, but the nativists remained unsatisfied. The National Origins Act of 1924 banned immigration from *National Origins Act of 1924* East Asia entirely and reduced the quota for Europeans from 3 to 2 percent. The quota would be based, moreover, not on the 1910 statistics but on the census of 1890, a year in which there had been far fewer southern and eastern Europeans in the country. What new immigration there was, in other words, would heavily favor northwestern Europeans. Five years later, a further restriction set a rigid limit of 150,000 immigrants a year. In the years that followed, immigration officials seldom permitted even half that number actually to enter the country.

To defenders of an older, more provincial America, the growth of large communities of foreign peoples, alien in speech, habits, and values, came to seem a direct threat to their own embattled way of life. Among other things, this provincial nativism helped instigate the rebirth of the Ku Klux Klan as a major force in American society. The first Klan, founded during Reconstruction, had died in the 1870s. But in 1915, a new group of white southerners met on Stone Mountain near Atlanta and established *Rise of the New Klan* a modern version of the society. Nativist passions had swelled in Georgia and elsewhere in response to the case of Leo Frank, a Jewish factory manager in Atlanta convicted in 1914 (on very flimsy evidence) of murdering a female employee; a mob stormed Frank's jail and lynched him. The premiere (also in Atlanta) of D. W. Griffith's film *The Birth of a Nation,* which glorified the early Klan, also helped inspire white southerners to form a new one.

At first the new Klan, like the old, was largely concerned with intimidating blacks. After World War I, however, concern about blacks gradually became secondary to concern about Catholics, Jews, and foreigners. At that point, membership in the Klan expanded rapidly and dramatically, not just in the small towns and rural areas of the South but in industrial cities in the North and Midwest as well. By 1924, there were reportedly 4 million members, including many women, organized in separate, parallel units. The largest state Klan was not in the South but in Indiana. Beginning in 1925, a series of scandals involving the organization's leaders precipitated a slow but steady decline in the Klan's influence.

Most Klan units (or "klaverns") tried to present their members as patriots and defenders of morality, and some did nothing more menacing than stage occasional parades and rallies. Often, however, the Klan also operated as a brutal, even violent, opponent of "alien" groups. Klansmen systematically terrorized blacks, Jews, Catholics, and foreigners. At times, they engaged in public whipping, tarring and feathering, arson, and lynching. What the Klan feared, however, was not simply "foreign" or "racially impure" groups, but anyone who posed a challenge to traditional values.

Religious Fundamentalism

Another cultural controversy of the 1920s involved the place of religion in contemporary society. By 1921, American Protestantism was already divided into two warring camps. On one side stood the modernists: mostly urban, middle-class people who were attempting to adapt religion to the teachings of modern science and to the realities of their modern, secular society. *Fundamentalists and Modernists*   On the other side stood the fundamentalists: provincial, largely (although far from exclusively) rural men and women fighting to preserve traditional faith and to maintain the centrality of religion in American life. The fundamentalists insisted the Bible was to be interpreted literally. Above all, they opposed the teachings of Charles Darwin, whose theory of evolution had openly challenged the biblical story of the Creation.

By the mid-1920s, to the great alarm of modernists, fundamentalist demands to forbid the teaching of evolution in public schools were gaining political strength in some states. In Tennessee in March 1925, the legislature adopted a measure making it illegal for any public school teacher "to teach any theory that denies the story of the divine creation of man as taught in the Bible."

The Tennessee law caught the attention of the fledgling American Civil Liberties Union (ACLU), founded in 1917 to defend pacifists, radicals, and conscientious objectors during World War I. The ACLU offered free counsel to any Tennessee educator willing to defy the law and become the defendant in a test case. A twenty-four-year-old biology teacher *Scopes Trial*   in the town of Dayton, John T. Scopes, agreed to have himself arrested. And when the ACLU decided to send the famous attorney Clarence Darrow to defend Scopes, the aging William Jennings Bryan (now an important fundamentalist spokesman) announced that he would travel to Dayton to assist the prosecution. Journalists from across the country flocked to Tennessee to cover the trial. Scopes had, of course, clearly and deliberately violated the law; and a verdict of guilty was a foregone conclusion, especially when the judge refused to permit "expert" testimony by evolution scholars. Scopes was fined $100, and the case was ultimately dismissed in a higher court because of a technicality. Nevertheless, Darrow scored an important victory for the modernists by calling Bryan himself to the stand to testify as an "expert on the Bible." In the course of the cross-examination, which was broadcast by radio to much of the nation, Darrow made Bryan's defense of biblical truths appear stubborn and foolish and finally maneuvered Bryan into admitting the possibility that not all religious dogma was subject to only one interpretation.

The Scopes trial put fundamentalists on the defensive. It discouraged many of them from participating openly in politics. But it did not resolve the conflict between fundamentalists and modernists, which continued to smolder.

The Democrats' Ordeal

The anguish of provincial Americans attempting to defend an embattled way of life proved particularly troubling to the Democratic Party during the 1920s. More than the

Republicans, the Democrats consisted of a diverse coalition of interest groups, including prohibitionists, Klansmen, and fundamentalists on one side and Catholics, urban workers, and immigrants on the other.

At the 1924 Democratic National Convention in New York City, a bitter conflict broke out over the platform when the party's urban wing attempted to win approval of planks calling for the repeal of prohibition and a denunciation of the Klan. Both planks narrowly failed. (The effort to condemn the Klan by name failed by one vote out of 1,085.) Even more damaging to the party was a deadlock in the balloting for a presidential candidate. Urban Democrats supported Alfred E. Smith, the Irish Catholic governor *Divided Democrats* of New York; rural Democrats backed William McAdoo, Woodrow Wilson's Treasury secretary, who had skillfully positioned himself to win the support of southern and western delegates suspicious of modern urban life but whose reputation had been tarnished by a series of scandals resulting from his work as an attorney for an unsavory oil tycoon. For 103 ballots, the convention dragged on, with Smith supporters chanting "No oil on Al," until finally both Smith and McAdoo withdrew. The party settled on a compromise: the corporate lawyer John W. Davis, who lost decisively to Calvin Coolidge.

A similar schism plagued the Democrats again in 1928, when Al Smith finally secured his party's nomination for president. He was not, however, able to unite his divided party—in part because of widespread anti-Catholic sentiment, especially in the South. He was the first Democrat since the Civil War not to carry the entire South. Elsewhere, he carried no states at all except Massachusetts and Rhode Island. Smith's opponent, and the victor in the presidential election, was a man who perhaps more than any other personified the modern, prosperous, middle-class society of the New Era: Herbert Hoover.

REPUBLICAN GOVERNMENT

For twelve years, beginning in 1921, both the presidency and the Congress rested in the hands of the Republican Party. For most of those years, the federal government enjoyed a warm and supportive relationship with the American business community. Yet the government of the New Era was more than the passive, pliant instrument that critics often described. It attempted to serve in many respects as an agent of economic change.

HARDING AND COOLIDGE

Nothing seemed more clearly to illustrate the unadventurous nature of 1920s politics than the characters of the two men who served as president during most of the decade: Warren G. Harding and Calvin Coolidge.

Harding, who was elected to the presidency in 1920, was an undistinguished senator from Ohio. He had received the Republican presidential nomination as a result of an agreement among leaders of his party, who considered him, as one noted, a "good second-rater." Harding appointed distinguished men to some important *Warren Harding* cabinet offices, and he attempted to stabilize the nation's troubled foreign policy. But he seemed baffled by his responsibilities, as if he recognized his own unfitness. "I am a man of limited talents from a small town," he reportedly told friends on one occasion. "I don't seem to grasp that I am President." Harding's intellectual limits were compounded by personal weaknesses: his penchant for gambling, illegal alcohol, and attractive women.

Harding lacked the strength to abandon the party hacks who had helped create his political success. One of them, Ohio party boss Harry Daugherty, he appointed attorney general. Another, New Mexico senator Albert B. Fall, he made secretary of the interior. Members of the so-called Ohio Gang filled important offices throughout the administration. Unknown to the public, Daugherty, Fall, and others were engaged in fraud and corruption.

Teapot Dome Scandal The most spectacular scandal involved the rich naval oil reserves at Teapot Dome, Wyoming, and Elk Hills, California. At the urging of Fall, Harding transferred control of those reserves from the Navy Department to the Interior Department. Fall then secretly leased them to two wealthy businessmen and received in return nearly half a million dollars in "loans" to ease his private financial troubles. Fall was ultimately convicted of bribery and sentenced to a year in prison; Harry Daugherty barely avoided a similar fate for his part in another scandal.

In the summer of 1923, only months before Senate investigations and press revelations brought the scandals to light, a tired and depressed Harding left Washington for a speaking tour in the West. In Seattle late in July, he complained of severe pain, which his doctors wrongly diagnosed as food poisoning. A few days later, in San Francisco, he died. He had suffered two major heart attacks.

In many ways, Calvin Coolidge, who succeeded Harding in the presidency, was utterly different from his predecessor. Where Harding was genial, garrulous, and debauched, Coolidge was dour, silent, even puritanical. In other ways, however, Harding and Coolidge were similar figures. Both took essentially passive approaches to their office.

Elected governor of Massachusetts in 1919, Coolidge had won national attention with *Calvin Coolidge* his tough, if laconic, response to the Boston police strike that year. That was enough to make him his party's vice presidential nominee in 1920. Three years later, after Harding's death, he took the oath of office from his father, a justice of the peace, by the light of a kerosene lamp.

If anything, Coolidge was even less active as president than Harding, partly as a result of his conviction that government should interfere as little as possible in the life of the nation. In 1924, he received his party's presidential nomination virtually unopposed. Running against John W. Davis, he won a comfortable victory: 54 percent of the popular vote and 382 of the 531 electoral votes. Coolidge probably could have won renomination and reelection in 1928. Instead, in characteristically understated fashion, he walked into a press room one day and handed each reporter a slip of paper containing a single sentence: "I do not choose to run for president in 1928."

GOVERNMENT AND BUSINESS

However passive the New Era presidents may have been, much of the federal government worked effectively and efficiently during the 1920s to adapt public policy to the widely accepted goal of the time: helping business and industry to operate with maximum efficiency and productivity. The close relationship between the private sector and the federal government forged during World War I continued. Secretary of the Treasury Andrew Mellon, a *Sharp Tax Reductions* wealthy steel and aluminum tycoon, worked to achieve substantial reductions in taxes on corporate profits, personal incomes, and inheritances. Largely because of his efforts, Congress cut them all by more than half. Mellon also worked closely with President Coolidge after 1924 on a series of measures to trim dramatically the already modest federal budget, even managing to retire half the nation's World War I debt.

The most prominent member of the cabinet was Commerce Secretary Herbert Hoover. During his eight years in the Commerce Department, Hoover constantly encouraged voluntary cooperation in the private sector as the best avenue to stability. But the idea of voluntarism did not require that the government remain passive; on the contrary, public institutions, Hoover believed, had a duty to play an active role in creating the new, cooperative order. Above all, Hoover became the champion of the concept of business "associationalism"—a concept that envisioned the creation of national organizations of businessmen in particular industries. Through these trade associations, private entrepreneurs could, Hoover believed, study and stabilize their industries and promote efficiency in production and marketing. *"Associationalism"*

Many progressives derived encouragement from the election of Herbert Hoover to the presidency in 1928. Hoover easily defeated Al Smith, the Democratic candidate. And he entered office promising bold new efforts to solve the nation's remaining economic problems. But Hoover had few opportunities to prove himself. Less than a year after his inauguration, the nation plunged into the severest and most prolonged economic crisis in its history—a crisis that brought many of the optimistic assumptions of the New Era crashing down and launched the nation into a period of unprecedented social innovation and reform. *Herbert Hoover*

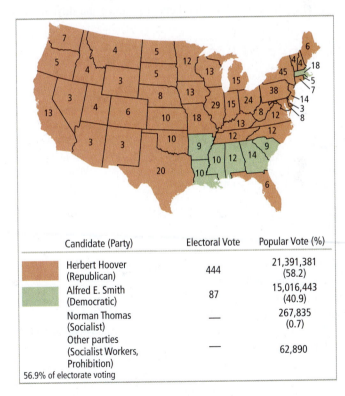

Candidate (Party)	Electoral Vote	Popular Vote (%)
Herbert Hoover (Republican)	444	21,391,381 (58.2)
Alfred E. Smith (Democratic)	87	15,016,443 (40.9)
Norman Thomas (Socialist)	—	267,835 (0.7)
Other parties (Socialist Workers, Prohibition)	—	62,890

56.9% of electorate voting

THE ELECTION OF 1928   The election of 1928 was highly one-sided. Herbert Hoover won over 58 percent of the popular vote to Alfred Smith's 41 percent. Smith carried only Massachusetts, Rhode Island, and some traditionally Democratic states in the South. • *Why did Smith do so poorly even in some parts of the South?*

CONCLUSION

The remarkable prosperity of the 1920s shaped much of what exuberant contemporaries liked to call the "New Era." In the years after World War I, America built a vibrant and extensive national culture. Its middle class moved increasingly into the embrace of the growing consumer culture. Politics were reorganized around the needs of a booming, interdependent industrial economy—rejecting many of the reform crusades of the previous generation but also creating new institutions to help promote economic growth and stability.

Beneath the glittering surface of the New Era, however, were great controversies and injustices. Although the prosperity of the 1920s was more widely spread than at any time in the nation's industrial history, more than half the population failed to achieve any real benefits from the growth. A new, optimistic, secular culture attracted millions of urban middle-class people. But many other Americans looked at it with alarm and fought against it with great fervor. The unprepossessing conservative presidents of the era suggested a time of stability, but in fact few eras in modern American history have seen so much political and cultural conflict.

The 1920s ended in a catastrophic economic crash that has colored the image of those years ever since. The crises of the 1930s should not obscure the real achievements of the New Era economy. Neither, however, should the prosperity of the 1920s obscure the inequity and instability in those years that helped produce the difficult years to come.

KEY TERMS/PEOPLE/PLACES/EVENTS

American Plan 548
Brotherhood of Sleeping
  Car Porters 548
Calvin Coolidge 560
flappers 555
Harlem Renaissance 556
Herbert Hoover 561

Issei 549
Ku Klux Klan 557
Langston Hughes 556
Lost Generation 556
Margaret Sanger 554
National Origins Act
  of 1924 557

Nisei 549
parity 551
Scopes trial 558
Teapot Dome 560
The Jazz Singer 554
Warren Harding 559
welfare capitalism 547

RECALL AND REFLECT

1. What was the impact of the automobile on American life?
2. How did labor fare during the 1920s? What particular problems did female, black, immigrant, and unskilled laborers face?
3. How did religion respond to the consumer culture of the 1920s?
4. What was the myth and what was the reality of the new professional woman of the 1920s?
5. What was the nature and extent of the nativism of the 1920s?

23 THE GREAT DEPRESSION

THE COMING OF THE DEPRESSION

THE AMERICAN PEOPLE IN HARD TIMES

THE DEPRESSION AND AMERICAN CULTURE

THE ORDEAL OF HERBERT HOOVER

LOOKING AHEAD

1. What were some of the causes of the Great Depression? What made it so severe, and why did it last so long?
2. What was the impact of the Depression on farmers, minorities, and women?
3. How did President Hoover and his administration try to deal with the Depression? What was the result of those efforts?

"WE IN AMERICA TODAY," Herbert Hoover proclaimed in August 1928, "are nearer to the final triumph over poverty than ever before in the history of any land." Only fifteen months later, those words would return to haunt him, as the nation plunged into the severest and most prolonged economic depression in its history—a depression that continued in one form or another for a full decade, not only in the United States but throughout much of the world.

1929

Stock market crash; Great Depression begins

Agricultural Marketing Act

1930

Hawley-Smoot Tariff

Drought begins in Dust Bowl

1931

Scottsboro defendants arrested

1932

Reconstruction Finance Corporation established

Bonus Army in Washington

Franklin D. Roosevelt elected president

1934

Southern Tenant Farmers Union organized

1935

American Communist Party proclaims Popular Front

1936

Pare Lorentz's *The Plow That Broke the Plains*

1939

Steinbeck's *The Grapes of Wrath*

1940

Wright's *Native Son*

THE COMING OF THE DEPRESSION

The sudden financial collapse in 1929 came as an especially severe shock because it followed so closely an era that appeared to offer economic miracles—miracles that seemed especially evident in the remarkable performance of the stock market.

In February 1928, stock prices began a steady ascent that continued, with only a few temporary lapses, for a year and a half. Between May 1928 and September 1929, the average price of stocks rose over 40 percent. Trading mushroomed from 2 or 3 million shares a day to over 5 million, and at times to as many as 10 or 12 million. In short, a widespread speculative fever grew steadily more intense, particularly once brokerage firms began encouraging the mania by offering absurdly easy credit to those buying stocks.

THE GREAT CRASH

In the autumn of 1929, the market began to fall apart. On October 29, "Black Tuesday," after a week of growing instability, all efforts to save the market failed. Sixteen million shares of stock were traded; the industrial index dropped 43 points (or nearly 10 percent), wiping out all the gains of the previous year; stocks in many companies became virtually worthless. Within a month, stocks had lost half their September value, and despite occasional, short-lived rallies, they continued to decline for several years after that.

Popular folklore has established the stock market crash as the beginning, and even the cause, of the Great Depression. Although October 1929 might have been the most visible early sign of the crisis, the Depression had earlier beginnings and other causes.

CAUSES OF THE DEPRESSION

Economists and historians have argued for decades about the causes of the Great Depression. But most agree on several things. They agree, first, that what is remarkable about the crisis is not that it occurred but that it was so severe and that it lasted so long, which most observers agree—even if they agree on little else—was the result of several factors.

One was a lack of diversification in the American economy in the 1920s. Prosperity had depended excessively on a few basic industries, notably construction and automobiles, which in the late 1920s began to decline. Expenditures on *Weaknesses in the U.S. Economy* construction fell from $11 billion in 1926 to under $9 billion in 1929. Automobile sales fell by more than a third in the first nine months of 1929. Newer industries were emerging to take up the slack—among them petroleum, chemicals, electronics, and plastics—but none had yet developed enough strength to compensate for this decline.

A second important factor was the maldistribution of purchasing power and, as a result, a weakness in consumer demand. As industrial and agricultural production increased, the proportion of the profits going to potential consumers was too small to create an adequate market for the goods the economy was producing. Even in 1929, after nearly a decade of economic growth, more than half the families in America lived on the edge of or below the minimum subsistence level.

A third major problem was the credit structure of the economy. Farmers were deeply in debt, and crop prices were too low to allow them to pay off what they owed. Small banks were in constant trouble as their customers defaulted on loans; large banks were in trouble, too. Although most American bankers were very conservative, some of the nation's biggest banks were investing recklessly in the stock market or making unwise loans. When the market crashed and the loans went bad, some banks failed and others made the crisis worse by contracting already scarce credit and calling in loans that borrowers could not pay.

A fourth factor was America's position in international trade. Late in the 1920s, European demand for American goods began to decline, partly because *Global Factors* European industry and agriculture were becoming more productive and partly because some European nations were having financial difficulties of their own. But it was also because the European economy was being destabilized by the international debt structure that had emerged in the aftermath of World War I.

This debt structure, therefore, was a fifth factor contributing to the Depression. When the war came to an end in 1918, all the European nations that had been allied with the United States owed large sums of money to American banks, sums much too large to be repaid out of their shattered economies, which is partly why the Allies had insisted on reparation payments from Germany and Austria. Reparations, they believed, would provide them with a way to pay off their own debts. But Germany and Austria were no more able to pay the reparations than the Allies were able to pay their debts.

The American government refused to forgive or reduce the debts. Instead, American banks began making large loans to European governments, which used them to pay off their earlier loans. Thus debts (and reparations) were being paid only by piling up new and greater debts. At the same time, American protective tariffs were making it difficult for Europeans to sell their goods in American markets. Without any source of foreign exchange with which to repay their loans, they began to default. The collapse of the international credit structure was one of the reasons the Depression spread to Europe after 1931. (See "America in the World: The Global Depression.")

THE GLOBAL DEPRESSION

The Great Depression began in the United States. But it did not end there. The American economy was the largest in the world, and its collapse sent shock waves across the globe. By 1931, the American depression had become a world depression, with important implications for the course of global history.

The origins of the worldwide depression lay in the pattern of debts that had emerged during and after World War I, when the United States loaned billions of dollars to European nations. In 1931, with American banks staggering and in many cases collapsing, large banks in New York began desperately calling in their loans from Germany and Austria. That precipitated the collapse of one of Austria's largest banks, which in turn created panic through much of central Europe. The economic collapse in Germany and Austria meant that those nations could not continue paying reparations to Britain and France (required by the Treaty of Versailles of 1919), which meant in turn that Britain and France could not continue paying off their loans to the United States. This spreading financial crisis was accompanied by a dramatic contraction of international trade, precipitated in part by the Hawley-Smoot Tariff in the United States, which established the highest import duties in history and stifled much global commerce. Depressed agricultural prices—a result of worldwide overproduction—also contributed to the downturn. By 1932, worldwide industrial production had declined by more than one-third, and world trade had plummeted by nearly two-thirds. By 1933, 30 million people in industrial nations were unemployed, five times the number of four years before.

But the Depression was not confined to industrial nations. Imperialism and

LOOKING FOR WORK IN LONDON, 1935 An unemployed London man wears a sign that seems designed to convince passersby that he is an educated, respectable person despite his present circumstances. (©Hulton Archive/Getty Images)

industrialization had drawn almost all regions of the world into the international industrial economy. Colonies and nations in Africa, Asia, and South America—critically dependent on exporting raw materials and agricultural goods to industrial countries—experienced a collapse in demand for their products and thus rising levels of poverty and unemployment. Some nations—among them the Soviet Union and China—remained relatively unconnected to the global economy and suffered relatively little from the Great Depression. But in most parts of the world, the Depression caused tremendous social and economic hardship.

It also created political turmoil. Among the countries hardest hit by the Depression was Germany, where industrial production declined by 50 percent and unemployment reached 35 percent in the early 1930s. The desperate economic conditions there contributed greatly to the rise of the Nazi Party and its leader, Adolf Hitler, who became chancellor in 1933. Japan suffered as well, dependent as it was on world trade to sustain its growing industrial economy and purchase essential commodities for its needs at home. And in Japan, as in Germany, economic troubles produced political turmoil and aided the rise of a new militaristic regime. In Italy, the fascist government of Benito Mussolini, which had first taken power in the 1920s, also saw militarization and territorial expansion as a way out of economic difficulties.

In other nations, governments sought solutions to the Depression through reform of their domestic economies. The most prominent example was the New Deal in the United States. But there were important experiments in other nations as well. Among the most common responses to the Depression around the world was substantial government investment in public works, such as roads, bridges, dams, public buildings, and other large projects. Among the nations that adopted this approach—in addition to the United States—were Britain, France, Germany, Italy, and the Soviet Union. Another response was the expansion of government-funded relief for the unemployed. All the industrial countries of the world experimented with various forms of relief, often borrowing ideas from one another in the process. And the Depression helped create new approaches to economics,

in the face of the apparent failure of classical models of economic behavior to explain, or provide solutions to, the crisis. The great British economist John Maynard Keynes revolutionized economic thought in much of the world. His 1936 book *The General Theory of Employment, Interest, and Money*, despite its bland title, created a sensation by arguing that the Depression was a result not of declining production but of inadequate consumer demand. Governments, he said, could stimulate their economies by increasing the money supply and creating investment—through a combination of lowering interest rates and public spending. Keynesianism, as Keynes's theories became known, began to have an impact in the United States in 1938, and in much of the rest of the world in subsequent years.

The Great Depression was an important turning point not only in American history but also in the history of the twentieth-century world. It transformed ideas of public policy and economics in many nations. It toppled old regimes and created new ones. And perhaps above all, it was a major factor in the coming of World War II. •

UNDERSTAND, ANALYZE, & EVALUATE

1. How did the 1919 Treaty of Versailles and the Hawley-Smoot Tariff contribute to the global depression of the 1930s?
2. How did the governments of European nations respond to the Depression?
3. What effect did the global depression have on economic theory? Why was Keynes's economic theory so revolutionary?

PROGRESS OF THE DEPRESSION

The stock market crash of 1929 did not so much cause the Depression, then, as help trigger a chain of events that exposed larger weaknesses in the American economy. During the next three years, the crisis grew steadily worse.

The most serious problem at first was the collapse of much of the banking system. Between 1930 and 1933, over 9,000 American banks either went bankrupt or closed their doors to avoid bankruptcy. Partly as a result of these banking closures, the nation's money supply shrank by perhaps a third or more between 1930 and 1933, which caused a decline in purchasing power and thus deflation. Manufacturers and merchants began reducing prices, cutting back on production, and laying off workers. Some economists argue that a severe depression could have been avoided if the Federal Reserve system had acted responsibly. But late in 1931, in a misguided effort to build international confidence in the dollar, it raised interest rates, which contracted the money supply even further.

The American gross national product plummeted from over $104 billion in 1929 to $76.4 billion in 1932—a 25 percent decline in three years. By 1932, according to the relatively crude estimates of the time, 25 percent of the American workforce was unemployed. (Some argue that the figure was even higher.) For the rest of the decade, unemployment averaged nearly 20 percent, never dropping below 15 percent. Up to another one-third of the workforce was "underemployed"—experiencing major reductions in wages, hours, or both.

THE AMERICAN PEOPLE IN HARD TIMES

Someone asked the British economist John Maynard Keynes in the 1930s whether he was aware of any historical era comparable to the Great Depression. "Yes," Keynes replied. "It was called the Dark Ages, and it lasted 400 years." The Depression did not last 400 years. It did, however, bring unprecedented economic despair to the United States and much of the Western world.

THE HUNGRY   Hundreds of men wait to be fed outside the Municipal Lodging House in New York City.
(© Bettmann/Corbis)

Unemployment and Relief

In the industrial Northeast and Midwest, cities were virtually paralyzed by unemployment. Cleveland, Ohio, for example, had an unemployment rate of 50 percent in 1932; Akron, 60 percent; Toledo, 80 percent. Unemployed workers walked through the streets day after day looking for jobs that did not exist. An increasing number of families turned to state and local public relief systems, just to be able to eat. But those systems, which in the 1920s had served only a small number of indigents, were totally unequipped to handle the heavy new demands. In many cities, therefore, relief simply collapsed. Private charities attempted to supplement the public relief efforts, but the problem was far beyond their capabilities as well.

In rural areas, conditions were in many ways worse. Farm income declined by 60 percent between 1929 and 1932. A third of all American farmers lost their land. In addition, a large area of agricultural settlement in the Great Plains suffered from a catastrophic natural disaster: one of the worst droughts in the history of the nation. Beginning in 1930, the region that came to be known as the "Dust Bowl," which stretched north from Texas into the Dakotas, experienced a steady decline *"Dust Bowl"* in rainfall and an accompanying increase in heat. The drought continued for a decade, turning what had once been fertile farm regions into virtual deserts. Severe winds blew dust across the eastern United States.

Many farmers, like many urban unemployed, left their homes in search of work. In the South, in particular, many dispossessed farmers—black and white—simply wandered from town to town, hoping to find jobs or handouts. Hundreds of thousands of families from the Dust Bowl (often known collectively as "Okies," though not all came from *"Okies"* Oklahoma) traveled to California and other states, where they found conditions little better than those they had left. Many worked as agricultural migrants, traveling from farm to farm, picking fruit and other crops at starvation wages.

DUST STORM, SOUTHWEST PLAINS, 1937   The dust storms of the 1930s were a terrifying experience for all who lived through them. Resembling a black wall sweeping in from the western horizon, such a storm engulfed farms and towns alike, blotting out the light of the sun and covering everything with a fine dirt. (© Bettmann/Corbis)

AFRICAN AMERICANS AND THE DEPRESSION

Most African Americans had not shared very much in the prosperity of the previous decade. But they did share in the hardships of the Great Depression.

As the Depression began, over half of all black Americans still lived in the South. Most were farmers. The collapse of prices for cotton and other staple crops left some with no income at all. Many left the land altogether—either by choice or because they had been evicted by landlords who no longer found sharecropping profitable. Some migrated to southern cities. But there, unemployed whites believed they had first claim to what work there was, and some now began to take positions as janitors, street cleaners, and domestic servants, displacing the African Americans who formerly occupied those jobs. By 1932, over half the blacks in the South were unemployed.

Unsurprisingly, therefore, many black southerners—perhaps 400,000 in all—left the South in the 1930s and journeyed to the cities of the North. But conditions there were little better. In New York, black unemployment was nearly 50 percent. In other cities, it was higher. Two million African Americans—half the total black population of the country— were on some form of relief by 1932.

Traditional patterns of segregation and disenfranchisement in the South survived the Depression largely unchallenged. But a few particularly notorious examples of racism did attract the attention of the nation. The most celebrated was the Scottsboro case. In *Scottsboro Case* March 1931, nine black teenagers were taken off a freight train in northern Alabama (in a small town near Scottsboro) and were arrested for vagrancy and disorder. Later, two white women who had also been riding the train accused them of rape. In fact, there was overwhelming evidence, medical and otherwise, that the women had not been raped at all; they may have made their accusations out of fear of being arrested themselves. Nevertheless, an all-white jury in Alabama quickly convicted all nine of the "Scottsboro boys" (as they were known to both friends and foes) and sentenced eight of them to death.

The Supreme Court overturned the convictions in 1932, and a series of new trials began. The International Labor Defense, an organization associated with the Communist Party, came to the aid of the accused youths and began to publicize the case. Although the white southern juries who sat on the case never acquitted any of the defendants, all of the accused eventually gained their freedom—although the last of the Scottsboro defendants did not leave prison until 1950.

HISPANICS AND ASIANS IN DEPRESSION AMERICA

Similar patterns of discrimination confronted many Mexicans and Mexican Americans. *Hispanic Workers Targeted* The Hispanic population of the United States had been growing steadily since early in the century, largely in California and other areas of the Southwest. Chicanos (Mexican Americans) filled many of the same menial jobs there that blacks had traditionally filled in other regions. Some farmed small, marginal tracts; others became agricultural migrants. It had always been a precarious existence, and the Depression made things significantly worse. Unemployed whites in the Southwest demanded jobs held by Hispanics, jobs that whites had previously considered beneath them. Thus Mexican unemployment rose quickly to levels far higher than those for whites. Some officials arbitrarily removed Mexicans from relief rolls or simply rounded up and deported them. Perhaps half a million Chicanos left the United States for Mexico in the first years of the Depression.

There were occasional signs of organized resistance by Mexican Americans themselves, most notably in California, where some formed a union of migrant farmworkers. But harsh repression by local growers and the public authorities allied with them prevented such organizations from having much impact. As a result, many Hispanics began to migrate to cities such as Los Angeles, where they lived in poverty comparable to that of urban blacks in the South and Northeast.

For Asian Americans, too, the Depression reinforced long-standing patterns of discrimination and economic marginalization. In California, where the *Plight of Asian Americans* largest Japanese American and Chinese American populations were, educated Asians had always found it difficult, if not impossible, to move into mainstream professions. Japanese American college graduates often found themselves working in family fruit stands. For those who found jobs in the industrial or service economy, employment was precarious; like blacks and Hispanics, Asians often lost jobs to white Americans desperate for work. Japanese farmworkers, like Chicano farmworkers, suffered from the increasing competition for even these low-paying jobs with white migrants from the Great Plains.

CHINATOWN, NEW YORK CITY A Chinese man carries a signboard through the streets of New York City's Chinatown bearing the latest news of the war between China and Japan, which in 1938 was well under way. Chinese Americans had the duel challenge in the 1930s of dealing both with large-scale unemployment and with continuing news of catastrophe from China, where most still had family members. (© Hulton Archive/Getty Images)

CONSIDER THE SOURCE

MR. TARVER REMEMBERS THE GREAT DEPRESSION

The Federal Writers' Project (FWP) was a New Deal program that employed authors and researchers during the Great Depression. Participants produced tourist guidebooks, ethnographies, oral histories, and many other kinds of documents. In 1940, an FWP writer interviewed a bank employee named Mr. Tarver.

Yes, I really went through the depression. [. . .] "There were thousands who went down during the panic—lost fortunes, homes, business, and in fact everything. Some have survived, and many never will. A great many were too old to begin building up again. In the kind of work I'm in I have been in position to know some of the devastating effects of it, and it certainly gets on your sympathy.

"I guess you would say I am recovering from it. When I say that though, I'm not boasting, but I'm deeply grateful for the good fortunes that have came my way. Then, too, I feel under everlasting obligations to some of my friends who have helped me to get where I am.

"I had not accumulated a great deal at the time of the panic, but I did have some savings and a good job. That was the trouble, my savings and my job went at the same time. Now that was real trouble. Nobody but my wife and I knew just what we did go through. [. . .]

I was making a fine salary, had a growing savings account, and a host of friends, and no serious troubles to worry about. My wife is just the smartest, thriftiest person you have ever seen. To her I owe a lot of my successes. She is fine with her needle and crocheting, and you never saw her idle. She made all her spending money that way. Even now since we have been in Washington she keeps it up. And her fruit cake! People here rave about it. She cooks an enormous amount of it every Christmas and sells it for

a big profit. She can't fill all the orders she gets. She is very resourceful and right now, if I were to die and not leave her a thing, she would manage some way. One of my hobbies was gardening and it proved to be a profitable one too. This place we rented had a fine garden spot, the finest in Dublin, so every one said. I worked in it early every morning and in the afternoon after banking hours. I sold lots of vegetables, and realized a lot on them—especially the early variety that brought a good price." [. . .]

"One morning we three were at the breakfast table when the phone rang. It was one of the fellows who worked at the bank.

"Tarver, he said, 'have you heard the news?'

"'What news? No, I haven't heard any news,' said I. What's it all about?'

"'Well,' he said, "hurry on down and see.'

"If you will excuse the expression, when he said that, the seat of my britches almost dropped out. I felt like it meant trouble of some kind. I had had a terrible feeling of uneasiness over the bank for some time. Banks had been closing all over the country. There had been a run on our bank some time previous to that, but we tided that over, and since then it had seemed stronger than ever.

"I hurried down and, sure enough, in front of the bank, there stood a crowd of employees, as blank expressions on their faces as I've ever seen. They were too dumbfounded to be excited even.

"The bank was closed and a notice to that effect on the door. We stood there just looking at each other until finally one said, 'Well, boys, guess we had better go on the inside and see if we can find out what it's all about. I guess there goes our jobs.'

[. . .] "Just as I was getting in the dumps about a regular job, I was notified to report at once, to act as assistant receiver for a defunct bank in Florida. They were feeling the depression there even more than we were in Georgia, and banks were closing every day.

[. . .] "Banks were still closing until it was hard to get enough receivers for them. Oh, we did work. Banks in neighboring towns were added to our work until we were liquidating six banks at one time, all in different places. I had to have another car then but was lucky to pick up a good used car almost at my own price. People had lost their cars as well as their homes, so it was no trouble to buy a good used one. Sometimes I would ride to all six of these banks in one day and when night came I would be completely given out. I couldn't stop even then, for there was scarcely a night that we didn't work."

UNDERSTAND, ANALYZE, & EVALUATE

1. Why was Mr. Tarver doubly affected by the banking crisis of the Great Depression? How did Mr. and Mrs. Tarver compensate for their losses in the job market?
2. How might the Great Depression have shaped the outlook of Mr. and Mrs. Tarver on work, leisure, and consumption for years, if not decades, to come?

Source: Mr. W. W. Tarver (White), Finance Officer in U.S. Treasury (Bank Conservator), 5001 Nebraska Ave., N.W., Washington, D.C., interviewed by Bradley. Library of Congress, *American Life Histories: Manuscripts from the Federal Writers' Project, 1936–1940.* http://memory.loc.gov/cgi-bin/query/r?ammem/wpa:@field%28DOCID+@lit%28wpa112060215%29%29.

Chinese Americans fared no better. The overwhelming majority worked, as they had for many years, in Chinese-owned laundries and restaurants. Those who moved outside the Asian community could rarely find jobs above the entry level. Chinese women, for example, might find work as stock girls in department stores but almost never as salesclerks. Educated Chinese men and women could hope for virtually no professional opportunities outside the world of the Chinatowns.

WOMEN AND FAMILIES IN THE GREAT DEPRESSION

The economic crisis strengthened the widespread belief that a woman's proper place was in the home. Many men and women believed that with employment so scarce, what work there was should go to men and that no woman whose husband was employed should accept a job. Indeed, from 1932 until 1937, it was illegal for more than one member of a family to hold a federal civil service job.

But the widespread assumption that married women, at least, should not work outside the home did not stop them from doing so. Both single and married women worked in the 1930s because they or their families needed the money. Some women did small jobs at home or sold food or goods to make ends meet. (See "Consider the Source: Mr. Tarver Remembers the Great Depression.") By the end of the Depression, 25 percent more women were working for wages than had been doing so at the beginning, despite considerable obstacles. Professional opportunities for women declined because unemployed men began moving into professions that had previously been considered women's fields. Female industrial workers were more likely to be laid off or to *Female Wage Earners* experience wage reductions than their male counterparts. But white women also had certain advantages in the workplace. The nonprofessional jobs that women traditionally held—salesclerks, stenographers, and other service positions—were less likely to disappear than the predominantly male jobs in heavy industry.

· **573**

Black women suffered massive unemployment, particularly in the South, because of a great reduction of domestic service jobs. As many as half of all black working women lost their jobs in the 1930s. Even so, at the end of the 1930s, 38 percent of black women were employed, as compared with 24 percent of white women. That was so because black women—both married and unmarried—had always been more likely to work than white women, less out of preference than out of economic necessity.

The Depression also worked to erode the strength of many family units. There was a *Declining Marriage Rate and Birthrate* decline in the divorce rate, but largely because divorce was now too expensive for some. More common was the informal breakup of families, particularly the desertion of families by unemployed men trying to escape the humiliation of being unable to earn a living. The marriage rate and the birthrate both declined for the first time since the early nineteenth century.

THE DEPRESSION AND AMERICAN CULTURE

The Great Depression was a traumatic experience for millions of Americans. Out of the crisis emerged probing criticisms of American life. But the Depression also produced powerful confirmations of more traditional values and reinforced many traditional goals. There was not one Depression culture, but many.

DEPRESSION VALUES

Prosperity and industrial growth had done much to shape American values in the 1920s. Yet even when hard times came, American social values seemed to change relatively little in response to the Depression. Instead, many people responded to hard times by redoubling their commitment to familiar ideas and goals. The Depression did not destroy the success ethic.

The survival of the ideals of work and individual responsibility was evident in many ways, not least in the reactions of those most traumatized by the Depression: people who suddenly found themselves without employment. Some expressed anger and struck out at the economic system. Many, however, seemed to blame themselves. At the same time, millions responded eagerly to reassurances that they could, through their own efforts, *Dale Carnegie* restore themselves to prosperity and success. Dale Carnegie's *How to Win Friends and Influence People* (1936), a self-help manual preaching individual initiative, was one of the best-selling books of the decade.

Yet the most popular cultural products of the 1930s diverted attention away from the Depression. And they came to Americans primarily through the two most powerful instruments of popular culture in the 1930s—radio and the movies. (For another powerful vehicle of escapist culture, see "Patterns of Popular Culture: The Golden Age of Comic Books.")

RADIO

Almost every American family had a radio in the 1930s. In cities and towns, radio consoles were as familiar a part of the furnishing of homes as tables and chairs. Even in remote rural areas without access to electricity, many families purchased radios and hooked them up to car batteries when they wished to listen.

Radio was often a community experience. Young people would place radios on their front porches and invite friends by to sit, talk, or dance. In poor urban neighborhoods, people would gather on a street or in a backyard to listen to sporting events or concerts. Within families, the radio often drew parents and children together to listen to favorite programs.

Although radio stations occasionally carried provocative programs, the staple of broadcasting was escapism, including comedies such as *Amos 'n'*   *Escapist Programming* *Andy* (with its demeaning picture of urban blacks) and adventures such as *Superman, Dick Tracy,* and *The Lone Ranger.* Radio brought a new kind of comedy to a wide audience. Jack Benny, George Burns and Gracie Allen, and other masters of elaborately timed repartee began to develop broad followings. Enormously popular, especially among women who were alone in the house during the day, were soap operas (so named because they were generally sponsored by soap companies, whose advertising was targeted at women).

Radio provided Americans with their first direct access to important public events. On-air coverage of news and sports expanded rapidly to meet the demand. Some of the most dramatic moments of the 1930s were a result of radio coverage of celebrated events: the World Series, the Academy Awards, political conventions. When the German dirigible *Hindenburg* crashed in flames in Lakehurst, New Jersey, in 1937, it   *The Hindenburg Crash* produced an enormous national reaction largely because of the live radio account by a broadcaster, overcome with emotion, who cried out, as he watched the terrible crash, "Oh the humanity! Oh the humanity!" The actor-director Orson Welles created another memorable event on Halloween night, 1938, when he broadcast a radio play about aliens landing in central New Jersey who had set off toward New York armed with terrible weapons. The play took the form of a news broadcast, and it created panic among some people who believed for a while that the events it described were real.

THE MOVIES

In the first years of the Depression, movie attendance dropped significantly. By the mid-1930s, however, most Americans had resumed their moviegoing habits in part because the movies (now with sound and, by the end of the decade, color) were becoming more appealing.

Hollywood continued to exercise tight control over its products in the 1930s through its resilient censor Will Hays, who ensured that most movies carried no sensational or controversial messages. The studio system—through which a few large movie companies exercised iron control over actors, writers, and directors—also worked to ensure that Hollywood films avoided controversy.

Neither the censor nor the studio system, however, could (or wished to) completely prevent films from exploring social questions. There were many serious films that portrayed the problems of the Depression—for example, King Vidor's *Our Daily Bread* (1932) and John Ford's adaptation of *The Grapes of Wrath* (1940). Gangster movies such as *Little Caesar* (1930) and *The Public Enemy* (1931) portrayed a dark, gritty, violent world with which few Americans were familiar, but their desperate stories were popular nevertheless with those engaged in their own difficult struggles.

But the most effective presentation of a social message came from the brilliant Italian-born director Frank Capra. Capra had a deep and somewhat romanticized love for his adopted country, and he translated that love into a vaguely populistic admiration for ordinary people. He contrasted the decency of small-town America   *Films of Frank Capra* and the common man with what he considered the grasping opportunism of the

THE GOLDEN AGE OF COMIC BOOKS

In the troubled years of the Great Depression (and later, World War II), many Americans sought release from their anxieties in fantasy. Movies, plays, books, radio shows, and other diversions drew people out of their own lives and into a safer or more glamorous or more exciting world. Beginning in 1938, one of the most popular forms of escape for many young Americans was the comic book.

In February 1935, Malcolm Wheeler-Nicholson founded the first comics magazine—what we now know as the "comic book"—titled *New Fun*. It was not successful, but Wheeler founded a new company, Detective Comics. He began in 1937 to design a new magazine called *Action Comics*. Wheeler ran out of money before he could publish anything, but the company continued without him. In 1938, the first issue of *Action Comics* appeared with a startling and controversial cover—a powerful man in a skintight suit lifting a car over his head. His name was Superman, and he became the most popular cartoon character of all time.

Within a year, Superman had a comic book named after him, which was selling over 1.2 million copies each issue. By 1940, there was a popular Superman radio show—introduced by a breathless announcer crying, "It's a bird! It's a plane! It's . . . Superman!" Soon, other publishers began developing new *superheroes* (a term invented by the creators of Superman) to capitalize on this growing popular appetite. In 1939, a second great comic book publisher appeared—Marvel Comics.

By the early 1940s, Superman had been joined by other superheroes: the Human Torch, the Sub-Mariner, Batman, the Flash,

and Wonder Woman, a character created in part to signal the importance of women to the war effort.

It is not hard to imagine why superheroes would be so appealing to Americans in the 1930s and 1940s—particularly to the teenage boys who were the largest single purchasers of comic books. Superman and other superheroes were idealized versions of the ideal boy—smart, good, "the perfect Boy Scout," as one fan put it. But they were also all-powerful, capable of righting wrong and preventing catastrophe. Even as the national economy faltered, comic book heroes modeled patriotic pride, resilience, and optimism. They operated with moral certainty when so much was uncertain. At a time when suffering was an ever-present reality in the world, superheroes offered a comforting escape from anxiety.

Many of the early comic book writers were young Jewish men, conscious of their outsider status in an American culture not yet wholly open to them. Almost all the characters they created had alter egos, identities they used while living within the normal world. Superman was Clark Kent, a "mild-mannered reporter." Batman was Bruce Wayne, a wealthy heir. All were part of mainstream American society, and they expressed in part the outsider's dream of assimilation. The superheroes themselves were outsiders too—but outsiders endowed with special powers and abilities unavailable to ordinary people.

In the last years of the Depression, the comic superheroes began battling the Axis powers. Marvel's Human Torch and Sub-Mariner joined forces against the German

SUPERMAN The most popular action figure in the history of comic books was Superman, whose superhuman powers were particularly appealing fantasies to Americans suffering through the Depression and, later, World War II. (© Hulton Archive/Getty Images)

navy. Superman fought spies and saboteurs at home. Captain America, a new character created in March 1941, was a frail young man rejected by the army who, after being given a secret serum by a military doctor, became extraordinarily powerful. The cover of the first issue of *Captain America* showed the title character punching Adolf Hitler in his headquarters in Germany.

The end of the war was also the end of this first golden age of American comic books. New comic books emphasized romance, mild sexuality, and, over time, violence and cruelty. But comic books never surpassed the heights of popularity that the superhero comics attained during the Depression and World War II. •

UNDERSTAND, ANALYZE, & EVALUATE

1. What could comic books offer readers suffering through the crisis of the Great Depression?
2. How and why have comic book superheroes changed over time?

city and the greedy capitalist marketplace. In *Mr. Deeds Goes to Town* (1936), a simple man from a small town inherits a large fortune, moves to the city, and—not liking the greed and dishonesty he finds there—gives the money away and moves back home. In *Mr. Smith Goes to Washington* (1939), a decent man from a western state is elected to the United States Senate, refuses to join in the self-interested politics of Washington, and dramatically exposes the corruption and selfishness of his colleagues. Capra's films, incredibly popular in the 1930s, helped audiences find solace in a vision of an imagined American past—in the warmth and goodness of idealized small towns and the decency of ordinary people.

More often, however, the commercial films of the 1930s, like most radio programs, were deliberately and explicitly escapist: lavish musicals such as *Gold Diggers of 1933,* "screwball" comedies such as Capra's *It Happened One Night*, or the many films of the Marx Brothers—films designed to divert audiences from their troubles and, often, indulge their fantasies about quick and easy wealth.

The 1930s were the first years of Walt Disney's long reign as the champion of animation and children's entertainment. After producing cartoon shorts for theaters in the late 1920s, many of them starring the newly created character Mickey Mouse, Disney began to produce feature-length animated films, starting in 1937 with *Snow White*. Other enormously popular films of the 1930s were adaptations of popular novels, such as *The Wizard of Oz* and *Gone with the Wind,* both released in 1939.

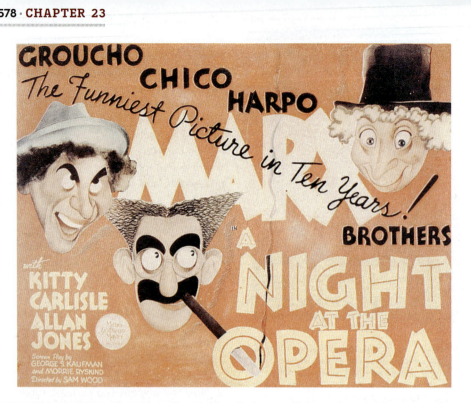

A NIGHT AT THE OPERA   The antic comedy of the Marx Brothers provided a popular and welcome escape from the hardships of the Great Depression. The Marx Brothers, shown here in a poster for one of their most famous films, effectively lampooned dilemmas that many Americans faced in their ceaseless, and usually unsuccessful, efforts to find an easy route to wealth and comfort. (© Everett Collection)

Hollywood did little to challenge the conventions of popular culture on issues of gender and race. Women in movies were portrayed overwhelmingly as wives and mothers, or if not, as sexually attractive flirts. Mae West portrayed herself in a series of successful films as an overtly sexual woman manipulating men through her attractiveness. Few films included important African American characters. Most of the black men and women who did appear in movies were portrayed as servants or farmhands or entertainers.

Stereotypes in Film

LITERATURE AND JOURNALISM

Much literature and journalism in the 1930s dealt directly or indirectly with the tremendous disillusionment, and the increasing radicalism, of the time.

Not all literature, of course, was challenging or controversial. The most popular books and magazines of the 1930s, in fact, were as escapist and romantic as many radio shows and movies. Two of the best-selling novels of the decade were romantic sagas set in earlier eras: Margaret Mitchell's *Gone with the Wind* (1936) and Hervey Allen's *Anthony Adverse* (1933). Leading magazines focused more on fashions, stunts, scenery, and the arts than on the social conditions of the nation. The new and enormously popular photographic journal *Life,* first published in 1936, had the largest readership of any publication in the United States other than *Reader's Digest.*

Life Magazine

It devoted some attention to politics and to the economic conditions of the Depression, but it was best known for stunning photographs of sporting and theater events, natural landscapes, and impressive public projects. One of its most popular features was "*Life* Goes to a Party," which took the chatty social columns of daily newspapers and turned them into glossy photographic glimpses of the rich and famous, but also ordinary people enjoying less lavish parties.

Other Depression writing, however, was frankly and openly challenging to the dominant values of American popular culture. Some of the most   *Depression-Era Fiction* significant literature offered corrosive portraits of the harshness and emptiness of American life: John Dos Passos's *U.S.A.* trilogy (1930–1936), which attacked what he considered the materialistic madness of American culture; in Richard Wright's *Native Son* (1940), the story of a young African American man broken by the system of racial oppression; Nathanael West's *Miss Lonelyhearts* (1933), the story of an advice columnist overwhelmed by the sadness he encounters in the lives of those who consult him; Jack Conroy's *The Disinherited* (1933), a harsh portrait of the lives of coal miners; and James T. Farrell's *Studs Lonigan* (1932), a portrait of a lost, hardened working-class youth. Perhaps the best-known depiction of Depression-era life is John Steinbeck's *The Grapes of Wrath* (1939). The novel's main characters are the Joad family, migrants from the Dust Bowl to California who encounter an unending string of calamities and failures. Their story offers a critique of the exploitative features of agrarian life in the West, as well as a tribute to the fortitude and heart of the community the Joads represent.

THE POPULAR FRONT AND THE LEFT

The Communist Party, a relatively small organization in the early twentieth century, flourished during the Great Depression. It had long been a harsh and unrelenting critic of American capitalism, largely hidden from the public world. But with the capitalist system's flaws exposed, the Depression brought the communists into the light. They created what came to be called the "Popular Front," a broad coalition of   *Popular Front Alliances* "antifascist" groups on the left. Not all members of the Popular Front considered themselves communists, but communism was its driving force. The Popular Front presented itself as an American organization, but it was in fact largely controlled by the Soviet Union. Over time, Stalin and the Communist Party softened their attitude toward President Franklin Roosevelt (elected in 1932), hoping that he would become an ally against Nazi Germany. To that end, the Popular Front formed loose alliances with "progressive groups," and it praised even some strong anticommunists such as the labor leader John L. Lewis. In its heyday, the Popular Front did much to enhance the reputation and influence of the Communist Party. It also helped mobilize writers, artists, and intellectuals behind a critical, democratic sensibility.

The Spanish Civil War of the mid-1930s showed how the left helped give meaning and purpose to individual lives. The war in Spain pitted the forces supporting Francisco Franco (who received aid from Hitler and Mussolini and was thus allied with fascism) against the existing republican government. A substantial group of young Americans— more than 3,000 in all—formed the Abraham Lincoln Brigade and trav-   *Lincoln Brigade* eled to Spain to join in what they considered a fight against the fascists. The American Communist Party was instrumental in creating the Lincoln Brigade, and directed many of its activities.

higher wages or better hours. But by mid-1931, economic conditions had deteriorated so much that the structure of voluntary cooperation had collapsed.

Hoover also attempted to use government spending as a tool for fighting the Depression. The president proposed to Congress an increase of $423 million—a significant sum by the standards of the time—in federal public works programs, and he encouraged state and local governments to fund public construction. But the spending was not nearly enough in the face of such devastating problems. And when economic conditions worsened, he became less willing to increase spending, worrying instead about keeping the budget balanced.

Even before the stock market crash, Hoover had begun to construct a program to assist the troubled agricultural economy. In April 1929, he proposed the Agricultural Marketing *Agricultural Marketing Act* Act, which established the first major government program to help farmers maintain prices. A federally sponsored Farm Board would make loans to national marketing cooperatives or establish corporations to buy surpluses and thus raise prices. At the same time, Hoover attempted to protect American farmers from international competition *Hawley-Smoot Tariff* by raising agricultural tariffs. The Hawley-Smoot Tariff of 1930 increased protection on seventy-five farm products. But neither the Agricultural Marketing Act nor the Hawley-Smoot Tariff ultimately helped American farmers significantly. Agricultural surpluses, combined with declining consumption, kept the farm economy in crisis.

By the spring of 1931, Herbert Hoover's political position had deteriorated considerably. In the 1930 congressional elections, Democrats won control of the House and made substantial inroads in the Senate. Many Americans blamed the president personally for the crisis and began calling the shantytowns that unemployed people established on the *"Hoovervilles"* outskirts of cities "Hoovervilles." Democrats urged the president to support more vigorous programs of relief and public spending. Hoover, instead, seized on a slight improvement in economic conditions early in 1931 as proof that his policies were working. The international financial panic of the spring of 1931 destroyed that illusion.

By the time Congress convened in December 1931, conditions had grown so desperate that Hoover supported a series of measures designed to keep endangered banks afloat and protect homeowners from foreclosure on their mortgages. Most important was a bill *The RFC* passed in January 1932 establishing the Reconstruction Finance Corporation (RFC), a government agency to provide federal loans to troubled banks, railroads, and other businesses. Unlike some earlier Hoover programs, the RFC operated on a large scale. In 1932, it had a budget of $1.5 billion for public works alone.

Nevertheless, the new agency failed to deal directly or forcefully enough with the real problems of the economy to produce any significant recovery. The RFC lent funds only to financial institutions with sufficient collateral; much of its money went to large banks and corporations. At Hoover's insistence, it helped finance only those public works projects that promised ultimately to pay for themselves (toll bridges, public housing, and others). Above all, the RFC did not have enough money to make any real impact on the Depression, and it did not even spend all the money it had.

POPULAR PROTEST

For the first several years of the Depression, most Americans were either too stunned or too confused to raise much effective protest. By the middle of 1932, however, dissident voices began to be heard.

In the summer of 1932, a group of unhappy farm owners gathered in Des Moines, Iowa, to establish a new organization: the Farmers' Holiday Association, which endorsed the withholding of farm products from the market—in effect a farmers' strike. The strike began in August in western Iowa, spread briefly to a few neighboring areas, and succeeded in blockading several markets; but in the end, it dissolved in failure.

A more celebrated protest movement emerged from American veterans. In 1924, Congress had approved the payment of a $1,000 bonus to all those who had served in World War I, the money to be paid beginning in 1945. By 1932, however, many veterans were demanding that the bonus be paid immediately. Hoover, concerned about balancing the budget, rejected their appeal. In June, more than 20,000 veterans, members of the self-proclaimed Bonus Expeditionary Force, or "Bonus Army," marched *The "Bonus Army"* into Washington, built crude camps around the city, and promised to stay until Congress approved legislation to pay the bonus. Some of the veterans departed in July, after Congress had voted down their proposal. Many, however, remained in Washington.

CLEARING OUT THE BONUS MARCHERS In July 1932, President Hoover ordered the Washington, D.C., police to evict the Bonus Marchers from some of the public buildings and land they had been occupying. After a series of skirmishes between police and the protesters, Hoover ordered the United States Army to complete the eviction. (© Bettmann/Corbis)

Their continued presence in Washington embarrassed President Hoover. Finally, in mid-July, he ordered police to clear the marchers out of several abandoned federal buildings in which they had been staying. A few marchers threw rocks at the police, and someone opened fire; two veterans fell dead. Hoover called the incident evidence of uncontrolled violence and radicalism, and he ordered the United States Army to assist the police in clearing out the buildings.

General Douglas MacArthur, the army chief of staff, carried out the mission himself and greatly exceeded the president's orders. He led the Third Cavalry, two infantry regiments, a machine-gun detachment, and six tanks down Pennsylvania Avenue in pursuit *Demise of the Bonus Army* of the Bonus Army. The veterans fled in terror. MacArthur followed them across the Anacostia River, where he ordered the soldiers to burn their tent city to the ground. More than 100 marchers were injured.

The incident dealt another serious blow to Hoover's already battered political standing. The "Great Engineer," the personification of the optimistic days of the 1920s, had become a symbol of the nation's failure to deal effectively with its startling reversal of fortune.

The Election of 1932

As the 1932 presidential election approached, few people doubted the outcome. The Republican Party dutifully renominated Herbert Hoover for a second term of office, but few delegates believed he could win. The Democrats, in the meantime, gathered jubilantly in Chicago to nominate the governor of New York, Franklin Delano Roosevelt.

Roosevelt had been a well-known figure in the party for many years already. A Hudson *Franklin Delano Roosevelt* Valley aristocrat, a distant cousin of Theodore Roosevelt, and a handsome, charming young man, he progressed rapidly: from a seat in the New York State legislature to a position as assistant secretary of the navy during World War I to his party's vice presidential nomination in 1920 on the ill-fated ticket with James M. Cox. Less than a year later, he was stricken with polio. Although he never regained use of his legs (and could walk only by using crutches and braces), he built up sufficient physical strength to return to politics in 1928. When Al Smith received the Democratic nomination for president that year, Roosevelt was elected to succeed him as governor. In 1930, he easily won reelection.

Roosevelt worked no miracles in New York, but he did initiate enough programs of government assistance to be able to present himself as a more energetic and imaginative *"A New Deal"* leader than Hoover. In national politics, he avoided divisive cultural issues and emphasized the economic grievances that most Democrats shared. As a result, he was able to assemble a broad coalition within the party and win his party's nomination. In a dramatic break with tradition, he flew to Chicago to address the Democratic National Convention in person and accept the nomination. In the course of his acceptance speech, Roosevelt aroused the delegates with his ringing promise: "I pledge you, I pledge myself, to a new deal for the American people." Neither then nor in the subsequent campaign did Roosevelt give much indication of what that program would be. But Herbert Hoover's unpopularity virtually ensured Roosevelt's election.

Roosevelt won by a landslide, receiving 57.4 percent of the popular vote to Hoover's 39.7, and carried every state except Delaware, Pennsylvania, Connecticut, Vermont, New Hampshire, and Maine. Democrats won large majorities in both houses of

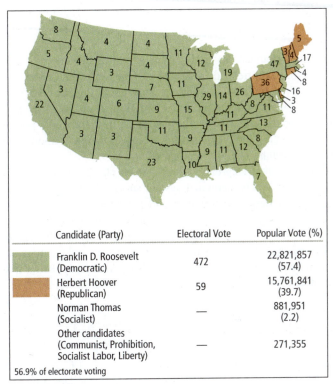

Candidate (Party)	Electoral Vote	Popular Vote (%)
Franklin D. Roosevelt (Democratic)	472	22,821,857 (57.4)
Herbert Hoover (Republican)	59	15,761,841 (39.7)
Norman Thomas (Socialist)	—	881,951 (2.2)
Other candidates (Communist, Prohibition, Socialist Labor, Liberty)	—	271,355

56.9% of electorate voting

THE ELECTION OF 1932 Like the election of 1928, the election of 1932 was exceptionally one-sided. But this time, the landslide favored the Democratic candidate, Franklin Roosevelt, who overwhelmed Herbert Hoover in all regions of the country except New England. Roosevelt obviously benefited primarily from popular disillusionment with Hoover's response to the Great Depression. • *But what characteristics of Roosevelt himself contributed to his victory?*

Congress. It was a convincing mandate, but it was not yet clear what Roosevelt intended to do with it.

THE "INTERREGNUM"

The period between the election and the inauguration (which in the early 1930s lasted more than four months) was a season of growing economic crisis. Presidents-elect traditionally do not involve themselves directly in government. But in a series of brittle exchanges with Roosevelt, Hoover tried to exact a pledge from the president-elect to maintain policies of economic orthodoxy. Roosevelt genially refused.

In February, only a month before the inauguration, a new crisis developed when the collapse of the American banking system suddenly and rapidly accelerated. *Banking Collapse* Depositors withdrew their money in panic; and one bank after another closed its doors and declared bankruptcy. Hoover again asked Roosevelt to give prompt public assurances that there would be no tinkering with the currency, no heavy borrowing, no unbalancing of the budget. Roosevelt again refused.

March 4, 1933, was, therefore, a day of both economic crisis and considerable personal bitterness. On that morning, Herbert Hoover rode glumly down Pennsylvania Avenue with a beaming, buoyant Franklin Roosevelt, who would shortly be sworn in as the thirty-second president of the United States.

CONCLUSION

The Great Depression changed many things in American life. It created unemployment on a scale never before experienced in the nation's history. It put enormous pressures on families, on communities, on state and local governments, and ultimately on Washington. The innovative but ultimately failed presidency of Herbert Hoover was unable to produce policies capable of dealing effectively with the crisis. In the nation's politics and culture, there were strong currents of radicalism and protest; and many middle-class Americans came to fear that a revolution might be approaching.

In reality, while the Great Depression shook much of American society and culture, it actually toppled very little. The capitalist system survived, damaged for a time but never truly threatened. The values of materialism and personal responsibility were shaken but never overturned. The American people in the 1930s were more receptive than they had been in the 1920s to evocations of community, generosity, and the dignity of common people. They were more open to experiments in government and business and even private lives than they had been in earlier years. But for most Americans, belief in the "American way of life" remained strong throughout the long years of economic despair.

KEY TERMS/PEOPLE/PLACES/EVENTS

Abraham Lincoln Brigade 579
Agricultural Marketing Act 582
Bonus Army 583
Dale Carnegie 574
Dust Bowl 569
Frank Capra 575

Franklin Delano Roosevelt 584
Great Depression 565
Hawley-Smoot Tariff 582
Hindenburg 575
Hoovervilles 582
John Dos Passos 579
John Steinbeck 579

Life magazine 578
Okies 569
Popular Front 579
Reconstruction Finance Corporation (RFC) 582
Richard Wright 579
Scottsboro case 570

RECALL AND REFLECT

1. Was the 1929 stock market crash the cause of the Depression? Why or why not?
2. How did farmers fare during the Depression? What environmental conditions contributed to their plight?
3. How did popular entertainment and the arts respond to the needs of Depression-era audiences?
4. What popular protests arose in response to the Depression? How successful were these protests?
5. How did Hoover's political beliefs affect his attempt to deal with the economic crisis of the Depression?

24 | THE NEW DEAL

LAUNCHING THE NEW DEAL
THE NEW DEAL IN TRANSITION
THE NEW DEAL IN DISARRAY
LIMITS AND LEGACIES OF THE NEW DEAL

LOOKING AHEAD

1. What emergency measures did Franklin Delano Roosevelt (FDR) take in his first hundred days as president?

2. Who were the major critics of FDR's New Deal, and how did their criticisms influence FDR's "Second New Deal"?

3. What were the principal achievements of the Second New Deal in 1935?

DURING HIS TWELVE YEARS IN office, Franklin Roosevelt became more central to the life of the nation than any president had ever been. More important, his administration constructed a series of reforms that fundamentally altered the federal government and its relationship to society. By the end of the 1930s, the New Deal (as the Roosevelt administration's program was called) had not ended the Great Depression; only World War II did that. But it had created many of the broad outlines of the political world we know today.

1933

"First New Deal" legislation

Prohibition ends

1934

American Liberty League founded

Long's Share-Our-Wealth Society established

1935

Supreme Court invalidates NRA

"Second New Deal" legislation, including Social Security and Wagner Acts

Lewis breaks with AFL

1936

Supreme Court invalidates Agricultural Adjustment Act

CIO established

Roosevelt reelected

Sit-down strikes

1937

Roosevelt's "Court-packing" plan

Supreme Court upholds Wagner Act

Severe recession

1938

Fair Labor Standards Act

LAUNCHING THE NEW DEAL

Roosevelt's first task upon taking office was to alleviate the panic that was creating the chaos in the financial system. He did so in part by force of personality and in part by rapidly constructing an ambitious and diverse program of legislation.

RESTORING CONFIDENCE

Much of Roosevelt's early success was a result of his ebullient personality. He was the first president to make regular use of the radio; and his friendly "fireside chats," during which he explained in simple terms his programs and plans to the people, helped build public confidence in the administration. But Roosevelt could not rely on image alone. On March 6, two days after taking office, he issued a proclamation closing all American banks for four days until Congress could meet in special session to consider banking reform legislation. So great was the panic about bank failures that the "bank holiday," as the president euphemistically described it, created a general sense of relief and hope.

Three days later, Roosevelt sent to Congress the Emergency Banking Act, a generally conservative bill designed primarily to protect the larger banks from being dragged down by the weakness of smaller ones. The bill provided for Treasury Department inspection of all banks before they would be allowed to reopen. It also provided federal assistance to some troubled institutions and a thorough reorganization of those banks in the greatest difficulty. Congress passed the bill within a few hours of its introduction. Whatever else the new law accomplished, it helped dispel the panic. Three-quarters of the banks in the Federal Reserve system reopened within the next three days, and $1 billion in hoarded currency and gold flowed back into them within a month. The immediate banking crisis was over.

On the morning after passage of the Emergency Banking Act, Roosevelt sent to Congress another measure—the Economy Act—designed to convince the public (and especially the business community) that the federal government was in safe, responsible hands. The act proposed to balance the federal budget by cutting the salaries of government employees and reducing pensions to veterans by as much as 15 percent. Like the banking bill, this one passed through Congress almost instantly, even though the cost cutting reduced the growth of the economy. Later that spring, Roosevelt signed the Glass-Steagall Act of June 1933, which gave the government authority to curb irresponsible speculation by banks. More important, perhaps, it established the Federal Deposit Insurance Corporation (FDIC), which guaranteed all bank deposits up to $2,500. Even if *Federal Deposit Insurance Corporation* a bank should fail, small depositors would be able to recover their money.

To restore confidence in the stock market, Congress passed the so-called Truth in Securities Act of 1933, requiring corporations issuing new securities to provide full and accurate information about them to the public. In June 1934, another act established the Securities and Exchange Commission (SEC) to police the stock market. Roosevelt also *Securities and Exchange Commission* signed a bill to legalize the manufacture and sale of beer with a 3.2 percent alcohol content—an interim measure pending the repeal of prohibition, for which a constitutional amendment (the Twenty-First) was already in process. The amendment was ratified later in 1933.

AGRICULTURAL ADJUSTMENT

These initial actions bought time for more comprehensive programs. The first was the Agricultural Adjustment Act, which Congress passed in May 1933. Under the provisions of the act, producers of seven basic commodities (wheat, cotton, corn, hogs, rice, tobacco,

THE NEW DEAL Of the many resources at Roosevelt's disposal was the impression of his sunny personality during dark times. It conveyed to many a sense of hope and optimism. In this political cartoon from about 1934, Roosevelt is seen steering the ship of state toward economic recovery. His detractors are shown grumbling under the cloud of depression. (© Granger, NYC—All Rights Reserved.)

and dairy products) would impose production limits on their crops. The government, through the Agricultural Adjustment Administration (AAA), would then tell individual *Agricultural Adjustment Administration*   farmers how much they should produce and would pay them subsidies for leaving some of their land idle. A tax on food processing (for example, the milling of wheat) would provide the funds for the new payments. Farm prices were to be subsidized up to the point of parity.

The AAA helped bring about a rise in prices for farm commodities in the years after 1933. Gross farm income increased by half in the first three years of the New Deal, and the agricultural economy as a whole emerged from the 1930s more stable and prosperous than it had been in many years. The AAA did, however, favor larger farmers over smaller ones. By distributing payments to landowners, not those who worked the land, the government allowed planters to reduce their acreage, evict tenants and sharecroppers, and fire field hands.

In January 1936, the Supreme Court struck down the crucial provisions of the AAA, arguing that the government had no constitutional authority to require farmers to limit production. But within a few weeks, the administration had secured passage of new legislation (the Soil Conservation and Domestic Allotment Act), which permitted the government to pay farmers to reduce production so as to "conserve soil," prevent erosion, and accomplish other secondary goals.

The administration launched several efforts to assist poor farmers as well. The Resettlement Administration, established in 1935, and its successor, the Farm Security *Farm Security Administration*   Administration, created in 1937, provided loans to help farmers cultivating submarginal soil to relocate to better lands. But the programs moved no more than a few thousand farmers. More effective was the Rural Electrification Administration, created in 1935, which worked to make electric power available for the first time to thousands of farmers through utility cooperatives.

INDUSTRIAL RECOVERY

Since 1931, leaders of the United States Chamber of Commerce and many others had been urging the government to adopt an antideflation program that would permit trade associations to cooperate in stabilizing prices within their industries. Existing antitrust laws clearly forbade such practices, and Herbert Hoover had refused to endorse suspension of the laws. The Roosevelt administration was more receptive. In exchange for relaxing antitrust provisions, however, New Dealers insisted on other provisions. Business leaders would have to recognize the workers' right to bargain collectively through unions and to ensure that the incomes of workers would rise along with prices. And to help create jobs and increase consumer buying power, the administration added a major program of public works spending. The result of these and many other impulses was the National Industrial Recovery Act, which Congress passed in June 1933.

At its center was a new federal agency, the National Recovery Administration (NRA), *National Recovery Administration*   under the direction of the flamboyant and energetic Hugh S. Johnson. Johnson called on every business establishment in the nation to accept a temporary "blanket code": a minimum wage of between 30 and 40 cents an hour, a maximum workweek of thirty-five to forty hours, and the abolition of child labor. At the same time, Johnson negotiated another, more specific set of codes with leaders of the nation's major industries. These industrial codes set floors below which no company would lower prices or wages in its search for a competitive advantage, and they included provisions for maintaining employment and production. He quickly won agreements from almost every major industry in the country.

From the beginning, however, the NRA stumbled. The codes themselves were hastily and often poorly written. Large producers consistently dominated the *Problems of the NRA* code-writing process and ensured that the new regulations would work to their advantage and to the disadvantage of smaller firms. And the codes at times did more than simply set floors under prices; they actively and artificially raised them—sometimes to levels higher than the market could sustain.

Other NRA goals also worked against recovery. Section 7(a) of the National Industrial Recovery Act promised workers the right to form unions and engage in collective bargaining and encouraged many workers to join unions for the first time. But Section 7(a) contained no enforcement mechanisms. The Public Works Administration (PWA), established to administer the National Industrial Recovery Act's spending programs, only gradually allowed the $3.3 billion in public works funds to trickle out.

Perhaps the clearest evidence of the NRA's failure was that industrial production actually declined in the months after the agency's establishment, despite the rise in prices that the codes had helped create. The NRA failed to increase the buying power for consumers, which made the higher prices an obstacle to growth. By the spring of 1934, the NRA was besieged by criticism. That fall, Roosevelt pressured Johnson to resign and established a new board of directors to oversee the NRA.

Then in 1935, the Supreme Court intervened with a case involving alleged NRA code violations by the Schechter brothers, who operated a wholesale poultry business confined to Brooklyn, New York. The Court ruled unanimously that the Schechters were not engaged in interstate commerce (and thus not subject to federal regulation) and, further, that Congress had unconstitutionally delegated legislative power to the president to draft the NRA codes. The justices struck down the legislation establishing the agency. Roosevelt denounced the justices for their "horse-and-buggy" interpretation of the interstate commerce clause. He was rightly concerned, for the reasoning in the Schechter case threatened many other New Deal programs as well. But many New Dealers—and many others— welcomed the NRA's demise.

REGIONAL PLANNING

The AAA and the NRA largely reflected the beliefs of New Dealers who favored economic planning but wanted private interests (farmers or business leaders) to dominate the planning process. But other reformers believed that the government itself should be the chief planning agent in the economy. Their most conspicuous *Tennessee Valley Authority* success was an unprecedented experiment in regional planning: the Tennessee Valley Authority (TVA).

Progressive reformers had agitated for years for public development of the nation's water resources as a source of cheap electric power. In particular, they had urged completion of a great dam at Muscle Shoals on the Tennessee River in Alabama—a dam begun during World War I but left unfinished when the war ended. But opposition from the utilities companies had blocked further progress on the dam.

In 1932, however, one of the great utility empires—that of the electricity magnate Samuel Insull—collapsed spectacularly amid widely publicized exposés of corruption. Hostility to the

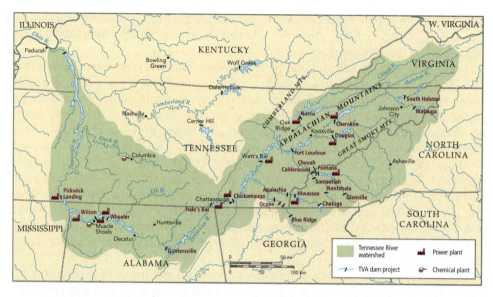

THE TENNESSEE VALLEY AUTHORITY The Tennessee Valley Authority was one of the largest experiments in government-funded public works and regional planning in American history to that point. The federal government had helped fund many projects in its history—canals, turnpikes, railroads, bridges, dams, and others. But never before had it undertaken a project of such great scope, and never before had it maintained such close control and ownership over the public works it helped create. This map illustrates the broad reach of the TVA within the Tennessee Valley region, which spanned seven states. TVA dams throughout the region helped control floods and also provided a source of hydroelectric power, which the government sold to consumers. Note the dam near Muscle Shoals, Alabama, in the bottom left of the map. It was begun during World War I, and efforts to revive it in the 1920s helped create the momentum that produced the TVA. • *Why were progressives so eager to see the government enter the business of hydroelectric power in the 1920s?*

utilities soon grew so intense that the companies were no longer able to block the public power movement. The result was legislation, supported by the president and enacted by Congress in May 1933, creating the Tennessee Valley Authority. The TVA was authorized to complete the dam at Muscle Shoals and build other dams in the region, and to generate and sell electricity from them to the public at reasonable rates. It was also intended to promote a comprehensive redevelopment of the entire region, encouraging the growth of local industries, supervising a substantial program of reforestation, and helping farmers improve productivity.

Opposition by conservatives ultimately blocked many of the ambitious social planning projects proposed by the more visionary TVA administrators, but the Authority revitalized the region in numerous ways. It improved water transportation, virtually eliminated flooding in the region, and provided electricity to thousands who had never before had it. Throughout the country, largely because of the "yardstick" provided by the TVA's cheap production of electricity, private power rates declined. Even so, the Tennessee Valley remained a generally impoverished region despite the TVA's efforts.

THE GROWTH OF FEDERAL RELIEF

The Roosevelt administration did not consider relief to the unemployed its most important task, but it recognized the necessity of doing something to help impoverished Americans survive until the government could revive the economy to the point where relief might not be necessary. Among Roosevelt's first acts as president was the establishment of the Federal Emergency Relief Administration (FERA), which provided cash grants to states to prop up bankrupt relief agencies. To administer the program, he chose the director of the New York State relief agency, Harry Hopkins. Both Hopkins and Roosevelt had misgivings about establishing a government "dole," but they felt somewhat more comfortable with another form of government assistance: work relief. Thus when it became clear that the FERA grants were not enough, the administration established a second program: the Civil Works Administration (CWA), which put more than 4 million people to work on temporary projects between November 1933 and April 1934. Some of the projects were of lasting value, such as the construction of roads, schools, and parks; others were little more than make-work. To Hopkins, however, the important things were pumping money into the economy and providing assistance to people with nowhere else to turn.

Roosevelt's favorite relief project was the Civilian Conservation Corps (CCC). The CCC created camps in national parks and forests and in other rural *Civilian Conservation Corps* and wilderness settings. There, young unemployed men from the cities worked in a semimilitary environment on such projects as planting trees, building reservoirs, developing parks, and improving agricultural irrigation.

Mortgage relief was a pressing need for millions of farm owners and homeowners. The Farm Credit Administration, which within two years refinanced *Mortgage Relief* one-fifth of all farm mortgages in the United States, was one response to that problem. The Frazier-Lemke Farm Bankruptcy Act of 1933 was another. It enabled some farmers to regain their land even after the foreclosure of their mortgages. Despite such efforts, however, 25 percent of all American farm owners had lost their land by 1934. Homeowners were similarly troubled, and in June 1933 the administration established the Home Owners' Loan Corporation, which by 1936 had refinanced the mortgages of more than 1 million householders. A year later, Congress established the Federal Housing Administration to insure mortgages for new construction and home repairs.

THE NEW DEAL IN TRANSITION

Seldom has an American president enjoyed such remarkable popularity as Franklin Roosevelt did during his first two years in office. But by early 1935, the New Deal faced fierce public criticism. (For reverberations of such praise and condemnation in the historical scholarship on Roosevelt, see "Debating the Past: The New Deal.") In the spring of 1935, partly in response to these growing attacks, Roosevelt launched an ambitious new program of legislation that has often been called the "Second New Deal."

THE CONSERVATIVE CRITICISM OF THE NEW DEAL

Despite his great popularity, Franklin Roosevelt had many conservative critics. Some of them detested him so bitterly that they would refuse to say his name—calling him "that man." Those critics included businessmen, financiers, wealthy families, and members of aristocratic society.

THE NEW DEAL

Contemporaries of Franklin Roosevelt debated the impact of the New Deal with ferocious intensity. Conservatives complained of a menacing tyranny of the state. Liberals celebrated the New Deal's progressive achievements. Some people on the left charged that the reforms of the 1930s were largely cosmetic and ignored the nation's fundamental problems. Although the conservative critique found relatively little scholarly expression until many years after Roosevelt's death, the liberal and left positions continued for decades to shape the way historians described the Roosevelt administration.

The dominant view from the beginning was an approving liberal interpretation, and its most important early voice was that of Arthur M. Schlesinger Jr. He argued in the three volumes of *The Age of Roosevelt* (1957–1960) that the New Deal marked a continuation of the long struggle between public power and private interests, a struggle Roosevelt had moved to a new level. Workers, farmers, consumers, and others now had much more protection than they had enjoyed in the past.

At almost the same time, however, other historians were offering more qualified assessments of the New Deal, although they remained securely within the liberal framework. Richard Hofstadter argued in 1955 that the New Deal gave American liberalism a "social-democratic tinge that had never before been present in American reform movements," but that its highly pragmatic approach lacked a central, guiding philosophy. James MacGregor Burns argued in 1956 that Roosevelt failed to make full use of his potential as a leader.

William Leuchtenburg's *Franklin D. Roosevelt and the New Deal* (1963) was the first systematic "revisionist" interpretation. Leuchtenburg challenged the views of earlier scholars who had proclaimed the New Deal a "revolution" in social policy. Leuchtenburg could muster only enough enthusiasm to call it a "halfway revolution," one that helped some previously disadvantaged groups (most notably farmers and workers) but that did little or nothing for many others (African Americans, sharecroppers, the urban poor).

Harsher criticisms soon emerged. Barton Bernstein in a 1968 essay concluded that the New Deal had saved capitalism, but at the expense of the least powerful. Ronald Radosh, Paul Conkin, and, later, Thomas Ferguson and Colin Gordon expanded on these criticisms. The New Deal, they contended, was part of the twentieth-century tradition of "corporate liberalism"—a tradition in which reform is closely wedded to the needs and interests of capitalism.

Most scholars in the 1980s and 1990s, however, seemed largely to have accepted the revised liberal view: that the New Deal was a significant and valuable chapter in the history of reform, but one that worked within rigid, occasionally crippling limits. Much of that work on the New Deal, therefore, focused on the constraints it faced. Some scholars (notably the sociologist Theda Skocpol) emphasized the issue of "state capacity"—the absence of a government bureaucracy with sufficient strength and expertise to shape or administer many programs. James T. Patterson, Barry Karl, Mark Leff, and others stressed the political constraints the New Deal encountered—the conservative inhibitions about government that remained strong in Congress and among the public. Frank Freidel, Ellis Hawley, Herbert Stein, and many others pointed as well to the ideological constraints affecting Franklin Roosevelt and his supporters—the limits of their own understanding of their time. Alan Brinkley, in *The End of Reform* (1995), described an ideological shift within New Deal liberalism that marginalized older concerns about wealth and monopoly power and replaced them with consumer-oriented Keynesianism. David Kennedy, in *Freedom from Fear* (1999), argued, by contrast, that the more aggressively anticapitalist measures of the early New Deal actually hampered recovery. Only when Roosevelt embraced the power of the market did prosperity begin to return.

The conservative attacks on the New Deal in the 2000s provided a newly powerful alternative view. A group of conservatives—among them Amity Schlaes and Burton Folsom—attacked the New Deal as a failure that created a vast bureaucracy and caused the Depression to last longer than it had to.

The phrase "New Deal liberalism" has come in the postwar era to seem synonymous with modern ideas of aggressive federal management of the economy, elaborate welfare systems, a powerful bureaucracy, and large-scale government spending. But many historians of the New Deal would argue that the modern idea of New Deal liberalism bears only a limited relationship to the ideas that New Dealers themselves embraced. •

UNDERSTAND, ANALYZE, & EVALUATE

1. How has the scholarly understanding of the New Deal changed over time?
2. Did the New Deal save capitalism? If so, how and why?

Roosevelt himself was among the most aristocratic presidents in American history. But he became the enemy of the very world that he came from. He was an alumnus of Harvard University, but the university president barely spoke to him when he went there to give a speech. He was, as many members of the American elite called him, a "traitor to his class." But even greater hatred came from conservative businessmen and financiers, who correctly accused New Dealers of imposing new regulations on the business and financial worlds. His critics were also infuriated by new taxes imposed by Roosevelt, even though high taxation reached only a few wealthy people.

The hatred of Roosevelt from conservatives took many forms. In 1935, a "whispering campaign" emerged from a New Deal effort to regulate the public utility industry. Stories circulated that the president was a drug addict, that he was insane, and that he was surrounded by psychiatrists at all times. Hamilton Fish Jr., a highly conservative member of Congress, said on the floor of the House of Representatives that "whom the gods would destroy, they make first mad."

Not all critics were as virulent in their hatred of the president. Walter Lippmann, a revered columnist, complained that Roosevelt was moving away from the nation's traditions. "We belong to a generation that has lost its way," he wrote. "Unable to develop the great truths which it inherited from the emancipators, it has returned to the heresies of absolutism, authority, and the domination of men by men." He added that the "enormous concentration of power in the hands of appointed officials . . . can lead only to waste, confusion, bureaucratic rigidity, and the loss of personal liberty." He charged that Roosevelt had become attracted to fascism and communism, instead of protecting the freedom of individuals.

Lewis Douglas, Roosevelt's first budget director, resigned in response to the president's determination to spend deficit funds to help provide relief to the unemployed. Al Smith, the former New York governor and twice the Democratic candidate, also turned against the president—partly because of jealousy, but also because he considered the New Deal much too far to the left. However, for the most part, the New Deal lacked a clear ideology and, instead, experimented in many ways, some that conservatives found offensive.

Conservative business leaders were the most committed leaders of the attack on the *Liberty League Established* New Deal. They formed a new organization called the Liberty League, led by the Du Pont family (owners of the nation's largest chemical company). Its goal was to arouse public opposition to what its members called the "dictatorial" policies of the New Deal and to what they considered its attacks on free enterprise. It was led by John Jacob Raskob (a former head of the Democratic National Committee, a former director of General Motors, and a trustee of Du Pont), who had abandoned the Democratic Party and joined the League. Within a year of its founding in 1934, there were more than 35,000 members of the League, reaching a peak of 125,000 in 1936. It also recruited college students from 345 institutions, gaining over 10,000 members. Many followers were northeastern industrialists. The League described itself as a "nonpartisan organization founded to defend the Constitution and defend the rights and liberties guaranteed by that Constitution." Its purpose was

> to teach the necessity of respect for the rights of persons and property as fundamental to every
> form of government . . . to teach the duty of government, to encourage and protect individual
> and group initiative and enterprise, to foster the right to work, earn, save and acquire property,
> and to preserve the ownership and lawful use of property when acquired.

The Liberty League attracted considerable attention, but it had relatively little impact on the New Deal. Its leaders tried to remain nonpartisan, even though its members were staunchly anti-Roosevelt. They became a target for the president's 1936 reelection campaign. Soon after Roosevelt's landslide victory, the League dissolved. Hatred of Roosevelt did not disappear, but there was little organized opposition after 1936.

THE POPULIST CRITICISM OF THE NEW DEAL

Roosevelt's critics on the far left also managed to produce alarm among some supporters of the administration. The Communist Party, the Socialist Party, and other radical and semiradical organizations were at times harshly critical of the New Deal. But like the conservatives, they failed to attract genuine mass support.

More menacing to the New Deal than either the far right or the far left was a group of dissident political movements that defied easy ideological classification. Some gained substantial public support within particular states and regions. And three men succeeded in mobilizing genuinely national followings. Dr. Francis E. Townsend, an elderly California physician, rose from obscurity to lead a movement of more than 5 million members with his plan for federal pensions for older adults. According to the Townsend *The Townsend Plan* Plan, all Americans over the age of sixty would receive monthly government pensions of $200, provided they retired (thus freeing jobs for younger, unemployed Americans) and spent the money in full each month (which would pump needed funds into the economy). By 1935, the Townsend Plan had attracted the support of many older men and women.

HUEY LONG Few public speakers could arouse a crowd more effectively than Huey Long of Louisiana, known to many as "the Kingfish" (a nickname borrowed from a scheming character on the popular radio show *Amos 'n' Andy*). It was Long's effective use of radio, however, that contributed most directly to his spreading national popularity in the early 1930s. (© Archive Photos/Getty Images)

Father Charles E. Coughlin, a Catholic priest in the Detroit suburb of Royal Oak, Michigan, achieved even greater renown through his weekly nationally *Father Charles Coughlin* broadcast radio sermons. He proposed a series of monetary reforms—remonetization of silver, issuing of greenbacks, and nationalization of the banking system—that he insisted would restore prosperity and ensure economic justice. At first a warm supporter of Roosevelt, Coughlin had become disheartened by late 1934 by what he claimed was the president's failure to deal harshly enough with the "money powers." In the spring of 1935, he established his own political organization, the National Union for Social Justice.

Most alarming to the administration was the growing national popularity of Senator Huey P. Long of Louisiana. Long had risen to power in his home state through his *Huey Long* strident attacks on the banks, oil companies, and utilities and on the conservative political oligarchy allied with them. Elected governor in 1928, he launched an assault on his opponents so thorough and forceful that they were soon left with virtually no political power. But he also maintained the overwhelming support of the Louisiana electorate, in part because of his flamboyant personality and in part because of his solid record of conventional progressive accomplishments: building roads, schools, and hospitals; revising the tax codes; distributing free textbooks; lowering utility rates. Barred by law from succeeding himself as governor, he ran in 1930 for a seat in the United States Senate and won easily.

Long, like Coughlin, supported Franklin Roosevelt for president in 1932. But within six months of Roosevelt's inauguration, Long had broken with the president. As an alternative to the New Deal, he advocated a drastic program of wealth redistribution, a program he ultimately named the Share-Our-Wealth Plan. The government, he claimed, could end the Depression easily by using the tax system to confiscate the surplus riches of the wealthiest men and women in America and distribute these surpluses to the rest of the population. That would, he claimed, allow the government to guarantee every family a minimum "homestead" of $5,000 and an annual wage of $2,500. In 1934, Long established his own national organization: the Share-Our-Wealth Society, which soon attracted a large following through much of the nation. A poll by the Democratic National Committee in the spring of 1935 disclosed that Long might attract more than 10 percent of the vote if he ran as a third-party candidate, possibly enough to tip a close election to the Republicans.

Members of the Roosevelt administration considered dissident movements—and the broad popular discontent they represented—a genuine threat. An increasing number of advisers were warning Roosevelt that he would have to do something dramatic to counter their strength.

THE "SECOND NEW DEAL"

Roosevelt launched the so-called Second New Deal in the spring of 1935 in response both to growing political pressures and to the continuing economic crisis. The new proposals represented a shift in the emphasis of New Deal policy. Perhaps the most conspicuous change was in the administration's attitude toward big business. Symbolically at least, the president was now willing to attack corporate interests openly. In March, for example, he proposed to Congress an act designed to break up the great utility holding companies. The Holding Company Act of 1935 was the result, although furious lobbying by the utilities led to amendments that sharply limited its effects.

Equally alarming to affluent Americans was a series of tax reforms proposed by the president in 1935. Apparently designed to undercut the appeal of Huey Long's Share-Our-Wealth Plan, the Roosevelt proposals called for establishing the highest and most progressive peacetime tax rates in history—although the actual impact of these rates was limited.

The Supreme Court decision in 1935 to strike down the National Industrial Recovery Act also invalidated Section 7(a) of the act, which had guaranteed workers the right to organize and bargain collectively. A group of progressives in Congress, led by Senator Robert E. Wagner of New York, introduced what became the National Labor Relations Act of 1935. The new law, popularly known as the Wagner Act, provided workers with a crucial enforcement mechanism missing from the 1933 law: the National Labor Relations *National Labor Relations Board* Board (NLRB), which would have power to compel employers to recognize and bargain with legitimate unions. The president was not entirely happy with the bill, but he signed it anyway. That was largely because American workers themselves had by 1935 become so important and vigorous a force that Roosevelt realized his own political future would depend in part on responding to their demands.

LABOR MILITANCY

The emergence of a powerful trade union movement in the 1930s occurred partly in response to government efforts to enhance the power of unions. It was also a result of the increased militancy of American workers after a lull during the 1920s. Business leaders

THE NEW DEAL · 599

and industrialists lost (at least temporarily) the ability to control government policies. Equally important, new and more powerful labor organizations emerged.

The American Federation of Labor (AFL) remained committed to the idea of the craft union: organizing workers on the basis of their skills. But that concept had little to offer unskilled laborers, who now constituted the bulk of the industrial workforce. During the 1930s, therefore, a newer concept of labor organization challenged the craft union ideal: industrial unionism. Advocates of this approach argued that all workers in a particular industry should be organized in a single union, regardless of what functions the workers performed. United in this way, workers would greatly increase their power.

Leaders of the AFL craft unions for the most part opposed the new concept. But industrial unionism found a number of important advocates, most prominent among them John L. Lewis, the leader of the United Mine Workers. At first, Lewis *John Lewis and the CIO* and his allies attempted to work within the AFL, but friction between the new industrial organizations Lewis was promoting and the older craft unions grew rapidly. At the 1935 AFL convention, Lewis became embroiled in a series of angry confrontations with craft union leaders before finally walking out. A few weeks later, he created the Committee on Industrial Organization. When the AFL expelled the new committee and all the industrial unions it represented, Lewis renamed the committee the Congress of Industrial Organizations (CIO) and became its first president.

The CIO expanded the constituency of the labor movement. It was more receptive to women and to African Americans than the AFL had been, in part because CIO organizing drives targeted previously unorganized industries (textiles, laundries, tobacco factories, and others) where women and minorities constituted much of the workforce. The CIO was also more militant than the AFL. By the time of the 1936 schism, it was already engaged in major organizing battles in the automobile and steel industries.

Organizing Battles

The United Auto Workers (UAW) gradually emerged preeminent in the early and mid-1930s. But although it was gaining recruits, it was making little progress in winning recognition from the corporations. In December 1936, however, autoworkers employed a controversial and effective new technique for challenging corporate opposition: the **sit-down strike.** Employees in several General Motors plants in Detroit simply sat down inside the plants, refusing either to work or to leave, thus preventing the company from using strikebreakers. The tactic spread to other locations, and by February 1937, strikers had occupied seventeen GM plants. The strikers ignored court orders and local police efforts to force them to vacate the buildings. When Michigan's governor refused to call up the National Guard to clear out the strikers, and when the federal government also refused to intervene on behalf of employers, General Motors relented. In February 1937, it became the first major manufacturer to recognize the UAW. Other automobile companies soon did the same.

In the steel industry, the battle for unionization was less easily won. In 1936, the Steel Workers Organizing Committee (SWOC), later the United Steelworkers of America, began a major organizing drive involving thousands of workers and frequent, at times bitter, strikes. In March 1937, to the surprise of almost everyone, United States Steel, the giant of the industry, recognized the union rather than risk a costly strike. But the smaller companies (known collectively as "Little Steel") were less accommodating. On Memorial Day 1937, a group of striking workers from Republic Steel gathered with their families

THE "MEMORIAL DAY MASSACRE" The bitterness of the labor struggles of the 1930s was nowhere more evident than in Chicago in 1937, when striking workers attempting to march on a Republic Steel plant were brutally attacked by Chicago police, who used clubs, tear gas, and guns to turn away the marchers. Ten strikers were killed and many others were injured. (© Carl Linde/AP Images)

for a picnic and demonstration in south Chicago. When they attempted to march peacefully (and legally) toward the steel plant, police opened fire on them. Ten demonstrators were killed; another ninety were wounded. Despite a public outcry against the "Memorial Day Massacre," the harsh tactics of Little Steel companies succeeded. The 1937 strike failed.

But the victory of Little Steel was among the last gasps of the kind of brutal strike-breaking that had proved so effective in the past. In 1937 alone, there were 4,720 strikes— *Rapid Union Growth* over 80 percent of them settled in favor of the unions. By the end of the year, more than 8 million workers were members of unions recognized as official bargaining units by employers (as compared with 3 million in 1932). By 1941, that number had expanded to 10 million and included the workers of Little Steel, whose employers had finally recognized the SWOC.

SOCIAL SECURITY

From the first moments of the New Deal, important members of the administration had been lobbying for a system of federally sponsored social insurance for elderly people and those who were unemployed—not just for humanitarian reasons, but also to keep those groups active in the nation's economy. In 1935, Roosevelt gave public support to what became the Social Security Act, which Congress passed the same year. It established several distinct programs. For older people, there were two types of assistance. Those who were presently destitute could receive up to $15 a month in federal assistance. More important for the future, many Americans presently working were incorporated into a pension system, to which they and their employers would contribute through a payroll tax; it would provide them with an income on retirement. Pension payments would provide only $10 to $85 a month to recipients. At first, payment was not to be distributed until 1942. But public pressure pushed the payment date back to 1937. Broad categories of workers (including domestic servants and agricultural laborers) were excluded from the program. But the act was a crucial first step in building the nation's most important social program for retired Americans.

In addition, the Social Security Act created a system of unemployment insurance, which employers alone would finance. It also established a system of federal aid to people with disabilities and a program of aid to dependent children.

The framers of the Social Security Act wanted to create a system of "insurance," not "welfare." And the largest programs (old-age pensions and unemployment insurance) were in many ways similar to private insurance programs. But the act also provided considerable direct assistance based on need—to low-income aging adults, to those with disabilities, to dependent children and their mothers. These groups were widely perceived to be small and genuinely unable to support themselves. But in later generations, the programs for these groups would expand until they assumed dimensions that the planners of Social Security had not foreseen.

New Directions in Relief

Social Security was designed primarily to fulfill long-range goals. But millions of unemployed Americans had immediate needs. To help them, the Roosevelt administration established in 1935 the Works Progress Administration (WPA). Like the Civil Works Administration and other earlier efforts, the WPA established a system of work relief for the unemployed. But it was much bigger than the earlier agencies.

Under the direction of Harry Hopkins, the WPA was responsible for building or renovating 110,000 public buildings and for constructing almost 600 *Harry Hopkins and the WPA* airports, more than 500,000 miles of roads, and over 100,000 bridges. In the process, the WPA kept an average of 2.1 million workers employed and pumped needed money into the economy.

The WPA also displayed remarkable flexibility and imagination. The Federal Writers' Project of the WPA, for example, gave unemployed writers a chance to do their work and receive a government salary. The Federal Art Project, similarly, helped painters, sculptors, and others continue their careers. The Federal Music Project and the Federal Theatre Project oversaw the production of concerts and plays, creating work for unemployed musicians, actors, and directors. Other relief agencies emerged alongside the WPA. The National Youth Administration (NYA) provided work and scholarship assistance to men and women of high school and college age. The Emergency Housing Division of the Public Works Administration began federal sponsorship of public housing.

The new welfare system dealt with men and women in very different ways. For men, the government concentrated mainly on work relief—on such programs as the CCC, the CWA, and the WPA. The principal government aid to women was not work relief but cash assistance—most notably through the Aid to Dependent Children program of Social Security, which was designed largely to assist single mothers. This disparity in treatment

WPA WORKERS ON THE JOB   The Works Progress Administration funded an enormous variety of work projects to provide jobs for unemployed individuals. The majority of WPA employees, however, worked on construction sites. (© Joseph Schwartz/Corbis)

reflected a widespread assumption that men should constitute the bulk of the paid work-force. Yet, millions of women were already employed by the 1930s.

THE 1936 "REFERENDUM"

By the middle of 1936—with the economy visibly reviving—there could be little doubt that Roosevelt would win a second term. The Republican Party nominated the moderate governor of Kansas, Alf M. Landon, who waged a relatively dull campaign. Roosevelt's dissident challengers now appeared powerless. One reason was the assassination of their most effective leader, Huey Long, in Louisiana in September 1935. Another reason was the ill-fated alliance among Father Coughlin, Dr. Townsend, and Gerald L. K. Smith (an intemperate henchman of Huey Long), who joined forces that summer to establish a new political movement—the Union Party, which nominated an undistinguished North Dakota congressman, William Lemke.

The result was the greatest landslide in American history to that point. Roosevelt polled just under 61 percent of the vote to Landon's 36 percent and carried every state except Maine and Vermont. The Democrats increased their already large majorities in both houses of Congress.

The election results demonstrated the party realignment that the New Deal had pro-duced. The Democrats now controlled a broad coalition of western and southern farmers, the urban working classes, the poor and unemployed, and white southerners, as well as traditional progressives and committed new liberals. New Deal aid flowing to black communities in northern cities helped pry that constituency from the Republican column. The resulting coalition constituted a substantial majority of the electorate. It would be decades before the Republican Party could again create a lasting majority coalition of its own.

THE NEW DEAL IN DISARRAY

Roosevelt emerged from the 1936 election at the zenith of his popularity. Within months, however, the New Deal was mired in serious new difficulties.

THE COURT FIGHT

The 1936 mandate, Franklin Roosevelt believed, made it possible for him to do something about the Supreme Court. No program of reform, he believed, could long survive the conservative justices, who had already struck down the NRA and the AAA.

In February 1937, Roosevelt sent a surprise message to Capitol Hill proposing an overhaul of the federal court system; included among the many provisions was one to add up to six new justices to the Supreme Court. The courts were "overworked," the president claimed, and needed additional manpower and younger blood to enable them to cope with their increasing burdens. But Roosevelt's real purpose was to give himself the opportunity to appoint new, liberal justices and change the ideological balance of the Court. (See "Consider the Source: Franklin D. Roosevelt Speaks on the Reorganization of the Judiciary.")

Conservatives were outraged at the "Court-packing plan," and even many Roosevelt supporters were disturbed by it. Still, Roosevelt might well *Reaction to "Court-Packing Plan"* have persuaded Congress to approve at least a compromise measure had not the Supreme Court itself intervened. Of the nine justices, three reliably supported the New Deal, and four reliably opposed it. Of the remaining two, Chief Justice Charles Evans Hughes often sided with the progressives, and Associate Justice Owen J. Roberts usually voted with the conservatives. On March 29, 1937, Roberts, Hughes, and the three progressive justices voted together to uphold a state minimum-wage law—in the case of *West Coast Hotel v. Parrish*—thus reversing a 5-to-4 decision of the previous year invalidating a similar law. Two weeks later, again by a 5-to-4 margin, the Court upheld the Wagner Act, and in May it validated the Social Security Act. Whatever the reasons for the decisions, the Court's newly moderate position made the Court-packing bill seem unnecessary. Congress ultimately defeated it.

On one level, Franklin Roosevelt had achieved a victory. The Court was no longer an obstacle to New Deal reforms. But the Court-packing episode did lasting political damage to the administration. From 1937 on, southern Democrats and other conservatives voted against Roosevelt's measures much more often than they had in the past.

RETRENCHMENT AND RECESSION

By the summer of 1937, the national income—which had dropped from $82 billion in 1929 to $40 billion in 1932—had risen to nearly $72 billion. Other economic indices also showed similar advances. Roosevelt seized on these improvements as a justification for trying to balance the federal budget. Between January and August 1937,

FRANKLIN D. ROOSEVELT SPEAKS ON THE REORGANIZATION OF THE JUDICIARY

Franklin D. Roosevelt made masterful use of the radio to explain his policies to the American people and win their support and affection. On Tuesday, March 9, 1937, he went on the air to defend his controversial proposal for reforming the courts. The president couched his appeal within a broader summary of the New Deal's accomplishments.

Tonight, sitting at my desk in the White House, I make my first radio report to the people in my second term of office.

I am reminded of that evening in March, four years ago, when I made my first radio report to you. We were then in the midst of the great banking crisis.

Soon after, with the authority of the Congress, we asked the Nation to turn over all of its privately held gold, dollar for dollar, to the Government of the United States.

Today's recovery proves how right that policy was. [. . .]

In 1933 you and I knew that we must never let our economic system get completely out of joint again—that we could not afford to take the risk of another great depression.

We also became convinced that the only way to avoid a repetition of those dark days was to have a government with power to prevent and to cure the abuses and the inequalities which had thrown that system out of joint.

We then began a program of remedying those abuses and inequalities—to give balance and stability to our economic system—to make it bomb-proof against the causes of 1929.

Today we are only part-way through that program—and recovery is speeding up to a point where the dangers of 1929 are again becoming possible, not this week or month perhaps, but within a year or two.

National laws are needed to complete that program. Individual or local or state effort alone cannot protect us in 1937 any better than ten years ago.

It will take time—and plenty of time—to work out our remedies administratively even after legislation is passed. To complete our program of protection in time, therefore, we cannot delay one moment in making certain that our National Government has power to carry through.

Four years ago action did not come until the eleventh hour. It was almost too late.

If we learned anything from the depression we will not allow ourselves to run around in new circles of futile discussion and debate, always postponing the day of decision.

The American people have learned from the depression. For in the last three national elections an overwhelming majority of them voted a mandate that the Congress and the President begin the task of providing that protection—not after long years of debate, but now.

The Courts, however, have cast doubts on the ability of the elected Congress to protect us against catastrophe by meeting squarely our modern social and economic conditions.

We are at a crisis in our ability to proceed with that protection. It is a quiet crisis. There are no lines of depositors outside closed banks. But to the far-sighted it is far-reaching in its possibilities of injury to America.

I want to talk with you very simply about the need for present action in this crisis—the need to meet the unanswered challenge of one-third of a Nation ill-nourished, ill-clad, ill-housed.

Last Thursday I described the American form of Government as a three horse team provided by the Constitution to the American people so that their field might be plowed. The three horses are, of course, the three branches of government—the Congress, the Executive and the Courts. Two of the horses are pulling in unison today; the third is not. Those who have intimated that the President of the United States is trying to drive that team, overlook the simple fact that the President, as Chief Executive, is himself one of the three horses.

It is the American people themselves who are in the driver's seat.

It is the American people themselves who want the furrow plowed.

It is the American people themselves who expect the third horse to pull in unison with the other two.

[. . .] [S]ince the rise of the modern movement for social and economic progress through legislation, the Court has more and more often and more and more boldly asserted a power to veto laws passed by the Congress and State Legislatures [. . .].

In the last four years the sound rule of giving statutes the benefit of all reasonable doubt has been cast aside. The Court has been acting not as a judicial body, but as a policy-making body.

When the Congress has sought to stabilize national agriculture, to improve the conditions of labor, to safeguard business against unfair competition, to protect our national resources, and in many other ways, to serve our clearly national needs, the majority of the Court has been assuming the power to pass on the wisdom of these acts of the Congress—and to approve or disapprove the public policy written into these laws. [. . .]

We have, therefore, reached the point as a nation where we must take action to save the Constitution from the Court and the Court from itself. We must find a way to take an appeal from the Supreme Court to the Constitution itself. We want a Supreme Court which will do justice under the Constitution and not over it. In our courts we want a government of laws and not of men.

[. . .] What is my proposal? It is simply this: whenever a Judge or Justice of any Federal Court has reached the age of seventy and does not avail himself of the opportunity to retire on a pension, a new member shall be appointed by the President then in office, with the approval, as required by the Constitution, of the Senate of the United States. [. . .]

Those opposing this plan have sought to arouse prejudice and fear by crying that I am seeking to "pack" the Supreme Court and that a baneful precedent will be established.

What do they mean by the words "packing the Court"?

UNDERSTAND, ANALYZE, & EVALUATE

1. According to President Roosevelt, what had been most important for economic reform and recovery? How did he assess this recovery?

2. How were the three branches of government supposed to work, in the president's view?

3. What criticism did the president level against the courts? What solution did he offer? Was this conflict between the executive branch and the United States Supreme Court unique to the New Deal?

Source: On the Reorganization of the Judiciary, Tuesday, March 9, 1937 [35:28] WH, Fireside Chats of Franklin D. Roosevelt, Franklin D. Roosevelt Presidential Library, Hyde Park, New York.

for example, he cut the WPA in half, laying off 1.5 million relief workers. A few weeks later, the fragile boom collapsed. The index of industrial production dropped from 117 in August 1937 to 76 in May 1938. Four million additional workers lost their jobs. Economic conditions were soon almost as bad as they had been in the bleak days of 1932–1933.

The recession of 1937, known to the president's critics as the "Roosevelt recession," *Sources of the "Roosevelt Recession"* was a result of many factors. But to many observers at the time, it seemed to be a direct result of the administration's unwise decision to reduce spending. And so in April 1938, the president asked Congress for an emergency appropriation of $5 billion for public works and relief programs, and government funds soon began pouring into the economy once again. Within a few months, another tentative recovery seemed to be under way.

At about the same time, Roosevelt sent a stinging message to Congress, vehemently denouncing what he called an "unjustifiable concentration of economic power" and asking for the creation of a commission to consider major reforms in the antitrust laws. In response, Congress established the Temporary National Economic Committee (TNEC), whose members included representatives of both houses of Congress and officials from several executive agencies. Later in 1938, the administration successfully supported one of its most ambitious pieces of labor legislation, the Fair Labor Standards Act, which for the first time established a national minimum wage and a forty-hour workweek and which also placed strict limits on child labor.

Despite these achievements, however, by the end of 1938 the New Deal had essentially *End of the New Deal* come to an end. Congressional opposition now made it difficult for the president to enact any major new programs. But more important, perhaps, the threat of world crisis hung heavy in the political atmosphere, and Roosevelt was gradually growing more concerned with persuading a reluctant nation to prepare for war than with pursuing new avenues of reform.

LIMITS AND LEGACIES OF THE NEW DEAL

The New Deal made major changes in American government, some of them still controversial today. It also left important problems unaddressed.

AFRICAN AMERICANS AND THE NEW DEAL

The New Deal was not hostile to black aspirations. Eleanor Roosevelt spoke throughout the 1930s on behalf of racial justice and put continuing pressure on her husband and others in the federal government to ease discrimination against blacks. The president himself appointed a number of African Americans to significant second-level positions in his administration, creating an informal network of officeholders that became known *The "Black Cabinet"* as the "Black Cabinet." Eleanor Roosevelt, Interior Secretary Harold Ickes, and WPA Director Harry Hopkins all made efforts to ensure that New Deal relief programs did not exclude blacks. By 1935 an estimated 30 percent of all African Americans were receiving some form of government assistance, even amid persistent racial discrimination against people of color by the administrators of aid. One result was a historic change in black electoral behavior. As late as 1932, most American blacks were voting Republican, as they had been doing since the Civil War. By 1936, more than 90 percent were voting Democratic.

African Americans supported Franklin Roosevelt, but they had few illusions that the New Deal represented a major turning point in American race relations. The president was, for example, never willing to risk losing the support of southern Democrats by supporting legislation to make lynching a federal crime or to ban the poll tax, one of the most potent tools by which white southerners kept blacks from voting.

New Deal relief agencies did not challenge, and indeed reinforced, existing patterns of discrimination. The CCC established separate black camps. The NRA codes tolerated paying blacks less than whites doing the same jobs. The WPA routinely relegated African Americans and Hispanic workers to the least-skilled and lowest-paying jobs; when funding ebbed, African Americans, like women, were among the first *Discrimination Reinforced* to be dismissed.

The New Deal was not hostile to African Americans, and it made some contributions to their progress. But it never made racial justice a significant part of its agenda.

THE NEW DEAL AND THE "INDIAN PROBLEM"

New Deal policy toward the Indian tribes marked a significant break from earlier approaches, largely because of the efforts of the extraordinary commissioner of Indian affairs, John Collier. Collier was greatly influenced by the work of twentieth-century anthropologists who advanced the idea of cultural relativism—the theory that every culture should be accepted and respected on its own terms.

Collier wanted to reverse the pressures on Native Americans to assimilate and instead allow them to remain Indians. He effectively promoted legislation—which became the Indian Reorganization Act of 1934—that restored to *John Collier's Advocacy* the tribes the right to own land collectively and to elect tribal governments. In the thirteen years after passage of the 1934 bill, tribal land increased by nearly 4 million acres, and Indian agricultural income increased from under $2 million in 1934 to over $49 million in 1947. Even with the redistribution of lands under the 1934 act, however, Indians continued to possess, for the most part, only territory whites did not want—much of it arid, some of it desert. And as a group, they continued to constitute the poorest segment of the population.

WOMEN AND THE NEW DEAL

Symbolically at least, the New Deal marked a breakthrough in the role of women in public life. Roosevelt appointed the first female member of the cabinet in the nation's history: Secretary of Labor Frances Perkins. He also named more than 100 *Frances Perkins* other women to positions at lower levels of the federal bureaucracy. But the administration was concerned not so much about achieving gender equality as about obtaining special protections for women.

The New Deal generally supported the widespread belief that in hard times women should withdraw from the workplace to open up more jobs for men. New Deal relief agencies offered relatively little employment for women. The Social Security program excluded domestic servants, waitresses, and other predominantly female occupations.

Repeating its handling of racial justice, the New Deal was not actively hostile to feminist aspirations, but it accepted prevailing cultural norms. There was not yet sufficient political pressure from women themselves to persuade the administration to do otherwise. Indeed, some of the most important supporters of policies that reinforced traditional gender roles (such as Social Security) were themselves women.

ELEANOR ROOSEVELT   First Lady Eleanor Roosevelt was among the first women to play an important role in politics and government. She oversaw Franklin Roosevelt's political campaigns before he became president as well as developing an important career of her own working on social programs in New York. When she moved to the White House, she championed human rights issues. In this photograph she is on the way to inspect a Washington, D.C., jail that had a reputation for being overcrowded and obsolete. (© Underwood & Underwood/Corbis)

THE NEW DEAL AND THE WEST

One part of American society that did receive special attention from the New Deal was the American West. The West received more government funds per capita through relief programs than any other region.

Except for the TVA, the largest New Deal public works programs—the great dams and power stations—were mainly in the West, both because the best locations for such facilities were there and because the West had the greatest need for new sources of water and power. The Grand Coulee Dam on the Columbia River was the largest public works project in American history to that point, and it provided cheap electric power for much of the Northwest. Its construction, and that of other, smaller dams and water projects, created a basis for economic development in the region. Without this enormous public investment by the federal government, much of the economic growth that transformed the West after World War II would have been much more difficult, if not impossible, to achieve.

THE NEW DEAL, THE ECONOMY, AND POLITICS

The most frequent criticisms of the New Deal involve its failure to revive or reform the American economy. New Dealers never fully recognized the value of government spending as a vehicle for recovery. The economic boom sparked by World War II—not the New Deal—finally ended the crisis.

Nevertheless, the New Deal did have a number of important and lasting effects on the American economy. It helped elevate new groups—workers and farmers in particular—to positions from which they could at times challenge the power of the corporations. It increased the regulatory functions of the federal government in ways that helped stabilize previously troubled areas of the economy: the stock market, the banking system, and others. And the administration helped establish the basis for new forms of federal fiscal policy, which in the postwar years would give the government tools for promoting and regulating economic growth.

The New Deal also created the rudiments of the American welfare state through its many relief programs and, above all, through the Social Security system. The conservative inhibitions New Dealers brought to this task ensured that the welfare system that ultimately emerged would be limited in its impact, would reinforce some traditional patterns of gender and racial discrimination, and would be expensive and cumbersome to administer. But for all its limits, the new system marked a historic break with the nation's traditional reluctance to offer public assistance to its neediest citizens.

Finally, the New Deal had a dramatic effect on the character of American politics. It took a weak and divided Democratic Party, which had been a minority force in American politics for many decades, and turned it into a mighty coalition that would dominate national party competition for more than thirty years. It turned the attention of many voters away from some of the controversial cultural issues that had preoccupied them in the 1920s and awakened an interest in economic matters of direct importance to the lives of citizens.

CONCLUSION

From the time of Franklin Roosevelt's inauguration in 1933 to the beginning of World War II eight years later, the federal government engaged in a broad and diverse series of experiments designed to relieve the distress of unemployment and poverty; to reform the economy to prevent future crises; and to bring the Great Depression itself to an end. It had only partial success in all those efforts.

Unemployment and poverty remained high throughout the New Deal, although many federal programs provided assistance to millions of people who would otherwise have had none. The structure of the American economy remained essentially the same as it had been in earlier years, although there were by the end of the New Deal some important new regulatory agencies in Washington—and an important new role for organized labor. The New Deal failed to end the Great Depression. But some of its policies kept the Depression from getting worse; others helped alleviate the suffering of people caught in its grip; and still others pointed the way toward more effective economic policies in the future.

Perhaps the most important legacy of the New Deal was to create a sense of possibilities among many Americans. The New Deal persuaded many citizens that the fortunes of individuals need not be left entirely to chance or to the workings of an unregulated market. Many Americans, Republicans and Democrats alike, emerged from the 1930s convinced that individuals deserved some protections from the unpredictability and instability of the modern economy. The New Deal—for all its limitations—had demonstrated the value of enlisting government in the effort to provide those protections.

KEY TERMS/PEOPLE/PLACES/EVENTS

Agricultural Adjustment
  Administration (AAA) 590
Charles E. Coughlin 597
Civilian Conservation
  Corps (CCC) 593
Congress of Industrial
  Organizations (CIO) 599
Court-packing plan 603
Eleanor Roosevelt 606
Farm Security
  Administration 590
Federal Deposit Insurance
  Corporation (FDIC) 589

fireside chats 588
Frances Perkins 607
Harry P. Hopkins 601
Huey Long 597
John Collier 607
John L. Lewis 599
Liberty League 596
National Labor Relations
  Board (NLRB) 598
National Recovery
  Administration (NRA) 590
New Deal 594
Second New Deal 598

Securities and Exchange
  Commission (SEC) 589
sit-down strike 599
Social Security Act 600
Tennessee Valley Authority
  (TVA) 591
Townsend Plan 596
Works Progress
  Administration (WPA) 601

RECALL AND REFLECT

1. What New Deal programs were aimed at agricultural and industrial recovery, and what was the effect of the programs in both areas?
2. What criticisms did critics on both the right and the left level at the New Deal? How did FDR and his administration respond to these criticisms?
3. What gains did organized labor make during the 1930s?
4. What was the impact of the New Deal on women?

25 THE GLOBAL CRISIS, 1921–1941

THE DIPLOMACY OF THE NEW ERA
ISOLATIONISM AND INTERNATIONALISM
FROM NEUTRALITY TO INTERVENTION

LOOKING AHEAD

1. What are some of the views that Americans expressed as the world crises of the 1930s expanded?
2. How did the economic crisis of the worldwide Great Depression help create new political orders in many nations?
3. What was the sequence of events between 1939 and 1941 that brought the United States into military involvement in World War II?

HENRY CABOT LODGE OF MASSACHUSETTS, Republican chair of the Senate Foreign Relations Committee, led the fight that defeated ratification of the Treaty of Versailles in 1919 and 1920. As a result, the United States declined to join the League of Nations. American foreign policy embarked instead on an independent course that for the next two decades would attempt, but ultimately fail, to expand American influence in the world without committing the United States to any lasting relationships with other nations.

Lodge was not an isolationist. He believed the United States should exert its influence internationally. But he believed, too, that the United States should remain unfettered by obligations to anyone else. He said in 1919:

> We are a great moral asset of Christian civilization.... How did we get there? By our own efforts. Nobody led us, nobody guided us, nobody controlled us.... I would keep America as she has been—not isolated, not prevent her from joining other nations for ... great purposes—but I wish her to be master of her own fate.

In the end, the limited American internationalism of the interwar years proved insufficient to protect the interests of the United States, to create global stability, or to keep the nation from becoming involved in the most catastrophic war in human history.

1924

Dawes Plan

1928

Kellogg-Briand Pact

1931

Japan invades
Manchuria

1933

U.S. recognizes
Soviet Union

Good Neighbor Policy

1937

Roosevelt's
"quarantine" speech

1938

Munich Conference

1939

Nazi–Soviet
nonaggression pact

Germany invades
Poland

1940

Tripartite Pact

America First
Committee founded

Roosevelt reelected

Destroyers-for-bases
deal

1941

Lend-lease plan

Atlantic Charter

Japan attacks Pearl
Harbor

U.S. enters
World War II

THE DIPLOMACY OF THE NEW ERA

Critics in the 1920s often described American foreign policy with a single word: *isolationism*. But in reality, the United States played a more active role in world affairs in the 1920s than it had at almost any previous time in its history.

REPLACING THE LEAGUE

By the time the Harding administration took office in 1921, American membership in the League of Nations was no longer a realistic possibility. But Secretary of State Charles Evans Hughes wanted to find a replacement for the League as a guarantor of world peace and stability.

The most important effort was the Washington Conference of 1921—an attempt to prevent a destabilizing naval armaments race among the United States, Britain, and Japan. Hughes proposed a plan for dramatic reductions in the fleets of all three nations and a ten-year moratorium on the construction of large warships. To the surprise of almost everyone, the conference ultimately agreed to accept most of Hughes's terms. The Five-Power Pact of February 1922 established limits for total naval tonnage and a ratio of armaments among the signatories. For every 5 tons of American and British warships, Japan would maintain 3 and France and Italy 1.75 each.

When the French foreign minister, Aristide Briand, asked the United States in 1927 to join an alliance against Germany, Secretary of State Frank Kellogg (who had replaced Hughes in 1925) proposed instead a multilateral treaty outlawing war as an instrument of national policy. Fourteen nations signed the agreement in Paris on August 27, 1928, amid wide international acclaim. Forty-eight other nations later joined the Kellogg-Briand Pact. It contained no instruments of enforcement.

DEBTS AND DIPLOMACY

The first responsibility of diplomacy, Hughes, Kellogg, and others agreed, was to ensure that American overseas trade faced no obstacles. The Allied powers of Europe were struggling to repay $11 billion in loans they had contracted with the United States during and shortly after the war. At the same time, Germany was attempting to pay the reparations levied by the Allies. The United States stepped in with a solution.

Charles G. Dawes, an American banker who became vice president under Coolidge in 1925, negotiated an agreement in 1924 among France, Britain, Germany, and the United States. Under the Dawes Plan, American banks would provide enormous   *The Dawes Plan* loans to Germany, which would use that money to pay reparations to France and Britain; Britain and France would agree to reduce the amount of those payments and, in turn, use those funds (as well as the large loans they themselves were receiving from American banks) to repay war debts to the United States. One historian said of this circular plan, "It would have made equal sense for the U.S. to have taken the money out of one drawer in the Treasury and put it into another." The flow of funds was able to continue only by virtue of the enormous debts the European nations were acquiring to American banks and corporations. The American economic involvement in Europe continued to expand until the worldwide depression shattered the system in 1931.

During the 1920s, American military forces maintained a presence in Nicaragua, Panama, and several other countries in the region, while United States investments in Latin America more than doubled. American banks offered large loans to Latin American governments, just as in Europe; and as with the Europeans, the Latin Americans had difficulty earning the money to repay them in the face of the formidable United States tariff barrier.

HOOVER AND THE WORLD CRISIS

By 1931, the world financial crisis had produced a rising nationalism in Europe and Japan. It soon toppled some existing political leaders and replaced them with powerful, belligerent governments committed to expansion. Herbert Hoover thus confronted the beginning of a process that would ultimately lead to war.

In Latin America, Hoover tried to repair some of the damage done by earlier American policies. He made a ten-week goodwill tour through Latin America before his inauguration. Once in office, he generally abstained from intervening in the internal affairs of neighboring nations and moved to withdraw American troops from Nicaragua and Haiti. He also announced a new policy: America would grant diplomatic recognition to any sitting government in the region without questioning the means it had used to obtain power. He even repudiated the Theodore Roosevelt Corollary to the Monroe Doctrine by refusing to permit American intervention when several Latin American countries defaulted on debt obligations in October 1931.

In Europe, the administration enjoyed few successes. When Hoover's proposed moratorium on debts failed to produce financial stability, he refused to cancel all war debts to the United States as many economists advised him to do. Several European nations promptly went into default. Efforts to extend the 1921 limits on naval construction fell victim to French and British fears of German and Japanese militarism.

The ineffectiveness of American diplomacy in Europe was particularly troubling in light of the rise of **fascism,** an ideology that rejected democratic forms of government in favor of concentrated state power under a dictator. Benito Mussolini's Fascist Party had

THE SINO-JAPANESE WAR, 1931–1941

Long before Pearl Harbor, well before war broke out in Europe in 1939, the first shots of what would become World War II had been fired in the Pacific in a conflict between Japan and China.

Having lived in almost complete isolation from the world until the nineteenth century, Japan emerged from World War I as one of the world's great powers, with a proud and powerful military and growing global trade. But the Great Depression created severe economic problems for the Japanese; and as in other parts of the world, the crisis strengthened the political influence of highly nationalistic armed forces. Out of the Japanese military emerged dreams of a new empire in the Pacific. Such an empire would, its proponents believed, give the nation access to fuel, raw material, markets for its industries, as well as land for its agricultural needs and its rapidly increasing population. Such an empire, they also argued, would free Asia from its exploitation by Europe and America and would create a "new world order based on moral principles."

During World War I, Japan had taken territory and economic concessions from China and had created a particularly strong presence in the northern Chinese region of Manchuria. There, in September 1931, a group of young, militant army officers seized on a railway explosion to justify a military campaign through which they conquered the entire province. Both the United States government and the League of Nations demanded that Japan evacuate Manchuria. The Japanese ignored them and for the next six years consolidated its control over the new territory.

On July 7, 1937, Japan began a wider war when it attacked Chinese troops at the Marco Polo Bridge outside Beijing. Over the next few weeks, Japanese forces overran a large part of southern China, including most of the port cities, killing many Chinese soldiers and civilians in the process. Particularly notorious was the Japanese annihilation of many thousands of civilians in the city of Nanjing (the number has long been in dispute, but estimates range from 80,000 to over 300,000) in an event that became known in China and the West as the "Rape of Nanjing," or the Nanjing Massacre. The Chinese government fled to the mountains. As in 1931, the United States and the League of Nations protested in vain.

China was a nation in turmoil. It was engaged in a civil war of its own—between the so-called Kuomintang, a nationalist party led by Chiang Kai-shek, and the Chinese Communist Party, led by Mao Zedong; and this internal struggle weakened China's capacity to resist. But beginning in 1937, the two rivals agreed to an uneasy truce and began fighting the Japanese together, with some success—bogging the Japanese military down in a seemingly endless war and imposing great hardships on the Japanese people at home. The Japanese government and military, however, remained determined to continue the war against China, whatever the sacrifices.

One result of the costs of the war in China was a growing Japanese dependence on the United States for steel and oil to meet civilian and military needs. In July 1941, in an effort to pressure the Japanese to stop their expansion, the Roosevelt administration made it impossible for the

Japanese to continue buying American oil. Japan now faced a choice between ending its war in China or finding other sources of fuel to keep its war effort (and its civilian economy) going. Japan chose to extend the war beyond China in a search for oil. The best available sources were in the Dutch East Indies. But the only way to secure that European colony, the Japanese believed, would be to neutralize the increasingly hostile United States in Asia. Visionary military planners in Japan began advocating a daring move to immobilize the Americans in the Pacific before expanding the war elsewhere—with an attack on the American naval base at Pearl Harbor. The first blow of World War II in America, therefore, was the culmination of more than a decade of Japanese efforts to conquer China. •

UNDERSTAND, ANALYZE, & EVALUATE

1. What were the goals of the Japanese militarists in the 1930s that led to the attacks on China?
2. Why was China unable to stop Japanese aggression in the 1930s?

been in control of Italy since the early 1920s and had become increasingly nationalistic and militaristic. Still more ominous was the growing power of the National Socialist (or Nazi) Party in Germany. By the late 1920s, the Weimar *Hitler and Mussolini in Europe* Republic, the nation's government since the end of World War I, had been largely discredited by, among other things, a ruinous inflation. Adolf Hitler, the leader of the Nazis, grew rapidly in popular favor and took power in 1933. He believed in, among other things, the genetic superiority of the Aryan (German) people and in extending German territory to provide *Lebensraum* (living space) for what he called the German "master race." He displayed a pathological anti-Semitism and a passionate militarism.

More immediately alarming to the Hoover administration was a major crisis in Asia—another early step toward World War II. The Japanese, suffering from an economic depression of their own, were concerned about the increasing power of the Soviet Union and

HITLER AND MUSSOLINI IN BERLIN   The German and Italian dictators (shown here reviewing Nazi troops in Berlin in the mid-1930s) acted publicly as if they were equals. Privately, Hitler treated Mussolini with contempt, and Mussolini complained constantly of being a junior partner in the relationship. (© Instituto Nazionale Luce/ Alinari/Getty Images)

THE SPANISH CIVIL WAR   Many Americans took up arms to help the republican forces fight against Franco and his army. The novelist Ernest Hemingway joined them in Spain as a reporter (and supporter of the republicans), and he spent much of his time talking with both American and Spanish troops. His novel *For Whom the Bell Tolls* was inspired by his experience in the civil war.   (Robert Capa/© International Center of Photography/Magnum Photos)

sailed the Yangtze River in China. But so reluctant was the Roosevelt administration to antagonize the isolationists that the United States eagerly seized on Japanese claims that the bombing had been an accident, accepted Japan's apologies, and overlooked the attack.

THE FAILURE OF MUNICH

In 1936, Hitler had moved the revived German army into the Rhineland, rearming an area that had been off-limits to German troops since World War I. In March 1938, German forces marched without opposition into Austria, and Hitler proclaimed a union (or *Anschluss*) between Austria, his native land, and Germany, his adopted one. Neither in America nor in most of Europe was there much more than a murmur of opposition.

Germany had by now occupied territory surrounding three sides of western Czechoslovakia, a region Hitler dreamed of annexing. In September 1938, he demanded that Czechoslovakia cede him the Sudetenland, a part of Czechoslovakia in which many ethnic Germans lived. Although Czechoslovakia was prepared to fight to stop Hitler, it needed assistance from other nations. But most Western governments, including the United States, were willing to pay almost any price to settle the crisis peacefully. On September 29, Hitler met with the leaders of France and Great Britain at Munich in an effort to resolve the crisis. The French and British agreed to accept the German demands in Czechoslovakia in return for Hitler's promise to expand no farther. Americans watched these events nervously—and the fear of war became a fixture of domestic thought and culture. (See "Patterns of Popular Culture: Orson Welles and the 'War of the Worlds.'")

The Munich agreement, which Roosevelt supported at the time, was the most prominent element of a policy that came to be known as **appeasement** and that came to be identified (not altogether fairly) with British prime minister Neville Chamberlain. Whoever was to blame, the policy was a failure. In March 1939, Hitler occupied the remaining areas of Czechoslovakia, violating the Munich agreement unashamedly. And in April, he began issuing threats against Poland.

At that point, both Britain and France assured the Polish government that they would come to its assistance in case of an invasion; they even tried, too late, to draw the Soviet Union into a mutual defense agreement. But the Soviet leader Josef Stalin, who had not even been invited to the Munich Conference, had decided he could expect no protection from the West. He signed a nonaggression pact with Hitler in August 1939, freeing the Germans, for a while, from the danger of a two-front war. Shortly after that, Hitler staged an incident on the Polish border to allow him to claim that Germany had been attacked, and on September 1, 1939, he launched a full-scale invasion of Poland.   *Invasion of Poland* Britain and France, true to their pledges, declared war on Germany two days later. World War II, already under way in Asia, had begun in Europe.

FROM NEUTRALITY TO INTERVENTION

"This nation will remain a neutral nation," the president declared shortly after the hostilities began in Europe, "but I cannot ask that every American remain neutral in thought as well." There was never any question that both he and the majority of the American people favored Britain, France, and the other Allied nations in the contest. The question was how much the United States was prepared to do to assist them.

NEUTRALITY TESTED

At the very least, Roosevelt believed, the United States should make armaments available to the Allied armies to counter the military advantage the large German munitions industry gave Hitler. In September 1939, he asked Congress to revise the Neutrality Acts and lift the arms embargo against any nation engaged in war. Congress maintained the prohibition on American ships entering war zones. But the 1939 law did permit belligerents to purchase arms on the same cash-and-carry basis that the earlier Neutrality Acts had established for the sale of nonmilitary materials.

After the German armies quickly subdued Poland, the war in Europe settled into a long, quiet lull that lasted through the winter and spring—a "phony war," some called it. But in the spring of 1940, Germany launched a massive invasion, known as the "blitzkrieg" (lightning war), to the west—first attacking Denmark and Norway, sweeping   *The Blitzkrieg* next across the Netherlands and Belgium, and driving finally deep into the heart of France. On June 10, Mussolini invaded France from the south as Hitler was attacking from the north. On June 22, France fell, and Nazi troops marched into Paris. A new French regime assembled in Vichy, largely controlled by the German occupiers; and   *Vichy Regime in France* in all of Europe, only the shattered remnants of the British and French armies—daringly rescued from the beaches of Dunkirk by a hastily organized armada of English boats, trawlers, and yachts—remained to oppose the Axis forces.

26 AMERICA IN A WORLD AT WAR

WAR ON TWO FRONTS
THE AMERICAN ECONOMY IN WARTIME
RACE AND ETHNICITY IN WARTIME AMERICA
ANXIETY AND AFFLUENCE IN WARTIME CULTURE
THE DEFEAT OF THE AXIS

LOOKING AHEAD

1. What was the impact of the war on the U.S. economy?
2. How was the military experience of the United States in World War II different in Europe and the Pacific?
3. How did the war affect life on the home front, especially for women, organized labor, and minorities?

THE ATTACK ON PEARL HARBOR thrust the United States into the greatest and most terrible war in the history of humanity, a war that changed the world as dramatically as any event of the twentieth century. World War II also transformed the United States in profound, if not always readily visible, ways. The war forced the American people to accept an unprecedented level of government control over their everyday lives. It transformed the roles of many women, reshaped the nation's industrial landscape, and thrust the United States into a position of global leadership that it has maintained ever since.

WAR ON TWO FRONTS

Whatever political disagreements and social tensions there may have been among the American people during World War II, there was striking unity of opinion about the conflict itself. But both unity and confidence faced severe tests in the first, troubled months of 1942.

CONTAINING THE JAPANESE

Ten hours after the strike at Pearl Harbor, Japanese airplanes attacked the American airfields at Manila in the Philippines, destroying much of America's remaining air power in the Pacific. Three days later, Guam, an American possession, fell. Wake Island and Hong Kong followed. The great British fortress of Singapore in Malaya surrendered in February 1942, the Dutch East Indies in March, and Burma in April. In the Philippines, exhausted Filipino and American troops gave up their defense of the islands on May 6. (The American commander, General Douglas MacArthur, vowed as he left, "I shall return.")

American strategists planned two broad offensives to turn the tide against the Japanese. One, under the command of MacArthur, would move north from Australia, through New Guinea, and eventually to the Philippines. The other, under Admiral Chester Nimitz, would move west from Hawaii toward major Japanese island outposts in the central Pacific. Ultimately, strategists predicted, the two offensives would come together to invade Japan itself.

The Allies achieved their first important victory in the Battle of the Coral Sea, just northeast of Australia, on May 7–8, 1942, when American forces turned back the previously unstoppable Japanese navy. An even more important turning point occurred a month later northwest of Hawaii, near the small American outpost at Midway Island. There, after an enormous four-day battle (June 3–6, 1942), the American navy, despite

TIME LINE

1942
Battle of Midway
Campaign in North Africa
Japanese Americans interned
Manhattan Project begins
CORE founded

1943
Americans capture Guadalcanal
Allied invasion of Italy
Soviet victory at Stalingrad

1944
Allies invade Normandy
Roosevelt reelected
Americans capture Philippines

1945
Roosevelt dies; Truman becomes president
Germany surrenders
U.S. drops atomic bombs on Hiroshima, Nagasaki
Japan surrenders

terrible losses, regained control of the central Pacific. The United States destroyed four Japanese aircraft carriers without losing one of its own.

The Americans took the offensive several months later in the southern Solomon Islands, to the east of New Guinea. In August 1942, American forces assaulted three of the islands: Gavutu, *Guadalcanal*   Tulagi, and Guadalcanal. A struggle of terrible ferocity continued at Guadalcanal for six months, inflicting heavy losses on both sides. In the end, however, the Japanese were forced to abandon the island—and with it their last chance of launching an effective offensive to the south. The Americans, with aid from the Australians and the New Zealanders, now began the slow, arduous process of moving toward the Philippines and Japan itself.

HOLDING OFF THE GERMANS

In the European war, the United States fought in cooperation with, among others, Britain and the exiled "Free French" forces in the west, and tried also to conciliate its new ally, the Soviet Union, which was now fighting Hitler in the east. The army chief of staff, General George C. Marshall, supported a plan for a major Allied invasion of France across the English Channel in the spring of 1943, and he placed a previously little-known general, *Dwight Eisenhower*   Dwight D. Eisenhower, in charge of planning the operation. The Soviet Union, which was absorbing the brunt of the German war effort, wanted the Allied invasion

WORLD WAR II IN NORTH AFRICA AND ITALY: THE ALLIED COUNTEROFFENSIVE, 1942-1943   The United States and Great Britain understood from the beginning that an invasion of France across the English Channel would eventually be necessary for a victory in the European war. In the meantime, however, they began a campaign against Axis forces in North Africa, and in the spring of 1943 they began an invasion across the Mediterranean into Italy. This map shows the points along the coast of North Africa where Allied forces landed in 1942—with American forces moving east from Morocco and Algeria and British forces moving west from Egypt. The two armies met in Tunisia and moved into Italy from there. • *Why were America and Britain reluctant to launch the cross-channel invasion in 1942 or 1943?*

to begin at the earliest possible moment. But the British wanted first to launch a series of Allied offensives around the edges of the Nazi empire—in northern Africa and southern Europe—before undertaking the invasion of France.

Roosevelt ultimately decided to support the British plan—in part because he was eager to get American forces into combat quickly and knew that a cross-channel invasion would take a long time to prepare. At the end of October 1942, the British opened a counter-offensive against General Erwin Rommel and the Nazi forces in northern Africa who were threatening the Suez Canal. In a major battle at El Alamein, they forced the Germans to retreat from Egypt. In early November, Anglo-American forces landed at Oran and Algiers in Algeria and at Casablanca in Morocco—areas under the Nazi-controlled French government at Vichy—and began moving east toward Rommel. The Germans threw the full weight of their forces in Africa against the inexperienced Americans and inflicted a serious defeat on them at the Kasserine Pass in Tunisia. General George S. Patton, however, regrouped and began an effective counteroffensive. With the help of Allied air and naval power and of British forces attacking from the east under Field Marshall Bernard Montgomery (the hero of El Alamein), the American offensive finally drove the last Germans from Africa in May 1943.

The North African campaign had tied up a large proportion of Allied resources, postponing the planned May 1943 cross-channel invasion of France, despite *Battle of Stalingrad* angry complaints from the Soviet Union. By now, however, the threat of a Soviet collapse seemed much diminished, for during the winter of 1942–1943, the Red Army had successfully held off a major German assault at Stalingrad in southern Russia. Hitler had committed such enormous forces to the battle, and had suffered such appalling losses, that he could not continue his eastern offensive.

The Soviet successes persuaded Roosevelt to agree, in a January 1943 meeting with Churchill in Casablanca, to a British plan for an Allied invasion of Sicily. Churchill argued that the operation in Sicily might knock Italy out of the war and tie up German divisions that would otherwise be stationed in France. On the night of July 9–10, 1943, American and British armies landed in southeastern Sicily; thirty-eight days later, they had conquered the island and were moving onto the Italian mainland. In the face of these setbacks, Mussolini's government collapsed *Italy Invaded* and the dictator himself fled north toward Germany. (He was later captured by Italian insurgents and hanged.) Mussolini's successor, Pietro Badoglio, quickly committed Italy to the Allies. Germany moved eight divisions into Italy and established a powerful defensive line south of Rome. The Allied offensive, which began on September 3, 1943, got bogged down at that line. Not until May 1944 did the Allies break through the German defenses to resume their northward advance. On June 4, 1944, they captured Rome.

The invasion of Italy delayed the invasion of France by as much as a year, deeply embittering Stalin but also giving the Soviets time to begin moving toward the countries of eastern Europe.

AMERICA AND THE HOLOCAUST

In the midst of this intensive fighting, the leaders of the American government confronted one of history's great tragedies: the Nazi campaign to exterminate the Jews of Europe, which became known as the Holocaust. As early as 1942, high officials in Washington had incontrovertible evidence that Hitler's forces were rounding up Jews and others

THE ST. LOUIS Many people consider the fate of the German liner *St. Louis* to be a powerful symbol of the indifference of the United States and other nations to the fate of European Jews during the Holocaust, even though its forlorn journey preceded both the beginning of World War II and the beginning of systematic extermination of Jews by the Nazi regime. The *St. Louis* carried a group of over 900 Jews fleeing from Germany in 1939, carrying exit visas of dubious legality cynically sold to them by members of Hitler's Gestapo. It became a ship without a port as it sailed from country to country—Mexico, Paraguay, Argentina, Costa Rica, and Cuba—where its passengers were refused entry time and again. Most of the passengers were hoping for a haven in the United States, but the American State Department refused to allow the ship even to dock as it sailed up the American eastern seaboard. Eventually, the *St. Louis* returned to Europe and distributed its passengers among Britain, France, Holland, and Belgium (where this photograph was taken, showing refugees smiling and waving as they prepared to disembark in Antwerp in June 1939). Less than a year later, all those nations except Britain fell under Nazi control. (© Bettmann/Corbis)

(including Poles, homosexuals, and communists) from all over Europe, transporting them to concentration camps in eastern Germany and Poland, and systematically murdering them. (The death toll would ultimately reach 6 million Jews and at least 4 million others.) News of the atrocities soon reached the public as well, and pressure began to build for an Allied effort to end the killing or at least to rescue some of the surviving Jews.

The American government consistently resisted almost all such demands. Although by mid-1944 Allied bombers were flying missions within a few miles of the most *U.S. Inaction* notorious death camp, at Auschwitz in Poland, the War Department argued that sending planes to destroy the crematoria was unfeasible. American officials also refused to destroy railroad lines leading to the camp. And the United States resisted pleas that it admit large numbers of Jewish refugees attempting to escape Europe.

More forceful action by the United States (and Britain, which was even less amenable to Jewish requests for assistance) might have saved at least some lives. That they did not take such action, it seems clear in retrospect, constituted a considerable moral failure. But policymakers justified their inaction by insisting that they needed to focus exclusively on the larger goal of winning the war. Any diversion of energy and attention to other purposes, they believed, would distract them from the overriding goal of victory.

THE AMERICAN ECONOMY IN WARTIME

Not since the Civil War had the United States been involved in so prolonged and consuming a military experience as World War II. American armed forces engaged in combat around the globe for nearly four years. American society, in the meantime, experienced changes that reached into every corner of the nation.

PROSPERITY AND THE RIGHTS OF LABOR

World War II had a profound impact on American domestic life by ending the Great Depression. By the middle of 1941, the economic problems of the 1930s—unemployment, deflation, industrial sluggishness—had vanished before the great wave of wartime industrial expansion.

The most important catalyst of the new prosperity was government spending, which after 1939 was pumping more money into the economy each year than   *Massive Government Spending* had all the New Deal relief agencies combined. In 1939, the federal budget had been $9 billion, the highest in American peacetime history. By 1945, it had risen to $100 billion. Largely as a result, the gross national product soared: from $91 billion in 1939 to $166 billion in 1945. Personal incomes in some regions grew by as much as 100 percent or more.

The West Coast, naturally, became the launching point for the war against Japan, and the government created large manufacturing facilities in California and elsewhere to serve the needs of the military. Altogether, the government made almost $40 billion worth of wartime capital investments (factories, military and transportation facilities, highways, power plants) in the West, more than in any other region. By the end of the war, the Pacific Coast had become the center of a growing American aircraft industry and an important shipbuilding center. Los Angeles, formerly a medium-sized city notable chiefly for its film industry, now became a major industrial center as well.

The war created a serious labor shortage. The armed forces took more than 16 million men and women out of the civilian workforce at the same time that the demand for labor was rising rapidly. Nevertheless, the supply of workers increased by almost 20 percent during the war—largely through the employment of many people previously considered inappropriate for the workforce: individuals who were very young or elderly, minorities, and, most important, several million women.

The war gave a substantial boost to union membership, which rose from about 10.5 million in 1941 to over 13 million in 1945. That was in part a result of labor's "maintenance-of-membership" agreement with the government,   *Union Membership Boosted* which ensured that the thousands of new workers pouring into unionized defense plants would be automatically enrolled in the unions. But the government also managed to win two important concessions from union leaders. One was the "no-strike" pledge, by which unions agreed not to stop production in wartime. Another was the so-called Little Steel formula, which set a 15 percent limit on wage increases.

Despite the no-strike pledge, nearly 15,000 work stoppages took place during the war, mostly wildcat strikes (strikes not authorized by the union leadership). When the United Mine Workers defied the government by striking in May 1943, Congress reacted by passing, over Roosevelt's veto, the Smith-Connally Act (the War Labor Disputes Act), which required that unions wait thirty days before striking and which empowered the president to seize a struck war plant. In the meantime, public animosity toward labor rose rapidly, and some states passed laws to limit union power.

STABILIZING THE BOOM AND MOBILIZING PRODUCTION

The fear of deflation, the central concern of the 1930s, gave way during the war to a fear of inflation, particularly after prices rose 25 percent in the two years before Pearl Harbor. *The Office of Price Administration* Fighting inflation was the task of the Office of Price Administration (OPA), which helped moderate what had been a serious problem during World War I. Even so, the agency was never popular. Black-marketing and overcharging grew in proportions far beyond OPA's policing capacity.

From 1941 to 1945, the federal government spent a total of $321 billion—twice as much as it had spent in the entire 150 years of its existence as a nation to that point, and ten times as much as the cost of World War I. The national debt rose from $49 billion in 1941 to $259 billion in 1945. The government borrowed about half the revenues it needed by selling $100 billion worth of bonds. Much of the rest it raised by radically increasing income-tax rates, through the Revenue Act of 1942. To simplify collection, Congress enacted a withholding system of payroll deductions in 1943.

In January 1942, to mobilize the wartime economy, the president created the War Production Board (WPB). Throughout its troubled history, the WPB was never able to win complete control over military purchases; the army and navy often circumvented the board. Nor was it able to satisfy the complaints of small business, which charged (correctly) that most contracts went to large corporations. Gradually, the president transferred much of the WPB's authority to a new office located within the White House: the Office of War Mobilization (OWM). But the OWM was only slightly more successful than the WPB.

Despite the administrative problems, however, the war economy managed to meet almost all of the nation's critical war needs. By the beginning of 1944, American factories were, in fact, producing more than the government needed. Their output was twice that of all the Axis countries combined.

WARTIME SCIENCE AND TECHNOLOGY

More than any previous American war, World War II was a watershed for technological and scientific innovation. That was so partly because the American government poured substantial funds into research and development beginning in 1940. In that year, *Government Financing of Research* the government created the National Defense Research Committee (which later became the Office of Scientific Research and Development). By the end of the war, the new agency had spent more than $100 million on research, more than four times the amount spent by the government on military research and development in the previous forty years.

In the first years of the war, all the technological advantages seemed to lie with the Germans and Japanese. Germany had made great advances in tanks and other mechanized armor in the 1930s, particularly during the Spanish Civil War, when it had helped arm Franco's forces. German submarine technology surpassed British and American capabilities in 1940. Japan had developed extraordinary capacity in its naval–air technology, as indicated by the successful raid on Pearl Harbor.

But Britain and America had advantages of their own. American techniques of mass production—the great automotive assembly lines in particular—were converted efficiently to military production in 1941 and 1942 and soon began producing airplanes, ships, tanks, and other armaments in much greater numbers than could the Germans and Japanese. Allied scientists and engineers moved quickly as well to improve Anglo-American aviation and naval technology, particularly submarines and tanks. By late 1942, Allied weaponry was at least as advanced as, and more plentiful than, that of the enemy. The Allies likewise enjoyed superiority in radar technology and developed effective naval mine detection systems.

Anglo-American antiaircraft technology—both on land and on sea—also improved, but never to the point where it could defeat bombing raids altogether. Germany made substantial advances in the development of rocket technology in the early years of the war and managed to launch some rocket-propelled bombs (the V1s and V2s) across the English Channel, aimed at London. The psychological effects of the rockets on the British people were considerable. But the Germans were never able to create a production technology capable of building enough such rockets to make a real difference in the balance of military power.

Beginning in 1942, British and American forces seized the advantage in the air war by producing new and powerful four-engine bombers in great numbers. At higher altitudes and with new navigation systems, they were able to conduct extensive bombing missions over Germany (and, later, Japan) with much less danger of being shot down.   *Long-Range Bombing* The Allies also benefited from a radio device that sent a sonic message to airplanes to tell them when they were within 20 yards of their targets, first introduced in December 1942.

The area in which the Allies had perhaps the greatest advantage was the gathering of intelligence, much of it through Britain's top-secret Ultra project. Some of the advantages the Allies enjoyed came from the capture of German and Japanese intelligence devices. More important, however, were the efforts of cryptologists, or code breakers. Much of Germany's coded communication made use of the so-called Enigma machine, which constantly changed the coding systems it used. In the first months of the war, Polish intelligence had developed an electromechanical computer. It was called the "Bombe," and it could decipher some Enigma messages. After the fall of Poland, British scientists, led by the brilliant computer pioneer Alan Turing, took the Bombe and greatly improved it. On April 15, 1940, the new, improved high-speed Bombe deciphered a series of German messages within hours (not days, as had previously been the case). A few weeks later, it began decrypting German messages at the rate of 1,000 a day, providing the British (and, later, the Americans) with a constant flow of information about enemy operations throughout the war. British scientists working for the intelligence services, meanwhile, built the first real programmable, digital computer—the Colossus II, which became   *The Colossus II* operational less than a week before the beginning of the Normandy invasion and which could decipher an enormous number of intercepted German messages almost instantly. The United States similarly developed the ability to crack a Japanese coding system.

RACE AND ETHNICITY IN WARTIME AMERICA

The war loosened many traditional barriers that had restricted the lives of minorities and women. There was so much demand for fighting men, so much demand for labor, and so much fluidity and mobility that the social and cultural barriers could not survive intact.

AFRICAN AMERICANS AND THE WAR

In the summer of 1941, A. Philip Randolph, president of the mostly African American Brotherhood of Sleeping Car Porters Union, began to insist that the   *A. Philip Randolph* government require companies receiving defense contracts to integrate their workforces.

To mobilize support for the demand, Randolph planned a massive march on Washington. The threat led Roosevelt to promise to establish what became the Fair Employment Practices Commission (FEPC) to investigate discrimination against African Americans in war industries.

The need for labor in war plants greatly increased the migration of African Americans from the rural South into industrial cities. The migration improved the economic conditions *Wartime Race Riots* of many African Americans. But it also created urban tensions and occasional violence. A terrible race riot in Detroit in 1943 killed thirty-four people, twenty-five of them black.

Despite such tensions, leading black organizations redoubled their efforts to challenge segregation. The Congress of Racial Equality (CORE), organized in 1942, mobilized mass popular resistance to discrimination in a way that the older, more conservative organizations had never done. Randolph, Bayard Rustin, James Farmer, and other, younger African American leaders helped organize sit-ins and demonstrations in segregated theaters and *CORE* restaurants. CORE also organized "Freedom Rides" to desegregate buses and bus terminals. Though often unsuccessful, these efforts strengthened a culture of civil rights activism in the black community.

Pressure for change also grew within the military. The armed forces maintained their traditional practice of limiting African Americans to the most menial assignments, keeping them in segregated training camps and units, and barring them entirely from the Marine Corps and the Army Air Force. But there were signs of change. By the end of the war, the number of black servicemen had increased sevenfold, to 700,000; some training camps were being at least partially integrated. African Americans were allowed to serve on ships with white sailors, and more black units were sent into combat. The changes did not come easily. In some of the partially integrated army bases—Fort Dix, New Jersey, for example—riots broke out when black soldiers protested mistreatment and segregation.

NATIVE AMERICANS AND THE WAR

Approximately 25,000 Indians served in the military during World War II. Many Native Americans saw combat. Others (mostly Navajo) became military "code talkers," speak-*Navajo "Code Talkers"* ing their own language (which enemy forces would be unlikely to understand) over the radio and the telephones. The war had important effects on the Indians who served in the military. It brought them into intimate contact (often for the first time) with white society, and it awakened among some of them a taste for the material benefits of life in capitalist America that they would retain after the war. Some never returned to the reservations but chose to remain in the non-Indian world and assimilate to its ways.

The war had important effects, too, on the Native Americans who stayed on the reservations. Little war work reached the tribes. Government subsidies dwindled. Talented young people left the reservations to serve in the military or work in war production, creating workforce shortages in some tribes. The wartime emphasis on national unity undermined support for the revitalization of tribal autonomy that the Indian Reorganization Act of 1934 had launched. New pressures emerged to eliminate the reservation system and to require the tribes to assimilate into white society. The pressures were so severe that John Collier, the energetic director of the Bureau of Indian Affairs who had done so much to promote the reinvigoration of the reservations, resigned in 1945.

MEXICAN AMERICAN WAR WORKERS

Large numbers of Mexican workers entered the United States in response to wartime labor shortages on the Pacific Coast and in the Southwest. The American and Mexican governments agreed in 1942 to a program by which *braceros* (contract laborers)   **Braceros Program** would be admitted to the United States for a limited time. Some worked as migrant farm laborers, but many Mexicans were able for the first time to find factory jobs. They formed the second-largest group of migrants (after African Americans) to U.S. cities in the 1940s. They concentrated mainly in the West but established significant Mexican communities in Chicago, Detroit, and other industrial cities.

The sudden expansion of Mexican American neighborhoods created tensions and occasional conflict. Anglo residents of Los Angeles became alarmed at the activities of Mexican American teenagers, many of whom joined street gangs (*pachucos*). The Mexican American youths were particularly distinctive because of their style of dress. At a time when fabric had been rationed for the war effort, they wore long, loose jackets with padded shoulders, baggy pants tied at the ankles, long watch chains, broad-brimmed hats, and greased, ducktail hairstyles. The outfit was known as a "zoot suit." In June 1943,   *Zoot Suits* animosity toward the "zoot-suiters"—driven partly by ethnic prejudice and partly by the apparent disregard of rationing—produced a four-day riot in Los Angeles. Anglo sailors in Long Beach invaded Mexican American communities and attacked zoot-suiters. The police did little to restrain the sailors, who grabbed Hispanic teenagers, tore off and burned their clothes, cut off their ducktails, and beat them. When Mexicans tried to fight back, the police moved in and arrested them. In the aftermath of the "zoot-suit riots," Los Angeles passed a law prohibiting zoot suits.

THE INTERNMENT OF JAPANESE AMERICANS

World War II produced considerable animosity toward the Japanese. After the attack on Pearl Harbor, government propaganda and popular culture combined to create an image of the Japanese as a devious, malign, and savage people. (See "Consider the Source: The Face of the Enemy.")

This racial animosity soon extended to Americans of Japanese descent. There were not many Japanese Americans in the United States—about 127,000, most of them concentrated in a few areas in California. About one-third were unnaturalized first-generation immigrants (Issei); two-thirds were naturalized or native-born citizens of the United States (Nisei). Because they generally kept to themselves and preserved traditional Japanese cultural patterns, it was easy for Anglo Americans to imagine (wrongly) that the Japanese Americans were engaged in conspiracies on behalf of their ancestral homeland.

In February 1942, in response to pressure from military officials and political leaders on the West Coast (including California attorney general Earl Warren) and recommendations from the War Department, the president authorized the army to "intern" the Japanese Americans. More than 100,000 people (Issei and Nisei alike) were rounded up, told to dispose of their property however they could (which often meant simply abandoning it), and taken to what the government euphemistically called "relocation   *"Relocation Centers"* centers." In fact, they were facilities little different from prisons, many of them located in the western mountains and desert. A group of innocent people (many of them citizens of the United States) were forced to spend up to three years in grim, debilitating isolation, barred from lucrative employment, provided with only minimal medical care, and deprived of decent schools for their children. The Supreme Court upheld the evacuation in the 1944

CONSIDER THE SOURCE

THE FACE OF THE ENEMY

During World War II, illustrators used caricature, symbolism, exaggeration, and juxtaposition to mobilize public opinion and behavior. The Japanese were frequent objects of such representation. Early in the war, an artist working under the auspices of the Work Projects Administration (WPA, formerly the Works Progress Administration) produced the poster, "Salvage Scrap to Blast the Jap." The second image, Arthur Szyk's cover for *Collier's* magazine in December 1942, depicts the Japanese prime minister Hideki Tojo.

UNDERSTAND, ANALYZE, & EVALUATE

1. The Americans and Japanese are represented by different animals in the WPA poster. What do those choices suggest about how people in the United States viewed the character of the two nations?
2. What event is artist Arthur Szyk depicting in the cartoon on the *Collier's* cover? What evidence can you find in the cartoon to support your choice?

U.S. NAVY POSTER "SALVAGE SCRAP TO BLAST THE JAP" (The Library of Congress)

ARTHUR SZYK, *COLLIER'S* COVER, DECEMBER 12, 1942 (© Private Collection/Peter Newark Military Pictures/Bridgeman Images/Reproduced with the cooperation of The Arthur Szyk Society, Burlingame, CA; www.syzk.org)

Korematsu decision; and although most of the Japanese Americans were released later that year, they were unable to win any significant compensation for their   **Korematsu v. U.S.** losses until Congress finally acted in the late 1980s.

CHINESE AMERICANS AND THE WAR

At the same time that the war undermined the position of Japanese Americans, the American alliance with China during World War II significantly enhanced both the legal and social status of Chinese Americans. In 1943, partly to improve relations with the government of China, Congress repealed the Chinese Exclusion Act, which had barred almost all Chinese immigration since its renewal in 1892. The new quota for Chinese immigrants was minuscule (105 a year), but a substantial number of Chinese women managed to gain entry into the country through other provisions covering war brides and fiancées. Over 4,000 Chinese women entered the United States in the first three years after the war. Permanent residents of Chinese descent were finally permitted to become citizens.

Racial animosity toward the Chinese did not disappear, but it did decline—in part because government propaganda and popular culture both began presenting positive images of the Chinese (in some measure to contrast them with the Japanese) and in part because Chinese Americans (like African Americans and other previously marginal groups) began taking jobs in war plants and other booming areas suffering from labor shortages. A higher proportion of Chinese Americans (22 percent of all adult males) was drafted than that of any other national group, and the entire Chinese community in most cities worked hard and conspicuously for the war effort.

ANXIETY AND AFFLUENCE IN WARTIME CULTURE

The war created considerable anxiety in American lives. Families worried about loved ones at the front, and as the war continued, many mourned relatives who had died in combat. Women struggled to support families in the absence of husbands and fathers. Businesses and communities struggled with shortages of goods and labor. People living on the two coasts, in particular, worried about enemy invasions and sabotage.

But the abundance of the war years also created a striking buoyancy in American life. Suddenly people had money to spend again and—despite the many shortages—at least some things to spend it on. In fact, consumerism became, as it had in   *Consumerism Reborn* the 1920s, one of the most powerful forces in American culture.

HOME-FRONT LIFE AND CULTURE

As part of the consumerist resurgence of the war years, Americans spent millions of dollars and hours on entertainment and leisure. Audiences equal to about half the nation's population attended movies each week. Radio ownership increased, and pictorial magazines such as *Life* flourished. Dance halls were packed with young people drawn to the seductive music of bands. Soldiers and sailors home on leave, or awaiting shipment abroad, were special fans of the dances, which became to many of them a symbol of the life they were leaving and fighting to protect. The most popular music was the relatively new jazz form known as swing, which had emerged from the African American musical imagination. Bandleaders such as Benny Goodman and Duke Ellington were among the most recognized figures in American popular culture, rivaling movie stars, and they sometimes hired black musicians to join their groups.

Much of what Americans read, heard, and saw during the war was managed by the government and military. At the center of the government's propaganda effort was the *The Office of War Information*   Office of War Information (OWI). The OWI issued posters, ran magazine advertisements, and produced films. These materials urged ordinary Americans to do their part—buy war bonds, conserve household resources, keep quiet about troop movements.

Government and military officials, meanwhile, censored the reports that journalists filed from the war zone. Correspondents happily refrained from printing anything that might compromise military strategy or effectiveness—they wanted the United States to win too, after all. But Roosevelt and others also believed that gory or depressing war news would sap the public's will, especially in the first two years of the war. It wasn't until September 1943 that officials allowed an image of American dead to appear in print. Federal officials had changed their minds, deciding that slightly more graphic war coverage would awaken a public growing complacent about the sacrifices being made on its behalf.

Hollywood films about the war—and there were hundreds of them—offered a relatively *The Celluloid War*   sanitized picture of the conflict. Whether of their own volition or in consultation with military officials, movie producers usually offered a picture of the soldier in line with journalistic reports and government propaganda. In many "platoon films," death came quickly and without blood and guts. Soldiers behaved courageously, missed home, and found maturity (rather than breakdown) through combat. Blacks didn't typically appear in these platoons—true to the reality of a Jim Crow army—but many other white ethnic groups did. In fact, a central point of many wartime pictures, as well as OWI propaganda posters, was that Jews, Polish Americans, Italian Americans, and other groups largely barred by the 1924 immigration restriction had become assimilated contributors to the American military machine.

The upshot of all this was a wartime popular culture saturated with combat imagery but which kept some of the worst realities of war obscured. This frustrated one of the central figures in the project of wartime information management. The beloved war correspondent Ernie Pyle, a popular and honest chronicler of the American GI before an audience of millions, believed that no one at home had really *seen* the war. After a Japanese sniper killed Pyle in April 1945, American soldiers found an unfinished column in his pocket. "You didn't see him lying so grotesque and pasty beside the gravel road in France," he wrote of the generic dead soldier. "We saw him, saw him by the multiple thousands. That's the difference."

LOVE, FAMILY, AND SEXUALITY IN WARTIME

For men at the front, the image of home both served as a motivational symbol and helped soften the rigors of combat. Letters and mementos from loved ones sustained the morale of millions of service members. They dreamed of music, food, movies, and other material comforts. Many also dreamed of women—wives and girlfriends, but also movie stars and entertainers, who became the source of one of the most popular icons of the front: the pinup. Sailors pasted pinups inside their lockers. Infantrymen carried them (along with pictures of wives, mothers, and girlfriends) in their knapsacks. Fighter pilots gave their planes female names and painted bathing beauties on their nose cones.

For the servicemen who remained in America, and for soldiers and sailors in cities far from home in particular, the company of friendly, "wholesome" women was, the military believed, critical to sustaining morale. The branches of the United Service Organization (known as USOs) recruited thousands of young women to serve as   *Importance of USOs* hostesses in their clubs. They were expected to dress nicely, dance well, and chat happily with lonely men. Other women joined "dance brigades," traveling by bus to military bases for social evenings with servicemen. The "USO girls" and the members of the dance brigades were forbidden to have any contact with men except at parties at the clubs or during dances. Clearly, such regulations were often violated. The military took elaborate measures to root out gay men and lesbians from their ranks—vigilantly searching for evidence of homosexuality and unceremoniously dismissing gay people with undesirable discharges. The services quietly tolerated illicit heterosexual relationships, which they believed were temporary, natural, and, for many men, necessary.

Wartime families also experienced change. The number of women in the workforce increased by nearly 60 percent during the war, as many women replaced male industrial workers serving in the military. These new wage-earning women were likely to be married and were, on the whole, older than most who had entered the workforce in the past.

Many factory owners continued to categorize jobs by gender, reserving the most lucrative positions for men. (Female work, like male work, was also categorized by race: black women

WOMEN AT WAR Many American women enlisted in the army and navy women's corps during World War II, but an equally important contribution to the war effort was their work in factories and offices—often in jobs that would have been considered inappropriate for them in peacetime but that they were now encouraged to assume because of the absence of so many men. (The Library of Congress)

were usually assigned more menial tasks, and paid at a lower rate, than their white counter-parts.) But some women began to take on heavy industrial jobs that had long been considered *"Rosie the Riveter"* "men's work." The famous wartime image of "Rosie the Riveter" symbol-ized the new importance of the female industrial worker. Women joined unions in substantial numbers and helped erode at least some of the prejudice, including the prejudice against mothers working, that had previously kept many of them from paid employment.

Most women workers during the war, however, were employed not in factories but in service-sector jobs. Above all, they worked for the government, whose bureaucratic needs expanded dramatically alongside its military and industrial needs. Even within the mili-*WAACs and WAVEs* tary, which enlisted substantial numbers of women as WAACs (army) and WAVEs (navy), most female work was clerical.

Many mothers whose husbands were in the military had to combine work with child care. The scarcity of child-care facilities or other community services meant that some women had no choice but to leave young children at home alone (or sometimes locked in cars in factory parking lots) or with relatives or neighbors while they worked.

Perhaps in part because of the family dislocations of the war, juvenile crime rose mark-edly. Young boys were arrested at increasing rates for car theft, burglary, vandalism, and vagrancy. For many children, however, the distinctive experience of the war years was not crime but work. More than a third of all teenagers between the ages of fourteen and eighteen were employed during the last years of the war, causing some reduction in high school enrollments.

The return of prosperity helped increase the marriage rate and lower the age at which people married, but many marriages were unable to survive the pressures of wartime separa-tion. The divorce rate rose rapidly. Even so, the rise in the birthrate that accompanied the increase in marriages was the first sign of what would become the great postwar "baby boom."

THE GROWTH OF WARTIME CONSERVATISM

Late in 1943, Franklin Roosevelt publicly suggested that "Dr. New Deal," as he called it, had served its purpose and should now give way to "Dr. Win-the-War." The statement reflected the president's own genuine shift in concern: victory was now more important than reform. But it reflected, too, the political reality that had emerged during the first two years of war.

The greatest assault on New Deal reforms came from conservatives in Congress, who seized on the war as a reason to do what many had wanted to do in peacetime: dismantle many of *Conservative Assault on the New Deal* the achievements of the New Deal. They were assisted by the end of mass unemployment, which decreased the need for such relief programs as the Civilian Conservation Corps and the Works Progress Administration (both of which Congress abol-ished). They were assisted, too, by their own increasing numbers. In the congressional elections of 1942, Republicans gained 47 seats in the House and 10 in the Senate.

Republicans approached the 1944 election determined to exploit what they believed was resentment of wartime regimentation and unhappiness with Democratic reform. They *Democrats Drop Wallace* nominated as their candidate the young and vigorous governor of New York, Thomas E. Dewey. Roosevelt was unopposed within his party, but Democratic leaders pressured him to abandon Vice President Henry Wallace, an advanced New Dealer and hero of the CIO. Roosevelt agreed to replace him with a more moderate figure, Senator Harry S. Truman of Missouri. Truman had won acclaim as chairman of the Senate War Investigating Committee (known as the Truman Committee), which compiled an impressive record uncovering waste and corruption in wartime production.

The election revolved around domestic economic issues and, indirectly, the president's health. He was, in fact, gravely ill, suffering from, among other things, advanced arteriosclerosis. But the campaign seemed momentarily to revive him. Roosevelt made several strenuous public appearances late in October, which dispelled popular doubts about his health and ensured his reelection. He captured 53.5 percent of the popular *Roosevelt Reelected* vote to Dewey's 46 percent, and 432 electoral votes to Dewey's 99. Democrats lost 1 seat in the Senate, gained 20 in the House, and maintained control of both.

THE DEFEAT OF THE AXIS

By the middle of 1943, America and its allies had succeeded in stopping the Axis advance in both Europe and the Pacific. In the next two years, the Allies themselves seized the offensive and launched a series of powerful drives that led the way to victory.

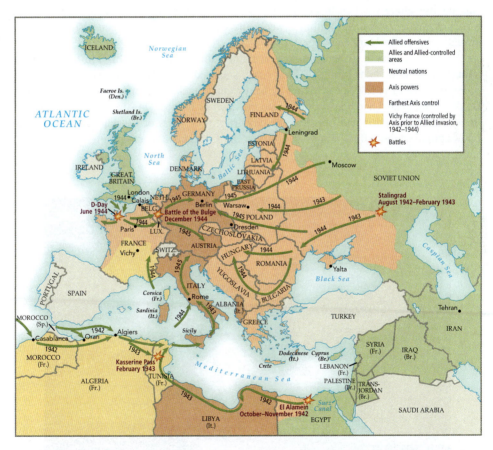

WORLD WAR II IN EUROPE: THE ALLIED COUNTEROFFENSIVE, 1943–1945 This map illustrates the final, climactic movements in the war in Europe—the two great offensives against Germany that began in 1943 and culminated in 1945. From the east, the armies of the Soviet Union, having halted the Germans at Stalingrad and Moscow, swept across eastern Europe toward Germany. From the west and the south, American, British, and other Allied forces moved toward Germany through Italy and—after the Normandy invasion in June 1944—through France. The two offensives met in Berlin in May 1945. Note, too, the northern routes that America and Britain used to supply the Soviet Union during the war. • *What problems did the position of the Allied forces at the end of the war help produce?*

THE EUROPEAN OFFENSIVE

By early 1944, American and British bombers were attacking German industrial installations and other targets almost around the clock, drastically cutting production and impeding transportation. A February 1945 incendiary raid on Dresden created a great firestorm that destroyed three-fourths of the previously undamaged city and killed approximately 135,000 people, almost all civilians.

An enormous offensive force had been gathering in England for two years before the spring of 1944: almost 3 million troops and perhaps the greatest array of naval vessels and armaments ever assembled in one place. On the morning of June 6, 1944 (D-Day), *D-Day* this vast invasion force moved into action. The landing came not at the narrowest part of the English Channel, where the Germans had expected and prepared for it, but along sixty miles of the Cotentin Peninsula on the coast of Normandy. While airplanes and battleships offshore bombarded the Nazi defenses, 4,000 vessels landed American, British, Canadian, and other troops and supplies on the beaches. (Three divisions of paratroopers had been dropped chaotically behind the German lines the night before.) Fighting was intense along the beach, but the superior manpower and equipment of the Allied forces gradually prevailed. Within a week, the German forces had been dislodged from virtually the entire Normandy coast.

For the next month, further progress remained slow. But in late July, in the Battle of Saint-Lô, General Omar Bradley's First Army smashed through the German lines. George S. Patton's Third Army, spearheaded by heavy tank attacks, then moved through the hole Bradley had created and began a drive into the heart of France. On August 25, Free French forces arrived in Paris and liberated the city from four years of German occupation. By mid-September the Allied armies had driven the Germans almost entirely out of France and Belgium.

THE NORMANDY INVASION This photograph, taken from a landing craft, shows American troops wading ashore and onto the Normandy beaches, where one of the decisive battles of World War II was taking shape. The invasion was launched despite threatening weather and rough seas. (© Popperfoto/Getty Images)

The great Allied drive came to a halt, however, at the Rhine River against a firm line of Nazi defenses. In mid-December, German forces struck in desperation along fifty miles of front in the Ardennes Forest. In the Battle of the Bulge (named for a   *Battle of the Bulge* large bulge that appeared in the American lines as the Germans pressed forward), they drove fifty-five miles toward Antwerp before they were finally stopped at Bastogne. It was the last major battle on the western front.

While the western Allies fought their way through France, Soviet forces swept westward into central Europe and the Balkans. In late January 1945, the Russians launched a great offensive toward the Oder River, inside Germany. By early   *Germany Invaded*

AUSCHWITZ, DECEMBER 1944   This photograph, taken near the end of World War II, shows a group of imprisoned children behind a barbed wire fence in one of the most notorious Nazi concentration camps. By the time this picture was taken, the Nazis had been driven out of Auschwitz and were under the control of Allied soldiers. (© Keystone/Getty Images)

spring, they were ready to launch a final assault against Berlin. General Omar Bradley, in the meantime, was pushing toward the Rhine from the west. Early in March, Bradley's forces captured the city of Cologne, on the river's west bank. The next day, they discovered and seized an undamaged bridge over the river at Remagen; Allied troops were soon pouring across the Rhine. In the following weeks, the British commander Montgomery, with a million troops, pushed into Germany in the north while Bradley's army, sweeping through central Germany, completed the encirclement of 300,000 German soldiers in the Ruhr.

The German resistance was now broken on both fronts. American forces were moving eastward faster than they had anticipated and could have beaten the Russians to Berlin and Prague. The American and British high commands decided, instead, to halt the advance along the Elbe River in central Germany to await the Russians. That decision enabled the Soviets to occupy eastern Germany and Czechoslovakia.

On April 30, with Soviet forces on the outskirts of Berlin, Adolf Hitler killed himself in his bunker in the capital. And on May 8, 1945, the remaining German forces surrendered unconditionally.

THE PACIFIC OFFENSIVE

In February 1944, American naval forces under Admiral Chester Nimitz won a series of victories in the Marshall Islands and cracked the outer perimeter of the Japanese Empire. Within a month, the navy had destroyed other vital Japanese bastions. American submarines, in the meantime, were decimating Japanese shipping and crippling Japan's domestic economy.

America's principal ally in Asia was China. To assist the Chinese forces, the army sent General Joseph W. Stilwell to help provide critical supplies to China by a land route through India and across the Himalayas. It was a brutal task, but in the fall of 1944, Stilwell's forces succeeded in constructing a road and pipelines across the mountains into China. More dangerously, the Japanese were also threatening the wartime capital of China in Chungking. Chiang Kai-shek, the Chinese premier, was reluctant to use his troops against the Japanese and seemed more concerned with attacking Chinese communists, who were also fighting the Japanese. After Stilwell left China, his successors continued to have trouble prodding Chiang to confront the Japanese.

The decisive battles of the Pacific war occurred not in China but at sea. In mid-June 1944, an enormous American armada struck the heavily fortified Mariana Islands and, after some of the bloodiest operations of the war, captured Tinian, Guam, and Saipan. On October 20, General MacArthur's troops landed on Leyte Island in the Philippines. The Japanese now employed virtually their entire fleet against the Allied invaders in three major encounters—which together constituted the decisive Battle of Leyte Gulf, the larg-
Battles of Leyte Gulf and Iwo Jima est naval engagement in history. American forces held off the Japanese onslaught and sank four Japanese carriers, all but destroying Japan's capacity to continue a serious naval war. In February 1945, American marines seized the tiny volcanic island of Iwo Jima, just 750 miles from Tokyo, but only after the costliest battle in the history of the Marine Corps.

The battle for Okinawa, an island only 370 miles south of Japan, gave evidence of the
Okinawa strength of the Japanese resistance in these last desperate days. Week after week, the Japanese sent kamikaze (suicide) planes against American and British ships, sacrificing

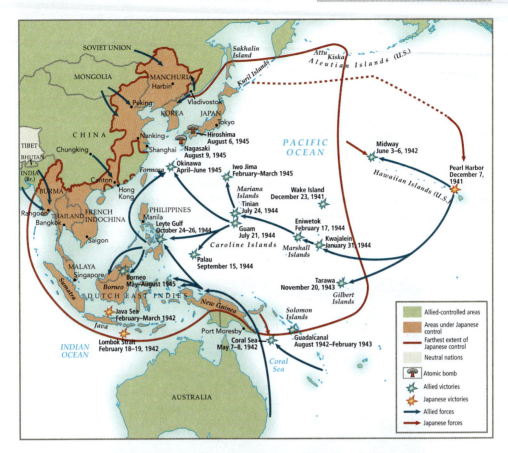

WORLD WAR II IN THE PACIFIC This map illustrates the changing fortunes of the two combatants in the Pacific phase of World War II. The long red line stretching from Burma around to Manchuria represents the eastern boundary of the vast areas of the Pacific that had fallen under Japanese control by the summer of 1942. The blue lines illustrate the advance of American forces back into the Pacific beginning in May 1942 and accelerating in 1943 and after, which drove back the Japanese forces. The American advance was a result of two separate offensives—one in the central Pacific, under the command of Chester Nimitz, which moved west from Hawaii; and the other, under the command of Douglas MacArthur, which moved north from Australia. By the summer of 1945, American forces were approaching the Japanese mainland and were bombing Tokyo itself. The dropping of two American atomic bombs, on Hiroshima and Nagasaki, finally brought the war to an end. • *Why did the Soviet Union enter the Pacific war in August 1945, as shown in the upper-left corner of the map?*

3,500 of them while inflicting great damage. Japanese troops on shore launched desperate nighttime attacks on the American lines. The United States and its allies suffered nearly 50,000 casualties before finally capturing Okinawa in late June 1945. Over 100,000 Japanese died in the siege.

It seemed likely that the same kind of bitter fighting would await the Americans when they invaded Japan. But there were also some signs early in 1945 that such an invasion might not be necessary. The Japanese had almost no ships or planes left with which to fight. The firebombing of Tokyo in March, in which American bombers *Tokyo Firebombed* dropped napalm on the city and created a firestorm in which over 80,000 people died,

THE DECISION TO DROP THE ATOMIC BOMB

There has been continuing disagreement since 1945 among historians—and many others—about how to explain and evaluate President Truman's decision to use the atomic bomb against Japan.

Truman himself, both at the time and in his 1955 memoirs, insisted that the decision was a simple and straightforward one. The alternative to using atomic weapons, he claimed, was an American invasion of

NAGASAKI SURVIVORS   A Japanese woman and child look grimly at a photographer as they hold pieces of bread in the aftermath of the dropping of the second American atomic bomb—this one on Nagasaki. (© Bettmann/Corbis)

mainland Japan that might have cost as many as a million American lives. That view has received considerable support from historians. Herbert Feis argued in *The Atomic Bomb and the End of World War II* (1966) that Truman made his decision on purely military grounds—to ensure a speedy American victory. David McCullough, the author of a popular biography of Truman published in 1992, also accepted Truman's own account of his actions largely uncritically, as did Alonzo L. Hamby in *Man of the People* (1995), an important scholarly study of Truman. "One consideration weighed most heavily on Truman," Hamby concluded. "The longer the war lasted, the more Americans killed."

Others have strongly disagreed. As early as 1948, British physicist P. M. S. Blackett wrote in *Fear, War, and the Bomb* that the destruction of Hiroshima and Nagasaki was "not so much the last military act of the second World War as the first major operation of the cold diplomatic war with Russia." The most important critic of Truman's decision is the historian Gar Alperovitz, the author of two influential books on the subject: *Atomic Diplomacy: Hiroshima and Potsdam* (1965) and *The Decision to Use the Atomic Bomb* (1995). Alperovitz dismissed the argument that the bomb was used to shorten the war and save lives. Japan was likely to have surrendered soon even if the bomb had not been used, he claimed. Instead, he argued, the United States used

the bomb less to influence Japan than to intimidate the Soviet Union, "to make Russia more manageable in Europe."

John W. Dower's *War Without Mercy* (1986) contributed, by implication at least, to another controversial explanation of the American decision: racism. The Japanese, many Americans came to believe during the war, were almost a subhuman species. Even many of Truman's harshest critics, however, note that it is, as Alperovitz has written, "all but impossible to find specific evidence that racism was an important factor in the decision to attack Hiroshima and Nagasaki."

The debate over the decision to drop the atomic bomb is an unusually emotional one, and it has inspired bitter professional and personal attacks on advocates of almost every position. It illustrates clearly how history has often been, and remains, a powerful force in the way societies define themselves. •

UNDERSTAND, ANALYZE, & EVALUATE

1. The United States dropped two atomic bombs on Japan, one on Hiroshima and the other on Nagasaki. Was dropping the bomb on Hiroshima necessary? Was it justifiable? Do the reasons for dropping the bomb on Hiroshima apply equally to the bombing of Nagasaki?

2. How might the war in the Pacific have been different if the United States had decided not to drop the bombs?

further weakened the Japanese will to resist. Moderate Japanese leaders, who had long since concluded the war was lost, were looking to end the fighting. But they continued to face powerful opposition from military leaders. Whether the moderates could ultimately have prevailed is a question historians continue to debate. In any case, their efforts became superfluous in August 1945, when the United States made use of a terrible new weapon it had been developing throughout the war.

THE MANHATTAN PROJECT AND ATOMIC WARFARE

Reports had reached the United States in 1939 that Nazi scientists had taken the first step toward the creation of an atomic bomb, a weapon more powerful than any previously devised. The United States and Britain immediately began a race to develop the weapon before the Germans did.

The search for the new weapon emerged from theories developed by atomic physicists, beginning early in the century, and particularly from some of the founding ideas of modern physics developed by Albert Einstein. Einstein's famous theory of relativity had revealed that matter could be converted into a tremendous force of energy. Einstein himself, who by then had left his native Germany and was living in the United States, warned Franklin Roosevelt of German interest in atomic weapons.

By the late 1930s and early 1940s, scientists at American universities were working to catch up with the Germans. Soon after the United States entered the war, the army took over the research and named it the Manhattan Project, because it was devised in the Manhattan Engineer District Office of the Army Corps of Engineers. Over the next three years, the government secretly poured nearly $2 billion into a massive scientific and technological effort conducted at hidden laboratories in Oak Ridge, Tennessee; Los Alamos, New Mexico; Hanford, Washington; and other sites. Scientists in Oak Ridge, who were charged with finding a way to create a nuclear chain reaction that could be feasibly replicated within the confined space of a bomb, began experimenting with plutonium—a derivative of uranium first discovered by scientists at University of California–Berkeley. Plutonium proved capable of providing a practical fuel for the weapon. Scientists in Los Alamos, under the direction of J. Robert Oppenheimer, were charged with the construction of the actual atomic bomb.

By 1944, despite many unforeseen problems, the Manhattan Project scientists pushed ahead much faster than anyone had predicted. Even so, the war in Europe ended before they were ready to test the first weapon. Just before dawn on July 16, 1945, in the desert *Atomic Test in New Mexico*   near Alamogordo, New Mexico, the scientists gathered to witness the first atomic explosion in history: the detonation of a plutonium-fueled bomb that scientists had named Trinity. The explosion—a blinding flash of light, perhaps brighter than any ever before seen on earth, followed by a huge, billowing mushroom cloud—created a vast crater in the barren desert. Watching the test, Oppenheimer was reminded of a passage from a Hindu scripture: "I am become death, the destroyer of worlds."

News of the explosion reached President Harry S. Truman (who had taken office in April on the death of Roosevelt) in Potsdam, Germany, where he was attending a conference of Allied leaders. He issued an ultimatum to the Japanese (signed jointly by the British), demanding that they surrender by August 3 or face utter devastation. When the Japanese failed to meet the deadline, Truman ordered the air force to use the new atomic weapons against Japan.

Controversy has continued for decades over whether Truman's decision to use the bombs was justified and what his motives were. Some have argued that the atomic attack was unnecessary—that had the United States agreed to the survival of the emperor before the bombs were used (which it ultimately did agree to after the bombings), or had it waited only a few more weeks, the Japanese would have surrendered. Others argue that nothing less than the atomic bombs could have persuaded the Japanese to surrender without a costly American invasion. (See "Debating the Past: The Decision to Drop the Atomic Bomb.")

Most of the nation's military and political leaders, however, seemed little concerned about such matters. Truman, who had not even known of the existence of the Manhattan Project until he became president, made what he apparently believed to be a simple military decision. A weapon was available that would end the war quickly; he could see no reason not to use it.

On August 6, 1945, an American B-29, the *Enola Gay,* dropped an atomic weapon on *Hiroshima Destroyed*   the Japanese industrial center at Hiroshima. With a single bomb, the United States completely incinerated a four-square-mile area at the center of the previously undamaged city. More than 80,000 civilians died, according to later American estimates.

Many more suffered the crippling effects of radioactive fallout or passed those effects on to their children in the form of birth defects.

The Japanese government, stunned by the attack, was at first unable to agree on a response. Two days later, on August 8, the Soviet Union declared war on Japan. And the following day, another American plane dropped another atomic weapon—this time on the city of Nagasaki—inflicting 100,000 deaths and terrible damage on yet another unfortunate community. Finally, the emperor intervened to break the   *Second Bomb and Surrender* stalemate in the cabinet, and on August 14 the government announced that it was ready to give up. On September 2, 1945, on board the American battleship *Missouri,* anchored in Tokyo Bay, Japanese officials signed the articles of surrender.

The most destructive war in human history had come to an end, and the United States had emerged from it not only victorious but also in a position of unprecedented power, influence, and prestige. It was a victory, however, that few could greet with unambiguous joy. Fourteen million combatants had died in the struggle. As many as 50 million or more civilians may have perished, making World War II by far the deadliest war in history. The United States had suffered only light casualties in comparison with some other nations (and particularly in comparison with Russia and Germany), but the cost had still been high: more than 400,000 dead, almost 700,000 injured. And the world continued to face an uncertain future, menaced by the threat of nuclear warfare and by an emerging antagonism between the world's two strongest nations—the United States and the Soviet Union—that would darken the peace for many decades to come.

CONCLUSION

The United States played a critical, indeed decisive, role in the war against Germany and Italy. It defeated Imperial Japan in the Pacific largely alone. But America's contributions to and sacrifices in the war paled next to those of its most important allies. Britain, France, and, above all, the Soviet Union paid a staggering price—in lives, treasure, and social unity—that had no counterpart in the United States. Most American citizens in the United States experienced a booming prosperity and only modest privations during the four years of American involvement in the conflict. There were, of course, jarring social changes during the war that even prosperity could not entirely offset: shortages, restrictions, regulations, family dislocations, and, perhaps most of all, the absence of millions of men and considerable numbers of women, who went overseas to fight.

American fighting men and women, of course, had very different experiences from those of the people who remained at home. They endured tremendous hardships, substantial casualties, and much fear and loneliness. They fought effectively and bravely. They helped liberate North Africa and Italy from German occupation. And in June 1944, finally, they joined British, French, and other forces in a great and successful invasion of France. It led less than a year later to the destruction of the Nazi regime and the end of the European war. In the Pacific, Americans turned back the Japanese offensive through a series of difficult naval and land battles. Ultimately, however, it was not the American army and navy that brought the war against Japan to a close. It was the unleashing of the most destructive weapon ever created—the atomic bomb—on the people of Japan that finally persuaded the leaders of that nation to surrender.

KEY TERMS/PEOPLE/PLACES/EVENTS

A. Philip Randolph 635
Battle of the Bulge 645
braceros 637
Colossus II 635
Congress of Racial Equality
  (CORE) 636
D-Day 644
Dwight D. Eisenhower 630

Guadalcanal 630
Harry S. Truman 650
Hiroshima 650
Holocaust 631
Korematsu v. U.S. 639
Manhattan Project 650
Office of Price Administration
  (OPA) 634

Office of War Information
  (OWI) 640
Okinawa 646
relocation centers 637
Rosie the Riveter 642
United Service Organization
  (USO) 641
zoot suits 637

RECALL AND REFLECT

1. List some of the measures that the federal government took to mobilize the nation for the war effort.
2. How did advances in technology affect the course of the military conflict?
3. How did the United States contribute to the Allied victory in Europe? How important were America's allies? Which allies were most important?
4. How did the war affect U.S. society—women, workers, African Americans, Japanese Americans, and immigrants?
5. Why did the United States bomb civilians in Japan and Europe in the last years of the war?

27 | THE COLD WAR

ORIGINS OF THE COLD WAR
THE COLLAPSE OF THE PEACE
AMERICA AFTER THE WAR
THE KOREAN WAR
THE CRUSADE AGAINST SUBVERSION

LOOKING AHEAD

1. What made the growing tension between the United States and the Soviet Union evolve into the Cold War?
2. What is the theory of containment, and how did it drive U.S. foreign policy and foreign interventions in the postwar era?
3. Why did the U.S. government and the American people believe that there was a threat of internal communist subversion?

EVEN BEFORE WORLD WAR II ENDED, there were signs of tension between the United States and the Soviet Union. Once the fighting was over, those tensions grew to create what became known as the "Cold War"—a long and dangerous rivalry between the two former allies that would cast its shadow over international affairs and American domestic life for more than four decades.

The Cold War took shape gradually over a five-year period, during which the relationship between the United States and the Soviet Union deteriorated and the United States crafted a new structure for American foreign policy—known as "containment"—that sought to keep communism from expanding.

1945
Yalta and Potsdam
Conferences
United Nations founded

1946
Atomic Energy
Commission
established

1947
Truman Doctrine
Marshall Plan proposed
National Security Act
Taft-Hartley Act

1948
Berlin blockade
Truman elected
president
Hiss case begins

1949
NATO established
Soviet Union explodes
A-bomb
Mao victorious in China

1950
NSC-68
Korean War begins
McCarthy's
anticommunism
campaign begins

1951
Truman fires
MacArthur

1952
American occupation of
Japan ends
Eisenhower elected
president

ORIGINS OF THE COLD WAR

Few issues in twentieth-century American history have aroused more debate than the origins of the Cold War. Some have claimed that Soviet duplicity and expansionism created the international tensions; others, that American provocations and global ambitions were at least equally to blame. (See "Debating the Past: The Cold War.")

SOURCES OF SOVIET–AMERICAN TENSION

At the heart of the rivalry between the United States and the Soviet Union in the 1940s—in addition to the basic ideological, economic, and political distinctions between the two societies—was a fundamental difference in the ways the great powers envisioned the postwar world. One vision, first openly outlined in the Atlantic Charter in 1941, was a world in which nations abandoned their traditional beliefs in military alliances and spheres of influence and governed their relations with one another through democratic processes, with an international organization serving as the arbiter of disputes and the protector of every nation's right of self-determination. At least in theory, that vision appealed to many Americans, including Franklin Roosevelt.

The other vision was that of the Soviet Union and, to some extent, Great Britain. Both Josef Stalin and Winston Churchill had signed the Atlantic Charter. But Churchill had always been uneasy about the implications of self-determination for Britain's own enormous empire. And the Soviet Union was determined to create a secure sphere for itself in Central and Eastern Europe as protection against possible future aggression from the West. Both Churchill and Stalin, therefore, tended to envision a postwar structure vaguely similar to the traditional European balance of power, in which the great powers would control areas of strategic interest to them. The United States, for its part, soon labored to establish and protect its own spheres of interest around the globe. When the two sides competed for influence and power in this way, the Cold War began.

WARTIME DIPLOMACY

Serious strains began to develop in the alliance with the Soviet Union in January 1943, when Roosevelt and Churchill met in Casablanca, Morocco, to discuss Allied strategy. The two leaders could not accept Stalin's most important demand—the immediate opening of a second front in Western Europe. But they tried to reassure Stalin by announcing that they would accept nothing less than the unconditional surrender of the Axis powers. They would not negotiate a separate peace with Hitler and leave the Soviets to fight on alone.

In November 1943, Roosevelt and Churchill traveled to Tehran, Iran, for their first meeting with Stalin. By now, however, Roosevelt's most effective bargaining tool—Stalin's need for American assistance against Germany—had been largely removed. The German advance against Russia had been halted; Soviet forces were now launching their own westward offensive. Nevertheless, the Tehran Conference seemed in *Tehran Conference* most respects a success. Stalin agreed to an American request that the Soviet Union enter the war in the Pacific soon after the end of hostilities in Europe. Roosevelt, in turn, promised that an Anglo-American second front would be established within six months.

On other matters, however, the origins of future disagreements were already visible. Most important was the question of Poland. Roosevelt and Churchill were willing to agree to a movement of the Soviet border westward, allowing Stalin to annex some historically Polish territory. But they differed sharply on the nature of the postwar government in the portion of Poland that would remain independent. Roosevelt and Churchill supported the claims of the Polish government-in-exile that had been functioning in London since 1940; Stalin wished to install another, pro-communist exiled government that had spent the war in Lublin, in the Soviet Union. The three leaders left the Tehran Conference with the issue unresolved.

YALTA

More than a year later, in February 1945, Roosevelt joined Churchill and Stalin again, for a peace conference in the Soviet city of Yalta. In return for Stalin's renewed promise to enter the Pacific war, Roosevelt agreed that the Soviet Union should receive some of the Pacific territory that Russia had lost in the 1904–1905 Russo-Japanese War.

The negotiators also agreed to a plan for a new international organization, one that had been hammered out during the previous summer at a conference in Washington, D.C. The new United Nations would contain a General Assembly, in which *United Nations Established* every member would be represented, and a Security Council, with permanent representatives of the five major powers (the United States, Britain, France, the Soviet Union, and China), each of which would have veto power. The Security Council would also have temporary delegates from several other nations. These agreements became the basis of the United Nations charter, drafted at a conference of fifty nations beginning April 25, 1945, in San Francisco. In sharp contrast to the American rejection of the League of Nations a generation before, the United States Senate ratified the charter in July by a vote of 80 to 2. (It was, many internationalists believed, a "second chance" to create a stable world order.)

THE COLD WAR

For more than a decade after the beginning of the Cold War, few historians saw any reason to challenge the official American interpretation of its origins. The breakdown of relations between the United States and the Soviet Union was, most agreed, a direct result of Soviet expansionism and of Stalin's violation of the wartime agreements forged at Yalta and Potsdam. The Soviet imposition of communist regimes in Eastern Europe was part of a larger ideological design to spread communism throughout the world. American policy was the logical and necessary response: a firm commitment to oppose Soviet expansionism and to keep American forces in a continual state of readiness.

Disillusionment with the official justifications for the Cold War began to find expression even in the late 1950s, when anticommunist sentiment in America remained strong and pervasive. William Appleman Williams's *The Tragedy of American Diplomacy* (1959) insisted that the Cold War was simply the most recent version of a consistent American effort in the twentieth century to preserve an "open door" for American trade in world markets. The confrontation with the Soviet Union, he argued, was less a response to Soviet aggressive designs than an expression of the American belief in the necessity of capitalist expansion.

As the Vietnam War grew larger and more unpopular in the 1960s, the scholarly critique of the Cold War quickly gained intensity. Walter LaFeber's *America, Russia, and the Cold War,* first published in 1967, maintained that America's supposedly idealistic internationalism at the close of the war was in reality an effort to ensure a postwar order shaped in the American image—with every nation open to American influence (and to American trade). That was why the United States was so apt to misinterpret Soviet policy, much of which reflected a perfectly reasonable commitment to ensure the security of the Soviet Union itself, as part of a larger aggressive design.

The revisionist interpretations of the Cold War ultimately produced a reaction of their own: what has come to be known as "postrevisionist" scholarship. The most important work in this school attempted to strike a balance between orthodoxy and revisionism and to identify areas of blame and patterns of misconceptions on both sides of the conflict. An important early statement of this approach was John Lewis Gaddis's *The United States and the Cold War, 1941–1947* (1972), which argued that "neither side can bear sole responsibility for the onset of the Cold War." Both sides had limited options, given their own political constraints and their own preconceptions. Other postrevisionist works—by Thomas G. Paterson, Melvyn Leffler, William Taubman, and others—have elaborated on ways in which the United States and the Soviet Union acted in response to genuine, if not necessarily accurate, beliefs about the intentions of the other. "The United States and the Soviet Union were doomed to be antagonists," Ernest May wrote in 1984. "There probably was never any real possibility that the post-1945 relationship could be anything but hostility verging on conflict."

Since the fall of the Soviet Union in 1991, scholars have had access to newly released Russian archives that have enriched—although not fundamentally altered—the way historians view the Cold War. John Lewis

Gaddis, in *We Now Know: Rethinking Cold War History* (1998) and *The Cold War* (2005), portrays a Cold War somewhat more dangerous than his own earlier studies, and those of many other scholars, had portrayed; and he argues that the strong anticommunist positions of Margaret Thatcher, Ronald Reagan, and Pope John Paul II had a larger impact on the weakening of the Soviet Union than was previously understood. Similarly assisted by newly released archives, Odd Arne Westad, in *The Global Cold War* (2005), roots the origins of the dangerous instability in the so-called Third World in the frequent interventions of both the Soviet Union and the United States in the Cold War era. •

UNDERSTAND, ANALYZE, & EVALUATE

1. What are the orthodox, revisionist, and postrevisionist arguments concerning the origins of the Cold War?
2. Was the Cold War inevitable?

On other issues, however, the Yalta Conference produced no real accord. Basic disagreement remained about the postwar Polish government. Stalin, whose armies now occupied Poland, had already installed a government composed of the pro-communist "Lublin" Poles. Roosevelt and Churchill insisted that the pro-Western "London" Poles must be allowed a place in the Warsaw regime. Roosevelt envisioned a government based on free, democratic elections—which both he and Stalin recognized the pro-Western forces would win. Stalin agreed only to a vague compromise by which an unspecified number of pro-Western Poles would be granted a place in the government. He said he would hold "free and unfettered elections" in Poland on an unspecified future date. They did not happen until 1989.

Dispute over Poland

Nor was there agreement about Germany. Roosevelt seemed to want a reconstructed and reunited Germany. Stalin wanted to impose heavy reparations on Germany and to ensure a permanent dismemberment of the nation. The final agreement was, like the Polish accord, vague and unstable. The decision on reparations would be referred to a future commission. The United States, Great Britain, France, and the Soviet Union would each control its own "zone of occupation" in Germany—the zones to be determined by the position of troops at the end of the war. Berlin, the German capital, was

YALTA, 1945 Churchill (*left*) and Stalin (*right*) were shocked at the physical appearance of Franklin Roosevelt (*center*) when he arrived for their critical meeting at Yalta. Roosevelt had enough energy to perform capably at the conference, but he was in fact gravely ill. Two months later, not long after he gave Congress what turned out to be an unrealistically optimistic report of the prospects for postwar peace, he died. (© Bettmann/Corbis)

already well inside the Soviet zone, but because of its symbolic importance, it would itself be divided into four occupied sectors. At an unspecified date, Germany would be reunited. As for the rest of Europe, the conference produced a murky accord on the establishment of governments "broadly representative of all democratic elements" and "responsible to the will of the people."

The Yalta accords, in other words, were less a settlement of postwar issues than a set of loose principles that sidestepped the most difficult questions. Roosevelt, Churchill, and Stalin returned home from the conference, each apparently convinced that he had signed an important agreement. But the Soviet interpretation of the accords differed so sharply from the Anglo-American interpretation that the illusion endured only briefly. In the weeks following the Yalta Conference, Roosevelt watched with growing alarm as the Soviet Union moved systematically to establish pro-communist governments in one *Soviets in Central and Eastern Europe* Central or Eastern European nation after another and as Stalin refused to make the changes in Poland that the president believed Stalin had promised. Still believing the differences could be settled, Roosevelt left Washington early in the spring for a vacation at his retreat in Warm Springs, Georgia. There, on April 12, 1945, he suffered a sudden massive stroke and died.

THE COLLAPSE OF THE PEACE

The new president, Harry S. Truman, had almost no familiarity with international issues. Nor did he share Roosevelt's apparent faith in Soviet flexibility. Truman sided with the many people inside the government who considered the Soviet Union fundamentally untrustworthy and viewed Stalin himself with suspicion and even loathing.

THE FAILURE OF POTSDAM

Truman had been in office only a few days before he decided to "get tough" with the Soviet Union. On April 23, he met with Soviet foreign minister Molotov and sharply chastised him for violations of the Yalta accords. In fact, Truman had little leverage. Russian forces already occupied Poland and much of the rest of Central and Eastern Europe. Germany was already divided among the Allies. The United States was still engaged in a war in the Pacific and was neither able nor willing to enter into a second conflict in Europe. Truman insisted that the United States should be able to get "85 percent" of what it wanted, but he was ultimately forced to settle for much less.

He conceded first on Poland. When Stalin made a few minor concessions to the pro-Western exiles, Truman recognized the Warsaw government, hoping that noncommunist forces might gradually expand their influence there. (Until the 1980s, they did not.) To settle other questions, Truman met in July at Potsdam, in Russian-occupied Germany, with Stalin and Churchill (who, after elections in Britain in the midst of the talks, was replaced as prime minister by Clement Attlee). Truman reluctantly accepted the adjustments of the Polish–German border that Stalin had long demanded; he refused, however, to permit the Russians to claim any reparations from the American, French, and British zones of Germany. This stance effectively confirmed that Germany would remain divided. The western zones ultimately united into one nation, friendly to the United States, and the Russian zone survived as another nation, with a pro-Soviet, communist government.

THE CHINA PROBLEM AND JAPAN

American hopes for an open, peaceful world "policed" by the great powers required a strong, independent China. But those hopes faced a major obstacle: the Chinese government of Chiang Kai-shek. Chiang was generally friendly to the   *Chiang versus Mao in China* United States, but his government was corrupt and incompetent, with feeble popular support. Ever since 1927, the nationalist government he headed had been engaged in a bitter rivalry with the communist armies of Mao Zedong. By 1945, Mao was in control of one-fourth of the population.

Some Americans urged the government to try to find a "third force" to support as an alternative to either Chiang or Mao. Truman, however, decided reluctantly that he had no choice but to continue supporting Chiang. For the next several years, the United States continued to pump money and weapons to Chiang, even as it was becoming clear that the cause was lost. But Truman was not prepared to intervene militarily to save the nationalist regime.

Instead, the American government began to consider an alternative to China as the strong, pro-Western force in Asia: a revived Japan. Abandoning the strict   *Support for Japan* occupation policies of the first years after the war (when General Douglas MacArthur had governed the nation), the United States lifted restrictions on industrial development and encouraged rapid economic growth in Japan. The vision of an open, united world was giving way in Asia, as it was in Europe, to an acceptance of a divided world with a strong pro-American sphere of influence.

THE CONTAINMENT DOCTRINE

By the end of 1945, a new American foreign policy was slowly emerging. It became known as **containment.** Rather than attempting to create a unified, "open" world, or to destroy communism where it already existed, the United States and its allies would work to prevent Soviet expansion.

The new doctrine emerged in part as a response to events in Europe in 1946. In Turkey, Stalin was trying to win control over the vital sea-lanes to the Mediterranean. In Greece, communist forces were threatening the pro-Western government; the British had announced they could no longer provide assistance. Faced with these challenges, Truman decided to enunciate a firm new policy. In doing so, he drew from the ideas of the American diplomat George F. Kennan, who had warned not long after the war that the only viable American response to Soviet power was "a long-term, patient but firm and vigilant containment of Russian expansive tendencies." On March 12, 1947, Truman appeared before Congress and used Kennan's warnings as the basis of what became known as the Truman Doctrine. "I believe," he argued, "that it must be the policy of the United States to   *Truman Doctrine* support free peoples who are resisting attempted subjugation by armed minorities or by outside pressures." In the same speech, he requested $400 million for aid to Greece and Turkey, which Congress quickly approved.

The American commitment ultimately helped reduce Soviet pressure on Turkey and helped the Greek government defeat the communist insurgents and, in the process, establish containment as a basis for American policy that survived for more than forty years.

THE CONSERVATIVE OPPOSITION TO CONTAINMENT

The containment doctrine attracted broad, bipartisan support for dealing with the Cold War. But not everyone believed that containment was the right way to deal with communism. Some Americans on the left believed that containment was an unnecessarily belligerent approach to the Soviet Union, that the United States could have made peace with the Russians. Wider opposition to containment came from conservative Americans, who believed that containment was too weak a response to communism—that, indeed, it was a kind of appeasement.

Among the conservatives who disdained containment were members of an anticommunist organization known as the John Birch Society. Its leader was *John Birch Society* Robert Welch, a man so fearful of communism that he believed that some of the most important leaders of American government were trying to undermine the United States and collaborating with the Soviets. Welch presented his opposition in *The Blue Book of the John Birch Society,* in which he argued that much of the American government was riddled with treason. "For years," he wrote, "we have been taken steadily down the road to Communism by steps supposedly designed . . . as ways of *fighting* Communism." Instead, he argued, it was communist Americans themselves who were undermining the nation. "Both the U.S. and Soviet governments are controlled by the same furtive conspiratorial cabal of internationalists, greedy bankers, and corrupt politicians," Welch wrote. "If left unexposed, the traitors inside the U.S. government would betray the country's sovereignty to the United Nations for a collectivist New World Order, managed by a 'one-world' socialist government." Among the sources of treason, Welch claimed, was the creation of the United Nations and other international institutions. Many Americans considered the John Birch Society an extremist organization, but the belief that communism was the greatest danger facing the United States was widely supported.

The opposition to containment reached some of the highest levels of the government. John Foster Dulles, who would soon become secretary of state in the Eisenhower administration, wrote the foreign policy plank in the Republican platform in 1952. "We charge that the leaders of the Administration in power lost the peace so dearly earned by World War II," Dulles charged. "They abandoned friendly nations such as Latvia, Lithuania, Estonia, Poland, and Czechoslovakia." Containment, they argued, was a policy of weakness that had allowed the communists to take over much of the world. Instead, those who opposed containment called for what was known as "rollback." Instead of containing communism, the United States should be pushing back the borders of communism, despite the possibility of another war. President Dwight Eisenhower, however, did not share Dulles's belief in rollback, and the government abided by the containment strategy throughout the 1950s and beyond—despite the fevered opposition to what some still considered to be treason.

THE MARSHALL PLAN

An integral part of the containment policy was a proposal to aid in the economic reconstruction of Western Europe. There were many motives: humanitarian concern for the European people; a fear that Europe would remain an economic drain on the United States if it could not quickly rebuild; and a desire for a strong European market for American goods. But above all, American policymakers believed that unless something could be done to strengthen the shaky pro-American governments in Western Europe, those governments might fall under the control of the growing domestic communist parties.

In June 1947, Secretary of State George C. Marshall announced a plan to provide economic assistance to all European nations (including the Soviet Union) that would join in drafting a program for recovery. Although Russia and its Eastern satellites predictably rejected the plan, sixteen Western European nations eagerly participated. Whatever isolationist opposition there was in the United States largely vanished after a sudden coup in Czechoslovakia in February 1948, which established a Soviet-dominated communist government. In April, Congress approved the creation of the Economic Cooperation Administration, the agency that would administer the Marshall Plan, as it became known. Over the next three years, the Marshall Plan channeled $13 billion of American aid into Europe, helping to spark a substantial economic revival. By the end of 1950, European industrial production had risen 64 percent, communist strength in the member nations had declined, and opportunities for American trade had revived.

MOBILIZATION AT HOME

In 1948, at the president's request, Congress approved a new military draft and revived the Selective Service System. In the meantime, the United States, having failed to reach agreement with the Soviet Union on international control of nuclear weapons, redoubled its own efforts in atomic research, elevating nuclear weaponry to a central place in its military arsenal. The Atomic Energy Commission, established in 1946, became the supervisory body charged with overseeing all nuclear research, civilian and military alike. And in 1950, the Truman administration approved the development of the new hydrogen bomb, a nuclear weapon far more powerful than those used in 1945.

The National Security Act of 1947 reshaped the nation's military and diplomatic institutions. A new Department of Defense would oversee all branches of the armed services, combining functions previously performed separately by the War and Navy Departments. A National Security Council (NSC), operating out *Creation of NSC, CIA, and Defense Department* of the White House, would govern foreign and military policy. A Central Intelligence Agency (CIA) would replace the wartime Office of Strategic Services and would be responsible for collecting information through both open and covert methods; as the Cold War continued, the CIA would also engage in secret political and military operations on behalf of American interests. The National Security Act, in other words, gave the president expanded powers with which to pursue the nation's international goals.

THE ROAD TO NATO

The United States also moved to strengthen the military capabilities of Western Europe. Convinced that a reconstructed Germany was essential to the needs of the West, Truman reached an agreement with England and France to merge the three western zones of occupation into a new West German republic (which would include the three non-Soviet sectors of Berlin, even though that city lay within the Soviet zone). Stalin responded quickly. On June 24, 1948, he imposed a tight blockade around the western sectors of Berlin. *Berlin Airlift* If Germany was to be officially divided, Stalin was implying, then the country's Western government would have to abandon the capital city in the heart of the Soviet-controlled eastern zone. Truman refused to do so. Unwilling to risk war through a military challenge to the blockade, he ordered a massive airlift to supply the city with food, fuel, and other needed goods. The airlift continued for more than ten months, transporting nearly 2.5 million tons of food and other material, keeping a city of 2 million people alive. In the spring of 1949, Stalin lifted the now ineffective blockade. And in October, the division of Germany into two nations—the Federal Republic in the west (with its new capital in Bonn) and the Democratic Republic in the East (with its capital in East Berlin)—became official.

DIVIDED EUROPE AFTER WORLD WAR II This map shows the sharp division that emerged in Europe after World War II between the area under the control of the Soviet Union and the area allied with the United States. In the east, Soviet control or influence extended into all the nations shaded brown—including the eastern half of Germany. In the west and south, the green-shaded nations were allied with the United States as members of the North Atlantic Treaty Organization (NATO). The countries shaded gold were aligned with neither of the two superpowers. The small map in the upper right shows the division of Berlin among the various occupying powers at the end of the war. Eventually, the American, British, and French sectors were combined to create West Berlin, a city governed by West Germany but entirely surrounded by communist East Germany. The airplane icons represent the airlift of supplies ordered by President Truman into the blockaded zones of West Berlin beginning in June 1948. • *How did the West prevent East Germany from absorbing West Berlin?*

The crisis in Berlin accelerated the consolidation of what was already in effect an alliance among the United States and the countries of Western Europe. On April 4, 1949, twelve nations signed an agreement establishing the North Atlantic Treaty Organization (NATO)—declaring that an armed attack against one member would be considered an attack against all. The NATO countries would, moreover, maintain a standing military force in Europe to defend against what they believed was the threat of a Soviet invasion. The formation of NATO eventually spurred the Soviet Union to create an alliance of its *Warsaw Pact* own with the communist governments in Eastern Europe, as formalized in 1955 by the Warsaw Pact.

REEVALUATING COLD WAR POLICY

In September 1949, the Soviet Union successfully exploded its first atomic weapon. The Russian nuclear capacity came years earlier than predicted, shocking and frightening many Americans. So did the collapse of Chiang Kai-shek's nationalist government in China, which occurred with startling speed in the last months of 1949. Chiang fled with his political allies and the remnants of his army to the offshore island of Formosa (Taiwan), and the entire Chinese mainland came under the control of a   *Communist Victory in China* communist government led by Mao Zedong that many Americans believed to be an extension of the Soviet Union. The United States refused to recognize the new communist regime.

The fall of China to communism was one of the most traumatic events of the Cold War. It accelerated the fear of communism, and it persuaded many Americans that the defeat was a result of weakness, and even treason. As a result, American friends of China formed what came to be known as the China Lobby. Among its eminent leaders were members of Congress, high-level military figures, and powerful journalists. They believed that the United States had not done enough to prevent the communists from taking over mainland China. The failure persuaded many Americans that the government—particularly members of the State Department—was responsible.

In this atmosphere of escalating crisis, Truman called for a thorough review of American foreign policy. The result, a National Security Council report, issued in 1950 and commonly known as NSC-68, outlined a shift in the American position. The first statements of the containment doctrine—the writings of George Kennan, the Truman Doctrine speech—had made distinctions between areas of vital interest to the United States and areas of less importance to the nation's foreign policy. The containment doctrine also called for sharing the military burden of protecting the Western nations. But NSC-68 argued that the United States could no longer rely on other nations to take the initiative in resisting communism. It must move on its own to stop communist expansion virtually anywhere it occurred, regardless of the intrinsic strategic or economic value of the lands in question. Among other things, the report called for a major expansion of American military power, with a defense budget almost four times the previously projected figure. (See "Consider the Source: National Security Council Paper No. 68.")

AMERICA AFTER THE WAR

The crises overseas were not the only frustrations the American people encountered after the war. The nation also faced serious, if short-lived, economic difficulties in adapting to peace. And it suffered from an exceptionally heated political climate that produced a new wave of insecurity and repression.

THE PROBLEMS OF RECONVERSION

Despite widespread predictions that the end of the war would return America to depression conditions, economic growth continued after 1945. Pent-up consumer demand from workers who had accumulated substantial savings during the war helped spur the boom. So did a $6 billion tax cut. The Servicemen's Readjustment Act of 1944, better known as   *GI Bill* the GI Bill of Rights, provided housing, education, and job-training subsidies to veterans and increased spending even further.

CONSIDER THE SOURCE

NATIONAL SECURITY COUNCIL PAPER NO. 68 (NSC-68)

On April 7, 1950, foreign policy experts in the Truman administration completed a top-secret report calling for an expansion of the American commitment to containing the Soviet Union. They based that call, as outlined in the selection below, on their dim view of Soviet character and on their understanding of international power relations in the previous four decades.

Within the past thirty-five years the world has experienced two global wars of tremendous violence. It has witnessed two revolutions—the Russian and the Chinese—of extreme scope and intensity. It has also seen the collapse of five empires—the Ottoman, the Austro-Hungarian, German, Italian, and Japanese—and the drastic decline of two major imperial systems, the British and the French. During the span of one generation, the international distribution of power has been fundamentally altered. For several centuries it had proved impossible for any one nation to gain such preponderant strength that a coalition of other nations could not in time face it with greater strength. The international scene was marked by recurring periods of violence and war, but a system of sovereign and independent states was maintained, over which no state was able to achieve hegemony.

Two complex sets of factors have now basically altered this historical distribution of power. First, the defeat of Germany and Japan and the decline of the British and French Empires have interacted with the development of the United States and the Soviet Union in such a way that power has increasingly gravitated to these two centers. Second, the Soviet Union, unlike previous aspirants to hegemony, is animated by a new fanatic faith, antithetical to our own, and seeks to impose its absolute authority over the rest of the world. Conflict has, therefore, become endemic and is waged, on the part of the Soviet Union, by violent or nonviolent methods in accordance with the dictates of expediency. With the development of increasingly terrifying weapons of mass destruction, every individual faces the ever-present possibility of annihilation should the conflict enter the phase of total war. [. . .]

Our overall policy at the present time may be described as one designed to foster a world environment in which the American system can survive and flourish. It therefore rejects the concept of isolation and affirms the necessity of our positive participation in the world community.

This broad intention embraces two subsidiary policies. One is a policy which we would probably pursue even if there were no Soviet threat. It is a policy of attempting to develop a healthy international community. The other is the policy of "containing" the Soviet system. These two policies are closely interrelated and interact on one another. Nevertheless, the distinction between them is basically valid and contributes to a clearer understanding of what we are trying to do.

UNDERSTAND, ANALYZE, & EVALUATE

1. What broader historical trends did the authors of this memorandum identify as precursors to global power relations after World War II?
2. How did Memorandum NSC-68 characterize the Soviet Union? How did it characterize the goals of the United States? How does this compare to the historical record presented to you in this text?

Source: U.S. Department of State, *Foreign Relations of the United States, 1950. National Security Affairs; Foreign Economic Policy* (Washington, D.C.: U.S. Government Printing Office, 1977), I, pp. 237, 252–253, 262–263, 264, 282, 290. Located in Elizabeth Cobbs Hoffman and Jon Gjerde (eds.), *Major Problems in American History. Volume II: Since 1865* (Boston: Houghton Mifflin Company, 2002), pp. 287–288.

The GI Bill expressed the progressive hopes of many Americans who wanted to see the government do more to assist its citizens. But it also expressed some of the enduring inequalities in American life. Few GI Bill benefits were available to women, even though many women had assisted the war effort in important ways. And while the GI Bill itself did not discriminate against African Americans, its provisions giving local governments jurisdiction allowed southern states, in particular, to deny or limit benefits to black veterans.

The flood of consumer demand contributed to more than two years of inflation, during which prices rose at annual rates of 14 to 15 percent. Compounding the economic difficulties was a sharp rise in labor unrest. By the end of 1945, major strikes had occurred in the automobile, electrical, and steel industries. In April 1946, John L. Lewis led the United Mine Workers out on strike, shutting down the coal fields for forty days. Truman finally forced coal production to resume by ordering government seizure of the mines.   *Inflation and Strikes* But in the process, he pressured mine owners to grant the union most of its demands. Almost simultaneously, the nation's railroads suffered a total shutdown—the first in the nation's history—as two major unions walked out on strike. By threatening to use the army to run the trains, Truman pressured the strikers back to work after only a few days.

Reconversion was particularly difficult for the millions of women and minorities who had entered the workforce during the war. With veterans returning home, employers tended to push women, African Americans, Hispanics, and others out of the plants to make room for white males. Some war workers, particularly women, left the workforce voluntarily, out of a desire to return to their former domestic lives. But as many as 80 percent of women workers, and virtually all black and Hispanic males, wanted to continue working. The postwar inflation, the pressure of a growing high-consumption society, the rising divorce rate (which left many women responsible for their own economic well-being)—all combined to create a high demand for paid employment among women. As women workers found themselves excluded from industrial jobs, therefore, they moved increasingly into other areas of the economy (above all, the service sector).

THE FAIR DEAL REJECTED

Days after the Japanese surrender, Truman submitted to Congress a twenty-one-point domestic program outlining what he later named the "Fair Deal." It called for an expansion of Social Security benefits, the raising of the legal minimum wage from 40 to 65 cents an hour, a program to ensure full employment through aggressive use of federal spending and investment, a permanent Fair Employment Practices Act, public housing and slum clearance, long-range environmental and public works planning, and government promotion of scientific research. Weeks later he added other proposals: federal aid to education, government health insurance and prepaid medical care, funding for the St. Lawrence Seaway, and nationalization of atomic energy.

But most of Truman's programs fell victim to the same public and congressional conservatism that had crippled the last years of the New Deal. Indeed, that conservatism seemed to be intensifying, as the November 1946 congressional elections suggested. Using the simple but devastating slogan "Had Enough?" the Republican Party won control of both houses of Congress, which quickly moved to reduce government spending and chip away at New Deal reforms. Its most notable action was its assault on the Wagner Act of 1935, in the form of the Labor-Management Relations Act of 1947, better known as the Taft-Hartley Act. It made illegal the closed shop (a workplace in which no one can be hired without first being a member of a union). And although it continued to permit the creation of union shops (in which workers must join a union after being hired), it permitted states to pass "right-to-work" laws

Taft-Hartley Act prohibiting even that. The Taft-Hartley Act also empowered the president to call for a ten-week "cooling-off" period before a strike by issuing an injunction against any work stoppage that endangered national safety or health. Outraged workers and union leaders denounced the measure as a "slave labor bill." Truman vetoed it. But both houses easily over-ruled him the same day. The Taft-Hartley Act did not destroy the labor movement. But it did damage weaker unions in relatively lightly organized industries such as chemicals and textiles, and it made much more difficult the organizing of workers who had never been union members at all, especially in the South and the West.

THE ELECTION OF 1948

Truman and his advisers believed that the American public was not ready to abandon the achievements of the New Deal, despite the 1946 election results. As they planned their strategy for the 1948 campaign, therefore, they hoped to appeal to enduring Democratic loyalties. Throughout 1948, Truman proposed one reform measure after another (including, on February 2, the first major civil rights bill of the century). To no one's surprise, Congress ignored or defeated them all, but the president was building campaign issues for the fall.

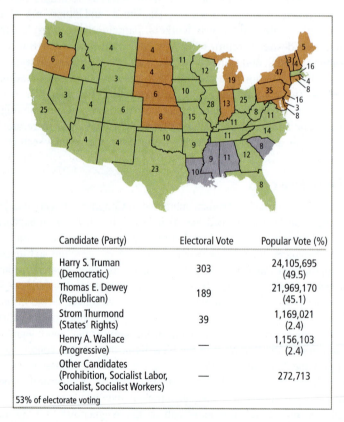

Candidate (Party)	Electoral Vote	Popular Vote (%)
Harry S. Truman (Democratic)	303	24,105,695 (49.5)
Thomas E. Dewey (Republican)	189	21,969,170 (45.1)
Strom Thurmond (States' Rights)	39	1,169,021 (2.4)
Henry A. Wallace (Progressive)	—	1,156,103 (2.4)
Other Candidates (Prohibition, Socialist Labor, Socialist, Socialist Workers)	—	272,713

53% of electorate voting

THE ELECTION OF 1948 Despite the widespread expectation that the Republican candidate, Thomas Dewey, would easily defeat Truman in 1948, the president in fact won a substantial reelection victory that year. This map shows the broad geographic reach of Truman's victory. Dewey swept most of the Northeast, but Truman dominated almost everywhere else. Strom Thurmond, the States' Rights candidate, carried four states in the South. • *What had prompted Thurmond to desert the Democratic Party and run for president on his own?*

There remained, however, the problems of Truman's personal unpopularity—the assumption among much of the electorate that he lacked stature and that his administration was weak and inept—and the deep divisions within the Democratic Party. At the Democratic National Convention that summer, two factions abandoned the party altogether. Angered by Truman's proposed civil rights bill and by the approval at the convention of a civil rights plank in the platform (engineered by Hubert Humphrey, the reform mayor of Minneapolis), some southern conservatives walked out and formed the States' Rights (Democratic or "Dixiecrat") Party, with Governor Strom Thurmond   *Divided Democratic Party* of South Carolina as its nominee. At the same time, some members of the party's left wing—contemptuous of what they considered Truman's ineffectual leadership and his excessively confrontational stance toward the Soviet Union—joined the new Progressive Party, whose candidate was Henry A. Wallace.

Many Democratic liberals who were unhappy with Truman were unwilling to leave the party. The Americans for Democratic Action (ADA), a coalition of anticommunist liberals, tried to entice Dwight D. Eisenhower, the popular war hero, to contest the nomination. Only after Eisenhower refused did liberals concede the nomination to Truman. The Republicans, in the meantime, once again nominated Governor Thomas E. Dewey of New York. Austere, dignified, and competent, he seemed to offer an unbeatable alternative to the president.

Only Truman seemed to believe he could win. As the campaign gathered momentum, he became more and more aggressive, turning the fire away from himself and toward Dewey and the "do-nothing, good-for-nothing" Republican Congress, which was, he told voters, responsible for fueling inflation and abandoning workers and common people. To dramatize his point, he called Congress into special session in July to give it a chance, he said, to enact the liberal measures the Republicans had recently written into their platform. Congress met for two weeks and, predictably, managed to pass almost nothing.

On election night, to the surprise of almost everyone, Truman won a narrow but decisive and dramatic victory: 49.5 percent of the popular vote to Dewey's   *Truman Defeats Dewey* 45.1 percent (with the two splinter parties dividing the small remainder evenly between them), and an electoral margin of 303 to 189. Democrats regained both houses of Congress by substantial margins.

THE FAIR DEAL REVIVED

Despite the Democratic victories, the Eighty-First Congress was little more hospitable to Truman's Fair Deal reform. Truman did win some important victories. Congress raised the legal minimum wage from 40 cents to 75 cents an hour. It approved an important expansion of the Social Security system, increasing benefits by 75 percent and extending them to 10 million additional people. And it passed the National Housing Act of 1949, which provided for the construction of 810,000 units of low-income housing accompanied by long-term rent subsidies.

But on other issues—national health insurance and aid to education, among them—Truman made little progress. Nor was he able to persuade Congress to accept the civil rights legislation he proposed in 1949, legislation that would make lynching a federal crime, provide federal protection of black voting rights, abolish the poll tax, and establish a new Fair Employment Practices Commission to curb discrimination in hiring. Southern Democrats filibustered to kill the bill.

Undeterred, Truman proceeded on his own to battle several forms of racial discrimination. He ordered an end to discrimination in the hiring of government employees. He began to dismantle segregation within the armed forces. And he allowed the Justice Department to become actively involved in court battles against discriminatory statutes. The Supreme Court, in the meantime, signaled its own growing awareness of the issue by ruling, in *Shelley v. Kraemer* (1948), that courts could not be used to enforce private "covenants" meant to bar blacks from residential neighborhoods.

THE NUCLEAR AGE

Looming over the many struggles of the postwar years was the image of the great and terrible mushroom clouds that had risen over Alamogordo in July 1945 and over the ruined Japanese cities of Hiroshima and Nagasaki. Americans greeted these terrible new instruments of destruction with fear and awe, but also with expectation. Postwar culture was torn between a dark image of the nuclear war that many Americans feared would result from the rivalry with the Soviet Union, and the bright image of a dazzling technological future that atomic power might help to produce.

The fear of nuclear weapons appeared widely in popular culture, but it was often dis-
Menace in Films   guised. The late 1940s and early 1950s were the heyday of *film noir,* a kind of filmmaking that originated in France and had been named for the dark lighting characteristic of the genre. American *film noir* portrayed the loneliness of individuals in an impersonal world—a staple of American culture for many decades—but also suggested the menacing character of the age, the looming possibility of vast destruction. Sometimes,

THE RED MENACE This 1949 movie poster suggests how much attention was directed to the threat of communism. The film told the story of a man and a woman who joined the Communist Party, only to become disillusioned when they watched the murder of a party member who had begun to doubt the party's principles. (© Republic Pictures/Photofest)

popular fears addressed nuclear fear explicitly—for example, the celebrated television show of the 1950s and early 1960s, *The Twilight Zone,* which featured dramatic portrayals of the aftermath of nuclear war; or postwar comic books, which depicted powerful superheroes saving the world from destruction.

Such images resonated with the public because awareness of nuclear weapons was increasingly built into their daily lives. Schools and office buildings held regular air-raid drills to prepare people for the possibility of nuclear attack. Radio stations regularly tested the Emergency Broadcast System, which stood in readiness for war. Fallout shelters stocked with water and canned goods sprang up in public buildings and private homes. Though few Americans went about their daily lives in a state of panic, anxiety simmered below the surface.

And yet, the United States was also an exuberant nation in these years, dazzled by its own prosperity and excited by the technological innovations transforming the nation, including nuclear power. The same scientific knowledge that could destroy the world, many believed, might also lead it into a glimmering future. The *New York Times,* only days after Hiroshima, expressed its own rosy view of the nuclear future: "This new knowledge . . . can bring to this earth not death but life, not tyranny and cruelty, but a divine freedom."

That kind of optimism soon became widespread. The "secret of the atom," many Americans predicted, would bring "prosperity and a more complete life." A public opinion poll late in 1948 revealed that approximately two-thirds of those questioned believed that, "in the long run," atomic energy would "do more good than harm."   *Nuclear Power* Nuclear power plants began to spring up in many areas of the country and were welcomed as the source of cheap and unlimited electricity, their potential dangers scarcely even discussed by those who celebrated their creation.

THE KOREAN WAR

Though the Cold War started in Europe, it quickly spread to Asia. On June 24, 1950, the armies of communist North Korea swept across their southern border and invaded the pro-Western half of the Korean peninsula. Within days, they had occupied much of South Korea, including Seoul, its capital. True to the dictates of containment, the United States almost immediately committed itself to the conflict.

THE DIVIDED PENINSULA

When World War II ended, both the United States and the Soviet Union had troops in Korea fighting the Japanese; neither army was willing to leave. Instead, they divided the nation, supposedly temporarily, along the 38th parallel. The Russians finally departed in 1949, leaving behind a communist government in the north with a strong, Soviet-equipped army. The Americans left a few months later, handing control to the pro-Western government of Syngman Rhee. Anticommunist but only nominally   *Syngman Rhee* democratic, he used his relatively small military primarily to suppress internal opposition.

The relative weakness of South Korea offered a strong temptation to nationalists in the North Korean government who wanted to reunite the country, particularly after the American government implied that it did not consider Korea within its own "defense perimeter." The Soviets and Chinese did not order the invasion, but they did not try to stop it. They supported the offensive once it began.

Almost immediately, on June 27, 1950, the president ordered limited American military assistance to South Korea, and on the same day he appealed to the United Nations to intervene. The Soviet Union was boycotting the Security Council at the time (to protest the council's refusal to recognize the new communist government of China) and was thus unable to exercise its veto power. As a result, American delegates were able to win UN agreement to a resolution calling for international assistance to the Rhee government. On June 30, the United States ordered its own ground forces into Korea, and Truman appointed General Douglas MacArthur to command the UN operations there. (Several other nations provided assistance and troops, but the "UN" armies were, in fact, overwhelmingly American.)

After a surprise American invasion at Inchon in September had routed the North Korean forces from the south and sent them back across the 38th parallel, Truman gave

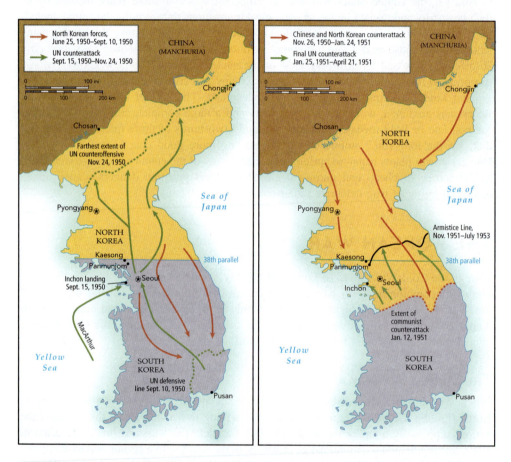

THE KOREAN WAR, 1950–1953 These two maps illustrate the changing fortunes of UN forces (which were mostly American) during the 1950–1953 Korean War. The map at the left shows the extent of the North Korean invasion of South Korea in 1950; communist forces for a time controlled all of Korea except a small area around Pusan in the southeast. On September 15, 1950, UN troops under Douglas MacArthur landed in force at Inchon and soon drove the North Koreans back across the border. MacArthur then pursued the North Koreans well into their own territory. The map at right shows the very different circumstances once the Chinese entered the war in November 1950. Chinese forces drove the UN army back below the 38th parallel and, briefly, deep into South Korea, below Seoul. The UN troops fought back to the prewar border between North and South Korea late in 1951, but the war then bogged down into a stalemate that continued for a year and a half. • *What impact did the Korean War have on American politics in the early 1950s?*

MacArthur permission to pursue the communists into their own territory. Hoping now to create "a unified, independent and democratic Korea," the president had moved beyond simple containment to an attempted rollback of communist power.

FROM INVASION TO STALEMATE

For several weeks, MacArthur's invasion of North Korea proceeded smoothly. On October 19, the capital, Pyongyang, fell to the UN forces. Victory seemed near—until the Chinese government, alarmed by the movement of American forces toward its *China Intervenes* border, intervened. In early November, eight divisions of the Chinese army entered the war. The UN offensive stalled and then collapsed. Through December 1950, outnumbered American forces were forced into a rapid, bitter retreat in numbingly cold temperatures. Within weeks, communist forces had pushed the Americans back below the 38th parallel once again and had recaptured the South Korean capital of Seoul. By mid-January 1951 the rout had ceased; and by March the UN armies had managed to regain much of the territory they had recently lost, taking back Seoul and pushing the communists north of the 38th parallel for the second time. With that, the war turned into a protracted stalemate.

From the start, Truman had been determined to avoid a direct conflict with China, which he feared might lead to a new world war. Once China *Truman–MacArthur Controversy* entered the war, he began seeking a negotiated solution to the struggle. But General MacArthur had ideas of his own. The United States was really fighting the Chinese, MacArthur argued. It should, therefore, attack China itself, if not through an actual invasion, then at least by bombing communist forces massing north of the Chinese border with conventional or even atomic weapons. In March 1951, he indicated his unhappiness with Truman's reluctance to invade China. In a public letter to House Republican Leader Joseph W. Martin, he concluded: "There is no substitute for victory." His position had wide popular support. Yet the release of the Martin letter struck the president as intolerable insubordination. On April 11, 1951, he relieved MacArthur of his command.

Sixty-nine percent of the American people supported MacArthur, a Gallup poll reported. When the general returned to the United States later in 1951, he was greeted with wild enthusiasm. Public criticism of Truman finally abated somewhat when a number of prominent military figures, including General Omar Bradley, publicly supported the president's decision. But substantial hostility toward Truman remained. In the meantime, the Korean stalemate continued. Negotiations between the opposing forces began at Panmunjom in July 1951, but the talks—and the war—dragged on until 1953.

LIMITED MOBILIZATION

The war in Korea produced only a limited American military commitment abroad. It also created only a limited economic mobilization at home.

Truman set up the Office of Defense Mobilization to fight inflation by holding down prices and discouraging high union wage demands. When these cautious regulatory efforts failed, the president took more drastic action. Railroad workers walked off the job in 1951, and Truman, who considered the workers' demands inflationary, ordered the government to seize control of the railroads. In 1952, during a nationwide steel strike, Truman seized the steel mills, citing his powers as commander in chief. But in a 6-to-3 decision, the Supreme Court ruled that the president had exceeded his authority, and Truman was forced to relent.

The Korean War significantly boosted economic growth by pumping new government funds into the economy at a point when many believed it was about to decline. But the war had other, less welcome effects. It came at a time of rising insecurity about America's position in the world and intensified anxiety about communism. As the long stalemate continued, producing 140,000 American dead and wounded, frustration turned to anger. The United States, which had recently won the greatest war in history, seemed unable to conclude what many Americans considered a minor border skirmish in a small country. They began to believe that something must be deeply wrong—not only in Korea but within the United States as well. Such fears contributed to the rise of the second major campaign of the century against domestic communism.

THE CRUSADE AGAINST SUBVERSION

Why did the American people develop a growing fear of internal communist subversion— a fear that by the early 1950s occasionally reached the point of hysteria? There are many possible answers but no single definitive explanation. (See "Debating the Past: McCarthyism.")

One factor was obvious: communism was not an imagined enemy. It had tangible shape, in Josef Stalin and the Soviet Union. Adding to the concern were the Korean stalemate, the "loss" of China, and the Soviet development of an atomic bomb. Searching for someone to blame, many began to believe that there was a communist conspiracy within American borders. But there were other factors as well, rooted in events in American domestic politics.

HUAC and Alger Hiss

Much of the anticommunist furor emerged out of the search by Republicans for an issue with which to attack the Democrats, and out of the efforts of the Democrats to take that issue away from them. Beginning in 1947, the House Un-American Activities Committee (HUAC) held widely publicized investigations to prove that, under Democratic rule, the government had tolerated (if not actually encouraged) communist subversion. The committee turned first to the movie industry, arguing that communists had infiltrated Hollywood and tainted American films with propaganda. Writers and producers, some of them former communists, were called to testify; and when some of them (the "Hollywood Ten") refused to answer questions about their political beliefs and those of their colleagues, they were sent to jail for contempt. Others were barred from employment in the industry when Hollywood, attempting to protect its public image, adopted a "blacklist" of those of "suspicious loyalty."

Alger Hiss More alarming to the public was HUAC's investigation into charges of disloyalty leveled against Alger Hiss, a former high-ranking member of the State Department. In 1948, Whittaker Chambers, a former communist agent, now a conservative editor at *Time* magazine, told the committee that Hiss had passed classified State Department documents to him in 1937 and 1938. When Hiss sued him for slander, Chambers produced microfilms of the documents (called the "pumpkin papers," because Chambers had kept them hidden in a pumpkin in his vegetable garden). Hiss could not be tried for espionage because of the statute of limitations (which protects individuals from prosecution for most crimes after seven years have passed). But largely because of the relentless efforts of Richard M. Nixon, a first-term congressman from California and a member of HUAC, Hiss was convicted of perjury and served several years in prison. The Hiss case not only discredited a prominent young diplomat, it also cast suspicion on a generation of liberal Democrats. It also transformed Nixon into a national figure and helped him win a Senate seat in 1950.

THE FEDERAL LOYALTY PROGRAM AND THE ROSENBERG CASE

Partly to protect itself against Republican attacks and partly to encourage support for the president's foreign policy initiatives, the Truman administration in 1947 initiated a widely publicized program to review the "loyalty" of federal employees. By 1951, more than 2,000 government employees had resigned under pressure and 212 had been dismissed.

The Federal Employee Loyalty Program helped launch a major assault on subversion throughout the government—and beyond. The attorney general established a widely cited list of supposedly subversive organizations. The director of the Federal Bureau of Investigation (FBI), J. Edgar Hoover, investigated and harassed alleged radicals. In 1950, Congress passed the McCarran Internal Security Act, which, among other restrictions on "subversive" activity, required that all communist organizations register with the government and publish their records. Congress easily overrode Truman's veto of the bill.

The successful Soviet detonation of an atomic bomb in 1949 suggested to some that there had been a conspiracy to pass American atomic secrets to the Russians. In 1950, Klaus Fuchs, a young British scientist, seemed to confirm those fears when he testified that he had delivered to the Russians details of the bomb's manufacture. The case ultimately moved to an obscure New York couple, Julius   *Julius and Ethel Rosenberg* and Ethel Rosenberg, members of the Communist Party. The government claimed the Rosenbergs had received secret information from Ethel's brother, a machinist on the Manhattan Project in New Mexico, and had passed it on to the Soviet Union through other agents (including Fuchs). The Rosenbergs were convicted and, on April 5, 1951, sentenced to death. After two years of appeals and public protests, they died in the electric chair on June 19, 1953. Historians now believe that Julius—but not Ethel—was guilty as charged.

All these factors—the HUAC investigations, the Hiss trial, the loyalty investigations, the McCarran Act, the Rosenberg case—combined with other concerns by the early 1950s to create a fear of communist subversion that seemed to grip the entire country. State and local governments, the judiciary, schools and universities, labor unions—all sought to purge themselves of real or imagined subversives. It was a climate that made possible the rise of an extraordinary public figure.

MCCARTHYISM

Joseph McCarthy was an undistinguished first-term Republican senator from Wisconsin until, in February 1950, in the midst of a speech in Wheeling, West Virginia, he lifted up a sheet of paper and claimed to "hold in my hand" a list of 205 known communists currently working in the American State Department. No person of comparable stature had ever made so bold a charge against the federal government. In the months to come, as McCarthy repeated and expanded on his accusations, he emerged as the nation's most prominent leader of the crusade against domestic subversion.

McCARTHYISM

The American Civil Liberties Union warned in the early 1950s, at the peak of what is now known as McCarthyism, that "the threat to civil liberties today is the most serious in the history of our country." It was expressing a view with which many Americans wholeheartedly agreed. But while there were unusually powerful challenges to freedom of speech and association in the late 1940s and early 1950s, there is wide disagreement about the causes and meaning of those challenges.

The simplest argument—and one that continues to attract scholarly support—is that the postwar Red Scare expressed real and legitimate concerns about communist subversion in the United States. William O'Neill, in *A Better World* (1982), and Richard Gid Powers, in *Not Without Honor* (1995), have both argued that anticommunism was a serious, intelligent, and patriotic movement, despite its excesses. The American Communist Party, according to this view, was an agent of Stalin and the Soviet Union within the United States, actively engaged in espionage and subversion. The effort to root communists out of public life was both understandable and justifiable—and the hysteria it sometimes produced was an unhappy but predictable by-product of an essentially rational and justifiable effort. "Anticommunism," Powers wrote, "expressed the essential American determination to stand against attacks on human freedom and foster the growth of democracy throughout the world. . . . To superimpose on this rich history the cartoon features of Joe McCarthy is to reject history for the easy comforts of moralism."

Most interpretations, however, have been less charitable. In the 1950s, in the midst of the Red Scare itself, an influential group of historians and social scientists began to portray the anticommunist fervor of their time as an expression of deep social maladjustment—an argument perhaps most closely associated with a famous essay by Richard Hofstadter, "The Paranoid Style in American Politics." There was, they argued, no logical connection between the modest power of actual communists in the United States and the hysterical form these scholars believed anticommunism was assuming. The explanation, therefore, had to lie in something other than reality, in a deeper set of social and cultural anxieties that had only an indirect connection with the political world as it existed. Extreme anticommunism, they claimed, was something close to a pathology; it expressed fear of and alienation from the modern world. A person afflicted with the "paranoid style," Hofstadter wrote,

> believes himself to be living in a world in which he is spied upon, plotted against, betrayed, and very likely destined for total ruin. He feels that his liberties have been arbitrarily and outrageously invaded. He is opposed to almost everything that has happened in American politics in the past twenty years.

Other scholars, writing not long after the decline of McCarthyism, rejected the sociocultural arguments of Hofstadter and others but shared the belief that the crusade against subversion was a distortion of normal public life. They saw the anticommunist crusade as an example of party politics run amok. Richard Freeland, in

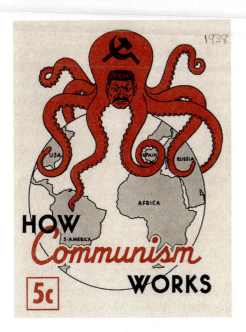

1938

HOW
Communism
WORKS

5¢

USA · SPAIN · RUSSIA · AFRICA · S-AMERICA

(Rare Book and Special Collection Division, The Library of Congress)

The Truman Doctrine and the Origins of McCarthyism (1971), argued that the Democrats began the effort to purge the government of radicals to protect themselves from attacks by the Republicans. Nelson Polsby, Robert Griffith, and others have noted how Republicans seized on the issue of communism in government in the late 1940s to reverse their nearly twenty-year exclusion from power. With each party trying to outdo the other in its effort to demonstrate its anticommunist credentials, it was hardly surprising that the crusade reached extraordinarily intense proportions.

Still other historians have emphasized the role of powerful government officials and agencies with a strong commitment to anti-communism—most notably J. Edgar Hoover and the FBI. Athan Theoharis and Kenneth

O'Reilly introduced the idea of an anticommunist bureaucracy in work published in the 1970s and 1980s. Ellen Schrecker's *Many Are the Crimes* (1998) likewise identified an interlocking cluster of official agencies committed to anticommunism and operating across many years—not just those dominated by McCarthy. Yet those agencies and individuals, she argued, whatever the sincerity of their anticommunist fervor, oversaw a period of repression that recklessly destroyed careers and lives, shattered the left, chilled dissent, and narrowed the terms of political debate.

Several scholars, finally, have presented an argument that does not so much challenge other interpretations as complement them. Anticommunist zealots were not alone to blame for the excesses of McCarthyism, they argue. It was also the fault of liberals—in politics, in academia, and, perhaps above all, in the media—who were so intimidated by the political climate, or so imprisoned within the conventions of their professions, that they found themselves unable to respond effectively to the distortions and excesses that they recognized around them. •

UNDERSTAND, ANALYZE, & EVALUATE

1. Why did the American public feel so threatened by communism? Who exploited the public's fears and why?
2. Was the public reaction to the Red Scare a logical response or disproportionate to the actual threat posed by communism?
3. How were party politics and McCarthyism connected? Do you find elements similar to McCarthyism in politics today?

Within weeks of his charges against the State Department, McCarthy leveled accusations at other agencies. After 1952, with the Republicans in control of the Senate and McCarthy now the chair of a special subcommittee, he conducted highly publicized investigations of alleged subversion in many areas of the government. McCarthy never produced conclusive evidence that any federal employee was a communist. But a growing constituency adored him nevertheless for his coarse, "fearless" assaults on a government establishment that many considered arrogant, effete, even traitorous. Republicans, in particular, rallied to his claims that the Democrats had been responsible for "twenty years of treason" and that only a change of parties could rid the country of subversion. McCarthy, in short, provided his followers with an issue into which they could channel a wide range of resentments: fear of communism, animosity toward the country's "eastern establishment," and frustrated partisan ambitions. For a time, McCarthy intimidated all but a few people from opposing him. Even the highly popular Dwight D. Eisenhower, running for president in 1952, did not speak out against him, although he disliked McCarthy's tactics and was outraged at, among other things, McCarthy's attacks on General George Marshall. Eventually his assaults against such respected figures and institutions drove McCarthy from popular favor—but not before **"McCarthyism"** came to define an era of hysterical and often unfounded accusations.

THE REPUBLICAN REVIVAL

Public frustration over the stalemate in Korea and popular fears of internal subversion combined to make 1952 a bad year for the Democratic Party. Truman, now deeply unpopular, withdrew from the presidential contest. The party united instead behind Governor Adlai E. Stevenson of Illinois. Stevenson's dignity, wit, and eloquence made him a beloved figure to many liberals and intellectuals. But those same qualities seemed only to fuel Republican charges that Stevenson lacked the strength or the will to combat communism sufficiently.

Stevenson's greatest problem, however, was the Republican candidate opposing him. Rejecting the efforts of conservatives to nominate Robert Taft or Douglas MacArthur, the Republicans turned to a man who had no previous identification with the party: General Dwight D. Eisenhower—military hero, commander of NATO, president of Columbia University—who won nomination on the first ballot. He chose as his running mate the young California senator who had gained national prominence through his crusade against Alger Hiss: Richard M. Nixon.

In the fall campaign, Eisenhower attracted support through his geniality and his statesmanlike pledges to settle the Korean conflict. Nixon (after surviving early accusations of financial improprieties, which he effectively neutralized in a famous television address, the Checkers speech) exploited the issue of domestic anticommunism by attacking the Democrats for "cowardice" and "appeasement." The response at the polls was overwhelm-
Eisenhower Elected   ing. Eisenhower won both a popular and an electoral landslide: 55 percent of the popular vote to Stevenson's 44 percent, 442 electoral votes to Stevenson's 89. Republicans gained control of both houses of Congress for the first time since 1946.

CONCLUSION

Even during World War II, when the United States and the Soviet Union were allies, it was evident to leaders in both nations that America and Russia had quite different visions of what the postwar world should look like. Very quickly after the war ended, the once fruitful relationship between the world's greatest powers quickly soured. Americans came to believe that the Soviet Union, like Hitler's Germany, harbored dangerous expansionist ambitions. Soviets came to believe that the United States was trying to protect its own dominance in the world by encircling the Soviet Union. The result of these tensions was what became known by the end of the 1940s as the Cold War.

In the early years of the Cold War, the United States constructed a series of policies designed to prevent both war and Soviet aggression. It helped rebuild the shattered economies of Western Europe through the Marshall Plan, to stabilize those nations and prevent them from becoming communist. America embraced a new foreign policy—known as containment—that committed it to keeping the Soviet Union from expanding its influence further into the world. The United States and Western Europe formed a strong and enduring alliance, NATO, to defend Europe against possible Soviet advances.

In 1950, the armed forces of communist North Korea launched an invasion of noncommunist South Korea; and to most Americans, the conflict quickly came to be seen as a test of American resolve. The Korean War was long, costly, and unpopular, with many military setbacks and frustrations. In the end, however, the United States—working through the United Nations—managed to drive the North Koreans out of South Korea and stabilize the original division of the peninsula.

The Korean War hardened American foreign policy into a much more rigidly anticommunist form. It undermined the Truman administration, and the Democratic Party, and helped strengthen conservatives and Republicans. It greatly bolstered an already powerful crusade against communists, and those believed to be communists, within the United States—a crusade often known as McCarthyism, because of the notoriety of Senator Joseph McCarthy of Wisconsin, the most celebrated leader of the effort.

America after World War II was indisputably the wealthiest and most powerful nation in the world. But in the harsh climate of the Cold War, neither wealth nor power could dispel deep anxieties and bitter divisions.

KEY TERMS/PEOPLE/PLACES/EVENTS

Alger Hiss 672
Central Intelligence Agency
  (CIA) 661
Cold War 653
containment 659
Douglas MacArthur 670
Fair Deal 665
GI Bill 663
House Un-American Activities
  Committee (HUAC) 672

John Birch Society 660
Julius and Ethel
  Rosenberg 673
Korean War 669
Mao Zedong 663
Marshall Plan 661
McCarthyism 676
North Atlantic Treaty
  Organization (NATO) 662
NSC-68 663

Syngman Rhee 669
Taft-Hartley Act 665
Truman Doctrine 659
United Nations 655
Warsaw Pact 662
Yalta Conference 657

RECALL AND REFLECT

1. How did American diplomats plan for the postwar world and settle postwar issues? How did opposing visions of the postwar world order thwart those efforts?
2. How did postwar economic problems affect American politics and society?
3. Why did the United States become involved in the war in Korea? What was the result of U.S. involvement in that war?
4. Why did the fear of communism at home reach such great proportions? What events helped fan that fear?

28

THE AFFLUENT SOCIETY

THE ECONOMIC "MIRACLE"

THE EXPLOSION OF SCIENCE AND
TECHNOLOGY

PEOPLE OF PLENTY

THE OTHER AMERICA

THE RISE OF THE CIVIL RIGHTS MOVEMENT

EISENHOWER REPUBLICANISM

EISENHOWER, DULLES, AND THE COLD WAR

LOOKING AHEAD

1. Why did the U.S. economy experience such a boom in the late 1950s and early 1960s? How did this boom affect American society?

2. Who constituted the "other America," who failed to share in the economic prosperity and affluence of the postwar era? Why were they left out?

3. What was the response to the Supreme Court decision in *Brown v. Board of Education*? How did the Court's decision affect African Americans and the early civil rights movement? How did it affect white southerners?

4. What policy guided foreign affairs under Eisenhower, and how was that policy implemented around the world?

IF AMERICA EXPERIENCED A GOLDEN age in the 1950s and early 1960s, as many Americans believed at the time and many continue to believe today, it was largely a result of two developments. One was a booming national prosperity, which profoundly altered the social, economic, and even physical landscape of the United States. The other was the continuing struggle against communism, a struggle that created considerable anxiety but that also encouraged many Americans to look even more approvingly at their own society. But if these powerful forces created a widespread sense of national purpose and self-satisfaction, they also helped blind many Americans to serious problems developing at home.

THE ECONOMIC "MIRACLE"

Perhaps the most striking feature of American society in the 1950s and early 1960s was the booming economic growth that made even the heady 1920s seem pale by comparison. It was a better-balanced and more widely distributed prosperity than that of thirty years earlier. It was not, however, as universal as some Americans liked to believe.

Economic Growth

By 1949, despite the continuing problems of postwar reconversion, an economic expansion had begun that would continue with only brief interruptions for almost twenty years. Between 1945 and 1960, the gross national product grew by 250 percent, from $200 billion to over $500 billion. Unemployment remained at about 5 percent or lower throughout the 1950s and early 1960s. Inflation, in the meantime, hovered around 3 percent a year or less.

The causes of this growth were varied. Part of the growth came from Americans throwing off the emotional shackles of the Great Depression. Buoyed by victory in the world war, Americans again began to believe in a brighter future, and they invested in it. Government spending, which had reached new levels from fighting a world war and the Great Depression, continued to stimulate growth through public funding of schools, housing, veterans' benefits, welfare, interstate highways, and, above all, the military. Economic growth peaked during the first half of the 1950s, when military spending was highest because of the Korean War. Additionally, trade agreements after the war began to open markets for goods and services like no other time in its history. Virtually untouched by the destruction of war, U.S. manufacturing and services reaped the initial rewards of international trade.

TIME LINE

1947
Levittown construction begins

1953
Korean War ends

1954
Brown v. Board of Education
Army–McCarthy hearings

1955
Montgomery bus boycott

1956
Federal Highway Act
Eisenhower reelected
Suez crisis

1957
Sputnik launched
Kerouac's *On the Road*
Little Rock desegregation crisis

1959
Castro seizes power in Cuba

1960
U-2 incident
Eisenhower's farewell address

1961
First American in space
U.S. severs diplomatic relations with Cuba

1969
Americans land on moon

The national birthrate reversed a long pattern of decline with what is commonly called the **Baby Boom,** which began during World War II and peaked in 1957. The nation's population rose almost 20 percent in the decade, from 150 million in 1950 to 179 million in 1960, which meant increased consumer demand and expanding economic growth.

Rapid suburban expansion—a 47 percent increase in the 1950s—helped stimulate growth in several important sectors of the economy. The number of privately owned cars more than doubled in a decade. Demand for new homes helped sustain a vigorous housing industry. The construction of roads stimulated the economy as well.

The combination of post–WWII economic growth, new standards of support from government spending, and a booming population led to a renewed American vitality for the next thirty years. And while that growth was far from equally distributed, the average American in 1960 had over 20 percent more purchasing power than in 1945 and more than twice as much as during the prosperous 1920s. The American people had achieved the highest standard of living of any society in the history of the world.

THE RISE OF THE MODERN WEST

No region experienced more dramatic changes than the American West. Its population expanded dramatically; its cities boomed; its industrial economy flourished. By the 1960s, some parts of the West were among the most important (and populous) industrial and cultural centers of the nation.

As during World War II, much of the growth of the West was a result of federal spending and investment—on the dams, power stations, highways, and other infrastructure projects that made additional economic development possible. Military contracts continued

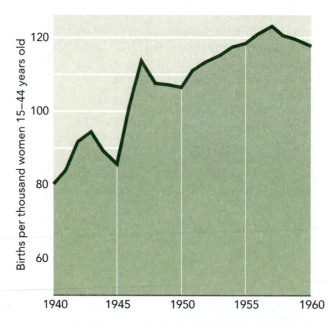

THE AMERICAN BIRTHRATE, 1940–1960   This chart shows how the American birthrate grew rapidly during and after World War II (following a long period of decline in the 1930s) to produce what became known as the "Baby Boom." At the peak of the Baby Boom, during the 1950s, the nation's population grew by 20 percent. • *What impact did the Baby Boom have on the nation's economy?*

to flow disproportionately to factories in California and Texas, many built with government funds during the war. The growing number of automobiles created new demands for petroleum and contributed to the rapid growth of oil fields in Texas and Colorado and of the metropolitan centers, among them Houston, Dallas, and Denver. State governments in the West invested heavily in their universities. The University of Texas and University of California systems, in particular, became among the nation's largest and created important centers of research. They helped attract technology-intensive industries to the region. Climate also contributed to growth in the West. Southern California, Nevada, and Arizona, in particular, attracted many migrants from the East because of their warm, dry climates. The growth of Los Angeles after World War II was a remarkable phenomenon: more than 10 percent of all new businesses in the United States between 1945 and 1950 began in Los Angeles. Its population rose by over 50 percent between 1940 and 1960.

CAPITAL AND LABOR

Booming corporations were reluctant to allow strikes to interfere with their operations; and since the most important labor unions were now so large and entrenched that they could not easily be suppressed or intimidated, leaders of large businesses made important concessions to them. By the mid-1950s, factory wages in most industries had risen substantially, to an average of $80 per week. In December 1955, the American Federation of Labor and the Congress of Industrial Organizations ended their twenty-year rivalry   *AFL and CIO Merge* and merged to create the AFL-CIO, under the leadership of George Meany.

But success also bred stagnation and corruption in some union bureaucracies. In 1957, the powerful Teamsters Union became the subject of a congressional investigation, and its president, David Beck, was charged with the misappropriation of union funds.

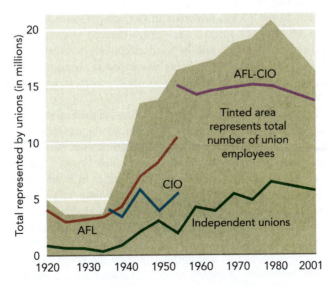

WORKERS REPRESENTED BY UNIONS, 1920–2001   This chart shows the number of workers represented by unions over an eighty-year period. Note the dramatic rise in the unionized workforce during the 1930s and 1940s, the slower but still significant rise in the 1960s and 1970s, and the steady decline that began in the 1980s. The chart, in fact, understates the decline of unionized labor in the postwar era, since it shows union membership in absolute numbers and not as a percentage of the rapidly growing workforce. • *Why did unions cease recruiting new members successfully in the 1970s, and why did they begin actually losing members in the 1980s?*

Beck ultimately stepped down to be replaced by Jimmy Hoffa, whom government investigators pursued for nearly a decade before finally winning a conviction against him in 1964 for jury tampering. The United Mine Workers, similarly, became tainted by violence and charges of corruption.

THE EXPLOSION OF SCIENCE AND TECHNOLOGY

In 1961, *Time* magazine selected as its "man of the year" not a specific person but "the American Scientist." The choice was an indication of the widespread fascination with which Americans in the age of atomic power viewed science and technology.

MEDICAL BREAKTHROUGHS

The twentieth century saw greater progress in the development of medical science than had occurred in all the centuries before it. A very large proportion of that progress occurred during and after World War II. Particularly important was the development of new antibacterial drugs capable of fighting infections that had once been all but untreatable.

To be sure, the development of antibiotics originated in the discoveries of Louis Pasteur and Jules-Francois Joubert. Working in France in the 1870s, they produced the first conclusive evidence that virulent bacterial infections could be defeated by other, more ordinary bacteria. Using their discoveries, the English physician Joseph Lister revealed the value of antiseptic solutions in preventing infection during surgery several years later.

But the practical use of antibacterial agents to combat disease did not begin until many decades later. In the 1930s, scientists in Germany, France, and England demonstrated the power of so-called sulfa drugs—drugs derived from an antibacterial agent known as sulfanilamide—which could be used effectively to treat streptococcal blood infections. New sulfa drugs were soon being developed at an astonishing rate and were frequently improved; they were enormously successful in treating what had once been a major cause of death.

In 1928, in the meantime, Alexander Fleming, an English medical researcher, accidentally discovered the antibacterial properties of an organism that he named penicillin. There was little progress in using penicillin to treat human illness, however, until a group of researchers at Oxford University, directed by Howard Florey and Ernest Chain, learned how to produce stable, potent penicillin in sizable enough quantities to make it a practical weapon against bacterial disease. The first human trials of the new drug, in 1941, were dramatically successful, but progress toward the mass availability of penicillin was stalled in England because of World War II. American laboratories further developed methods for the mass *Treatments for Bacterial Infections* production and commercial distribution of penicillin, which became widely available to doctors and hospitals around the world by 1948. Since then, a wide range of new antibiotics of highly specific character have been developed so that bacterial infections are now among the most successfully treated of all human illnesses.

Immunization—the development of vaccines that can protect humans from contracting both bacterial and viral diseases—also progressed dramatically. The first great immunological triumph was the development of the smallpox vaccine by the English researcher Edward Jenner in the late eighteenth century. A vaccine effective against typhoid was developed by an English bacteriologist, Almroth Wright, in 1897 and was in wide use by World War I. Vaccination against tetanus became widespread just before and during World War II. Medical scientists also developed a vaccine against another major killer, tuberculosis, in the 1920s; but controversy over its safety stalled its adoption, especially in the United States, for many years. It was not widely used in the United States until after World War II, when it largely eliminated tuberculosis until a limited recurrence began in the 1990s.

Viruses are much more difficult to prevent and treat than bacterial infections, and progress toward vaccines against viral infections—except for smallpox—was relatively slow. Not until the 1930s, when scientists discovered how to grow viruses in tissue cultures, could researchers study them with any real effectiveness. Gradually, they discovered how to produce forms of a virus capable of triggering antibodies that would protect vaccinated people from contracting disease. An effective vaccine against yellow fever was developed in the late 1930s, and one against influenza—one of the great killers of the early twentieth century—appeared in 1945.

A particularly dramatic postwar triumph was the development of a vaccine against polio. In 1954, the American scientist Jonas Salk introduced an effective   *Polio Vaccine* vaccine against the disease that had killed or crippled thousands of children and adults (among them Franklin Roosevelt). It was provided free to the public by the federal government beginning in 1955. After 1960, an oral vaccine developed by Albert Sabin— usually administered in a sugar cube—made widespread vaccination even easier. By the early 1960s, these vaccines had virtually eliminated polio from American life and from much of the rest of the world.

Advancements made in mass production and administration of resources expanded the use and availability of the previous decades' discoveries. As a result, both infant mortality and the death rate among young children declined significantly in the first twenty-five years after the war (although not by as much as in Western Europe). Average life expectancy in that same period rose by five years, to seventy-one. These medical advances have saved millions, but overuse of antibacterial agents and time has led to genetic mutations in once controlled diseases. These "super bugs" resist traditional medical solutions, and their defeat represents the next great challenge of the medical field.

PESTICIDES

Scientists also developed new kinds of chemical pesticides to protect crops from destruction by insects and to protect humans from such insect-carried diseases as typhus and   *DDT* malaria. Perhaps the most famous of the new pesticides was dichlorodiphenyltrichloroethane, generally known as DDT, a compound discovered in 1939 by the Swiss chemist Paul Muller. He had discovered that although DDT seemed harmless to human beings and other mammals, it was extremely toxic to insects. American scientists learned of Muller's discovery in 1942, just as the army was grappling with the insect-borne tropical diseases— especially malaria and typhus—that threatened American soldiers.

DDT was first used on a large scale in Italy in 1943–1944 during a typhus outbreak, which it quickly helped end. Soon DDT was being sprayed in mosquito-infested areas of Pacific islands where American troops were fighting the Japanese. The incidence of malaria dropped precipitously. DDT quickly gained a reputation as a miraculous tool for controlling insects, and it undoubtedly saved thousands of lives. Only later did it become evident that DDT had long-term toxic effects on animals and humans.

the crime. Later that day he was mysteriously murdered by a Dallas nightclub owner, Jack Ruby, as he was being moved from one jail to another. Most Americans at the time accepted the conclusions of a federal commission appointed by President Johnson to investigate the assassination. The commission, chaired by Chief Justice Earl Warren, found that both Oswald and Ruby had acted alone, that there was no larger conspiracy. *Warren Commission*   In later years, however, many Americans came to believe that the Warren Commission report had ignored evidence of a wider conspiracy behind the murders. Controversy over the assassination continues still.

LYNDON JOHNSON

The Kennedy assassination was a national trauma—a defining event for almost everyone old enough to be aware of it. At the time, however, much of the nation took comfort in the personality and performance of Kennedy's successor in the White House, Lyndon Baines Johnson. Johnson was a native of the poor "hill country" of west Texas and had risen to become majority leader of the U.S. Senate by dint of extraordinary, even obsessive, effort and ambition. Having failed to win the Democratic nomination for president in 1960, he surprised many who knew him by agreeing to accept the vice presidential nomination on the ticket with Kennedy. The events in Dallas thrust him into the White House.

Johnson's rough-edged, even crude, personality could hardly have been more different from Kennedy's. But like Kennedy, Johnson was a man who believed in the active use of power. Between 1963 and 1966, he compiled the most impressive legislative record of any president since Franklin Roosevelt. He was aided by the tidal wave of emotion that

THE JOHNSON TREATMENT   Lyndon Johnson was legendary for his powers of persuasion—for a combination of charm and intimidation that often worked on even the most experienced politicians. He is shown here in the Oval Office meeting with his old friend Senator Richard Russell of Georgia and demonstrating one of his most powerful and unsettling techniques: moving so close to the person with whom he was talking as to be almost touching him. (Lyndon Baines Johnson Library)

followed the death of Kennedy, which helped win support for many New Frontier proposals. But Johnson also constructed a greater and more far reaching reform program of his own, one that he ultimately labeled the "Great Society." And he won   *"Great Society"* approval of much of it through the same sort of skillful lobbying in Congress that had made him an effective majority leader.

Johnson's first year in office was, by necessity, dominated by the campaign for reelection. There was little doubt that he would win—particularly after the Republican Party nominated the very conservative Senator Barry Goldwater of Arizona. In the November 1964 election, the president received a larger plurality, over 61 percent, than any candidate before or since. Goldwater, with his hard-line stance against communism and government expansion, managed to carry only his home state of Arizona and five states in the Deep South. Nevertheless, the failed Goldwater campaign mobilized many right-wing activists who would propel the growth of conservative political strength for decades to come. Record Democratic majorities in both houses of Congress, many of whose members had been swept into office only because of the margin of Johnson's victory, ensured that the president would be able to fulfill many of his goals.

THE ASSAULT ON POVERTY

For the first time since the New Deal, the federal government took steps in the 1960s to create important new social welfare programs. The most important of these was Medicare, which provides federal aid to elderly individuals for medical expenses.   *Medicare and Medicaid* Its enactment in 1965 came at the end of a bitter twenty-year debate between those who believed in the concept of national health assistance and those who denounced it as "socialized medicine." But Medicare pacified many critics. For one thing, it avoided the stigma of "welfare" by making Medicare benefits available to all elderly Americans, regardless of need (just as Social Security had done with pensions). That created a large middle-class constituency for the program. It also defused the opposition of the medical community by allowing doctors serving Medicare patients to practice privately and (at first) to charge their normal fees; Medicare simply shifted responsibility for paying those fees from the patient to the government. In 1966, Johnson steered to passage the Medicaid program, which extended federal medical assistance to welfare recipients and other indigent people of all ages.

Medicare and Medicaid were early steps in a much larger assault on poverty—one that Kennedy had been planning in the last months of his life and that Johnson launched only weeks after taking office. The centerpiece of this "war on poverty," as Johnson called it, was the Office of Economic Opportunity (OEO), which created an array of new educational, employment, housing, and health-care programs. But the OEO was controversial from the start, in part because of its commitment to the idea of "Community Action."

Community Action was an effort to involve members of poor communities themselves in the planning and administration of the programs designed to help   *Community Action Programs* them. The Community Action programs provided jobs for many poor people and gave them valuable experience in administrative and political work. But despite its achievements, the Community Action approach proved impossible to sustain. Administrative failures damaged the program. So did the apparent excesses of a few agencies, which damaged the popular image of the Community Action programs and indeed the war on poverty as a whole.

The OEO spent nearly $3 billion during its first two years of existence, and it helped reduce poverty in some areas. But it fell far short of eliminating poverty altogether. That was in part because of the weaknesses of the programs themselves and in part because funding for them, inadequate from the beginning, dwindled as the years passed and a costly war in Southeast Asia became the nation's first priority.

CITIES, SCHOOLS, AND IMMIGRATION

Closely tied to the antipoverty program were federal efforts to promote the revitalization of decaying cities and to strengthen the nation's schools. The Housing Act of 1961 offered $4.9 billion in federal grants to cities for the preservation of open spaces, the development of mass-transit systems, and the subsidization of middle-income housing. In 1966, Johnson established a new cabinet agency, the Department of Housing and Urban Development (whose first secretary, Robert Weaver, was the first African American ever to serve in the cabinet). Johnson also inaugurated the Model Cities Program, which offered federal subsidies for urban redevelopment pilot programs.

Kennedy had fought for federal aid to public education, but he had failed to overcome two important obstacles. Many Americans feared that aid to education was the first step *Federal Aid to Education* toward federal control of the schools, and Catholics insisted that federal assistance must extend to parochial as well as public schools. Johnson managed to circumvent both objections with the Elementary and Secondary Education Act of 1965 and a series of subsequent measures. The bills extended aid to all types of schools and based the aid on the economic conditions of the students, not on the needs of the schools themselves.

The Johnson administration also supported the Immigration Act of 1965, one of the most important pieces of legislation of the 1960s. For decades since the 1920s, *Immigration Act of 1965* the law maintained a strict limit on the number of newcomers admitted to the country each year (170,000). But the 1965 act eliminated the "national origins" system established in the 1920s, which gave preference to immigrants from northern Europe over those from other parts of the world. It continued to restrict immigration from some parts of Latin America, but it allowed people from all parts of Europe, Asia, and Africa to enter the United States on an equal basis. By the early 1970s, the character of American immigration had changed dramatically. The numbers of immigrants grew significantly, with members of new national groups—and particularly large groups of Asians—entering the United States and transforming the character of the American population.

LEGACIES OF THE GREAT SOCIETY

Taken together, the Great Society reforms significantly increased federal spending. For a time, rising tax revenues from the growing economy nearly compensated for the new expenditures. In 1964, Johnson managed to win passage of the $11.5 billion tax cut that Kennedy had first proposed in 1962. The cut increased the federal deficit, but substantial economic growth over the next several years made up for much of the revenue initially lost. As Great Society programs began to multiply, however—particularly as they began to compete with the escalating costs of America's military ventures—the federal budget rapidly outpaced increases in revenues. In 1961, the federal government had spent $94.4 billion. By 1970, that sum had risen to $196.6 billion.

The high costs of the Great Society, and the failures of some of it, weakened the popularity of the federal efforts to solve social problems. But the Great Society was also responsible for some remarkable achievements. It significantly reduced hunger in America. It made medical care available to millions of elderly and poor people who would otherwise have had great difficulty affording it. It contributed to the greatest reduction in poverty in American history. In 1959, according to the most widely accepted estimates, 21 percent of the American people lived below the officially established poverty line (a level that did not survive for very long). In 1969, only 12 percent remained below that line. Much of that progress was a result of economic growth, but some of it was a direct result of Great Society programs.

THE BATTLE FOR RACIAL EQUALITY

By the early 1960s, African Americans forced issues of racial justice and equality to the forefront of American politics. While scholars debate the origins and legacies of the modern civil rights movement, none challenge how deeply it influenced the nation's history in the late twentieth century. (See "Debating the Past: The Civil Rights Movement.")

EXPANDING PROTESTS

John Kennedy was sympathetic to the cause of racial justice, but he was far from a committed crusader. Like presidents before him, he feared alienating southern voters and powerful southern Democrats in Congress. His administration hoped to contain the racial problem by enforcing existing laws and using executive orders—not proposing new legislation.

But the pressure for change was growing uncontainable even before Kennedy took office. Throughout the 1950s, African Americans in northern cities had grown increasingly active in opposing discrimination. They demanded progress in housing, jobs, and education. Protests grew in the 1960s, especially in the South. This restiveness soon spread. In February 1960, black college students in Greensboro, North Carolina, staged a sit-in at a segregated Woolworth's lunch counter; and in the following months, such demonstrations spread throughout the South, forcing many merchants to integrate their facilities. In the fall of 1960, some of those who had participated in the sit-ins formed the Student Nonviolent Coordinating Committee (SNCC)—a student branch of Martin Luther King Jr.'s Southern Christian Leadership Conference; SNCC worked to keep the spirit of resistance alive.

In 1961, an interracial group of students, working with the Congress of Racial Equality (CORE), began what they called "freedom rides." Traveling by bus *Freedom Rides* throughout the South, they tried to force the desegregation of bus stations. They were met in some places with such savage violence on the part of some white southerners that Attorney General Robert Kennedy finally dispatched federal marshals to help keep the peace and ordered the integration of all bus and train stations.

Events in the Deep South in 1963 helped bring the growing movement to something of a climax. In April, Martin Luther King Jr. helped launch a series of nonviolent demonstrations in Birmingham, Alabama. Police Commissioner Eugene "Bull" Connor personally supervised a brutal effort to break up the peaceful marches, arresting hundreds of demonstrators and using attack dogs, tear gas, electric cattle prods, and fire hoses—at times even against small children—in full view of television cameras. Two months later,

THE CIVIL RIGHTS MOVEMENT

The civil rights movement was one of the most important events in the modern history of the United States. It helped force the dismantling of legalized segregation and disenfranchisement of African Americans and also served as a model for other groups mobilizing to demand dignity and rights. And like all important events in history, it has produced scholarship that examines the movement in a number of different ways.

The early histories of the civil rights movement remain widely accepted. They rest on a heroic narrative of moral purpose and personal courage by which great men and women inspired ordinary people to rise up and struggle for their rights. This narrative generally begins with the *Brown* decision of 1954 and the Montgomery bus boycott of 1955, continues through the civil rights campaigns of the early 1960s, and culminates in the Civil Rights Acts of 1964 and 1965. Among the central events in this narrative are the March on Washington of 1963, with Martin Luther King Jr.'s famous "I Have a Dream" speech, and the assassination of King in 1968, which has often symbolized the end of the movement and the beginning of a different, more complicated period of the black freedom struggle. The key element of these narratives is the central importance to the movement of a few great leaders, most notably King himself. Among the best examples of this narrative are Taylor Branch's powerful studies of the life and struggles of King, *Parting the Waters* (1988), *Pillar of Fire* (1998), and *At Canaan's Edge* (2006), as well as David Garrow's important study, *Bearing the Cross* (1986).

Few historians would deny the importance of King and other leaders to the successes of the civil rights movement. But a number of scholars have argued that the leader-centered narrative obscures the vital contributions of ordinary people in communities throughout the South, and the nation, to the struggle. John Dittmer's *Local People: The Struggle for Civil Rights in Mississippi* (1994) and Charles Payne's *I've Got the Light of Freedom* (1995) both examine the day-to-day work of the movement's rank and file in the early 1960s and argue that their efforts were at least as important as those of King and other leaders. The national leadership helped bring visibility to these struggles, but King and his circle were usually present only briefly, if at all, for the actual work of communities in challenging segregation. Only by understanding the local origins of the movement, these and other scholars argue, can we understand its true character.

Scholars also disagree about the time frame of the movement. Rather than beginning the story in 1954 or 1955 (as in Robert Weisbrot's excellent 1991 synthesis *Freedom Bound* or in William Chafe's remarkable 1981 local study *Civilities and Civil Rights,* which examined the Greensboro sit-ins of 1961), a number of scholars have tried to move the story into both earlier periods and later ones. Robin Kelly's *Race Rebels* (1994) emphasizes the important contributions of working-class African Americans, some of them allied for a time with the Communist Party, to the undermining of racist assumptions starting in the 1930s. These activists organized some of the earliest civil rights demonstrations—sit-ins, marches, and other efforts to challenge segregation—well before the conventional dates for the beginning of the movement. Gail O'Brien's *The Color of the Law* (1999) examines a 1946 "race riot" in Columbia, Tennessee, arguing for its importance as a signal of the early growth of African American militancy and the movement of that militancy from the streets into the legal system.

Other scholars have looked beyond the 1960s and have incorporated events outside the orbit of the formal "movement" to explain

BROWN V. BOARD OF EDUCATION This photograph, taken for an Atlanta newspaper, illustrated the long and dangerous walk that Linda Brown, one of the plaintiffs in the famous desegregation case that ultimately reached the Supreme Court, had to travel each day on her way to a segregated school in Topeka, Kansas. An all-white school was located close to her home, but to reach the black school she had to attend required a long walk and a long bus ride each day. Not only does the picture illustrate the difficulties segregation created for Linda Brown, it was also part of a broad publicity campaign launched by the supporters of the case. (Photo by Carl Iwasaki/© Time & Life Pictures/Getty Images)

the history of the civil rights struggle. A growing literature on northern, urban, and relatively radical activists has suggested that focusing too much on mainstream leaders and the celebrated efforts in the South in the 1960s diverts our view from the equally important challenges facing northern African Americans and the very different tactics and strategies that they often chose to pursue their goals. The enormous attention historians have given to the life and legacy of Malcolm X—among them Alex Haley's influential *Autobiography of Malcolm X* (1965), Michael Eric Dyson's *Making Malcolm* (1996), and Manning Marable's important biography, *Malcolm X: A Life of Reinvention* (2012)—is an example of this, as is the increasing attention scholars have given to black radicalism in the late 1960s and beyond and to such militant groups as the Black Panthers. Other literature has extended the civil rights struggle even further, into the 1980s and beyond, and has brought into focus such issues as the highly disproportionate number of African Americans sentenced to death within the criminal justice system. Randall Kennedy's

Race, Crime, and the Law (1997) is a particularly important study of this issue.

Even *Brown v. Board of Education* (1954), the great landmark of the legal challenge to segregation, has been subject to reexamination. Richard Kluger's narrative history of the *Brown* decision, *Simple Justice* (1975), is a classic statement of the traditional view of *Brown* as a triumph over injustice. But others have been less certain of the dramatic success of the ruling. James T. Patterson's *Brown v. Board of Education: A Civil Rights Milestone and Its Troubled Legacy* (2001) argues that the *Brown* decision long preceded any national consensus on the need to end segregation and that its impact was far less decisive than earlier scholars have suggested. Michael Klarman's *From Jim Crow to Civil Rights* (2004) examines the role of the Supreme Court in advancing civil rights and suggests, among other things, that the *Brown* decision may actually have retarded racial progress in the South for a time because of the enormous backlash it created. Charles Ogletree's *All Deliberate Speed* (2004) and Derrick Bell's *Silent Covenants* (2004) both argue that the Court's decision did not provide an effective enforcement mechanism for desegregation and in many other ways failed to support measures that would have made school desegregation a reality. Stephen Tuck's *We Ain't What We Ought to Be: The Black Freedom Struggle from Emancipation to Obama* (2011) concludes his bro-ad narrative of the road to racial equality by focusing on the continued activism of African Americans into the present.

As the literature on the African American freedom struggles of the twentieth century has grown, historians have begun to speak of civil rights *movements,* rather than a single, cohesive movement.   •

UNDERSTAND, ANALYZE, & EVALUATE

1. If historians now speak of plural civil rights *movements,* what are these movements?
2. Why are the contributions of local grassroots workers so often overlooked, in studies of the civil rights movement as well as in accounts of other great events in American history?

Governor George Wallace stood in the doorway of the Foster Auditorium at the University of Alabama to prevent the court-ordered enrollment of several black students. Only after the arrival of federal marshals did he give way. The same night, NAACP official Medgar Evers was murdered in Mississippi. And in September, the bombing of the Sixteenth Street Baptist Church in Birmingham killed four African American children.

A NATIONAL COMMITMENT

The events in Alabama and Mississippi were a warning to the president that he could no longer avoid the issue of race. In an important television address the night of the University of Alabama confrontation, Kennedy spoke eloquently of the "moral issue" facing the nation. Days later, he introduced new legislative proposals prohibiting segregation in "public accommodations" (stores, restaurants, theaters, hotels), barring discrimination in employment, and increasing the power of the government to file suits on behalf of school integration.

To generate support for the legislation, and to dramatize the power of the growing movement, more than 200,000 demonstrators marched down the Mall in
March on Washington   Washington, D.C., in August 1963 and gathered before the Lincoln Memorial for the largest civil rights demonstration in the nation's history to that point.

MARTIN LUTHER KING JR. IN WASHINGTON Moments after completing his memorable speech during the August 1963 March on Washington, King waves to the vast and enthusiastic crowd that had gathered in front of the Lincoln Memorial to demand "equality and jobs." (© AP Images)

Martin Luther King Jr., in one of the greatest speeches of American politics, aroused the crowd with a litany of resonant American images prefaced again and again by the phrase "I have a dream."

The assassination of President Kennedy three months later gave new impetus to civil rights legislation. The ambitious measure that Kennedy had proposed in June 1963 was stalled in the Senate after having passed through the House of Representatives with relative ease. Early in 1964, after Lyndon Johnson had applied both public *Civil Rights Act of 1964* and private pressure, supporters of the measure finally mustered the two-thirds majority necessary to end a filibuster by southern senators; and the Senate passed the most important civil rights bill of the twentieth century.

THE BATTLE FOR VOTING RIGHTS

Having won a significant victory in one area, the civil rights movement shifted its focus to another: voting rights. During the summer of 1964, thousands of civil rights workers, black and white, northern and southern, spread throughout the South, but primarily into Mississippi, to work on behalf of black voter registration and participation. The campaign was known as "Freedom Summer," and it produced a violent *"Freedom Summer"* response from many southern whites. Three of the first freedom workers to arrive in the South—two whites, Andrew Goodman and Michael Schwerner, and one African American, James Chaney—were murdered. Local law enforcement officials were involved in the crime.

The Freedom Summer also produced the Mississippi Freedom Democratic Party (MFDP), an integrated alternative to the regular state Democratic party organization. Under the leadership of Fannie Lou Hamer and others, the MFDP challenged the regular party's right to its seats at the Democratic National Convention that summer. (See "Consider the Source: Fannie Lou Hamer on the Struggle for Voting Rights.") President Johnson, with King's help, managed to broker a compromise by which members of the MFDP could be seated as observers, with promises of party reforms later on, while the regular party retained its official standing. Many MFDP members rejected the agreement and left the convention embittered.

A year later, in March 1965, King helped organize a major demonstration in Selma, Alabama, to press for the right of blacks to register to vote. Selma sheriff Jim Clark led local police in a vicious attack on the demonstrators, which was televised nationally. Two northern whites participating in the Selma march were murdered in the course of the effort there. The widespread national outrage that followed the events in Alabama helped push Lyndon Johnson to win passage of the Voting Rights Act of 1965, which provided federal protection to African Americans attempting to exercise their *Selma and the Voting Rights Act* right to vote. But important as such gains were, they failed to satisfy the rapidly rising expectations of civil rights activists as the focus of the movement began to move from political to economic issues.

THE CHANGING MOVEMENT

By 1966, of African Americans 69 percent lived in metropolitan areas and 45 percent lived outside the South. Although the economic condition of most Americans was improving, in many poor urban black communities things were getting significantly worse. Indeed, more than half of all nonwhite Americans lived in poverty at the beginning of the 1960s.

CONSIDER THE SOURCE

FANNIE LOU HAMER ON THE STRUGGLE FOR VOTING RIGHTS

Fanny Lou Hamer shone a harsh spotlight on racial terror in her native state of Mississippi during her speech before the Credentials Committee of the Democratic National Convention in Atlantic City, New Jersey, in August 1964. With this testimony, Hamer tried—unsuccessfully—to unseat the all-white Mississippi delegation and seat members of the Mississippi Freedom Democratic Party (MFDP). Four years later, the MFDP succeeded in winning seats at the Convention.

Mr. Chairman, and to the Credentials Committee, my name is Mrs. Fannie Lou Hamer, and I live at 626 East Lafayette Street, Ruleville, Mississippi, Sunflower County, the home of Senator James O. Eastland, and Senator Stennis.

It was the 31st of August in 1962 that eighteen of us traveled twenty-six miles to the county courthouse in Indianola to try to register to become first-class citizens.

We was met in Indianola by policemen, Highway Patrolmen, and they only allowed two of us in to take the literacy test at the time. After we had taken this test and started back to Ruleville, we was held up by the City Police and the State Highway Patrolmen and carried back to Indianola where the bus driver was charged that day with driving a bus the wrong color.

After we paid the fine among us, we continued on to Ruleville, and Reverend Jeff Sunny carried me four miles in the rural area where I had worked as a timekeeper and sharecropper for eighteen years. I was met there by my children, who told me that the plantation owner was angry because I had gone down to try to register.

After they told me, my husband came, and said the plantation owner was raising Cain because I had tried to register. Before he

quit talking the plantation owner came and said, "Fannie Lou, do you know—did Pap tell you what I said?"

And I said, "Yes, sir."

He said, "Well I mean that." He said, "If you don't go down and withdraw your registration, you will have to leave." Said, "Then if you go down and withdraw," said, "you still might have to go because we are not ready for that in Mississippi."

And I addressed him and told him and said, "I didn't try to register for you. I tried to register for myself."

I had to leave that same night.

On the 10th of September 1962, sixteen bullets was fired into the home of Mr. and Mrs. Robert Tucker for me. That same night two girls were shot in Ruleville, Mississippi. Also Mr. Joe McDonald's house was shot in.

And June the 9th, 1963, I had attended a voter registration workshop; was returning back to Mississippi. Ten of us was traveling by the Continental Trailway bus. When we got to Winona, Mississippi, which is Montgomery County, four of the people got off to use the washroom, and two of the people—to use the restaurant—two of the people wanted to use the washroom.

The four people that had gone in to use the restaurant was ordered out. During this time I was on the bus. But when I looked through the window and saw they had rushed out I got off of the bus to see what had happened. And one of the ladies said, "It was a State Highway Patrolman and a Chief of Police ordered us out."

I got back on the bus and one of the persons had used the washroom got back on the bus, too.

As soon as I was seated on the bus, I saw when they began to get the five people in a highway patrolman's car. I stepped off of

718 ·

the bus to see what was happening and somebody screamed from the car that the five workers was in and said, "Get that one there." When I went to get in the car, when the man told me I was under arrest, he kicked me.

I was carried to the county jail and put in the booking room. They left some of the people in the booking room and began to place us in cells. I was placed in a cell with a young woman called Miss Ivesta Simpson. After I was placed in the cell I began to hear sounds of licks and screams, I could hear the sounds of licks and horrible screams. And I could hear somebody say, "Can you say, 'yes, sir,' nigger? Can you say 'yes, sir'?"

And they would say other horrible names. She would say, "Yes, I can say 'yes, sir.'"

"So, well, say it."

She said, "I don't know you well enough."

They beat her, I don't know how long. And after a while she began to pray, and asked God to have mercy on those people.

And it wasn't too long before three white men came to my cell. One of these men was a State Highway Patrolman and he asked me where I was from. I told him Ruleville and he said, "We are going to check this."

They left my cell and it wasn't too long before they came back. He said, "You are from Ruleville all right," and he used a curse word. And he said, "We are going to make you wish you was dead."

I was carried out of that cell into another cell where they had two Negro prisoners. The State Highway Patrolmen ordered the first Negro to take the blackjack.

The first Negro prisoner ordered me, by orders from the State Highway Patrolman, for me to lay down on a bunk bed on my face.

I laid on my face and the first Negro began to beat. I was beat by the first Negro until he was exhausted. I was holding my hands behind me at that time on my left side, because I suffered from polio when I was six years old.

After the first Negro had beat until he was exhausted, the State Highway Patrolman ordered the second Negro to take the blackjack.

The second Negro began to beat and I began to work my feet, and the State Highway Patrolman ordered the first Negro who had beat me to sit on my feet—to keep me from working my feet. I began to scream and one white man got up and began to beat me in my head and tell me to hush.

One white man—my dress had worked up high—he walked over and pulled my dress—I pulled my dress down and he pulled my dress back up.

I was in jail when Medgar Evers was murdered.

All of this is on account of we want to register, to become first-class citizens. And if the Freedom Democratic Party is not seated now, I question America. Is this America, the land of the free and the home of the brave, where we have to sleep with our telephones off the hooks because our lives be threatened daily, because we want to live as decent human beings, in America?

Thank you.

UNDERSTAND, ANALYZE, & EVALUATE

1. What tactics were used to prevent Hamer from registering to vote?
2. Why did the Highway Patrolmen choose black prisoners to beat Hamer?
3. When the television networks broadcast this speech, the level of public support for the Mississippi Freedom Democratic Party rose sharply. What aspects of Hamer's speech were so effective?

Source: Fannie Lou Hamer, "Testimony Before the Credentials Committee," Democratic National Convention, August 22, 1964. Copyright © 1964 by Fannie Lou Hamer. All rights reserved. Used with permission.

The great publicity of the civil rights movement in the South intensified antidiscrimination efforts in northern cities. Those cities had no Jim Crow laws but much segregation. Many African American leaders (and their white supporters), having struggled in relative obscurity in the 1940s and 1950s, began to move the battle against job discrimination to a new level. They argued that the only way for employers to prove they were not discriminating against African Americans was to demonstrate that they were hiring minorities. If necessary, they should adopt positive measures to recruit minorities. Lyndon Johnson gave his support to the concept of **affirmative action** in 1965. Over the next decade, affirmative action guidelines gradually extended to virtually all institutions doing business with or receiving funds from the federal government (including schools and universities)—and to many others as well. Discrimination based on gender also began to receive federal interest. When "sex" was added at the last minute to Title VII of the 1964 Civil Rights Act, many thought it was an attempt to kill the bill. Regardless, the result added federal authority to begin dismantling the entrenched discrimination of women in the workplace and higher education.

A symbol of the movement's new direction, and of the problems it would cause, was a major campaign in the summer of 1966 in Chicago, in which King played a prominent role. Organizers of the Chicago campaign hoped to direct national attention to housing and employment discrimination in northern industrial cities. But the Chicago campaign evoked vicious and at times violent opposition from white residents and failed to attract wide attention or support in the way events in the South had done.

URBAN VIOLENCE

Well before the Chicago campaign, the problem of urban poverty had thrust itself into national prominence when riots broke out in African American neighborhoods in major cities. There were disturbances in the summer of 1964, most notably in New York City's Harlem. The most serious race riot since the end of World War II occurred the following summer in the Watts section of Los Angeles. In the midst of a traffic arrest, a white police officer struck a protesting black bystander with his club. The incident triggered a storm of anger and a week of violence. Thirty-four people died during the uprising, which was eventually quelled by the National Guard. In the summer of 1966, forty-three additional outbreaks occurred, the most serious in Chicago and Cleveland. And in the summer of 1967, eight major disorders took place, including the largest of them all—a racial clash in Detroit in which forty-three people died.

Televised images of the violence alarmed millions of Americans and created both a new sense of urgency and a growing sense of doubt among some whites who had embraced the cause of racial justice only a few years before. A special Commission on Civil Disorders, ordered by the president in response to the riots, issued a celebrated report in the spring of 1968 recommending massive spending to eliminate the abysmal conditions of the ghettoes. To many white Americans, however, the riots exposed the need for stern measures to stop violence and lawlessness.

BLACK POWER

Disillusioned with the ideal of peaceful change through cooperation with whites, an increasing number of African Americans turned to a new approach to the racial issue: the philosophy of **black power.** Black power meant many different things. But in all its forms, it suggested a shift away from the goals of assimilation and toward increased awareness of racial distinctiveness.

Perhaps the most enduring impact of the black-power ideology was a social and psychological one: instilling racial pride in African Americans. But black power took political forms as well, and it created a deep schism within the civil rights movement. Traditional black organizations that emphasized cooperation with sympathetic whites— groups such as the NAACP, the Urban League, and King's Southern Christian Leadership Conference—now faced competition from more radical groups. The Student Nonviolent Coordinating Committee and the Congress of Racial Equality had both begun as relatively moderate interracial organizations. By the mid-1960s, however, these and other groups were calling for more radical and occasionally even violent action against white racism and were openly rejecting the approaches of older, more established black leaders.

The most radical expressions of the black-power idea came from such revolutionary organizations as the Black Panthers, based in Oakland, California, and the separatist group the Nation of Islam, which denounced whites as "devils" and appealed to African Americans to embrace the Islamic faith and work for complete racial separation. The most celebrated of the Black Muslims, as whites often termed them, was Malcolm Little, who adopted the name Malcolm X ("X" to denote his lost African   *Malcolm X* surname). Malcolm X left the Nation of Islam in 1964 and founded the Muslim Mosque, Inc., which he hoped would allow him to work with other civil rights leaders. After a pilgrimage to Mecca, he returned with a new hope that racial problems could be overcome. He died in 1965 when gunmen, presumably under orders from rivals within the Nation of Islam, assassinated him. But he remained a major figure in many African American communities long after his death, attaining a stature comparable to that of Martin Luther King Jr.

"FLEXIBLE RESPONSE" AND THE COLD WAR

In international affairs as much as in domestic reform, the optimistic liberalism of the Kennedy and Johnson administrations dictated a more active and aggressive approach to dealing with the nation's problems than that of the 1950s.

DIVERSIFYING FOREIGN POLICY

The Kennedy administration entered office convinced that the United States needed to be able to counter communist aggression in more flexible ways than the atomic-weapons-oriented defense strategy of the Eisenhower years. In particular, Kennedy was unsatisfied with the nation's ability to meet communist threats in "emerging areas" of the Third World—the areas in which, Kennedy believed, the real struggle against communism would be waged in the future. He gave enthusiastic support to the expansion of the Special Forces (or "Green Berets," as they were soon known)—soldiers trained specifically to fight guerrilla conflicts and other limited wars.

Kennedy also favored expanding American influence through peaceful means. To repair the badly deteriorating relationship with Latin America, he proposed an "Alliance for Progress"—a series of projects for peaceful development and stabilization of the nations of that region. Kennedy also inaugurated the Agency for International Development

Map labels:

CHINA

NORTH VIETNAM

BURMA

Lao Cai

Dien Bien Phu • Thai Nguyen
Red R.
Black R.
• Hanoi

Haiphong

Gulf of Tonkin

Hainan

Luang Prabang · PLAIN OF JARS
Mekong R.
Thanh Hoa

LAOS

Vinh

Vientiane

Dong Hoi
Partition Line 1954
DMZ (Demilitarized Zone)

South China Sea

Udon Thani   Phanom

THAILAND

Sepone
Khe Sanh
Hue
Phu Bai
Da Nang
Hoi An

FRIENDSHIP HIGHWAY
Ping R.
Yom R.
Po Sak R.

Takhli

Don Muang   Ratchasima   Udon Ratchathani
Mun R.
Mekong R.

Chulai
My Lai
Quang Ngai
Dak To

Kon Tum   Ankhe
Pleiku   Qui Nhon
CENTRAL HIGHLANDS

Bangkok

CAMBODIA
Battambang

Tonle Sap

SOUTH VIETNAM

Pursat

Kompong Cham

Nha Trang

1970—U.S. and South Vietnam troops entered Viet Cong strongholds inside Cambodia

Phnom Penh
Mekong R.
Tay Ninh

Bo Duc
Da Lat   Camranh Bay
Phanrang

Gulf of Thailand

Song Be

Saigon
PLAIN OF REEDS

Sihanoukville

Cantho
Mekong River Delta

0   200 mi
0   200   400 km

■ U.S. bases

→ U.S. and South Vietnam invasion of Cambodia

→ Ho Chi Minh Trail (communist supply route)

THE WAR IN VIETNAM AND INDOCHINA, 1964–1975 Much of the Vietnam War was fought in small engagements in widely scattered areas and did not conform to traditional notions of combat. But as this map shows, there were traditional battles and invasions and supply routes as well. The red arrows in the middle of the map show the general path of the Ho Chi Minh Trail, the main supply route by which North Vietnam supplied its troops and allies in the south. The blue arrow in southern South Vietnam indicates the point at which American troops invaded Cambodia in 1970. • *What is there in the geography of Indochina, as presented on this map, that helps explain the great difficulty the American military had in securing South Vietnam against communist attacks?*

moved the Ho Chi Minh Trail to make it elusive to American bombers. Far from breaking the north's resolve, the bombing seemed actually to strengthen popular commitment to the war.

Another important part of the American strategy was the "pacification" program, whose purpose was to push the Viet Cong from particular regions and then *"Pacification" Program* "pacify" those regions by winning the "hearts and minds" of the people. Routing the Viet Cong was often possible, but the subsequent pacification was more difficult. Gradually, the pacification program gave way to a more heavy-handed relocation strategy, through which American troops uprooted villagers from their homes, sent them fleeing to refugee camps or into the cities (producing by 1967 more than 3 million refugees), and then destroyed the vacated villages and surrounding countryside. "It became necessary to destroy the village in order to save it," an American military official famously said of one such action, thus revealing the flawed assumptions of the pacification program.

As the war dragged on and victory remained elusive, some American officers and officials urged the president to expand the military efforts. But Johnson resisted—in part because he remembered the Korean War. He feared drawing China directly into the Vietnam War, and he was beginning to encounter obstacles and frustrations at home.

THE WAR AT HOME

Few Americans, and even fewer influential ones, had protested the American involvement in Vietnam as late as the end of 1965. But as the war dragged on inconclusively, political support for it began to erode.

By the end of 1967, American students opposed to the war (and to the military draft) had become a significant political force. Enormous peace marches in New York, Washington, D.C., and other cities drew broad public attention to the antiwar movement. (Music also raised awareness; see "Patterns of Popular Culture: The Folk-Music Revival.") In the meantime, a growing number of journalists, particularly reporters who had spent time in Vietnam, helped sustain the movement with their frank revelations about the brutality and apparent futility of the war.

Senator J. William Fulbright of Arkansas, chair of the Senate Foreign Relations Committee, also turned against the war and in January 1966 began to stage highly publicized and occasionally televised congressional hearings to air criticisms of it. Other members of Congress joined Fulbright in opposing Johnson's policies—including, in 1967, Robert F. Kennedy, brother of the slain president, now a senator from New York. Even within the administration, the consensus seemed to be crumbling. Robert McNamara, who had done much to help extend the initial American involvement in Vietnam, quietly left the government, disillusioned, in 1968. His successor as secretary of defense, Clark Clifford, became a quiet but powerful voice within the administration on behalf of a cautious scaling down of the commitment.

In the meantime, Johnson's commitment to fighting the war while continuing his Great Society reforms helped cause a rise in inflation, from the 2 percent level it had occupied through most of the early 1960s to 3 percent in 1967, 4 percent in 1968, and 6 percent in 1969. In August 1967, Johnson asked Congress for a tax increase to avoid even more ruinous inflation. In return, congressional conservatives demanded a $6 billion reduction in the funding for Great Society programs. The president accepted the reduction as a way to mollify congressional conservatives unnerved by economic troubles and critical of social welfare programs.

THE FOLK-MUSIC REVIVAL

Two impulses of the 1960s—the renewed interest among young people in the politics of the left, and the search for an "authentic" alternative to what many considered the artificial, consumerist culture of modern America—helped produce the revived popularity of folk music in that turbulent era. Although the harder, harsher, and more sensual music of rock 'n' roll was more visible and more popular in the 1960s, folk music more clearly expressed many of the political ideas and aspirations that were welling up in the youth culture of the time.

The folk-music tradition, like most American musical traditions, had many roots. It drew from some of the black musical traditions of the South, and from the white country music of Appalachia. And it drew most immediately from a style of music developed by musicians associated with the Communist Party's Popular Front in the 1930s. Woody Guthrie, Pete Seeger, the Weavers, and others whose music would become popular again in the 1960s began their careers singing in Popular Front and union rallies during the Great Depression. Their music, like the Popular Front itself, set out to seem entirely American, rooted in the nation's folk traditions.

Folk music remained alive in the 1940s and 1950s, but it had only a modest popular following. Pete Seeger and the Weavers continued to perform and to attract attention on college campuses. Harry Belafonte and the Kingston Trio recorded slick, pop versions of folk songs in an effort to bring them to mass audiences. In 1952, Folkway Records released the *Anthology of American Folk Music*, a collection of eighty-four performances recorded in the 1920s and 1930s that became an inspiration and an important source of material to many younger folk musicians. Folk-music festivals—at Berkeley, Newport, and Chicago—began to proliferate beginning in 1959. And an important community of folk musicians lived and performed together in the 1950s and early 1960s in New York City's Greenwich Village.

As the politics of the 1960s became more heated, and as young people in particular became politically aroused, it was folk music that most directly reflected their new values and concerns. Peter, Paul, and Mary—although only intermittently political—became icons to much of the New Left, beginning with their 1962 recording of "If I Had a Hammer," a song first performed at Communist Party rallies in the 1940s by Pete Seeger and the Weavers. Bob Dylan, whose own politics were never wholly clear to the public, had a large impact on the 1960s left, even inadvertently providing a name to the most radical offshoot of Students for a Democratic Society (SDS), the Weathermen, who named themselves after a line from one of his songs: "You don't need a weatherman to know which way the wind blows."* Joan Baez, whose politics were no secret to anyone, was actively engaged in the antiwar movement and was arrested several times for participating in militant protests.

But it was not just the overt political messages of folk musicians that made them so important to young Americans in the 1960s. In addition, folk was a kind of music that seemed to reflect the "authenticity" the youth culture was attempting to find. In truth, neither the musicians themselves nor the young Americans attracted to them had much real connection with the traditions they were trying to evoke. The audiences

COFFEEHOUSE MUSIC   The Feejon Coffee House in Manhattan was popular among young writers, poets, and others in the late 1950s, in part because it was a gathering place for folk musicians, two of whom are shown here performing at right.   (© John Orris/Getty Images)

for folk music—a product of rural and working-class traditions—were overwhelmingly urban, middle-class people. But the message of folk music—that there is a "real" America rooted in values of sharing and community, hidden beneath the crass commercialism of modern culture—resonated with the yearnings of many people in the 1960s (and beyond) for an alternative to their own troubled world. When young audiences responded to Woody Guthrie's famous ballad "This Land Is Your Land," they were expressing a hope for a different America—more democratic, more honest, and more natural than the land they knew.   •

UNDERSTAND, ANALYZE, & EVALUATE

1. What did folk music, with roots in the musical traditions of blacks, rural folk, and working-class people, offer that made it so appealing to and popular with urban, middle-class audiences?
2. What similarities between the 1930s and the 1960s might help explain the popularity of folk music during both those decades?
3. What musical style or form today continues the folk-music tradition of expressing a political message and reflecting the search for "authenticity"?

THE TRAUMAS OF 1968

By the end of 1967, the twin crises of the war in Vietnam and the deteriorating racial situation at home had produced great social and political tensions. In the course of 1968, those tensions burst to the surface and seemed to threaten national chaos. (The year 1968 was turbulent elsewhere in the world as well; see "America in the World: 1968.")

1968

The year 1968 was one of the most turbulent in the postwar history of the United States. Much of what made it so traumatic were specifically American events—the growing controversy over the war in Vietnam, the assassinations of Martin Luther King Jr. and Robert Kennedy, racial unrest across the nation's cities, student protests on campuses throughout America. But the turmoil of 1968 was not confined to the United States. There were tremendous upheavals in many parts of the globe that year.

The most common form of turbulence around the world in 1968 was student unrest. In France, a student uprising in May far exceeded in size and ferocity anything that occurred in the United States. It attracted the support of French workers and briefly paralyzed Paris and other cities. It contributed to the downfall of the government of Charles de Gaulle a year later. In England, Ireland, Germany, Italy, the Netherlands, Mexico, Canada, Japan, and South Korea, students and other young people demonstrated in great numbers, and at times with violence, against governments, universities, and other structures of authority. Elsewhere, there was more widespread protest, as in Czechoslovakia, where hundreds of thousands of citizens took to the streets in support of what became known as "Prague Spring." It caused a demand for greater democracy and a repudiation of many of the oppressive rules and structures imposed on the nation by its Soviet-dominated communist regimes. Russian tanks rolled into the city to crush the uprising.

Many people have tried to explain why so much instability emerged in so many nations at the same time. One factor that contributed to the worldwide turbulence of 1968 was simple numbers. The postwar Baby Boom had created a very large age cohort in many nations, and by the late 1960s it was coming of age. In the industrial West, the sheer size of the new generation produced a tripling of the number of people attending colleges and universities. In fewer than twenty years it also created a heightened sense of the power of youth. The long period of postwar prosperity and relative peace in which this generation had grown up contributed to heightened expectations of what the world should offer them—and a greater level of impatience than previous generations had demonstrated with the obstacles that stood in the way of their hopes. A new global youth culture emerged that was in many ways at odds with the dominant culture of older generations. It valued nonconformity, personal freedom, and even rebellion.

A second force contributing to the widespread turbulence of 1968 was the power of global media. Satellite communication introduced in the early 1960s made it possible to transmit live news across the world. Videotape technology and the creation of lightweight portable television cameras enabled media organizations to respond to events much more quickly and flexibly than in the past. The audience for these televised images was by now global and enormous, particularly in industrial nations but even in the poorest areas of the world. Protests in one country were suddenly capable of inspiring protests in others. Demonstrators in Paris, for example, spoke openly of how campus protests in the United States in 1968—for example, the student uprising at Columbia University in New York the previous month—had helped motivate French students to rise up as well. Just as American students were protesting against what they considered antiquated, paternalistic features of their universities, French students demanded an end to the rigid, autocratic character of their own academic world.

In most parts of the world, the 1968 uprisings came and went without fundamentally altering institutions and systems. But many changes came in the wake of these protests. Universities around the globe undertook significant reforms. Religious observance in mainstream churches and synagogues in the West declined dramatically after 1968. New concepts of personal freedom gained legitimacy, helping to inspire social movements in the years that followed—among them the dramatic growth of feminism in many parts of the world and the emergence of the gay and lesbian rights movement. The events of 1968 did not produce a revolution in the United States or in most of the rest of the world, but it did help launch a period of dramatic social, cultural, and political changes that affected the peoples of many nations. •

UNDERSTAND, ANALYZE, & EVALUATE

1. What factors combined to produce the turbulence that resulted in the uprisings of 1968?
2. Did the demonstrators of 1968 succeed or fail to achieve their objectives? What were the long-term effects of the 1968 uprisings?

THE TET OFFENSIVE

On January 31, 1968, the first day of the Vietnamese New Year (Tet), communist forces launched an enormous, concerted attack on American strongholds throughout South Vietnam. A few cities, most notably Hue, fell temporarily to the communists. But what made the Tet offensive so shocking to the American people, who saw vivid reports of it on television, was the sight of communist forces in the heart of Saigon, setting off bombs, shooting down South Vietnamese officials and troops, and holding down fortified areas (including, briefly, the American embassy). The Tet offensive also suggested to the American public something of the brutality of the fighting in Vietnam. In the midst of the fighting, television cameras recorded the sight of a South Vietnamese officer shooting a captured and defenseless young Viet Cong soldier in the head in the streets of Saigon.

American forces soon dislodged the Viet Cong from most of the positions they had seized. And during the battle they had inflicted enormous casualties on the communists and permanently depleted the ranks of the NLF, forcing North Vietnamese troops to take on a much larger share of the subsequent fighting, but such accomplishments registered little with the American public who felt betrayed by an administration that had sworn the war was nearly over. Tet may have been a military victory for the United States, but it was a political defeat for the administration.

In the following weeks, opposition to the war grew substantially. Leading newspapers and magazines, television commentators, and mainstream politicians began taking public stands against the conflict. Public opposition to the war almost doubled, and Johnson's personal popularity rating had slid to 35 percent, the lowest of any president since Harry Truman.

THE POLITICAL CHALLENGE

Beginning in the summer of 1967, dissident Democrats tried to mobilize support behind an antiwar candidate who would challenge Lyndon Johnson in the 1968 primaries.

When Robert Kennedy turned them down, they recruited Senator Eugene McCarthy of Minnesota. A brilliantly orchestrated campaign by young volunteers in the New Hampshire primary produced a startling showing by McCarthy in March; he nearly defeated the president.

A few days later, Robert Kennedy entered the campaign, embittering many McCarthy supporters but bringing his own substantial strength among minorities, poor people, and workers to the antiwar cause. Polls showed the president trailing badly in the next scheduled primary, in Wisconsin. On March 31, 1968, Johnson went on television to announce a limited halt in the bombing of North Vietnam—his first major concession to the antiwar forces. And then, stunningly, he declared that he was withdrawing from the presidential contest.

Robert Kennedy quickly established himself as the champion of the Democratic primaries, winning one election after another. In the meantime, however, Vice President Hubert Humphrey, with the support of President Johnson, entered the contest and began to attract the support of party leaders and of the many delegations that were selected not by popular primaries but by state party organizations. He soon overtook Kennedy as the front-runner in the race.

ASSASSINATIONS AND POLITICS

On April 4, Martin Luther King Jr., who had traveled to Memphis, Tennessee, to lend his *Assassination of Dr. King* support to striking black sanitation workers in the city, was shot and killed while standing on the balcony of his motel. The assassin, James Earl Ray, who was captured two months later in London, had no apparent motive. Subsequent evidence suggested that he had been hired by others to do the killing, but he himself never revealed the identity of his employers.

King's tragic death produced a great outpouring of grief. Among some African Americans, it also produced anger. In the days after the assassination, major riots broke out in more than sixty American cities. Forty-three people died.

Late in the night of June 6, Robert Kennedy appeared in the ballroom of a Los Angeles hotel to acknowledge his victory in that day's California primary. As he left the ballroom after his victory statement, Sirhan Sirhan, a young Palestinian apparently enraged by pro-Israeli remarks Kennedy had recently made, emerged from a crowd and shot him in the head. Early the next morning, Kennedy died. The shock of this second tragedy in two *Assassination of Robert Kennedy* months—and only five years after the assassination of John Kennedy—cast a pall over the remainder of the presidential campaign.

When the Democrats finally gathered in Chicago in August, for a convention in which Hubert Humphrey was now the only real contender, even the most optimistic observers predicted turbulence. Inside the hall, delegates bitterly debated an antiwar plank in the party platform that both Kennedy and McCarthy supporters favored. Miles away, in a downtown park, thousands of antiwar protesters staged demonstrations. On the third night of the convention, as the delegates began their balloting on the now virtually inevitable nomination of Hubert Humphrey, demonstrators and police clashed in a bloody riot in the streets of Chicago. Hundreds of protesters were injured as police attempted to disperse them with tear gas and billy clubs. Aware that the violence was being televised to the nation, the demonstrators taunted the authorities with the chant, "The whole world is watching!" And Hubert Humphrey, who had spent years dreaming of becoming his party's candidate for president, finally got the nomination but from a badly fractured party that would make it difficult for him to manage his campaign.

THE CONSERVATIVE RESPONSE

The turbulent events of 1968 persuaded some observers that American society was in the throes of revolutionary change. In fact, however, the response of many Americans to the turmoil was to question the social changes of the prior decade and take a conservative political turn.

The most visible sign of the conservative backlash was the surprising success of the campaign of George Wallace for the presidency. Wallace had been one of the leading spokesmen for the defense of segregation when, as governor of Alabama, he had attempted to block the admission of black students to the University of Alabama in *George Wallace* 1963. In 1968, he became a third-party candidate for president, basing his campaign on a host of conservative grievances. He denounced the forced busing of students to achieve racial integration in public schools, the proliferation of government regulations and social programs, and what he called the permissiveness of authorities toward crime, race riots, and antiwar demonstrations. There was never any serious chance that Wallace would win the election, but his standing in the polls rose at times to over 20 percent.

At the same time, a more effective effort to mobilize the conservative middle in favor of order and stability was under way within the Republican Party. Richard Nixon, whose

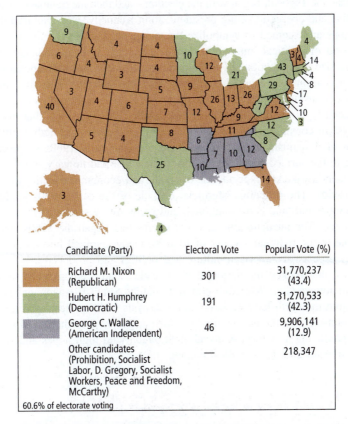

Candidate (Party)	Electoral Vote	Popular Vote (%)
Richard M. Nixon (Republican)	301	31,770,237 (43.4)
Hubert H. Humphrey (Democratic)	191	31,270,533 (42.3)
George C. Wallace (American Independent)	46	9,906,141 (12.9)
Other candidates (Prohibition, Socialist Labor, D. Gregory, Socialist Workers, Peace and Freedom, McCarthy)	—	218,347

60.6% of electorate voting

THE ELECTION OF 1968 The 1968 presidential election, which Richard Nixon won, was almost as close as the election of 1960, which he lost. Nixon might have won a more substantial victory had it not been for the independent candidacy of Governor George C. Wallace, who attracted many of the same conservative voters to whom Nixon appealed. • *How does the distribution of Democratic and Republican strength in this election compare to that in 1960?*

political career had seemed at an end after his losses in the presidential race of 1960 and *Nixon Elected*   a California gubernatorial campaign two years later, reemerged as the spokesperson for what he called the "silent majority." By offering a vision of stability, law and order, government retrenchment, and "peace with honor" in Vietnam, he easily captured the nomination of his party for the presidency. And despite a last-minute surge by Humphrey, Nixon hung on to eke out a victory almost as narrow as his defeat in 1960. He received 43.4 percent of the popular vote to Humphrey's 42.3 percent (a margin of only about 500,000 votes), and 301 electoral votes to Humphrey's 191. George Wallace, who like most third-party candidates faded in the last weeks of the campaign, still managed to poll 12.9 percent of the popular vote and to carry five southern states with a total of 46 electoral ballots. Nixon had hardly won a decisive personal mandate. But the election made clear that a majority of the American electorate was more interested in restoring stability than in promoting social change.

CONCLUSION

Perhaps no decade of the twentieth century created more powerful and enduring images in America than the 1960s. It began with the election—and then the traumatic assassination—of an attractive and energetic young president, John Kennedy, who captured the imagination of millions and seemed to symbolize the rising idealism of the time. It produced a dramatic period of political innovation, led by President Lyndon Johnson, who greatly expanded the size and functions of the federal government and its responsibility for the welfare of the nation's citizens. He called it the Great Society. This time also saw the emergence of a sustained and enormously powerful civil rights movement that won a series of crucial legal victories, including two major civil rights acts that dismantled the Jim Crow system constructed in the late nineteenth and early twentieth centuries.

The spirit of dynamism and optimism that made the early 1960s so productive also helped bring to the surface problems and grievances that had no easy solutions. The civil rights movement awakened expectations of social and economic equality that laws alone could not provide. The peaceful, interracial crusade of the early 1960s gradually turned into a much more militant, confrontational, and increasingly separatist movement toward the decade's end. The idealism among white youths that began the 1960s, and played an important role in the political success of John Kennedy, evolved into an angry rebellion against many aspects of American culture and politics and produced a large upsurge of student protest that rocked the nation at the decade's end. Perhaps most of all, a small and largely unnoticed Cold War commitment to defend South Vietnam against communist aggression from the north led to a large and disastrous war that destroyed the presidency of Lyndon Johnson, sent thousands of young men and women to their deaths, and showed no signs of producing a victory. A decade that began with high hopes and soaring ideals ended with division and deep disillusionment.

KEY TERMS/PEOPLE/PLACES/EVENTS

affirmative action 720	Community Action	freedom rides 713
Bay of Pigs 722	programs 711	Freedom Summer 717
black power 720	Cuban missile crisis 722	George Wallace 733

Great Society 711
Gulf of Tonkin
 Resolution 725
Immigration Act
 of 1965 712
John Kennedy 708
Lyndon Johnson 710

Malcolm X 721
March on Washington 716
Medicaid 711
Medicare 711
New Frontier 709
Ngo Dinh Diem 724
Richard Nixon 733

Robert Kennedy 732
Tet offensive 731
Viet Cong (National
 Liberation Front) 724
Voting Rights Act 717

RECALL AND REFLECT

1. What were the political effects of John Kennedy's assassination?
2. How did increasing radicalism affect the successes and the setbacks of the civil rights movement?
3. What was the military strategy of the United States in Vietnam? What were the U.S. aims in that conflict? Why did the United States ultimately fail in Vietnam?
4. What accounted for growing opposition to the war in Vietnam?
5. What events made 1968 such a turbulent year both in the United States and elsewhere in the world? How did these events affect U.S. politics?

30 THE CRISIS OF AUTHORITY

THE YOUTH CULTURE

THE MOBILIZATION OF MINORITIES

THE NEW FEMINISM

ENVIRONMENTALISM IN A TURBULENT
    SOCIETY

NIXON, KISSINGER, AND THE VIETNAM WAR

NIXON, KISSINGER, AND THE WORLD

POLITICS AND ECONOMICS IN THE NIXON
    YEARS

THE WATERGATE CRISIS

LOOKING AHEAD

1. What were some of the characteristics of the social and cultural revolutions of the 1960s and 1970s?

2. How did the U.S. strategy in Vietnam change under Nixon? What was the result of the change in strategy?

3. What was the Watergate scandal and how did it affect the presidency?

THE ELECTION OF RICHARD NIXON in 1968 was the result of more than the unpopularity of Lyndon Johnson and the Vietnam War. It was the result, too, of a broad popular reaction against what many Americans considered an assault on the foundations of their society and culture. In Richard Nixon such Americans found a man who seemed to match their mood. A product of a hardworking, middle-class family, Nixon projected an image of stern dedication to traditional values. Yet the presidency of Richard Nixon, far from returning calm and stability to American politics, coincided with, and helped produce, more years of crisis.

THE YOUTH CULTURE

Many conservatives in the 1960s and 1970s were alarmed by what they saw as a pattern of social and cultural anger by younger Americans. The protesters gave vent to two related impulses. One, emerging from the political left, was to create a great new community of "the people," which would rise up to break the traditional power of elites and force the nation to end the war, pursue racial and economic justice, and transform its political life. The other, at least equally powerful impulse was the vision of personal "liberation." It found expression in part through the efforts of many groups—African Americans, Indians, Hispanics, women, gay people, and others—to define and assert themselves and make demands on the larger society. It also found expression through the efforts of individuals to create a new culture—one that would allow them to escape from what some considered the dehumanizing pressures of the modern "technocracy."

THE NEW LEFT

Among the products of the racial crisis and the war in Vietnam was a radicalization of many American students. In the course of the 1960s, they formed what became known as the New Left. In 1962, a group of students (most of them white and many of them from the University of Michigan) gathered in Michigan to form Students for a Democratic Society (SDS), which became the most prominent organization of the New Left. Their declaration of beliefs, the Port Huron Statement, expressed their disillusionment with the society they had inherited and their determination to build a new politics. In the following years, SDS became the leading organization of student radicalism.

Since most members of the New Left were students, much of their radicalism centered for a time on issues related to the modern university. A 1964 dispute at the University

TIME LINE

1963
Friedan's *The Feminine Mystique*

1964
Free Speech Movement begins

1966
National Organization for Women formed

1968
Turmoil in universities

1969
Rock concert in Woodstock, NY

1970
Cambodian incursion
Kent State and Jackson State shootings

1971
Pentagon Papers published
Nixon imposes wage–price controls

1972
Nixon visits China
SALT I
"Christmas bombing" of North Vietnam
Watergate burglary
Nixon reelected

1973
U.S. withdraws from Vietnam
Arab oil embargo
Agnew resigns
Supreme Court decides *Roe v. Wade*

1974
Nixon resigns; Ford becomes president

1975
South Vietnam falls

CONSIDER THE SOURCE

DEMANDS OF THE NEW YORK HIGH SCHOOL STUDENT UNION

Like high school students across the country, young New Yorkers formed a union and demanded reform in the city's school system. Their demands from 1970 reflected the growing call among young Americans for greater control over public institutions and leaders and a new focus on the needs and aspirations of historically disadvantaged groups.

1—No suspensions, involuntary transfers, exclusion from classes, detention, harassment of students. Due process for students.

2—No cops in schools, no narcos, security guards, plain clothesmen, informers.

3—No program cards, hall checks, ID's, passes.

4—An end to commercial and general diplomas, one diploma for every student upon graduation.

5—Open admissions to colleges, a college education free for everyone who wants one.

6—Jobs and housing for every student who wants them on graduating, dropping out, or leaving home. The army is not a decent job.

7—No military recruiting in schools, no military assemblies, literature, no sending names to draft boards or recruiters. An immediate end to the draft.

8—Black and Latin departments controlled by Black and Latin students.

9—Community control of the schools and every other community facility. Students are part of the community.

10—POWER! Student control of curriculum, publications, assemblies, clubs, student government, dress, etc. The right to organize politically.

11—We support the fifteen points of the Black and Puerto Rican Citywide HS Council.

UNDERSTAND, ANALYZE, & EVALUATE

1. What might have inspired the students' demand for "due process"? What other evidence of an anti-authoritarian sentiment can you detect here?

2. How did the civil rights and the black power movements shape this Student Union? What are some of the rights movements covered in this chapter that were *not* reflected in this statement?

3. What role did the Vietnam War play for these students—what made this a possibly quite personal issue?

Source: *New York High School Free Press* (an underground newspaper), No. 8, reprinted in John Birmingham, *Our Time Is Now: Notes from the High School Underground* (New York: Praeger, 1970), p. 178.

of California at Berkeley over the rights of students to engage in political activities on campus—the Free Speech Movement—was the first major outburst of what *Free Speech Movement* was to be nearly a decade of campus turmoil. The antiwar movement greatly inflamed and expanded the challenge to the universities; and beginning in 1968, campus demonstrations, riots, and building seizures became almost commonplace. At Columbia University in New York, students seized the offices of the president and others and occupied them for several days until local police forcibly ejected them. Over the next several years, hardly any major university was immune to some level of disruption. Small groups of especially dogmatic radicals—among them the "Weathermen," an offshoot of SDS—were responsible for a few cases of arson and bombing that destroyed campus buildings and claimed several lives. Protests also erupted in high schools, where students voiced similar demands for greater control over the curriculum on the subjects taught to them and over disciplinary policy. (See "Consider the Source: Demands of the New York High School Union.")

Not many people accepted the radical political philosophy of the New Left. But many supported the position of SDS and other groups on particular issues, and above all on the Vietnam War. Between 1967 and 1969, student activists organized some of the largest political demonstrations in American history to protest the war.

A related issue that helped fuel the antiwar movement was opposition to the military draft. The gradual abolition of many traditional deferments—for *Opposition to the Draft* graduate students, teachers, husbands, fathers, and others—swelled the ranks of those faced with conscription (and thus likely to oppose it). Of the almost 2 million drafted, about 7,000 draft-age Americans simply refused induction, accepting what were occasionally long terms in jail as a result. Thousands of others fled to Canada, Sweden, and elsewhere (where they were joined by deserters from the armed forces) to escape conscription.

THE COUNTERCULTURE

Closely related to the New Left was a new youth culture openly scornful of the values and conventions of middle-class society. The most visible characteristic of the **counterculture,** as it became known, was a change in personal styles. As if to display their contempt for conventional standards, young Americans flaunted long hair, shabby or flamboyant clothing, and a rebellious disdain for traditional speech and decorum. Also important to the counterculture was a new, more permissive view of sex and drugs.

Like the New Left, the counterculture challenged modern American society, attacking what it claimed were its banality, its hollowness, its artificiality, its isolation from nature. The most committed adherents of the counterculture—the hippies, who came to dominate the Haight-Ashbury neighborhood of San Francisco and other places, and the social dropouts, many of whom retreated to rural communes—rejected modern society altogether and attempted to find refuge in a simpler, more "natural" existence. But even those whose commitment to the counterculture was less intense shared the idea of personal fulfillment through rejecting the inhibitions and conventions of middle-class culture and giving fuller expression to personal instinct and desire.

The counterculture was only an exaggerated expression of impulses coursing through the larger society. Long hair and outlandish clothing became the badge not only of hippies and radicals but of an entire generation. The widespread use of marijuana, the freer attitudes toward sex, the iconoclastic (and often obscene) language—all spread far beyond the true devotees of the counterculture.

One of the most powerful elements of the new youth society was rock music. Its growing influence in the 1960s was a result in part of the phenomenal popularity of the Beatles, the English group whose first visit to the United States in 1964 created a remarkable sensation. For a time, most rock musicians—like most popular musicians before them—concentrated largely on uncontroversial romantic themes. By the late 1960s, however, rock had begun to reflect many of the new iconoclastic values of its time. The Beatles, for example, abandoned their once simple and seemingly innocent style for a new, experimental, even mystical approach that reflected the growing popular fascination with drugs and Eastern religions. Other groups, such as the Rolling Stones, turned even more openly

WOODSTOCK In the summer of 1969, more than 400,000 people gathered for a music festival on a farm near Woodstock, New York. The gathering became a symbol of the youth movement of the sixties. (© Shelly Rustin/ Black Star)

to themes of anger, frustration, and rebellion. Many popular musicians used their music to express explicit political radicalism as well—especially some of the leading folk singers of the era, such as Bob Dylan and Joan Baez. Rock's driving rhythms, its undisguised sensuality, its often harsh and angry tone—all made it an appropriate vehicle for expressing the themes of the social and political unrest of the late 1960s.

A powerful symbol of the fusion of rock music and the counterculture was the massive *Woodstock* music festival at Woodstock, New York, in the summer of 1969, where 400,000 people gathered on a farm for nearly a week. Despite heavy rain, mud, inadequate facilities, and impossible crowding, the attendees remained peaceful and harmonious. Champions of the counterculture spoke rhapsodically at the time of how Woodstock represented the birth of a new youth culture, the "Woodstock nation." Four months later, however, another large rock concert—at the Altamont racetrack near San Francisco, featuring the Rolling Stones and attended by 300,000 people—exposed a darker side of the youth culture. Altamont became a brutal and violent event at which four people died, several accidentally or from drug overdoses but one because of injuries inflicted by members of a Hells Angels motorcycle gang, who were serving as security guards at the concert and who brutally beat and stabbed a number of people.

THE MOBILIZATION OF MINORITIES

The growth of African American protest encouraged other minorities to assert themselves and demand redress of their grievances. For Indians, Hispanic Americans, gay men and lesbians, and others, the late 1960s and 1970s were a time of growing self-expression and political activism.

Seeds of Indian Militancy

Few minorities had deeper or more justifiable grievances against the prevailing culture than did American Indians—or Native Americans, as they began defiantly to call themselves in the 1960s. Indians were the least prosperous, least healthy, and least stable ethnic group in the nation. And while African Americans attracted the attention (for good or for ill) of many whites, Indians for years had remained largely ignored.

For much of the postwar era, federal tribal policies tried to incorporate Indians into mainstream American society whether Indians wanted to assimilate or not. Two laws passed in 1953 established the basis of this policy, which became known as "termination." Through termination, the federal government withdrew all official rec- *Termination Policy* ognition of the tribes as legal entities; they were no longer administratively separate from state governments and were subject to the same local jurisdictions as non–Native American residents. At the same time, the government encouraged Indians to assimilate into the white world and worked to funnel Native Americans into cities, where, presumably, they would adapt themselves to the larger society and lose their cultural distinctiveness.

Despite some individual successes, the new policies were a disastrous failure on the whole. Indians themselves fought so bitterly against these policies that in 1958, the Eisenhower administration barred further terminations. In the meantime, the struggle against termination mobilized a new generation of Indian militants and breathed life into the principal Native American organization, the National Congress of American Indians, which had been created in 1944.

The Democratic administrations of the 1960s made no effort to revive termination. Instead, they made modest efforts to restore at least some degree of tribal autonomy such as funneling Office of Economic Opportunity money to tribal organizations through the Community Action programs. In the meantime, the tribes themselves began to fight for greater self-determination. The new militancy benefited from the rapid increase in the Indian population, which was growing much faster than that of the rest of the nation (nearly doubling between 1950 and 1970 to a total of about 800,000).

The Indian Civil Rights Movement

In 1961, more than 400 members from 67 tribes gathered in Chicago and issued the Declaration of Indian Purpose, which stressed the "right to choose our own way of life" and the "responsibility of preserving our precious heritage." Another example of a growing Indian self-consciousness, the National Indian Youth Council, created in the aftermath of the 1961 Chicago meeting, promoted the idea of Indian nationalism and intertribal unity. In 1968, a group of young, militant Indians established the American Indian Movement (AIM), which drew support from urban areas *American Indian Movement* and reservations alike.

The new activism produced results. In 1968, Congress passed the Indian Civil Rights Act. It guaranteed reservation Indians protections by the Bill of Rights, *Indian Civil Rights Act* but also recognized the legitimacy of tribal laws within the reservations. In 1968, Indian fishermen, citing old treaty rights, clashed with Washington State officials on the Columbia River and in Puget Sound. The following year, members of several tribes occupied the abandoned federal prison on Alcatraz Island in San Francisco Bay, claiming the site "by right of discovery."

In response, the Nixon administration appointed Louis Bruce, a Mohawk-Sioux, as commissioner of Indian affairs in 1969; and in 1970, the president promised both

THE OCCUPATION OF ALCATRAZ Alcatraz, an island in San Francisco Bay, once housed a large federal prison that by the late 1960s had been abandoned. In 1969, a group of Indian activists occupied the island and claimed it as Indian land—precipitating a long standoff with authorities. (© AP Images)

increased tribal self-determination and an increase in federal aid. But the protests continued. In November 1972, nearly a thousand demonstrators, most of them Lakota Sioux, forcibly occupied the building of the Bureau of Indian Affairs in Washington, D.C., for six days. In February 1973, members of AIM seized the town of Wounded Knee, South Dakota, the site of the 1890 massacre of Sioux by federal troops. For two months, they occupied the town, demanding that the government honor its long-forgotten treaty obligations.

The Indian civil rights movement, like other civil rights movements of the same time, fell far short of winning full equality for Native Americans. But it helped the tribes win a series of new legal rights and protections that, together, gave them a stronger position than they had enjoyed at any previous time in the twentieth century.

Latino Activism

The fastest-growing minority group in the United States in the 1970s was Latinos, or Hispanic Americans. Large numbers of Mexicans had entered the country during World War II in response to the wartime labor shortage, and many had remained in the cities of the Southwest and the Pacific Coast. By 1960, Los Angeles had a bigger Mexican population than any place except Mexico City.

But the greatest expansion in the Latino population of the United States was yet to *Growing Latino Population* come. In 1960, the census reported slightly more than 3 million Latinos living in the United States. By 1970, that number had grown to 9 million and by 2000 to 35 million. By 2010, the number passed 50 million. Hispanics constituted more than a third of all legal immigrants to the United States after 1960.

Large numbers of Puerto Ricans (who were entitled to American citizenship by birth) migrated to eastern urban areas, particularly New York City, where they formed one of the poorest communities in the city. South Florida's substantial Cuban population began with a wave of middle-class refugees fleeing the Castro regime in the early 1960s. These first Cuban migrants quickly established themselves as a successful and highly assimilated part of Miami's middle class. In 1980, a second, much poorer wave of Cuban immigrants—the so-called Marielitos, named for the port from which they left Cuba—arrived in Florida when Castro temporarily relaxed exit restrictions. Later in the 1980s, large numbers of immigrants (both legal and illegal) began to arrive from Central and South America—from Guatemala, Nicaragua, El Salvador, Peru, and other countries.

Like African Americans and Indians, many Latinos responded to the highly charged climate of the 1960s by strengthening their ethnic identification and by organizing for political and economic power. Affluent Hispanics in Miami filled influential positions in the professions and local government; in the Southwest, Latino voters elected Mexican Americans to seats in Congress and to governorships. A Mexican American political organization, La Raza Unida, exercised influence in Southern California and elsewhere in the Southwest in the 1970s and beyond. One of the most visible efforts to organize Hispanics occurred in California, where an Arizona-born farmworker of Mexican descent, César Chávez, created an effective *César Chávez* union of largely Mexican itinerant farmworkers: the United Farm Workers (UFW).

For most Latinos, however, the path to economic and political power was more difficult. Mexican Americans and others were slow to develop political influence in proportion to their numbers. In the meantime, Latinos formed one of the poorest segments of the United States population.

KENNEDY AND CHÁVEZ César Chávez, leader of the United Farm Workers, endured a hunger strike in 1968 in the spirit of nonviolent protest against the treatment of field workers. Robert F. Kennedy, just beginning his campaign for the presidency, visited the union leader to show his support. At this point, Chávez had been fasting for several weeks. (Photo by Michael Rougier/© Time & Life Pictures/Getty Images)

Gay Liberation

Another important liberation movement to emerge in the 1960s was the effort by gay men and lesbians to win political and economic rights and social acceptance. Homosexuality has been a generally unacknowledged reality throughout Western civilization. Nonheterosexual men and women were forced for generations to suppress their sexual preferences, to exercise them surreptitiously, or to live within isolated and often persecuted communities. But by the late 1960s, the liberating impulses that had affected other groups helped mobilize gay men and lesbians to fight for their own rights.

On June 27, 1969, police officers raided the Stonewall Inn, a gay nightclub in New York City's Greenwich Village, and began arresting patrons simply for frequenting the place. The raid was not unusual, but the response was. Gay onlookers taunted the police and then attacked them. Someone started a blaze in the Stonewall Inn itself, almost trapping the police inside. Rioting continued throughout Greenwich Village (the center of New York's gay community) through much of the night.

The "Stonewall Riot" marked the growth of the gay liberation movement—one of the *Stonewall Riot* most controversial challenges to traditional values and assumptions of its time. New organizations—among them the Gay Liberation Front, founded in New York in 1969—sprang up around the country. Public discussion and media coverage of homosexuality, long subject to an unofficial taboo, quickly and dramatically increased. Gay activists had some success in challenging the long-standing assumption that homosexuality was aberrant behavior; many argued that no sexual preference was any more normal than another. One victory came when the American Psychiatric Association stopped categorizing homosexuality as a mental illness in 1974.

Most of all, however, the gay liberation movement transformed the outlook of many gay men and lesbians themselves. It helped them "come out," express their preferences openly and unapologetically, and demand from society a recognition that gay relationships could be as significant and worthy of respect as heterosexual ones. By the early 1980s, the gay liberation movement had made remarkable strides. Even the ravages of the AIDS epidemic, which, in the beginning at least, affected the gay community more disastrously than any other group, failed to halt the growth of gay liberation. Indeed, it not only strengthened the gay community, but it also helped Americans understand and humanize those suffering, which in turn slowly led to increased acceptance.

By the early twenty-first century, gay men and lesbians had achieved many of the same milestones that other oppressed minorities had attained in earlier decades. Openly gay politicians won election to public office. Universities established gay and lesbian studies programs. Laws prohibiting discrimination on the basis of sexual preference made slow, halting progress at the state and local levels. But gay liberation produced a powerful *Backlash against Gay Liberation* backlash as well. President Bill Clinton's 1993 effort to end the ban on gay men and lesbians serving in the military met a storm of criticism from members of Congress and within the military itself. Clinton retreated to a "Don't Ask, Don't Tell" policy and even signed the Defense of Marriage Act (DOMA) in 1996 that allowed states to refuse to recognize same-sex marriages granted under the laws of other states. Conservative voters in some cities and states approved referendum questions on their ballots outlawing civil rights protections for gay men and lesbians, and, during a bitter debate over gay rights in the 2004 presidential campaign, voted state bans on gay marriage. Antigay violence continued periodically in communities around the country.

At the same time, however, support for gay rights grew stronger in many parts of the country. In 2010, President Obama and the Congress repealed the "Don't Ask, Don't Tell" policy that forced people in the military to hide their homosexuality. And in June 2015, the Supreme Court affirmed the right of same-sex couples to wed in all 50 states.

THE NEW FEMINISM

Women constitute over 50 percent of the United States population. But during the 1960s and 1970s, many women began to identify with minority groups as they renewed demands for a liberation of their own.

THE REBIRTH

The 1963 publication of Betty Friedan's *The Feminine Mystique* is often cited as one of the first events of contemporary women's liberation. A writer for women's *Betty Friedan* magazines in the 1950s, Friedan traveled around the country interviewing women who had graduated with her from Smith College in 1947. Most of these women were living out the dream that postwar American society had promised them: they were affluent wives and mothers living in comfortable suburbs. And yet many of them were deeply frustrated and unhappy, with no outlets for their intelligence, talent, and education. Friedan's book did not so much cause the revival of feminism as help give voice to a movement that was already stirring.

By the time *The Feminine Mystique* appeared, President Kennedy had already established the President's Commission on the Status of Women, which brought national

Note: People 15 years old and older beginning in 1980 and people 14 years old and older as of the following year for previous years. Before 1989, data are for civilian workers only.

MEDIAN EARNINGS BY GENDER, 1960–2009 U.S. Census Bureau data comparing the median earnings of full-time, year-round workers show changes in the gender wage gap over time. • *If the Equal Pay Act barred employers from paying women less than men for the same work, what factors might account for the differences in median earnings of men and women?* (U.S. Census Bureau, Current Population Survey, 1961 to 2009 Annual Social and Economic Supplements) attention to sexual discrimination. Also in 1963, the Kennedy administration helped win passage of the Equal Pay Act, which barred the pervasive practice of paying women less than men for the same work in some fields. A year later, Congress incorporated into the Civil Rights Act of 1964 an amendment—Title VII—that extended to women many of the same legal protections against discrimination that were being extended to African Americans and other minorities.

In 1966, Friedan joined with other feminists to create the National Organization for Women (NOW), which was to become the nation's largest and most influential feminist organization. NOW responded to the complaints of women by demanding greater educational opportunities for women and denouncing the domestic ideal and the traditional concept of marriage. But the heart of the movement was an effort to address the needs of women in the workplace.

WOMEN'S LIBERATION

By the late 1960s, new and more radical feminist demands were also attracting a large following, especially among younger, white, educated women. Many of them drew inspiration from the New Left and the counterculture. Some were involved in the civil rights movement; others, in the antiwar crusade. Many had found that even within those movements, they faced discrimination and exclusion and were subordinated to male leaders.

In its most radical form, the new feminism rejected the whole notion of marriage, family, and even heterosexual relationships (a vehicle, some women claimed, of male domination). Few women embraced such extremes. But by the early 1970s, large numbers of women were coming to see themselves as an exploited group banding together against oppression and developing a culture of their own. In cities and towns across the country, feminists opened women's bookstores, bars, and coffee shops. They founded feminist newspapers and magazines. They created women's health clinics, centers to assist victims of rape and abuse, day-care centers, and, particularly after 1973, abortion clinics.

EXPANDING ACHIEVEMENTS

In 1971, the government extended its affirmative action guidelines to include women—linking sexism with racism as an officially acknowledged social problem. Women made rapid progress, in the meantime, in their efforts to move into the economic and political mainstream. The nation's all-male educational institutions began to crack open their doors to women. (Princeton and Yale did so in 1969, and many others soon did the same.) In 1972, Congress approved legislation (known as Title IX) requiring universities to support male and female athletic programs at equal levels.

Women were also becoming an important force in business and the professions. Nearly half of all married women held jobs by the mid-1970s, and almost 90 percent of all women with college degrees worked. The two-career family, in which both the husband and the wife maintained active professional lives, slowly became a widely accepted middle-class norm. (It had been common within much of the working class for decades.) There were also important symbolic changes, such as the refusal of many women to adopt their husbands' surnames when they married and the use of the term "Ms." in place of "Mrs." or "Miss" to signal the irrelevance of a woman's marital status in the professional world.

By the mid-1980s, women were serving in both houses of Congress, on the Supreme Court, in numerous federal cabinet positions, as governors of several states, and in many other political positions. In 1981, Ronald Reagan named the first female Supreme Court justice, Sandra Day O'Connor; in 1993, Bill Clinton named the second, Ruth Bader Ginsburg. In 1984, the Democratic Party chose a woman, Representative   *Women in Government* Geraldine Ferraro of New York, as its vice presidential candidate. Madeleine Albright (under Clinton) and Condoleezza Rice (under George W. Bush) became the first women to serve as secretary of state. And in 2008, Hillary Clinton nearly became the Democratic candidate for president. She, too, became secretary of state in the Obama administration. In academia, women were expanding their presence in traditional scholarly fields; they were also creating new fields—women's and gender studies, which in the 1980s and 1990s were among the fastest-growing areas of American scholarship.

In 1972, Congress approved the Equal Rights Amendment (ERA) to the Constitution and sent it to the states. For a while, ratification seemed almost   *The Equal Rights Amendment* certain. By the late 1970s, however, the momentum behind the amendment had died because of a rising chorus of objections to it from people (including many antifeminist women) who feared that it would disrupt traditional social patterns. In 1982, the ten years allotted for ratification expired.

THE ABORTION ISSUE

A major goal of American feminism since the 1920s has been the effort by women to win greater control of their own sexual and reproductive lives. In its least controversial form, this impulse helped produce an increasing awareness beginning in the 1970s of the problems of rape, sexual abuse, and domestic abuse. The dissemination of contraceptives and birth-control information became more widespread and less controversial than it had been earlier in the century. A related issue, however, stimulated as much popular controversy as any question of its time: abortion.

Abortion had once been legal in much of the United States, but by the beginning of the twentieth century, it was banned by statute in most of the country and remained so into the 1960s (although many abortions continued to be performed quietly, and often dangerously, out of sight of the law). The women's movement created strong new pressures for the legalization of abortion. Several states had abandoned restrictions on abortion by the end of the 1960s. And in 1973, the Supreme Court's decision in   **Roe v. Wade** *Roe v. Wade,* based on an implied but not specified "right to privacy" first protected by the Court only a few years earlier in *Griswold v. Connecticut,* invalidated all laws prohibiting abortion during the "first trimester"—the first three months of pregnancy. But even then, the issue remained far from settled.

ENVIRONMENTALISM IN A TURBULENT SOCIETY

Like feminism, environmentalism entered the 1960s with a long history but relatively little public support. Also like feminism, environmentalism profited from the turbulence of the era and emerged by the 1970s as a powerful force in American life. The rise of this new movement was in part a result of the intensifying level of environmental degradation in advanced industrial societies of the late twentieth century. It was a result, too, of the growth of ecology, a science that provided environmentalists with new and powerful arguments.

The New Science of Ecology

Until the mid-twentieth century, most people who considered themselves environmentalists based their commitment on aesthetic or moral grounds. They wanted to preserve nature because it was too beautiful to despoil, because it was a mark of divinity on the world, or because it permitted humans a spiritual experience that would otherwise be unavailable to them. Other groups took their cue from the late President Theodore Roosevelt. These conservationists wanted to protect the environment for use in outdoor activities like camping and hunting. In the course of the twentieth century, however, scientists in much of the world began to create a new rationale for environmentalism. They called it ecology.

Ecology is the science of the interrelatedness of the natural world. It addresses such problems as air and water pollution, the destruction of forests, the extinction of species, and toxic wastes, which are not separate, isolated problems. All elements of the earth's environment are intimately and delicately linked. Damaging any one of those elements, therefore, risks damaging all the others.

Among the early contributions to popular knowledge of ecology was the work of writer and naturalist Aldo Leopold. During a career in forest management, Leopold sought to apply the new scientific findings on ecology to his interactions with the natural world. And in 1949, he published a classic of environmental literature, *The Sand County Almanac,* in which he argued that humans had a responsibility to understand and maintain the balance of nature, that they should behave in the natural world according to a code that he called the "land ethic." By then, the science of ecology was spreading widely in the scientific community. Among the findings of ecologists were such now-common ideas as the "food *Rachel Carson*   chain," the "ecosystem," "biodiversity," and "endangered species." Rachel Carson's sensational 1962 book, *Silent Spring,* which revealed the dangers of pesticides, was based solidly on the ideas of ecologists and did at least as much as Leopold's work to introduce those ideas to a larger public.

Environmental Advocacy

Among the major environmental organizations were the Wilderness Society, the Sierra Club, the National Audubon Society, the Nature Conservancy, the National Wildlife Federation, and the National Parks and Conservation Association. All of these organizations predated the rise of modern ecological science, but the growth of environmental threats and scientific efforts to address them kept these organizations engaged like never before. They found allies among such groups as the American Civil Liberties Union, the League of Women Voters, the National Council of Churches, and even the AFL-CIO.

Out of these organizations emerged a new generation of environmental activists able to contribute to the legal and political battles of the movement. Scientists provided the necessary data. Lawyers fought battles with government agencies and in the courts.

Many other forces contributed to what became the environmental movement. Lady Bird Johnson, the first lady, helped raise public awareness of the landscape with her energetic "beautification" campaign in the mid-1960s—a campaign unconnected to any ecological concepts, but one that reflected a growing popular dismay at the despoiling of the landscape by rapid economic growth. Members of the counterculture contributed to environmental awareness with their romanticization of the natural world and their repudiation of the "technocracy."

But perhaps the greatest force behind environmentalism was the condition of the environment itself. By the 1960s, the damage to the natural world from postwar population and economic growth was becoming hard to ignore. Water pollution—which had been a problem in some areas of the country for many decades—was becoming so *Pollution* widespread that almost every major city was dealing with the unpleasant sight and odor, as well as the health risks, of polluted rivers and lakes. In Cleveland, Ohio, for example, the Cuyahoga River actually burst into flame from time to time from the petroleum waste being dumped into it; the city declared the river an official fire hazard.

Perhaps more alarming was the growing awareness that the air itself was becoming unhealthy, that toxic fumes from factories, power plants, and, most of all, automobiles were poisoning the atmosphere. Weather forecasts and official atmospheric information began to refer to "smog" levels—using a relatively new word formed from a combination of "smoke" and "fog," which became an almost perpetual fact of daily life in such cities as Los Angeles and Denver. In 1969, a damaged oil-well platform off Santa Barbara, California, spewed hundreds of thousands of gallons of crude oil into the ocean just off the popular beaches of this affluent city. This oil spill had a tremendous impact on the environmental consciousness of millions of Americans. Another, much larger spill—indeed, the largest in American history—occurred off the coast of Alaska in 1989 when the giant tanker *Exxon Valdez* hit a reef in Prince William Sound. The damage it caused to the nearby shoreline and wildlife also greatly increased environmental consciousness. In April 2010, the Deepwater Horizon oil rig exploded forty-one miles off the Louisiana coast, killing eleven. Over the next three months, chemical dispersants used to control the spill and 5 million gallons of crude oil spread into *Major Oil Spills* the Gulf of Mexico, destroying sea life and damaging the coastline. The long-term effects are still unknown.

Environmentalists brought to public attention many long-term dangers and helped create a broad and powerful movement.

Earth Day and Beyond

On April 22, 1970, people all over the United States participated in the first "Earth Day." Originally proposed by Wisconsin senator Gaylord Nelson as a series of teach-ins on college campuses, Earth Day gradually took on a much larger life. Carefully managed by people who wanted to avoid associations with the radical left, it had a less threatening quality than antiwar demonstrations and civil rights rallies seemed to have. According to some estimates, over 20 million Americans participated in Earth Day observances, making Earth Day, possibly, the largest single demonstration in the nation's history.

The cautious, centrist character of Earth Day and related efforts to popularize environmentalism helped create a movement that was for a time less divisive than other, more controversial causes. Gradually, environmentalism became more than simply a series of demonstrations and protests. It became part of the consciousness of the vast majority of Americans—absorbed into popular culture, built into primary and secondary education, and endorsed by almost all politicians (even if many of them actually opposed some environmental goals).

It also became part of the fabric of public policy. In 1970, Congress passed and President Nixon signed the National Environmental Protection Act, which created a new agency—the Environmental Protection Agency—to enforce antipollution *EPA Established* standards on businesses and consumers. The Clean Air Act, also passed in 1970, and the Clean Water Act, passed in 1972, became additional tools in the government's arsenal of weapons against environmental degradation.

Different administrations displayed varying levels of support for environmental goals, and new environmental problems continued to emerge even as older ones sometimes found solutions. Environmentalism became simultaneously a movement, a set of public policies, and a broad national ideal—and it was the combination of all those aspects that made it a powerful force in American life.

NIXON, KISSINGER, AND THE VIETNAM WAR

Richard Nixon assumed office in 1969 committed not only to restoring stability at home but to creating a new and more stable order in the world. Central to his hopes for international stability was a resolution of the stalemate in Vietnam. Yet the new president felt no freer than his predecessor to abandon the American commitment there.

VIETNAMIZATION

Despite Nixon's own deep interest in international affairs, he brought with him into government a man who at times seemed to overshadow the president himself in the *Henry Kissinger* conduct of diplomacy: Henry Kissinger, a Harvard professor whom Nixon appointed as his special assistant for national security affairs. Kissinger quickly established dominance over Secretary of State William Rogers and Secretary of Defense Melvin Laird. Together, Nixon and Kissinger set out to find an acceptable solution to the stalemate in Vietnam.

The new Vietnam policy moved along several fronts. One was the move to "Vietnamize" the conflict—that is, train and equip the South Vietnamese military to assume the burden of combat in place of American forces. In the fall of 1969, Nixon announced the withdrawal of 60,000 American ground troops from Vietnam. By the fall of 1972, relatively few American soldiers remained in Indochina. From a peak of more than 540,000 in 1969, the number had dwindled to about 60,000.

Vietnamization (and the decreased draft calls it produced) did help quiet domestic opposition to the war for a time. It did nothing, however, to break the stalemate in the negotiations with the North Vietnamese in Paris. The new administration decided that new military pressures would be necessary to do that.

ESCALATION

By the end of 1969, Nixon and Kissinger had decided that the most effective way to tip the military balance in South Vietnam's favor was to destroy bases in Cambodia and Laos that the U.S. military believed were the launching points for many North Vietnamese attacks. (Laos, Cambodia, and Vietnam are neighboring states in the peninsula of Indochina.) Very early in his presidency, Nixon secretly ordered the air force to bomb these bases; on April 30, 1970, the president announced that he was sending U.S. ground troops across the border into Cambodia to destroy them.

Literally overnight, the Cambodian invasion restored the dwindling antiwar movement to vigorous life. The first days of May saw widespread and vocal antiwar demonstrations. A mood of crisis was already mounting when, on May 4, four college students were killed and nine injured after members of the National Guard opened fire on antiwar demonstra-
Kent State and Jackson State tors at Kent State University in Ohio. Ten days later, police killed

two African American students at Jackson State University in Mississippi during a demonstration there.

The clamor against the war spread into the government and the press. Congress angrily repealed the Gulf of Tonkin Resolution in December. Then, in June 1971, first the *New York Times* and later other newspapers began publishing excerpts from a secret study of the war prepared by the Defense Department during the Johnson administration. The so-called Pentagon Papers were leaked to the press by former Defense official   *Pentagon Papers* Daniel Ellsberg. They provided evidence that the government had been dishonest, both in reporting the military progress of the war and in explaining its own motives for American involvement. The administration went to court to suppress the documents, but the Supreme Court ruled that the press had the right to publish them.

Morale and discipline among American troops in Vietnam were rapidly deteriorating in the waning years of the war. In 1971 Lieutenant William Calley was tried and convicted of overseeing a massacre of more than 100 unarmed South Vietnamese civilians in 1968 near the village of My Lai. It attracted wide public attention to the dehumanizing impact of the war on those who fought it—both Americans and Vietnamese. Less publicized were other, more widespread problems among American troops in Vietnam: desertion, drug addiction, racism, refusal to obey orders, even the killing of unpopular officers by enlisted men.

By 1971, polls indicated that nearly two-thirds of Americans supported withdrawal from Vietnam. President Nixon, however, believed that a defeat in Vietnam would cause unacceptable damage to the nation's credibility. The FBI, the CIA, the White House itself, and other federal agencies increased their efforts to discredit and harass antiwar and radical groups, often through illegal means.

In Indochina, meanwhile, the fighting raged on. American bombing in Vietnam and Cambodia increased. In March 1972, the North Vietnamese mounted their biggest offensive since 1968 (the so-called Easter offensive). American and South Vietnamese   *Easter Offensive* forces managed to halt the communist advance, but it was clear that without American support, the South Vietnamese would not have succeeded. At the same time, Nixon ordered American planes to bomb targets near Hanoi, the capital of North Vietnam, and Haiphong, its principal port, and called for the mining of seven North Vietnamese harbors.

"PEACE WITH HONOR"

As the 1972 presidential election approached, the administration stepped up its effort to produce a breakthrough in negotiations with the North Vietnamese. In April, the president dropped his longtime insistence on the removal of North Vietnamese troops from the south before any American withdrawal. Meanwhile, Henry Kissinger met privately in Paris with the North Vietnamese foreign secretary, Le Duc Tho, to work out terms for a cease-fire. On October 26, only days before the presidential election, Kissinger announced that "peace is at hand."

Several weeks later (after the election), negotiations broke down once again. Although both the American and the North Vietnamese governments were ready to accept the Kissinger–Tho plan for a cease-fire, President Nguyen Van Thieu of South Vietnam balked, still insisting on a full withdrawal of North Vietnamese forces from the south. Kissinger tried to win additional concessions from the communists to meet Thieu's objections, but on December 16 talks broke off.

The next day, December 17, American B-52s began the heaviest and most destructive air raids of the entire war on Hanoi, Haiphong, and other North Vietnamese targets.

Civilian casualties were high, and fifteen American B-52s were shot down by the North Vietnamese; in the entire war to that point, the United States had lost only one of the "*Christmas Bombing*" giant bombers. On December 30, Nixon terminated the "Christmas bombing." The United States and the North Vietnamese returned to the conference table; and on January 27, 1973, they signed an "agreement on ending the war and restoring peace in Vietnam." Nixon claimed that the Christmas bombing had forced the North Vietnamese to relent. At least equally important, however, was the enormous American pressure on Thieu to accept the cease-fire.

The terms of the Paris accords were little different from those Kissinger and Tho had accepted in principle a few months before. Nor were they much different from the peace plan Johnson had proposed in 1968. There would be an immediate cease-fire. The North Vietnamese would release several hundred American prisoners of war. The Thieu regime would survive for the moment, but North Vietnamese forces already in the south would remain there. An undefined committee would work out a permanent settlement.

THE EVACUATION OF SAIGON A harried U.S. official struggles to keep panicking Vietnamese from boarding an already overpacked helicopter on the roof of the U.S. embassy in Saigon. The hurried evacuation of Americans took place only hours before the arrival of North Vietnamese troops, signaling the final defeat of South Vietnam. (© AP Images)

DEFEAT IN INDOCHINA

American forces were hardly out of Indochina before the Paris accords began to collapse. In March 1975, the North Vietnamese launched a full-scale offensive against the now greatly weakened forces of South Vietnam. Thieu appealed to Washington for assistance. The president (now Gerald Ford) appealed to Congress for additional funding; Congress refused. Late in April 1975, communist forces marched into Saigon, shortly *Fall of Saigon* after officials of the Thieu regime and the staff of the American embassy had fled the country in humiliating disarray. The communist forces quickly occupied the capital, renamed it Ho Chi Minh City, and began the process of reuniting Vietnam under the government based in Hanoi. At about the same time, the Lon Nol regime in Cambodia fell to the murderous forces of the Khmer Rouge—whose brutal policies led to the death of more than a third of the country's people over the next several years.

Such were the dismal results of more than a decade of direct American military involvement in Vietnam. More than 1.2 million Vietnamese soldiers had died in combat, along with countless civilians throughout the region. A beautiful land had been ravaged, its agrarian economy left in ruins; until an economic revival began in the early 1990s, Vietnam remained for more than a decade one of the poorest nations in the world. The United States had paid a heavy price as well. The war had cost the nation almost $150 billion in direct costs and much more indirectly. It had resulted in the deaths of over 57,000 young Americans and the injury of 300,000 more. And the nation had suffered a blow to its confidence and self-esteem from which it did not soon recover.

NIXON, KISSINGER, AND THE WORLD

The continuing war in Vietnam provided an unhappy backdrop to what Nixon considered his larger mission in world affairs: the construction of a new international order. The president had become convinced that the old assumptions of a "bipolar" world—in which the United States and the Soviet Union were the only real great powers—were now obsolete. America must adapt to the new "multipolar" international structure, in which China, Japan, and Western Europe were becoming major, independent forces. Nixon had a considerable advantage over many other politicians in changing the assumptions behind American foreign policy. His long anticommunist record gave him credibility among many conservatives for his effort to transform American relations with communist China and the Soviet Union.

THE CHINA INITIATIVE AND SOVIET–AMERICAN DÉTENTE

For more than twenty years, ever since the fall of Chiang Kai-shek in 1949, the United States had treated China, the most populous nation on earth, as if it did not exist. Instead, America recognized the regime-in-exile on the small island of Taiwan as the legitimate government of China. Nixon and Kissinger wanted to forge a new relationship with the Chinese communists—in part to strengthen them as a counterbalance to the Soviet Union. The Chinese, for their part, were eager to end China's own isolation from the international arena.

In July 1971, Nixon sent Henry Kissinger on a secret mission to Beijing. When Kissinger returned, the president made the startling announcement that he would visit China himself within the next few months. That fall, with American approval, the United

NIXON IN CHINA   President Nixon's 1972 visit to China was an important step in normalizing relations between the United States and the People's Republic of China. Here, Nixon toasts the developing relationship with Prime Minister Zhou Enlai. (© Universal Images Group/Getty Images)

Nations admitted the communist government of China and expelled the representatives of the Taiwan regime. Finally, in February 1972, Nixon paid a formal visit to China. It erased much of the deep animosity between the United States and the Chinese communists. Nixon did not yet formally recognize the communist regime, but in 1972 the United States and China began low-level diplomatic relations.

The initiatives in China coincided with an effort by the Nixon administration to improve relations with the Soviet Union, an initiative known by the French word **détente.** In 1971, American and Soviet diplomats produced the first Strategic Arms Limitation Treaty (SALT I), which froze the arsenals of some nuclear missiles (ICBMs) on both sides at present levels. In May of that year, the president traveled to Moscow to sign the agreement. The next year, the Soviet premier, Leonid Brezhnev, visited Washington.

DEALING WITH THE THIRD WORLD

The policies of rapprochement with communist China and détente with the Soviet Union reflected Nixon's and Kissinger's belief in the importance of stable relationships among the great powers. But, as America's experience in Vietnam already illustrated, the so-called Third World remained the most volatile and dangerous source of international tension. Since the end of World War I, the United States and the European powers had lost or withdrawn control over former colonies. The result was a number of newly independent but economically fragile and politically unstable nations around the globe. (See "America in the World: The End of Colonialism.")

The Nixon–Kissinger policy toward the Third World tried to maintain the status quo without involving the United States too deeply in local disputes. In 1969 and 1970, the *Nixon Doctrine* president described what became known as the Nixon Doctrine, by which the United States would "participate in the defense and development of allies and friends" but would leave the "basic responsibility" for the future of those "friends" to the nations themselves. In practice, the Nixon Doctrine meant a declining American interest in contributing to Third World development. There was also a growing contempt for the United Nations, where underdeveloped nations were gaining influence through their sheer numbers. And there was increasing American support for authoritarian regimes attempting to withstand radical challenges from within.

In 1970, for example, the CIA poured substantial funds into Chile to help support the government against a communist challenge. When the Marxist candidate for president, Salvador Allende, came to power through an open election despite *Allende Overthrown* American efforts, the United States began funneling more money to opposition forces in Chile to help destabilize the new government. In 1973, a military junta seized power from Allende, who was subsequently murdered. The United States developed a friendly relationship with the new, repressive military government of General Augusto Pinochet.

In the Middle East, conditions grew more volatile in the aftermath of a 1967 war in which Israel had occupied substantial new territories, dislodging many Palestinian Arabs from their homes. The refugees were a source of considerable instability in Jordan, Lebanon, and the other surrounding countries into which they moved. In October 1973, on the Jewish high holy day of Yom Kippur, Egyptian and Syrian forces attacked Israel. For ten days, the Israelis struggled to recover from the surprise attack; finally, they launched an effective counteroffensive against Egyptian forces in the Sinai. At that point, the United States intervened, placing heavy pressure on Israel to accept a cease-fire rather than press its advantage.

The Yom Kippur War demonstrated the growing dependence of the United States and its allies on Arab oil. A brief but painful embargo in 1973–1974 by the Arab members of the Organization of the Petroleum Exporting Companies (OPEC) against *OPEC Embargo* the United States and other allies that supported Israel provided an ominous warning of the costs of dependence on foreign oil. It also prompted Congress to pass fuel economy standards, requiring automakers to raise average mileage from 13.5 miles per gallon to 27. (The standard has since been raised to 54.5 mpg by 2025.)

POLITICS AND ECONOMICS IN THE NIXON YEARS

Nixon ran for president in 1968, promising a return to more conservative social and economic policies and a restoration of law and order. Once he was in office, however, his domestic policies sometimes continued and even expanded the liberal initiatives of the previous two administrations.

DOMESTIC INITIATIVES

Many of Nixon's domestic policies were a response to what he believed to be the demands of his constituency—the "silent majority" of conservative, mostly *"Silent Majority"* middle-class people who, he believed, wanted to reduce federal interference in local affairs. He tried, unsuccessfully, to persuade Congress to pass legislation prohibiting school desegregation through the use of forced busing. He forbade the Department of Health, Education, and Welfare (now called the Department of Health and Human Services) to cut off federal funds from school districts that had failed to comply with court

THE END OF COLONIALISM

On July 4, 1946, less than a year after the close of World War II, a ceremony in Manila marked what Senator Millard Tydings of Maryland called "one of the most unprecedented, most idealistic, and most far-reaching events in all recorded history." On that day, the United States voluntarily ended nearly five decades of colonial control of the Philippines, which it had acquired as part of the spoils from the 1898 Spanish-American War. Philippine independence was only a small part of a dramatic change in the political structure of the world. The close of World War II marked not only the defeat of fascism in Germany, Italy, and Japan, but also the beginning of the end of the formal system of imperialism that European powers had maintained for centuries. The repudiation of colonialism was driven in part by the heightened belief in democracy and self-determination that the war helped strengthen through much of the world. It was also driven by the weakness of the European powers after World War II and their inability to sustain control over their increasingly restive colonies. Like most great geopolitical changes, the drive for colonial independence was turbulent and often violent.

The United States had been a latecomer to the imperialist system. But even its peaceful divestiture of the Philippines reflected the challenges many imperial powers and postcolonial nations faced in renegotiating colonial relationships. America was not quite as ready to cede military presence and economic influence in the region as it was to give up political responsibility over the islands. Philippine independence came with important caveats: that the United States maintained control of Fillipino military bases and that required (through the Bell Trade Act, passed by Congress in 1946) that the Philippines not engage in any direct economic competition with the United States and that it revise its constitution to allow American interests free and

unfettered access to the nation's natural resources. Many Filipinos argue that their nation did not achieve full independence until 1991, when the Philippine Senate refused to ratify a treaty that would have extended the American lease on the Subic Bay naval base (once the largest U.S. Navy installation in the Pacific). A year later, the United States closed the base and left, marking the first time in 400 years that the Philippines (once a Spanish possession) was not home to a foreign military power.

England's imperial holdings were the vastest in the world, and the existence of the British Empire was deeply embedded in England's economic life and national self-image. But it, too, withdrew from most of its colonies in the decades after World War II—beginning in 1947 with its largest and most important colony, India. The British Raj—as the colonial government was known—withdrew from South Asia in response to a growing independence movement on the subcontinent. As often happened as colonial rule ended, suppressed conflicts in the native population quickly emerged—in the case of India, between Hindus and Muslims. The price of Indian independence, therefore, was the partition of the country into India and Pakistan (and, several decades later, Bangladesh).

A year later, the British gave up its World War I mandate of Palestine (ceding the territory to the United Nations and allowing for the creation of Israel) as well as many of its holdings in Southeast Asia, including Burma and Ceylon. Malaya followed in 1957 and Singapore in 1965. In 1982, England passed the Canada Act, effectively severing Canada from the United Kingdom and culminating a move toward full Canadian self-government that had begun several decades earlier. In 1997, England returned one of its last important overseas territories, Hong Kong, to the control of China, bringing nearly to an end the era of the British Empire.

The dissolution of the British Empire did not always proceed smoothly. The Suez Crisis of 1956, in which the combined efforts of Britain, France, and Israel failed to halt Egypt's nationalization of the Suez Canal, dealt a decisive blow to England's status as a major power in the Middle East. In 1982, England's dispute over the tiny Falkland Islands erupted into war with Argentina, which claimed the islands (just off its coast) as its own. After the deaths of 258 English and 649 Argentine soldiers, England maintained its control of the Falklands, although Argentina continues to assert its right to the islands.

Despite these controversies, the dissolution of the British Empire proceeded relatively smoothly compared to the experience of the French, who became engaged in several major conflicts after 1945. In late 1946, Vietnamese nationalists rose up against the French colonial government that had recently reoccupied the region after the defeat of Japan in World War II. France's effort to return to Vietnam culminated ultimately in its defeat at Dien Bien Phu in 1954 and its subsequent withdrawal from Indochina. France also became embroiled in, and tried to suppress by force, a number of other violent colonial uprisings—in Madagascar, Cameroon, and, most notably, Algeria. The Algerian War (1954–1962) was a particularly bloody and costly conflict, taking on aspects of a civil war and involving guerrilla warfare, torture, acts of terrorism, and, eventually, the collapse of the French government in 1958. Algeria ultimately won its independence.

The end of the colonial system had its greatest impact on Africa. European powers had carved up almost all of sub-Saharan Africa in the nineteenth century. In the decades after World War II, almost all the African colonies won their independence, even if not always easily: Morocco (1956), Ghana (1957), the Congo (1960), Nigeria (1960), Uganda (1962), Kenya (1963), and Gambia (1965). African nationalism was troubled for decades by political instability and, in some countries, extreme poverty. The Caribbean also saw many new independent nations born in the postwar era, including Jamaica (1961), Trinidad and Tobago (1962), Barbados (1966), and Guyana (1966).

The most recent epicenter of independence movements has been in the lands that used to comprise the former Soviet Union. A long and costly war in Afghanistan began in the 1970s as the Soviet Union struggled to retain control of the nation in the face of powerful local insurgencies. The war was one of the principal factors in the unraveling of the Soviet Empire that began in 1991. Many of the former Soviet republics—which considered themselves colonies of Russia—soon separated from Russia and became independent nations. These included Estonia, Latvia, and Lithuania—the formerly independent Baltic nations seized by the Soviet Union during World War II. Other former Soviet possessions that became independent nations included Ukraine, Moldavia, Armenia, Georgia, Azerbaijan, Kazakhstan, Uzbekistan, Tajikistan, and Turkmenistan. Russia continues to deal with the problems of empire. A vicious conflict with Chechnya, an Islamic area of Russia insisting on independence, created terror and instability for years.

The end of colonialism was one of the most epochal global changes of the last several centuries—a change that brought to an end a system that was based on the assumption of European (and American) superiority over non-Western peoples. Despite the many problems new postcolonial nations have encountered since their independence, few, if any, such nations would choose to become colonies again. Although formal colonialism came to an end in the post–World War II era, other aspects of imperialism did not. Many former colonies, which comprise much of the nonindustrialized world, still struggle with the indirect exercise of economic power that wealthy Western nations continue to exert over them. •

UNDERSTAND, ANALYZE, & EVALUATE

1. How did the experience of World War II contribute to the end of colonialism?
2. What have been the effects of colonialism—and the end of colonialism—on Africa? Why have the effects been so pronounced on that continent, more so than in other areas of the world?

orders to integrate. At the same time, he began to reduce or dismantle many of the social programs of the Great Society and the New Frontier. In 1973, he abolished the Office of Economic Opportunity—a centerpiece of the antipoverty program of the Johnson years.

Yet Nixon's domestic policies had progressive and creative elements as well. He signed legislation creating the Environmental Protection Agency and establishing the most stringent environmental regulations in the nation's history. He ordered the first affirmative action program for workers on federally funded projects. One of the administration's boldest efforts was an attempt to overhaul the nation's welfare system. Nixon proposed replacing the existing system with what he called the Family Assistance Plan (FAP). It would, in effect, have created a guaranteed annual income for all Americans: $1,600 in federal grants, which could be supplemented by outside earnings up to $4,000. The FAP won approval in the House in 1970, but the bill failed in the Senate. Nixon also became the first president since Truman to propose a plan for national health insurance, which likewise made no progress in Congress.

FROM THE WARREN COURT TO THE NIXON COURT

Of all the liberal institutions that aroused the enmity of the conservative silent majority in the 1950s and 1960s, none evoked more anger and bitterness than the Supreme Court
Warren Court Rulings under Chief Justice Earl Warren. The Warren Court's rulings on racial matters disrupted traditional social patterns in both the North and the South. Its defense of civil liberties directly contributed to the increase in crime, disorder, and moral decay in the eyes of many Americans. In *Engel v. Vitale* (1962), the Court ruled that prayers in public schools were unconstitutional, sparking outrage among religious fundamentalists and others. In *Roth v. United States* (1957), the Court sharply limited the authority of local governments to curb pornography. In a series of other decisions, the Court greatly strengthened the civil rights of criminal defendants and, many Americans believed, greatly weakened the power of law enforcement officials to do their jobs. For example, in *Gideon v. Wainwright* (1963), the Court ruled that every felony defendant was entitled to a lawyer, regardless of his or her ability to pay. In *Escobedo v. Illinois* (1964), it ruled that a defendant must be allowed access to a lawyer before questioning by police. In *Miranda v. Arizona* (1966), the Court confirmed the obligation of authorities to inform a criminal suspect of his or her rights. By 1968, the Warren Court had become the target of Americans who felt the United States had shifted too far toward helping poor, dispossessed, and criminal individuals at the expense of the middle class.

Nixon promised to give the Court a more conservative cast. When Chief Justice Earl Warren retired early in 1969, Nixon replaced him with a federal appeals court judge of conservative leanings, Warren Burger. At about the same time, Associate Justice Abe Fortas resigned his seat after the disclosure of a series of alleged financial improprieties. To replace him, Nixon named Clement F. Haynsworth, a respected federal circuit court judge from South Carolina. But Haynsworth came under fire from Senate liberals, black organizations, and labor unions for his conservative record on civil rights. The Senate rejected him. Nixon's next choice was G. Harrold Carswell, a Florida federal appeals court judge of little distinction. He, too, was rejected.

Nixon angrily denounced the votes. But he was careful thereafter to choose men of standing within the legal community to fill vacancies on the Supreme Court: Harry Blackmun, a moderate jurist from Minnesota; Lewis F. Powell Jr., a respected lawyer from Virginia; and William Rehnquist, a member of the Nixon Justice Department.

The new Court, however, fell far short of what the president and many conservatives had expected. Rather than retreating from its commitment to social reform, the Court in many areas actually moved further toward it. In *Swann v. Charlotte-Mecklenburg Board of Education* (1971), it ruled in favor of forced busing to achieve racial balance in schools. Despite intense and occasionally violent opposition of local communities as diverse as Boston and Louisville, Kentucky, the judicial commitment to integration was not overturned. In *Furman v. Georgia* (1972), the Court overturned existing capital punishment statutes and established strict new guidelines for such laws in the future. In *Roe v. Wade* (1973), one of the most controversial decisions in the Court's modern history, it struck down laws forbidding abortions in the first three months of pregnancy.

Burger Court Rulings

In other decisions, however, the Burger Court did demonstrate a more conservative temperament than the Warren Court had shown. Although the justices approved busing as a tool for achieving integration, they rejected, in *Milliken v. Bradley* (1974), a plan to transfer students across municipal lines (in this case, between Detroit and its suburbs) to achieve racial balance. While the Court upheld the principle of affirmative action in its celebrated 1978 decision, *Bakke v. Board of Regents of California,* it established restrictive new guidelines for such programs in the future. In *Stone v. Powell* (1976), the Court agreed to certain limits on the right of a defendant to appeal a state conviction to the federal judiciary.

THE 1972 LANDSLIDE

Nixon entered the presidential race in 1972 with substantial strength. His energetic reelection committee had collected enormous sums of money. The president himself used the powers of incumbency to strengthen his political standing in strategic areas. And Nixon's foreign policy successes, especially his trip to China, increased his stature in the eyes of the nation.

Nixon was most fortunate in 1972, however, in his opposition. George Wallace, partly at Nixon's urging, entered the Democratic primaries and helped divide the party until a would-be assassin shot the Alabama governor during a rally at a Maryland shopping center in May. Paralyzed from the waist down, Wallace was unable to continue campaigning. In the meantime, the most liberal factions of the party succeeded in establishing their candidate, Senator George S. McGovern of South Dakota, as the front-runner for the nomination. An outspoken critic of the war and a forceful advocate of liberal positions on many social and economic issues, McGovern profited greatly from party reforms (which he himself had helped draft) that gave increased influence to women, minorities, and young people in the selection of the Democratic ticket. But in the process, the McGovern campaign came to be associated with aspects of the turbulent 1960s that many middle-class Americans were eager to reject.

George McGovern

On election day, Nixon won reelection by one of the largest margins in history: 60.7 percent of the popular vote to McGovern's 37.5 percent and an electoral margin of 520 to 17. The Democratic candidate carried only Massachusetts and the District of Columbia. But serious problems, some beyond the president's control and others of his own making, lurked in the wings.

THE TROUBLED ECONOMY

Although it was a political scandal that would ultimately destroy the Nixon presidency, the most important issue of the early 1970s was the beginning of a long-term transformation

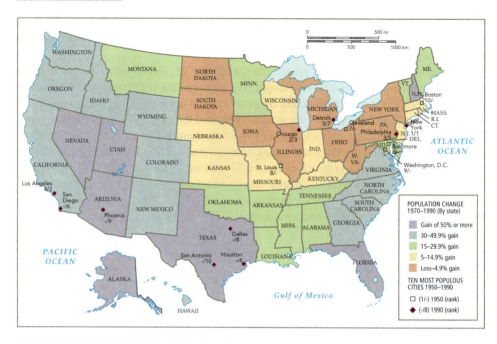

GROWTH OF THE SUNBELT, 1970-1990 One of the most important demographic changes of the last decades of the twentieth century was the shift of population out of traditional population centers in the Northeast and Midwest and toward the states of the so-called Sunbelt—most notably the Southwest and the Pacific Coast. This map gives a dramatic illustration of the changing concentration of population between 1970 and 1990. The orange states are those that lost population, while the purple and blue states are those that made significant gains (30 percent or more). • *What was the impact of this population shift on the politics of the 1980s?*

of Scientology; the Unification Church of the Reverend Sun Myung Moon; even the tragic People's Temple, whose members committed mass suicide in their jungle retreat in Guyana in 1978. But the most important impulse of the religious revival was the growth of evangelical Christianity.

Surging Evangelicalism Evangelicals have in common a belief in personal conversion (being "born again" through direct communication with Jesus). Evangelical religion had been the dominant form of Christianity in America through much of its history. In its modern form, it became increasingly visible during the early 1950s, when evangelicals such as Billy Graham and Pentecostals such as Oral Roberts began to attract huge national (and international) followings for their energetic revivalism.

By the late 1970s, evangelical Christians had become more visible and more politically assertive. More than 70 million Americans now described themselves as born-again Christians. Christian evangelicals owned newspapers, magazines, radio stations, and television networks. They operated their own schools and universities. Three modern presidents—Jimmy Carter, Bill Clinton, and George W. Bush—have identified themselves as evangelicals.

Some evangelical Christians supported racial and economic justice and world peace of the type espoused by civil rights leaders like Rev. Martin Luther King. But many others had a different political focus. Alarmed by what they considered the spread of immorality and disorder in American life, they were concerned about the way a secular culture was intruding into their communities, schools, and families. Many evangelical men and women, for example, feared that the growth of feminism posed a threat to the traditional family, and they resented the way in which government policies advanced the goals of the women's movement. Particularly alarming to them were Supreme Court decisions eliminating all religious observance from schools and, later, the decision guaranteeing women the right to an abortion.

By the late 1970s, the "Christian right" had become a powerful political force. Jerry Falwell, a fundamentalist minister in Virginia with a substantial television audience, launched a highly visible movement he called the Moral Majority. He founded Liberty University in Lynchburg, Virginia, to train men and women according to conservative Christian principles. The Pentecostal minister Pat Robertson began a political movement of his own and, in the 1990s, launched an organization known as the *Christian Coalition* Christian Coalition. These and other organizations of the Christian right opposed federal interference in local affairs; denounced abortion, divorce, feminism, and homosexuality; defended unrestricted free enterprise; and supported a strong American posture in the world. Some denied the scientific doctrine of evolution and instead urged the teaching in schools of the biblical story of the Creation or—beginning in the early twenty-first century—the idea of "intelligent design." Their goal was a new era in which "Christian values" once again dominated American life.

The role of religion in the growth of conservatism was not limited to evangelical Christians. In the 1970s, the Catholic Church began to make a strong case for tradition as well. The Church fought most aggressively against abortion, thus joining the evangelical right in one of the most controversial issues of the time. Not all Catholics were or are conservatives; many priests and parishioners took strong liberal positions. But in the political world, Catholics became strong allies of the right, joining evangelicals in fighting for many conservative issues.

Mormons, too, began to emerge as an important element of the right. For many years, Mormons did not publicize their conservatism. But like Catholics, many Mormons began to take openly conservative stances in the 1970s on some of the controversial battles of the time. Some of these Mormons, wealthy and successful businesspeople, became conservative political politicians in various parts of the country. (In 2012, two wealthy Mormons—Mitt Romney and Jon Huntsman, both former governors—were candidates for the presidency.)

THE EMERGENCE OF THE NEW RIGHT

Religious issues were only a part—although an important part—of what became known as the New Right—a diverse but powerful movement that enjoyed rapid growth in the 1970s and early 1980s. It had begun to take shape after the 1964 election, in which Barry Goldwater had suffered his shattering defeat. Energetic organizers responded to that disaster by building a new and powerful set of right-wing institutions to help conservatives campaign more effectively in the future. Beginning in the 1970s, largely because of these organizational advances, conservatives found themselves almost always better funded and organized than their opponents. By the late 1970s, there were right-wing think tanks, consulting firms, lobbyists, foundations, and colleges and universities. Conservatives also succeeded in building mechanisms to raise money, mobilize activists, and project their ideas to a broad audience. Building from a list compiled by Richard Viguerie after the 1964 Goldwater campaign, the right built a direct-mail operation that ultimately reached millions of conservative voters. Evangelicals such as Pat Robertson used cable television to reach the conservative faithful. Conservative radio hosts such as Rush Limbaugh created shows that attracted a vast national audience.

Another factor in the revival of the right was the emergence in the late 1960s and early *Ronald Reagan* 1970s of Ronald Reagan. Once a moderately successful actor, he had moved into politics in the early 1960s and in 1964 delivered a memorable television speech on behalf of Goldwater. After Goldwater's defeat, Reagan worked quickly to seize the leadership of the conservative wing of the party. In 1966, with the support of a group of wealthy conservatives, he won the first of two terms as governor of California.

The presidency of Gerald Ford also played an important role in the rise of conservatism. Ford, probably without realizing it, touched on some of the right's rawest nerves. He appointed as vice president Nelson Rockefeller, the liberal Republican governor of New York and an heir to one of America's great fortunes; many conservatives had been demonizing Rockefeller and his family for more than twenty years. Ford proposed an amnesty program for draft resisters, embraced the hated Nixon–Kissinger policies of détente, presided over the fall of Vietnam, and agreed to cede the Panama Canal to Panama. When Reagan challenged Ford in the 1976 Republican primaries, the president survived, barely, only by dumping Nelson Rockefeller from the ticket and replacing him with Kansas Senator Robert Dole, a steadfast conservative. He also agreed to a platform largely written by conservatives.

THE TAX REVOLT

At least equally important to the success of the New Right was a new and potent conservative issue: the tax revolt. It had its public beginnings in 1978, when Howard Jarvis, a conservative activist in California, launched the first successful major citizens' tax revolt with Proposition 13, *Proposition 13* a referendum question on the state ballot rolling back property tax rates. Because property taxes were the most important source of funding for schools, Proposition 13 began the slow deterioration of much of the great California education system. Similar antitax movements soon began in other states and eventually spread to national politics.

In Proposition 13 and similar initiatives, members of the right succeeded in separating the issue of taxes from the issue of what taxes supported. Instead of attacking popular programs such as Social Security, they attacked taxes themselves and argued that much of the money government raised through taxes was wasted. Virtually no one liked to pay taxes, and as the economy grew weaker and the relative burden of paying taxes grew heavier, that resentment naturally rose.

THE CAMPAIGN OF 1980

By the time of the crises in Iran and Afghanistan, Jimmy Carter was in desperate political trouble—his standing in popularity polls lower than that of any president in history. Senator Edward Kennedy, younger brother of John and Robert Kennedy, challenged him in the primaries. And while Carter managed to withstand the confrontation and win his party's nomination, his campaign aroused little popular enthusiasm. The stage was set for sweeping political change.

The Republican Party, in the meantime, rallied enthusiastically behind the man who, four years earlier, had nearly stolen the nomination from Gerald Ford. Ronald Reagan was a sharp critic of the excesses of the federal government. He linked his campaign to the spreading tax revolt by promising substantial tax cuts. He also championed a restoration of American "strength" and "pride" in the world.

On election day 1980, the anniversary of the seizure of the hostages in Iran, Reagan swept to victory, winning 51 percent of the vote to 41 percent for Jimmy Carter and

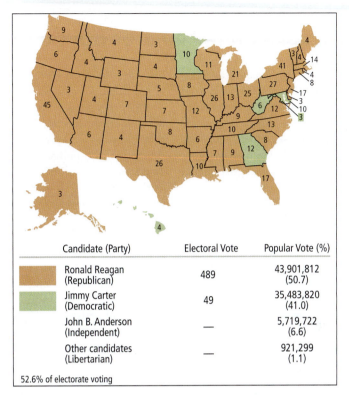

Candidate (Party)	Electoral Vote	Popular Vote (%)
Ronald Reagan (Republican)	489	43,901,812 (50.7)
Jimmy Carter (Democratic)	49	35,483,820 (41.0)
John B. Anderson (Independent)	—	5,719,722 (6.6)
Other candidates (Libertarian)	—	921,299 (1.1)

52.6% of electorate voting

THE ELECTION OF 1980 Although Ronald Reagan won only slightly more than half of the popular vote in the 1980 presidential election, his electoral majority was overwhelming—a reflection to a large degree of the deep unpopularity of President Jimmy Carter in 1980. • *What had made Carter so unpopular?*

7 percent for John Anderson—a moderate Republican congressman from Illinois who had mounted an independent campaign. The Republican Party won control of the Senate for the first time since 1952; and although the Democrats retained a modest majority in the House, the lower chamber, too, seemed firmly in the hands of conservatives.

On the day of Reagan's inauguration, the American hostages in Iran were released after their 444-day ordeal. The government of Iran, desperate for funds to support its floundering war against neighboring Iraq, had ordered the hostages freed in return for a release of billions in Iranian assets that the Carter administration had frozen in American banks. Americans welcomed the hostages home with demonstrations of joy and patriotism seldom seen since the end of World War II. But while the celebration in 1945 had marked a great American triumph, the euphoria in 1981 marked something quite different—a troubled nation grasping for reassurance. Ronald Reagan set out to provide it.

THE "REAGAN REVOLUTION"

Ronald Reagan assumed the presidency in January 1981, promising a revolution in government more fundamental than any since the New Deal of fifty years before. (See "Consider the Source: Excerpts from Reagan's First Inaugural Address.") While his eight years in office produced a significant shift in public policy, they brought nothing so

CONSIDER THE SOURCE

RONALD REAGAN ON THE ROLE OF GOVERNMENT

In this excerpt from his first inaugural address, on January 20, 1981, Ronald Reagan laid out his central vision for the role of government in society. Questioning the ability of government to solve society's social and economic ills, Reagan argued that the key to the nation's future lay in reducing the role of government in everyday life.

The economic ills we suffer have come upon us over several decades. They will not go away in days, weeks, or months, but they will go away. They will go away because we as Americans have the capacity now, as we've had in the past, to do whatever needs to be done to preserve this last and greatest bastion of freedom.

In this present crisis, government is not the solution to our problem; government is the problem. From time to time we've been tempted to believe that society has become too complex to be managed by self-rule, that government by an elite group is superior to government for, by, and of the people. Well, if no one among us is capable of governing himself, then who among us has the capacity to govern someone else? All of us together, in and out of government, must bear the burden. The solutions we seek must be equitable, with no one group singled out to pay a higher price.

We hear much of special interest groups. Well, our concern must be for a special interest group that has been too long neglected. It knows no sectional boundaries or ethnic and racial divisions, and it crosses political party lines. It is made up of men and women who raise our food, patrol our streets, man our mines and factories, teach our children, keep our homes, and heal us when we're sick—professionals, industrialists, shopkeepers, clerks, cabbies, and truck drivers.

They are, in short, "We the people," this breed called Americans.

Well, this administration's objective will be a healthy, vigorous, growing economy that provides equal opportunities for all Americans with no barriers born of bigotry or discrimination. Putting America back to work means putting all Americans back to work. Ending inflation means freeing all Americans from the terror of runaway living costs. All must share in the productive work of this "new beginning," and all must share in the bounty of a revived economy. With the idealism and fair play which are the core of our system and our strength, we can have a strong and prosperous America, at peace with itself and the world.

So, as we begin, let us take inventory. We are a nation that has a government—not the other way around. And this makes us special among the nations of the Earth. Our government has no power except that granted it by the people. It is time to check and reverse the growth of government, which shows signs of having grown beyond the consent of the governed.

It is my intention to curb the size and influence of the Federal establishment and to demand recognition of the distinction between the powers granted to the Federal Government and those reserved to the States or to the people. All of us need to be reminded that the Federal Government did not create the States; the States created the Federal Government.

Now, so there will be no misunderstanding, it's not my intention to do away with government. It is rather to make it work—work with us, not over us; to stand by our side, not ride on our back. Government can and must provide opportunity, not smother it; foster productivity, not stifle it.

If we look to the answer as to why for so many years we achieved so much, prospered as no other people on Earth, it was because here in this land we unleashed the energy and individual genius of man to a greater extent than has ever been done before. Freedom and the dignity of the individual have been more available and assured here than in any other place on Earth. The price for this freedom at times has been high, but we have never been unwilling to pay that price.

It is no coincidence that our present troubles parallel and are proportionate to the intervention and intrusion in our lives that result from unnecessary and excessive growth of government. It is time for us to realize that we're too great a nation to limit ourselves to small dreams. We're not, as some would have us believe, doomed to an inevitable decline. I do not believe in a fate that will fall on us no matter what we do. I do believe in a fate

that will fall on us if we do nothing. So, with all the creative energy at our command, let us begin an era of national renewal. Let us renew our determination, our courage, and our strength. And let us renew our faith and our hope.

UNDERSTAND, ANALYZE, & EVALUATE

1. What does Reagan mean when he says, in the opening lines of the second paragraph, that "government is the problem"?
2. Why did Reagan's call for a curb on the government's role in society and the economy strike such a popular chord in the 1980s?
3. According to Reagan, who has been treated unfairly under the previous administration? Whom are the disadvantaged?

Source: The Ronald Reagan Presidential Library, National Archives and Records Administration, www.reagan.utexas.edu/archives/speeches/1981/12081a.htm.

fundamental as many of his supporters had hoped or his opponents had feared. But Reagan succeeded brilliantly in making his own engaging personality the central fact of American politics in the 1980s. He also benefited from the power of the diverse coalition that had united behind him.

THE REAGAN COALITION

The Reagan coalition included a relatively small but highly influential group of wealthy Americans firmly committed to unfettered capitalism. They believed that the "market" offered the best solutions to most problems, and they shared a deep hostility to most (although not all) government interference in markets. Central to this group's agenda in the 1980s was opposition to what it scorned as the "redistributive" economic politics of the government (especially its highly progressive tax structure) and hostility to the rise of what they believed were "antibusiness" government regulations. Reagan courted these free-market conservatives carefully and effectively, and in the end *Free-Market Conservatives* it was their interests his administration most effectively served.

A second element of the Reagan coalition consisted of a small but influential group of intellectuals commonly known as "neoconservatives," who gave to the *Neoconservatives* right something it had not had in many years—a firm base among "opinion leaders," people with access to the most influential public forums of ideas. Many of these people had once been liberals and, before that, socialists. But during the turmoil of the 1960s, they had become alarmed by what they considered a dangerous and destructive radicalism.

RONALD AND NANCY REAGAN   The president and the first lady greet guests at a White House social event. Nancy Reagan was committed to making the White House, and her husband's presidency, seem more glamorous than those of most recent administrations. But she also played an important, if usually quiet, policy role in the administration.   (Photo by Dirck Halstead/© Time & Life Pictures/Getty Images)

Neoconservatives were sympathetic to the complaints and demands of capitalists, but their principal concern was to reassert legitimate authority and reaffirm Western democratic, anticommunist values and commitments. They considered themselves soldiers in a battle to "win back the culture"—from the crass, radical ideas that had polluted it.

Neoconservatives also strongly dissented from the new foreign policy orthodoxies of liberals and the left in the aftermath of the Vietnam War. They utterly rejected the idea that America should be a less interventionist nation, that it should work to ease tensions with the Soviet Union, and that it should tolerate radical regimes. Instead, they argued for an escalation of the Cold War as part of an effort to destabilize the Soviet Union. They insisted that the Vietnam War was an appropriate American commitment and that its abandonment was a terrible mistake. They believed that the United States had a special role to play in the world and should be willing to use military intervention to secure its vision. These ideas strongly influenced the foreign policy of the Reagan administration. The same ideas (and some of the same people) resurfaced in the early twenty-first century to help shape the international policies of the George W. Bush administration.

These groups formed an uneasy alliance with the broad grassroots conservative movement, but collectively formed the New Right. It shared a fundamental distrust of the "eastern establishment": a suspicion of its motives and goals and a sense that it exercised a dangerous, secret power in American life. These populist conservatives expressed the kinds of concerns that outsiders—non-elites—have traditionally voiced in American society: an opposition to centralized power and influence and a fear of living in a world where distant, hostile forces are controlling society and threatening individual freedom and community autonomy. It was a testament to Ronald Reagan's political skills and personal charm that he was able to generate enthusiastic support from these populist conservatives while at the same time appealing to more elite conservative groups whose concerns were in many ways antithetical to those of the New Right.

REAGAN IN THE WHITE HOUSE

Even many people who disagreed with Reagan's policies found themselves drawn to his attractive and carefully honed public image. He turned seventy years old a few weeks after taking office and was the oldest man ever to serve as president. But through most of his presidency, he appeared to be vigorous, resilient, even youthful. When wounded in an assassination attempt in 1981, he joked with doctors on his way into surgery and appeared to bounce back from the ordeal with remarkable speed. Even when things went wrong, as they often did, the blame seldom seemed to attach to Reagan himself (inspiring some Democrats to refer to him as the "Teflon president").

Reagan was not much involved in the day-to-day affairs of running the government; he surrounded himself with tough, energetic administrators who insulated him from many of the pressures of the office and who apparently relied on him largely for general guidance, not specific decisions. At times, the president revealed a startling ignorance about the nature of his own policies or the actions of his subordinates. But Reagan did make active use of his office to generate public support for his administration's programs.

"SUPPLY-SIDE" ECONOMICS

Reagan's 1980 campaign for the presidency had promised to restore the economy to health by a bold experiment that became known as "supply-side"—or, to its critics, "trickle-down"— economics. Eventually, it was called "Reaganomics." Supply-side economics *Reaganomics* operated from the assumption that the woes of the American economy were in large part a result of excessive taxation, which left inadequate capital available to investors to stimulate growth. The solution, therefore, was to reduce taxes, with particularly generous benefits to corporations and wealthy individuals, in order to encourage new investments.

In its first months in office, the new administration hastily assembled a legislative program based on the supply-side idea. It proposed $40 billion in budget reductions and managed to win congressional approval of almost all of them. In addition, the president proposed a bold three-year, 30 percent reduction on both individual and corporate *Tax Cuts* tax rates. In the summer of 1981, Congress passed it, too, after lowering the reductions to 25 percent. Reagan suceeded thanks to a disciplined Republican majority in the Senate and a Democratic majority in the House that was weak and riddled with defectors.

Reagan appointees in the executive branch of government aimed to reduce the role of government in American economic life. **Deregulation,** an idea many Democrats had begun to embrace in the Carter years, became almost a religion in the Reagan administration. Secretary of the Interior James Watt, a major figure in the antienvironmental Sagebrush Rebellion, opened up public lands and water to development and led a charge to reverse older conservationist policies. The Environmental Protection Agency (before some of its directors were indicted for corruption) relaxed or entirely eliminated enforcement of major environmental laws and regulations.

By early 1982, the nation had sunk into a severe recession. The Reagan economic program was not directly to blame for the problems, but neither did it offer a quick solution. During 1982, unemployment reached 11 percent, one of the highest levels since the 1930s. But before the recession could do great damage to Reagan, the economy recovered more rapidly and impressively than almost anyone had expected. By late 1983, unemployment had fallen to 8.2 percent, and it declined steadily for several years after that. The gross national product (GNP) grew 3.6 percent in a year, the largest increase since the mid-1970s. Inflation fell below 5 percent. The economy continued to grow, and both inflation and unemployment remained low through most of the decade.

The recovery was a result of many things. Prior years of tight money policies by the Federal Reserve Board had helped lower inflation; perhaps equally important, the Fed had lowered interest rates early in 1983 in response to the recession. A worldwide "energy glut" and the virtual collapse of the OPEC cartel had produced at least a temporary end to the inflationary pressures of spiraling fuel costs. And staggering federal budget deficits were pumping billions of dollars into the flagging economy. As a result, consumer spending and business investment both increased. The stock market rose up from its doldrums of the 1970s and began a sustained and historic boom. In August 1982, the Dow Jones Industrial Average stood at 777. Five years later it had passed 2,000. Despite a frightening crash in the fall of 1987, the market continued to grow for more than another decade. The Dow Jones average passed 18,000 in 2015.

THE FISCAL CRISIS

The economic revival did little at first to reduce the staggering, and to many Americans alarming, federal budget deficits (the gap between revenue and spending in a single year) or to slow the growth in the national debt (the debt the nation accumulates over time as a result of its annual deficits). By the mid-1980s, this growing fiscal crisis had become one of the central issues in American politics. Having entered office promising a balanced *Record Budget Deficits* budget within four years, Reagan presided over record budget deficits and accumulated more debt in his eight years in office than the American government had accumulated in its entire previous history. Before the 1980s, the highest single-year budget deficit in American history had been $66 billion (in 1976). Throughout the 1980s, the annual budget deficit consistently exceeded $100 billion (and in 1991 peaked at $268 billion). The national debt rose from $907 billion in 1980 to nearly $3.5 trillion by 1991. Much larger deficits—and debt—were soon to come.

The enormous deficits had many causes. The budget suffered from enormous increases in the costs of "entitlement" programs (especially both Social Security and Medicare), a result of the aging of the population and dramatic increases in the cost of health care. The 1981 tax cuts, the largest in American history, also contributed to the deficit. The massive increase in military spending on which the Reagan administration insisted added much more to the federal budget than its cuts in domestic spending removed.

In the face of these deficits, the administration proposed further cuts in "discretionary" domestic spending, which included many programs aimed at the poorest (and politically weakest) Americans. By the end of Reagan's third year in office, funding for domestic programs had been cut nearly as far as Congress (and, apparently, the public) was willing to tolerate, and still no end to the rising deficit was in sight. By the late 1980s, many fiscal conservatives were calling for a constitutional amendment mandating a balanced budget—a provision the president himself claimed to support. But Congress never approved the amendment.

REAGAN AND THE WORLD

Relations with the Soviet Union, which had been steadily deteriorating in the last years of the Carter administration, grew still chillier in the first years of the Reagan presidency. The president spoke harshly of the Soviet regime (which he once called the "evil empire"), accusing it of sponsoring world terrorism and declaring that any armaments negotiations must be linked to negotiations on Soviet behavior in other areas. Although the president had long denounced the SALT II arms control treaty as unfavorable to the United States, he continued to honor its provisions. But the president proposed the most ambitious (and potentially most expensive) new military program in many years: the Strategic Defense Initiative (SDI), *Strategic Defense Initiative* widely known as "Star Wars" (after the popular movie of that name). Reagan claimed that SDI, through the use of lasers and satellites, could provide an effective shield against incoming missiles and thus make nuclear war obsolete. The Soviet Union claimed that the new program would elevate the arms race to new and more dangerous levels and insisted that any arms control agreement should begin with an American abandonment of SDI.

The escalation of Cold War tensions and the slowing of arms control initiatives helped produce an important popular movement in Europe and the United States calling for a "nuclear freeze," an agreement between the two superpowers not to expand their atomic arsenals. In what many believed was the largest mass demonstration in American history, nearly a million people rallied in New York City's Central Park in 1982 to support the freeze. Perhaps partly in response to this growing pressure, the administration began tentative efforts to revive arms control negotiations in 1983.

The administration created a new policy known as the Reagan Doctrine, designed to help resist communism and anti-Americanism in the Third World. *Reagan Doctrine* The United States sent soldiers and money to aid guerrillas and resistance movements in countries with anti-American governments—among them Grenada, El Salvador, and Nicaragua. But Reagan generally backed away from more serious warfare. In 1982, when the Israeli army invaded Lebanon, American peacekeeping forces entered Beirut to stabilize the nation. But when a terrorist bombing of a U.S. military barracks in Beirut led to the death of 241 marines, Reagan quickly withdrew the American forces. There were other terrorist events against America and other nations by attacking bombs, ships, and diplomatic buildings—the beginning of what would become a long battle against terrorism.

Reagan approached the campaign of 1984 at the head of a united Republican Party firmly committed to his candidacy. The Democrats nominated former vice president Walter Mondale. Mondale brought momentary excitement to the Democratic campaign by selecting a woman, Representative Geraldine Ferraro of New York, to be his running mate and the first female candidate ever to appear on a national ticket. But Reagan's triumphant campaign scarcely took note of his opponents and spoke instead of what he claimed was the remarkable revival of American fortunes and spirits under his leadership, *Reagan Reelected* or what he sometimes called "Morning in America." He won 59 percent of the vote and carried every state but Mondale's native Minnesota and the District of Columbia.

AMERICA AND THE WANING OF THE COLD WAR

Many factors contributed to the collapse of the Soviet Empire. The long, stalemated war in Afghanistan proved at least as disastrous to the Soviet Union as the Vietnam War had been to America. The government in Moscow failed to address a long-term economic decline in the Soviet republics and the Eastern-bloc nations. Restiveness with the heavy-handed policies of communist police states was growing throughout much of the Soviet Empire. But the most visible factor at the time was the emergence of Mikhail Gorbachev, who succeeded to the leadership of the Soviet Union in 1985 and, to the surprise of almost everyone (probably including himself), very quickly became the most revolutionary figure in world politics in decades.

Mikhail Gorbachev

THE FALL OF THE SOVIET UNION

Gorbachev transformed Soviet politics with two dramatic new initiatives: *glasnost* (openness), the dismantling of many of the repressive mechanisms that had been conspicuous features of Soviet life for over half a century, and *perestroika* (reform), an effort to restructure the rigid and unproductive Soviet economy by introducing, among other things, such elements of capitalism as private ownership and the profit motive. He also began to transform Soviet foreign policy.

Glasnost and Perestroika

The severe economic problems at home evidently convinced Gorbachev that the Soviet Union could no longer sustain its extended commitments around the world. As early as

THE FALL OF THE BERLIN WALL   The Berlin Wall is widely considered to have "fallen" on November 9, 1989. Starting on that date and in the days and weeks that followed, people used sledgehammers and picks to tear down the wall, often keeping the broken pieces as souvenirs of this symbolic conclusion of the Cold War.
(© DIZ München GmbH/Alamy)

1987, he began reducing the Soviet presence in Eastern Europe. And in 1989, in the space of a few months, every communist state in Europe—Poland, Hungary, Czechoslovakia, Bulgaria, Romania, East Germany, Yugoslavia, and Albania—either overthrew its government or forced it to transform itself into an essentially noncommunist (and in some cases, actively anticommunist) regime. Perhaps the most dramatic event of this extraordinary revolution was the tearing down of the infamous Berlin Wall.

Not all international protests against communism were so successful. In May 1989, students in China launched a mass movement calling for greater democratization. But in June, hard-line leaders seized control of the government and sent military forces to crush the uprising. The result was a bloody massacre on June 3, 1989, in Tiananmen Square in Beijing, in which an unknown number of demonstrators died. The assault   *Tiananmen Square* crushed the democracy movement and restored hard-liners to power. It did not, however, stop China's efforts to modernize and even Westernize its economy.

But China was an exception to the widespread movement toward democratization. Early in 1990, the government of South Africa, long an international pariah for its rigid enforcement of "apartheid" (a system designed to protect white supremacy, much like the Jim Crow system had done in the American South) legalized the chief black party in the nation, the African National Congress (ANC), which had been banned for decades. The government also released from prison the leader of the ANC, Nelson Mandela, who had been in jail for twenty-seven years. Over the next several years, the South African government repealed its apartheid laws. And in 1994, there were national elections in which all South Africans could participate. As a result, Nelson Mandela became the first black president of South Africa.

In 1991, communism began to collapse in the Soviet Union itself. An unsuccessful coup by hard-line Soviet leaders on August 19 precipitated a dramatic unraveling of communist power. Within days, the coup itself collapsed in the face of resistance from the   *Collapse of the USSR* public and crucial elements within the military. By the end of August, many of the republics of the Soviet Union had declared independence; the Soviet government was clearly powerless to stop the fragmentation. Gorbachev himself finally resigned as leader of the now virtually powerless Communist Party and Soviet government, and the Soviet Union ceased to exist.

The last years of the Reagan administration coincided with the first years of the Gorbachev regime; and while Reagan was skeptical of Gorbachev at first, he gradually became convinced that the Soviet leader was sincere in his desire for reform. In 1988, the two superpowers signed a treaty eliminating American and Soviet intermediate-range nuclear forces (INF) from Europe—the most significant arms control agreement of the nuclear age. At about the same time, Gorbachev ended the Soviet Union's long and frustrating military involvement in Afghanistan.

THE FADING OF THE REAGAN REVOLUTION

For a time, the dramatic changes around the world and Reagan's personal popularity deflected attention from a series of scandals that might well have destroyed another administration, including revelations of illegal and ethical lapses in the Environmental Protection Agency, the CIA, the Department of Defense, the Department of Labor, the Department of Justice, and the Department of Housing and Urban Development. A more serious scandal emerged within the savings and loan industry, which the Reagan administration had helped deregulate in the early 1980s. By the end of the decade, the industry was in chaos, and the government was forced to step in to prevent a complete collapse. The cost of the debacle to the public eventually ran to more than half a trillion dollars.

But the most politically damaging scandal of the Reagan years came to light in
Iran-Contra Scandal   November 1986, when the White House conceded that it had sold
weapons to the revolutionary government of Iran as part of a largely unsuccessful
effort to secure the release of several Americans being held hostage. Even more damaging was the revelation that some of the money from the arms deal with Iran had
been covertly and illegally funneled into a fund to aid the contras, a loose group of
commandos who fought against the anti-American government after the 1979 revolution in Nicaragua.

In the months that followed, aggressive reporting and a series of congressional hearings
exposed a widespread pattern of covert activities orchestrated by the White House and dedi-
cated to advancing the administration's foreign policy aims through secret and at times illegal
means. The Iran-contra scandal, as it became known, did serious damage to the Reagan
presidency—even though the investigations never tied the president himself to the most serious
violations of the law.

THE PRESIDENCY OF GEORGE H. W. BUSH

The fraying of the Reagan administration helped the Democrats regain control of the
United States Senate in 1986 and fueled hopes in the party for a presidential victory in
1988. Michael Dukakis, a three-term governor of Massachusetts, eventually captured the
nomination. Vice President George H. W. Bush was the largely unopposed Republican
candidate. Neither candidate succeeded in creating public enthusiasm.

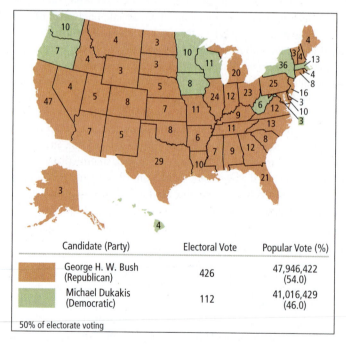

Candidate (Party)	Electoral Vote	Popular Vote (%)
George H. W. Bush (Republican)	426	47,946,422 (54.0)
Michael Dukakis (Democratic)	112	41,016,429 (46.0)

50% of electorate voting

THE ELECTION OF 1988 Democrats had high hopes going into the election of 1988, but Vice President
George H. W. Bush won a decisive victory over Michael Dukakis, who did only slightly better than Walter
Mondale had done four years earlier. • *What made it so difficult for a Democrat to challenge the Republicans
in 1988 after eight years of a Republican administration?*

Beginning at the Republican National Convention, Bush made his campaign a long, relentless attack on Dukakis, tying him to all the unpopular social and cultural stances Americans had come to identify with "liberals." Bush won a substantial victory in November: 54 percent of the popular vote to Dukakis's 46 percent, and 426 electoral votes to Dukakis's 112. But Bush carried few Republicans into office with him; the Democrats retained secure majorities in both houses of Congress. The broad popularity Bush enjoyed during much of his first three years in office was partly a result of his subdued, unthreatening public image. But it was primarily due to the wonder and excitement with which Americans viewed the dramatic events in the rest of the world. Bush moved cautiously at first in dealing with the changes in the Soviet Union. But like Reagan, he eventually cooperated with Gorbachev and reached a series of significant arms control agreements with the Soviet Union in its waning years.

On domestic issues, the Bush administration was less successful. His administration inherited a staggering burden of debt and a federal deficit that had been growing dramatically for nearly a decade. Constantly concerned about the right wing of his own party, Bush aggressively opposed current laws governing abortion and affirmative action that damaged his ability to work with the Democratic Congress.

Despite this political stalemate, Congress and the White House managed on occasion to agree on significant measures. In 1990, the president agreed to a significant tax increase as part of a multiyear "budget package" designed to reduce the deficit—thus violating his own 1988 campaign pledge of "no new taxes."

But the most serious domestic problem facing the Bush administration was one for which neither the president nor Congress had any answer: a recession that began late in 1990 and became more serious in 1991 and 1992.

THE GULF WAR

The fall of the Soviet Union left the United States in the unanticipated position of being the only real superpower in the world. It forced the Bush administration to consider what to do with America's formidable political and military power.

The events of 1989–1991 suggested two possible answers. One was that the United States would reduce its military strength dramatically and concentrate its energies and resources on pressing domestic problems. The other was that America would continue to use its power actively, not to fight communism but to defend its regional and economic interests. The answer came quickly. In 1989, the administration ordered an invasion of Panama, which overthrew the unpopular military leader Manuel Noriega (under indictment in the United States for drug trafficking) and replaced him with an elected, pro-American regime. And in 1990, that same impulse drew the United States into the turbulent politics of the Middle East.

On August 2, 1990, the armed forces of Iraq invaded and quickly overwhelmed the emirate of Kuwait, the small oil-rich neighbor of Iraq. Saddam Hussein, *Saddam Hussein* the militaristic leader of Iraq, soon announced that he was annexing Kuwait. The Bush administration soon agreed to lead other nations in a campaign to force Iraq out of Kuwait—through the pressure of economic sanctions if possible, through military force if necessary. Within a few weeks, Bush had persuaded virtually every important government in the world, including the Soviet Union and almost all the Arab and Islamic states, to join in a United Nations–sanctioned trade embargo of Iraq.

At the same time, the United States and its allies (including the British, French, Egyptians, and Saudis) began deploying a large military force along the border between Kuwait and Saudi Arabia, a force that ultimately reached 690,000 troops (425,000 of them American). And on January 16, American and allied air forces began a massive bombardment of Iraqi troops in Kuwait and of military and industrial installations in Iraq itself.

The allied bombing continued for six weeks. On February 23, allied (primarily American) forces under the command of General Norman Schwarzkopf began a major ground offensive to the north of the Iraqi forces. The allied armies encountered almost no resistance and suffered only light casualties (141 fatalities). Estimates of Iraqi deaths in the war were 100,000 or more. On February 28, Iraq announced its acceptance of allied terms for a cease-fire, and the brief Persian Gulf War was over.

THE ELECTION OF 1992

President Bush's popularity reached a record high in the immediate aftermath of the Gulf War. But the glow of that victory faded quickly as the recession worsened in late 1991. That gave Bill Clinton, the young five-term Democratic governor of Arkansas, an opportunity to emerge as the early front-runner. Clinton survived a bruising primary campaign and a series of damaging personal controversies to win his party's nomination.

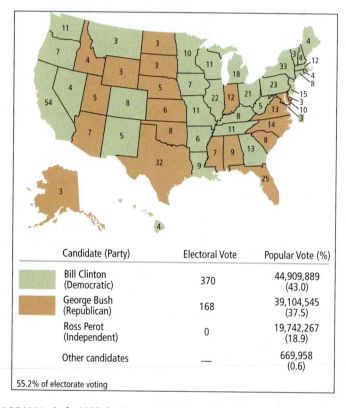

Candidate (Party)	Electoral Vote	Popular Vote (%)
Bill Clinton (Democratic)	370	44,909,889 (43.0)
George Bush (Republican)	168	39,104,545 (37.5)
Ross Perot (Independent)	0	19,742,267 (18.9)
Other candidates	—	669,958 (0.6)

55.2% of electorate voting

THE ELECTION OF 1992   In the 1992 election, for the first time since 1976, a Democrat captured the White House. And although the third-party candidacy of Ross Perot deprived Bill Clinton of an absolute majority, he nevertheless defeated George Bush by a decisive margin in both the popular and electoral votes. • *What factors had eroded President Bush's once-broad popularity by 1992? What explained the strong showing of Ross Perot?*

Complicating the campaign was the emergence of Ross Perot, a blunt, forthright Texas billionaire who became an independent candidate by tapping popular resentment of the federal bureaucracy and by promising tough, uncompromising leadership to deal with the fiscal crisis. At several moments in the spring, Perot led both Bush and Clinton in public opinion polls. But in July, as he began to face hostile scrutiny from the media, he abruptly withdrew from the race. Early in October, he reentered and soon regained much (although never all) of his early support.

After a campaign in which the economy was the principal issue, Clinton won a clear, but hardly overwhelming, victory over Bush and Perot. He received 43 percent   *Clinton Elected* of the vote in the three-way race, to the president's 38 percent and Perot's 19 percent (the best showing for a third-party or independent candidate since Theodore Roosevelt in 1912). Clinton won 370 electoral votes to Bush's 168; Perot won none. Democrats also retained control of both houses of Congress.

CONCLUSION

America in the late 1970s was, by the standards of its own recent history, an unusually troubled nation—numbed by the Watergate scandals, the fall of Vietnam, and perhaps most of all the nation's increasing economic difficulties. The unhappy presidencies of Gerald Ford and Jimmy Carter provided little relief from these accumulating problems and anxieties. Indeed, in the last year of the Carter presidency, the nation's future seemed particularly bleak in light of severe economic problems, a traumatic seizure of American hostages in Iran, and a Soviet invasion of Afghanistan.

In the midst of these problems, American conservatives slowly and steadily prepared for a political revolution. A coalition of disparate but impassioned groups on the right—including a large movement known as the "New Right," with vaguely populist impulses—gained strength from the nation's troubles and from their own success in winning support for a broad-ranging revolt against taxes. Their efforts culminated in the election of 1980, when Ronald Reagan became the most conservative man in at least sixty years to be elected president of the United States.

Reagan's first term was a dramatic contrast to the troubled presidencies that had preceded it and signaled a reversal or at least a modification of ruling economic and social policies. He won substantial victories in Congress (cutting taxes, reducing spending on domestic programs, building up the military). Perhaps equally important, he made his own engaging personality one of the central political forces in national life. Easily reelected in 1984, he seemed to have solidified the conservative grip on national political life. In his second term, however, a series of scandals and misadventures—and the president's own declining energy—limited the administration's effectiveness. Nevertheless, Reagan's personal popularity remained high, and the economy continued to prosper—factors that propelled his vice president, George H. W. Bush, to succeed him in 1989.

Bush's presidency was not as successful as Reagan's had been, and the perception of his disengagement with the nation's growing economic problems contributed to Bush's defeat in 1992. But a colossal historic event overshadowed most domestic concerns during Bush's term in office: the collapse of the Soviet Union and the fall of communist regimes all over Europe. The United States was to some degree a dazzled observer of this process. But the end of the Cold War also propelled the United States into the possession of unchallenged global preeminence—and drew it increasingly into the role of international arbiter and peacemaker. The Gulf War of 1991 was the most dramatic example of the new global role the United States would now increasingly assume as the world's only true superpower.

KEY TERMS/PEOPLE/PLACES/EVENTS

Ayatollah Ruhollah
  Khomeini 770
Bill Clinton 786
Camp David accords 769
Christian Coalition 773
deregulation 779
George H. W. Bush 784
Gerald Ford 774
glasnost 782

Iran-contra scandal 784
Jimmy Carter 768
Mikhail Gorbachev 782
neoconservatives 777
New Right 773
perestroika 782
Reagan Doctrine 781
Reaganomics 779
Ronald Reagan 774

Saddam Hussein 785
Sagebrush Rebellion 771
stagflation 767
Strategic Defense
  Initiative (SDI) 781
Sunbelt 771
Tiananmen Square 783

RECALL AND REFLECT

1. Did the Ford and Carter presidencies fail to repair the damage done to the reputation of the presidency by the Watergate scandal and Nixon's resignation? If so, why?
2. Why did the American electorate become increasingly conservative during the 1970s and 1980s? What are some examples that testify to this increasing conservatism?
3. What philosophy guided foreign policy under Reagan? How did the rise of Mikhail Gorbachev alter Reagan's foreign policy toward the Soviet Union?

32

THE AGE OF GLOBALIZATION

A RESURGENCE OF PARTISANSHIP

SCIENCE AND TECHNOLOGY IN THE NEW ECONOMY

A CHANGING SOCIETY

AMERICA IN THE WORLD

LOOKING AHEAD

1. How did increasing partisanship affect governing during the late 1900s and early 2000s? How does it continue to affect the relationship between the president and Congress?

2. How did the growth of the "new economy" affect how Americans worked and lived?

3. How was the American population changing at the turn of the century? What characterizes it, and what key challenges does it confront?

4. How did the terrorist attack of September 11, 2001, affect the United States and begin a new era in American foreign policy?

ON AN EARLY TUESDAY morning in 2001, a commercial airliner crashed into the side of one of two tallest buildings in New York, the North Tower of the World Trade Center. Within thirty minutes, another commercial airliner struck the South Tower. Before the steel girders in both towers buckled and collapsed from the tremendous heat of the burning wreckage, Americans learned of even more disasters. A plane flew into the Pentagon in Washington, D.C., and another crashed a few hundred miles away in a field not far from Pittsburgh, after passengers apparently seized the cockpit and prevented the hijackers from reaching their unknown target. In these four, almost simultaneous, catastrophes, nearly 3,000 people died.

The events of September 11 and their aftermath sparked significant changes in American life. And yet there was at least one great continuity between the world of the 1990s and the world that seemed to begin on September 11, 2001. The United States in the last years of the twentieth century and the first years of the twenty-first, more than at any other time in its history, was becoming more and more deeply entwined in a new age of globalism—an age that combined great promise with great peril.

1992
Bill Clinton elected

1993
NAFTA ratified

1995
Government shutdown

1996
Welfare reform passed
Defense of Marriage Act
Clinton reelected

1997
Balanced budget agreement

1998
Lewinsky scandal breaks
Clinton impeached by House

1999
Clinton acquitted by Senate

2000
George W. Bush wins contested election

2001
9/11 attacks
U.S. defeats Taliban regime in Afghanistan

2003
U.S. invades Iraq

2004
Abu Ghraib scandal
Bush reelected

2005
Hurricane Katrina

2007
"Tea Party" fields candidates
Troop "surge" in Iraq
Mortgage crisis

2008
The Great Recession
Obama elected nation's first African American president

2010
Affordable Care Act signed
Deepwater Horizon (BP) oil spill

2011
Osama bin Laden killed by U.S. Special Forces
Occupy Wall Street

2012
Obama reelected
Sandy Hook school shooting

2013
Border bill passes Senate, fails in the House

2015
Obergefell v. Hodges

A RESURGENCE OF PARTISANSHIP

When Bill Clinton took the presidential oath of office in January 1993, little did he or any other American realize that partisan politics would become a crippling problem. Beginning with Clinton and continuing through the administration of President Barack Obama, Democrats and Republicans regularly chose ideological purity over political compromise, effectively gumming up the machinery of the federal government and nearly bringing it to the brink of shutting down on more than one occasion. At times the political divides occurred within a party: conservative Republicans refusing the hand of negotiation to their more liberal brethren on matters of higher taxes, raising the national debt ceiling, or supporting national health insurance. Like few periods in American history, the turn of the twenty-first century showcased bitter splits between the parties that fundamentally affected how the White House and Congress functioned.

LAUNCHING THE CLINTON PRESIDENCY

Bill Clinton entered office as the first Democratic president since Jimmy Carter and the first self-proclaimed "activist" president, meaning a president seeking to expand the active role of the federal government in solving social problems, since Lyndon Johnson. Indeed, his domestic agenda was more ambitious than that of any president since the 1960s. But Clinton also had significant political weaknesses. Having won the vote of well under half the electorate, he had no powerful mandate for change.

The new administration began with a series of missteps and misfortunes in its first months. The president's effort to end the longtime ban on gay men and lesbians serving in the military met with ferocious resistance, and he was forced to settle for a compromise known as "Don't Ask, Don't Tell," which forbade recruiters to ask recruits about their sexual preferences but also forbade servicemen and servicewomen to reveal them. Several of his early appointments became so controversial he had to withdraw them. Then Vince Foster, a longtime friend of the president who served as a deputy White House counsel and previous legal partner of First Lady Hillary Rodham Clinton, committed suicide in the summer of 1993. His death sparked an escalating inquiry into some banking and real estate ventures involving the Clintons in the early 1980s, which became known as the Whitewater affair. An independent counsel began examining these issues in 1993. (The Clintons were ultimately cleared of wrongdoing in Whitewater in 2000.)

Despite its many problems, the Clinton administration had some important achievements in its first year. The president narrowly won approval of a budget that marked a significant turn away from some of the policies of the Reagan–Bush years, especially the focus on reducing personal and corporate taxes. It included a substantial tax increase on the wealthiest Americans, a sizable reduction in many areas of government spending, and a major expansion of tax credits to low-income working people.

Clinton was a committed advocate of free trade. After a long and difficult battle against, among others, Ross Perot, the AFL-CIO, and many Democrats in Congress, he secured passage of the North American Free Trade Agreement (NAFTA), which eliminated   *Free-Trade Agreements* most trade barriers among the United States, Canada, and Mexico. Later he won approval to sign a global accord that created the World Trade Organization (WTO), an international organization charged with negotiating agreements and settling disputes among its members.

The president's most notable and ambitious initiative was a major reform of the nation's health-care system. Early in 1993, he appointed a task force, chaired by the first lady. The presidential task force proposed a sweeping reform designed to guarantee coverage to every American and hold down the costs of medical care. But there was substantial opposition from those who believed the reform would transfer too much power to the government. Well-funded opposition doomed the plan. The foreign policy of the Clinton administration was at first cautious and tentative. Yugoslavia, a nation created after World War I out of a group of small Balkan countries, dissolved again into several different countries in the wake of the 1989 collapse of its communist government. Bosnia was among the new nations, and it quickly became embroiled in a bloody civil war between its two major ethnic groups: one Muslim, the other Serbian and Christian, backed by the neighboring Serbian republic. All efforts by the other European nations and the United States to negotiate an end to the struggle failed until 1995, when the American negotiator Richard Holbrooke finally brought the warring parties together and crafted an agreement to partition Bosnia.

THE REPUBLICAN RESURGENCE

The trials of the Clinton administration, and the failure of health-care reform in particular, proved damaging to the Democratic Party as it faced the congressional elections of 1994. For the first time in over forty years, Republicans gained control of both houses of Congress.

Throughout 1995, the Republican Congress, under the aggressive leadership of House Speaker Newt Gingrich, worked at a sometimes feverish pace to construct   *Newt Gingrich* what they called a "Contract with America," an ambitious and even radical legislative program. The Republicans proposed a series of measures to transfer important powers from the federal government to the states; pushed for dramatic reductions in federal spending, including a major restructuring of the Medicare program, to reduce costs; and attempted to scale back a wide range of federal regulatory functions.

President Clinton responded to the 1994 election results by shifting his own activist agenda conspicuously to the center—announcing his own plan to cut taxes and balance the budget. But the presidential politics of 1996 made compromise between the president and Congress very difficult. In November 1995 and again in January 1996, the federal government literally shut down for several days because the president and Congress could not agree on a budget. Republican leaders refused to pass a "continuing resolution" (to allow government operations to continue during negotiations) in hopes of pressuring the president to agree to their terms. That proved to be an epic political blunder. Public opinion turned quickly and powerfully against the Republican leadership and much of its agenda. Newt Gingrich emerged as one of the most unpopular political leaders in the nation, while President Clinton slowly improved his standing in public opinion polls.

By the time the 1996 campaign began in earnest, President Clinton was in a commanding position to win reelection. Unopposed for the Democratic nomination, he faced a Republican opponent—Senator Robert Dole of Kansas—who inspired little enthusiasm even within his own party. Clinton benefited from the disastrous errors by congressional Republicans in 1995 and early 1996. But his greatest strength came from the remarkable success of the American economy and the marked reduction in the federal deficit. Like Reagan in 1984, he could campaign as the champion of peace, prosperity, and national well-being.

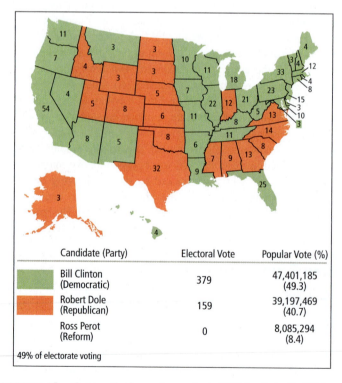

Candidate (Party)	Electoral Vote	Popular Vote (%)
Bill Clinton (Democratic)	379	47,401,185 (49.3)
Robert Dole (Republican)	159	39,197,469 (40.7)
Ross Perot (Reform)	0	8,085,294 (8.4)

49% of electorate voting

THE ELECTION OF 1996 Ross Perot received many fewer votes in 1996 than he had in 1992, and President Clinton came much closer than he had four years earlier to winning a majority of the popular vote. Once again, Clinton defeated his Republican opponent, this time Robert Dole, by a decisive margin in both the popular and electoral votes. • *After the 1994 Republican landslide in the congressional elections, Bill Clinton had seemed permanently weakened. What explains his political revival?*

In a flurry of activity in the spring and summer of 1996, Congress passed several important bills. The most dramatic was a welfare reform bill that ended the fifty-year federal guarantee of assistance to families with dependent children and turned most of the responsibility for allocating federal welfare funds to the states. Most of all, it shifted the bulk of welfare benefits away from those without jobs and toward low-wage workers.

Clinton's buoyant campaign flagged slightly in the last weeks, but the president neverthe-less received just over 49 percent of the popular vote to Dole's 41 percent; Ross Perot, running now as the candidate of what he called the Reform Party, received just over 8 percent of the vote. Clinton won 379 electoral votes to Dole's 159; Perot won none, as was *Clinton Reelected* the case in the 1992 election. But the Democrats failed to regain either house of Congress.

CLINTON TRIUMPHANT AND EMBATTLED

The first Democratic president to win two terms as president since Franklin Roosevelt, Bill Clinton began his second administration with serene confidence. He proposed a rela-tively modest domestic agenda. He negotiated effectively with the Republican leadership on a plan for a balanced budget, which passed with much fanfare late in 1997. By the end of 1998, the federal budget was generating its first surplus in thirty years.

Clinton's renewed popularity was critical to his political survival in the turbulent year that followed, when the most serious crisis of his presidency suddenly erupted. Clinton had been the target of accusations of corruption and scandal since his first weeks in office: the investigation into Whitewater, charges of corruption against members of his cabinet and staff, accusations of illegalities in financing his 1996 campaign, and a civil suit for sexual harassment filed early in his first term by a former Arkansas state employee, Paula Jones.

In early 1998, inquiries associated with the Paula Jones case led to charges that the president had had a sexual relationship with a twenty-two-year-old White House intern, Monica Lewinsky. The most damaging charge was that he had lied about it in his depo-sition before Jones's attorneys. Those revelations produced a new investigation by the independent counsel in the Whitewater case, Kenneth Starr, a former judge and official in the Reagan Justice Department.

Clinton forcefully denied the charges, and a majority of the public strongly backed him. His popularity soared to record levels and remained high throughout the year that followed. In the meantime, a federal judge dismissed the Paula Jones case, which had launched the scandal.

But the scandal revived again with great force in August 1998, when Lewinsky struck a deal with the independent counsel and testified about her relationship with Clinton. Starr then subpoenaed Clinton himself, who—faced with the prospect of speaking *The Starr Report* to a grand jury—finally admitted that he and Lewinsky had had what he called an "improper relationship." A few weeks later, Starr submitted a lengthy and salacious report to Congress on the results of his investigation, recommending that Congress impeach the president.

IMPEACHMENT, ACQUITTAL, AND RESURGENCE

On December 19, 1998, the House, voting on strictly partisan lines, narrowly approved two counts of impeachment: lying to the grand jury and obstructing justice. The matter then moved to the Senate, where a trial of the president—the first since the trial of Andrew Johnson in 1868—began in early January. It ended with a decisive acquittal of the presi-dent. Neither of the charges attracted even a majority of the votes, let alone the two-thirds necessary for conviction.

Still, the trial dampened public support for the president and stiffened congressional opposition to any of his initiatives. Indeed, the last two years of the Clinton presidency were relatively quiet. The president had no real hope of major domestic achievements in the face of a hostile Republican Congress. Overseas, however, he was more active.

In 1999, the president faced another crisis in the Balkans. This time, the conflict *Kosovo* involved a province of Serbian-dominated Yugoslavia—Kosovo—most of whose residents were Albanian Muslims. A savage civil war erupted there in 1998 between Kosovo nationalists and Serbians. In May 1999, NATO forces—dominated and led by the United States—began a major bombing campaign against the Serbians, which after little more than a week led the leader of Yugoslavia, Slobodan Milosevic, to agree to a cease-fire. Serbian troops withdrew from Kosovo entirely, replaced by NATO peacekeeping forces. A precarious peace returned to the region.

Buoyed by his success overseas and a rising economy, Clinton actually finished his eight years in office with his popularity higher than it had been when he had begun. No president in the years since has experienced the same approval ratings. Indeed, despite politicians' use of new technology and polling data to connect with the public, the relationship between the elected and the voter has steadily deteriorated.

THE ELECTION OF 2000

The 2000 presidential election was one of the most extraordinary in American history—not because of the campaign that preceded it but because of the sensational controversy over its results, which preoccupied the nation for more than five weeks after the actual voting.

The two men who had been the front-runners for their parties' nominations a year before the election captured these nominations with only slight difficulty: Republican George W. Bush, son of the former president and a second-term governor of Texas, and Democrat Al Gore, former Tennessee senator and vice president under Clinton.

Both men ran cautious, centrist campaigns. In the congressional races, Republicans maintained control of the House of Representatives by a scant five seats, while the Senate split evenly between Democrats and Republicans. (Among the victors in the Senate races was First Lady Hillary Rodham Clinton, who won in New York.) In the presidential race, Gore won the national popular vote by the thin margin of about 540,000 votes out of *Florida Disputed* about 100 million cast (a difference of 0.5 percent). But on election night, both candidates remained short of the 270 electoral votes needed for victory because the Florida results were too close to call.

After a mandatory recount over the next two days, Bush led Gore in the state by fewer than 300 votes. The technology of voting soon became central to the dispute. The Gore campaign asked for hand recounts in three critical counties, which the Florida Supreme Court unanimously supported.

The battle over the ballots continued between the candidates in the news and the courts until the U.S. Supreme Court ruled on December 12. Voting 5 to 4, along ideological lines, the conservative majority ruled that the Florida Supreme Court's order for a recount was unconstitutional; insisted that according to U.S. Code any revised recount order be completed by December 12 (the same day that the ruling was issued and therefore impossible to execute); and argued that the standards for evaluating punch-card ballots were too arbitrary and unfair to withstand constitutional scrutiny. With Florida's results certified, Bush's victory in Florida—and thus nationally—stood.

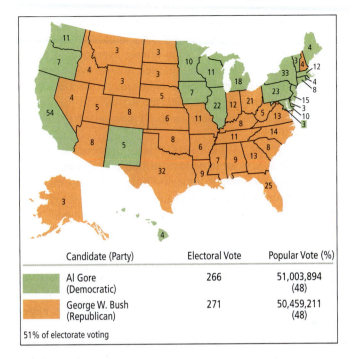

Candidate (Party)	Electoral Vote	Popular Vote (%)
Al Gore (Democratic)	266	51,003,894 (48)
George W. Bush (Republican)	271	50,459,211 (48)

51% of electorate voting

THE ELECTION OF 2000 The 2000 presidential election was one of the closest and most controversial in American history. It also starkly revealed a new pattern of party strength, which had been developing over the previous decade. Democrats swept the Northeast and most of the industrial Midwest and carried all the states of the Pacific Coast. Republicans swept the South, the plains states, and the mountain states (with the exception of New Mexico) and held on to a few traditional Republican strongholds in the Midwest. • *Compare this map to those of earlier elections, in particular the election of 1896 (Chapter 19). How did the pattern of party support change over the course of the twentieth century?*

THE PRESIDENCY OF GEORGE W. BUSH

George W. Bush assumed the presidency in January 2001 burdened by both the controversies surrounding his election and the widespread perception, even among some of his own supporters, that he was ill-prepared for the office. Nevertheless, Bush moved forcefully to enact an ambitious and controversial agenda.

Having campaigned as a moderate, Bush spent his first term as president governing as a staunch conservative and relying on the most conservative members of his party for support. He won passage of the largest tax cut in American history—$1.35 trillion. Critics noted that the massive tax cuts of 2001 went disproportionately to wealthy   *Bush Tax Cuts* Americans, reflecting the view of White House economists that the best way to ensure growth was to put money into the hands of people most likely to invest.

Bush's other major domestic accomplishment was a controversial education reform bill, known as "No Child Left Behind," which tied federal funding in schools to the success of students in taking standardized tests. Still other proposals—an effort to privatize some aspects of the Social Security system, for example—never attracted significant support in Congress. Nonetheless, for most of the first three years of his presidency, George W. Bush was revered by many Americans because of his resolute stance against terrorism. Even the Iraq War, which began in 2003 and initially enjoyed widespread backing, helped sustain his popularity for a time.

As the 2004 election approached, Karl Rove, the president's political adviser, encouraged the administration to take increasingly conservative positions to mobilize the party's conservative constituency in what almost everyone agreed was likely to be a very close election. The electorate was divided almost evenly throughout the campaign, and in the end turnout proved decisive. Although the Democrats turned out in much higher numbers than they had in 2000, the increase in the Republican vote was even larger. Bush won a narrow victory, with 51 percent of the popular vote and an electoral vote margin of 35.

The 2004 election was one of the last successful moments in the Bush administration. The public's recent turn against the war in Iraq contributed to the rapidly declining approval ratings of the president himself—ratings that by mid-2008 had reached the lowest level of presidential approval in the history of polling. Perhaps even more *Hurricane Katrina* damaging to Bush's popularity was the government's weak response to Hurricane Katrina, a Category 3 hurricane of tremendous force that ravaged the Gulf Coast of Louisiana and Mississippi in late August 2005. The storm leveled many communities along the coast and crippled the city of New Orleans. Some of the levees that protected the city failed, causing massive flooding and destruction. While local, state, and federal governance fumbled the initial evacuation and recovery of southern Louisiana, the administration took the brunt of the blame. The Federal Emergency Management Agency (FEMA) failed to handle the disaster effectively and arguably made it worse. The political fallout from Hurricane Katrina, along with scandals in the Justice Department, revelations of violations of civil liberties, revulsion from aggressive interviewing tactics used against suspected terrorists, and declining economic prospects, culminating in a disastrous financial crisis beginning in early 2008—all contributed to the growing unpopularity of the president.

Bush managed some significant victories despite these setbacks. He won confirmation of two justices that he proposed for the Supreme Court: John Roberts, who succeeded William Rehnquist as chief justice; and Samuel Alito, who succeeded the retiring Sandra Day O'Connor. Both were fierce conservatives, inspiring hopes among some and fears among others that the Court would veer more sharply to the political right.

THE ELECTION OF 2008

The 2008 presidential election was the first since 1952 that did not include an incumbent president or vice president. Both parties began the campaign with large fields of candidates, but by the spring of 2008 the contest had narrowed considerably. Senator John McCain of Arizona emerged from the early primaries with his nomination ensured. In the Democratic race, the primaries quickly eliminated all but two candidates: Senator Hillary Rodham Clinton of New York, the former first lady, and Senator Barack Obama of Illinois, a young, charismatic politician and the son of an African father and a white American mother. As the first woman and the first African American to have a realistic chance of being elected president, Clinton and Obama attracted great enthusiasm. The passions driving both campaigns led to a primary contest that lasted much longer than usual. Not until the last primaries in June was it clear that Obama would be the nominee.

As the nomination campaigns were heating up, a series of financial problems erupted that imperiled the state of the economy. Indeed, by early 2008 the nation confronted its worst financial crisis since the Great Depression. The problem had several causes. For years, financial institutions had been developing new credit instruments intended to make borrowing easier and cheaper, which had lured millions of people into taking on large and risky mortgages. One such instrument, called an adjustable rate mortgage (ARM), offered homebuyers mortgages with initially low interest rates that would increase in later years. Other loans, called "jumbo loans," extended credit to people who lacked the financial means needed to pay them back. These new business practices were made possible with the repeal in 1999 of a centerpiece of New Deal legislation, the Glass-Steagall Act. Glass-Steagall had been passed in 1933 to prevent irresponsible banking practices by mandating layers of government oversight designed to catch fraud or risky investment strategies. Consumers responded to these new means of financing home purchases by snapping them up. Not surprisingly, the sale of houses, many of which were based on these risky mortgages, soared for a while, causing a "housing bubble"—a rapid rise in housing prices fueled by high demand. But the bubble eventually burst. The price of homes soon leveled off and even dipped. Those with ARMs saw them reset at much higher rates and struggled to make the higher payments. They and many owners of jumbo loans sought to sell their homes but couldn't because the market value of the home had often sunk below the value of the mortgages held, forcing some to walk away from their property and default on their loans. Foreclosures skyrocketed across the country. Many of the nation's largest banks had invested heavily in the securities that backed these risky loans; now, with the collapse of the housing market, they lost vast sums of money.

The so-called Great Recession of 2008, influenced by the loan crisis, also pushed down wages and triggered widespread job layoffs. The increased unemployment *Great Recession of 2008* rate further accelerated the downward economic spiral. Many Americans simply could not meet basic financial obligations such as the repayment of home, car, or school loans or credit card debt. There was also less money available for investing, or economic growth. Predictably, the Great Recession fueled outrage among those most affected: blue-collar and trades workers, manufacturers, and the poor. Popular anger surfaced in art, literature, and especially contemporary music. Rap, one of the newest and most successful forms of popular music, chronicled lives of despair and called for economic change. (See "Patterns of Popular Culture: Rap.")

By mid-September 2008, the financial crisis suggested an economy spinning out of control. Secretary of the Treasury Henry Paulson, supported by other economic leaders, stepped in. He proposed a massive use of federal funds to help the government bail out banks that were failing. Both the Bush administration and eventually the Obama administration won congressional support for $750 billion in the form of the Troubled Asset Relief Program (TARP) to shore up the tottering financial institutions. The bailout kept the economy from collapsing, but it remained very weak for several years, with exceptionally high unemployment rates.

This extraordinary crisis formed the backdrop against which the two presidential candidates fought out the last two months of their campaign. Neither offered clear or convincing solutions to the crisis, but most voters came to believe that Obama would likely be a better steward of the economy than McCain. Obama benefited both from the unpopularity of George W. Bush and from his success at persuading voters that McCain would continue Bush's policies. Obama held on to—and indeed increased—his lead through late September and October, helped by a heavily financed and highly disciplined campaign.

RAP

The long musical lineage of rap includes elements of the disco and street funk of the 1970s; of the fast-talking jive of black radio DJs in the 1950s; of the onstage patter of Cab Calloway and other African American stars of the first half of the twentieth century. It contains reminders of tap and break dancing—even of the boxing-ring poetry of Muhammad Ali.

Rap's most important element is its words. Rap is as much a form of language as a form of music. It bears a distant resemblance to some traditions of African American pulpit oratory, which also included forms of spoken song. It draws from some of the verbal traditions of urban black street life, including the "dozens"—a ritualized trading of insults particularly popular among young black men.

But rap is also the product of a distinctive place and time: the South Bronx in the 1970s and 1980s and the hip-hop culture that was born there and that soon dominated the appearance and public behavior of many young black males. "Hip hop is how you walk, talk, live, see, act, feel," said one Bronx hip-hopper. Some elements of hip-hop culture faded, and by the 1990s the most popular element of hip-hop culture was rap, which had by then been developing for nearly twenty years.

Beginning in the early 1970s, Bronx DJs began setting up their equipment on neighborhood streets and staging block parties, where they not only played records but also put on shows of their own—performances that featured spoken rhymes, jazzy phrases, and pointed comments about the audience, the neighborhood, and themselves. Gradually, the DJs began to bring "rappers" into shows— young men who developed the DJ style into a much more elaborate form of performance,

usually accompanied by dancing. As rap grew more popular in the inner city, record promoters began signing some of its new stars. In 1979, the Sugarhill Gang's "Rapper's Delight" became the first rap single to be played on mainstream commercial radio and the first to become a major hit. In the early 1980s, Run-DMC became the first national rap superstars. From there, rap moved quickly to become one of the most popular and commercially successful forms of popular music. In the 1990s and early 2000s, rap recordings routinely sold millions of copies.

Rap has taken many forms. There have been white rappers (Eminem, House of Pain), female rappers (Missy Elliott, Queen Latifah), even religious rappers and children's rappers. But it has always been primarily a product of the young male culture of the inner city, and some of the most successful rap has conveyed the frustration and anger that these men have felt about their lives—"a voice for the oppressed people," one rap artist said, "that in many other ways don't have a voice." In 1982, the rap group Grandmaster Flash and the Furious Five released a rap called "The Message," a searing description of the ghetto and the lack of educational and economic opportunities.

In the late 1980s, the Compton and Watts neighborhoods of Los Angeles—two of the most distressed minority communities in the city—produced their own style, known as West Coast rap, with such groups as Ice Cube, Ice-T, Tupac Shakur, and Snoop Doggy Dog. West Coast rap often had a harsh, angry character, and at its extremes (the so-called gangsta' rap), it could be strikingly violent and highly provocative. Scandals erupted over controversial lyrics—Ice-T's "Cop Killer," which some

KANYE WEST Testifying to the continued popularity of rap, as of 2014 rapper Kanye West remains one of the best-selling artists of all time, having sold well over 21 million albums and 66 million digital downloads in the United States alone. *Time* magazine has named West one of the 100 most influential people in the world. He is a rapper, songwriter, record producer, film director, entrepreneur, and fashion designer. (© Getty Images Entertainment/Getty Images)

critics believed advocated murdering police; and the sexually explicit lyrics of 2 Live Crew and other groups, which critics accused of advocating violence against women.

But it was not just the lyrics that caused the furor. Rap artists were almost all products of tough inner-city neighborhoods, and the rough-edged styles many took with them into the public eye made many people uncomfortable. Some rappers got caught up in highly publicized trouble with the law. Several—including two of rap's biggest stars, Tupac Shakur and Notorious B.I.G.—were murdered. The business of rap, particularly the confrontational business style of Death Row Records (founded by Dr. Dre, a veteran of the first major West Coast rap group NWA), was a source of public controversy as well.

These controversies at times unfairly dominated the image of rap as a whole. Some rap is angry and cruel, as are many of the realities of the world from which it comes. But much of it is explicitly positive, some of it deliberately gentle. Chuck D and other successful rappers use their music to exhort young black men to avoid drugs and crime, to take responsibility for their children, to get an education. And the form, if not the content, of the original rappers has spread widely through American culture. Rap came to dominate the music charts in America, and its styles made their way onto *Sesame Street* and other children's shows, into television commercials, Hollywood films, and the everyday language of millions of people, young and old, black and white. It became another of the arresting, innovative African American musical traditions that have shaped American culture for more than a century. •

UNDERSTAND, ANALYZE, & EVALUATE

1. What other African American musical forms have helped shape American popular culture?

2. If rap is so closely associated with the inner-city culture where it originated, what accounts for its widespread popularity and commercial success? What other forms or styles of popular music enjoy a popularity that extends far beyond its cultural origins?

3. Do you think rap's popularity will endure? Why or why not?

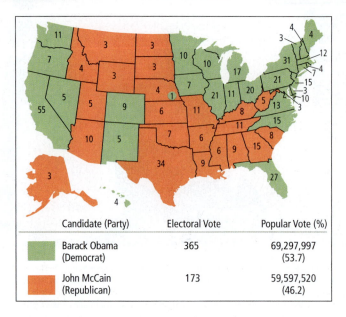

Candidate (Party)	Electoral Vote	Popular Vote (%)
Barack Obama (Democrat)	365	69,297,997 (53.7)
John McCain (Republican)	173	59,597,520 (46.2)

THE ELECTION OF 2008   The election of 2008 produced a decisive victory for Barack Obama. Democrats won majorities in both the House and the Senate, only to see the Republicans win a majority of the House two years later. • *Compare this map to the election of 2000 map. Which states did Bush win that went to Obama in 2008?*

On November 4, 2008, Barack Obama won a decisive victory, winning the popular vote 53 percent to 46 percent and the electoral vote by an even larger margin. Obama became the first Democratic candidate since Lyndon Johnson to win so large a victory.

OBAMA AND HIS OPPONENTS

The global exuberance that Obama's election created in 2008 did not linger for long. The first two years of his presidency coincided with the worst period of the economic crisis. But large supportive Democratic majorities in both houses of Congress strengthened Obama's ability to enact broad reforms. During those years, Obama passed a large stimulus package of $800 billion to support state and local budgets, public works, and other investments that he hoped would generate economic growth. He and his congressional allies also succeeded in passing significant financial regulations that were designed to avoid another crisis like the one that began in 2008. Even more important, he oversaw the passage of the Affordable *Affordable Care Act*   Care Act, a broad health-care bill that would ensure that almost all Americans would have access to insurance, regardless of their means. Yet Obama's legislation, and especially his health-care initiative, triggered fear among many Republicans about a federal government becoming too powerful and overstepping its limits. Indeed, only one Republican congressman supported the health-care bill. For Obama, who had built much of his presidential bid around the idea of bipartisanship and conciliation, the polarization of the two parties was a significant setback. Many Republican state's attorneys sued to stop the health bill. Judges were divided as to whether the bill was constitutional, and only favorable rulings by the Supreme Court in June 2012 and 2015 preserved it.

The 2010 midterm congressional campaigns were dominated by the emergence of a new *Tea Party*   social movement—the Tea Party movement, a vigorous conservative effort to reduce the national debt, lower taxes, and limit the role of government. This broad movement attracted mostly white men and women, largely from the middle class. It viewed

Obama and his peers as dangerous enemies to a stronger, more prosperous America. It helped send a large majority of anti-Obama Republicans to the House and reduced the majority of Democrats in the Senate. For the next two years, President Obama struggled to get proposals passed by Congress because nearly every Republican summarily rejected them.

In September 2011, another movement emerged—Occupy Wall Street *Occupy Wall Street* (OWS). But this movement preached a radically different agenda than the Tea Party movement. Significantly smaller and younger than the Tea Party, OWS argued for stricter financial regulation, progressive taxation, stronger support for unions, more resources to reduce unemployment, assaults on economic inequality, and the end of what it believed were unnecessary and failed wars. Its rallying cry was "We are the 99%," referring to the growing gap of income equality between the richest 1 percent and the rest of Americans. They symbolically demonstrated their grievances by camping in Zuccotti Park in the Wall Street area of lower Manhattan. Soon after, similar demonstrations took place in many other places in the United States and around the world. OWS, never a broad-based popular movement, quickly lost steam and was largely extinguished by 2013. Yet it served as an emblem of popular concern over the unsteady recent history of the economy and the ability of politicians to solve crises in general.

Obama and the Challenge of Governing

The election of 2012—the most expensive campaign in history—pitted President Obama against Mitt Romney, a former governor of Massachusetts. The campaign was not only expensive but also raucous and at times quite angry. As election day neared, the presidential debates in October became the most important part of the campaign. In the first debate, most viewers saw President Obama as tired and uninterested—a stigma that gave Romney a significant boost in the polls. But in the next two, a more energetic and commanding Obama captured support and slowly built a lead.

Still, the race was up in the air until the very end. The polls showed Obama with a persistent lead during the final weeks of the campaign, but only a razor-thin one. Enormous amounts of campaign money and effort flooded into the few states that were still up for grabs—among them Ohio, Virginia, Florida, Wisconsin, Iowa, and New Hampshire. On election night, it became clear that these states had tilted toward Obama in the last few days. He won all of them. His victory was close in popular votes, but his electoral college votes gave him a large lead with 332 votes. The Democrats also won several new senators, giving the party a majority. The House of Representatives remained Republican, but the majority was now smaller.

The political gridlock of Obama's presidency continued after his reelection. Many of his initiatives faced serious obstacles or simply did not come to pass. A major disappointment for Obama and his supporters involved the failure to enact meaningful gun control measures despite a series of horrific shootings occurring during his *Sandy Hook Shooting* terms in office, including the shooting of twenty children and six adults at the Sandy Hook Elementary School in Newtown, Connecticut, on December 14, 2012. Despite the president's promise to exert "whatever power this office holds" to generate such gun control reform, the Congress resisted enacting any such legislation. The National Rifle Association and the conservative wing of the Republican Party successfully warded off any change on the federal level of the right of Americans to buy and use guns.

The gridlock of the House also dashed any hopes President Obama had of gaining a deal on immigration. After his second inaugural, Obama and his strategists hoped to cement their gains among the Latino population revealed in the general election. Many Republicans, as well, believed that their party should reach out to this growing sector of the population by pushing through an immigration reform bill. On June 27, 2013, the Senate, in a rare show of bipartisanship, passed the Border Security, Economic Opportunity, and Immigration Modernization Act of 2013 as a comprehensive package of provisions, including a path to U.S. citizenship for illegal immigrants already in the country. But powerful conservative Republican opposition in the House, based largely on the idea that illegal immigrants should not be granted citizenship, doomed the bill and it died in Congress. Obama responded by issuing an executive order, through which he sought to implement many of the provisions of the bill over the howls of protest from House Republicans. A federal judge eventually intervened in December 2014, ruling that the president's actions were unconstitutional. This decision, along with lawsuits filed by individual states, has effectively killed the reform, at least for the immediate future.

The fate of the immigration bill embodied the challenge of governing in the early twenty-first century. President Obama had whipped up popular support for a bill tackling a pressing social issue and rallied the Senate to pass it—only to see it twist in the wind of partisan debate in the House and eventually die there. As Clinton and Bush had before him, Obama confronted the painful realities of political leadership in modern America, where fealty to political ideology often trumped any desire to compromise with a member of the opposite party or even with those in the same party.

SCIENCE AND TECHNOLOGY IN THE NEW ECONOMY

The last three decades have seen remarkable changes in American life—some a result of the end of the Cold War, some the changing character of the American population, and some a product of a rapidly evolving culture. But most of these changes were at least in part a product of the dramatic transformation of American trade and industry. Indeed, this "new economy" represented a profound shift in the nation's financial history. Throughout much of the twentieth century, manufacturing had powered the nation's economy. Making cars, rubber, steel, and airplanes, for example, had provided many workers with steady jobs and decent wages and benefits as well as entry into the middle class. But in the face of the sluggish growth and persistent inflation of the last decades of the 1900s, many American corporations began making drastic changes in the way they ran their businesses. They invested heavily in new technology to make themselves more efficient and productive and, more significantly, aggressively reduced their labor costs, which were among the highest in the world and which many economists and business leaders believed had made the United States uncompetitive against the emerging economies that relied on low-wage workers. Businesses now took a much harder line against unions. And nonunion companies became more successful in staving off unionization drives. Some companies actually moved their operations to areas of the country where unions were weak and wages low—the American South and Midwest in particular. Others simply relocated much of their production out of the United States, to such nations as Mexico and China, where there were large available pools of unorganized cheap labor.

At the same time, the digital revolution took hold. The rapid development of the personal computer and the Internet profoundly reshaped how companies operated and organized themselves, rewarding in particular college-educated workers skilled in software design and application. It also redefined how people communicated, worked, shopped, and spent their free time.

THE DIGITAL REVOLUTION

The dramatic growth in the use of computers and other digital devices was among the most significant innovations of the late twentieth century. The development of the micro-processor, first introduced in 1971 by Intel, represented a notable advance in the technology of integrated circuitry. A microprocessor miniaturized the central processing unit (CPU) of a computer, making it possible for a small machine to perform calculations that in the past only very large machines could do. Considerable technological innovation was needed before the microprocessor could actually become the basis of what was first known as a "minicomputer" and later a personal computer or "PC." In 1977, Apple launched its Apple II personal computer, the first such machine to be widely available to the public. Several years later, International Business Machines (IBM) entered the personal computer market with the first PC. So that it could focus its internal resources on developing computer hardware, IBM had engaged a small software development company, Microsoft, to design an operating system for its new computer. No PC could operate without it. The PC, and its software, made its debut in August 1981 and immediately became enormously successful. Three years later, Apple introduced its Macintosh computer. For a time, Apple could not match IBM's marketing power. By the late-1980s, the PC had established its dominance in the booming personal computer market, but IBM was replaced by Microsoft as the dominant computer company in the world. The computer revolution created thousands of new, lucrative businesses: computer manufacturers themselves, makers of the tiny silicon chips that ran the computers, and makers of software.

THE INTERNET

Out of the computer revolution emerged another dramatic source of information and communication: the Internet—a vast, geographically far-flung network of computers that allows people to communicate with others all over the world. It had its beginning in 1963, in the U.S. government's Advanced Research Projects Agency (ARPA), which funneled federal funds into scientific research projects. In the early 1960s, J. C. R. Licklider, the head of ARPA's Information Processing Techniques Office, launched a program to link together computers over large distances. It was known as ARPANET. For several years, ARPANET served mainly as a way for groups of people to exchange information and collaborate with one another through the remote use of a small handful of computer networking facilities. Gradually, however, both the size and the uses of the network expanded.

Two new important technologies made ARPANET's expansion possible. The first was a system for transmitting large quantities of data in "packets" that took advantage of ARPANET's indirect structure. The second was the development of the Transmission Control Protocol/Internet Protocol (TCP/IP), which not only provided a way to deliver addresses to machines and networks but also provided protection against lost data packets on the network.

By 1971, ARPANET linked twenty-three computers, which served mostly research labs and universities. Gradually, interest in the system began to spread and the number of devices connected to it grew. In the early 1980s, the Defense Department, an early partner in the development of ARPANET, withdrew from the project for security reasons. The network, soon renamed the Internet, was then free to develop independently. In 1989, Tim Berners-Lee, a British scientist working at a laboratory in Geneva, introduced the World Wide Web, which helped establish an orderly system for both the distribution and retrieval of electronic information over the Internet. By 2012, there were well over a

TWENTY-FOUR-HOUR NEWS CYCLE The digital revolution has contributed to a vast change in the reporting of news events and political commentary. Politicians now have much less control over how their messages are transmitted and received. (© Ian Dagnall/Alamy)

billion computers in use in the world (and many more now-obsolete ones). Virtually all of them are connected to the Internet.

The development of the Internet, along with the emergence of the computer industry and digital technology, made possible an enormous range of new products and services that quickly became central to economic life: digital music, video, and cameras; iPods, smartphones, and tablets; and Facebook, Instagram, YouTube, and Vine. These modern industries employed hundreds of thousands of people (many of them from outside the United States) and created new consumer needs and appetites.

Breakthroughs in Genetics

Computers helped create new scientific breakthroughs in genetics. Early discoveries in genetics by Gregor Mendel, Thomas Hunt Morgan, and others laid the groundwork for more dramatic breakthroughs—the discovery of DNA by the British scientists Oswald Avery, Colin MacLeod, and Maclyn McCarty in 1944; and in 1953, the dramatic discovery by the American biochemist James Watson and the British biophysicist Francis Crick of the double-helix structure of DNA, and thus of the key to identifying genetic codes. From these discoveries emerged the new science—and, ultimately, the new industry—of genetic engineering, through which new medical treatments and new techniques for hybridization of plants and animals have already become possible.

Scientists began to identify specific genes in humans and other living things. But the identification of genes was painfully slow; and in 1989, in an effort to accelerate the process, the federal government appropriated $3 billion to fund the National Center for *Human Genome Project* the Human Genome. The Human Genome Project formally began its mission to identify and classify all of the more than 100,000 genes in 1990 and declared its work complete in 2003.

But genetic research was (and continues to be) a source of great controversy. Many people feared that the new science might alter aspects of human life that previously seemed beyond human control. Some critics opposed genetic research on religious grounds, seeing it as an interference with "God's plan" for human nature. Still others complained that it equipped humans with immoral powers such that, for example, parents could "design" their children and "order" certain desirable traits. And a particularly heated controversy emerged over the ways in which scientists obtained genetic material. One of the most promising sources of genetic research comes from stem cell material from human embryos, but the research deeply offends those who believe that the embryo is an early-aged human life deserving of protection from harm. In 2001, President Bush issued an executive order banning federal funding of research using new sources of human stem cells. President Obama reversed the order in 2009.

A CHANGING SOCIETY

The American population changed dramatically in the late twentieth and early twenty-first centuries. It grew larger, older, and more racially and ethnically diverse. It debated the success and scope of earlier landmark events, such as the civil rights movement and the right to an abortion. At the same time, the nation's citizenry confronted powerful new challenges, such as the spread of AIDS, the debate over gay rights and same-sex marriage, and the prospect of dwindling natural resources.

A Shifting Population

Decreasing birthrates and growing life spans contributed to one of the most important characteristics of the American population in the early twenty-first century: its increasing agedness. The enormous "Baby-Boom" generation—people born in the first ten years after World War II—drove the median age steadily upward (from 34 in 1996 to 37 in 2011 to a projected 39 by 2035). It had important implications for the workforce. In the last twenty years of the twentieth century, the number of people aged 25–54 (known statistically as the prime workforce) grew by over 26 million. In the first ten years of the twenty-first century, the number of American-born workers in that age group did not grow at all. This combination of fewer Americans working and more of them retired put enormous stress on the Social Security and Medicare systems to continue to fulfill their financial obligations.

The slowing growth of the native-born population, and the workforce shortages it helped create, was one reason for the rapid growth of immigration. In 2011, the number of foreign-born residents of the United States was the highest in American history—more than 40 million people. These immigrants came from a wider variety of backgrounds than ever before, as a result of the 1965 Immigration Reform Act, which eliminated national origins as a criterion for admission. The growing presence of the foreign-born contributed to a significant drop in the percentage of white residents in the United States—from 90 percent in 1965 to 80 percent in 2008. (Relative to the overall population, non-Hispanic whites constituted just over 65 percent.) Latinos and Asians were by far the largest groups of immigrants in these years. But others came in significant numbers from Africa, the Middle East, Russia, and eastern Europe.

African Americans in the Post–Civil Rights Era

The civil rights movement and other liberal efforts of the 1960s had two very different effects on African Americans. On one hand, they increased opportunities for advancement to those in a position to take advantage of them. And they helped make possible the election of the first black American to the White House, an event unthinkable to all but

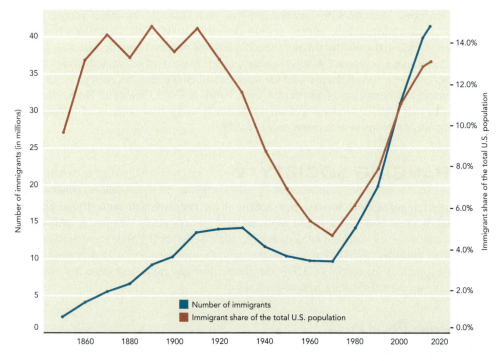

U.S. IMMIGRANT POPULATION AND SHARE OVER TIME, 1850–PRESENT   This chart shows the tremendous increase in immigration to the United States in the decades since the Immigration Reform Act of 1965. • *At what point since 1850 was the immigrant share of the total U.S. population highest? When was the last time that the immigrant share was at its current level?* (Source of data: Migration Policy Institute and U.S. Census Bureau.)

the most optimistic freedom fighter during the King years. On the other hand, as the industrial economy declined and government services dwindled, there was a growing sense of helplessness and despair among large groups of poor nonwhites who continued to find themselves barred from upward mobility.

By the early twenty-first century, the black middle class constituted over half of the African *Growth of Black Middle Class*   American population; progress was remarkable in the decades after the high point of the civil rights movement. Disparities between black and white professionals did not vanish, but they diminished substantially. African American families moved into more affluent urban communities and, in many cases, into suburbs—at times as neighbors of whites, more often into predominantly black communities. The percentage of black high school graduates going on to college was virtually the same as that of white high school graduates by the early twenty-first century (although a smaller proportion of blacks than whites managed to complete high school). And African Americans were making rapid strides in many professions. A generation earlier, they had been barred from many jobs because of segregation. Over half of all employed African Americans in the United States had skilled white-collar jobs in 2010. There were few areas of American life from which blacks were any longer entirely excluded.

But the rise of the black middle class also accentuated the increasingly desperate plight of less fortunate African Americans. Economic growth and the activist programs of the 1960s and beyond had never reached them. A third of the nation's black population was categorized as impoverished, often described as the "underclass." As more successful *Plight of Impoverished People*   blacks moved out of the inner cities, the poor were left behind in their decaying neighborhoods. Less than half of young inner-city blacks finished high school in 2010; more than 60 percent were unemployed. The black family structure changed as well from the dislocations of urban poverty. There was a radical increase in the number of single-parent, female-headed black households. In 1970, 59 percent of all black children under eighteen years old lived with both their parents (already down from 70 percent a decade earlier). In 2010, only 35 percent of black children lived in such households, compared to 77 percent of non-Hispanic white children.

Nonwhites were also disadvantaged by many other factors in the changing social and economic climate of the late twentieth and early twenty-first centuries. Among them was Clinton's revision of federal welfare policies and a growing impatience with affirmative action. There was also a steady decline in the number of unskilled jobs in the economy. Not surprisingly, then, many blacks openly questioned the long-term successes of the civil rights movement. A steady rise in the rate of the incarceration of young black men prompted calls for better schools and intervention programs as well as a review of the justice system as a whole. Signs of popular despair surfaced during moments of racial tension, especially after the use of questionable policing tactics left black men dead, as in the case of Eric Garner in New York City in July 2014 and eighteen-year-old Michael Brown in Ferguson, Missouri, in August 2014. In these highly publicized cases, hundreds of blacks took to the streets, demanding fairer treatment by local police and decrying a lack of racial respect between Americans of different colors.

THE ABORTION DEBATE

Among the principal goals of the growing power of conservatism as it became more assertive in the late twentieth century was a challenge to feminism and its achievements. Leaders of the New Right had campaigned successfully against the proposed Equal Rights Amendment to the Constitution. And they played a central role in the most divisive issue of the late 1980s and 1990s: abortion rights.

For women who choose to terminate unwanted pregnancies, the Supreme Court's decision in *Roe v. Wade* (1973) had seemed to settle the question. By the 1980s, abortion was the most commonly performed surgical procedure in the country. But at the same time, critics of abortion began to build a powerful grassroots movement. The "right-to-life" or "pro-life" movement, as it called itself, found its most fervent supporters among Catholics; and *Right-to-Life Movement* indeed, the Catholic Church itself lent its institutional authority to the battle against legalized abortion. Religious doctrine also motivated the anti-abortion stance of Mormons, evangelical Christians, and other groups. The opposition of other anti-abortion activists had less to do with religion than with their commitment to traditional notions of family and gender relations. To them, abortion was a particularly offensive part of a much larger assault by feminists on the role of women as wives and mothers. It was also, many foes contended, a form of murder. Fetuses, they claimed, were human beings who had a "right to life" from the moment of conception.

Although the right-to-life movement was persistent in its demand for a reversal of *Roe v. Wade* or, barring that, a constitutional amendment banning abortion, it also attacked abortion in more-limited ways and at its most vulnerable points. Starting in the late 1970s, Congress and many state legislatures began barring the use of public funds to pay for abortions, thereby making them almost inaccessible for many poor women in some states. The Reagan and the two Bush administrations imposed further restrictions on federal funding and even on the right of doctors in federally funded clinics to give patients any information on abortion. Extremists in the right-to-life movement began picketing, occupying, and at rare times even bombing abortion clinics. Several anti-abortion activists murdered doctors who performed abortions; others subjected physicians to campaigns of terrorism and harassment. The shifting composition of the Supreme Court between 1981 and 2010 (during which time new conservative justices were appointed to the Court) renewed the right-to-life movement's hopes for a reversal of *Roe v. Wade*.

The changing judicial climate of the late twentieth and early twenty-first centuries mobilized defenders of abortion as never before. They called themselves the "pro-choice" *Pro-Choice Movement* movement because they were defending not so much abortion itself as every woman's right to choose whether and when to bear a child. The pro-choice movement was in many parts of the country at least as strong as, and in some areas much stronger than, the right-to-life movement.

With the election of President Clinton in 1992, a vocal supporter of "choice," the immediate threat to *Roe v. Wade* faded. Clinton's reelection in 1996 was evidence that the pro-choice movement maintained considerable political strength. But abortion rights remained highly vulnerable. Clinton's successor, George W. Bush, openly opposed abortion. Whereas Clinton had refused to sign the Partial-Birth Abortion Ban Act, Bush, to great fanfare, inked it into law in 2003. The legislation forbade physicians from performing a medical procedure called "intact dilation and extraction." The Supreme Court upheld the constitutionality of the law in *Gonzales v. Carhart* in 2007. Barack Obama supported the right to abortion when he became president, but judicial struggles over whether and to what extent society has an obligation to protect it continued. In 2007, the state of Massachusetts amended its Reproductive Health Facility Act (originally passed in 2003) to create a 35-foot buffer zone around reproductive centers that offered abortions. Its intent was to provide patients entering an abortion clinic a greater measure of safety and relief from confrontational protesters. The Supreme Court, however, declared this law unconstitutional in 2014. In *McCullen v. Coakley*, *McCullen v. Coakley* the Court ruled that the 35-foot protective zone violated the right of abortion opponents to protest peacefully and unfairly limited their free speech.

AIDS AND MODERN AMERICA

Two new and deadly epidemics ravaged many American communities beginning in the 1980s. One was a dramatic increase in drug use, which penetrated nearly every community in the nation. The enormous demand for drugs, and particularly for "crack" cocaine in the late 1980s and early 1990s, spawned what was in effect a multibillion-dollar industry. Drug use declined significantly among middle-class people beginning in the late 1980s, largely because of educational campaigns, but the epidemic declined much more slowly in the poor urban neighborhoods, where it was doing the most severe damage.

The drug epidemic was related to another scourge of the late twentieth and early twenty-first centuries: the rapid spread of a new and lethal disease first documented in 1981 and soon named AIDS (acquired immune deficiency syndrome). AIDS is the product of the human immunodeficiency virus (HIV), which is transmitted by the exchange of bodily fluids (blood or semen). The virus gradually destroys the body's immune system and makes its victims highly vulnerable to a number of diseases (particularly to various forms of cancer and pneumonia) to which they would otherwise have a natural resistance. During the early history of the disease, those infected with the virus (that is, those who identified as "HIV-positive") and became ill were almost certain to die. The first American victims of AIDS (and for many years the group among whom cases remained the most numerous) were gay men. But by the late 1980s, as the gay community began to implement aggressive education and intervention programs, the most rapid increase in the spread of the disease occurred among heterosexuals, many of them intravenous drug users who spread the virus by sharing contaminated hypodermic needles.

In the mid-1990s, AIDS researchers, after years of frustration, finally began discovering effective treatments for the disease. By taking a combination of powerful drugs on a rigorous schedule, among them a group known as protease inhibitors, even people with advanced cases of AIDS experienced dramatic improvement—so much so that in many cases there were no measurable quantities of the virus left in their bloodstreams. Currently a diagnosis of AIDS is not the near-certain death sentence it was in the late nineties; rather, new medication regimes permit those living with AIDS to successfully manage the disease and live mostly normal lives. Every president has steadily increased federal funding for AIDS research and education and for the care of individuals living with AIDS, both domestically and abroad. President George W. Bush provided $15 billion to fight AIDS in Africa, where the epidemic was rampant and the poor had little access to drugs. In the budget for 2015, President Obama called for $30.4 billion to combat AIDS.

The Centers for Disease Control and Prevention (CDC) estimates that 1.3 million Americans currently suffer from AIDS, nearly one in seven not even realizing that they are infected. But the United States represents only a tiny proportion of the worldwide total of people afflicted with HIV, an estimated 35 million people. Over two-thirds of those cases are concentrated in Africa.

GAY AMERICANS AND SAME-SEX MARRIAGE

In the late twentieth century, inspired in part by the success of AIDS activists in winning political support and funding, many gay men and lesbians began to lobby for greater protections under the law, particularly the right to marry. Until the 1990s, the issue of same-sex marriage was not a national political issue. But in 1993, Hawaii's Supreme Court ruled in *Baehr v. Lewin* that the state needed a compelling reason to bar same-sex marriage. In response, Congress easily passed the Defense of Marriage Act (DOMA) in 1996   *DOMA* with rare bipartisan support. President Clinton signed it into law. DOMA exempted states from being required to recognize same-sex marriages from other states. It also defined marriage as being between a man and a woman and denied same-sex married couples the ability to be classified as "spouses" for federal purposes, such as the filing of joint tax returns, Social Security survivor benefit claims, adoption papers, and immigration applications. Gay rights activists identified more than 1,000 protections and responsibilities of marriage denied them by DOMA. Thirty states quickly followed suit with similar laws.

Almost immediately, gay men and lesbians and their supporters took to the courts in protest. They typically argued that DOMA and related state laws violated the Equal Protection Clause of the Fourteenth Amendment of the U.S. Constitution. They gained many victories. By 2013, eleven states had passed new legislation making same-sex marriage legal. That year as well the U.S. Supreme Court struck down the section of DOMA defining marriage as being between two people of the opposite sex, so that all married couples living in states where same-sex marriage is legal are classified as spouses by the federal government. The tide against same-sex marriage appeared to be turning. By early 2015, state and federal courts had overturned legal barriers to same-sex marriage in twenty-six states. Finally, on June 26, 2015, the Supreme Court, in a close 5-4 decision, ruled that the ability of same-sex couples to marry was a right guaranteed by the Constitution. Writing for the majority, Justice Anthony Kennedy proclaimed that "No longer may this liberty be denied."

Driving the radical change in the legal status of same-sex marriage, in addition to the guidance and political savvy of its advocates, was a profound shift in public opinion about the issue. Indeed, broad popular support for same-sex marriage grew steadily since the

SAME-SEX MARRIAGE, 2015

The debate over the right of people of the same sex to marry legally and enjoy the full range of benefits accorded to married couples under federal and state law hit a fever pitch in early January 2015.

Nearly four years earlier, Cari Searcy and Kimberly McKeand, a same-sex couple who were legally married in California under that state's laws, wanted Searcy to be able to adopt McKeand's eight-year-old biological son, under a provision of Alabama's adoption code that allows a person to adopt her "spouse's child." But Searcy's petition was denied in December 2011 based on the Alabama Sanctity of Marriage Amendment and the closely related Alabama Marriage Protection Act. Both laws declared that "Marriage is inherently a unique relationship between a man and a woman," that "No marriage license shall be issued in the State of Alabama to parties of the same sex," and that "The State of Alabama shall not recognize as valid any marriage of parties of the same sex that occurred or was alleged to have occurred as a result of the law of any jurisdiction regardless of whether a marriage license was issued." Therefore, because Alabama does not recognize the legality of same-sex plaintiffs' marriage, Searcy failed to qualify as a "spouse" for adoption purposes. Searcy appealed the denial of her adoption petition to the Alabama Court of Civil Appeals, which ruled against her and affirmed the decision of the probate court.

In federal court, Searcy sued the attorney general of Alabama, Luther Strange, and sought to declare these two Alabama state laws unconstitutional on the grounds that they violated the due-process clause and equal protection clause of the Fourteenth Amendment. Callie Granade, a federal judge for the U.S. District Court in Alabama (Southern Division), agreed in January 2015. She ordered the state to begin to issue marriage licenses to same-sex couples immediately, though the order was delayed while Attorney General Strange appealed to the U.S. Supreme Court for a stay. But once the High Court refused to hear the case, on February 9, Granade's order took effect. Some counties obliged, but others didn't, heeding the encouragement of Alabama's Supreme Court justice, Roy Moore, to ignore the federal ruling. Then, in March 2015, the state's Supreme Court ruled 7 to 1 that all probate justices (county officials officially charged with the management of marriage licenses) must cease issuing marriage licenses to same-sex couples. In June, the U.S. Supreme Court ruled that gay marriage bans such as Alabama's were unconstitutional.

In the following excerpt from Judge Granade's ruling, she clarifies why she ruled in favor of same-sex marriage.

Defendant contends that Alabama has a legitimate interest in protecting the ties between children and their biological parents and other biological kin. However, the Court finds that the laws in question are not narrowly tailored to fulfill the reported interest. The Attorney General does not explain how allowing or recognizing same-sex marriage between two consenting adults will prevent heterosexual parents or other biological kin from caring for their biological children. He proffers no justification for why it is that the provisions in question single out same-sex couples and prohibit them, and them alone, from marrying in order to meet that goal. Alabama does not exclude from marriage any other couples who are either unwilling or unable to biologically procreate. There is no law prohibiting infertile couples, elderly couples, or couples who do not wish to procreate from marrying. Nor does the state prohibit recognition of marriages between such couples from other states. The attorney general fails to demonstrate any rational, much less compelling, link between its prohibition and non-recognition of same-sex marriage and its goal of having more children raised in the biological family structure the state wishes to promote. There has been no evidence presented that these marriage laws have any effect on the choices of couples to have or raise children, whether they are same-sex couples or opposite-sex couples. In sum, the laws in question are an irrational way of promoting biological relationships in Alabama.…

If anything, Alabama's prohibition of same-sex marriage detracts from its goal of promoting optimal environments for children. Those children currently being raised by same-sex parents in Alabama are just as worthy of protection and recognition by the State as are the children being raised by opposite-sex parents. Yet Alabama's Sanctity laws harms the children of same-sex couples for the same reasons that the [U.S.] Supreme Court found that the Defense of Marriage Act harmed the children of same-sex couples. Such a law "humiliates … thousands of children now being raised by same-sex couples. The law in question makes it even more difficult for the children to understand the integrity and closeness of their own family and its concord with other families in their community and in their daily lives." [Windsor, 133 S. Ct. at 2694] Alabama's prohibition and non-recognition of same-sex marriage "also brings financial harm to children of same-sex couples," [id at 2695] because it denies the families of these children a panoply of benefits that the State and the federal government offer to families who are legally wed. Additionally, these laws further injures those children of all couples who are themselves gay or lesbian, and who will grow up knowing that Alabama does not believe they are as capable of creating a family as their heterosexual friends.

For all of these reasons, the court finds that Alabama's marriage laws violate the Due Process Clause and Equal Protection Clause of the Fourteenth Amendment to the United States Constitution.

UNDERSTAND, ANALYZE, & EVALUATE

1. How does Judge Granade's ruling reflect—or not reflect—changing popular attitudes toward gay men and lesbians?
2. How is the definition of a "family" being redefined?
3. In what ways do the actions of Judge Roy Moore and the Alabama Supreme Court evoke tensions between the state and civil rights protesters of the 1950s and 1960s? Or are the civil rights of black Americans and gay and lesbian Americans two very different issues?
4. In his dissenting opinion in *Obergefell v. Hodges,* Supreme Court Justice John Roberts said, "The fundamental right to marry does not include a right to make a state change its definition of marriage." What does the decision in *Searcy v. Strange* have to say about the state's definition of marriage?

Source: *Searcy v. Strange*, Civil Action No. 14-0208-CG-N (S.D. Ala. Jan. 25, 2015), https://scholar.google.com/scholar_case?case=14084561318965877067&hl=en&as_sdt=6&as_vis=1&oi=scholarr (accessed March 19, 2015).

end of the twentieth century, primarily among younger generations of Americans. Still, there was no national consensus about the legality of same-sex marriage, and many southern and midwestern states had laws on the books preventing same-sex marriage or were engaged in heated legal battles over it. For example, in January 2015 in Alabama, a federal judge ruled in favor of same-sex marriage. (See "Consider the Source: Same-Sex Marriage, 2015.") But less than two months later, Alabama's Supreme Court, by a vote of 7 to 1, forbade county officials from issuing a marriage license to any same-sex couple. Ultimately the decision by the U.S. Supreme Court broke the legal stalement and compelled Alabama (and all states with gay marriage bans) to issue the licenses.

THE GLOBAL ENVIRONMENTAL MOVEMENT

An international movement for well over a century, environmentalism has grown rapidly throughout the world in the late twentieth and early twenty-first centuries. What began as a series of localized efforts to preserve wilderness sites and to clean up air and water has evolved into a broad effort to deal with concerns that affect, and threaten, the entire globe.

During the 1960s, 1970s, and 1980s, while long-standing American environmental associations such as the Wilderness Society, the Sierra Club, and the National Audubon Society were being rejuvenated, organizations elsewhere in the world sought to create an international environmental movement. The World Wildlife Fund (WWF), created in Switzerland in 1961, eventually attracted more than 5 million supporters in over 150 countries and now claims to be the world's largest independent conservation organization. Greenpeace was founded in Canada in 1971 to oppose U.S. nuclear testing off the coast of Alaska. It, too, has grown into an international organization, with 2.8 million financial supporters worldwide and a presence in forty nations.

Nongovernmental organizations (NGOs) such as Greenpeace and WWF were not the only institutions to recognize environmental concerns. In June 1972, the United Nations (UN) held its first Conference on the Human Environment in Stockholm, Sweden. Representatives of 113 countries attended the conference to discuss issues of global environmental importance—including the role of chlorofluorocarbons (CFCs), a chemical compound used in refrigerants and aerosol sprays, in depleting the ozone layer. After the conference, the UN created the United Nations Environment Programme (UNEP) to help coordinate international efforts for environmentalism and encourage sustainable development in poorer nations around the world.

The world's first "Green" parties—political parties explicitly devoted to environmental concerns (and often to other issues of social justice)—appeared in 1972, beginning in New Zealand (the Values Party) and Tasmania (the United Tasmania Group). Since then, Green parties have proliferated throughout the world, including in the United States. The most powerful Green party to date has been *Die Grünen* in Germany, founded in 1980. *Die Grünen* allied with the Social Democratic Party in a governing coalition from 1998, and in 2000, this coalition successfully passed the Nuclear Exit Law, which set a timetable of twenty years for Germany's eventual abandonment of nuclear power and a switch to renewable energy.

Large-scale ecological catastrophes have often helped galvanize the global environmental movement. Among the more significant of these events was the Bhopal disaster of 1984, in which a gas leak at a Union Carbide pesticide plant in Bhopal, India, resulted in the deaths of between 3,000 and 15,000 people. Two years later, a nuclear reactor accident in the Soviet city of Chernobyl, in Ukraine, caused fifty-six direct deaths, with predictions of many thousands more deaths to follow as a result of exposure. The area around Chernobyl itself is expected to be partially contaminated for 24,000 years, the radioactive half-life of plutonium-239. A less catastrophic nuclear accident at Three Mile Island, Pennsylvania, in 1979 heightened antinuclear sentiment in the United

States. In 1989, the oil tanker *Exxon Valdez* ran aground on Bligh Reef in Prince William Sound, Alaska, and spilled approximately 10.9 million gallons of crude oil. Eventually covering thousands of square miles of ocean water (and 1,300 miles of Alaska shoreline) in oil, the spill killed hundreds of thousands of animals instantly and devastated the fragile ecosystem of the sound. The 2010 explosion of the Deepwater Horizon well about 50 miles southeast of the Mississippi Delta caused the largest marine oil spill in history.

In developed, industrialized nations, environmental advocacy has largely focused on energy policy, conservation, clean technologies, and changing individual and social attitudes about consumption (as in the recycling movement). The growth of environmentalism is often linked to issues of human and democratic rights and freedom from First World exploitation. For example, the Green Belt Movement in Kenya, begun in 1977 by Wangari Maathai, encouraged Kenyan women to plant over 30 million trees across the nation to address the challenges of deforestation, soil erosion, and lack of water. The Green Belt Movement became an important human rights and women's rights organization, focused on reducing poverty and promoting peaceful democratic change through environmental conservation and protection. Maathai won the 2004 Nobel Peace Prize for her achievements.

Over the past two decades, the environmental movement has grown even more global in scope, with multilateral environmental treaties and worldwide summits becoming the principal strategies of advocates. In 1997, an international effort to reduce global warming by mandating the lowering of greenhouse gas emissions culminated in the Kyoto Protocol (which the United States did not join). While the George W. Bush administration rejected most efforts to limit carbon emissions, other leading Americans helped bring the issue of global warming to wide attention both in the United States and around the world. Perhaps most notable has been former vice president Al Gore, whose 2006 film *An Inconvenient Truth* may have done more to raise awareness of the threat of global warming than any other recent event—both in the United States and in many other nations. As a result of his efforts, Gore won the 2007 Nobel Peace Prize—an honor he shared with others, appropriately, given the global character of the movement he has championed. His cowinner was the Intergovernmental Panel on Climate Change, launched in Switzerland in 1988 and affiliated with the United Nations. •

UNDERSTAND, ANALYZE, & EVALUATE

1. Why are environmental movements in developing nations often linked to issues of human rights and protection from exploitation by developed nations? How do developed nations threaten the environment of developing nations?
2. What is the current status of UN initiatives to reduce carbon omissions, such as the Kyoto Protocol?

THE CONTEMPORARY ENVIRONMENTAL MOVEMENT

The environmental movement in the United States continued to expand in the decades after the 1980s. It drew inspiration from the older international environmental movement, which organized in the 1960s and steadily grew in political power. (See "America in the World: The Global Environmental Movement.") After the first Earth Day, domestic environmental issues gained increasing attention and support. Although the federal government displayed only intermittent interest in the subject, environmentalists won a series of significant battles, mostly at the local level. They blocked the construction of roads, airports, and other projects that they claimed would be ecologically dangerous, taking advantage of new legislation protecting endangered species and environmentally fragile regions.

In the late 1980s, the environmental movement began to mobilize around a new and ominous challenge—"global warming." It produced a steady rise in the earth's temperature as a result of emissions from the burning of fossil fuels (most notably coal and oil). Although considerable controversy has continued for years over the pace, and even the reality, of global warming, by the early twenty-first century a growing consensus began to emerge—in part as a result of the leadership of significant public figures, such as former vice president Al Gore, who won a Nobel Peace Prize in 2007 for his efforts to draw attention to the problem. In 1997, representatives of the major industrial nations met in Kyoto, Japan, and agreed to a broad treaty establishing steps toward reducing carbon emissions and thus slowing or reversing global warming. The Clinton administration formally signed the Kyoto Protocol, but nothing came of it. Reading the hand-

Kyoto Protocol   writing on the wall, Clinton never even submitted it for ratification because the Senate had earlier passed the Byrd-Hagel Resolution by a vote of 95 to 0 that rejected the treaty's key tenets. President George W. Bush, while proclaiming grave concern over climate concern, refused to support the Kyoto Protocol because it excluded developing countries like China and India. Since 2009, President Obama has met with mixed success on climate change issues. While major international agreements have not materialized during his presidency, the president did champion and sign legislation raising fuel efficiency in passenger cars and trucks in 2012 and has since directed the Environmental Protection Agency to regulate coal ash, a major CO_2 emitter primarily used in creating electricity, to intense political scrutiny.

DEEPWATER HORIZON DISASTER   In 2010, a BP (British Petroleum) offshore well, Deepwater Horizon, suffered a crippling explosion that sent approximately 5 million barrels of oil into the Gulf of Mexico. This photograph shows the attempt to cap the well. The oil leaked for months, destroying local fisheries, and the effects to the environment from the oil and the dispersants used to clean it up are still unknown. The event galvanized the global environmental movement. (© Julie Dermansky/Corbis)

AMERICA IN THE WORLD

The celebration of the beginning of a new millennium on January 1, 2000, was an important moment not just because of the change in the calendar. It was notable above all as a global event—a shared and for the most part joyous experience that united the world in its exuberance. But if the millennium celebrations suggested the bright promise of an interconnected world, other events at the dawn of the new century suggested its dark perils. Indeed, the United States' increasing role as an economic and military superpower triggered fears among many Americans about a foreign policy that was too aggressive and trade initiatives that took advantage of low-wage workers in other countries and unfairly benefited large international businesses. The rise of mass protests over America's global economic policies and terrorism painfully brought home the dangers of living in the twenty-first century.

OPPOSING THE "NEW WORLD ORDER"

In the United States and other industrial nations, opposition to globalization—or to what President George H. W. Bush once called the "new world order"—took several forms. To many Americans on both the political left and right, the nation's increasingly interventionist foreign policy was deeply troubling. Critics on the left charged that the United States was using military action to advance its economic interests—in the 1991 Gulf War and, above all, in the Iraq War that began in 2003. Critics on the right criticized humanitarian interventions in Somalia in 1993 and the Balkans in the late 1990s as too costly and risky. Others complained that the United States was ceding its sovereignty to international organizations, such as United Nations–led peacekeeping missions.

Labor unions insisted that the rapid expansion of free-trade agreements led to the export of jobs from advanced nations to less developed ones. Other groups attacked working conditions in new manufacturing countries on humanitarian grounds, arguing that the global economy was creating new classes of "slave laborers" working in conditions that few Western nations would tolerate. Environmentalists argued that globalization, in exporting industry to low-wage countries, also exported industrial pollution and toxic waste into nations that had no effective laws to control them, and contributed significantly to global warming. And still others opposed global economic arrangements on the grounds that they enriched and empowered large multinational corporations and threatened the freedom and autonomy of individuals and communities.

Varied opponents of globalization found a common enemy in the multinational institutions that policed and advanced the global economy. Among them were the World Trade Organization, which monitored the enforcement of the General Agreement on Tariffs and Trade (GATT) treaties of the 1990s; the International Monetary Fund (IMF), which controlled international credit and exchange rates; and the World Bank, which made money available for development projects in many countries. In November 1999, when leaders of leading industrial nations gathered for their annual meeting in Seattle, Washington, tens of thousands protested—most of them peacefully. But some of them clashed with police, smashed store windows, and all but paralyzed the city. A few months later, a smaller but still substantial demonstration disrupted meetings of the IMF and the World Bank in Washington, D.C. And in July 2001, at a meeting of the same leaders in Genoa, Italy, an estimated 50,000 demonstrators clashed violently with police in a melee that left one protester dead and several hundred injured. The participants in the meeting responded to the demonstrations by pledging $1.2 billion to fight the AIDS epidemic in developing countries, and by deciding to hold future meetings in remote locations far from major cities.

PROTESTING THE WTO IN SEATTLE, 1999 Thousands of demonstrators rallied at the site of the 1999 World Trade Organization meeting to protest the WTO's role in the globalization of the economy and, they believed, the exploitation of working people. They succeeded in postponing the opening of the conference. In this photograph, a protester faces Seattle police in a cloud of tear gas, waiting to be arrested. (© Andy Clark/Reuters/Corbis)

Defending Orthodoxy

Outside the industrialized West, the impact of globalization sparked other controversies. Many citizens of nonindustrialized nations resented the way the world economy had left them in poverty. In their view, the developed world exploited and oppressed them. In some parts of the nonindustrialized world—particularly in some of the Islamic nations of the Middle East—the increasing reach of globalization created additional grievances, rooted not just in economics but also in religion and culture.

The Iranian Revolution of 1979, in which orthodox Muslims ousted a despotic government, was one of the first large and visible manifestations of a phenomenon that eventually reached across much of the Islamic world. It threatened the stability of the globe. Militants used isolated incidents of violence and mayhem, designed to disrupt societies and governments and to create fear among their peoples. Such tactics are known to the world as terrorism.

The Rise of Terrorism

The term **terrorism** was used first during the French Revolution in the 1790s to describe the actions of radical Jacobins against the French government. It continued to be used intermittently throughout the nineteenth and early twentieth centuries to describe the use of violence as a form of intimidation against peoples and governments. But the widespread understanding of terrorism as an important fact of modern life is largely a product of the end of the twentieth century and the beginning of the twenty-first.

Acts of what came to be called terrorism have occurred in many parts of the world. Irish revolutionaries engaged in terrorism regularly against the English through much of the twentieth century. Jews used it in Palestine against the British before the creation of Israel, and Palestinians have used it frequently against Jews in Israel—particularly in the past several decades. Revolutionary groups in Italy, Germany, Japan, and France have engaged in terrorist acts intermittently over the past several decades.

The United States, too, has experienced terrorism for many years, much of it against American targets abroad—including the bombing of the Marine barracks in Beirut in 1983; the explosion that brought down an American airliner over Lockerbie, Scotland, in 1988; the bombing of American embassies in 1998; and the assault on the U.S. naval vessel *Cole* in 2000. Terrorist incidents were relatively rare, *Terrorist Incidents before 9/11* but not unknown, within the United States itself prior to September 11, 2001. Militants on the American left performed various acts of terror in the 1960s and early 1970s. In February 1993, a bomb exploded in the parking garage of the World Trade Center in New York, killing six people and causing serious, but not irreparable, structural damage to the towers. Several men connected with militant Islamic organizations were convicted of the crime. In April 1995, a van containing explosives blew up in front of a federal building in Oklahoma City, killing 168 people. Timothy McVeigh, a former Army soldier who had become part of a militant antigovernment movement of the American right, was convicted of the crime and eventually executed in 2001.

SEPTEMBER 11, 2001 A New York City symbol stands against a sky filled with the thick smoke from the destruction of another American symbol, New York City's World Trade Center towers, a few hours after terrorists crashed two planes into them. (© Daniel Hulshizer/AP Images)

Most Americans, however, considered terrorism a problem mainly confined to other nations. One of the many results of the terrible events of September 11, 2001, was to jolt the American people out of their complacency and alert them to the presence of continuing danger. Predictably, that awareness increased dramatically in the years following September 11. New security measures changed the way in which Americans traveled. New government regulations altered immigration policies and affected the character of international banking. Warnings of possible new terrorist attacks created widespread tension and uneasiness.

THE WAR ON TERROR

In the aftermath of September 11, 2001, the United States government launched what President Bush called a "war on terror." The attacks on the World Trade Center and the Pentagon, government intelligence indicated, had been planned and orchestrated by Middle Eastern agents of a powerful terrorist network known as Al Qaeda. Its leader, Osama bin Laden—until *Osama bin Laden and Al Qaeda* 2001 little known outside the Arab world—quickly became one of the most notorious figures in the world. The militant Taliban government of Afghanistan had sheltered and supported Al Qaeda previously, and most reports placed bin Laden in continued care. In 2001, NATO, led by the United States, began a sustained campaign of bombing against the regime and sent in ground troops. Afghanistan's Taliban regime quickly collapsed, and its leaders—along with the Al Qaeda fighters allied with them—fled the capital, Kabul. American and anti-Taliban Afghan troops pursued them into the mountains but failed to capture bin Laden and the other leaders of his organization.

American forces in Afghanistan rounded up several hundred people with suspected connections to the Taliban and Al Qaeda and moved these prisoners (and eventually *Guantánamo* others) to a facility at the American military base in Guantánamo, Cuba. They were among the first suspected terrorists to be handled under new standards established by the federal government in dealing with terrorism after September 11, 2001. They were held for months, and in some cases years, without access to lawyers, without facing formal charges, and were subjected to intensive interrogation, and at times torture. Many critics denounced the dangers to basic civil liberties that they believed the war on terror had created. Others argued that the new tactics were necessary to protect Americans. President Obama, in his first month in the White House, pledged to close the prison at Guantánamo. But he soon found that the promise was difficult to keep.

THE IRAQ WAR

In his State of the Union address to Congress in January 2002, President Bush spoke of an "axis of evil," which included the nations of Iraq, Iran, and North Korea—all countries with anti-American regimes that either possessed or were thought to be trying to acquire nuclear weapons. Although Bush did not say so at the time, many people around the world interpreted these words to mean that the United States would soon try to topple the government of Saddam Hussein in Iraq.

For over a year, the Bush administration slowly built a public case for invading Iraq. Much of that case rested on two claims. One was that Iraq was supporting terrorist groups that were hostile to the United States. The other, and eventually the more important, was that Iraq either had or was developing what came to be known as "weapons of mass *Weapons of Mass Destruction* destruction," which included nuclear weapons and agents of chemical and biological warfare. Less central to these arguments, at least in the United

States, was the charge that the Hussein government was responsible for major violations of human rights. Except for the last, none of these claims turned out to be accurate.

In March 2003, American troops, with support from Great Britain and several other countries and partial authorization from the United Nations, invaded Iraq and quickly toppled the Hussein regime. Hussein himself went into hiding but was eventually captured in December 2003. He was executed in Iraq on December 30, 2006. In May 2003, shortly after the American capture of Baghdad, President Bush made a dramatic appearance on an aircraft carrier off the coast of California, where he declared victory in the Battle of Iraq, praised the military and allies in the war effort, and warned, weakly, of the "difficult work to do in Iraq" while standing in front of a large sign reading "Mission Accomplished."

In the following months, however, events in Iraq suggested that the mission had only just begun. Of the more than 4,800 American soldiers killed in Iraq as of 2014, over 4,000 of them died after the "mission accomplished" speech. And despite significant efforts by the United States and its allies to hand over authority to an Iraqi government and to restore order to the country, insurgents continued to disrupt the recovery with persistent attacks and terrorist actions throughout the fragile nation.

Support for the war in the United States steadily declined in the years after the first claim of victory. The failure to find evidence of the weapons of mass destruction, whose existence the president had claimed, was a hammer blow to the war's credibility. Another blow came from reports of the torture and humiliation of Iraqi prisoners by American soldiers   *Abu Ghraib* at the Abu Ghraib prison in Baghdad and other sites in Iraq and around the world.

The invasion of Iraq was the most visible evidence of a basic change in the structure of American foreign policy under the presidency of George W. Bush. Ever since the late 1940s, the containment policy had become the cornerstone of America's role in the world. The United States had worked to maintain stability in the world by containing, but not often directly threatening or attacking, its adversaries. Even after the Cold War ended, the United States continued to demonstrate a level of constraint, despite its now unchallenged military preeminence. In the administrations of George H. W. Bush and Bill Clinton, for example, American leaders worked closely with the United Nations and NATO to achieve U.S. international goals and resisted taking unilateral military action.

There had always been those who criticized these constraints. They believed that America should do more than maintain stability and should move actively to topple undemocratic regimes and destroy potential enemies of the United States. In the administration of George W. Bush, these critics took control of American foreign policy and began to reshape it. The legacy of containment was largely repudiated. Instead, the public   *Bush's Foreign Policy Doctrine* stance of the American government was that the United States had the right and the responsibility to fight tyranny and spread freedom throughout the world—not just by exhortation and example but also, when necessary, by military force. In Latvia in May 2005, President Bush spoke of the decision at the end of World War II not to challenge Soviet domination of Eastern Europe. That decision had rested on the belief that such a challenge would lead the United States into another war. The controversial agreement negotiated at Yalta in 1945 by Roosevelt, Churchill, and Stalin, which failed to end the Soviet occupation of Poland and other Eastern European nations, was, the president said, part of an "unjust tradition" by which powerful governments sacrificed the interests of small nations. "This attempt to sacrifice freedom for the sake of stability," the president continued, "left a continent divided and unstable." The lesson, Bush suggested, was that the United States and other great powers should value stability less and freedom more, and should be willing to take greater risks in the world to end tyranny and oppression.

AMERICA AFTER THE IRAQ WAR

The end of the American combat role in Iraq was already under way in the last year of the Bush administration. Obama brought it to an end in 2010. At the same time, he com-
Escalation in Afghanistan   mitted significant additional troops to the war in Afghanistan, where Americans had been fighting since 2001. Obama escalated the Afghan war in 2011. For almost ten years, a major goal of American foreign policy was to find Osama bin Laden, the head of Al Qaeda, the organization behind the destruction of 9/11. In May 2011, Navy Seals found and killed bin Laden. Shortly afterward, leaders from countries of the North Atlantic Treaty Organization drafted a plan for the withdrawal of international forces from Afghanistan and facilitated peace talks between the Afghan government and the Taliban. Obama ordered nearly all American troops to leave the country and cease combat operations by the close of 2014, in effect ending American involvement in the conflict.

Despite the end of the Iraq War and the killing of bin Laden, conflict in the Middle East continued to dominate American foreign policy. Obama had appointed Hillary Clinton as his
Hillary Clinton as Secretary of State   secretary of state, and together they tried to create peace between Israel and Palestine—an effort that made little or no progress. Elsewhere they sought to improve relationships damaged by the Iraq War and to build new international trade opportunities as well. But increasing turmoil in the Middle East, and the growing power of China, created new challenges. The United States intervened in a civil war in Libya and helped end the regime of the long-standing leader Muammar Qadaffi. And in 2012, Obama and Clinton sought to stop Iran from creating nuclear weapons—an effort that remained unfinished.

DRONES Unmanned combat air vehicles (UCAVs), also known as drones, have become weapons of choice during many U.S. military engagements throughout the world. Pilots operate these vehicles from remote sites, a practice that was unimaginable when the international laws of war were last drafted in 1949. In calling for an examination of this practice, critics have cited the unintended killing of civilians in Pakistan and the targeting of three American citizens by U.S. drones in Yemen, as well as the potential for foreign governments to develop drones and follow the American precedent. (© Kirsty Wigglesworth/AP Images)

Syria, a country locked in violent civil war since 2011, experienced a new and terrifying level of bloodshed. Opponents of the Ba'ath government sought the *Syrian Civil War* ouster of President Bashar al-Assad and his repressive regime. Assad unleashed the army in response, killing an estimated 120,000 of his own people by September 2013. The displacement of hundreds of thousands of Syrians into neighboring countries threatened to further destabilize the region. Assad's use of chemical weapons triggered a strong condemnation by the United States and its European allies. Working with Russia, a traditional ally of the Assad regime, the United States and Europe brokered a deal to remove the stockpile of chemical weapons from the country. Obama, aware of his nation's unwillingness to become involved in another ground war, resisted calls for sending troops to dislodge Assad. The violent struggle continued in 2015 with no sign of abatement in sight.

A key element in the Syrian conflict has been the rise of rebel groups committed not only to overthrowing the Assad government but also violently resisting Western backers of the ruling regime and attacking Western influence over traditional Islamic society. Most notably, ISIS (the Islamic State of Iraq and Syria), a powerful and deadly opposition force, has *ISIS* recently embarked on campaigns of terror against Western nations, including the public execution of American and British citizens uploaded to social media websites around the world. In 2015, ISIS serves as a symbol of the persistent instability of the region and a reminder of the continuing threat of terrorism.

Turmoil in the Middle East and the threat of terrorism are not the only focal points of current American foreign policy. In a bold move that reignited memories of the Cold War, Russia, under the leadership of President Vladimir Putin, annexed the *Vladimir Putin* Ukrainian territory of Crimea in March 2014. Putin inserted military troops to support Russian separatists and quickly established a firm grip over the local government and untrammeled access to the city and Bay of Sevastopal, home to Russia's Black Sea fleet. Ignoring a flurry of international peace initiatives and sanctions imposed by the United States, its allies, and the United Nations, Putin tightened his hold over Crimea and even implemented sanctions of his own: he eliminated most agricultural imports from countries opposing him. The relationship between Russia and America remains tense, with no resolution satisfactory to both countries over the issue of Crimea in sight. It reminds us that major conflicts between the United States and countries in central and eastern Europe did not end with the fall of the Berlin Wall or collapse of the Soviet Union but persist in the form of nations like Russia intent on aggressively expanding its sphere of international influence.

CONCLUSION

The United States in the first decade of the twenty-first century was a nation beset with many problems and anxieties. U.S. foreign policy after the attacks of September 11, 2001, had not only divided the American people but had also deeply alienated much of the world. Crises in the Middle East made it impossible to ignore the persistent threat of terrorism and extremism while conflict with Russia brought back Cold War fears of instability in eastern and central Europe. The American economy was struggling as early as 2007 and, in the fall of 2008, experienced the worst economic crisis since the Great Depression. By 2014 the economy had improved but some polls indicated a continuing sense of uncertainty about the future among many Americans. Gridlock continued at the federal level, making it difficult to achieve sweeping reform in several key areas. Political divisions—not only among politicians, but also among voters—were as great in 2015 as they had been in many years.

The United States remains the wealthiest and most powerful nation in the world, and it continues to cherish great ideals and great hopes. Moving forward into an uncertain future, Americans are burdened with serious problems and great challenges, but they are also armed with extraordinary resilience and energy that has allowed the nation—through its long and turbulent history—to endure, to flourish, and to imagine and strive for a better future.

KEY TERMS/PEOPLE/PLACES/EVENTS

Affordable Care Act 800
Afghan war 820
AIDS 808
Al Qaeda 818
Barack Obama 796
Defense of Marriage Act
  (DOMA) 809
George W. Bush 795

Great Recession
  of 2008 797
Guantánamo 818
Hillary Rodham
  Clinton 796
Human Genome
  Project 804
Iraq War 795

new world order 815
9/11 attacks 817
Occupy Wall Street
  (OWS) 801
Osama bin Laden 818
Tea Party 800
terrorism 816
Vladimir Putin 821

RECALL AND REFLECT

1. How has partisanship affected how presidents governed in the last twenty-five years?
2. How has America's relationship to the rest of the world changed as a result of the war on terror and in particular the Iraq War?
3. How did the digital revolution affect the American economy?
4. What were the key causes of the Great Recession?

APPENDIX

The Declaration of Independence

The Constitution of the United States

Presidential Elections

THE DECLARATION OF INDEPENDENCE

In Congress, July 4, 1776,

THE UNANIMOUS DECLARATION OF THE THIRTEEN UNITED STATES OF AMERICA

When, in the course of human events, it becomes necessary for one people to dissolve the political bands which have connected them with another, and to assume, among the powers of the earth, the separate and equal station to which the laws of nature and of nature's God entitle them, a decent respect to the opinions of mankind requires that they should declare the causes which impel them to the separation.

We hold these truths to be self-evident, that all men are created equal; that they are endowed by their Creator with certain unalienable rights; that among these, are life, liberty, and the pursuit of happiness. That, to secure these rights, governments are instituted among men, deriving their just powers from the consent of the governed; that, whenever any form of government becomes destructive of these ends, it is the right of the people to alter or to abolish it, and to institute a new government, laying its foundation on such principles, and organizing its powers in such form, as to them shall seem most likely to effect their safety and happiness. Prudence, indeed, will dictate that governments long established, should not be changed for light and transient causes; and, accordingly, all experience hath shown, that mankind are more disposed to suffer, while evils are sufferable, than to right themselves by abolishing the forms to which they are accustomed. But, when a long train of abuses and usurpations, pursuing invariably the same object, evinces a design to reduce them under absolute despotism, it is their right, it is their duty, to throw off such government and to provide new guards for their future security. Such has been the patient sufferance of these colonies, and such is now the necessity which constrains them to alter their former systems of government. The history of the present King of Great Britain is a history of repeated injuries and usurpations, all having, in direct object, the establishment of an absolute tyranny over these States. To prove this, let facts be submitted to a candid world:

He has refused his assent to laws the most wholesome and necessary for the public good.

He has forbidden his governors to pass laws of immediate and pressing importance, unless suspended in their operation till his assent should be obtained; and, when so suspended, he has utterly neglected to attend to them.

He has refused to pass other laws for the accommodation of large districts of people, unless those people would relinquish the right of representation in the legislature; a right inestimable to them, and formidable to tyrants only.

He has called together legislative bodies at places unusual, uncomfortable, and distant from the depository of their public records, for the sole purpose of fatiguing them into compliance with his measures.

He has dissolved representative houses repeatedly for opposing, with manly firmness, his invasions on the rights of the people.

He has refused, for a long time after such dissolutions, to cause others to be elected; whereby the legislative powers, incapable of annihilation, have returned to the people at large for their exercise; the state remaining, in the meantime, exposed to all the danger of invasion from without, and compulsions within.

He has endeavored to prevent the population of these States; for that purpose, obstructing the laws for naturalization of foreigners, refusing to pass others to encourage their migration hither, and raising the conditions of new appropriations of lands.

He has obstructed the administration of justice, by refusing his assent to laws for establishing judiciary powers.

He has made judges dependent on his will alone, for the tenure of their offices, and the amount and payment of their salaries.

He has erected a multitude of new offices, and sent hither swarms of officers to harass our people, and eat out their substance.

He has kept among us, in time of peace, standing armies, without the consent of our legislatures.

He has affected to render the military independent of, and superior to, the civil power.

He has combined, with others, to subject us to a jurisdiction foreign to our Constitution, and unacknowledged by our laws; giving his assent to their acts of pretended legislation:

For quartering large bodies of armed troops among us:

For protecting them by a mock trial, from punishment, for any murders which they should commit on the inhabitants of these States:

For cutting off our trade with all parts of the world:

For imposing taxes on us without our consent:

For depriving us, in many cases, of the benefit of trial by jury:

For transporting us beyond seas to be tried for pretended offences:

For abolishing the free system of English laws in a neighboring province, establishing therein an arbitrary government, and enlarging its boundaries, so as to render it at once an example and fit instrument for introducing the same absolute rule into these colonies:

For taking away our charters, abolishing our most valuable laws, and altering, fundamentally, the powers of our governments:

For suspending our own legislatures, and declaring themselves invested with power to legislate for us in all cases whatsoever.

He has abdicated government here, by declaring us out of his protection, and waging war against us.

He has plundered our seas, ravaged our coasts, burnt our towns, and destroyed the lives of our people.

He is, at this time, transporting large armies of foreign mercenaries to complete the works of death, desolation, and tyranny, already begun, with circumstances of cruelty and perfidy scarcely paralleled in the most barbarous ages, and totally unworthy the head of a civilized nation.

He has constrained our fellow citizens, taken captive on the high seas, to bear arms against their country, to become the executioners of their friends, and brethren, or to fall themselves by their hands.

He has excited domestic insurrections amongst us, and has endeavored to bring on the inhabitants of our frontiers, the merciless Indian savages, whose known rule of warfare is an undistinguished destruction of all ages, sexes, and conditions.

In every stage of these oppressions, we have petitioned for redress, in the most humble terms; our repeated petitions have been answered only by repeated injury. A prince, whose character is thus marked by every act which may define a tyrant, is unfit to be the ruler of a free people.

Nor have we been wanting in attention to our British brethren. We have warned them, from time to time, of attempts made by their legislature to extend an unwarrantable jurisdiction over us. We have reminded them of the circumstances of our emigration and settlement here. We have appealed to their native justice and magnanimity, and we have conjured them, by the ties of our common kindred, to disavow these usurpations, which would inevitably interrupt our connections and correspondence. They, too, have been deaf to the voice of justice and consanguinity. We must, therefore, acquiesce in the necessity which denounces our separation, and hold them as we hold the rest of mankind, enemies in war, in peace, friends.

We, therefore, the representatives of the United States of America, in general Congress assembled, appealing to the Supreme Judge of the world for the rectitude of our intentions, do, in the name, and by the authority of the good people of these colonies, solemnly publish and declare, that these united colonies are, and of right ought to be, free and independent states: that they are absolved from all allegiance to the British Crown, and that all political connection between them and the state of Great Britain is, and ought to be, totally dissolved; and that, as free and independent states, they have full power to levy war, conclude peace, contract alliances, establish commerce, and to do all other acts and things which independent states may of right do. And, for the support of this declaration, with a firm reliance on the protection of Divine Providence, we mutually pledge to each other our lives, our fortunes, and our sacred honor.

The foregoing Declaration was, by order of Congress, engrossed, and signed by the following members:

John Hancock

NEW HAMPSHIRE
Josiah Bartlett
William Whipple
Matthew Thornton

CONNECTICUT
Roger Sherman
Samuel Huntington
William Williams
Oliver Wolcott

NEW YORK
William Floyd
Philip Livingston
Francis Lewis
Lewis Morris

NEW JERSEY
Richard Stockton
John Witherspoon
Francis Hopkinson
John Hart
Abraham Clark

MASSACHUSETTS BAY
Samuel Adams
John Adams
Robert Treat Paine
Elbridge Gerry

PENNSYLVANIA
Robert Morris
Benjamin Rush
Benjamin Franklin
John Morton
George Clymer
James Smith
George Taylor
James Wilson
George Ross

DELAWARE
Caesar Rodney
George Read
Thomas M'Kean

MARYLAND
Samuel Chase
William Paca
Thomas Stone
Charles Carroll, of
  Carrollton

RHODE ISLAND
Stephen Hopkins
William Ellery

VIRGINIA
George Wythe
Richard Henry Lee
Thomas Jefferson
Benjamin Harrison
Thomas Nelson Jr.
Francis Lightfoot Lee
Carter Braxton

NORTH CAROLINA
William Hooper
Joseph Hewes
John Penn

SOUTH CAROLINA
Edward Rutledge
Thomas Heyward Jr.
Thomas Lynch Jr.
Arthur Middleton

GEORGIA
Button Gwinnett
Lyman Hall
George Walton

Resolved, That copies of the Declaration be sent to the several assemblies, conventions, and committees, or councils of safety, and to the several commanding officers of the continental troops; that it be proclaimed in each of the United States, at the head of the army.

THE CONSTITUTION OF THE UNITED STATES[1]

We the People of the United States, in Order to form a more perfect Union, establish Justice, insure domestic Tranquility, provide for the common defence, promote the general Welfare, and secure the Blessings of Liberty to ourselves and our Posterity, do ordain and establish this CONSTITUTION for the United States of America.

Article I

Section 1.
All legislative Powers herein granted shall be vested in a Congress of the United States, which shall consist of a Senate and House of Representatives.

Section 2.
The House of Representatives shall be composed of Members chosen every second Year by the People of the several States, and the Electors in each State shall have the Qualifications requisite for Electors of the most numerous Branch of the State Legislature.

No Person shall be a Representative who shall not have attained to the Age of twenty-five Years, and been seven Years a Citizen of the United States, and who shall not, when elected, be an Inhabitant of that State in which he shall be chosen.

[Representatives and direct Taxes[2] shall be apportioned among the several States which may be included within this Union, according to their respective Numbers, which shall be determined by adding to the whole Number of free Persons, including those bound to Service for a Term of Years, and excluding Indians not taxed, three fifths of all other Persons.][3] The actual Enumeration shall be made within three Years after the first Meeting of the Congress of the United States, and within every subsequent Term of ten Years, in such Manner as they shall by Law direct. The Number of Representatives shall not exceed one for every thirty Thousand, but each State shall have at Least one Representative; and until such enumeration shall be made, the State of New Hampshire shall be entitled to chuse three, Massachusetts eight, Rhode-Island and Providence Plantations one, Connecticut five, New York six, New Jersey four, Pennsylvania eight, Delaware one, Maryland six, Virginia ten, North Carolina five, South Carolina five, and Georgia three.

When vacancies happen in the Representation from any State, the Executive Authority thereof shall issue Writs of Election to fill such Vacancies.

The House of Representatives shall chuse their Speaker and other Officers; and shall have the sole Power of Impeachment.

Section 3.
The Senate of the United States shall be composed of two Senators from each State, chosen by the Legislature thereof, for six Years; and each Senator shall have one Vote.

Immediately after they shall be assembled in Consequence of the first Election, they shall be divided as equally as may be into three Classes. The Seats of the Senators of the first

1 This version, which follows the original Constitution in capitalization and spelling, was published by the United States Department of the Interior, Office of Education, in 1935.
2 Altered by the Sixteenth Amendment.
3 Negated by the Fourteenth Amendment.

Class shall be vacated at the Expiration of the second Year, of the second Class at the Expiration of the fourth Year, and of the third Class at the Expiration of the sixth Year, so that one-third may be chosen every second Year; and if Vacancies happen by Resignation, or otherwise, during the Recess of the Legislature of any State, the Executive thereof may make temporary Appointments until the next Meeting of the Legislature, which shall then fill such Vacancies.

No Person shall be a Senator who shall not have attained to the Age of thirty Years, and been nine Years a Citizen of the United States, and who shall not, when elected, be an Inhabitant of that State for which he shall be chosen.

The Vice President of the United States shall be President of the Senate, but shall have no vote, unless they be equally divided.

The Senate shall chuse their other Officers, and also a President pro tempore, in the absence of the Vice President, or when he shall exercise the Office of President of the United States.

The Senate shall have the sole Power to try all Impeachments. When sitting for that purpose they shall be on Oath or Affirmation. When the President of the United States is tried, the Chief Justice shall preside: And no person shall be convicted without the Concurrence of two thirds of the Members present.

Judgment in Cases of Impeachment shall not extend further than to removal from Office, and disqualification to hold and enjoy any Office of honor, Trust, or Profit under the United States: but the Party convicted shall nevertheless be liable and subject to Indictment, Trial, Judgment, and Punishment, according to Law.

Section 4.
The Times, Places and Manner of holding Elections for Senators and Representatives, shall be prescribed in each State by the Legislature thereof; but the Congress may at any time by Law make or alter such Regulations, except as to the Places of Chusing Senators.

The Congress shall assemble at least once in every Year, and such Meeting shall be on the first Monday in December, unless they shall by Law appoint a different Day.

Section 5.
Each House shall be the Judge of the Elections, Returns and Qualifications of its own Members, and a Majority of each shall constitute a Quorum to do Business; but a smaller number may adjourn from day to day, and may be authorized to compel the Attendance of absent Members, in such Manner, and under such Penalties, as each House may provide.

Each House may determine the Rules of its Proceedings, punish its Members for disorderly Behaviour, and, with the Concurrence of two thirds, expel a Member.

Each House shall keep a Journal of its Proceedings, and from time to time publish the same, excepting such Parts as may in their Judgment require Secrecy; and the Yeas and Nays of the Members of either House on any question shall, at the Desire of one fifth of those Present, be entered on the Journal.

Neither House, during the Session of Congress, shall, without the Consent of the other, adjourn for more than three days, nor to any other Place than that in which the two Houses shall be sitting.

Section 6.
The Senators and Representatives shall receive a Compensation for their Services, to be ascertained by Law, and paid out of the Treasury of the United States. They shall in all Cases, except Treason, Felony, and Breach of the Peace, be privileged from Arrest during

their Attendance at the Session of their respective Houses, and in going to and returning from the same; and for any Speech or Debate in either House, they shall not be questioned in any other Place.

No Senator or Representative shall, during the Time for which he was elected, be appointed to any civil Office under the Authority of the United States, which shall have been created, or the Emoluments whereof shall have been increased, during such time; and no Person holding any Office under the United States shall be a Member of either House during his continuance in Office.

Section 7.

All Bills for raising Revenue shall originate in the House of Representatives; but the Senate may propose or concur with Amendments as on other bills.

Every Bill which shall have passed the House of Representatives and the Senate, shall, before it become a Law, be presented to the President of the United States; If he approve he shall sign it, but if not he shall return it, with his Objections, to that House in which it shall have originated, who shall enter the Objections at large on their Journal, and proceed to reconsider it. If after such Reconsideration two thirds of that House shall agree to pass the bill, it shall be sent, together with the objections, to the other House, by which it shall likewise be reconsidered, and if approved by two thirds of that House, it shall become a Law. But in all such Cases the Votes of both Houses shall be determined by Yeas and Nays, and the Names of the Persons voting for and against the Bill shall be entered on the Journal of each House respectively. If any Bill shall not be returned by the President within ten Days (Sundays excepted) after it shall have been presented to him, the Same shall be a Law, in like Manner as if he had signed it, unless the Congress by their Adjournment prevent its Return, in which Case it shall not be a Law.

Every Order, Resolution, or Vote to which the Concurrence of the Senate and House of Representatives may be necessary (except on a question of Adjournment) shall be presented to the President of the United States; and before the Same shall take Effect, shall be approved by him, or being disapproved by him, shall be repassed by two thirds of the Senate and House of Representatives, according to the Rules and Limitations prescribed in the Case of a Bill.

Section 8.

The Congress shall have Power To lay and collect Taxes, Duties, Imposts and Excises, to pay the Debts and provide for the common Defence and general Welfare of the United States; but all Duties, Imposts and Excises shall be uniform throughout the United States;

To borrow money on the credit of the United States;

To regulate Commerce with foreign Nations, and among the several States, and with the Indian Tribes;

To establish an uniform rule of Naturalization, and uniform Laws on the subject of Bankruptcies throughout the United States;

To coin Money, regulate the Value thereof, and of foreign Coin, and fix the Standard of Weights and Measures;

To provide for the Punishment of counterfeiting the Securities and current Coin of the United States;

To establish Post Offices and post Roads;

To promote the Progress of Science and useful Arts, by securing for limited Times to Authors and Inventors the exclusive Right to their respective Writings and Discoveries;

To constitute Tribunals inferior to the Supreme Court;

To define and punish Piracies and Felonies committed on the high Seas, and Offenses against the Law of Nations;

To declare War, grant Letters of Marque and Reprisal, and make Rules concerning Captures on Land and Water;

To raise and support Armies, but no Appropriation of Money to that Use shall be for a longer Term than two Years;

To provide and maintain a Navy;

To make Rules for the Government and Regulation of the land and naval forces;

To provide for calling forth the Militia to execute the Laws of the Union, suppress Insurrections and repel Invasions;

To provide for organizing, arming, and disciplining the Militia, and for governing such Part of them as may be employed in the Service of the United States, reserving to the States respectively, the Appointment of the Officers, and the Authority of training the Militia according to the discipline prescribed by Congress;

To exercise exclusive Legislation in all Cases whatsoever, over such District (not exceeding ten Miles square) as may, by Cession of particular States, and the acceptance of Congress, become the Seat of the Government of the United States, and to exercise like Authority over all Places purchased by the Consent of the Legislature of the State in which the Same shall be, for the Erection of Forts, Magazines, Arsenals, Dock-yards, and other needful Buildings;—And

To make all Laws which shall be necessary and proper for carrying into Execution the foregoing Powers, and all other Powers vested by this Constitution in the Government of the United States, or in any Department or Officer thereof.

Section 9.

The Migration or Importation of such Persons as any of the States now existing shall think proper to admit, shall not be prohibited by the Congress prior to the Year one thousand eight hundred and eight, but a tax or duty may be imposed on such Importation, not exceeding ten dollars for each Person.

The privilege of the Writ of Habeas Corpus shall not be suspended, unless when in Cases of Rebellion or Invasion the public Safety may require it.

No bill of Attainder or ex post facto Law shall be passed.

No capitation, or other direct, Tax shall be laid unless in Proportion to the Census or Enumeration herein before directed to be taken.

No Tax or Duty shall be laid on Articles exported from any State.

No Preference shall be given by any Regulation of Commerce or Revenue to the Ports of one State over those of another: nor shall Vessels bound to, or from, one State, be obliged to enter, clear, or pay Duties in another.

No Money shall be drawn from the Treasury, but in Consequence of Appropriations made by Law; and a regular Statement and Account of the Receipts and Expenditures of all public Money shall be published from time to time.

No Title of Nobility shall be granted by the United States: And no Person holding any Office of Profit or Trust under them, shall, without the Consent of the Congress, accept of any present, Emolument, Office, or Title, of any kind whatever, from any King, Prince, or foreign State.

Section 10.

No State shall enter into any Treaty, Alliance, or Confederation; grant Letters of Marque and Reprisal; coin Money; emit Bills of Credit; make any Thing but gold and silver Coin a Tender in Payment of Debts; pass any Bill of Attainder, ex post facto Law, or Law impairing the Obligation of Contracts, or grant any Title of Nobility.

No State shall, without the Consent of the Congress, lay any Imposts or Duties on Imports or Exports, except what may be absolutely necessary for executing its inspection Laws; and the net Produce of all Duties and Imposts, laid by any State on Imports or Exports, shall be for the use of the Treasury of the United States; and all such Laws shall be subject to the Revision and Control of the Congress.

No state shall, without the Consent of Congress, lay any duty of Tonnage, keep Troops, or Ships of War in time of Peace, enter into any Agreement or Compact with another State, or with a foreign Power, or engage in War, unless actually invaded, or in such imminent Danger as will not admit of delay.

Article II

Section 1.

The executive Power shall be vested in a President of the United States of America. He shall hold his Office during the Term of four years, and, together with the Vice President, chosen for the same Term, be elected, as follows:

Each State shall appoint, in such Manner as the Legislature thereof may direct, a Number of Electors, equal to the whole Number of Senators and Representatives to which the State may be entitled in the Congress: but no Senator or Representative, or Person holding an Office of Trust or Profit under the United States, shall be appointed an Elector.

[The Electors shall meet in their respective States, and vote by Ballot for two persons, of whom one at least shall not be an Inhabitant of the same State with themselves. And they shall make a List of all the Persons voted for, and of the Number of Votes for each; which List they shall sign and certify, and transmit sealed to the Seat of the Government of the United States, directed to the President of the Senate. The President of the Senate shall, in the Presence of the Senate and House of Representatives, open all the Certificates, and the Votes shall then be counted. The Person having the greatest Number of Votes shall be the President, if such Number be a Majority of the whole Number of Electors appointed; and if there be more than one who have such Majority, and have an equal Number of Votes, then the House of Representatives shall immediately chuse by Ballot one of them for President; and if no Person have a Majority, then from the five highest on the List the said House shall in like Manner chuse the President. But in chusing the President, the Votes shall be taken by States, the Representation from each State having one Vote; a quorum for this Purpose shall consist of a Member or Members from two-thirds of the States, and a Majority of all the States shall be necessary to a Choice. In every Case, after the Choice of the President, the Person having the greatest Number of Votes of the Electors shall be the Vice President. But if there should remain two or more who have equal votes, the Senate shall chuse from them by Ballot the Vice President.][4]

The Congress may determine the Time of chusing the Electors, and the Day on which they shall give their Votes; which Day shall be the same throughout the United States.

No person except a natural-born Citizen, or a Citizen of the United States, at the time of the Adoption of this Constitution, shall be eligible to the Office of President; neither shall

4 Revised by the Twelfth Amendment.

any Person be eligible to that Office who shall not have attained to the Age of thirty-five years, and been fourteen Years a Resident within the United States.

In Case of the Removal of the President from Office, or of his Death, Resignation, or Inability to discharge the Powers and Duties of the said Office, the same shall devolve on the Vice President, and the Congress may by Law provide for the Case of Removal, Death, Resignation, or Inability, both of the President and Vice President, declaring what Officer shall then act as President, and such Officer shall act accordingly, until the disability be removed, or a President shall be elected.

The President shall, at stated Times, receive for his Services a Compensation, which shall neither be increased nor diminished during the Period for which he shall have been elected, and he shall not receive within that Period any other Emolument from the United States, or any of them.

Before he enter on the execution of his Office, he shall take the following Oath or Affirmation:—"I do solemnly swear (or affirm) that I will faithfully execute the Office of President of the United States, and will, to the best of my Ability, preserve, protect, and defend the Constitution of the United States."

Section 2.

The President shall be Commander in Chief of the Army and Navy of the United States, and of the Militia of the several States, when called into the actual Service of the United States; he may require the Opinion, in writing, of the principal Officer in each of the executive Departments, upon any subject relating to the Duties of their respective Offices, and he shall have Power to Grant Reprieves and Pardons for Offenses against the United States, except in Cases of Impeachment.

He shall have Power, by and with the Advice and Consent of the Senate, to make Treaties, provided two-thirds of the Senators present concur; and he shall nominate, and by and with the Advice and Consent of the Senate, shall appoint Ambassadors, other public Ministers and Consuls, Judges of the supreme Court, and all other Officers of the United States, whose Appointments are not herein otherwise provided for, and which shall be established by Law: but the Congress may by Law vest the Appointment of such inferior Officers, as they think proper, in the President alone, in the Courts of Law, or in the Heads of Departments.

The President shall have Power to fill up all Vacancies that may happen during the Recess of the Senate, by granting Commissions which shall expire at the End of their next Session.

Section 3.

He shall from time to time give to the Congress Information of the State of the Union, and recommend to their Consideration such Measures as he shall judge necessary and expedient; he may, on extraordinary occasions, convene both Houses, or either of them, and in Case of Disagreement between them, with respect to the Time of Adjournment, he may adjourn them to such Time as he shall think proper; he shall receive Ambassadors and other public Ministers; he shall take care that the Laws be faithfully executed, and shall Commission all the Officers of the United States.

Section 4.

The President, Vice President and all civil Officers of the United States, shall be removed from Office on Impeachment for, and Conviction of, Treason, Bribery, or other high Crimes and Misdemeanors.

Article III

Section 1.

The judicial Power of the United States, shall be vested in one supreme Court, and in such inferior Courts as the Congress may from time to time ordain and establish. The Judges, both of the supreme and inferior Courts, shall hold their Offices during good Behaviour, and shall, at stated Times, receive for their Services, a Compensation, which shall not be diminished during their Continuance in Office.

Section 2.

The judicial Power shall extend to all Cases, in Law and Equity, arising under this Constitution, the Laws of the United States, and Treaties made, or which shall be made, under their Authority;—to all Cases affecting ambassadors, other public ministers and consuls;—to all cases of admiralty and maritime Jurisdiction;—to Controversies to which the United States shall be a Party;—to Controversies between two or more States;—between a State and Citizens of another State;[5]—between Citizens of different States—between Citizens of the same State claiming Lands under Grants of different States, and between a State, or the Citizens thereof, and foreign States, Citizens, or Subjects.

In all Cases affecting Ambassadors, other public Ministers and Consuls, and those in which a State shall be Party, the supreme Court shall have original Jurisdiction. In all the other Cases before mentioned, the supreme Court shall have appellate Jurisdiction, both as to Law and Fact, with such Exceptions, and under such Regulations as the Congress shall make.

The trial of all Crimes, except in Cases of Impeachment, shall be by Jury; and such Trial shall be held in the State where the said Crimes shall have been committed; but when not committed within any State, the Trial shall be at such Place or Places as the Congress may by Law have directed.

Section 3.

Treason against the United States, shall consist only in levying War against them, or in adhering to their Enemies, giving them Aid and Comfort. No Person shall be convicted of Treason unless on the Testimony of two Witnesses to the same overt Act, or on Confession in open Court.

The Congress shall have power to declare the Punishment of Treason, but no Attainder of Treason shall work Corruption of Blood, or Forfeiture except during the Life of the Person attained.

Article IV

Section 1.

Full Faith and Credit shall be given in each State to the public Acts, Records, and judicial Proceedings of every other State. And the Congress may by general Laws prescribe the Manner in which such Acts, Records and Proceedings shall be proved, and the Effect thereof.

Section 2.

The Citizens of each State shall be entitled to all Privileges and Immunities of Citizens in the several States.

5 Qualified by the Eleventh Amendment.

A Person charged in any State with Treason, Felony, or other Crime, who shall flee from Justice, and be found in another State, shall on demand of the executive Authority of the State from which he fled, be delivered up, to be removed to the State having Jurisdiction of the crime.

No Person held to Service or Labour in one State, under the Laws thereof, escaping into another, shall, in Consequence of any Law or Regulation therein, be discharged from such Service or Labour, but shall be delivered up on Claim of the Party to whom such Service or Labour may be due.

Section 3.

New States may be admitted by the Congress into this Union; but no new State shall be formed or erected within the Jurisdiction of any other State; nor any State be formed by the Junction of two or more States, or parts of States, without the Consent of the Legislatures of the States concerned as well as of the Congress.

The Congress shall have Power to dispose of and make all needful Rules and Regulations respecting the Territory or other Property belonging to the United States; and nothing in this Constitution shall be so construed as to Prejudice any Claims of the United States, or of any particular State.

Section 4.

The United States shall guarantee to every State in this Union a Republican Form of Government, and shall protect each of them against Invasion; and on Application of the Legislature, or of the Executive (when the Legislature cannot be convened) against domestic Violence.

Article V

The Congress, whenever two-thirds of both Houses shall deem it necessary, shall propose Amendments to this Constitution, or, on the Application of the Legislatures of two-thirds of the several States, shall call a Convention for proposing Amendments, which, in either Case, shall be valid to all Intents and Purposes, as part of this Constitution, when ratified by the Legislatures of three-fourths of the several States, or by Conventions in three-fourths thereof, as the one or the other Mode of Ratification may be proposed by the Congress; Provided that no Amendment which may be made prior to the Year One thousand eight hundred and eight shall in any Manner affect the first and fourth Clauses in the Ninth Section of the first Article; and that no State, without its Consent, shall be deprived of its equal Suffrage in the Senate.

Article VI

All Debts contracted and Engagements entered into, before the Adoption of this Constitution, shall be as valid against the United States under this Constitution, as under the Confederation.

This Constitution, and the Laws of the United States which shall be made in Pursuance thereof; and all Treaties made, or which shall be made, under the Authority of the United States, shall be the supreme Law of the Land; and the Judges in every State shall be bound thereby, any Thing in the Constitution or Laws of any State to the Contrary notwithstanding.

The Senators and Representatives before mentioned, and the Members of the several State Legislatures, and all executive and judicial Officers, both of the United States and of the several States, shall be bound by Oath or Affirmation to support this Constitution; but no religious Tests shall ever be required as a qualification to any Office or public Trust under the United States.

Article VII

The Ratification of the Conventions of nine States shall be sufficient for the Establishment of this Constitution between the States so ratifying the same.

Done in Convention by the Unanimous Consent of the States present the Seventeenth Day of September in the Year of our Lord one thousand seven hundred and Eighty seven, and of the Independence of the United States of America the Twelfth. In Witness whereof We have hereunto subscribed our Names.[6]

George Washington
President and deputy from Virginia

NEW HAMPSHIRE
John Langdon
Nicholas Gilman

MASSACHUSETTS
Nathaniel Gorham
Rufus King

CONNECTICUT
William Samuel Johnson
Roger Sherman

NEW YORK
Alexander Hamilton

NEW JERSEY
William Livingston
David Brearley
William Paterson
Jonathan Dayton

PENNSYLVANIA
Benjamin Franklin
Thomas Mifflin
Robert Morris
George Clymer
Thomas FitzSimons
Jared Ingersoll
James Wilson
Gouverneur Morris

DELAWARE
George Read
Gunning Bedford Jr.
John Dickinson
Richard Bassett
Jacob Broom

MARYLAND
James McHenry
Daniel of St. Thomas Jenifer
Daniel Carroll

VIRGINIA
John Blair
James Madison Jr.

NORTH CAROLINA
William Blount
Richard Dobbs Spaight
Hugh Williamson

SOUTH CAROLINA
John Rutledge
Charles Cotesworth
    Pinckney
Charles Pinckney
Pierce Butler

GEORGIA
William Few
Abraham Baldwin

Articles in Addition to, and Amendment of, the Constitution of the United States of America, Proposed by Congress, and Ratified by the Legislatures of the Several States, Pursuant to the Fifth Article of the Original Constitution.[7]

[Article I]

Congress shall make no law respecting an establishment of religion, or prohibiting the free exercise thereof; or abridging the freedom of speech, or of the press; or the right of the people peaceably to assemble, and to petition the Government for a redress of grievances.

[Article II]

A well regulated Militia, being necessary to the security of a free State, the right of the people to keep and bear Arms shall not be infringed.

6 These are the full names of the signers, which in some cases are not the signatures on the document.
7 This heading appears only in the joint resolution submitting the first ten amendments.

[Article III]

No Soldier shall, in time of peace, be quartered in any house, without the consent of the Owner, nor in time of war, but in a manner to be prescribed by law.

[Article IV]

The right of the people to be secure in their persons, houses, papers, and effects, against unreasonable searches and seizures, shall not be violated, and no Warrants shall issue, but upon probable cause, supported by Oath or affirmation, and particularly describing the place to be searched, and the persons or things to be seized.

[Article V]

No person shall be held to answer for a capital or otherwise infamous crime, unless on a presentment or indictment of a Grand Jury, except in cases arising in the land or naval forces, or in the Militia, when in actual service in time of War or public danger; nor shall any person be subject for the same offence to be twice put in jeopardy of life or limb; nor shall be compelled in any criminal case to be a witness against himself, nor be deprived of life, liberty, or property, without due process of law; nor shall private property be taken for public use, without just compensation.

[Article VI]

In all criminal prosecutions, the accused shall enjoy the right to a speedy and public trial, by an impartial jury of the State and district wherein the crime shall have been committed, which district shall have been previously ascertained by law, and to be informed of the nature and cause of the accusation; to be confronted with the witnesses against him; to have compulsory process for obtaining witnesses in his favour, and to have the Assistance of Counsel for his defense.

[Article VII]

In suits at common law, where the value in controversy shall exceed twenty dollars, the right of trial by jury shall be preserved, and no fact tried by a jury, shall be otherwise reexamined in any Court of the United States, than according to the rules of the common law.

[Article VIII]

Excessive bail shall not be required, nor excessive fines imposed, nor cruel and unusual punishments inflicted.

[Article IX]

The enumeration of the Constitution, of certain rights, shall not be construed to deny or disparage others retained by the people.

[Article X]

The powers not delegated to the United States by the Constitution, nor prohibited by it to the States, are reserved to the States respectively, or to the people.

[Amendments I–X, in force 1791.]

[Article XI][8]

The Judicial power of the United States shall not be construed to extend to any suit in law or equity, commenced or prosecuted against one of the United States by Citizens of another State, or by Citizens or Subjects of any Foreign State.

[Article XII][9]

The Electors shall meet in their respective States and vote by ballot for President and Vice-President, one of whom, at least, shall not be an inhabitant of the same State with themselves; they shall name in their ballots the person voted for as President, and in distinct ballots the person voted for as Vice-President, and they shall make distinct lists of all persons voted for as President, and of all persons voted for as Vice-President, and of the number of votes for each, which lists they shall sign and certify, and transmit sealed to the seat of the government of the United States, directed to the President of the Senate;— The President of the Senate shall, in the presence of the Senate and House of Representatives, open all the certificates and the votes shall then be counted;—The person having the greatest number of votes for President, shall be the President, if such number be a majority of the whole number of Electors appointed; and if no person have such majority, then from the persons having the highest numbers not exceeding three on the list of those voted for as President, the House of Representatives shall choose immediately, by ballot, the President. But in choosing the President, the votes shall be taken by states, the representation from each state having one vote; a quorum for this purpose shall consist of a member or members from two-thirds of the states, and a majority of all the states shall be necessary to a choice. And if the House of Representatives shall not choose a President whenever the right of choice shall devolve upon them, before the fourth day of March next following, then the Vice-President shall act as President, as in the case of the death or other constitutional disability of the President.—The person having the greatest number of votes as Vice-President, shall be the Vice-President, if such number be a majority of the whole number of Electors appointed, and if no person have a majority, then from the two highest numbers on the list, the Senate shall choose the Vice-President; a quorum for the purpose shall consist of two-thirds of the whole number of Senators, and a majority of the whole number shall be necessary to a choice. But no person constitutionally ineligible to the office of President shall be eligible to that of Vice-President of the United States.

[Article XIII][10]

Section 1.
Neither slavery nor involuntary servitude, except as a punishment for crime whereof the party shall have been duly convicted, shall exist within the United States, or any place subject to their jurisdiction.

Section 2.
Congress shall have power to enforce this article by appropriate legislation.

8 Adopted in 1798.
9 Adopted in 1804.
10 Adopted in 1865.

[Article XIV][11]

Section 1.

All persons born or naturalized in the United States, and subject to the jurisdiction thereof, are citizens of the United States and of the State wherein they reside. No State shall make or enforce any law which shall abridge the privileges or immunities of citizens of the United States; nor shall any State deprive any person of life, liberty, or property, without due process of law; nor deny to any person within its jurisdiction the equal protection of the laws.

Section 2.

Representatives shall be apportioned among the several States according to their respective numbers, counting the whole number of persons in each State, excluding Indians not taxed. But when the right to vote at any election for the choice of electors for President and Vice-President of the United States, Representatives in Congress, the Executive and Judicial officers of a State, or the members of the Legislature thereof, is denied to any of the male inhabitants of such State, being twenty-one years of age, and citizens of the United States, or in any way abridged, except for participation in rebellion, or other crime, the basis of representation therein shall be reduced in the proportion which the number of such male citizens shall bear to the whole number of male citizens twenty-one years of age in such State.

Section 3.

No person shall be a Senator or Representative in Congress, or elector of President and Vice-President, or hold any office, civil or military, under the United States, or under any State, who, having previously taken an oath, as a member of Congress, or as an officer of the United States, or as a member of any State legislature, or as an executive or judicial officer of any State, to support the Constitution of the United States, shall have engaged in insurrection or rebellion against the same, or given aid or comfort to the enemies thereof. But Congress may by a vote of two-thirds of each House, remove such disability.

Section 4.

The validity of the public debt of the United States, authorized by law, including debts incurred for payment of pensions and bounties for services in suppressing insurrection or rebellion, shall not be questioned. But neither the United States nor any State shall assume or pay any debts or obligation incurred in aid of insurrection or rebellion against the United States, or any claim for the loss or emancipation of any slave; but all such debts, obligations, and claims shall be held illegal and void.

Section 5.

The Congress shall have the power to enforce, by appropriate legislation, the provisions of this article.

[Article XV][12]

Section 1.

The right of citizens of the United States to vote shall not be denied or abridged by the United States or by any State on account of race, color, or previous condition of servitude—

Section 2.

The Congress shall have power to enforce this article by appropriate legislation.

11 Adopted in 1868.
12 Adopted in 1870.

[Article XVI][13]

The Congress shall have power to lay and collect taxes on incomes, from whatever source derived, without apportionment among the several States, and without regard to any census or enumeration.

[Article XVII][14]

The Senate of the United States shall be composed of two Senators from each State, elected by the people thereof, for six years; and each Senator shall have one vote. The electors in each State shall have the qualifications requisite for electors of the most numerous branch of the State legislatures.

When vacancies happen in the representation of any State in the Senate, the executive authority of such State shall issue writs of election to fill such vacancies: *Provided,* That the legislature of any State may empower the executive thereof to make temporary appointments until the people fill the vacancies by election as the legislature may direct.

This amendment shall not be so construed as to affect the election or term of any Senator chosen before it becomes valid as part of the Constitution.

[Article XVIII][15]

Section 1.
After one year from the ratification of this article the manufacture, sale, or transportation of intoxicating liquors within, the importation thereof into, or the exportation thereof from the United States and all territory subject to the jurisdiction thereof for beverage purposes is hereby prohibited.

Section 2.
The Congress and the several States shall have concurrent power to enforce this article by appropriate legislation.

Section 3.
This article shall be inoperative unless it shall have been ratified as an amendment to the Constitution by the legislatures of the several States, as provided in the Constitution, within seven years from the date of the submission hereof to the States by the Congress.

[Article XIX][16]

The right of citizens of the United States to vote shall not be denied or abridged by the United States or by any State on account of sex.

Congress shall have power to enforce this article by appropriate legislation.

[Article XX][17]

Section 1.
The terms of the President and Vice-President shall end at noon on the 20th day of January, and the terms of Senators and Representatives at noon on the 3d day of January,

---

13 Adopted in 1913.
14 Adopted in 1913.
15 Adopted in 1918.
16 Adopted in 1920.
17 Adopted in 1933.

of the years in which such terms would have ended if this article had not been ratified; and the terms of their successors shall then begin.

Section 2.
The Congress shall assemble at least once in every year, and such meeting shall begin at noon on the 3d day of January, unless they shall by law appoint a different day.

Section 3.
If, at the time fixed for the beginning of the term of the President, the President elect shall have died, the Vice-President elect shall become President. If a President shall not have been chosen before the time fixed for the beginning of his term or if the President elect shall have failed to qualify, then the Vice-President elect shall act as President until a President shall have qualified; and the Congress may by law provide for the case wherein neither a President elect nor a Vice-President elect shall have qualified, declaring who shall then act as President, or the manner in which one who is to act shall be selected, and such person shall act accordingly until a President or Vice-President shall have qualified.

Section 4.
The Congress may by law provide for the case of the death of any of the persons from whom the House of Representatives may choose a President whenever the right of choice shall have devolved upon them, and for the case of the death of any of the persons from whom the Senate may choose a Vice-President whenever the right of choice shall have devolved upon them.

Section 5.
Sections 1 and 2 shall take effect on the 15th day of October following the ratification of this article.

Section 6.
This article shall be inoperative unless it shall have been ratified as an amendment to the Constitution by the legislatures of three-fourths of the several States within seven years from the date of its submission.

[Article XXI][18]

Section 1.
The eighteenth article of amendment to the Constitution of the United States is hereby repealed.

Section 2.
The transportation or importation into any State, Territory, or possession of the United States for delivery or use therein of intoxicating liquors, in violation of the laws thereof, is hereby prohibited.

Section 3.
This article shall be inoperative unless it shall have been ratified as an amendment to the Constitution by conventions in the several States, as provided in the Constitution, within seven years from the date of the submission hereof to the States by the Congress.

18 Adopted in 1933.

[Article XXII][19]

No person shall be elected to the office of the President more than twice, and no person who has held the office of President, or acted as President, for more than two years of a term to which some other person was elected President shall be elected to the office of the President more than once.

But this Article shall not apply to any person holding the office of President when this Article was proposed by the Congress, and shall not prevent any person who may be holding the office of President, or acting as President, during the term within which this Article becomes operative from holding the office of President or acting as President during the remainder of such term.

This article shall be inoperative unless it shall have been ratified as an amendment to the Constitution by the legislatures of three-fourths of the several states within seven years from the date of its submission to the states by the Congress.

[Article XXIII][20]

Section 1.
The District constituting the seat of Government of the United States shall appoint in such manner as the Congress may direct:

A number of electors of President and Vice-President equal to the whole number of Senators and Representatives in Congress to which the District would be entitled if it were a State, but in no event more than the least populous State; they shall be in addition to those appointed by the States, but they shall be considered, for the purposes of the election of President and Vice-President, to be electors appointed by a State; and they shall meet in the District and perform such duties as provided by the twelfth article of amendment.

Section 2.
The Congress shall have power to enforce this article by appropriate legislation.

[Article XXIV][21]

Section 1.
The right of citizens of the United States to vote in any primary or other election for President or Vice President, for electors for President or Vice President, or for Senator or Representative in Congress, shall not be denied or abridged by the United States or any state by reason of failure to pay any poll tax or other tax.

Section 2.
The Congress shall have the power to enforce this article by appropriate legislation.

[Article XXV][22]

Section 1.
In case of the removal of the President from office or of his death or resignation, the Vice President shall become President.

---

19 Adopted in 1951.
20 Adopted in 1961.
21 Adopted in 1964.
22 Adopted in 1967.

Section 2.

Whenever there is a vacancy in the office of the Vice President, the President shall nominate a Vice President who shall take office upon confirmation by a majority vote of both Houses of Congress.

Section 3.

Whenever the President transmits to the President Pro Tempore of the Senate and the Speaker of the House of Representatives his written declaration that he is unable to discharge the powers and duties of his office, and until he transmits to them a written declaration to the contrary, such powers and duties shall be discharged by the Vice President as Acting President.

Section 4.

Whenever the Vice President and a majority of either the principal officers of the executive departments or of such other body as Congress may by law provide, transmit to the President Pro Tempore of the Senate and the Speaker of the House of Representatives their written declaration that the President is unable to discharge the powers and duties of his office, the Vice President shall immediately assume the powers and duties of the office as Acting President.

Thereafter, when the President transmits to the President Pro Tempore of the Senate and the Speaker of the House of Representatives his written declaration that no inability exists, he shall resume the powers and duties of his office unless the Vice President and a majority of either the principal officers of the executive departments or of such other body as Congress may by law provide, transmit within four days to the President Pro Tempore of the Senate and the Speaker of the House of Representatives their written declaration that the President is unable to discharge the powers and duties of his office. Thereupon Congress shall decide the issue, assembling within forty-eight hours for that purpose if not in session. If the Congress, within twenty-one days after receipt of the latter written declaration, or, if Congress is not in session, within twenty-one days after Congress is required to assemble, determines by two-thirds vote of both Houses that the President is unable to discharge the powers and duties of his office, the Vice President shall continue to discharge the same as Acting President; otherwise, the President shall resume the powers and duties of his office.

[Article XXVI][23]

Section 1.

The right of citizens of the United States, who are eighteen years of age or older, to vote shall not be denied or abridged by the United States or by any State on account of age.

Section 2.

The Congress shall have power to enforce this article by appropriate legislation.

[Article XXVII][24]

No law varying the compensation for the services of the Senators and Representatives shall take effect until an election of Representatives shall have intervened.

23 Adopted in 1971.
24 Adopted in 1992.

PRESIDENTIAL ELECTIONS

Year	Candidates	Parties	Popular Vote	Percentage of Popular Vote	Electoral Vote	Percentage of Voter Participation
1789	George Washington (Va.)*				69	
	John Adams				34	
	Others				35	
1792	George Washington (Va.)				132	
	John Adams				77	
	George Clinton				50	
	Others				5	
1796	John Adams (Mass.)	Federalist			71	
	Thomas Jefferson	Democratic-Republican			68	
	Thomas Pinckney	Federalist			59	
	Aaron Burr	Dem.-Rep.			30	
	Others				48	
1800	Thomas Jefferson (Va.)	Dem.-Rep.			73	
	Aaron Burr	Dem.-Rep.			73	
	John Adams	Federalist			65	
	C. C. Pinckney	Federalist			64	
	John Jay	Federalist			1	
1804	Thomas Jefferson (Va.)	Dem.-Rep.			162	
	C. C. Pinckney	Federalist			14	
1808	James Madison (Va.)	Dem.-Rep.			122	
	C. C. Pinckney	Federalist			47	
	George Clinton	Dem.-Rep.			6	

*State of residence at time of election.

(continued)

Year	Candidates	Parties	Popular Vote	% of Popular Vote	Electoral Vote	% Voter Participation
1812	James Madison (Va.)	Dem.-Rep.			128	
	De Witt Clinton	Federalist			89	
1816	James Monroe (Va.)	Dem.-Rep.			183	
	Rufus King	Federalist			34	
1820	James Monroe (Va.)	Dem.-Rep.			231	
	John Quincy Adams	Dem.-Rep.			1	
1824	John Q. Adams (Mass.)	Dem.-Rep.	108,740	30.5	84	26.9
	Andrew Jackson	Dem.-Rep.	153,544	43.1	99	
	William H. Crawford	Dem.-Rep.	46,618	13.1	41	
	Henry Clay	Dem.-Rep.	47,136	13.2	37	
1828	Andrew Jackson (Tenn.)	Democratic	647,286	56.0	178	57.6
	John Quincy Adams	National Republican	508,064	44.0	83	
1832	Andrew Jackson (Tenn.)	Democratic	687,502	55.0	219	55.4
	Henry Clay	National Republican	530,189	42.4	49	
	John Floyd	Independent			11	
	William Wirt	Anti-Mason	33,108	2.6	7	
1836	Martin Van Buren (N.Y.)	Democratic	765,483	50.9	170	57.8
	W. H. Harrison	Whig			73	
	Hugh L. White	Whig	739,765	49.1	26	
	Daniel Webster	Whig			14	
	W. P. Magnum	Independent			11	
1840	William H. Harrison (Ohio)	Whig	1,274,624	53.1	234	80.2
	Martin Van Buren	Democratic	1,127,781	46.9	60	
	J. G. Birney	Liberty	7,069	—	—	

Year	Candidates	Parties	Popular Vote	Percentage of Popular Vote	Electoral Vote	Percentage of Voter Participation
1844	James K. Polk (Tenn.)	Democratic	1,338,464	49.6	170	78.9
	Henry Clay	Whig	1,300,097	48.1	105	
	J. G. Birney	Liberty	62,300	2.3	—	
1848	Zachary Taylor (La.)	Whig	1,360,967	47.4	163	72.7
	Lewis Cass	Democratic	1,222,342	42.5	127	
	Martin Van Buren	Free-Soil	291,263	10.1	—	
1852	Franklin Pierce (N.H.)	Democratic	1,601,117	50.9	254	69.6
	Winfield Scott	Whig	1,385,453	44.1	42	
	John P. Hale	Free-Soil	155,825	5.0	—	
1856	James Buchanan (Pa.)	Democratic	1,832,955	45.3	174	78.9
	John C. Frémont	Republican	1,339,932	33.1	114	
	Millard Fillmore	American	871,731	21.6	8	
1860	Abraham Lincoln (Ill.)	Republican	1,865,593	39.9	180	81.2
	Stephen A. Douglas	Democratic	1,382,713	29.4	12	
	John C. Breckinridge	Democratic	848,356	18.1	72	
	John Bell	Union	592,906	12.6	39	
1864	Abraham Lincoln (Ill.)	Republican	2,213,655	55.0	212	73.8
	George B. McClellan	Democratic	1,805,237	45.0	21	
1868	Ulysses S. Grant (Ill.)	Republican	3,012,833	52.7	214	78.1
	Horatio Seymour	Democratic	2,703,249	47.3	80	
1872	Ulysses S. Grant (Ill.)	Republican	3,597,132	55.6	286	71.3
	Horace Greeley	Democratic; Liberal Republican	2,834,125	43.9	66	
1876	Rutherford B. Hayes (Ohio)	Republican	4,036,298	48.0	185	81.8
	Samuel J. Tilden	Democratic	4,300,590	51.0	184	
1880	James A. Garfield (Ohio)	Republican	4,454,416	48.5	214	79.4
	Winfield S. Hancock	Democratic	4,444,952	48.1	155	

(continued)

Year	Candidate	Party	Popular vote	%	Electoral vote	Voter participation
1884	**Grover Cleveland (N.Y.)**	Democratic	4,874,986	48.5	219	77.5
	James G. Blaine	Republican	4,851,981	48.2	182	
1888	**Benjamin Harrison (Ind.)**	Republican	5,439,853	47.9	233	79.3
	Grover Cleveland	Democratic	5,540,309	48.6	168	
1892	**Grover Cleveland (N.Y.)**	Democratic	5,556,918	46.1	277	74.7
	Benjamin Harrison	Republican	5,176,108	43.0	145	
	James B. Weaver	People's	1,041,028	8.5	22	
1896	**William McKinley (Ohio)**	Republican	7,104,779	51.1	271	79.3
	William J. Bryan	Democratic People's	6,502,925	47.7	176	
1900	**William McKinley (Ohio)**	Republican	7,207,923	51.7	292	73.2
	William J. Bryan	Dem.-Populist	6,358,133	45.5	155	
1904	**Theodore Roosevelt (N.Y.)**	Republican	7,623,486	57.9	336	65.2
	Alton B. Parker	Democratic	5,077,911	37.6	140	
	Eugene V. Debs	Socialist	402,283	3.0	—	
1908	**William H. Taft (Ohio)**	Republican	7,678,908	51.6	321	65.4
	William J. Bryan	Democratic	6,409,104	43.1	162	
	Eugene V. Debs	Socialist	420,793	2.8	—	
1912	**Woodrow Wilson (N.J.)**	Democratic	6,293,454	41.9	435	58.8
	Theodore Roosevelt	Progressive	4,119,538	27.4	88	
	William H. Taft	Republican	3,484,980	23.2	8	
	Eugene V. Debs	Socialist	900,672	6.0	—	
1916	**Woodrow Wilson (N.J.)**	Democratic	9,129,606	49.4	277	61.6
	Charles E. Hughes	Republican	8,538,221	46.2	254	
	A. L. Benson	Socialist	585,113	3.2	—	

Year	Candidates	Parties	Popular Vote	Percentage of Popular Vote	Electoral Vote	Percentage of Voter Participation
1920	Warren G. Harding (Ohio)	Republican	16,152,200	60.4	404	49.2
	James M. Cox	Democratic	9,147,353	34.2	127	
	Eugene V. Debs	Socialist	919,799	3.4	—	
1924	Calvin Coolidge (Mass.)	Republican	15,725,016	54.0	382	48.9
	John W. Davis	Democratic	8,386,503	28.8	136	
	Robert M. La Follette	Progressive	4,822,856	16.6	13	
1928	Herbert Hoover (Calif.)	Republican	21,391,381	58.2	444	56.9
	Alfred E. Smith	Democratic	15,016,443	40.9	87	
	Norman Thomas	Socialist	267,835	0.7	—	
1932	Franklin D. Roosevelt (N.Y.)	Democratic	22,821,857	57.4	472	56.9
	Herbert Hoover	Republican	15,761,841	39.7	59	
	Norman Thomas	Socialist	881,951	2.2	—	
1936	Franklin D. Roosevelt (N.Y.)	Democratic	27,751,597	60.8	523	61.0
	Alfred M. Landon	Republican	16,679,583	36.5	8	
	William Lemke	Union	882,479	1.9	—	
1940	Franklin D. Roosevelt (N.Y.)	Democratic	27,244,160	54.8	449	62.5
	Wendell L. Willkie	Republican	22,305,198	44.8	82	
1944	Franklin D. Roosevelt (N.Y.)	Democratic	25,602,504	53.5	432	55.9
	Thomas E. Dewey	Republican	22,006,285	46.0	99	
1948	Harry S. Truman (Mo.)	Democratic	24,105,695	49.5	303	53.0
	Thomas E. Dewey	Republican	21,969,170	45.1	189	
	J. Strom Thurmond	States' Rights Democratic	1,169,021	2.4	39	
	Henry A. Wallace	Progressive	1,156,103	2.4	—	
1952	Dwight D. Eisenhower (N.Y.)	Republican	33,936,252	55.1	442	63.3
	Adlai E. Stevenson	Democratic	27,314,992	44.4	89	

Year	Candidate	Party	Popular Vote	Percentage	Electoral Vote	Voter Participation
1956	Dwight D. Eisenhower (N.Y.)	Republican	35,575,420	57.6	457	60.6
	Adlai E. Stevenson	Democratic	26,033,066	42.1	73	
	Other	—			1	
1960	John F. Kennedy (Mass.)	Democratic	34,227,096	49.7	303	64.0
	Richard M. Nixon	Republican	34,108,546	49.6	219	
	Other	—			15	
1964	Lyndon B. Johnson (Tex.)	Democratic	43,126,506	61.1	486	61.7
	Barry M. Goldwater	Republican	27,176,799	38.5	52	
1968	Richard M. Nixon (N.Y.)	Republican	31,770,237	43.4	301	60.6
	Hubert H. Humphrey	Democratic	31,270,533	42.3	191	
	George Wallace	American Independent	9,906,141	12.9	46	
1972	Richard M. Nixon (N.Y.)	Republican	47,169,911	60.7	520	55.2
	George S. McGovern	Democratic	29,170,383	37.5	17	
	Other	—			1	
1976	Jimmy Carter (Ga.)	Democratic	40,828,587	50.0	297	53.5
	Gerald R. Ford	Republican	39,147,613	47.9	240	
	Other	—	1,575,459	2.1	1	
1980	Ronald Reagan (Calif.)	Republican	43,901,812	50.7	489	52.6
	Jimmy Carter	Democratic	35,483,820	41.0	49	
	John B. Anderson	Independent	5,719,722	6.6	—	
	Ed Clark	Libertarian	921,188	1.1	—	
1984	Ronald Reagan (Calif.)	Republican	54,455,075	59.0	525	53.3
	Walter Mondale	Democratic	37,577,185	41.0	13	
1988	George H. W. Bush (Tex.)	Republican	47,946,422	54.0	426	50.0
	Michael S. Dukakis	Democratic	41,016,429	46.0	112	
1992	William J. Clinton (Ark.)	Democratic	44,909,889	43.0	370	55.2
	George W. Bush	Republican	39,104,545	38.0	168	
	Ross Perot	Independent	19,742,267	19.0	0	

(continued)

Year	Candidates	Parties	Popular Vote	Percentage of Popular Vote	Electoral Vote	Percentage of Voter Participation
1996	William J. Clinton (Ark.)	Democratic	47,401,185	49.3	379	49.0
	Robert Dole	Republican	39,197,469	40.7	159	
	Ross Perot	Reform	8,085,294	8.4	—	
2000	George W. Bush (Tex.)	Republican	50,459,211	47.89	271	51.0
	Albert Gore Jr.	Democratic	51,003,894	48.41	266	
	Ralph Nader	Green	2,834,410	2.69	—	
2004	George W. Bush (Tex.)	Republican	62,028,285	50.73	286	60.0
	John Kerry	Democratic	59,028,109	48.27	251	
	Ralph Nader	Independent	463,647	0.38	0	
2008	Barack Obama (Ill.)	Democratic	69,297,997	53.7	365	61.7
	John McCain	Republican	59,597,520	46.2	173	
2012	Barack Obama (Ill.)	Democratic	65,915,796	51	332	54.9
	Mitt Romney	Republican	60,933,500	47	206	

GLOSSARY

abolitionist An advocate for the end of a state-approved practice or institution; the term is used most often in connection with the eradication of slavery.

affirmative action A policy that favors groups that historically have faced discrimination; examples include hiring, awarding contracts, and college admissions.

American System An economic plan of the early- to mid-nineteenth century designed to bolster and unify the American economy by raising protective tariffs, developing the transportation system, and establishing a strong national bank.

antebellum The period before a war; the term is commonly used to describe the pre–Civil War United States.

Antinomianism A Christian belief that salvation comes from God's grace alone and not from good works.

appeasement A foreign policy that accepts (rather than opposes) the aggressive moves of another state or actor.

artisan An independent, skilled craftsperson.

Atlantic World The peoples and empires around the Atlantic Ocean rim that became interconnected in the sixteenth century.

Baby Boom A period of increased birthrate; the term is used most often to describe such a demographic trend from 1946 to 1964.

Black Codes State laws that developed after the Civil War in the former Confederate states to limit the political power and mobility of black Americans.

black power A philosophy of racial empowerment and distinctiveness as opposed to assimilation into white culture; became popular during the Civil Rights movement of the 1960s.

brinksmanship The attempt to gain a negotiating advantage by pushing a situation to the edge of war or other disaster.

capitalist Owner of material or financial assets useful for the accumulation of additional wealth.

charter A formal order from a governmental leader or body, like the king of a court, often granting the recipient power over a body of land, a business, or a people.

checks and balances A system that grants the various branches of government the power to oversee or constrain other branches, so that no part grows too powerful.

colonization A process by which a country or territory falls, usually by force, under the control of of a hostile country or territory.

conquistador A European (especially Spanish and Portuguese) conqueror of the Americas (particularly Mexico and Peru) during the fifteenth and sixteenth centuries.

conscription The practice of requiring citizens to serve in the military or other national service; the draft.

conservationist A proponent of the protection of land for carefully managed development, as opposed to a preservationist, who seeks to protect nature from development altogether.

consumerism An increased focus on purchasing goods for personal use; the protection or promotion of consumer interests.

containment The Cold War strategy that called for preventing the spread of communism, by force or by other means.

counterculture A way of life opposed to the prevailing culture; the term typically refers to the revolution in lifestyles, values, and behavior among some young people of the 1960s.

covenant A Puritan belief that an individual's relationship with God and with others rested on mutual respect, duty, and consent.

Creole A person of European or African ancestry born in the Americas; also, a person of mixed European and African ancestry.

crop-lien system A credit system widely used in the South after the Civil War in which farmers promised a portion of their future crops in exchange for supplies from local merchants.

cult of domesticity The early-nineteenth-century belief that women were the guardians of family and religious virtue within the home.

cult of honor A set of beliefs that emphasized respect, reputation, and the protection of women; often associated with white southern males in the nineteenth century.

deism The belief that God created but does not actively control the universe.

deregulation The process of removing government controls over industries such as airlines, trucking, electricity supply, and banking, with the intention of stimulating competition and innovation.

détente The easing of hostilities between countries, used especially in connection with the Cold War in the 1970s.

Dollar Diplomacy Foreign policies, especially those of the Taft administration in Latin America, that privilege American economic interests.

embargo A ban on trade with another country, especially the refusal to allow foreign ships to unload goods at port.

encomienda The right to extract tribute and labor from the natives on large tracts of land in Spanish America; also the name given to the land and village in such tracts.

eugenics The pseudo-scientific movement that attributed genetic weakness to various races and ethnicities; also describes efforts to control or isolate supposed hereditary traits through selective breeding, sterilization, immigration restriction, and other forms of social engineering.

evangelist A devout person who aims to convert others to the faith through preaching and missionary work.

factory system A method of manufacturing involving powered machinery, usually run by water, that allowed the use of unskilled labor and greater output than in the artisan tradition.

fascism A term originating with Mussolini's Fascist Party and applying to any antidemocratic regime with a supreme leader, intolerance of dissent, faith in militarism over diplomacy, and a belief in national or ethnic superiority.

federalism A political system that traditionally divides powers between state and federal governments that together constitute a federation.

globalization The process of interaction and exchange between peoples and ideas from different parts of the globe.

gospel of wealth A philosophy popularized by Andrew Carnegie that assigns moral failure to the poor and personal virtue to the wealthy, and directs the rich to devote their resources to the common good. The concept developed by Andrew Carnegie that the wealthy should use their excess resources for the good of the community.

greenbacks Paper currency not backed by gold or silver.

horizontal integration A corporate combination where a group of businesses that do the same thing are consolidated.

impeachment The process of charging a public official with misconduct, with the potential for punishment including loss of office.

imperialism The process whereby an empire or nation pursues military, political, or economic advantage by extending its rule over external territories and peoples.

impressment The act of forcing people to serve in a navy or other military operation; the term is most commonly used in connection with the actions of British fleets against American sailors in the early 1800s.

indentured servitude The condition of being bound to an employer for a specific period of time, usually in exchange for the cost of passage to a new land. The labor practice was most commonly used in Britain's American colonies.

Industrial Revolution The transformation of an economy based on increasingly mechanized production.

isolationism A foreign policy that avoids forging alliances or lending support to other nations, especially in wartime.

jeremiad A sermon of despair at society's lost moral virtue, usually warning about dire consequences in the world and the afterlife.

jingoes A term coined in the late nineteenth century to refer to advocates for expanded U.S. economic, political, and military power in the world.

long drive A journey over grasslands that allowed western cattle ranchers to deliver their animals to railroad centers.

Lowell System A factory system used to mass-produce textiles, primarily in New England, that relied on young women workers who lived in factory communities.

Manifest Destiny An ideology holding that God or fate intended the United States to expand its dominion across the North American continent.

manumission The act of freeing slaves.

McCarthyism A form of anticommunism developed by Senator Joseph McCarthy in the early 1950s that recklessly persecuted alleged communists, often without evidence.

mercantilism An economic theory popular in Europe from the sixteenth through eighteenth centuries holding that nations were in competition with one another for wealth, and that the state should maximize its wealth by limiting imports and establishing new colonies that would provide access to precious minerals, spices, and slaves.

mestizo A person of mixed European and American descent, traditionally in Spanish-speaking territories and nations.

middle grounds Places where European and Indian cultures interacted and where neither side had a military advantage.

middle passage The name given to the route used by slave ships between Africa and the Americas.

monopoly A business entity that controls an industry or market sector without competition.

muckraker A journalist who exposes scandal, corruption, and injustice; the term was especially popular during the progressive era.

nativism A belief in the superiority of native-born inhabitants over immigrants; in particular, an anti-immigrant movement that began in the early 1800s in the United States and crested with the passage of immigration restriction in 1924.

nullification A theory that individual states, as the original creators of the federal government, possess the right to invalidate federal laws if they find them unconstitutional.

Open Door The metaphor Secretary of State John Hay used in 1898 to characterize the access to Chinese markets he desired for the United States; it was later expanded to refer to a policy of granting equal trade access to all countries.

popular sovereignty A term coined by Stephen A. Douglas to adjudicate the expansion of slavery in the western territories by allowing settlers to decide the status of slavery for their territory.

Populism A reform movement of the 1890s that promoted federal government policies to redistribute wealth and power from national elites to common people; more generally, refers to a political doctrine that supports the rights of the people over the elite.

primogeniture The English system of inheritance in which estates were passed down to first-born sons.

Quasi War The name given to the undeclared war between the United States and France of 1798–1799.

Reconstruction The process by which the federal government, between 1865 and 1877, controlled the former Confederate states and set the conditions for their readmission to the Union.

Red Scare A period of intense popular fear and government repression of real or imagined leftist radicalism; usually associated with the years immediately following World War I.

republicanism A system of governance in which power derives from the people, rather than from a ruling family, aristocratic class, or some other supreme authority.

secession The act of asserting independence by withdrawing membership from a political state; it refers in particular to the South's withdrawal from the United States.

separation of powers The partitioning of authority to distinct branches of a government.

sharecropping A farming system in which large landowners rent their fields to farmers, usually families, in return for a share of the crop's production.

sit-down strike A planned labor stoppage in which workers assume their positions in a factory or other workplace but refuse to perform their duties, thus preventing the use of strike-breakers.

slave codes Laws passed in the British colonies or in American states granting white masters absolute authority over the enslaved; these included laws depriving slaves of property, free movement, and legal defenses.

Social Darwinism The belief that societies are subject to the laws of natural selection and that some societies or peoples are innately superior to others.

socialism A political theory that advocates government (rather than private) ownership and management of the means of production and distribution.

social justice A movement that seeks justice for whole groups or societies rather than individuals.

sovereignty The authority to govern; popular sovereignty refers to the idea that the source of this authority is the people, who confer authority through elections.

spoils system A process whereby elected officials give out government jobs as reward for political favors.

Sunbelt The southeastern and southwestern regions of the United States.

temperance Self-restraint, especially concerning drink; the temperance movement pushed for bans on the sale and consumption of alcohol.

terrorism The use of violence as a form of intimidation against peoples and governments.

theocracy A form of government in which political power is believed to derive from a deity, and in which religious and government structures are intertwined.

transcendentalism A philosophical and literary movement of the early nineteenth century that sought beauty and truth in nature and the individual, rather than in formalized education, politics, or religion.

triangular trade A simplified description of the complex trade networks of the Atlantic World; the triangle metaphor refers to the trade in rum, slaves, and sugar among New England, Africa, and the West Indies.

Turner thesis The theory articulated by Frederick Jackson Turner in 1893 that westward expansion into the frontier had defined and continually renewed American ideas about democracy and individualism.

vertical integration The arrangement by which a company takes ownership of businesses in various stages of production and distribution within the same industry.

virtual representation British political theory holding that members of Parliament represented all British subjects, not just those from the specific region that had elected them.

welfare capitalism A corporate strategy for discouraging labor unrest by improving working conditions, hours, wages, and other elements of workers' lives.

yellow journalism Sensationalist reporting, particularly in newspapers of the late nineteenth and early twentieth centuries, so named for the color of a character in one of the papers' comic strips.

INDEX

AAA; *see* Agricultural Adjustment
    Administration
Abortion, 747, 759, 773, 807–808
Abraham Lincoln Brigade, 579
ACLU; *see* American Civil Liberties Union
ADA; *see* Americans for Democratic Action
Adams, Charles Francis, Jr., 489
Addams, Jane, 492
Advertising
    in 1920s, 551–554
    in 1950s, 687
    railroad, 420
    television, 688
AEF; *see* American Expeditionary Forces
Affirmative action, 720, 746, 758, 759, 807
Affordable Care Act, 800
Afghan war, 818, 820
Afghanistan, Soviets in, 757, 771, 783
AFL; *see* American Federation of Labor
AFL-CIO, 681, 748, 791
Africa
    AIDS epidemic, 809
    European colonies, 470–471
    former colonies, 757
    migration from, 433
African American women
    in cities, 428
    clubs, 494
    employment, 365, 366i, 428, 574, 641–642
    during Reconstruction, 365
    teachers, 493
    unemployment, 574
African Americans; *see also* Civil rights;
    Reconstruction; Slavery; Voting rights
    Black Cabinet, 606
    black nationalism, 539
    black power, 720–721
    in cities, 428, 539, 695, 698
    citizenship rights, 358–359
    in Congress, 363
    education, 356i, 364, 373–374, 806
    employment, 372–373, 428
    entertainers, 445
    families, 365, 807
    in Great Depression, 570
    Harlem Renaissance, 539, 556
    incomes, 364–365
    lynchings, 375, 378, 378i, 502, 539,
      606–607

    middle-class, 698, 806
    migration to cities, 428, 539, 570,
      636, 695
    migration to North, 538m, 539, 570
    military service, 538–539, 636, 665, 698
    music, 693–694, 798–799
    New Deal and, 606–607
    in New South, 372–375, 378
    performers, 377
    police shootings, 807
    poor, 365, 695, 717, 806–807
    populism and, 462
    post–civil rights era, 805–807
    reformers, 501–502
    Spanish-American War, 473, 475i,
      476, 483
    union members, 599
    wages, 440
    workers, 548
    World War I and, 527
    World War II and, 635–636
    writers, 539, 556, 579
African National Congress (ANC), 783
Agnew, Spiro, 763
Agrarian revolt, 460–462, 464
Agricultural Adjustment Administration (AAA),
    589–590
Agricultural Marketing Act, 582
Agriculture; *see also* Rural life
    child labor, 421
    commercial, 399–401
    dryland farming, 399
    exports, 551
    in Great Depression, 569, 570, 580, 582–583
    irrigation, 399
    migrant workers, 571, 695
    New Deal and, 589–590, 593
    in 1920s, 551, 565
    in 1950s, 695
    organizations, 459, 460, 493
    overproduction, 401
    parity, 551
    prices, 399, 402
    research, 551, 683
    sharecropping, 364, 365, 373, 373m, 695
    in South, 373
    technology, 551
    tenant farmers, 373, 580, 695
    in West, 386, 398–402

Aguinaldo, Emilio, 482, 483
AIDS, 744, 808–809, 815
Aiken, Howard, 545
AIM; *see* American Indian Movement
Airplanes
    bombers, 635
    early, 408
    mail delivery, 545
    manufacturing, 633
    in 1920s, 545
    in World War I, 408, 530
    in World War II, 635
Al Qaeda, 789, 818, 820
Alabama
    civil rights movement, 713, 716, 717
    Montgomery bus boycott, 697–698
    same-sex marriage case, 810–811
    Scottsboro case, 570, 580
Alabama claims, 368
Alaska, 368, 481
Albright, Madeleine, 747
Alcohol; *see* Prohibition; Temperance
Alcott, Louisa May, 413, 417, 447
Aldrich, Nelson W., 459
Aldrin, Edwin "Buzz," 685–686, 686i
Alger, Horatio, 413, 416–417
Algeria, 757
Alito, Samuel, 796
Allen, Hervey, *Anthony Adverse*, 578
Allende, Salvador, 755
Allies
    in interwar period, 612–613
    in World War I, 524–525, 527, 529–530,
        536, 565
    in World War II, 622, 623, 624, 625,
        630–631, 635, 643–646, 655
Alperovitz, Gar, 649
Altgeld, John Peter, 424
AMA; *see* American Medical Association
Ambrose, Stephen, 762
America First Committee, 622–623
American Civil Liberties Union (ACLU), 540,
    558, 674, 748
American Expeditionary Forces (AEF),
    529–530
American Federation of Labor (AFL), 422–423,
    424, 499, 538, 548, 599, 681
American Indian Movement (AIM),
    741–742
American Medical Association (AMA),
    492–493, 555
American Plan, 548

American Protective Association, 431
American Socialist Party, 419
American Telephone and Telegraph, 546
Americans for Democratic Action (ADA), 667
Anarchism, 423, 540
ANC; *see* African National Congress
Anderson, John, 775
Anthropology, 450
Anticommunism; *see also* Cold War
    historians' views, 674–675
    House Un-American Activities Committee,
        672–673
    John Birch Society, 660
    liberals, 667
    McCarthyism, 673–676, 699–700
    in 1930s, 580
    Red Scare, 540, 672–676
    suspected subversives, 672–676
Anti-Imperialist League, 479, 480–481
Anti-Saloon League, 503
Anti-Semitism, 557–558
Antitrust laws, 459, 505, 515
Apollo program, 685–686
Appeasement, 619
Apple Computer, 803
Arab-Israeli wars, 701, 702, 755
Arapahoe Indians, 382, 395
Arbenz Guzmán, Jacobo, 702
Architecture, skyscrapers, 436
Arizona, territory, 386
Arkansas, school desegregation, 696–697, 697i
Armory Show, 448
Arms control treaties, 754, 768, 770,
    771, 781, 783
Armstrong, Neil, 685–686
Army, U.S.; *see also* Military; World War II
    black soldiers, 473, 475i, 476, 483, 636
    modernization, 485
    Philippines occupation, 482–483
    World War I, 527–532
Army–McCarthy hearings, 699–700
Art
    Ashcan school, 448
    museums, 434
    Rocky Mountain school, 390
    in urban age, 448
    Western subjects, 390, 393
Arthur, Chester A., 457, 457i, 458
Ashcan school, 448
Asia; *see also specific countries*
    migration from, 433
    Open Door, 484, 520

Asian Americans; *see also* Chinese Americans; Japanese Americans
  discrimination against, 571–573
  in Great Depression, 571–573
  immigrants, 805
  migrant workers, 695
  workers, 549, 571
Assad, Bashar al-, 821
Assembly line production, 409, 409*i*, 634
Associated Press; *see* Newspapers
Associationalism, 561
Astronauts, 685
AT&T, 447–448, 684
Atlanta Compromise, 374
Atlantic and Pacific Tea Company (A&P), 441
Atlantic Charter, 624, 625, 654
Atomic bombs; *see also* Nuclear weapons
  development, 649–650
  Soviet, 662
  survivors, 648*i*
  Truman's decision to use, 648–649, 650–651
Atomic Energy Commission, 661
Attlee, Clement, 658
Auschwitz, 632, 645*i*
Austro-Hungarian Empire, 524
Automobile industry; *see also* Ford, Henry
  assembly lines, 409
  growth, 544, 687
  history, 408
  unions, 599
Automobiles
  development, 407–408
  economic impact, 544
  fuel economy standards, 755
  interstate highways, 689
  in 1920s, 551
  road trips, 689, 690–691
Aviation; *see* Airplanes
Axis powers, 625, 643–644, 655; *see also* World War II

Baby Boom, 680, 680*i*, 730, 805
Badoglio, Pietro, 631
Baez, Joan, 728
Bakke v. Board of Regents of California, 759
Ball, Lucille, 689*i*
Ballinger, Richard A., 510
Banks
  failures, 565, 567, 572–573, 585, 588
  federal deposit insurance, 589
  Federal Reserve system, 515, 568, 760, 780

mortgage crisis, 797
New Deal and, 588
Barbados, 377
Barbed wire, 399
Barton, Bruce, *The Man Nobody Knows*, 553*i*
Baruch, Bernard, 532
Baseball
  early, 444*i*, 444–445
  professional, 445
Basketball, 445
Batista, Fulgencio, 702
Battle of the Bulge, 645
Battles; *see specific battles and wars*
Bay of Pigs, 722
Beard, Charles A., 404, 450
Beard, Mary, 404
Beatles, 739
Beats, 692
Beck, David, 681–682
Begin, Menachem, 769, 770*i*
Belknap, William W., 367
Bell, Alexander Graham, 405, 447, 546
Bell, Derrick, 715
Bell Labs, 684
Bell System, 447–448
Bellamy, Edward, *Looking Backward*, 419
Bellow, Saul, 692
Bellows, George, 448, 449*i*
Berlin, 657–658, 661
Berlin Wall, 722, 782*i*, 783
Berners-Lee, Tim, 803
Bernstein, Barton, 594
Bessemer, Henry, 406
Bierstadt, Albert, 390
Bill of Rights, 540
Billington, Ray Allen, 392
Bin Laden, Osama, 818, 820
Birth control, 554, 747
Birth rates, in 1950s, 680, 680*i*
Bison (buffalo), 381, 394*i*, 395
Bissell, George, 407
Black Cabinet, 606
Black Codes, 358
Black nationalism, 539
Black Panthers, 721
Black power, 720–721
Blackett, P. M. S., 649
Blaine, James G., 457, 458
Bolshevik Revolution, 527, 536, 540
Bonds
  Liberty, 532
  during World War II, 634

Bonus Army, 583*i*, 583–584
Booth, John Wilkes, 355–357
Borah, William, 501
Bosch, Juan, 723
Boss Tweed; *see* Tweed, William M.
Boston
    Back Bay, 434
    police, 538, 560
    subway, 436
Bourbons (Redeemers), 371–372, 375
Bourke-White, Margaret, 533*i*, 580
Bowers, Henry, 431
Boxer Rebellion, 484
Boxing, 445, 449*i*
Braceros (contract laborers), 637
Bradley, Omar, 644, 646, 671
Branch, Taylor, 714
Brandeis, Louis, 504–505, 513, 515–516, 540
Brezhnev, Leonid, 754, 768, 770
Briand, Aristide, 612
Brinkley, Alan, 595
Brinksmanship, 700
Bristow, Benjamin H., 367
British Empire; *see also* England
    dissolution, 756–757
    India, 470, 471*i*, 756
    in nineteenth century, 470–471
    in Pacific, 472
Brooklyn Bridge, 436
Brotherhood of Sleeping Car Porters, 548,
    635–636
Browder v. Gayle, 697
Brower, David, 691
Brown, Linda, 715*i*
Brown, Michael, 807
Brown v. Board of Education of Topeka, 696,
    715, 715*i*
Bruce, Louis, 741–742
Bryan, William Jennings
    anti-imperialism, 468, 472, 481
    "Cross of Gold" speech, 465*i*, 466, 467
    presidential candidacies, 454, 466, 467*m*,
        481, 510
    Scopes trial, 558
Buffalo, 381, 394*i*, 395
Buffalo Bill; *see* Cody, Buffalo Bill
Bull Moose Party, 512
Bunau-Varilla, Philippe, 521
Burchard, Samuel, 458
Bureau of Indian Affairs, 394–395, 398, 607,
    636, 741–742
Bureau of Reclamation, 691

Bureaucracies, 692
Burger, Warren, 758
Burke-Wadsworth Act, 622
Burnham, Daniel, 434
Burns, James MacGregor, 594
Bush, George H. W.
    foreign policy, 785–786, 819
    presidency, 784–787
Bush, George W.
    cabinet, 747
    domestic policies, 795–796, 797, 805, 808
    foreign policy, 809, 819
    Iraq War, 795, 796, 815, 818–820
    presidential elections, 794, 796
    religious beliefs, 772
    war on terror, 818
Bush, Vannevar, 545
Business; *see also* Corporations; Industry
    associationalism, 561
    corruption, 489
    management, 411
    in 1950s, 681, 699
    regulation, 504–505, 515
    trusts, 412, 419, 459, 489, 489*i*, 504–505

California; *see also* Los Angeles; San Francisco
    Alcatraz, 741, 742*i*
    American settlers, 383
    annexation to U.S., 382–383
    film industry, 552–553
    Gold Rush, 383, 384, 387
    immigrants, 384, 384*i*
    Indians, 382
    labor laws, 499
    migration to, 681
    Proposition 13, 774
    Reagan as governor, 774
    Spanish colony, 382
Californios, 382–383
Calley, William, 751
Cambodia, 726*m*, 750–751, 753
Camp David Accords, 769, 770*i*
Canada
    immigration, 432*i*, 432–433
    self-government, 756
Canals, Panama, 521, 769, 774
Capitalism
    conservatism, 412–413, 466
    critics, 418–419, 422
    progressive reforms, 504–505
    welfare, 547–548
Capitalists, 412–413

Capra, Frank, 552, 575–577
Caribbean islands; *see also specific islands*
  colonies, 478, 757
  U.S. influence, 521, 522, 522*m*,
    523, 723, 723*m*
Carlisle Indian Industrial School, 450
Carnegie, Andrew, 411, 413, 414–415, 423, 479
Carnegie, Dale, 574
Carnegie Institution, 451
Carpetbaggers, 356, 362, 363*i*, 369
Carranza, Venustiano, 523
Carson, Rachel, 748
Carter, Jimmy, 770*i*
  presidency, 768–771, 774–775
  religious beliefs, 772
Cartoons, 479*i*, 638, 638*i*
Castro, Fidel, 702, 703*i*, 743
Catholic Church
  abortion issue, 773, 807
  Democratic supporters, 559
  missions in California, 382
Catt, Carrie Chapman, 495
Cattle ranching, 388–390, 389*m*, 400–401
CCC; *see* Civilian Conservation Corps
Centers for Disease Control and Prevention
    (CDC), 809
Central America; *see* Latin America; *and
    specific countries*
Central Intelligence Agency (CIA), 661,
    701–702, 722, 724, 755
Central Pacific Railroad Company, 385
Central Park, New York City, 434, 444, 446
Central Powers, 524, 527
Cervera, Pascual, 476
Chafe, William, 714
Chain, Ernest, 682
Challenger space shuttle, 686
Chamberlain, Joseph, 491
Chamberlain, Neville, 619
Chambers, Whittaker, 672
Chaney, James, 717
Charitable organizations, 438
Chávez, César, 743, 743*i*
Cheyenne Indians, 382, 389, 395
Chiang Kai-shek, 614, 616, 646, 659, 663
Chicago
  Columbian Exposition of 1893, 434
  Haymarket bombing, 423
  Hull House, 492
  "Memorial Day Massacre," 599–600, 600*i*
  race riots, 539
  skyscrapers, 436

suburbs, 435
Chicanos; *see* Mexican Americans
Child labor
  in agriculture, 421
  in industry, 421
  in mining, 506*i*
  regulation, 421, 494, 499, 516, 606
  in textile industry, 421*i*
  wages, 420
Children
  mortality rates, 683
  during World War II, 642
China
  Boxer Rebellion, 484
  civil war, 614, 646, 659
  communist government, 663
  democracy movement, 783
  Korean War, 669–672, 670*m*, 676, 679, 700
  relations with U.S., 753–754, 754*i*, 770
  Sino-Japanese War, 614–615, 616
  trade, 484
  Western powers and, 471, 484
  in World War II, 646, 647*m*
Chinese Americans; *see also* Asian Americans
  in Great Depression, 571
  immigrants, 383–386, 384*i*, 639
  workers, 573
  World War II and, 639
Chinese Exclusion Act, 386, 431, 639
Chinese workers, global migration, 433
Chopin, Kate, 448
Christian Coalition, 773
Christianity; *see* Catholic Church; Protestants;
    Social Gospel
Chun Duck Chin, 384*i*
Chun Jan Yut, 384*i*
Church of Jesus Christ of Latter-day Saints
    (Mormons), 386, 773, 807
Churchill, Winston
  Atlantic Charter, 624, 625, 654
  postwar vision, 654–655
  Potsdam conference, 650, 656, 658
  World War II and, 622, 631
  Yalta Conference, 655–658, 657*i*, 819
CIA; *see* Central Intelligence Agency
Cinema; *see* Films
CIO; *see* Congress of Industrial Organizations
Cities; *see also specific cities*
  African Americans, 539, 695, 698
  black migration, 428, 539, 570, 636, 695
  Chinatowns, 385
  crime, 438

Cities—*(Cont.)*
  economies, 696
  ethnic groups, 428–431, 445
  federal programs, 712
  fire departments, 437
  "ghettoes," 695–696, 806–807
  government reforms, 497
  growth, 427–429
  housing, 435*i*, 435–436
  immigrants, 429–431, 435–436
  industries, 406, 696
  leisure activities, 444–447
  life in, 433–440
  mass transit, 436
  Mexican Americans, 695–696
  political machines and bosses, 438–440
  pollution, 437
  poverty, 436, 437, 438, 695–696, 806–807
  public spaces, 434, 444
  race riots, 720, 732
  sanitation, 437, 451
  schools, 450
  settlement houses, 491–492
  skyscrapers, 436
  violence, 438
  western, 681
Citizenship
  of African Americans, 358–359
  Fourteenth Amendment, 358–359
City beautiful movement, 434
Civil rights
  of Indians, 741–742
  Supreme Court cases, 758
Civil Rights Act of 1866, 358
Civil Rights Act of 1964, 717
  Title VII, 720, 746
Civil Rights Cases (1883), 374
Civil rights movement
  causes, 698
  Freedom Summer, 717
  historians' views, 714–715
  King's leadership, 698, 713, 714, 717, 720
  legacy, 805–806
  March on Washington, 714, 716*i*, 716–717
  in 1940s, 636
  in 1950s, 696–698
  in 1960s, 713–720
Civil War
  aftermath, 352–354
  casualties, 352
  economic and social effects, 352
  foreign powers and, 368

  veterans' pensions, 456
Civil Works Administration (CWA), 593, 601
Civilian Conservation Corps (CCC), 593,
  601, 607, 642
Clark, Champ, 512–513
Clark, Dick, 694
Clark, Jim, 717
Class divisions; *see* Middle class
Clayton Antitrust Act, 515
Clean Air Act, 749
Clean Water Act, 749
Clemenceau, Georges, 536
Cleveland, Grover
  presidency, 424, 458, 462, 464
  presidential elections, 458, 459
Clifford, Clark, 727
Climate change, 813, 814, 815
Clinton, Bill
  domestic policies, 744, 790–793,
    807, 808, 809
  foreign policy, 791, 794, 819
  presidency, 747, 814
  presidential elections, 786–787,
    792–793, 808
  religious beliefs, 772
  scandals and impeachment, 791, 793–794
Clinton, Hillary Rodham
  as First Lady, 791
  presidential candidacy (2008), 747, 796
  as secretary of state, 820
  as senator, 794
Clubwomen, 494
Cochise, 397
Code breakers, 635
Cody, Buffalo Bill, 390–391
Cohan, George M., 534–535
Cold War; *see also* Anticommunism; Nuclear
  weapons
  alliances, 661–662
  arms race, 684–685, 781
  containment policy, 653, 659–660,
    663, 669, 700
  Cuban missile crisis, 722–723
  détente, 754, 774
  division of Europe, 658, 661–662, 662*m*
  Eisenhower's policies, 700–702
  end of, 656–657, 782–783
  fall of China, 663
  historians' views, 656–657
  Korean War, 669–672, 670*m*, 676, 679, 700
  Middle East crises, 701–702
  in 1950s, 700–703

in 1960s, 721, 722
origins, 653–658
Reagan and, 778, 781, 783
Colfax, Schuyler, 367
Colleges; *see* Universities
Collier, John, 607, 636
Collins, Michael, 685–686
Colombia, Panama Canal and, 521
Colonies, 471; *see also* British Empire;
    Imperialism; Spanish Empire
Colorado
mining, 387
statehood, 386
Colossus II, 635
Columbia space shuttle, 686
Columbia University, 738
Comic books, 576–577, 577*i*
Commerce Department, 561
Committee on Public Information (CPI), 533
Communist Party, 570, 579–580, 596, 674;
    see also Anticommunism
Community Action programs, 711
Compromise of 1877, 369–370
Computers, 545, 684, 802–804
Concentration policy, 394
Coney Island, 446
Congress
African American members, 363
direct election of senators, 462, 497
House Un-American Activities Committee,
    672–673
McCarthyism, 673–676, 699–700
Watergate investigations, 761, 763
women in, 527
Congress of Industrial Organizations (CIO),
    599, 681
Congress of Racial Equality (CORE), 636,
    713, 721
Conkin, Paul, 594
Conkling, Roscoe, 457, 458
Connor, Eugene "Bull," 713
Conroy, Jack, 579
Conscription
in peacetime, 622, 661
during Vietnam War, 739
during World War I, 527
Conservationists, 507–509, 510, 748
Conservatives
abortion issue, 807–808
capitalists, 412–413, 466
free-market, 777
gay rights issues, 744

John Birch Society, 660
neo-, 777–778
on New Deal, 593–596, 642
New Right, 773, 778–779
in 1960s, 733
in 1970s, 771–774
in postwar period, 659–660, 665, 711
religious, 772–773
Sagebrush Rebellion, 771, 779
silent majority, 734, 755
Tea Party, 800–801
during World War II, 642–643
Constitution, U.S.; *see also specific amendments*
Bill of Rights, 540
interstate commerce clause, 591
Consumerism
mass consumption, 440–443
in 1920s, 551–554, 555–556
in 1950s, 686–687
during World War II, 639
Containment policy, 653, 659–660, 663, 669,
    700, 819
Conwell, Russell H., 413
Coolidge, Calvin
Boston police strike and, 538, 560
presidency, 551, 559, 560
Coolies, 383
CORE; *see* Congress of Racial Equality
Corporations; *see also* Business
consolidation, 412
history, 410–412
holding companies, 412, 598
power, 425
Corruption
Agnew case, 763
in business, 489
in Grant administration, 367
payola scandals, 694
political machines and bosses, 439–440, 497
in Reconstruction governments, 363
in unions, 681–682
Cortina, Juan, 383
Coughlin, Charles E., 597, 602, 617
Counterculture, 739–740, 748
Court-packing plan, 603, 604–605
Courts; *see* Supreme Court
Cowboys, 390–391, 393
Cox, Archibald, 761
Cox, James M., 541, 584
Coxey, Jacob S., 463–464
Coxey's Army, 463*i*, 464
CPI; *see* Committee on Public Information

Crane, Stephen, 448
Crédit Mobilier, 367
Creel, George, 533
Crile, G. W., 451
Crime
    in cities, 438
    organized, 556, 702
    during World War II, 642
Crop-lien system, 365, 373, 373m
Cuba
    Bay of Pigs, 722
    economy, 482
    migration from, 743
    revolution, 702, 703i
    Spanish-American War, 454–455, 473,
        476–478, 477m
    U.S. occupation, 482
    war of independence, 454–455,
        472–473, 475
Cuban Americans, 743
Cuban missile crisis, 722–723
Culture; see also Art; Music; Popular culture
    exports, 552
    of Great Depression, 574–579, 580
    high, 448
    in 1920s, 551–558
    in 1950s, 686–694
    during World War II, 639–643
Custer, George A., 395, 396
CWA; see Civil Works Administration
Czechoslovakia
    communist government, 661
    Prague Spring, 730
    Sudetenland, 618–619

Daimler, Gottfried, 408
Dakota Territory
    Black Hills gold rush, 388
    reservations, 394, 396
Dalrymple, Louis, 520i
Darrow, Clarence, 558
Darwinism
    evolution, 449, 558
    imperialism and, 468
    Scopes trial, 558
    social, 412–413, 449
Daugherty, Harry, 560
Davis, David, 369–370
Davis, Henry, 354
Davis, John W., 559, 560
Dawes, Charles G., 613
Dawes Plan, 613

Dawes Severalty Act, 397–398
Dawley, Alan, 501
D-Day, 644, 644i
DDT, 683
De Leon, Daniel, 418–419
Dean, James, 692–693
Dean, John, 761
Debs, Eugene V., 424, 504, 514, 535
Debt
    of federal government, 780, 785
    during World War II, 634
Defense Department, 661
Defense of Marriage Act (DOMA), 744,
        809, 811
Democratic Party
    civil rights movement and, 717,
        718–719
    in late nineteenth century, 455–456, 458,
        464, 465–466
    New Deal and, 602–603, 606, 609
    in 1920s, 558–559
    in postwar period, 667
    in South, 370, 456
Deng Xiaoping, 770
Department stores, 441, 441i, 442–443
Depressions, 463–464; see also Great
        Depression
Deregulation, 779–780
Détente, 754, 774
Detroit
    Motown Records, 694
    race riots, 636
DeVoto, Bernard, 691
Dewey, George, 476
Dewey, John, 450
Dewey, Thomas E., 642–643, 667
Díaz, Porfirio, 523
Dies, Martin, 580
Dillingham, William P., 503–504
Dingley Tariff, 467
Dinosaur National Monument, 691
Diplomacy; see also Treaties
    Bush doctrine, 819
    of Clinton administration, 791, 794
    Dollar Diplomacy, 522
    in 1860s and 1870s, 368
    of Eisenhower, 700–702, 703
    human rights issues, 769
    interwar period, 611–619
    Monroe Doctrine, 472
    multilateral, 819
    neutrality, 618–619, 623

in 1960s and 1970s, 721–723, 753–755, 768, 769–770
in 1980s, 781, 782–783
of Obama administration, 820–821
Open Door, 484, 520
relations with China, 753–754, 770
relations with Latin America, 520–521, 613, 721–722, 755, 781
of F. Roosevelt, 614–615, 616–618, 655–658
of T. Roosevelt, 519–521
Truman Doctrine, 659
during World War II, 655–658
Dirigibles, 575
Diseases; *see also* Medicine
  AIDS, 744, 808–809, 815
  bacterial infections, 682
  in cities, 437
  germ theory, 451
  infectious, brought by Europeans, 382
  influenza, 532, 683
  malaria, 683
  polio, 584, 683
  smallpox, 382, 682
  vaccines, 682–683
  viral, 683
Disney, Walt, 577, 687
Disneyland, 687
Dittmer, John, 714
Divorce rates, 494, 642, 665
Dole, Robert J., 774, 792, 793
Dollar Diplomacy, 522
DOMA; *see* Defense of Marriage Act
Dominican Republic, 521, 523, 723
Dos Passos, John, 579
Douglas, Lewis, 596
Dower, John W., 649
Draft laws; *see* Conscription
Drake, Edwin L., 407
Dreiser, Theodore, 448
  Sister Carrie, 438
Drones, 820*i*
Drugs
  abuse, 808, 809
  antibiotics, 682, 683
Du Bois, W. E. B., 356, 502
Du Pont, 596
Dukakis, Michael, 784–785
Dulles, John Foster, 660, 700, 702
Dunning, William A., 356
Dust Bowl, 569, 569*i*, 579
Dylan, Bob, 728

Dyson, Michael Eric, 715

Earth Day, 749
Eastern Europe; *see also* Cold War; *and specific countries*
  fall of communism, 782–783
  Soviets and, 655, 656, 658, 702–703, 819
Echo Park, 691
Eckford, Elizabeth, 697*i*
Ecology, 748
Economics; *see also* Depressions; Industry
  of cities, 696
  Keynesian policies, 567, 699
  mass consumption, 440–443
  in 1920s, 537–538, 544–551, 565
  in 1950s, 679–682, 686–689
  in 1960s and 1970s, 759–760, 767–768, 769
  in 1980s, 779–781
  in 1990s, 802
  in post-Reconstruction era, 372–373
  in postwar period, 663–666, 671–672, 686–687
  in Reconstruction South, 364–365
  of West, 386–390, 680–681
  during World War II, 633–634
Economy Act, 589
Edison, Thomas A., 405–406, 446
Education; *see also* Literacy; Universities
  of African Americans, 356*i*, 364, 373–374, 806
  desegregation, 696–697, 755, 758, 759
  federal aid, 712
  of Indians, 450
  medical, 451, 493
  "No Child Left Behind," 795
  prayer in schools, 758
  professional, 493
  public schools, 450
  racial segregation, 364, 374, 450, 493, 715*i*
  school shootings, 801
  universal, 450
  of women, 452, 493, 554, 746
  youth culture and, 737–739
Egypt, 702, 755, 768, 769
Eighteenth Amendment, 503, 556–557
Einstein, Albert, 650
Eisenhower, Dwight D.
  election of 1948 and, 667
  foreign policy, 660
  Horatio Alger Award, 417
  McCarthyism and, 676
  on military–industrial complex, 703, 704–705

Eisenhower, Dwight D.—(*Cont.*)
  presidency, 691, 696–697, 698–705, 741
  presidential elections, 676, 684, 699
  in World War II, 630
Elections; *see also* Voting rights
  municipal, 497
  primary, 497–498
  recall, 498
  secret ballots, 496–497, 498
  turnout, 456, 498
Elections, by year
  1868, 366
  1872, 367
  1876, 369–370, 370m
  1880, 457
  1884, 458
  1888, 458
  1892, 459, 461
  1896, 454, 465–466, 467m
  1900, 481, 498
  1904, 509
  1908, 509, 510
  1912, 498, 504, 512–514, 513m
  1916, 515–516, 525, 526m
  1920, 537, 541, 560
  1924, 559, 560
  1928, 559, 560, 561, 561m
  1932, 584–585, 585m
  1936, 596, 602–603
  1940, 623
  1944, 642–643
  1948, 666m, 666–667
  1952, 676, 684
  1956, 699
  1960, 708, 709m
  1964, 711, 773–774
  1968, 731–734, 733m, 736
  1972, 751, 759
  1976, 768m, 768–769
  1980, 774–775, 775m
  1984, 781
  1988, 784m, 784–785
  1992, 786m, 786–787, 790
  1996, 792m, 792–793, 808
  2000, 794, 795m
  2004, 796
  2008, 796, 797, 800, 800m
  2012, 801
Electoral College, election of 1876, 369–370, 370m
Electricity, 405–406, 409, 590, 591–592
Elementary and Secondary Education Act of
    1965, 712

Ellsberg, Daniel, 751
Ellwood, I. L., 399
Emancipation
  aftermath, 352–354, 360, 364–365
  Thirteenth Amendment, 358
Emergency Banking Act, 588
Energy sources; *see also* Oil industry
  coal, 406, 506–507
  hydropower, 591–592, 691
  nuclear, 669, 812–813
Enforcement Acts, 369
Engel v. Vitale, 758
England; *see also* British Empire; World War I;
      World War II
  Labour Party, 490
  Suez crisis, 702, 757
  U.S. Civil War and, 368
Enigma machine, 635
Environmental Protection Agency (EPA), 749,
    758, 780
Environmentalism
  conservative opposition, 771, 779–780
  dam controversies, 691
  global movement, 812–813
  in 1960s and later, 747–750, 813–814
  organizations, 691
EPA; *see* Environmental Protection Agency
Equal Pay Act, 746
Equal Rights Amendment (ERA), 555, 747, 807
Equality; *see* Inequality
ERA; *see* Equal Rights Amendment
Ervin, Sam J., 761
Escobedo v. Illinois, 758
Espionage Act of 1917, 533
Ethnic groups, 420, 430–431, 445; *see also*
      Asian Americans; Hispanics; Immigrants
Eugenics, 503–504
Europe; *see also* Eastern Europe; Immigrants,
      European; World War I; World War II;
      and specific countries
  alliances, 524
  Cold War division, 658, 661–662, 662m
  industrialization, 432
  Marshall Plan, 660–661
  population growth, 432
  social democracy, 490–491
Evers, Medgar, 716
Executive branch; *see also* Presidents
  civil service, 458
  female cabinet members, 747
  patronage, 457
Exports, 551, 552; *see also* Trade

Fair Deal, 665, 667–668
Fair Employment Practices Commission
　　(FEPC), 636, 667
Fair Labor Standards Act, 606
Falklands War, 757
Fall, Albert B., 560
Falwell, Jerry, 773
Families
　　African American, 365, 807
　　in Great Depression, 574
　　single-parent, 807
　　of slaves, 365
　　suburban, 687–688
　　in World War II, 642
Far West; see West
Farm Credit Administration, 593
Farm Security Administration, 580, 590
Farmer, James, 636
Farmers' Alliances, 460–461
Farmers' Holiday Association, 582–583
Farming; see Agriculture
Farrell, James T., 579
Fascism, 567, 613–615; see also Nazi
　　Germany
Faubus, Orval, 697
FBI; see Federal Bureau of Investigation
FDIC; see Federal Deposit Insurance Corporation
Federal Art Project, 580, 601
Federal Bureau of Investigation (FBI), 673, 675
Federal Communications Commission, 554
Federal Deposit Insurance Corporation
　　(FDIC), 589
Federal Emergency Management Agency
　　(FEMA), 796
Federal Emergency Relief Administration
　　(FERA), 593
Federal government; see also Congress;
　　Executive branch; Supreme Court
　　budgets, 532, 560, 633, 699, 760, 793
　　debt, 780, 785
　　deficits, 780–781, 785
　　expansion, 516
　　in late nineteenth century, 456–459
　　loyalty program, 673
　　in 1920s, 559–561
　　racial segregation, 515
　　regulatory function, 609
　　women in, 607
Federal Highway Act of 1956, 691, 699
Federal Housing Administration (FHA), 593
Federal Reserve Act, 515
Federal Reserve system, 568, 760, 780

Federal Trade Commission Act, 515
Federal Writers' Project (FWP), 572–573,
　　580, 601
Feis, Herbert, 649
FEMA; see Federal Emergency
　　Management Agency
Feminism, 745–747; see also Women's rights
FEPC; see Fair Employment Practices
　　Commission
FERA; see Federal Emergency Relief
　　Administration
Ferguson, Thomas, 594
Ferraro, Geraldine, 747, 781
FHA; see Federal Housing Administration
Field, Cyrus W., 405
Fifteenth Amendment, 359, 369, 375
Filipino Americans, 549
Films
　　American industry, 552–553, 672
　　animated, 577
　　The Birth of a Nation, 557
　　documentaries, 580
　　film noir, 668
　　in 1930s, 575–578, 580
　　in 1950s, 692–693
　　silent, 446
　　sound, 377, 554
　　during World War II, 640
Fireside chats, 588
Fish, Hamilton, 366, 368, 580
Fish, Hamilton, Jr., 595
Fitzgerald, F. Scott, The Great Gatsby, 556
Five-Power Pact, 612
Flappers, 555, 555i
Fleming, Alexander, 682
Florey, Howard, 682
Florida
　　Cuban Americans, 743
　　election of 2000, 794
Foch, Ferdinand, 529
Folk music, 728–729
Folsom, Burton, 595
Foner, Eric, 357
Food
　　in late nineteenth century, 440
　　prices, 551
　　safety, 506
Football, 445
Foraker Act, 478
Ford, Gerald
　　presidency, 753, 764, 767–769, 774
　　as vice president, 763

Ford, Henry, 408, 409, 548
Foreign relations; *see* Diplomacy; Imperialism
Fortas, Abe, 758
Foster, Vince, 791
Fourteen Points, 535–536
Fourteenth Amendment, 358–359, 374
France; *see also* World War I; World War II
  colonies, 471, 701, 757
  D-Day invasion, 644, 644*i*
  events of 1968, 730–731
  Paris Expositions, 490*i*
  social democracy, 491
  Suez crisis, 702, 757
  Vichy regime, 619, 631
  in Vietnam, 701
Franco, Francisco, 579, 617
Frank, Leo, 557
Franklin, John Hope, 356
Franz Ferdinand, Archduke, 524
Frazier-Lemke Farm Bankruptcy Act, 593
Free silver, 464, 465, 467
Free speech, 540–541, 808
Free Speech Movement, 737–738
Freedmen's Bureau, 353–354, 356*i*, 358, 364
Freedom rides, 713
Freedom Summer, 717
Freeland, Richard, 674–675
Freidel, Frank, 595
Frick, Henry Clay, 411, 423, 424
Friedan, Betty, 745, 746
Frontier, 391–393; *see also* West
Fuchs, Klaus, 673
Fulbright, J. William, 727
Furman v. Georgia, 759
FWP; *see* Federal Writers' Project

Gaddis, John Lewis, 656–657
Gagarin, Yuri, 685
Galveston, Texas, 497
Garfield, James, 457–458
Garland, Hamlin, *Jason Edwards*, 402
Garner, Eric, 807
Garrow, David, 714
Garvey, Marcus, 539
Gast, John, *American Progress*, 391*i*
Gay liberation, 744–745; *see also*
  Homosexuals
Gender relations; *see also* Families;
  Marriage; Women
  in African American families, 365
  at end of nineteenth century, 494, 495–496
  in Great Depression, 573

  in 1920s, 554–555
  in suburban families, 687–688
  in World War I, 528
  in World War II, 640–642
General Federation of Women's Clubs, 494
General Motors, 409, 599, 699
Genetic research, 545, 804–805
George, Henry, 419
Georgia, Sea Islands, 353
Germ theory of disease, 451
German Americans, 535
Germany; *see also* Nazi Germany;
    World War I
  Allied occupation, 657–658
  colonies, 471, 472
  division, 658, 661
  Great Depression, 566–567
  Green Party, 812
  reparations, 565, 566, 613
  social democracy, 491
  Weimar Republic, 615
Geronimo, 397
"Ghettoes," 695–696, 806–807
Ghost Dance, 397
GI Bill of Rights, 663–665
Gideon v. Wainwright, 758
Gingrich, Newt, 791
Ginsburg, Ruth Bader, 747
Glasnost, 782
Glass-Steagall Act, 589, 797
Glavis, Louis, 510
Glenn, John, 685
Glidden, Joseph H., 399
Global migration, 432–433; *see also*
    Immigration; Migration
Global warming, 813, 814, 815
Globalization, 815, 816*i*; *see also* Trade
Gold reserves, 464, 467
Gold rushes
  Black Hills, 388
  California, 383, 384, 387
Gold standard, 466, 467
Goldwater, Barry, 711, 773–774
Gompers, Samuel, 422, 479, 499, 548
Gonzales v. Carhart, 808
Good Neighbor Policy, 617
Goodman, Andrew, 717
Gorbachev, Mikhail, 782–783, 785
Gordon, Colin, 594
Gordy, Berry, 694
Gore, Al, 794, 813, 814
Gospel of wealth, 413, 414–415

Governments; *see* Federal government; State governments
Grady, Henry, 372
Graham, Billy, 417
Grand Coulee Dam, 608
Grangers, 459, 460
Grant, Ulysses S., presidency, 366–369
Great Depression; *see also* New Deal
  bank failures, 565, 567, 572–573, 585, 588
  causes, 565
  culture, 574–579, 580
  effects, 568–574
  end of, 633
  Hoover's policies, 581–582, 585
  impact, 567
  politics, 579–585
  progress of, 567–568
  public relief, 569, 570, 592–593, 601–602
  responses, 567, 581–582
  stock market crash and, 564
  values, 574
  worldwide, 565, 566–567
The Great Gatsby (Fitzgerald), 556
Great Lakes region, steel industry, 406–407, 411
Great Migration, 539
Great Plains; *see also* West
  climate, 399
  Dust Bowl, 569, 569*i*, 579
  Plains Indians, 381–382
Great Recession of 2008, 796–797, 800
Great Society, 711–713, 727, 758
Great War; *see* World War I
Greeley, Horace, 367, 369
Green, Samuel, 548
Green parties, 812
Greenbacks, 367–368
Greenpeace, 812
Griffith, D. W., *The Birth of a Nation*, 446, 557
Griffith, Robert, 675
Griswold v. Connecticut, 747
Guadalcanal, 630
Guam, 478, 481, 629
Guantánamo, 818
Gulf of Tonkin Resolution, 725
Gulf War (1991), 785–786, 815
Gun control, 801; *see also* Weapons
Guthrie, Woody, 729

Hailey, Royce, 690
Haiti, U.S. troops, 523, 613
Haley, Alex, 715
Half-Breeds, 457

Hamby, Alonzo L., 649
Hamer, Fannie Lou, 717, 718–719
Hamilton, Grant, 465*i*
Hampton Institute, 450
Hancock, Winfield Scott, 457
Hanna, Marcus A., 465, 466, 505
Harding, Warren G., presidency, 535, 541, 559–560, 612
Harlem Renaissance, 539, 556
Harrington, Michael, *The Other America*, 694–695
Harrison, Benjamin, 458–459
Harrison, William Henry, grandson, 458
Harvard University, 595
Hawaii, 483*m*
  annexation to U.S., 468–469
  native population, 469
  Pearl Harbor, 468–469, 615, 625, 626*i*, 637
  as territory, 481
Hawley, Ellis, 595
Hawley-Smoot Tariff, 566, 582
Hay, John, 473, 484, 521
Hayes, Rutherford B., 369–370, 422, 457, 469
Haymarket bombing, 423
Hays, Samuel, 500
Hays, Will, 575
Haywood, William ("Big Bill"), 504, 535
Health; *see also* Diseases; Medicine
  in cities, 437
  improvements, 440
  public, 437, 451
Health care programs
  Affordable Care Act, 800
  Clinton reforms, 791
  Medicare and Medicaid, 711
  Sheppard-Towner Act, 555
Hearst, William Randolph, 447, 472, 474, 475, 617
Hemingway, Ernest, 618*i*
Hepburn Railroad Regulation Act, 506
Hetch Hetchy dam, 509
Hewitt, Abram S., 406
High culture, 448; *see also* Art; Culture; Literature
Higher education; *see* Universities
Hindenburg, 575
Hine, Lewis, 421*i*, 506*i*, 547*i*
Hip-hop culture, 798
Hiroshima, 648–649, 650–651
Hispanics
  in Great Depression, 570–571
  immigrants, 805
  immigration reform and, 801–802

Hispanics—(*Cont.*)
migrant workers, 571, 743
migration to cities, 695–696, 742–743
New Deal and, 607
political power, 743
poor, 695, 743
population growth, 742
in West, 382–383, 570–571
workers, 420, 549–550
Hispaniola, 549; *see also* Haiti
Hiss, Alger, 672–673
Historians
on civil rights movement, 714–715
on Cold War, 656–657
on McCarthyism, 674–675
on New Deal, 594–595
on progressivism, 500–501
on Reconstruction, 356–357
scientific method, 450
on Truman's atom bomb decision, 648–649
on Watergate, 762–763
on West, 392–393
Hitchcock, Alfred, 553
Hitler, Adolf, 615*i*; *see also* Nazi Germany
beliefs, 615
in comic books, 577
death, 646
eastern offensive, 631
Munich conference, 619
rise of, 567, 615
HIV, 808–809
Ho Chi Minh, 701, 724
Hoffa, Jimmy, 682
Hofstadter, Richard, 500, 594, 674
Holbrooke, Richard, 791
Holding companies, 412
Holding Company Act, 598
Holmes, Oliver Wendell, Jr., 540–541
Holocaust, 631–632, 645*i*
Home Owners' Loan Corporation, 593
Homer, Winslow, 448
Homestead Act, 386
Homestead Strike, 423–424, 464
Homosexuals
AIDS epidemic, 808–809
gay liberation, 744–745
marriages, 744, 809–811
in military, 641, 744, 790–791
Hooper, William, 469
Hoover, Herbert
as commerce secretary, 561

foreign policy, 613, 615–616
presidency, 559, 561, 563, 581–585, 590, 613
World War I and, 532
Hoover, J. Edgar, 540, 673, 675
Hoovervilles, 582
Hopkins, Harry, 593, 601, 606
Hopper, Edward, 448
Horizontal integration, 411
House, Edward M., 514
House Un-American Activities Committee (HUAC), 672–673
Housing
bubble, 797
in cities, 435*i*, 435–436
mortgages, 593, 797
in 1950s, 680, 687
segregated, 687
Housing Act of 1961, 712
Howard, Oliver O., 354
Howells, William Dean, 448
HUAC; *see* House Un-American Activities Committee
Hubble Space Telescope, 686
Huerta, Victoriano, 523
Hughes, Charles Evans, 525, 603, 612, 613
Hughes, Langston, 556
Hull, Cordell, 617
Hull House, 492
Human Genome Project, 804
Human rights, 769
Humphrey, Hubert, 667, 732, 734
Hungary, 702
Huntsman, Jon, 773
Hurricane Katrina, 796
Hussein, Saddam, 785, 818–819

I Love Lucy, 689*i*
IBM, 684, 803
ICBMs, 685, 754
ICC; *see* Interstate Commerce Commission
Ickes, Harold, 606
Idaho, statehood, 386
Illinois; *see* Chicago
IMF; *see* International Monetary Fund
Immigrant labor force
braceros, 637
Chinese, 383–386
in late nineteenth century, 419–420, 424–425
need for, 431

Immigrants
  assimilation, 431
  Chinese, 383–386, 384*i*, 639
  in cities, 429–431, 435–436
  criminals, 438
  ethnic communities, 430–431, 445
  Japanese, 549
  Mexican, 549–550, 742
  military service, 527–529
  share of population, 805, 806*i*
  in West, 383–386
Immigrants, European
  in cities, 429–431
  countries of origin, 420, 430*i*
  quotas, 557
Immigration
  from 1861 to 1900, 419–420, 428–431, 429*i*
  Chinese Exclusion Act, 386, 431, 639
  motives, 420, 431, 432
  nativism, 504, 557–558
  quotas, 557, 639
  reforms, 712, 801–802
  restrictions, 431, 456, 503–504, 557
  in twenty-first century, 801–802, 805
Immigration Act of 1965, 712
Immigration Reform Act of 1965, 805
Immigration Restriction League, 431
Impeachment
  of Bill Clinton, 793–794
  of Andrew Johnson, 362
  Nixon investigation, 763
Imperialism; *see also* British Empire; Colonies;
    Spanish Empire
  American, 455, 468–472, 478–484, 756
  end of, 756
  European, 468, 470–471, 484
  Japanese, 614–615, 625
  labor migration and, 433
  opponents, 479–481
Income taxes, 515, 598, 634
Incomes; *see also* Wages
  around 1900, 420
  in industrial age, 440
  of middle class, 440
  in 1920s, 544, 545–546, 547, 548
  in 1930s, 569
  in post-Reconstruction South, 372
  in Reconstruction South, 364–365
  of women, 745*i*, 746
  during World War II, 633
Indentured servants
  Chinese, 383, 433

  in nineteenth century, 433
India
  Bhopal disaster, 812
  British rule, 470, 471*i*, 756
Indian Civil Rights Act, 741
Indian Peace Commission, 394
Indian policies
  assimilation, 398, 741
  concentration, 394–395
  Dawes Act, 397–398
  in New Deal, 607
  reservations, 394–395, 396, 636
  termination, 741
Indian Reorganization Act, 607, 636
Indian Territory, reservations, 394
Indians
  agriculture, 607
  assimilated, 636
  code-talkers, 636
  conflicts with whites, 395–397
  education, 450
  infectious diseases, 382
  iron and steel production, 411
  New Deal and, 607
  Plains, 381–382, 393–398
  poor, 695
  religions, 397
  rights movement, 741–742, 742*i*
  treaties, 394, 396
  tribal sovereignty, 394, 607, 636, 741–742
  wars with United States, 395, 396–397
  wars with white settlers, 382
  white attitudes, 607
  World War II and, 636
Indigenous peoples; *see* Indians
Individualism, 412–413
Industrial Workers of the World (IWW),
    504, 535
Industry; *see also* Business; Corporations; *and
    specific industries*
  assembly lines, 409, 409*i*
  in cities, 406, 696
  consolidation, 411–412, 418*i*, 545
  foreign competition, 760
  growth, 404–412
  horizontal integration, 411
  labor force, 409, 419–420, 696
  military–industrial complex, 703,
    704–705
  mill towns, 372–373
  New Deal and, 590–591
  in 1920s, 544, 545–548, 565

Industry—(*Cont.*)
    production techniques, 408–409
    research and development, 408
    restructuring, 760, 802
    in South, 372–373
    technologies, 405–408
    vertical integration, 411
    in World War I, 532–533
    in World War II, 633, 634, 635–636, 642
Inequality; *see also* Poverty
    Carnegie's defense, 414–415
    Occupy Wall Street protests, 801
Inflation
    in 1920s, 537–538
    in 1950s, 679
    in 1960s and 1970s, 760, 767–768, 769
    in 1980s, 780
    in postwar period, 665, 671
    during World War II, 634
Initiatives, 497
Insull, Samuel, 591
Intel, 803
Intelligence; *see also* Central Intelligence Agency
    Soviet spies, 673
    U-2 crisis, 703
    in World War II, 635
Interchangeable parts, 409
Interest groups, 498
Interior Department, 510, 560
International Monetary Fund (IMF), 815
Internet, 802, 803–804
Interstate Commerce Act, 459, 506
Interstate Commerce Commission (ICC), 459, 506
Interstate highways, 689, 691, 699
Inventions; *see* Technology
Iran
    coup against Mossadegh, 701–702
    hostage crisis, 770–771, 775
    nuclear program, 820
    revolution (1979), 816
    terrorism and, 818
Iran-contra scandal, 784
Iraq, Gulf War, 785–786, 815
Iraq War, 795, 796, 815, 818–820
Iron industry, 406, 411, 544
ISIS (Islamic State of Iraq and Syria), 821
Isolationism, 612, 617–618, 622–623
Israel
    founding, 701, 756
    relations with Egypt, 768, 769
    wars, 701, 702, 755
Issei, 549, 637

Italy
    fascism, 567, 613–615, 617
    Tripartite Pact, 625
    in World War II, 631
Iwo Jima, Battle of, 646
IWW ("Wobblies"), 504, 535

Jackson State University, 750–751
James, William, 450
Japan; *see also* World War II
    alliance with Germany and Italy, 625
    atomic bombings, 648*i*, 648–649, 650–651
    Great Depression, 567, 614
    imperialism, 614–615, 625
    military technology, 634
    navy, 520, 629–630, 646
    postwar growth, 659
    relations with United States, 520
    Russo-Japanese War, 520, 655
    Sino-Japanese War, 614–615, 616
    surrender, 651
    Tokyo firebombing, 647–649
Japanese Americans; *see also* Asian Americans
    in Great Depression, 571
    internment, 637–639
    Issei and Nisei, 549, 637
    workers, 549
Jarvis, Howard, 774
The Jazz Singer, 554
Jenner, Edward, 682
Jews
    anti-Semitism, 557–558
    comic book writers, 576
    Holocaust, 631–632, 645*i*
    immigrants, 430
    Reform Judaism, 431
    refugees, 632*i*
    on Supreme Court, 515–516
Jim Crow laws, 375
Jingoes, 468, 481
John Birch Society, 660
John Paul II, Pope, 657
Johns Hopkins University, 451, 493
Johnson, Andrew
    impeachment, 362
    presidency, 357–362, 364, 368
    as vice president, 357
Johnson, Hiram, 501
Johnson, Hugh S., 590, 591
Johnson, Lady Bird, 748
Johnson, Lyndon B., 710*i*
    foreign policy, 723

Great Society, 711–713, 727, 758
   presidency, 709, 710–713, 717
   Vietnam War, 725–727, 731–732
Jolson, Al, 377, 554
Jones, Paula, 793
Jones Act, 478
Joseph, Chief, 397
Joubert, Jules-Francois, 682
Journalism; see Muckrakers; News media;
     Newspapers; Press freedom
Judaism; see Jews
Judd, G. P., 469
Juvenile delinquency, 692

Kamehameha I, king of Hawaii, 469
Kamehameha III, king of Hawaii, 469
Kansas
   cattle drives, 389
   segregated schools, 696, 715i
Karl, Barry, 594–595
Kearney, Denis, 385
Kearny, Stephen W., 382
Keating-Owen Act, 516
Kellogg, Frank, 612, 613
Kellogg-Briand Pact, 612
Kelly, Robin, 714
Kelly, William, 406
Kennan, George F., 659, 663, 724
Kennedy, David, 595
Kennedy, Edward, 774
Kennedy, John F.
   assassination, 709–710, 717
   foreign policy, 721–723, 724–725
   presidency, 708–709, 712, 713, 716, 745–746
Kennedy, Joseph P., 622, 708
Kennedy, Randall, 715
Kennedy, Robert F., 713, 727, 732, 743i
Kent State University, 750
Keppler, Joseph, 489i
Kerouac, Jack, On the Road, 690, 692
Keynes, John Maynard, 567, 568, 699
Khomeini, Ruhollah, Ayatollah, 770
Khrushchev, Nikita, 703, 722
King, Martin Luther, Jr., 698, 713, 714, 716i,
   717, 720, 732
Kissinger, Henry, 750, 751, 753, 754, 768, 774
Klan; see Ku Klux Klan
Klarman, Michael, 715
Kluger, Richard, 715
Knights of Labor, 422, 423, 462
Knox, Philander C., 522
Koch, Howard, 620–621

Kolko, Gabriel, 500
Korean War, 669–672, 670m, 676, 679, 700
Korematsu v. U.S., 637–639
Kroc, Ray, 690–691
Ku Klux Klan, 368–369, 557–558, 559
Kutler, Stanley I., 763
Kuwait, Gulf War, 785–786
Kyoto Protocol, 813, 814

La Follette, Robert, 498, 512
Labor force; see also Child labor; Immigrant
     labor force; Indentured servants; Slavery;
     Strikes; Unemployment; Unions; Wages;
     Women in workforce
   agricultural, 571, 695
   industrial, 409, 419–425
   leisure time, 443
   in 1920s, 545–550
   in postwar period, 665
   racial and ethnic discrimination, 548–550,
     696, 720
   racial integration, 635–636
   regulations, 606
   segregation, 387
   in West, 387, 388
   white-collar, 440, 692
   working conditions, 372, 387, 420–421,
     499–501, 548
   during World War II, 633, 635–636, 637
Labor laws
   on child labor, 421, 494, 516, 606
   in nineteenth century, 421, 424
   progressive reforms, 499–501
Labor-Management Relations Act (Taft-Hartley
     Act), 665–666
LaFeber, Walter, 656
Laird, Melvin, 750
Lamar, Howard, 392
Land policies
   in Reconstruction South, 364
   in West, 386, 501, 507–509, 510
Land-grant institutions, 450, 451
Landon, Alf M., 602
Lange, Dorothea, 580, 581i
Laos, 726m, 750–751
Latin America; see also Spanish Empire; and
     specific countries
   CIA-supported coups, 702, 755
   Good Neighbor Policy, 617
   Monroe Doctrine, 472
   Roosevelt Corollary, 521, 613
   U.S. policies, 520–521, 613, 721–722, 755, 781

Lawyers, 493
Le Duc Tho, 751
League of Nations
    covenant, 536, 537
    Japan and, 614, 617
    opponents, 611
    proposal, 536
    replacing, 612
    Wilson's support, 541
League of Women Voters, 555
Lease, Mary E., 461i
Lebanon, 781
Leff, Mark, 594–595
Leffler, Melvyn, 656
Legal system; see Regulation; Supreme Court
Leisure activities
    in consumer society, 443–447
    gender differences, 444
    in 1950s, 688–691
    during World War II, 639–640
Lemke, William, 602
Lend-lease, 623
Lenin, V. I., 527
Leopold, Aldo, 748
Lesbians, Boston marriages, 494; see also
        Homosexuals
Leuchtenburg, William, 594
Levitt, William, 687
Levittown, 687
Lewinsky, Monica, 793
Lewis, John L., 579, 599, 665
Lewis, Sinclair, 556
Leyte Gulf, Battle of, 646
Liberal Republicans, 367, 369
Liberalism
    anticommunism, 667
    New Deal, 594, 595
    in 1960s, 708–713
Liberty bonds, 532
Liberty League, 596
Libya, 820
Life expectancies, 440, 683
Life magazine, 578–579, 623, 639
Liliuokalani, Queen, 469
Limbaugh, Rush, 773
Lincoln, Abraham
    assassination, 355–357
    Civil War and, 352, 353i
    portrait, 355i
    Reconstruction and, 354, 355
Lincoln, Mary Todd, 355
Lincoln Brigade, 579

Lindbergh, Charles, 408, 622–623
Lippmann, Walter, 595
Lister, Joseph, 682
Literacy, voting rights and, 375
Literature; see also Popular culture
    in Great Depression, 578, 579
    Harlem Renaissance, 539, 556
    in 1920s, 556
    in 1950s, 692
    realism, 448
    sentimental novels, 446
    in urban age, 448
    Western novels, 390
Little Bighorn, 396, 396i
Little Crow, 395
Little Women (Alcott), 417
Litwack, Leon, 357
Lloyd, Henry Demarest, 490
Lloyd George, David, 536
Lodge, Henry Cabot, 537, 611
Long, Huey P., 597i, 597–598, 602
Long drives, 388, 389m, 390
Lorentz, Pare, 580
Los Angeles
    growth, 681
    Hispanics, 742
    industry, 633
    Watts riots, 720
    zoot-suit riots, 637
Lost Generation, 556
Louisiana, Long as governor, 597
Lusitania, 525
Lynchings, 375, 378, 378i, 502, 539, 606–607

Maathai, Wangari, 813
MacArthur, Arthur, 482
MacArthur, Douglas
    Bonus Army and, 584
    father, 482
    Korean War, 670–671
    occupation of Japan, 659
    in World War II, 629, 646
Maceo, Antonio, 476
Madero, Francisco, 523
Magazines, 578–579, 623, 639, 682
Mahan, Alfred Thayer, 468
Maine, U.S.S., 473, 475
Manchuria, 614, 616–617
Mandela, Nelson, 783
Mangas Colorados, 397
Manhattan Project, 650, 673
Manifest Destiny, 468

Manufacturing; *see* Industry
Mao Zedong, 614, 659, 663
Marable, Manning, 715
March on Washington, 714, 716*i*, 716–717
Marconi, Guglielmo, 405
Marriage
    Boston marriages, 494
    companionate, 554
    same-sex, 744, 809–811
    during World War II, 640, 642
Marshall, George C., 630, 660, 676
Marshall Plan, 660–661
Martí, José, 472
Marx Brothers, 577, 578*i*
Massachusetts; *see* Boston
Massachusetts Institute of Technology, 451
May, Ernest, 656
McAdoo, William, 559
McCain, John, 796, 797, 800
McCarran Internal Security Act, 673
McCarthy, Eugene, 732
McCarthy, Joseph, 673–676, 699–700
McCarthyism, 673–676, 699–700
McCord, James W., 761
McCormick, Richard, 500
McCullen v. Coakley, 808
McCullough, David, 649
McDonald's, 690–691
McGerr, Michael, 501
McGovern, George S., 759
McKay, Claude, 539
McKeand, Kimberly, 810
McKinley, William
    assassination, 505
    cartoon, 479*i*
    in Congress, 459
    presidency, 454, 466–467, 484–485
    presidential elections, 454, 465, 466,
        467*m*, 481
    Spanish-American War, 472–473, 476–479
McKinley Tariff, 459, 465, 467
McNamara, Robert, 727
McNary-Haugen Bill, 551
McVeigh, Timothy, 817
Meany, George, 681
Meat Inspection Act, 506
Media; *see* News media; Radio; Television
Medicaid, 711
Medicare, 711
Medicine; *see also* Diseases; Health
    advances, 451, 682–683
    AIDS treatments, 809

    education, 451, 493
    nursing, 493
    as profession, 492–493
    vaccines, 682–683
Mellon, Andrew, 560
"Memorial Day Massacre," 599–600, 600*i*
Men; *see* Gender relations
Mencken, H. L., 556
Mendel, Gregor, 545, 804
Mercury Theater, 620–621
Mexican Americans; *see also* Hispanics
    braceros, 637
    in California and Texas, 382–383
    in cities, 695–696
    in Great Depression, 570–571
    immigrants, 549–550, 742
    migrant workers, 695, 743
    street gangs, 637
    workers in World War II, 637
Mexico
    Pershing expedition, 523
    Veracruz incident, 523
    Zimmermann Telegram, 525–526
MFDP; *see* Mississippi Freedom Democratic Party
Microsoft, 803
Middle class
    African Americans, 698, 806
    in cities, 438
    growth, 440
    leisure time, 443
    in 1920s, 551, 554
    in 1950s, 686–689
    professionals, 492–493
    progressivism, 500
    silent majority, 734, 755
Middle East; *see also specific countries*
    in Cold War, 701–702
    conflicts, 820–821
    refugees, 755
    terrorism, 781, 821
Migration; *see also* Immigrants; West, settle-
        ment of
    to California, 681
    to cities, 428–429, 432, 570, 636, 637, 695
    global, 432–433
    to North, 538*m*, 539, 570
    reverse, 399
Miles, Nelson, 397, 476
Military; *see also* Army; Conscription; Navy
    African Americans, 527, 538–539,
        636, 665, 698
    ban on homosexuals, 641, 744, 790–791

Military—(*Cont.*)
  immigrants in, 527–529
  Joint Chiefs of Staff, 485
  modernization, 485
  segregation, 527, 636, 667–668
  terrorist attacks on, 781
  women in, 642
Military–industrial complex, 703, 704–705
Milligan, Ex parte, 362
Milliken v. Bradley, 759
Milosevic, Slobodan, 794
Mining
  child labor, 506*i*
  gold rushes, 383, 384, 387–388
  unions, 505–506, 599, 633, 665, 682
Minstrel shows, 374, 376*i*, 376–377, 445
Miranda v. Arizona, 758
Mississippi Freedom Democratic Party (MFDP),
  717, 718–719
Mitchell, Margaret, *Gone with the Wind*, 578
Molly Maguires, 421–422
Mondale, Walter, 781
Monetary policy
  bimetallism, 464
  Federal Reserve system, 515
  gold reserves, 464, 467
  gold standard, 466, 467
  in 1930s, 568
  in 1970s, 769
  in 1980s, 780
  of Nixon, 760
  silver question, 464, 467
Monopolies; *see also* Antitrust laws
  critics of, 419
  in oil industry, 411
  power, 412, 413, 419
  telephone, 447–448
Monroe Doctrine, 472
  Roosevelt Corollary, 521, 613
Montana
  Little Bighorn, 396, 396*i*
  mining, 388
  statehood, 386
Montgomery, Bernard, 631, 646
Moon landings, 685–686, 686*i*
Moran, Thomas, 390
Morgan, J. P., 411, 412, 505, 509
Morgan, Thomas Hunt, 545, 804
Mormons, 386, 773, 807
Morrill Act, 450
Mossadegh, Mohammed, 701–702
Motown Records, 694

Movies; *see* Films
Mowry, George, 500
Muckrakers, 489, 497
Muir, John, 507, 508, 509
Mukden Incident, 616
Muller, Paul, 683
Munich conference, 619
Murphy, Charles Francis, 499
Music
  folk, 728–729
  jazz, 639–640
  minstrel shows, 374, 376*i*, 376–377, 445
  rap, 797, 798–799
  rock 'n' roll, 693–694, 739–740
  World War I songs, 534–535
Mussolini, Benito, 567, 613–615, 615*i*, 619, 631

NAACP (National Association for the
  Advancement of Colored People), 502,
  502*i*, 539, 716
NAFTA; *see* North American Free Trade
  Agreement
Nagasaki, 648*i*, 648–649, 651
Naismith, James A., 445
NASA; *see* National Aeronautics and Space
  Administration
Nasser, Gamal Abdel, 702
Nation of Islam, 721
National Aeronautics and Space Administration
  (NASA), 685–686
National American Woman Suffrage Associa-
  tion (NAWSA), 495
National Association of Colored Women, 494,
  502
National Association of Manufacturers, 493
National Broadcasting Company, 554
National Cash Register Company, 409*i*
National Consumers League (NCL), 443
National Defense Research Committee, 634
National Farm Bureau Federation, 493
National forests and parks, 507*m*, 507–509, 510
National Greenback Party, 368
National Industrial Recovery Act, 590–591, 598
National Labor Relations Act (Wagner Act),
  598, 603, 665
National Labor Relations Board (NLRB), 598
National Organization for Women (NOW), 746
National Origins Act of 1924, 557
National parks, 691
National Reclamation Act, 507
National Recovery Administration (NRA),
  590–591, 607

National Rifle Association (NRA), 801
National Security Act of 1947, 661
National Security Council (NSC)
  establishment, 661
  NSC-68, 663, 664
National War Labor Board, 532–533
National Woman's Party, 496, 555
National Youth Administration (NYA), 601
Nationalism
  black, 539
  New, 511, 513
Native Americans; *see* Indians
Nativism, 504, 557–558
NATO (North Atlantic Treaty Organization),
  661–662, 794, 818, 820
Navajo code-talkers, 636
Navy, U.S.
  Great White Fleet, 520
  growth, 519
  integrated ships, 636
  Pacific bases, 481, 756
  Pearl Harbor base, 468–469, 615, 625, 626*i*
  Spanish-American War, 476
  Veracruz incident, 523
  in World War I, 527, 530–531
  in World War II, 629–630, 646–647
NAWSA; *see* National American Woman
    Suffrage Association
Nazi Germany; *see also* World War II
  atomic bomb research, 649–650
  blitzkrieg, 619
  expansion, 618–619
  Holocaust, 631–632, 645*i*
  military technology, 634, 635
  reparations, 657, 658
  Soviet Union and, 580, 619, 623
  surrender, 646
  Tripartite Pact, 625
Nazi Party, 615
NCL; *see* National Consumers League
Nebraska, statehood, 386
Nelson, Gaylord, 749
Neoconservatives, 777–778
Neutrality Acts, 617–619
Nevada
  mining, 387–388
  statehood, 386
New Deal
  African Americans and, 606–607
  conservative criticism, 593–596, 642
  end of, 606, 642
  Federal Art Project, 580, 601

  Federal Writers' Project, 572–573,
    580, 601
  historians' views, 594–595
  industrial recovery, 590–591
  launching, 588–593
  legacy, 587, 608–609, 699
  political realignment, 602–603, 606, 609
  populist criticism, 596–598
  public works projects, 582, 590, 591–592,
    593, 601, 606, 608
  recession and, 603–606
  regional planning, 591–592
  relief programs, 592–593
  Second, 598
  Social Security Act, 600–601
  Works Progress Administration, 580, 601,
    602*i*, 605, 607, 642
New England; *see specific states*
New Freedom, 513, 515
New Frontier, 709, 711
New Left, 728, 737–739
New Mexico
  annexation to U.S., 382
  Hispanic residents, 382
  Indians, 382
  territory, 386
New Nationalism, 511, 513
New Right, 773, 778–779
New South, 371–375, 378
"New woman," 494
New World Order, 815
New York City
  Central Park, 434, 444, 446
  Chinatown, 571*i*
  expansion, 434
  Feejon Coffee House, 729*i*
  Great Depression, 568*i*
  mass transit, 436
  Puerto Ricans, 743
  skyscrapers, 436
  Stonewall Riot, 744
  Tammany Hall, 369, 439*i*, 440, 458,
    499, 501
New York High School Student Union, 738
New York Journal, 472, 474–475
New York Times, 751
New York Tribune, 367
New York World, 472, 474–475
News media
  election predictions, 684
  freedom of press, 640
  television, 684, 688, 698, 730

Newspapers
  chains, 447
  in late nineteenth century, 447
  mass-circulation, 447
  telegraph and, 447
  yellow journalism, 472, 474–475
Nez Percé, 396–397
Ngo Dinh Diem, 701, 724–725
Nicaragua
  canal projects, 521
  contras, 784
  treaty, 523
  U.S. troops, 522, 613
Nimitz, Chester, 629, 646
9/11 attacks, 789, 817i, 818
1920s
  culture, 551–558
  economy, 537–538, 544–551, 565
  gender relations, 554–555
  as New Era, 543
  politics, 558–561
  technology, 544–545
1950s; see also Postwar period
  affluence, 686–687
  Cold War, 700–703
  economic "miracle," 679–682
  Korean War, 669–672, 670m, 676, 679, 700
  margins of society, 694–696
  politics, 698–700
  popular culture, 688–689, 692–694, 698
  poverty, 694–696
  science and technology, 682–686
  youth culture, 692–693
1960s and 1970s; see also Vietnam War
  economy, 759–760, 767–768, 769
  environmentalism, 747–750
  events of 1968, 729–734
  foreign relations, 721–723, 753–755, 768, 769–770
  politics, 731–734, 755, 758–759, 767, 771–775
  religions, 771–773
  rights movements, 740–747
  youth culture, 730, 737–740
1980s
  economy, 779–781
  foreign relations, 781, 782–783
  politics, 775–779
Nineteenth Amendment, 496, 541
Nisei, 549, 637
Nixon, Richard M.
  China visit, 753–754, 754i
  in Congress, 672–673
  domestic policies, 741–742, 749, 755, 758, 760
  foreign policy, 753–755
  impeachment investigation, 763
  pardon, 767
  presidential elections, 708, 733–734, 759
  resignation, 764, 764i
  Supreme Court appointments, 758–759
  as vice president, 676
  Vietnam War, 750–752
  Watergate, 761–764
Nixon Doctrine, 754–755
NLRB; see National Labor Relations Board
Noriega, Manuel, 785
Norris, Frank, 448
Norris, George, 501
North, black migration, 538m, 539, 570; see also
    specific states
North Africa, in World War II, 630m, 631
North American Free Trade Agreement
    (NAFTA), 791
North Atlantic Treaty Organization (NATO),
    661–662, 794, 818, 820
North Dakota, statehood, 386
North Korea; see Korean War
North Vietnam; see Vietnam
Northern Securities Company, 505
NOW; see National Organization for Women
Noyce, Florence, 495i
NRA; see National Recovery Administration;
    National Rifle Association
NSC; see National Security Council
NSC-68, 663, 664
Nuclear power, 669, 812–813
Nuclear weapons; see also Atomic bombs
  arms control treaties, 754, 768, 770, 771,
    781, 783
  brinksmanship, 700
  fears, 668–669
  hydrogen bombs, 684–685
  ICBMs, 685, 754
  research, 661, 669, 684–685
Nurses, 493
NYA; see National Youth Administration
Nye, Gerald, 617, 622–623

Obama, Barack
  Affordable Care Act, 800
  cabinet, 747
  domestic policies, 745, 800–802, 805, 808, 814
  foreign policy, 820–821
  presidential elections, 796, 797, 800, 801

O'Brien, Gail, 714
Ocala Demands, 460, 462
Occupational Safety and Health Administration, 437
Occupy Wall Street (OWS), 801
O'Connor, Sandra Day, 747, 796
Office of Economic Opportunity (OEO), 711
Office of Price Administration (OPA), 634
Office of War Information (OWI), 640
Office of War Mobilization (OWM), 634
Ogletree, Charles, 715
Oil embargo, 755, 760
Oil industry
    early discoveries, 407, 407i
    monopolies, 411
    spills, 749, 813, 814i
    Teapot Dome scandal, 560
Okies, 569, 579, 581i
Okinawa, 646–647
Oklahoma territory, 386; see also Indian
    Territory
Olmsted, Frederick Law, 434
O'Neill, William, 674
OPA; see Office of Price Administration
OPEC; see Organization of Petroleum Exporting
    Countries
Open Door, 484, 520
Oppenheimer, J. Robert, 650
O'Reilly, Kenneth, 675
The Organization Man (Whyte), 692
Organization of Petroleum Exporting Countries
    (OPEC), 755, 760, 768, 769, 780
Orlando, Vittorio, 536
Oswald, Lee Harvey, 709–710
The Other America (Harrington), 694–695
Otto, Nicolaus August, 407–408
"Over There" (Cohan), 534–535
OWI; see Office of War Information
OWM; see Office of War Mobilization
OWS; see Occupy Wall Street

Pacific Islands; see also Hawaii
    Guam, 478, 481, 629
    Samoa, 469, 472
    U.S. territories, 481–482, 483m
    in World War II, 629–630, 646–649, 647m
Pahlevi, Mohammed Reza, Shah, 702
Palmer, A. Mitchell, 540
Palmer Raids, 540
Panama, U.S. invasion, 785
Panama Canal, 521, 769, 774
Panic of 1873, 367, 369

Panic of 1893, 463–464
Panic of 1907, 509, 512
Paris Expositions, 490i
Paris Peace Conference, 536
Parity, 551
Parks, Rosa, 697
Parmet, Herbert, 762
Parties; see Political parties
Partisanship, 790–791, 800–802
Pasteur, Louis, 682
Paterson, Thomas G., 656
Patronage, 457
Patten, Simon, 443–444
Patterson, James T., 594–595, 715
Patton, George S., 631
Paul, Alice, 496, 555
Paulson, Henry, 797
Payne, Charles, 714
Payne-Aldrich Tariff, 510
Payola scandals, 694
Peace Corps, 722
Pearl Harbor, 468–469, 615, 625, 626i, 637
Peirce, Charles S., 450
Pendleton Act, 458
Pennsylvania
    oil drilling, 407i
    steel industry, 406–407, 423–424
Pennsylvania Railroad, 407, 411
Pensions, 596; see also Social Security system
Pentagon Papers, 751
People's Party, 459, 461, 466; see also Populism
Perestroika, 782
Perkins, Frances, 607
Perot, Ross, 787, 791, 793
Pershing, John J., 523, 529, 530
Pesticides, 683
Petroleum; see Oil industry
Philadelphia, Wanamaker's department store,
    442–443
Philanthropy, 413, 414–415, 434, 450–451
Philippines, 483m
    independence, 484, 756
    revolt against U.S. rule, 482–483
    as Spanish colony, 472
    Spanish-American War, 476, 478–479
    U.S. occupation, 482–484
    in World War II, 629, 646
Phillips, Sam, 693
Photography
    of Great Depression, 580
    Life magazine, 578–579
Pinchot, Gifford, 507, 509, 510

Pinkerton Detective Agency, 423
Pinochet, Augusto, 755
Plains Indians, 381–382, 393–398
Planter class, 371
Platt Amendment, 482
Plessy v. Ferguson, 374, 696
Poland
    Auschwitz, 632, 645*i*
    Soviets and, 655, 657, 658
    World War II, 619, 655
Police forces, 438, 538, 560
Political machines and bosses, 438–440, 496,
        497, 498; *see also* Tammany Hall
Political parties; *see also specific parties*
    declining influence, 498
    green, 812
    in late nineteenth century, 455–456
    in late twentieth century, 790–791
    loyalties, 456
    New Deal realignment, 602–603, 606, 609
    in 1950s, 698–699
    People's Party, 459, 461, 466
Political systems, 496–498; *see also* Constitution
Pollution, 748–749, 815; *see also*
    Environmentalism
Polsby, Nelson, 675
Pomeroy, Earl, 392
Popular culture; *see also* Films; Music; Sports
    Alcott's novels, 413, 417, 447
    Alger's novels, 413, 416*i*, 416–417
    comic books, 576–577
    cowboys, 390–391
    dime novels, 446
    entertainment, 376–377
    in Great Depression, 574–579
    leisure activities, 443–447, 639–640,
        688–691
    minstrel shows, 374, 376*i*, 376–377, 445
    in 1950s, 688–689, 692–694, 698
    in postwar period, 668–669
    radio, 574–575, 620–621
    sentimental novels, 446
    television, 688
    theater, 445
    vaudeville, 445
    Wild West shows, 390–391
    in World War I, 533, 534–535
    in World War II, 639–640
    yellow journalism, 472, 474–475
Popular Front, 579, 580, 728
Population growth
    age distribution, 805

    environmental costs, 748–749
    in 1950s, 680
Populism
    Coxey's Army, 463–464
    Democrats and, 466
    of farmers, 460–462
    ideas, 462, 466, 497
    New Deal and, 596–598
    People's Party, 459, 461, 466
    reformers, 462
Pornography, 758
Postwar period; *see also* Cold War; 1950s
    economy, 663–666, 671–672, 686–687
    families, 687–688
    Marshall Plan, 660–661
    politics, 659–660, 665, 667, 711
    popular culture, 668–669
    Red Scare, 672–676
Potsdam conference, 650, 656, 658
Potter, Daniel, 686
Poverty
    of African Americans, 365, 695, 717,
      806–807
    aid programs, 601
    in developing world, 816
    of Indians, 607
    of minority groups, 695, 743, 806–807
    in 1920s, 565
    in 1930s, 592–593
    in 1950s, 694–696
    reducing, 711–712, 713
    in rural areas, 580, 695
    urban, 436, 437, 438, 695–696, 806–807
Powderly, Terence V., 422
Powell, Lewis F., Jr., 758
Powers, Francis Gary, 703
Powers, Richard Gid, 674
Pragmatism, 449–450
Presidents, 661; *see also* Elections; *and*
    individual names
Presley, Elvis, 693, 693*i*
Press; *see* Newspapers
Press freedom, 640
Printing technology, 447
Professions, 492–493
Progressive Party, 490, 512, 515, 667
Progressivism; *see also* Social democracy
    beliefs, 488–489
    economic reforms, 504–505, 513
    historians' views, 500–501
    immigration restrictions, 503–504
    impact, 487–488

labor laws, 499–501
political reforms, 496–498
public support, 511–512
of T. Roosevelt, 505, 511
settlement houses, 491–492
Social Gospel, 491
social justice, 489–491
sources, 498–502
Taft and, 510
tariff rates, 510, 514–515
temperance movement, 503, 556
western, 501
of Wilson, 512–513, 514–515
woman suffrage, 495–496
Prohibition, 503, 556–557, 559, 589
Proposition 13, 774
Prostitutes, 385, 388
Protestants
evangelical, 772–773
fundamentalists, 449, 558
liberal, 449
Public health, 437, 451; see also Diseases;
Health
Public Health Service, 437
Public Works Administration (PWA), 591, 601
Public works projects, 582, 590, 591–592, 593,
601, 606, 608
Puck magazine, 439i, 457i, 479i, 520i
Puerto Rico
annexation to U.S., 478
migration from, 695, 743
Spanish colony, 478
as territory, 478, 481
Pulitzer, Joseph, 472, 474
Pullman strike, 424, 464
Pure Food and Drug Act, 506
Putin, Vladimir, 821
PWA; see Public Works Administration
Pyle, Ernie, 640

Qadaffi, Muammar, 820

Race relations; see also African Americans
Atlanta Compromise, 374
Ku Klux Klan, 368–369, 557–558, 559
police shootings of blacks, 807
post-Reconstruction era, 374–375, 378
Race riots
in 1919, 539
in 1960s, 720, 732
in twenty-first century, 807
during World War II, 636

Racial discrimination; see also Civil rights
movement
in employment, 548–550, 696, 720
in government employment, 667–668
in New Deal, 606
in professional organizations, 493
Racial segregation
desegregated schools, 696–697, 755, 758, 759
of federal government, 515
of housing, 687
Jim Crow laws, 375
of labor force, 387
of military, 527, 636, 667–668
of New Deal programs, 607
of schools, 364, 374, 450, 493, 715i
Racism
anti-Chinese, 385–386
in popular culture, 445, 446
Radical Republicans, 354–355, 356, 358, 366
Radio
commercial, 545, 554, 694
disk jockeys, 694
FDR's use of, 588, 604–605
in Great Depression, 574–575, 576,
620–621
ownership, 639
payola scandals, 694
shortwave, 544–545
"War of the Worlds," 620i, 620–621
Radosh, Ronald, 594
Railroads
advertising, 420
Chinese workers, 385
corporations, 411, 419
expansion, 410, 410m
failures, 463
farmers and, 401
government financing, 410
industry and, 406–407, 410
monopolies, 505
regulation, 459, 506
in rural areas, 550m
in South, 372
in Southwest, 382
strikes, 422, 424, 464, 665, 671
transcontinental, 385, 399
tycoons, 410
in West, 394i, 398–399, 401
Ranching, 388–390, 389m, 400–401
Randolph, A. Philip, 548
Randolph, Edmund, 635–636
Range wars, 389–390

Rankin, Jeannette, 527
Rap music, 797, 798–799
Raskob, John Jacob, 596
Ray, James Earl, 732
RCA, 684
Reagan, Ronald
  as California governor, 774
  coalition, 777–779
  foreign policy, 657, 778, 781, 783
  on government role, 776–777
  Horatio Alger Award, 417
  presidency, 747, 775–777, 778i, 779–781,
    783–784
  presidential elections, 768, 774–775, 781
Reagan Doctrine, 781
Reaganomics, 779–780
Recessions; see also Depressions
  in 1920s, 537–538, 544
  of 1937, 603–606
  in 1980s, 780
  of 2008, 796–797, 800
Reconstruction
  congressional, 359–362
  end of, 368–370
  Freedmen's Bureau, 353–354, 358, 364
  historians' views, 356–357
  land redistribution, 353–354, 364
  legacy, 371
  loyalty oaths, 354
  plans, 354, 358
  politics of, 354–355, 358–362
  Radical, 358–362
  readmission to Union, 359, 361m
  state governments, 354–355, 358, 359,
    362–363, 369
  views of, 351, 352–353, 363i
Reconstruction Finance Corporation
    (RFC), 582
The Red Menace, 668i
Red Scare, 540, 672–676
Redeemers (Bourbons), 371–372, 375
Referenda, 497
Reformers; see also Populism; Progressivism
  African American, 501–502
  anti-corruption campaigns, 440
  women, 493–496, 500–501, 503
Regulation; see also Labor laws
  business, 504–505, 515
  deregulation, 779–780
  railroad, 459, 506
  stock market, 589
Rehnquist, William, 758, 796

Religions; see also Catholic Church; Jews;
    Protestants
  of Indian tribes, 397
  Mormons, 386, 773, 807
  in 1920s, 558
  in 1970s, 771–773
Relocation centers, 637–638
Remington, Frederick, 393
Republic Steel, 599–600
Republican Party
  Contract with America, 791
  Eisenhower era, 698–699
  in late nineteenth century, 455–456,
    457–458, 459, 465
  in 1920s, 559–560
  Radical, 354–355, 356, 358, 366
  in South, 370
Research and development, 408; see also
    Medicine; Science; Technology
RFC; see Reconstruction Finance Corporation
Rhee, Syngman, 669
Rhodes, Cecil, 470–471
Rice, Condoleezza, 747
Richardson, Elliot, 763
Richmond, 353i
Riesman, David, 692
Rights; see also Civil rights; Voting rights;
    Women's rights
  Bill of Rights, 540
  of homosexuals, 744–745
  human, 769
  movements in 1960s and 1970s, 740–747
  privacy, 747
  of unions, 598
Right-to-life movement, 807–808
Riis, Jacob, 436
Roads
  interstate highways, 689, 691, 699
  Route 66, 690, 690i
  in rural areas, 550m
Roberts, John, 796
Roberts, Owen J., 603
Robertson, Pat, 773
Rock 'n' roll, 693–694, 739–740
Rockefeller, John D., 411, 412
Rockefeller, Nelson, 774
Rockefeller Institute for Medical Research, 451
Rocky Mountain school, 390
Rodgers, Daniel, 501
Roe v. Wade, 747, 759, 807–808
Roebling, John A., 436
Rogers, William, 750

Rolling Stones, 739–740
Roman Catholic Church; *see* Catholic Church
Rommel, Erwin, 631
Romney, Mitt, 773, 801
Roosevelt, Eleanor, 606, 608*i*
Roosevelt, Franklin Delano; *see also*
    New Deal
  Atlantic Charter, 624, 625, 654
  Black Cabinet, 606
  career, 584
  civil rights and, 636
  death, 650, 658
  election of 1920 and, 541
  foreign policy, 614–615, 616–618,
    655–658
  health, 584
  judicial reforms, 603, 604–605
  personality, 588, 589*i*
  postwar vision, 657
  presidency, 587–588, 593–596
  presidential elections, 584–585, 602–603,
    623, 642–643
  World War II and, 619–626, 631, 637, 642
  Yalta Conference, 655–658, 657*i*, 819
Roosevelt, Theodore
  Bull Moose Party, 512, 513–514
  environmental policies, 507–509
  foreign policy, 519–521, 520*i*
  on immigration, 504
  imperialism and, 479
  muckrakers and, 489
  Panama Canal, 521
  post-presidency, 510–512, 511*i*
  presidency, 505–509, 519–521
  progressivism, 505, 511
  Spanish-American War, 472, 476, 481
  "Square Deal," 506
  as vice president, 481, 505
  The Winning of the West, 393
Roosevelt Corollary, 521, 613
Root, Elihu, 485
Rosenberg, Julius and Ethel, 673
Rosie the Riveter, 642
Roth v. United States, 758
Rough Riders, 476
Rove, Karl, 796
Ruby, Jack, 710
Rural Electrification Administration, 590
Rural life; *see also* Agriculture
  electric power, 590
  isolation, 402
  poverty, 580, 695

transportation, 550*m*
Russell, Richard, 710*i*
Russia; *see also* Soviet Union
  Bolshevik Revolution, 527, 536, 540
  Crimean annexation, 821
  World War I and, 527
Russo-Japanese War, 520, 655
Rustin, Bayard, 636

Sabin, Albert, 683
Sabotage Act, 533
Sacco, Nicola, 540
Sadat, Anwar, 769, 770*i*
Sagebrush Rebellion, 771, 779
St. Louis, 632*i*
Salinger, J. D., 692
Salk, Jonas, 683
Salvation Army, 438, 491
Same-sex marriage, 744, 809–811
Samoa, 469, 472
San Francisco
  Chinatown, 385
  Chinese immigrants, 384*i*
  counterculture, 739
  earthquake, 509
Sandy Hook shooting, 801
Sanger, Margaret, 554
Savings and loan industry, 783–784
Scalawags, 362
Schell, Jonathan, 762
Schlaes, Amity, 595
Schlesinger, Arthur M., Jr., 594, 762
Schools; *see* Education
Schrecker, Ellen, 675
Schwarzkopf, Norman, 786
Schwerner, Michael, 717
Science; *see also* Medicine
  atomic bomb research, 649–650
  ecology, 748
  engineering and, 408
  evolution, 449
  genetics, 545, 804–805
  research, 451, 634, 683
  social sciences and, 450
  space program, 685–686
  during World War II, 634
Scientific management, 408–409
SCLC; *see* Southern Christian Leadership
    Conference
Scopes, John T., 558
Scopes trial, 558
Scottsboro case, 570, 580

SDI; *see* Strategic Defense Initiative
SDS; *see* Students for a Democratic Society
Sea power, 468, 612; *see also* Navy, U.S.
Searcy, Cari, 810
SEC; *see* Securities and Exchange Commission
Second New Deal, 598
Securities and Exchange Commission (SEC), 589
Sedition Act of 1918, 533–535
Seeger, Pete, 728
Segregation; *see* Racial segregation
Selective Service Act, 527, 661
Sentimental novels, 446
September 11; *see* 9/11 attacks
Serbia, World War I and, 524
Settlement houses, 491–492
Seventeenth Amendment, 497
Seward, William H., 357, 368
Seymour, Horatio, 366
Shafter, William R., 476
Sharecropping, 364, 365, 373, 373m, 695
Shaw, Anna Howard, 495
Sheldon, Charles, 491
Shelley v. Kraemer, 668
Shepard, Alan, 685
Sheppard-Towner Act, 555
Sherman, John, 479
Sherman, William T., 353
Sherman Antitrust Act, 459, 505
Sherman Silver Purchase Act, 464
Sierra Club, 691, 748, 812
Silent majority, 734, 755
Silver question, 464, 467
Sinclair, Upton, 448, 506
Singer, Isaac, 411
Sino-Japanese War, 614–615, 616
Sioux Indians, 382, 395, 396, 397, 742
Sirhan, Sirhan, 732
Sirica, John J., 761
Sit-down strikes, 599
Sixteenth Amendment, 515
Skocpol, Theda, 594
Skyscrapers, 436
Slavery, 358, 365; *see also* Emancipation
Sloan, John, 448
Smallpox, 382, 682
Smith, Alfred E., 559, 561, 584, 596
Smith, Gerald L. K., 602
Smith, Henry Nash, 392
Smith-Connally Act, 633
Smith-Lever Act, 516
SNCC; *see* Student Nonviolent Coordinating Committee

Social Darwinism, 412–413, 449
Social democracy, 490–491, 594
Social Gospel, 491
Social justice, 489–491, 511
Social sciences, 450, 492
Social Security Act, 600–601, 603
Social Security system, 607, 609, 665, 667, 699
Social workers, 492
Socialism
    in nineteenth century, 418–419
    in twentieth century, 504, 580
Socialist Labor Party, 418–419
Socialist Party, 504, 535, 580, 596
Sociology, 450
Soil Conservation and Domestic
        Allotment Act, 590
South; *see also* Reconstruction; Slavery; *and
        specific states*
    agriculture, 373
    post-Reconstruction era, 371–375, 378
    segregated schools, 696
    Sunbelt, 771, 772m
South Africa, 471, 783
South America; *see* Latin America
South Dakota, statehood, 386
South Korea; *see* Korean War
South Vietnam; *see* Vietnam
Southern Christian Leadership Conference
        (SCLC), 698, 713
Southern Tenant Farmers Union (STFU), 580
Sovereignty, tribal, 394, 607, 636, 741–742
Soviet Union; *see also* Cold War; Russia;
        Stalin, Josef
    American Communist Party and, 579, 580
    atomic and nuclear weapons, 662,
        673, 684
    Berlin blockade, 661
    Chernobyl disaster, 812
    collapse, 656–657, 757, 782–783
    Cuba and, 702, 722–723
    films, 552
    relations with United States, 616
    space program, 685
    sphere of influence, 655, 656, 702–703, 819
    spies, 673
    treaty with Nazi Germany, 580, 619
    U-2 crisis, 703
    Warsaw Pact, 662
    in World War II, 623, 630–631, 645–646,
        651, 655
Space program, 685–686
Spanish Civil War, 579, 618i, 618, 634

Spanish Empire
in Caribbean, 478
rebellions, 472
Spanish-American War
background, 472–473
black troops, 473, 475i, 476, 483
in Cuba, 454–455, 473, 476–478, 477m
in Philippines, 476
Specie Resumption Act, 367
Spencer, Herbert, 413
Spock, Benjamin, 688
Sports
baseball, 444i, 444–445
basketball, 445
boxing, 445, 449i
football, 445
professional, 445
radio broadcasts, 575
televised, 688
Sputnik, 685
"Square Deal," 506
Stagflation, 767
Stalin, Josef; see also Soviet Union
Atlantic Charter, 654
Cold War and, 661
postwar vision, 654–655, 657
Potsdam conference, 650, 656, 658
Roosevelt and, 579, 616
treaty with Nazi Germany, 580, 619
World War II and, 631, 655
Yalta Conference, 655–658, 657i, 819
Stalingrad, Battle of, 631
Stalwarts, 457–458
Stampp, Kenneth, 356
Standard Oil, 411, 412, 489
Stanton, Edwin M., 361, 362
Stanton, Elizabeth Cady, 495
Starr, Kenneth, 793
State governments
Reconstruction, 354–355, 358, 359,
362–363, 369
reforms, 497–498
Statue of Liberty, 474
Steel industry
in Great Lakes region, 406–407, 411
in 1920s, 544
strikes, 423–424, 464, 538, 599–600, 671
technology, 406–407
unions, 599–600
Steel Workers Organizing Committee (SWOC),
599–600
Steffens, Lincoln, 489

Stein, Gertrude, 556
Stein, Herbert, 595
Steinbeck, John, 579
Stephens, Alexander H., 358
Stephens, Uriah S., 422
Stevens, Robert, 699–700
Stevens, Thaddeus, 354
Stevenson, Adlai E., 676, 684, 699
STFU; see Southern Tenant Farmers Union
Stilwell, Joseph W., 646
Stimson, Henry, 616
Stock market
in 1920s, 564, 780
regulation, 589
Stone v. Powell, 759
Stonewall Riot, 744
Strategic Defense Initiative (SDI), 781
Strikes
after World War I, 538
cooling off periods, 666
failed, 425
farmers, 582–583
general, 422–423
Homestead, 423–424, 464
mining, 505–506
in postwar period, 665, 671
Pullman, 424, 464
railroad, 422, 424, 464, 665, 671
sit-down, 599
steel industry, 423–424, 464, 538, 599–600,
671
violence, 538, 600
during World War II, 633
Student Nonviolent Coordinating Committee
(SNCC), 713, 721
Students for a Democratic Society (SDS), 728,
737, 739
Submarines
nuclear missiles, 685
in World War I, 525–526, 530–531
in World War II, 623–625, 634, 646
Suburbs
families, 687–688
growth, 680, 687
housing, 435
integration, 806
politics, 771
Suez crisis, 702, 757
Suffrage; see Voting rights
Sugar plantations, 469, 478, 482
Sumner, Charles, 354, 369
Sumner, William Graham, 413, 449

Sunbelt, 771, 772m
Superman, 576, 577i
Supply-side economics, 779–780
Supreme Court
    Brown v. Board, 696, 715
    Burger court, 758–759
    civil liberties, 540–541
    civil rights cases of 1883, 374
    Court-packing plan, 603, 604–605
    desegregation cases, 696, 697
    election of 2000 and, 794
    justices, 747, 758
    Korematsu decision, 637–639
    New Deal cases, 590, 591, 598, 603
    Pentagon Papers case, 751
    Plessy v. Ferguson, 374, 696
    racial discrimination cases, 668
    Reconstruction and, 362
    Roberts court, 796
    Roe v. Wade, 747, 759, 807–808
    same-sex marriage cases, 809, 811
    Scottsboro case, 570, 580
    Wabash case, 459
    Warren court, 696, 758
    Watergate case, 763–764
Swann v. Charlotte-Mecklenburg Board of
    Education, 759
Swift, Gustavus, 411
SWOC; see Steel Workers Organizing
    Committee
Syria, 755, 821
Szyk, Arthur, 638, 638i

Taft, William Howard
    as Philippines governor, 483–484
    presidency, 510, 522
    presidential election, 512, 513–514
Taft-Hartley Act, 665–666
Taiwan, 663, 754
Taliban, 818, 820
Tammany Hall, 369, 439i, 440, 458, 499, 501
Tarbell, Ida, 489
Tariffs
    McKinley, 459, 465, 467
    in 1920s, 565, 566
    in 1930s, 582
    reducing rates, 458, 510, 514–515
TARP; see Troubled Asset Relief Program
Taubman, William, 656
Taxes; see also Tariffs
    income, 515, 598, 634
    in 1920s, 560

    opposition, 774
    poll, 375, 606–607
    reducing, 779, 795
Taylor, Frederick Winslow, 409
Taylorism, 408–409
Tea Party, 800–801
Teachers, 493
Teamsters Union, 681–682
Teapot Dome, 560
Technology; see also Transportation; Weapons
    agricultural, 551
    barbed wire, 399
    communications, 405, 447–448
    computers, 545, 684, 802–804
    construction, 436
    digital revolution, 802–804
    electricity, 405–406, 409, 590
    electronic, 684
    industrial, 405–408
    Internet, 802, 803–804
    inventions, 405
    iron and steel production, 406–407
    medical, 451
    military, 634
    in 1920s, 544–545
    in 1950s, 683–684
    printing, 447
    research and development, 408
    telegraph, 447
    in World War I, 530–531
    in World War II, 634–635
Tehran Conference, 655
Tejanos, 383i
Telegraph, 447
Telephone, 405, 447–448, 545, 546, 546i
Television
    broadcasting, 684, 688
    commercials, 688
    development, 688
    news, 684, 688, 698, 730
    programming in 1950s, 688–689, 689i,
        690, 690i
    The Twilight Zone, 669
Teller Amendment, 473
Temperance
    supporters, 456, 496, 503
    WCTU, 503
Temporary National Economic Committee
    (TNEC), 606
Tenant farmers, 373, 580, 695
Tenements, 435i, 436
Tennessee, Scopes trial, 558

Tennessee Valley Authority (TVA), 591–592, 592*m*
Terrorism
  in Middle East, 781, 821
  in 1920s, 540
  9/11 attacks, 789, 817*i*, 818
  rise of, 816–818
  war on, 818
Tet offensive, 731
Texas
  cattle ranching, 388
  Hispanic residents, 383
Textile industry
  child labor, 421*i*
  female workers, 420
  growth, 440
  in South, 372
  wages, 440
Thatcher, Margaret, 657
Theater, 445
Theoharis, Athan, 675
Thieu, Nguyen Van, 751, 753
Third World
  former colonies, 754, 756–757
  Nixon Doctrine, 754–755
Thirteenth Amendment, 358
Thomas, Clarence, 417
Thomas, Norman, 580
Thurmond, Strom, 667
Tiananmen Square, 783
Tilden, Samuel J., 369–370
Time magazine, 623, 682
TNEC; *see* Temporary National Economic Committee
Tobacco industry, 372
Tojo, Hideki, 625, 638
Tourism, 390; *see also* Travel
Townsend, Francis E., 596, 602
Townsend Plan, 596
Trade; *see also* Tariffs
  with China, 484
  exports, 551, 552
  free-trade agreements, 791, 815
  in 1920s, 565
Trade unions; *see* Unions
Transportation; *see also* Automobiles; Railroads
  airplanes, 408, 530, 545, 633, 635
  bridges, 436
  canals, 521
  freight ships, 406
  public mass, 435, 436, 697
  roads, 550*m*, 690

  in rural areas, 550*m*
  steamboats, 406
Travel
  by automobile, 689, 690–691
  tourism, 390
  vacations, 689
Treasury Department, 588
Treaties
  arms control, 754, 768, 770, 771, 781, 783
  with Indians, 394, 396
Treaty of Paris, 479, 481
Treaty of Portsmouth, 520
Treaty of Versailles, 536–537, 566, 611
Trench warfare, 530, 531*i*
Triangle Shirtwaist Company Fire, 499, 499*i*
Triple Alliance, 524
Triple Entente, 524
Troubled Asset Relief Program (TARP), 797
Trujillo, Rafael, 723
Truman, Harry S.
  atom bomb decisions, 648–649, 650–651
  Korean War and, 669–672, 676
  Potsdam conference, 650, 656, 658
  presidency, 650, 658–659, 661, 663, 665–668, 673, 701
  presidential election, 666–667
  as vice president, 642–643
Truman Doctrine, 659
Trusts, 412, 419, 459, 489, 489*i*, 504–505; *see also* Antitrust laws
Truth in Securities Act of 1933, 589
Tuck, Stephen, 715
Turing, Alan, 635
Turner, Frederick Jackson, 392–393, 450
Turner thesis, 392–393
Tuskegee Institute, 374
TVA; *see* Tennessee Valley Authority
Twain, Mark, 391, 479
Tweed, William M., 440
Twenty-First Amendment, 589
Tydings, Millard, 756

U-2 crisis, 703
UAW; *see* United Auto Workers
Underwood-Simmons Tariff, 514–515
Unemployment
  in Great Depression, 566*i*, 566–567, 568, 568*i*, 569, 574, 580, 592–593
  in 1950s, 679
  in 1980s, 780
  in Panic of 1893, 463–464
  in recession of 2008, 797

Unemployment insurance, 601
UNEP; *see* United Nations Environment
    Programme
UNIA; *see* Universal Negro Improvement
    Association
Union Pacific Railroad Company, 367
Union Party, 602
Unions; *see also* Strikes
    black, 548, 635–636
    company, 548
    corruption, 681–682
    craft, 421–422, 548, 599
    decline, 802
    establishment, 422–423
    industrial, 599
    membership, 681*i*
    migrant workers, 743
    militancy in 1930s, 598–600
    New Deal and, 591, 598
    in 1920s, 548
    in 1950s, 681–682
    in nineteenth century, 421–425
    objectives, 422–423
    populism and, 462
    in postwar period, 665–666, 671
    power, 491
    progressivism and, 499
    racial discrimination, 548
    radical, 464, 504, 535
    rights to organize, 598
    right-to-work laws, 665–666
    trade policy and, 815
    women's, 494
    World War I and, 532–533, 535, 538
    World War II and, 633
United Auto Workers (UAW), 599
United Mine Workers, 505–506, 633, 665, 682
United Nations
    Chinese membership, 753–754
    establishment, 655
    Korean War, 670
    opponents, 660
United Nations Environment Programme
    (UNEP), 812
United Service Organization (USO), 641
United States Chamber of Commerce, 493, 590
United States Forest Service, 507, 510
United States Steel Corporation, 411, 509, 512, 599
United Steelworkers of America, 599
UNIVAC, 684
Universal Negro Improvement Association
    (UNIA), 539

Universities
    African American, 373–374
    coeducational, 746
    desegregation, 716
    female students, 452, 493, 554, 746
    land-grant institutions, 450, 451
    private, 450–451
    sports, 445
    state, 681
    student protests, 737–739, 750–751
University of California at Berkeley, 737–738
Urban areas; *see* Cities
Urban bosses; *see* Political machines and
    bosses
USO; *see* United Service Organization
Utah, statehood, 386

Valentino, Rudolph, 553*i*
Vanderbilt, Cornelius, 410, 418*i*
Vanzetti, Bartolomeo, 540
Vaudeville, 445
Vaux, Calvert, 434
Veblen, Thorstein, 492
Venezuela, 521
Veracruz incident, 523
Vertical integration, 411
Vichy regime, 619, 631
Viet Cong (National Liberation Front), 724, 725,
    727, 731
Vietnam
    Diem assassination, 724–725
    division, 701
    French colony, 757
Vietnam War, 726*m*
    atrocities, 751
    Christmas bombing, 751–752
    Easter offensive, 751
    fall of Saigon, 752*i*, 753
    Gulf of Tonkin Resolution, 751
    Nixon's policies, 750–752
    peace accords, 752
    protests, 727, 738, 739, 750–751
    Tet offensive, 731
    U.S. strategies, 725–727
    U.S. troops, 725
Vietnamization, 750
Viguerie, Richard, 773
Villa, Pancho, 523
Violence; *see also* Race riots
    in cities, 438
    school shootings, 801
    in strikes, 538, 600, 600*i*

Virgin Islands, 523

Virginia, freed slaves, 360

Von Richthofen, Walter Baron, *Cattle Raising on the Plains in North America*, 400–401

Voting rights; *see also* Elections
of African Americans, 354, 359, 374–375, 606–607, 717
Fifteenth Amendment, 359, 369, 375
literacy requirements, 375
poll taxes, 375
restrictions, 374–375
of women, 495*i*, 495–496, 541

Voting Rights Act, 717

WAACs and WAVEs, 642

Wabash, St. Louis, and Pacific Railway Co. v. Illinois, 459

Wade, Benjamin E., 354

Wade-Davis Bill, 354–355, 358

Wages; *see also* Incomes
of African Americans, 440
in industry, 409, 424, 440
minimum, 590, 603, 606, 665, 667, 699
in 1920s, 548
in 1950s, 681
of women, 420, 440

Wagner, Robert E., 598

Wagner Act, 598, 603, 665

Walker, James, *Tejano Ranchers*, 383*i*

Wallace, George, 716, 733, 734, 759

Wallace, Henry A., 623, 642, 667

Wanamaker, John, 442–443

War Industries Board (WIB), 532

"War of the Worlds," 620*i*, 620–621

War on terror, 818

War Production Board (WPB), 634

Ward, Lester Frank, 417–418

Warren, Earl, 637, 696, 710, 758

Warren Commission, 710

Warsaw Pact, 662

Washington, Booker T., 374, 502

Washington, statehood, 386

Washington Conference of 1921, 612

Washington Post, 761

Watergate, 761–764

Watson, John B., 554

Watt, James (Interior Secretary), 779–780

WCTU; *see* Women's Christian Temperance Union

Wealth
capitalists, 412–413
housing, 435
philanthropy, 413, 414–415, 434, 450–451
self-made men, 413, 416–417

Weapons; *see also* Atomic bombs; Nuclear weapons
gun control, 801
of mass destruction, 818–819
in World War I, 530
in World War II, 634–635

Weathermen, 728, 739

Weaver, James B., 459, 461

Webb, Walter Prescott, 392

Weimar Republic, 615

Weisbrot, Robert, 714

Welch, Robert, 660

Welfare capitalism, 547–548

Welfare programs, 609, 758, 793, 807

Welles, Orson, 575, 620*i*, 620–621

Wells, H. G., 620–621

Wells-Barnett, Ida B., 375, 502–503

West; *see also* Indian Territory
agriculture, 386, 398–402
cities, 681
economy, 386–390, 680–681
ethnic groups, 381–386, 387
federal policies, 386, 501, 507–509, 510
as frontier, 391–393
labor force, 550
New Deal and, 608
paintings, 390
Plains Indians, 381–382, 393–398
progressivism, 501
railroads, 398–399, 401
ranching, 388–390, 389*m*, 400–401
romantic images, 390–393
Sunbelt, 771, 772*m*

West, settlement of
in antebellum period, 380
farmers, 386, 398–399
historians' views, 392–393
Homestead Act, 386
Indian resistance, 395–397
motives, 386
railroads, 398–399

West, Kanye, 799*i*

West, Mae, 578

West, Nathanael, 579

West Indies; *see* Caribbean islands

West Virginia, USS, 626*i*

Westad, Odd Arne, 657

Weyler, Valeriano, 472

Wheeler, Burton, 622–623

Wheeler-Nicholson, Malcolm, 576

Whiskey Ring, 367
Whistler, James McNeil, 448
White, William Allen, 490–491
Whites; *see also* Race relations
  relations with Indians, 395–397, 607
  supporters of civil rights movement, 698
Whyte, William H., Jr., *The Organization Man*, 692
WIB; *see* War Industries Board
Wiebe, Robert, 500
Wild West shows, 390–391
Willard, Frances, 503
Williams, William Appleman, 656
Willkie, Wendell, 623
Wilson, Charles, 699
Wilson, Woodrow, 514*i*
  foreign policy, 522–523
  Fourteen Points, 535–536
  international vision, 526, 535–536
  presidency, 514–516, 522–523
  presidential elections, 512–514, 515–516, 525
  progressivism, 512–513, 514–515
  stroke, 537
  Treaty of Versailles, 536–537
  World War I and, 524–527, 532
Wisconsin, progressivism, 498
Wister, Owen, *The Virginian*, 390
Women; *see also* African American women; Gender relations
  clubs, 494
  in Congress, 527
  as consumers, 441–443, 551–553, 555
  discrimination against, 745–746
  domestic roles, 494
  education, 452, 493, 554, 746
  feminism, 745–747
  flappers, 555, 555*i*
  in Great Depression, 573–574
  incomes, 745*i*, 746
  lesbians, 494
  middle-class, 551, 554
  military service, 642
  motherhood, 554, 642, 687–688
  New Deal and, 601–602, 607
  nurses, 493
  in politics, 746–747
  Populists, 461*i*
  professional, 493, 554
  public roles, 494, 501
  reformers, 493–496, 500–501, 503
  settlement houses, 491–492
  single, 494
  sports, 445
  union members, 599
  in West, 388
  in World War II, 641–642
  writers, 448
Women in workforce
  African Americans, 365, 366*i*, 428, 574, 641–642
  increased participation, 746
  in industry, 372, 420
  in 1920s, 548, 554, 555
  in 1930s, 573–574
  in postwar period, 665, 687–688
  telephone operators, 447
  textile industry, 420
  Triangle Shirtwaist Company Fire, 499, 499*i*
  wages, 420, 440
  in World War I, 533*i*
  in World War II, 633, 641*i*, 641–642, 665
Women's Christian Temperance Union (WCTU), 503
Women's rights; *see also* Feminism
  in early twentieth century, 496
  Equal Rights Amendment, 555, 747, 807
  in 1920s, 555
  in 1960s and later, 745–747
  voting, 495*i*, 495–496, 541
Women's Trade Union League (WTUL), 494
Wood, Leonard, 476, 482
Woodstock, 740, 740*i*
Woolworth, F. W., 441
Workers; *see* Labor force; Unions
Workingmen's Party of California, 385–386
Works Progress Administration (WPA), 580, 601, 602*i*, 605, 607, 642
World Bank, 815
World Economic Conference, 616
World Trade Organization (WTO), 791, 815
World War I
  alliances, 524–525
  armistice, 530
  casualties, 531–532
  cultural impact, 555–556
  dissent, 504, 533–535
  financing, 532, 565
  organizing economy, 532–533
  Paris Peace Conference, 536
  posters, 528, 528*i*, 533
  preparedness, 525
  profiteering, 617
  propaganda, 533

reparations, 565, 566, 613
songs, 533, 534–535
trench warfare, 530, 531*i*
United States and, 524–527, 532
veterans, 583–584
Western Front, 529*m*, 529–530
World War II
beginning, 619
casualties, 640, 651
cultural impact, 639–643
end of, 651
in Europe, 630*m*, 630–631, 643*m*,
643–646, 655
German invasions, 619
intelligence, 635
London bombings, 622*i*, 635
minority group experiences, 636–639
in North Africa, 630*m*, 631
in Pacific, 629–630, 646–649, 647*m*
Pearl Harbor attack, 615, 625, 626*i*, 637
science and technology, 634–635
U.S. economy, 633–634
U.S. entry, 625–626
veterans, 663–665

World Wildlife Fund (WWF), 812
Wounded Knee, 397, 742
Wovoka, 397
WPA; *see* Works Progress Administration
WPB; *see* War Production Board
Wright, Almroth, 683
Wright, Richard, 579
Wright, Wilbur and Orville, 408
WTO; *see* World Trade Organization
WTUL; *see* Women's Trade Union League
WWF; *see* World Wildlife Fund
Wyoming, statehood, 386

X, Malcolm, 721

Yalta Conference, 655–658, 657*i*, 819
Yellow journalism, 472, 474–475
Yosemite National Park, 509
Youth culture, 692–693, 730, 737–740

Zhou Enlai, 754*i*
Zimmermann, Arthur, 525–526
Zimmermann Telegram, 525–526
Zoot suits, 637